Paul J.J. Welfens

Innovations in Macroeconomics

With 99 Figures and 23 Tables

 Springer

Professor Dr. Paul J.J. Welfens
University of Wuppertal
EIIW - European Institute
for International Economic Relations
Rainer-Gruenter-Straße 21
42119 Wuppertal
Germany
welfens@eiiw.uni-wuppertal.de

Library of Congress Control Number: 2006936075

ISBN-10 3-540-32859-9 Springer Berlin Heidelberg New York
ISBN-13 978-3-540-32859-9 Springer Berlin Heidelberg New York

Springer is part of Springer Science+Business Media

springer.com

© Springer-Verlag Berlin Heidelberg 2007

Production: LE-TEX Jelonek, Schmidt & Vöckler GbR, Leipzig
Cover-design: Erich Kirchner, Heidelberg

SPIN 11684336   43/3100YL - 5 4 3 2 1 0   Printed on acid-free paper

Preface

This book deals with the role of innovations in macroeconomics, and it presents innovations in macroeconomic theory. Growth and structural change are key issues here, but we also touch upon links between exchange rate dynamics and innovations. The approaches and ideas presented are not integrated into a large comprehensive model. Rather, we present analytical building blocks in selected fields of Schumpeterian Macroeconomics, including new insights about trade, growth, exchange rate dynamics, innovations and policy options.

An important starting point in chapter A is a generalization of the Solow growth model and a long term analysis of the link between process innovations and the price level as well as the exchange rate, which is shown to critically depend on the income elasticity of the demand for money. Moreover, we discuss the long term Phillips curve in the context of a growth model and can thereby gain some new insights. The theoretical reflections presented suggest the need for new empirical work. We also consider the role of foreign direct investment flows. Chapter B is an attempt to bridge the medium term analysis with the long run growth analysis. It is argued that individuals will partly base consumption – and thus savings – on current income and expected steady state income. While this approach is closely related to the permanent income hypothesis, its specific implications are quite interesting. Chapter C takes a closer look at some integration issues. Chapter D puts the focus on both growth in open economies and the real exchange rate. The analysis in chapter E is again devoted to open economy topics, where we present a Mundell-Fleming-Schumpeter model with product innovations. Chapter F focuses on the link between stock market dynamics and the exchange rate, and the framework presented is new and works rather satisfactorily from an empirical perspective. Chapter G starts with the traditional optimum growth framework and then proceeds by looking at the topic of endogenous growth (or quasi-endogenous growth). Chapter H involves trade, structural change and growth in open economies, while chapter I looks at the role of innovations in a digital market economy. Chapter J puts the focus on EU innovation policy and raises some critical questions about the EU economic policy. Finally, chapter K considers some aspects of monetary integration and growth including basic policy implications. In a rather simple approach, we explain why the integration of global financial markets has brought about a global fall of the interest rate along with a higher stock market price index. Essentially, there is an interplay between Asian capital inflows into the US and an increasing international bonds substitutability concerning Dollar-denominated and Euro-denominated assets (the start of the Euro has created a European bonds market which effectively offers better substitutes to the Dollar bonds than was the case for the previous DM-$ comparison). We also look at some other monetary issues. As regards the link between economic policy measures and economic development, one should emphasize that policy makers rarely make the crucial distinction between changes in the level of the growth path and the growth rate itself. This distinction is quite important in the context of the basic and modified neoclassical growth model.

Possibly the most important shift of analytical emphasis is the idea that one should take a look at various modelling approaches whereby the choice of model depends on the time horizon and the specific initial situation. From a policy perspective medium term models could be quite useful, however there is no adequate model which bridges the short run and the long run. One of the new ideas presented here is to link the short term and long run aspects in a new medium term Keynes-Solow model. In this approach, it is emphasized that both aggregate demand and aggregate supply determine the dynamics of actual income. In a medium term perspective, this approach can also be applied to hybrid growth modelling; in reality there is rarely a case for which only the demand side or only the supply side is valid.

Some of the analytical elements presented are refinements or extensions of existing approaches; other contributions aim at clarifying apparent inconsistencies in the literature. An important aspect here is the inconsistency, implying for instance that Poland or China export mainly capital goods to the USA and EU15, while reality is characterized by trade flows of machinery and equipment in the opposite direction between neoclassical growth theory and neoclassical (Heckscher-Ohlin-Samuelson) trade theory. Economics is a scientific field in which competition among researchers stimulates the specialization of scientists as well as the exploration of narrow islands. Little research is devoted to building intellectual bridges between islands in order to analyze the combined insights or to combine possible variants of models developed on each island. A few bridges are presented here.

In market economies, innovation dynamics have played a crucial role since the Industrial Revolution. Schumpeterian Economics has analyzed some of these developments on the basis of an evolutionary approach which is useful in many fields. At the other end of the spectrum, there are innovation researchers who persue a rather narrow focus on invention and novel products or on new process technologies in certain sectors. This is unsatisfactory in the sense that innovation dynamics should be combined with macroeconomic analysis, including growth analysis and models of stabilization policy. The new growth theory has delivered some interesting results including aspects related to product differentiation and spillover effects. In a different context, real business cycle models have shown that technological changes are able to generate economic cycles in a quasi-Walrasian world with no frictions in markets. However, the latter is a contradiction in itself since every innovation automatically creates information asymmetries which, in turn, take us away from competitive market clearing.

From an input perspective, one can measure innovation dynamics to some extent using the ratio of expenditures on research and development (R&D) to Gross Domestic Product or R&D expenditures per capita, from an output perspective through the number of (international) patents or patent applications per capita. In the second half of the 20th century, the R&D-GDP ratio increased continuously in OECD countries as did the number of patent applications per capita. At the start of the 21st century the R&D-GDP ratio in the leading OECD country, Sweden, reached 4%, in Japan 3%, and in the US and the EU-15 it was close to 2.5%, up from about 1% in the early 1960s. It is not only impressive to observe how strongly R&D expenditures have increased, but one must also consider the R&D-GDP ratio in comparison with the investment-GDP ratio, which is around 20% in leading OECD countries. As much as investment in machinery and equipment is the basis for the accumulation of a physical capital stock, the stream of R&D expenditures amounts to the accumulation of an R&D stock, which obviously contributes to the output of individual firms and the overall economy. Patent applications also increased in OECD countries in the 1980s and 1990s. However, many innovations cannot easily be patented; software is a difficult field in this respect.

Patenting behaviour can also change considerably as market structures change. With respect to this, the case of liberalization in European fixed-line telecommunications is interesting. Apparently, privatized former state-owned monopolies have intensified patenting which is natural in an environment that has become more competitive and more internationalized. (At the same time it seems that innovation activities have shifted away from network operators to the equipment industry.) Changes in patenting behaviour make interpretation of growth in patent applications rather difficult.

The results of innovation efforts are not simply patents, but what matters most are two types of innovations:

- Process innovations which imply cutting costs and thus bringing about a higher equilibrium output in markets; even modelling the simple case of endogenous technological progress in the context of a macroeconomic production function is not easy. Special problems occur if the industry has static or dynamic scale economies, a field not analyzed much in this book.
- Product innovations increase the willingness to pay on the demand side. This is a field of particular interest here, specifically in the case of open economies. Schumpeterian competition – based on product innovations – in a two-country model no longer allows for the assumption that the law of one price will hold.

As discussed in Industrial Economics literature, existing innovation-related literature in economics is divided on the one hand into innovation analysis. On the other hand, there is a niche in macroeconomic analysis, with some strands in the new growth literature looking into process innovations including technology spillovers. This is done, for example, in models by ROMER and LUCAS. GROSSMAN/HELPMAN have emphasized the role of product differentiation and hence product innovation broadly defined. However, those are rare efforts which indeed concern only part of macroeconomic analysis. This book seeks to add some building blocks to the existing literature, offering a particular focus on open economies in which the role of foreign direct investment and network effects in telecommunications is emphasized.

Moreover, we are interested in integrating innovations into short-term financial market analysis and medium-term models of the Mundell Fleming type. By doing so, we wish to link product innovations with modified long-term growth modelling. It must be emphasized, however, that we will not present comprehensive macroeconomic foundations for the innovations in our analysis. We present new ideas and building blocks for more realistic macroeconomic modelling on issues such as real exchange rate dynamics, fiscal and monetary policies in economies with foreign direct investment, and issues related to the use of telecommunications and the internet.

At the bottom line, it certainly is desirable to combine the analytical blocks developed here to a more comprehensive two-sector growth model for an open economy, but this ambitious goal is beyond the scope of this book. Our more modest aim is to suggest consistent improvement in Macroeconomics including approaches valid for a situation with unemployment. (In this context, a theoretical basis for OKUN's Law is presented.) A key element in the approach presented is that the law of one price is not assumed to hold strictly. This, however, is not really surprising for a world economy in which many innovative firms in many countries contribute to imperfect competition in global markets. Moreover, in part of the analysis presented here we look into convergence dynamics and product upgrading. At the same time, we integrate unemployment into some of the models.

It would be a true surprise if this book is liked by very many, as the approaches presented are to some degree unorthodox and also bridge Real Economics and Monetary Economics, which in the standard literature are rather distinct fields. The book should, however, have a lasting impact by encouraging economists and policymakers to take a fresh look at important macroeconomic topics and issues.

I am quite grateful to have had the opportunity to present some of my ideas to seminars at the IMF and the AICGS/the Johns Hopkins University in 2004 as well as at the Research Committee on International Economics and Economic Policy (Ausschuss für Außenwirtschaftstheorie und -politik) of the Verein für Sozialpolitik at the 2004 Paderborn meeting. Moreover, I would like to express my gratitude for the excellent research support of Dora Borbély, Jens Perret and Andre Jungmittag (EIIW at the University of Wuppertal) as well as Albrecht Kauffmann (EIIW Center at the University of Potsdam). I am also grateful for discussions with many colleagues during a conference at Chulalongkorn University in Bangkok in 2001 as well as within the scope of the 2005 workshop "The EU and Asean Facing Economic Globalization", jointly organized by Jean Monnet Chairs at the University of Wuppertal and the University of Birmingham as well as the Center for European Studies, Bangkok. With respect to stimulus of research, I would also like to mention the intellectual support of my colleagues in the EU 5th framework project: *"Changes in Industrial Competitiveness as a Factor of Integration: Identifying Challenges of the Enlarged Single European Market"* (Contract No. HPSE-CT-2002-00148), with special gratitude going to Anna Wziontek-Kubiak (CASE, Warsaw) who offered valuable criticism during the project meetings at CEPS, Brussels in November 2004 and November 2005. Finally, I am grateful to Jackson Janes from AICGS/The John Hopkins University who organized a seminar in Washington with SAIS in January 2006. My basic policy perception for continental Europa is that weak growth in the Euro zone and in Germany in particular has reasons which can easily be identified. The usual caveat holds here: I am solely responsible for the analysis. The editorial support by Michael Agner, Stephanie Kullmann, and Christian Schröder is deeply appreciated.

Wuppertal and Washington, August 2006   *Paul J.J. Welfens*

Table of Contents

A. Globalization, Specialization and Innovation Dynamics............................1
  A.1 Introduction..1
  A.2 Approaches in Modern Macroeconomics 3
  A.3 Human Capital, Physical Capital and Innovations in Open Economies......7
  A.4 A Critique of the Heckscher-Ohlin-Samuelson Approach.......................11
  A.5 Solving the Leontief Paradox?...14
  A.6 Variations on the Solow Model: Some New Insights for a Monetary
     Economy...20
     A.6.1 A Generalization of the Solow Growth Model.................................20
     A.6.2 Aspects of Empirical Analysis of Economic Development..............28
  A.7 Technological Progress and the Long Run Price Level 34
     A.7.1 Process Innovations 34
     A.7.2 The Model 36
     A.7.2.1 True Long Run Equilibrium in the Money Market.......................36
     A.7.2.2 Long Run Growth Perspective 38
     A.7.3 Conclusions for Analysis of Process Innovations in a Monetary
         Economy 42
     A.7.4 Solow Model and Role of Money for Growth..................................42
     A.7.5 Monetary Growth Model and Tobin Paradox..................................52
     A.7.6 Technological Progress Cycles...55
     A.7.7 Equilibrium and Terms of Trade Aspects in a Simple Open
         Economy Growth Model..57
     A.7.8 International Macroeconomics, FDI and Fiscal and Monetary
         Policy..58
     A.7.9 Long Run Phillips Curve in a Growing Economy 62
     A.7.10 Variable Output Elasticity of Capital 63
  A.8 Foreign Direct Investment and Innovation...65
     A.8.1 Innovation Dynamics and Multinational Companies 65
     A.8.2 Modified Multiplier in Macro Model with FDI Outflows.................77
  A.9 Output Dynamics: Interaction of the Demand Side and the Supply Side .81
  A.10 Growth Accounting Under Unemployment and Okun's Law.................82
  A.11 Innovation, Trade and Foreign Investment 86
  A.12 Conclusions..92
  Appendix A.1: Aggregation in a Two-Sector Growth Model: A Modified
             Solow Approach with Cobb-Douglas Production Functions...94
  Appendix A.2: Two Sector Model..98
  Appendix A.3: Labor Markets with Tradables and Nontradables.....................99
  Appendix A.4: Product Innovations with Schumpeterian Intermediate
             Products: A Simple Formula 102
  Appendix A.5: Medium-term Output and Wage Policies in an
             Open Economy 103

**B. Savings, Investment and Growth: New Approaches for Macro-
economic Modelling** **109**
  B.1 Introduction 109
  B.2 A Medium-term Keynes-Solow Model 111
    B.2.1 Capital Accumulation Dynamics and Profit Maximization 113
    B.2.2 Chosing a Consistent Investment Function and a New
           Consumption Function 115
    B.2.3 Multiplier Analysis 117
  B.3 Conclusions and Possible Extensions 126

C. Economic Integration, Technological Progress and Growth **129**
  C.1 Rich Countries vs. Poor Countries and Economic Integration 129
  C.2 Set-up of the Model 132
    C.2.1 Convergence in a Hybrid Growth Model with Trade and R&D 134
    C.2.2 Profit Maximization in the Hybrid Growth Model 137
  C.3 Asymmetric Foreign Direct Investment in a Two-Country Growth
       Model 138
  C.4 Policy Conclusions 140
  Appendix C.1: Basic Neoclassical Model 142
  Appendix C.2: General Approach and Simulations 142

**D. Impact of the Real Exchange Rate on Trade, Structural Change and
Growth** **146**
  D.1 Introduction 146
  D.2 Reputation, Market Size and Relative Price Effects: A Quasi-Balassa-
       Samuelson Effect 147
  D.3 Real Exchange Rate Dynamics and Economic Effects 150
    D.3.1 Real Exchange Rate and Trade 150
    D.3.2 Real Exchange Rate and Structural Change 150
    D.3.3 Real Exchange Rate and Growth 152
    D.3.3.1 Growth and FDI in a Modified Neoclassical Framework 152
    D.3.3.2 Negative International Spillovers? 157
  D.4 Real Effective Exchange Rate Dynamics in Selected EU
       Countries 158
  D.5 Wages, Prices and the Real Exchange Rate 158
  D.6 Towards an Integrated Macroeconomic Approach 159
  D.7 Medium Term Approach to Product Innovations, Output and the
       Exchange Rate 165
  D.8 Economic Catching-up and Long Term Real Exchange Rate Dynamics 172
  D.9 Policy Implications 176

**E. Macroeconomic Aspects of Opening up, Unemployment, Growth and
Transition** **178**
  E.1 Introduction 178
  E.2 Growth, Trade and Innovation 181
    E.2.1 New Production Function for Open Economies 181

E.2.2 Towards an Integrated Macroeconomic Approach 183
E.3 Growth, Resource Dynamics, Balassa-Samuelson Effects and
      Unemployment 196
   E.3.1 Growth, Natural Resources and Economic Welfare 196
   E.3.2 The Balassa-Samuelson Effect, Unemployment and Exports 197
   E.3.3 Wage Bargaining as Inherent Source of Unemployment? 200
E.4 Product Innovation and Macroeconomic Developments: Schumpeter
      and the Mundell-Fleming Model 206
   E.4.1 The Role of Risk and Innovation 206
   E.4.2 Endogenous Product Innovations in Countries with Similar
          Development Levels 207
E.5 Conclusions and Policy Implications 208
Appendix E.1: Maximization of Total Quasi-Income of Workers through
          Trade Unions 210
Appendix E.2: Mathematical Appendix 213
Appendix E.3: Reflections on EU Eastern Enlargement 215
Appendix E.4: Fiscal Multiplier in a Hybrid Approach 221
Appendix E.5: Reconsidering Aggregate Output in a Two-Sector
          Approach 221

**F. Productivity Shocks, Innovations, Stock Market Dynamics and
   Growth** **224**
   F.1 Introduction 224
   F.2 Traditional and New Approaches to the Exchange Rate and Stock
        Market Dynamics 229
      F.2.1 Stylized Facts of Exchange Rates and Stock Market Prices 229
      F.2.2 A Short-Term Analysis of Financial Market Dynamics and
             Technology Shocks 237
   F.3 Hybrid Model: Combining Interest Parity and Augmented Money
        Market Equilibrium 243
   F.4 Capital Asset Pricing Model and Product Innovations 245
   F.5 Consumption, Volatility and Growth 249
   F.6 Policy Issues and Conclusions 251
   Appendix F.1: Slope of Equilibrium Lines 253
   Appendix F.2: International Bonds Market Integration, Interest Rates and
             Stock Market Volatility 254

G. Innovation Dynamics and Optimum Growth **258**
   G.1 Introduction 258
   G.2 Endogenous Growth, Innovation and Maximum Consumption
        per Capita 261
      G.2.1 Optimum Endogenous Growth 261
      G.2.1.1 Role of Government Consumption 262
      G.2.1.2 New Political Economy 263
      G.2.1.3 High Population Growth vs. Ageing Societies 265
      G.2.1.4 Unemployment and Growth 266

G.2.2 Optimum Growth and Endogenous Growth Modeling in Open
      and Closed Economies 267
G.2.3 Biased Technological Progress and Optimum Growth................... 272
G.3 Policy Implications 273
Appendix G.1: Optimum Quantity of Money.. 276
Appendix G.2: Specialization, Technological Progress and Factor Price
              Ratios 277
Appendix G.3: Endogenous Progress in the Capital Goods Sector 278
Appendix G.4: Simple Differential Equation and Bernoulli Differential
              Equation 280

H. Trade, Structural Change and Growth in an Open Monetary
Economy **282**
H.1. Introduction... 282
H.2. Exchange Rate Dynamics, Relative Prices, Employment and Growth .. 284
      H.2.1 Nominal Exchange Rate, Real Exchange Rate and True Long Run
            Money Market Equilibrium... 284
      H.2.2 Real Exchange Rate, Growth Path and Steady State 289
      H.2.3 Investment, Real Exchange Rate and Employment........................ 293
      H.2.4 Technology, Exchange Rate Changes and the Relative Tradable
            Price 296
H.3 Real Exchange Rate Dynamics and Economic Effects............................ 299
Appendix H.1: Statistical Measures of Structural Change............................ 302
Appendix H.2: Indicators Measuring Structural Change............................... 304

I. Innovations in the Digital Economy: Promotion of R&D and Growth in
Open Economies **305**
I.1 Introduction 305
I.2 Innovations and New Economic Structures in the Digital Economy 308
      I.2.1 Selected Innovation Traits in OECD Countries 308
      I.2.2 Innovation System and Innovation Record 320
      I.2.3 High Technology, ICT Growth and Modernization of the Eco-
            nomic System.. 322
I.3 Theory of Innovation Policy.. 331
      I.3.1 The Standard Case 331
      I.3.1.1 Intermediate Traded Products, R&D Subsidies and Rent-Shifting 333
      I.3.1.2 Macroeconomic Approach: A Schumpeter-Mundell-Flemming
            Model 336
      I.3.1.3 Empirical Insights from the Analysis of Innovation, Growth and
            Structural Change 339
I.4 Policy Conclusions 340
      I.4.1 General Policy Conclusions for Innovation Policy in Open
            Economies 340
      I.4.2 Specific Policy Conclusions for Germany 341
      I.4.2.1 R&D Promotion for Medium Technologies and High-tech
            Industry... 341

I.4.2.2 Skill Upgrading and Reform of the Education System 342
I.4.2.3 Problems with Immigration of Unskilled Labour 342
I.4.2.4 Improving Knowledge Transfer from University to the Business
            Community 343
I.4.2.5 Keeping Skilled Workers and Innovation Leadership in the
            Region 344
I.4.2.6 A European Policy Perspective 345
Appendix I.1: Optimum Product Innovation under Uncertainty 346
Appendix I.2: Product Innovations and Network Effects in a Simple Model 347
Appendix I.3: NACE (EU classification) rev. 1.1 Classification at the
            2-digit level (in parts) 351
Appendix I.4: Model for Digital Innovation 351

J. EU Innovation Policy: Analysis and Critique 358
J.1 Introduction 358
J.2 Innovation Policy in the EU 360
J.3 Innovation Dynamics in OECD Countries 361
    J.3.1 Innovation, Specialization and Growth: Empirical Analysis
            for EU-15 and USA 361
    J.3.2 Comparative Innovation Dynamics 362
    J.3.3 Acceleration of Innovation Dynamics 367
    J.3.4 Specialization in Innovation and ICT Network Perspectives 369
    J.3.5 Openness, Taxation and Growth 374
J.4 Recommendations for Future EU Innovation Policy 376

**K. Financial Market Integration, Interest Rates and Economic
Development 379**
K.1 Introduction 379
K.2 Financial Market Integration in the EU 386
    K.2.1 From Basic Theory to Endogeneous Growth Approaches 386
    K.2.2 Current Account Dynamics: A New Approach 390
    K.2.3 Monetary Integration, Financial Market Integration and Welfare
            Effects 392
K.3 Integration of Financial Markets in the Euro Zone and Global
            Dynamics 397
K.4 Policy Conclusions 398
K.5 FDI and Information and Communication Technology in the
            Dornbusch Model 400
K.5.1 Basics of the Dornbusch Model 400
K.5.2 The Modified Dornbusch Model 401
K.5.3 Conclusions 411
Appendix K.1: Aspects of Transition and Trend Growth in a Setup with
            Technology Shifts 413
Appendix K.2: Uncertainty, Savings and Product Innovations 413
Appendix K.3: A Macro-Model with Unemployment and Endogenous
            Taxation 415

References 418

List of Figures 426

List of Tables 431

A. Globalization, Specialization and Innovation Dynamics

A.1 Introduction

Economic globalization means the combined growth of trade and foreign direct investment (FDI) on a worldwide scale. FDI grew particularly in the 1980s and 1990s, when the role of multinational companies started to grow strongly for various reasons:

- Privatization in many countries around the globe has created a larger menu for international mergers and acquisitions. For example, the infrastructure sector in Europe, Asia, Latin America and Africa has become strongly shaped by multinational companies.
- Regional integration in North America (NAFTA), Latin America (MERCOSUR), Europe (EU, most notably the full establishment of the EU single market in 1992) and Asia (ASEAN) created larger regional markets which in turn, raised the optimum firm size – this in turn implied strong motives for mergers and acquisitions, including international M&As.
- Opening up and systemic transformation in China in the 1980s and in Eastern Europe as well as the former Soviet Union have enlarged both the opportunities for trade and foreign direct investment.

About 1/3 of OECD countries' trade is intra-company trade, that is, trade within multinational companies (MNCs), so that foreign direct investment is crucial for three reasons:

- international trade – which includes trade in intermediate products; and growing intra-industrial trade whose expansion is linked to the rise of per capita income (the demand for differentiated products is a positive function of per capita income, y; and y can be raised by foreign direct investment inflows). Trade, in turn, can be reinforced by regional and global trade liberalization
- capital formation in the host country;
- international technology transfer: as markets for both patents and technologies are quite imperfect, the bulk of technology transfer is either intra-MNC technology transfer or – similar to the exchange of hostages – cross-licensing among MNCs.

There are various types of trade. International differences in preferences, differences in productivity, economies of scale and geographical proximity can all explain international trade. Regional integration schemes also stimulate trade which in turn could raise economic growth through higher investment-GDP ratios or through efficiency gains. LEVINE/RENELT (1992) found that a higher degree of economic openness raises the availability of physical capital but leaves efficiency unchanged. KORMENDI/MEGUIRE (1985) found weak empirical evidence that a higher trade share raises growth through increased efficiency. SHEEHEY (1995) finds that a higher degree of openness – as proxied by the export share – stimulates economic growth and contributes to improved efficiency. This, however, leaves open the question which sectors particularly benefit from economic opening up and trade. As regards foreign direct investment inflows (FDI) such investments could go to the tradables sector – giving a long term stimulus to exports – or the nontradables sector. In both cases, imports of machinery and equipment could increase if the host country is poorly endowed with capital. Foreign investors (e.g., from the US or Germany) often have a tendency to indeed import machinery and equipment from the country where the headquarters is located or use the same supplier from a third country which has successfully specialized as a producer and exporter of machinery and equipment.

Convergence issues and technology dynamics have been found to be interdependent in recent empirical analysis. JUNGMITTAG (2004) shows for the EU15 countries that technological specialization contributes to economic growth. Indeed, there are technological differences among OECD countries so that the assumption of identical production functions across countries – a basic ingredient of the Heckscher-Ohlin approach – cannot easily be defended unless there is technological convergence across countries. Empirical analysis has also shown that OECD countries absolutely abundant in skilled labor are net exporters in R&D-intensive industries and – with relatively weak evidence – that countries with a large domestic market will be net exporters of scale intensive goods (TORSTENSSON, 1998). Economic opening up of eastern Europe has, however, revealed that some of the small transition countries (Hungary and Czech Republic in 2001) have a positive revealed comparative advantage in scale intensive goods (BORBÉLY, 2004).

As regards international economic convergence it is clear that there can be no full convergence in a simple neoclassical framework unless capital intensities have converged in open economies with free trade. According to neoclassical theory, changes in capital intensity are associated with changes in the structure of output and trade. Is it possible to easily classify the structure of output and trade? Furthermore, can standard models of trade explain international trade dynamics? This trade is characterized by trade growing faster than national output and by intra-industrial trade gaining in relative importance in the long run. Moreover, trade with intermediate products seems to be growing relatively fast, namely in the context of growing vertical foreign direct investment.

Free trade brings equalization of relative goods prices and this in turn will bring about equalization of relative factor prices. This is the basic message of the Heckscher-Ohlin-Samuelson (HOS) model which assumes competition in goods markets and factor markets – so that capital K and labor L are rewarded in accordance with their respective marginal product – and considers two goods produced in both countries with identical technologies under autarky. There is factor mobility within each country, but there is no international factor mobility; opening this up leads only to trade. After economic opening up there will be structural change in accordance with changes in the relative price. This is the standard model in economics which is useful for analyzing some of the effects of economic opening up as well as trade liberalization. It is also useful to some extent, for understanding the effects of regional integration – see for example, the case of the EU where considerable economic catching-up has occurred without much migration. This holds at least for the case of southern EU enlargement in the 1980s when Greece (1981) and later Spain and Portugal (1986) joined the Community. However, the HOS approach has certain deficiencies as we will see. Taking a broader look at global trade liberalization is quite useful in this context.

The economic opening up of China has increased the global supply of unskilled workers, and this process will continue as long as there is excess supply in China's agriculture (so well into the middle of the 21st century). China's opening up will thus lead to a fall in wages, at least of the wages of unskilled workers worldwide. The relative fall of unskilled workers' wages in the 1980s and 1990s in the US, the UK and a few other countries has been interpreted in this sense, or it has been attributed to biased technological progress. That is, in model with unskilled labor, skilled labor ("human capital") and capital, the progress rate for unskilled labor is relatively high, and this then reduces the relative wage of unskilled workers worldwide. It is not really clear to which extent biased technological progress or the economic opening up of China has brought about the relative fall of unskilled labor (e.g., WOOD, 1999). To some extent one also could argue that the economic opening up of Eastern Europe and the former Soviet Union has increased the global supply of unskilled labor. (There is a caveat since one may argue that Eastern Europe and the former Soviet Union represent a well-educated labor force.)

A.2 Approaches in Modern Macroeconomics

Modern macroeconomics to a large extent has switched towards approaches which rely on explicit micro foundation and intertemporal optimization analysis. Such work is useful for many issues as it allows the understanding of the models mechanics to some extent. In a survey of modern open economy macroeconomics LANE (2002) points out the important role of the Obstfeld-Rogoff Redux model (OBSTFELD/ROGOFF, 1995) and concludes (p.48): "Although the impact effects of shocks on real variables in many cases are largely similar to those predicted by traditional reduced-form models, the intertemporal nature of the recent models also allows the tracking of dynamic effects. More importantly, the solid micro foundations embedded in these models permits welfare analysis, which can generate some surprising results. In turn, welfare analysis opens the door to rigorous policy evaluation, providing new foundations for the analysis of international policy interdependence. In related fashion, the stochastic versions of these new models are well-designed for making meaningful comparisons across different policy regimes. As is readily apparent…many welfare results are highly sensitive to the precise denomination of price stickiness, the specification of preferences and financial structure. For this reason, any policy recommendations emanating from this literature must be highly qualified."

There is, however, no doubt that models with explicit optimization behaviour often are quite useful. Even if the real world is not characterized by fully flexible prices, a dynamic general equilibrium model with optimizing agents and full price flexibility – e.g. BAXTER/KING (1993) – can be quite useful. This is because it gives a better understanding of fiscal policy transmission effects in a setting with very high price flexibility. So if the expansion of information and communication technology should bring about generally greater price flexibility one can thus get a better idea about the potential relevance of fiscal policy in the age of the digital economy. In the BAXTER/KING model, fiscal policy has a negative wealth effect implied by tax financed, rising government expenditure which brings about a reduction of private consumption along with an increase in labour supply, so that output and employment increase while the wage rate falls – this is a potentially crucial "wealth effect". This view is in sharp contrast to the Keynesian model which implies that expansionary fiscal policy will raise output, consumption and employment. One should note, however, that the BAXTER/KING results rely on the assumption that government's fiscal policy means a rise of government consumption. The alternative, that fiscal policy is exclusively or partly a rise of R&D subsidies and hence a double impulse – namely a rise of aggregate demand (as new R&D equipment is purchased) and a rise of the level of technology (assuming that higher R&D capital stocks translates into a higher level of labour-saving technology or product innovations), is not discussed. In a world economy which is more and more characterized by Schumpeterian competition and where government plays a crucial role with respect to R&D expenditures and human capital formation – complementary to R&D – one should indeed consider the implications of such a supply-side fiscal policy. As we will show some key aspects can be easily highlighted in the context of a neoclassical model; a modified Solow model makes clear that long term expectations with respect to long run equilibrium output must take into account implications of modern growth models. With respect to monetary policy – analyzed in a new neoclassical synthesis approach by LINNEMANN/SCHABERT (2003) – there are also interesting aspects in this context. From the perspective adopted here the most interesting policy perspectives concern a KEYNES-SOLOW model with money as the production function. An adequately specified growth model helps to avoid the TOBIN paradox according to which the introduction of money in a growth model implies a lower steady state capital intensity and hence a lower per captia income than the non-monetary SOLOW growth model (the KEYNES-SOLOW model developed here allows, in principle, the linking of the long run equilibrium solution of various growth models into a consistent medium term modelling).

To some extent there is a trade-off between analytical rigor and relevance. Ideally one would look for an intertemporal optimization framework with differentiated goods and price adjustment costs as well as process innovations. However, it does not really make sense to use very complex models when simple macro modelling gives complex analytical results. The microeconomic underpinning is, however, quite useful in the field of welfare analysis. KING (1993) has voiced harsh criticism about the viability of the traditional Keynesian IS-LM model since it neglects the role of expectations; in his view rational expectations are a key ingredient of modern macroeconomics. PALACIO-VERA (2005) has argued that recent approaches that drop the LM curve and replace it through an interest rate reaction function – as suggested by ROMER (2000) - are not really consistent with reality and do not consistently cover the interdependence of supply and demand. With respect to the real world one may point out that adjustment cost functions for investors – see e.g. ABEL/BLANCHARD, 1983 – are important and that nominal price stickiness in the form of CALVO (1983) and YUN (1996) is useful for analyzing certain issues; the approach of YUN (1996) implies that profit maximization of symmetrical firms leads to a condition which states that the deviation of current inflation π_t from the steady state inflation $\pi\#$ – we dub this excess inflation - is a positive function of the deviation of real money balances from its steady state value m# (weighted with the level of consumption C); moreover, the expected inflation rate for t+1 positively affects "excess inflation".

A useful new neoclassical synthesis is the GOODFRIEND/KING (1997) approach and a rather simple hybrid model is the analysis of GOODFRIEND (2004). Basically, the model of GOODFRIEND (2004) refers to a closed economy and puts the focus on intertemporal optimization. Households maximize utility which refers to present consumption C_1 and future consumption C_2, at the same time households consider the work-leisure trade off (with leisure time F and working time L adding up to unity) which leads to a labour supply function L^s which positively depends on the real wage rate w=: W/P (W is nominal wage, P the price level of consumption goods) and negatively on consumption. Firms use a mark-up μ and are active in a regime with monopolistic competition.

The household's utility function is given by $U(C_1, C_2)$ where utility refers to consumption in period 1 and period 2. Assuming given expected real income Y_1 and Y_2 the budget constraint for households – able to save or borrow at interest rate r - can be stated as $C_1+C_2/(1+r)=Y_1+Y_2/(1+r)$ which implies with a logarithmic utility function $U(C_1,C_2) = \ln C_1 + [1/(1+\rho)]\ln C_2$. Here ρ is the time preference rate. The well-known result is $C_2/C_1 = [1+r]/[1+\rho]$. Hence consumption will rise over time if the real interest rate exceeds the time preference rate. Labour supply – based on a logarithmic utility function (and taking into account the constraint that leisure time plus working time adds up to unity) is given by $L^s = 1 - [C/w]$ where w is the real wage rate W/P (with W denoting the nominal wage rate and P he price of consumer goods). Labour productivity is denoted as α and a constant mark-up $\mu - P/k'$ is assumed; note that marginal costs $k'=W/\alpha$ and hence $\mu = \alpha/[W/P]= \alpha/w$. The equilibrium wage then is $w\# = \alpha/\mu\#$ and the equilibrium labour supply is equal to $L^s = 1- [\alpha L/(\alpha/\mu)] = 1/[1+\mu\#]$. Equilibrium consumption is $C\# = \alpha/[1+\mu]$. The role of the interest rate becomes clear from the equilibrium expression $(1+r\#)= (1+\rho)(\alpha_2/\alpha_1)$ so that a rise of labour productivity over time will raise the long run real interest rate. Inflation π is determined by the expected trend inflation rate $E(\pi)$ plus a term reflecting the impact of actual and future mark-up rates $\pi = f(\mu_1, E\mu_2) + E(\pi)$. This model is indeed useful as a primer for analyzing inflation problems and monetary policy effectiveness in a closed economy. However, in the following analysis we rarely will deal with inflation and we often adopt a more conventional approach which we modify in various ways.

With respect to the GOODFRIEND approach one should note one simple interesting modification with respect to the role of productivity growth: If we assume that consumers anticipate that real consumption expenditures will raise aggregate output and hence individual income (as the rational central planner would do), we will use a modified condition for utility maximization:

$$C_2/C_1 = [1+r]/[1+\rho]\{(1-\partial Y/\partial C_1)/(1-\partial Y/\partial C_2)\} \tag{1}$$

The additional term is {…} which is positive as $\partial Y/\partial C_i$ is positive (for i=1,2); basically, there are two possible interpretations as one may consider an economy with consumption plus investment and look at first at a situation with initial unemployment and full employment in period 2; or at full employment in both periods. In a model with initial unemployment $\partial Y/\partial C_1$ this indicates by how much quasi-equilibrium output – as defined by the goods market equilibrium condition – is raised through a rise of C and a fall of L. In a permanent full employment economy $\partial Y/\partial C_2$ is the marginal product of labour in the overall economy occurring as a consequence of higher consumption and hence lower labour input.

Taking logs (and using $\ln[1+x]\approx x$) in the modified equilibrium condition for households gives:

$$\ln (C_2/C_1)= (r-\rho)[\partial Y/\partial C_2 - \partial Y/\partial C_1] \tag{2}$$

Interpreting $\partial Y/\partial C_i$ as the marginal product of the consumption goods sector we can argue that the ratio C_2/C_1 will rise over time if productivity – see the term […] on the RHS of the equation - is increasing over time.

One should note that complex dynamic optimization analyis does not always give crucial additional insights and certainly model-building will consider the relative analytical benefit from increased complexity; e.g. the message from the simple (GOODFRIEND) household optimization approach does not differ much from the continuous optimization analysis (see e.g. DIXIT, 1990, ch. 10) when households maximize discounted utility U – depending on consumption C – over an infinite time span (from t=0 to ∞): The representative household maximizes $\int U(c)\ e^{,-\rho t}\ dt$ subject to the constraint $dK/dt = F(K) -\delta K - C$; here C is consumption at point t, δ the depreciation rate of capital K and F(K) is a simple production function with standard properties. The Hamiltonian is $H= U(C)\ e^{,-\rho t}+\pi'[F(K) -\delta K - C]$ and the conditions dH/dC= 0 and $d\pi'/dt = -\partial H/\partial K$ lead to the optimum consumption plan described by $d\ln C/dt = [F'(K) – (\rho+\delta)]/\varepsilon$. Note that we have assumed (with $\varepsilon>0$) a convenient utility function $U(C)= C^{1-\varepsilon}/1-\varepsilon$ so that the parameter $\varepsilon = - CU''/U'$. As long as the marginal product of capital exceeds $\rho+\delta$ consumption will increase over time. Since one can show that the capital stock K will finally reach a steady state K# it is clear that consumption then will be stationary and hence dlnC/dt=0 if $F'(K)=\rho+\delta$; the latter indeed is the condition for profit maximization if we replace the time preference rate by the real interest rate.

Certainly, the GOODFRIEND setup is an interesting approach. However, there are alternative models which refer both to the closed and the open economy. An important aspect emphasized in the following analysis is the focus on medium term and long run policy perspectives. In ageing societies – with longevity increasing – long term decision-making might indeed become more important. Modern information and communication technology also could reinforce the emphasis on long run planning (WELFENS, 2005).

As long as the basic behavioural functions are in line with well established empirical findings one should not worry too much about explicit microeconomic foundations since taking into account the broad range of alternative utility functions used in modern Economics allows various aggregate functions to be derived rather easily. From an evolutionary perspective one also should emphasize that behavioural patterns rarely are characterized by strict profit maximization. Often managers in firms will simply want to achieve certain benchmarks, e.g. realize the same benchmark as the industry leader. Whether or not the industry leader itself is a profit-maximizing company remains to be seen. Finally, what looks like alternative approaches at first sight could in effect be complementary modelling efforts; e.g. in a period of turbulence many individuals will place less emphasis on long run equilibrium perspectives but rather on short term adjustment. As economic developments converge to normal dynamics in the medium term a more long term orientation might become more common again.

A.3 Human Capital, Physical Capital and Innovations in Open Economies

An important element of growth dynamics is human capital formation. This has been emphasized by various authors, including LUCAS (1988) and GOULD/ /RUFFIN (1995). The mechanics of integrating human capital are rather simple if we follow MANKIW ET AL. (1992) as well as GOULD/RUFFIN. Output can be consumed, invested in physical capital formation or invested in the formation of human capital so that the equilibrium condition for the goods market reads (δ denotes the depreciation rate; s' and s" are positive parameters):

$$dK/dt + \delta K + dH/dt + \delta H = [s'+s'']Y \qquad (A.I)$$

The share of output devoted to gross physical capital formation is s' and the share devoted to human capital formation is s". The aggregate production function is given by $y(t) = A(t) f(k(t), h(t)$ where L is labor, $y=:Y/L$, $k=:K/L$, $H=:H/L$ and A is the level of technology, so that the dynamic equations for dk/dt and for dh/dt are – with $s=:s'+s''$, $n=:dlnL/dt$, $a=:dln\Lambda/dt$ given by

$$dk/dt = (s-s'') f(k,h) - [n+a+\delta]k \qquad (A.II)$$

$$dh/dt = s'' f(k,h) - [n+a+\delta]h \qquad (A.III)$$

Equilibrium requires – this is an important modification compared to MANKIW ET AL. – that the marginal product of H (f_h) is equal to the marginal product of K (f_k); hence

$$f_k = f_h \qquad (A.IV)$$

Indeed WIILLIS (1986) and McMAHON (1991) have provided some evidence that the rate of return to physical capital is similar to the rate of return to schooling (on human capital and growth see also ROMER, 1990a and STOKEY, N.L., 1991). If we assume that the common rate of return is equal to the real interest rate r the slope of the schedule for dk/dt= 0 – implying a steady state value k# – is given by

$$dk/dh = [s'/r]/[n+a+\delta-s'r] \qquad\qquad (A.V)$$

The slope for the dh/dt= 0 schedule is given by

$$dk/dh = [s''/r]/[n+a+\delta-s''r] \qquad\qquad (A.VI)$$

Due to stability requirements, one may assume that the curve indicating dk/dt=0 is steeper than that for dk/dt=0. If the savings rate s'' is chosen in such a way that dk/dt=0 curve and the dh/dt=0 curve intersect on the fk=fh curve, we get a combination of k and h representating a steady state. GOULD and RUFFIN implement the model on the basis of a Cobb-Douglas function in which A is Harrod-neutral progress with respect to L.

$$Y = K^{\beta}H^{\beta'} (AL^{1-\beta-\beta'} \qquad\qquad (A.VII)$$

The steady state values are given by

$$k\# = s'^{\,1-\beta'} s''^{\beta'}/[n+a+\delta]^{\,1/1-\beta-\beta'} \qquad\qquad (A.VIII)$$

$$h\# = s'^{\,1-\beta} s''^{\beta}/[n+a+\delta]^{1/1--\beta-\beta'} \qquad\qquad (A.IX)$$

If the rate of return on physical capital is equal to the rate of return on human capital, the implication is that

$$\beta' k\# = \beta h\# \qquad\qquad (A.X))$$

and taking into account the steady state solutions gives:

$$s'/s'' = \beta/\beta' \qquad\qquad (A.XI)$$

Moreover, since s= s'+s'', one obtains:

$$s' = s\beta/(\beta+\beta') \qquad\qquad (A.XII)$$

$$s'' = s\beta'/(\beta+\beta') \qquad\qquad (A.XIII)$$

Note that in the steady state, we have

$$\ln y(t) = \ln A_0 + at +[(\beta+\beta')(1-\beta-\beta')\ln[s/(n+a+\delta)] \qquad\qquad (A.XIV)$$

Considering the economy in the vicinity of the steady state, we have in the vicinity of the steady state:

$$d\ln(y(t))/dt = \lambda[\ln(y\#) – \ln(y_0)] \qquad\qquad (A.XV)$$

The adjustment speed $\lambda=(n+a+\delta)(1-\beta-\beta')$. The solution of the differential equation is (with e' denoting the Euler number):

$$\ln(y\#) – \ln(y_0) = (1 - e'^{-\lambda t})\ln(y\#) – (1 - e'^{-\lambda t})\ln(y_0) \qquad\qquad (A.XVI)$$

Next we substitute $\ln y(t) = \ln A_0 + at +[(\beta+\beta')(1-\beta-\beta')\ln[s/(n+a+\delta)]$ in this equation and obtain:

$$\ln[y(t)/y(0)] = C + (1 - e^{,-\lambda t})[(\beta+\beta')(1-\beta-\beta')\ln[s/(n+a+\delta)] - \qquad \text{(A.XVII)}$$

$$(1 - e^{,-\lambda t})\ln(y_0)$$

Note that C is defined as $C = (1 - e^{,-\lambda t})(\ln A_0 + at)$.

GOULD/RUFFIN use the MANKIW ET AL. equation for $\ln[y(t)/y(0)]$ in a modified form, adding a term $\eta \ln H_0$ to capture additional effects of human capital. They find a significant positive effect for H_0. GOULD/RUFFIN discuss how economic openness affects growth, and they argue that in an open economy model both countries can benefit from the human capital stock in both countries. The authors rightly emphasize that endogenous two-sector growth model in open economies could be characterized by higher growth due to adjustment pressure from free trade leading to a shift of resources to the dynamic sector. One also should note that in the model of GROSSMAN/HELPMAN (1991) – with two factors, three sectors, including an R&D sector – the innovation sector reinforces the profitability of high technology goods and effectively stimulates human capital formation which in turn implies reduced costs of R&D and hence higher innovation dynamics (on some two-sector aspects, see the appendix). Free trade/trade liberalization in a country which has a comparative advantage in R&D will contribute in this endogenous growth setting to higher growth while the country with a comparative disadvantage will experience a lower growth rate as resources move out of the innovation sector. In their empirical analysis, GOULD/RUFFIN find that the human capital variable has a higher effect on growth than in a closed economy. There is, however, not a simple explanation for this.

Here one might consider a new explanation for a link between human capital accumulation and growth in open economies:

- a higher stock of human capital implies a higher demand for differentiated products, as we assume that people's love for variety is a positive function of the level of education; thus, there is a human capital-based positive STIGLITZ effect (by implication one should consider a STIGLITZ utility function with a finite number of goods n'; human capital accumulation will raise the number of varieties produced which means that the number of additional new varieties will exceed the number of basic varieties dropped from the production assortment).

- Given rising demand for product varieties, firms will indeed reinforce innovations and launch new product innovations. Those will fetch higher prices than standard products, but it is also true that the price of existing varieties will fall as new and superior alternatives emerge. We assume that at least part of the old varieties will survive – at reduced market-clearing prices –, namely due to "second-tier economies of scale" which indeed must be exploited by producers facing declining prices for older product varieties. Second tier economies of scale refer to the fact that all sophisticated products can be decomposed into basic intermediate products which may can be produced under static or dynamic economies of scale (tier one economies of scale would refer to economies of scale in the production of final goods). If product innovations esentially emply that the overall number of product varieties which exist in the market is rising, there will be increasing opportunities for exploiting scale economies in the production of intermediate products, provided that all existing varieties require at least one unit of the respective component (e.g., a computer chip). As all standardized economies of scale products are quite price sensitive, those intermediate products are naturally product-cycle trade goods. The more intensive price competition is, the more important international outsourcing and offshoring (the latter involving foreign direct investment – typically for the production of technology-intensive components) is. The implication here is that human capital formation can generate "SCHUMPETER-STIGLITZ effects" in combination with economies of sacle and growing international trade in intermediate products.

The hypothesis stated here implies that increasing human capital formation in OECD countries and Newly Industrializing Countries indeed stimulates international trade and foreign direct investment – including technology transfer – so that human capital formation in open economies should bring a higher growth effect than in closed economies.

As regards advantages in the production of scale intensive products, one may assume that large economies such as the US or Germany have favourable production conditions in scale-intensive sectors. While the US is richly endowed with capital, it is not clear that the country has a special advantage in producing machinery & equipment since machinery & equipment are not scale-intensive. Rather, it is knowledge-intensive so that relatively small economies with a relative abundance of skilled labor should be particularly competitive in the production of innovative machinery & equipment (this sector represents highly customized Schumpeterian products). This points to the particular importance of education policy in small open economies. From this perspective, small open economies specialized in knowledge-intensive production – and active in innovations in the tradables goods sector – could benefit from specialization patterns which emphasize both human capital formation and skilled labor. The endogenous growth effects associated with such specialization could explain why many small open economies have achieved relatively high per capita incomes so that there is no large gap between the per capita income of the US and that of many leading small OECD countries. Taking into account trade in scale-intensive products – with some of them also being knowledge-intensive (e.g., aircraft, software) – and assuming that the largest economy, the US, has sufficient economic leverage (i.e., a large home market) and political leverage to specialize in the Schumpeterian scale-intensive products, it would be natural to expect that the US has a clear leadership in per capita income among OECD countries. Markets, which are characterized both by scale economies and high R&D intensity, will be characterized by monopolistic competition and high Schumpeterian rents which effectively imply a rather high US per capita income. Taking these considerations into account one also should not be surprised to find that the US is not generally specialized in capital-intensive goods – this is potentially important in understanding the Leontief paradox. Even more important could be the fact that the high capital intensity of the US partly reflects high capital intensity in infrastructure sectors which largely represent the nontradables sector. One should, however, consider the generally trade-promoting effect of infrastructure investment; lower transportation costs typically also imply lower transportation costs to the next international airport or sea port.

The issues explored subsequently are rather simple as we often will rely on the one sector neoclassical growth model and augmented versions of the Mundell Flemming model (while incorporating product innovations). The notion of competitiveness used subsequently is not simply the ability to sell but the ability to generate long term revenues: Thus we are interested not only in quantity of product X sold in the market but in the long term evolution of export unit values as well. Countries may be specialized in various product groups – e.g. capital intensive, knowledge-intensive etc. If a country is specialized in product groups where a stable comparative advantage can be combined with improved export unit values we consider this as a clear indication of international competitiveness. Improving export unit values in the long run is linked to innovativeness. Explaining dynamic specialization patterns in a Schumpeterian world with foreign direct investment is a crucial challenge in Economics. Later we will present many statistics on (modified) RCA and export unit values in selected OECD countries.

A.4 A Critique of the Heckscher-Ohlin-Samuelson Approach

The workhorse of International Economics is the HOS approach which helps to understand the dynamics of trade and structural change in countries which differ in terms of relative factor endowments. Following the Heckscher-Ohlin-Samuelson approach (simple two country model with factors labor and capital) the country richly endowed with unskilled labor – country I which is assumed to have a relatively low per capita income – will specialize in labor intensive products. The export of labor-intensive products will start and expand which effectively implies a gradual rise in the wage-real interest ratio. As a result, the supply of unskilled labor in country II which imports the labor intensively produced good will increase. Country II in turn, will specialize in the production and export of goods which use capital intensively; the relatively poor country I, will import capita intensive goods which will effectively reduce the supply price of capital – the factor price ratio, namely the ratio of the real interest rate to the real wage rate will fall. Factor Price Equalization will occur in the long run.

The HOS approach has its problems since it assumes that the capital intensity in country I and II are given, while the Factor Price Ratio is changing. This is, of course, inconsistent since profit maximization implies that the capital intensity $k=:K/L$ (K is capital, L is labor) is a positive function of the wage-real interest rate ratio. Thus, the equalization of factor prices should cause an equalization of capital intensities across countries. As capital intensities have differed initially, there must be some accumulation of capital in the medium term. In particular the poor country must raise the capital intensity faster than the rich country. This holds since per capita income $y=: f(k)$, and technologies in both countries are assumed to be identical in the HOS model. With a linear homogenous production function and competition in goods and factor markets we have y= w + rk where w is the real wage rate and r the real interest rate so that w/r=w*/r* implies – with * denoting foreign variables – f(k(w/r)=f*(k*(w*/r*) and hence y=y*). This is difficult to reconcile with the neoclassical growth theory which suggests in a context of a model – with s, n and δ denoting the exogenous savings rate, the growth rate of the population and the capital depreciation rate, respectively - with a simple Cobb-Douglas function y=bk$^\beta$ and y*=bk*$^\beta$ that in long term equilibrium per capita income is given in the home country I by

$$y=b\{s/[n+\delta]\}^{\beta/1-\beta} \tag{A.1}$$

For the foreign country II we have

$$y^*=b\{s^*/[n^*+\delta^*]\}^{\beta/1-\beta} \tag{A.2}$$

As technologies are assumed to be identical in both countries, ß*=ß, δ*=δ and b*=b. The problem is that there is no mechanism which suggests an endogenous convergence of s/n=s*/n*; unless one assumes that both the savings rate and the growth rate of the population depend on per capita income or capital intensity.

Taking a look at the EU and China or at the US and China: should one expect that relatively poor Poland or China will mainly export investment goods to the EU15 (or the US) while the EU (or the US) will mainly export consumer goods? This is exactly what the HOS approach in combination with standard neoclassical growth theory suggests: In a dynamic perspective – with capital accumulation and growth – the HOS approach indeed raises a serious problem, namely that the neoclassical growth model is stable only if one assumes that the capital intensity of investment goods are higher than that of consumption goods. By implication, the rich country – with a high capital intensity – will mainly or exclusively export consumption goods. The poor country – with a low capital intensity – will mainly or exclusively export investment goods. This is obviously, totally unrealistic.

How can one reconcile neoclassical trade theory and neoclassical growth theory? The obvious and realistic way is as follows. Start with the observation that a country is likely to specialize in production and export of machinery and equipment if the domestic market for capital goods is relatively large and competitive. The first requirement implies that there is a high overall capital intensity which implies that workers and managers in this economy have much experience and expertise with modern machinery and equipments. Note that we do not say anything about the relative capital intensity of the production of sector 1 (investment good) or of sector 2 (consumption good). However, there are two constraints, namely that overall capital stock K=K'+K" where K' is the capital stock in sector 1 and K" the capital stock employed in sector 2 and we have a similar restriction for labor, namely L=L'+L". Assume that the production of investment goods can be written in country I, richly endowed with capital, as

$$Y' = b'K'^{\beta'} L'^{1-\beta'} \tag{A.3}$$

and output in the consumption goods industry is

$$Y" = b"K"^{\beta"} L"^{1-\beta"}$$ (A.4)

We assume $0<\beta'<1$ and $0<\beta"<1$ and that capital intensity in the consumption goods sector is higher than in the investment goods sector (Country I which is capital rich and has a higher per capita income than country II will then increase output of consumption goods and export in particular consumption goods while country II – the poor country – would specialize in the production of investment goods). Now, let us assume that there are cross-sectoral spillovers in the sense that using capital goods in the consumption goods sector – or cumulated past investment experience – generates useful knowledge for sector 1 where optimal combination of K' and L' can indeed be achieved only by using all experiences in the sector using investment goods intensively: the consumption goods sector. That is, there are positive cross-sector productivity spillover effects. We may thus replace the parameter b' in equation (A.3) by the term $bK"^{\sigma}$ where $K"^{\sigma}$ reflect the cross-sector spillover effect. Hence, the effective production function for the investment goods sector reads:

$$Y' = bK"^{\sigma} K'^{\beta'} L'^{1-\beta'}$$ (A.5a)

Effectively the overall capital stock K (K= K'+ K" so that we write $Y'= b[K-K']^{\sigma} K'^{\beta'} L'^{1-\beta'}$) affects the production of investment goods which at a sectoral level is reflecting the concept of learning by doing (ARROW, 1962) and is also similar to the approach of ROMER (1986) which, however, has its focus on the aggregate production function. The emphasis here on the sectoral spillover effect is indeed, crucial as we will also show in our subsequent discussion of the Leontief paradox which can be solved by the mechanism presented here. As regards the positive cross-sectoral productivity effect in the investment goods sector one will have to carefully study empirically, whether the spillover is mainly related to the use of capital equipment or both to the use of equipment in sector 2 and to the past cumulated production in sector 1 (suggesting a virtuous circle of producing investment goods where the benefits could obviously be related to the size of the economy). This question has also been important in the debate about the New Economy where the evidence suggests that technological progress and learning by doing effects are very fast in the production of information and communication technology (ICT) while the use of ICT is less dynamic in terms of productivity growth. Note also that the productivity spillovers could be enhanced through the presence of human capital.

For simplicity we assume the special case that K'=K" (and we assume that L'>L" so that apparent capital intensity in sector 1 is lower than in the consumption sector) so that we can rewrite the above equation

$$Y" = b K'^{\sigma+\beta'} L'^{1-\beta'}$$ (A.5b)

The approach presented is plausible and can solve the above-mentioned inconsistency. The apparent capital intensity in the investment goods sector is lower than in the consumption goods sector, but the effective capital goods intensity in the investment goods sector is higher than in the consumption goods sector. Factor proportion theory now suggests that the capital-rich country will specialize toward production and export of investment goods (so the US or EU15 will export investment goods to Poland or China).

A.5 Solving the Leontief Paradox?

Our simple approach could also shed light on the Leontief paradox - dealing with application of the HOS approach to the US: The empirical analysis of LEONTIEF (1953, 1956) found that the US – a country which is obviously relatively capital abundant – has a comparative advantage in labor intensive products: labor intensive products, including machinery and equipment, are exported while capital intensive goods (from the UK and other countries) are imported. As is well known, LEONTIEF did not really analyze figures for the factor intensity of other countries exporting to the US, rather he looked at import-competing industries and their relative factor contents as a means to indirectly detect the factor intensity of imported products. The assumption was, of course, that production technology in the US and abroad was the same. However, correct analysis of effective factor content might well reveal that certain goods were misspecified in terms of effective factor intensities. Indeed, taking import competing firms and sectors, respectively, as a substitute for analyzing exports of foreign countries can be quite misleading. As capital intensities differ across countries cross-sectoral national spillover effects will differ. The US, having the highest absolute capital stock among all industrialized countries, might be shaped by the following spillover mechanism: A high capital intensity in the US consumption goods sector generates relatively high learning-by-doing effects for the US investment goods industry whose effective capital intensity thus is higher than the statistically-measured capital intensity. Taking into account such spillover effects, the US investment goods sector is capital intensive and not labor intensive (We disregard the influence of human capital which already has been discussed in the literature as a mechanism to explain the Leontief Paradox.). Moreover, the spillover effects relevant for the US import-competing industries are different from the spillovers relevant for the UK export industry. If we consider the sector machinery and equipment in the UK, the relatively small capital stock of the UK will generate positive spillover effects while the productivity of machinery and equipment in the US benefits from the overall US capital stock – that is there is the direct effect of the capital stock of the sector employed in machinery and equipment plus the spillover effect from the capital stock in the consumption goods industry of the US in which the investment goods sector will differ across countries. Thus importing competing sectors' factor contents can be quite misleading when the task is to assess the effective relative factor proportions and the effective factor content of exports of supplier countries, respectively.

RCAs in Machinery and Equipment

Taking a closer look at the revealed comparative advantage (RCA) in the field of machinery and equipment (M&E) we can clearly see that Germany and some other EU15 countries, have a positive RCA in machinery and equipment while China and east European accession countries have a negative RCA in this field. Assuming that sectoral patents (PATM&E) also affect competitiveness we can run a cross-country regression:

$$RCAM\&E = a_0 + a_1PATM\&E + a_2K'/K'^* + a_3L'/L'^* + a_4K + \varepsilon \qquad (A.6)$$

We expect a positive sign for a_4; however, K also is an implicit indicator for the size of the home market and hence for opportunities to exploit economies of scale so that production of scale-intensive goods is favored by a high GDP. A more refined specification thus is to consider $a_4K+a_5K^2$ where a_5 is expected to be negative which implies a critical size K^c beyond which K contributes to an unfavourable RCA in M&E.

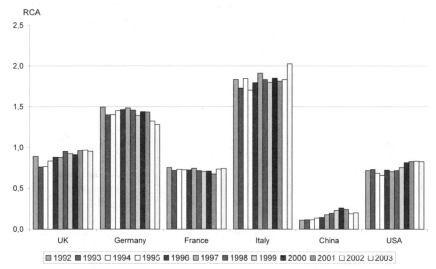

Fig. 1. RCAs for Machinery & Equipment in Selected Countries, 1992-2003

Regarding further options to come up with a refined and more realistic HOS model, it is clear that an obvious assumption which should be relaxed is that technologies are the same in both countries. If country II has a high capital intensity – and if machinery and equipment is not falling like manna from heaven – one may assume that country II has a technological advantage in the production of capital goods, and as international technology transfer is costly and since patents exist – those provide necessary incentives for innovations – one should not assume that the technology in both countries is identical. Even more important, the types of goods that can be produced are not the same in country I and II. This assumption has dramatic implications as the price index $P=p_1^\alpha p_2^{1-\alpha}$ and in country II – producing by assumption a third high technology good – the price index is $P^* = p_{1*}^{\alpha^*} p_{2*}^{\alpha^{*'}} p_3^{1-\alpha^*-\alpha^{*'}}$. If the high-technology good is a tradable good, we still could have a uniform international relative price, namely $=p_1/p_2 ==p_{1*}/p_{2*}$. However, it is clear that in a comprehensive way, namely taking into account not only goods 1 and 2 but also the high-tech good 3 - there is no common relative price. Hence, there can be no factor prize equalization. If good 3 is capital intensive the fact that it is employed in a high-technology sector naturally means that the rate of return on capital in this sector is above the average rate of return. The marginal product of capital expressed in units of the consumption good – say good 1 – must be relatively high either because the relative price of the high-technology good will reflect a Schumpeterian monopoly element or because investors in risky innovative sectors demand and get a risk premium R so that the marginal product of capital in the high-technology sector is not equal to r* but to r*+R. It is also clear that there cannot be such a thing as the law of one price in the simplistic form P=eP*.

Innovation is not really considered in the HOS model. As regards innovation we distinguish between product innovations – that is novel products – and process innovations which bring about a reduction of costs. A product innovation means that the demand curve is rotating to the right in p-q-space.

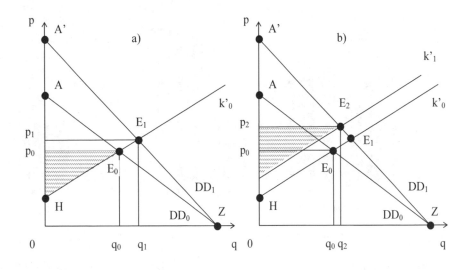

Fig. 2. Product Innovations and Changes of Costs

If the marginal costs curve is upward-sloping, the effect is a rise of the equilibrium price and of the equilibrium output. If product innovations were costly profit-maximizing firms would undertake any possible product innovation as such innovations raise (residual) profits. Compare the triangle P_1E_1H and the initial triangle p_0E_0H in the following graph. Product innovations are however not costly, rather it is necessary to incur some additional costs which could be purely fixed costs (the case of pharmaceuticals) or which might raise marginal costs as more complex production technologies become necessary – see the diagram in part b) which shows both an upward rotation of the demand curve and an upward shift of the marginal costs curve. Thus, there is a problem of optimal product innovations. In reality, product innovations often go along with process innovations as new products can often be built only on new machinery and equipment which embody new technologies. Firms in technology intensive sectors will normally further consider an optimization problem, namely that expenditures on research and development (R&D) have to be split between projects with a focus on product innovations and projects with a focus on process innovations.

Innovations are a key feature of the modern economy. At the same time it is true that – according to DUNNING (1977) – multinational companies are characterized by ownerspecific advantages which typically are technological advantages. As multinational companies have become increasingly important in the 20th century and since foreign direct investment (FDI) inflows and FDI outflows globally are very asymmetrically distributed, it must be true that technologies differ across countries. Taking a look at the EU15 or the EU25 also reveals considerable differences in FDI per capita or FDI relative to GDP. Given the growing role of foreign direct investment it would seem natural to incorporate FDI in a refined HOS model and to also consider differences in technologies across countries and their effects on income, inflation and employment – or one might want to study technological catching-up dynamics. This, however, is not so easy.

The modelling challenge is compounded further by the existence of nontradable goods. One might even study a model without trade but with foreign direct investment flowing from country I to II (or from II to I) where all FDI accrues only to the nontradables sector. If FDI inflows are greenfield investments, one may anticipate both a boost to capital accumulation and technology transfer. If FDI inflows are merely international mergers and acquisitions, there might only be a modest technology transfer. As FDI inflows raise capital intensity of the overall economy, this will affect the relative factor prices. Now, suppose that FDI inflows occur in an economy which has also opened up to trade. Then FDI inflows in the nontradables sector will raise the wage-real interest ratio which undermines the international competitiveness in a country which initially is characterized as richly endowed with labor. However, if capital accumulation in country II is faster than in country I, one still has to anticipate that labor-intensive exports of country I will increase – in international economics it is the relative factor endowment which matters. Problems become more complex if investment is associated with a certain bias in technological progress, a topic which we will largely ignore in the analysis. To put it differently, we will concentrate on Harrod-neutral, that is, laboraugmenting technological progress.

A final element which makes the analysis of structural change and growth difficult is the role of intermediate products. In the New Growth Theory intermediate products are considered to be a source of growth. International trade with intermediate products facilitates exploitation of economies of scale and allows at the same time, to build more product varieties which in some models itself, is conducive to growth. The problem which really occurs in a simple two country model with two intermediate goods and two final goods – with country I and country II each exporting one intermediate product and one final product – is that it is very difficult to define in certain cases which country is specialized in exports in which way. Take as a starting point the case that country I is producing and exporting automobiles (A' sector) while country II is producing computers (C'-sector) and exporting both computers and engines for automobiles (intermediate product sector a') to be produced in I. Country I is also producing and exporting computer chips (c-sector) which are used in the production of computers in country II. Assume that the initial valued-added in the A-industry and the C-industry and in the a-industry and the c-industry are as follows where the share in value-added of the final product is in brackets.

Table 1. Dynamics of Specialization in the Case of Trade in Intermediate Products (1/2 of final product is assumed to be exported)

SITUATION in t_o	COUNTRY I	COUNTRY II
A-industry	Automobiles (A'=70%)	Engines (a=30%)
C-industry	Chips (c=20%)	Computers (C'=80%)

SITUATION in t_n	COUNTRY I	Country II
A-industry	Automobiles (A'= 40%)	Engines (a=60%)
C-industry	Chips (c=70%)	Computers (C'=30%)

One may characterize both countries by saying that country I is strongly specialized in the export of automobiles while country II is strongly specialized in the export of computers. Now assume that some years later we observe the following picture: Based on sales, one would argue that specialization has not changed, but based on value-added, one could indeed argue that country I is strongly specialized in the export of computers while country II is strongly specialized in the export of automobiles. Specialization in production and specialization of exports could diverge, namely to the extent that the growth rate of the number of computers is relatively high in country II in t_n: The share of value-added in the global computer sector has fallen, but the share of computer exports in country II's overall exports could rise. This will happen if the number of computers exported rises strongly while the number of engines exported falls. The situation indeed would be even more paradoxical if the supply of intermediate products came from subsidiaries (abroad) of the firm producing the respective final product. In the case of Germany, statistics for the 1990s show that a high share of imports is indeed built into export products. The share of imported intermediate products increased from 27% in 1991 to 38% in 2002, in the case of the automotive industry where international outsourcing through vertical FDI is often observed. In the case of the computer industry the share of imported intermediate products even rose from about 45% in the mid-1980s to 57% in 1991, and to 80% in 2002. If in the period 1980-2002 Germany's exports of computers increased relative to overall exports should one argue that Germany's export specialization with respect to computers was re-inforced? Probably not. Obviously, one can classify trade specialization only if one takes into account the global input-output table. Here one finds a challenge for all statistical offices of the world, and probably one for the World Bank as well.

How would the international income distribution be if intermediate products traded would represent close to 50% of the respective value-added in both sectors? The answer is that it depends which sector is characterized by the higher Schum-peterian mark-up factor in final production. It is well-known that the firm produc-ing the final product – say in the automotive industry – normally has a higher profit rate than the supplier firms, a fact which might partly be related to the size of the firm at different stages of the overall production process. If the Schumpete-rian mark-up factor is positively related to technology intensity (one good is me-dium technology, the other high tech), the country with the final production of the high-technology good has bright prospects to have a lead in international per cap-ita income comparison provided value-added of the high-tech sector is relatively large. One might think of the computer sector as being a high tech sector. How-ever, a caveat is necessary to the extent that the intermediate product is the real high-technology element of the computer. In this case, Schumpeterian rents will accrue to the chip makers while firms assembling the final product will not get much of a Schumpeterian rent. Thus it is not surprising that computers produced in Poland, Malaysia or Thailand are not generating very high incomes for those working in that industry. This could, however, change in the long run if firms which assemble computers today should be able to upgrade technological and en-trepeneurial skills adequately. This statement holds in a broader sense as the ex-ample of Toyota tells us. Toyota started as producers of textiles, then became a producer of textile machinery and finally became the world's leading and most profitable car producer.

Assume a poor country with low capital intensity k wants to catch up with country II which is rich and has a high capital intensity k*. To which extent does it make a difference whether catching-up is through the import of capital goods or FDI inflows? Capital accumulation can accelerate through the import of capital goods; in the extreme case that the country is producing only consumer goods and all imported goods are capital accumulation is governed by (with J denoting im-ports):

$$dK/dt + \delta K = J \qquad (A.7)$$

Assume that $J=j(q^*)Y$ where q^* is defined as eP^*/P which in effect is the inter-national relative price of capital goods. We assume that output is produced accord-ing to a Cobb-Douglas function so that

$$Y= K^{\beta}L^{1-\beta} \qquad (A.8)$$

or

$$y = k^{\beta} \qquad (A.9)$$

Then – assuming that population growth at a constant rate n - we have a simple modified neoclassical growth model whose steady state is:

$$k\# = \{j(q^*)/[n+\delta]\}^{1/1-\beta} \qquad (A.10)$$

Per capita GDP is y=f(k) which is equal to gross national product. With no government expenditures exports X will be equal to (1-c)Y where c is the consumption-expenditure ratio. The balance of payments constraints reads:

P(1-c)Y = eP*jY. Therefore the real exchange rate P/eP* is given by j/s. If both goods are identical so that one cannot distinguish between capital goods and consumption goods it must hold under free trade that P=eP* and hence j=s.

Next, assume that the same amount of capital goods comes through FDI inflows. Then all machines and firms, respectively, are owned by foreigners who decide about the structure of production. In the steady state national output per capita will be equal to y=$\{j(q^*)/[n+\delta]\}^{\beta/1-\beta}$, but national income obviously is equal to y"=(1-ß)y. From this perspective, it seems natural that countries prefer trade with incentives for both investment and savings rather than free FDI inflows. This however, holds only under the assumption that the technology is the same both in the case of free trade (and not FDI) and in a system where capital accumulation is dominated by FDI inflows. Assume that in a regime with trade y=f(k) while in a system with FDI inflows we have per capita output according to y=F(K**/K)f(k) where the technology transfer factor F is larger than unity; K** is that of the overall capital stock K in country I which is owned by foreigner. A simple specification could be y=[1+ K**/K]f(k); if the technology transfer effect is larger than ß it would make sense for society to fully rely on foreign investors.

A.6 Variations on the Solow Model: Some New Insights for a Monetary Economy

A.6.1 A Generalization of the Solow Growth Model

Sustained economic growth is crucial for the well-being of individuals but also for the power of nations. As regards these two aspects of growth, it is clear that these are two distinct categories. A government which wants to impress its trading partners (or potentially adverse countries) will point to the size of the overall gross national income as well as its growth rate. Individual well-being is, however, related to per capita income and the growth rate of per capita income. Strictly speaking, we should use purchasing power figures in international comparisons, and we ultimately are interested in per capita consumption which leads to the issue of optimum growth.

Growth analysis is of key importance for both countries eager at catching up with rich countries and for the leading economies which want to stay ahead of "follower countries". Moreover, as short term cyclical dynamics are superseded by long run growth dynamics, one should be interested in long run growth issues even if one adopts the policy perspective of politicians with a medium term time horizon. This holds not in the least since the steady state solutions implied by growth models will certainly affect expectations of individual investors and consumers.

Growth models have a long term perspective while traditional macro models typically adopt a medium term perspective. It is not easy to reconcile the different approaches. Standard macro models are useful for business cycle analysis and for gaining an understanding into policy impacts in the short run and medium run. The enormous speed of financial markets and the considerable role of asset markets to some extent suggest putting more emphasis on short-term approaches and medium term models. At the same time, it is true that financial markets also represent a relatively large volume of medium and long term transactions as can be seen from the average maturity in bonds markets in countries with low inflation rates and stable governments. It is thus true that under high inflation, maturity will strongly decline.

Are there arguments why one should consider the implications of growth models? A classical argument is that the production potential and hence the production function will be a limiting factor of economic development in the long run. From this perspective, the accumulation of capital and knowledge is quite crucial. The latter in turn is linked to innovations. Another important argument for considering growth models is the phenomenon of ageing societies which is a global challenge, as ageing will characterize the majority of countries and people in the world economy in the 21st century. Rising longevity could imply that people – households, investors and politicians – will become more interested in long run economic perspectives. Thus growth theory could be quite useful. Moreover, there has been considerable analytical progress in recent years, and this includes endogenous growth models which go well beyond the standard SOLOW growth model. There are also typical caveats to neoclassical growth models, however, they are not really justified. The basic SOLOW model assumes a linear-homogenous production function Y(K,L) where K and L represent capital and labor, respectively, and then explores the implication of goods market equilibrium in the sense of sY=dK/dt – savings S=sY where s is the savings rate. The basic finding is that there is a unique long run steady state solution for capital intensity k=:K/L which is associated with a steady state equilibrium per capita income y=:Y/L. The higher the savings rate, the higher the steady state value for both k and y. The model can be easily extended to include technological progress which often is assumed to be Harrod neutral, as it is labor saving. The steady state variable determined in the model with an exogenous growth rate of the level of technology (A) then is k'=: K/(AL) where AL is dubbed labor in efficiency units. If one uses a Cobb-Douglas production function Y=$K^{ß}$ (AL) $^{1-ß}$ – where ß is the output elasticity of capital and y'=: Y/(AL) – we can write y'=$k'^{ß}$ and with k'# denoting the steady state value of k' we get y'#= $k'\#^{ß}$. The steady state value in a setting with an exogenous growth rate of the population n and an exogenous progress rate dlnA/dt=a is simply given by k'# = [s/(n+a)] $^{1/1-ß}$. This implies Y/L = [s/(n+a)] $^{ß/1-ß}$ $A_0e'^{at}$ (e' is the Euler number and A_0 the initial level of A).

Hence, the level of the growth path positively depends on s and negatively on the sum of n and a, while the long run growth rate is given by a. It is clear that a rise in the progress rate a thus reduces the growth path, but the growth rate will increase which will be the dominant effect on per capita income in the long run. This in a nutshell is what the SOLOW model says. (Note that we have disregarded capital depreciation which, however, is not difficult to include in the analysis.) The SOLOW model is a non-monetary growth model.

The SOLOW Model as an Analytical Starting Point

The neoclassical SOLOW growth model is elegant on the one hand, but it also is rather simple on the other hand. The latter does not, however, rule out our considering interesting modifications. While it is often claimed that the SOLOW model does not consider institutional aspects, it is quite easy to integrate at least two basic aspects. Write the production function – based on a Cobb-Douglas function with capital K, labor input L and the level of labor-saving technology A – as

$$Y = Z'K^{\beta}(\lambda\,AL)^{1-\beta} \qquad\qquad\qquad (A.I)$$

Therefore per capita income $Y/L=: y$ is given by

$$y = Z'\,k^{\beta}(\lambda\,A)^{1-\beta} \qquad\qquad\qquad (A.II)$$

Here Z' represents the quality of the basic political and economic institutional network which facilitates coordination in markets and within firms. Hence transaction costs aspects in markets and in firms are relevant here. The variable λ indicates the effort of the average worker. It is obvious that this effort is not only influenced by wages – here we have a bridge to the efficiency wage theory – but by the social security system as well; if there are generous benefits which can be obtained by those who are unemployed, the effort parameter will be low. The growth rate of per capita output therefore (with g denoting growth rates and a signifying g_A) is given by

$$g_y = g_{Z'} + \beta g_k + (1-\beta)(g_{\lambda} + a) \qquad\qquad (A.III)$$

Thus the growth rate of per capita income is the sum of the growth of the institutional quality factor Z', of the growth rate of the capital intensity (weighted with ß) and of the growth rate of working efforts plus the rate of non-emboddied technological progress (weighted with 1-ß). For transition countries, in particular those moving from a distorted socialist planned economy – with a poor institutional quality index and a weak labor motivation factor λ (not least due to an expanding socialist shadow economy), one may expect a transitory growth bonus until Z' in eastern European countries and λ have achieved quasi-equilibrium values which roughly could be assumed to be equal to EU15 average. Once this growth bonus is fully exploited, growth is simply the weighted sum of the growth of capital intensity k and the growth rate of technological progress.

If the basic politico-economic institutional network weakens so that its quality deteriorates, the parameter Z' falls. For example, if an integration club such as the EU25 (or individual member countries) should move towards a less consistent politico-economic system, this implies a fall of the level of per capita income. Moreover, if the social security system becomes too generous in the sense of weakening λ, the effect on per capita output will also be negative. (In a model with heterogeneous labor, one would have to modify the analysis since the unemployment insurance system allows workers laid off to move to new jobs with relatively high productivity instead of quickly accepting the next best job to come.) Let us adopt the standard assumption of the neoclassical growth model, namely that labor and technology growth with a constant rate, that is $L(t) = L_0 e^{'nt}$ and $A(t) = A_0 e^{'at}$ (n and a are assumed to be exogenous positive parameters). Within a simple growth equilibrium model which assumes that savings S=sY and imposes the goods market equilibrium condition S=dK/dt (hence there is no depreciation of capital) the steady state capital ratio k' is derived from the differential equation (with y'=: Y/[AL}):

$$dk'/dt = sy' - (n+a)k' \qquad (A.IV)$$

This gives the steady state capital stock ratio k' as:

$$k'\# = [sZ' \lambda^{1-\beta}/(n+a)]^{1/1-\beta} \qquad (A.V)$$

Here (note that # denotes the steady state) we can see that the savings rate s – the crucial variable in the SOLOW model – and both Z' and λ will affect the level of the growth path of k'. The long run growth rate of k=:K/L and per capita income y will be given, of course, by the progress rate a. An important phenomenon of the 1980s and 1990s is that many Asian countries launched a rather successful economic catching up process certainly interrupted by the Asian crisis of 1997. The US and Western European countries still are leading countries in terms of per capita income, however, there is some international real income convergence (unfortunately leaving out most of Africa).

With respect to the growth rate of per capita income, the EU and the US were roughly at par in the 1980s and 1990s. The US growth rate of real GNP exceeded that of the EU, however, since the US recorded considerable population growth while that of the EU was very low. Germany, France and Japan have almost caught up with the US in terms of per capita income.

From the perspective of the neoclassical growth model, catching up at some point of time t can be brought about by two mechanisms, namely by a rise of the relative per capita income level (while the long run growth rate remain constant) and/or by a relative rise of the growth rate of technological progress (while the level of the growth path is unchanged). Both Germany and the US have experienced several shifts in the trend growth rate of progress as has been suggested by JUNGMITTAG (2006 b) and by BEN-DAVID, LUMSDAINE, PAPEL (2003) for the case of the USA. In a world economy in which the ratio of research and development relative to national income is increasing over the long run – while the role of multinational companies (often representing technological ownership specific advantages) is rising at the same time – the progress rate is likely to play an increasingly important role over time. However, it is unclear to which extent the trend of the progress rate is stable across countries. Moreover, product innovations are likely to affect the speed of process innovations, as novel products can often be produced only on new machinery and equipment.

If two countries are to have the same level of the growth path and the same long run growth rate, the neoclassical growth model requires that a whole set of parameters should coincide across countries. It is not really clear which mechanisms could bring about such convergence of parameters, including convergence of the savings rate, the rate of capital depreciation and the growth rate of technological progress. The very existence of multinational companies is based on technological advantages of the respective companies, and there is no free lunch for firms (not being a subsidiary) in foreign countries to quickly get access to foreign multinationals' latest technologies. Here innovations mean process innovations, but equally important are product innovations which allow firms to temporarily fetch higher prices in world markets. The conventional idea of most textbooks that the law of one price is valid in a simple form is not really convincing in a world with heterogeneous products. There are other departures from the standard neoclassical models in reality, namely that there is unemployment in many countries for many years – to which extent can unemployment be considered in a long run growth model and how will long run inflation and long run unemployment interact with economic growth?

In the following tables and graphs we take a quick look at selected data which are an interesting background for the subsequent analysis. We can see that per capita GNP growth is relatively similar across countries, while the growth rates of GNP and of population are rather different.

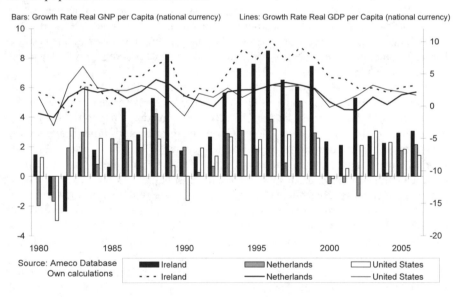

Source: Ameco Database

Fig. 3. Annual Growth Rate of Real GNP and GNP per Capita, 1980-2005 (US, Ireland and Netherlands)

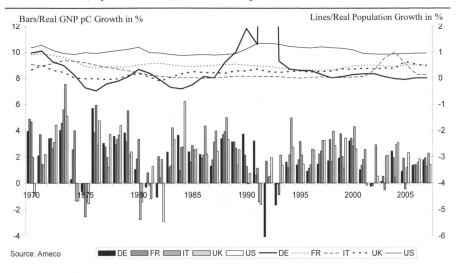

Source: Ameco Database

Fig. 4. Growth Rate of Real GNP per Capita and Population in Selected Countries, 1970-2005 (US, UK, France, Germany, UK, Italy)

Table 2. UN Projections of Growth Rates of Population for US, UK, France, Germany, UK, Italy, Turkey, China, India, Pakistan, World, 2000-2050

	2000	2005	2010	2015	2020	2025	2030	2035	2040	2045	2050
US	5.40	4.95	4.71	4.31	3.90	3.45	3.08	2.72	2.38	2.10	1.92
UK	1.73	1.70	1.42	1.49	1.75	1.88	1.62	1.20	0.90	0.79	0.85
France	1.85	2.05	1.72	1.31	0.99	0.72	0.48	0.22	-0.10	-0.41	-0.64
Germany	0.84	0.42	0.01	-0.23	-0.28	-0.38	-0.56	-0.77	-0.90	-0.88	-0.87
Italy	0.72	0.65	0.14	-0.62	-1.19	-1.44	-1.57	-1.70	-1.91	-2.22	-2.57
Turkey	8.97	7.27	6.68	5.84	5.00	4.37	3.66	2.87	2.15	1.56	1.02
China	4.48	3.29	2.94	2.84	2.22	1.23	0.35	-0.24	-0.66	-1.15	-1.74
India	9.14	8.06	7.24	6.51	5.69	4.76	3.84	3.12	2.69	2.17	1.59
Pakistan	13.15	10.72	10.92	10.41	9.45	8.34	7.40	6.61	5.86	5.11	4.28
World	6.91	6.23	5.85	5.50	4.97	4.32	3.72	3.22	2.81	2.37	1.89

Source: UN

As we can see, the growth rate of the population is declining in many countries, but the cross-country differences are considerable. Asia's economic weight will be reinforced both through high per capita growth and sustained growth of the population.

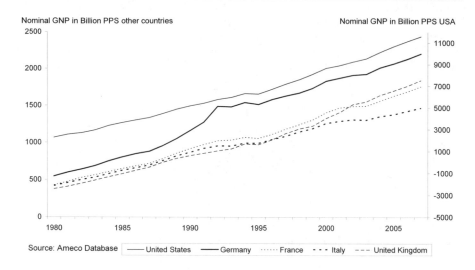

Source: Ameco Database

Fig. 5. GNP (PPP figures) in the US, UK, France, Germany, Italy, 1980-2005

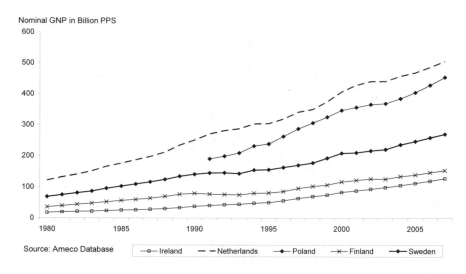

Source: Ameco Database

Fig. 6. GNP (PPP figures) in the Netherlands, Sweden, Finland, Ireland, Poland, 1980-2005

Foreign Direct Investment and Technology

Economic catching up in Europe was rather impressive for several countries in the 1960s and 1970s, but there were also impressive catching-up dynamics in the period from 1990 to 2005. It is rather unclear which forces explain these phenomena.

When one discusses economic catching-up across countries, it is important to make a distinction between GNP per capita and GDP per capita. Foreign direct investment inflows contribute to a rise of GDP and GNP, but the rise of GNP is likely to be lower, since subsidiaries of multinational companies will transfer profits to the parent companies abroad. Therefore, it is an important fact that per capita foreign direct investment inflows differ considerably across countries.

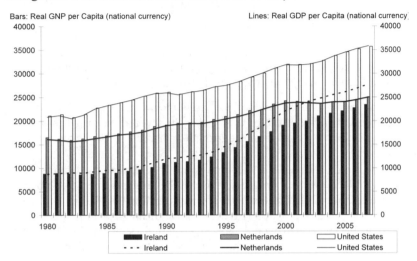

Source: Ameco Database

Fig. 7. Per Capita GDP and Per Capita GNP of the US, Ireland and the Netherlands, 1980-2005

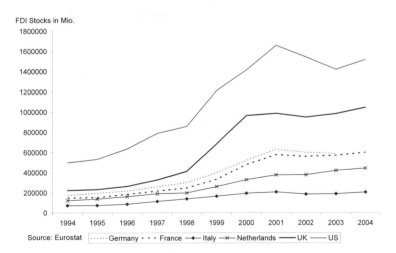

Source: Ameco Eurostat

Fig. 8. Foreign Direct Investment Stocks Per Capita in Selected Countries

A.6.2 Aspects of Empirical Analysis of Economic Development

The basic neoclassical growth model – based on a Cobb-Douglas production function $Y=K^{\beta}(AL)^{1-\beta}$ – and a savings function $S=sY(1-\tau)$, reinvestment δK and an exogenous growth rate of the level of labor-augmenting technology $A(t)$, namely a, and an exogenous growth rate of the population L, namely n, leads to the following steady state solution for per capita income $Y/L=y$:

$$y\# = \{s[1-\tau]/[n+\delta+a]\}^{\beta/1-\beta}\,e^{\prime at} \qquad\qquad (A.VI)$$

If one considers this model as an adequate approach to reality all medium term changes in y can be explained by the interaction of two basic elements provided that s, τ, n and δ are not correlated with a and also independent of time t:

- If there is an increase in the level of per capita income the underlying reason is a rise of s (or ß) or a fall of τ, δ or n. A rise in the level of the growth path must not be confused with a change of the growth path itself – this brings us to the next point.
- If there is a structural break in the time series the reason is a change in the growth rate of technological progress; a rise of the progress rate a will go along with a once-and-for-all fall of the level of the growth path and a fall of the progress rate a will go along with a rise of the level of the growth path. An additional test to be performed would look at a (period) sub-sample of the data, namely whether the coefficient for the progress rate has increased in the regression.

The following graph makes a clear distinction between a rise of the level of the growth path occurring in period t' and a rise of the growth rate occurring in period t" (see the arch ED). If both a rise of the level of the growth path and of the progress rate itself should occur we would see a picture such as the arch C'D'.

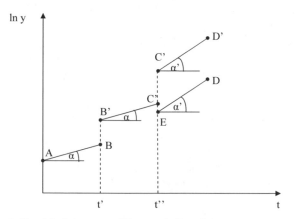

Fig. 9. Empirical Aspects of Economic Development

The initial stage of economic catching-up in poor countries typically is one during which the savings rate is increasing and the growth rate of the population falling which implies that the level of the growth path is raised over time. Often only in a later stage of economic catching-up will technological progress enter the picture and the international transfer of technology through various mechanisms and domestic innovation policy may well interact.

One may study the impact of economic opening up – that is of trade and capital flows – on both the parameters relevant only for the level of the growth path and for the growth rate of technological progress. In the literature this distinction is rarely made.

Population Growth, Progress and Economic Dynamics

Population growth increased in Europe after the Industrial Revolution; after the introduction of the modern welfare state it has considerably reduced and few European countries expect long term population growth. By contrast the US is expected to have sustained population growth and to face ageing problems much later than Japan and the EU (with eastern European population growth falling faster than in EU15). The demographical dynamics and ageing of the population clearly represents mayor challenges for policy makers in Europe and Japan. McMORROW/RÖGER (2003, p.35) argue that ageing will affect savings in various ways:

"On the positive side, ageing would be expected to boost savings rates due to: increased savings for retirement by forward-looking (not liquidity constrained) worker households; lower dissaving in retirement. On the negative side, ageing would be expected to deplete savings due to an increasing share of low savings retirees, higher expected future labor income and lower investment needs. In addition, the overall net effect of ageing on savings is further complicated by the interest rate effects. Regarding the latter, given that lifetime wealth calculations are affected and that the substitution and income effects can be different depending on the level of the inter-temporal elasticity of substitution, interest rate changes can easily have positive or negative effects on savings."

A refined neoclassical model is useful when considering some of the key aspects of changes in the growth rate of the population. We assume a standard Cobb-Douglas production function $Y=K^{\beta}(AL)^{1-\beta}$ and an exogenous growth rate of technology (A; $d\ln A/dt=:a$) and an exogenous growth rate of the population ($n=d\ln L/dt$). By assumption savings $S= s(1-\tau)(1-hu)Y$ where u is the structural unemployment rate – long term unemployed have a negative savings rate - and h a positive parameter; τ is the income tax rate. Imposing the equilibrium condition that gross investment (δ is the depreciation rate) equals savings, that is $dK/dt +\delta K = S$, we obtain the differential equation for $k'=:K/(AL)$:

$$dk'/dt = s(1-\tau)(1-hu)k'^{\beta} - (n+a+\delta)k' \qquad (A.VII)$$

The steady state solution for the ratio of capital to labor in efficiency units is:

$$k'\# = \{s(1-\tau)(1-hu)/(n+a+\delta)\}^{1/1-\beta} \qquad \text{(A.VIII)}$$

Thus y'=: Y/(AL) in the steady state is given by:

$$y'\# = \{s(1-\tau)(1-hu)/(n+a+\delta)\}^{\beta/1-\beta} \qquad \text{(A.IX)}$$

With e' denoting the Euler number we get for labor productivity y=: Y/L the result

$$y\# = \{A_0 s(1-\tau)(1-hu)/(n+a+\delta)\}^{1/1-\beta} e'^{at} \qquad \text{(A.X)}$$

A_0 is the initial level of technology. Denoting $\beta/(1-\beta)=\beta'$ per capita output in the steady state thus is governed by

$$\ln y(t) = \{\ln A_0 + \beta'[\ln s -\tau - hu - \ln(n+a+\delta)]\}+ at \qquad \text{(A.XI)}$$

Note that the elasticity of y with respect to the investment-output rate (read s) is $\beta/(1-\beta)$ which is 0.5 if we assume $\beta= 1/3$ as is typical for many OECD countries; raising the investment-GDP ratio from 20% to 21% (an increase by 5%) thus – from a theoretical perspective - should result in an increase of per capita income by 2.5% which is line with empirical findings reported subsequently for the US and the EU. If the empirical findings were larger or smaller the only explanation would be that s is affecting the progress rate; e.g. the apparent elasticity of y with respect to s could exceed $\beta/1-\beta$ if the progress rate a were a negative function of the investment-output ratio s (as s is raised it becomes more difficult for firms to organize investment projects in a way that all investment projects reflect a high rate of embodied technological progress – if empirical findings suggest an elasticity much above 0.5 one might indeed assume that such an effect plays a major role; using a''' as a positive parameter the implication is that a=a_0 –a'''s and from this perspective raising the savings rate would thus not be a prime task for government since one has to consider the potentially negative effect of s on the progress rate and the trend growth rate, respectively). The semi-elasticity of per capita income with respect to the income tax rate is given by –β' and the same applies for the unemployment rate if h is unity. In the latter case a reduction of the unemployment rate by 5 percentage points will raise the long run level of per capita income by 2.5%; based on an annual per capita income of 20 000 € this implies an increase by 500 € (of which government – including social security – would typically get 200 € in Euro zone countries). The long run gain would be much larger if one were to assume that the progress rate is a negative function of the unemployment rate u, that is we have a progress function a=a_0 – a#u. While it is true that the positive effect of lowering u on the level of the growth rate would be weakened by such a specification of the progress function, the implied increase of the trend growth rate a – after a fall of the structural unemployment rate – will more than offset this effect on the level of the growth path.

The expression {…} determines the level of the growth path. We have assumed that hu and τ are close to zero, so than we can use the approximation $\ln(1+x) \approx x$. The impact of a rise of n obviously is a fall of the level of the growth rate. However, reality is more complex and a particularly important aspect concerns the link between the growth rate of the population n and the progress rate a and the savings rate s. Considering such an impact leads to a quasi-endogenous growth model which is quite simple but offers some interesting insights.

Now let us assume that n affects the savings rate and the progress rate. Depending on the social security system, government may influence savings in a way which amounts to a negative link between the growth rate of the population and the savings rate. We also assume that the growth rate of the population positively affects the progress rate which we model (with a_0 and a_1 as positive parameters) as

$$a = a_0 + a_1 n \tag{A.XII}$$

The justification for a positive parameter a_1 is the idea that a rise of the growth rate of the population will bring more competition and implies that a larger pool of new ideas is available – both effects could raise the progress rate. As an alternative to the specification presented we could introduce an additional term $a_2 n^2$ (with $a_2 < 0$) so that there is a critical rate n beyond which n will negatively affect the progress rate - say, because having very many children will undermine the ability of the family to ensure a decent education for all kids. For the sake of simplicity we focus on the simple equation above. As regards the impact on savings we use – assuming n to be positive and using a positive parameter h' - the following function for the savings rate:

$$s = s_0\, e^{,h'/n} \tag{A.XIII}$$

The steady state is now determined by

$$\ln y(t) = \ln A_0 + \text{ß'}[\ln s_0 + h/n - \tau - hu - \ln(n + a_0 + a\ln + \delta)] + [a_0 + a_1 n]t \tag{A.IX}$$

To shed more light on the impact of n on the long run per capita (or labor productivity) we assume that $a_0 + \delta = 1$ so that we can write:

$$\ln y(t) = \ln A_0 + \text{ß'}[\ln s_0 + h'/n - \tau - hu - (n + a_1 n)] + [a_0 + a_1 n]t \tag{A.X}$$

The semi-elasticity of per capita income with respect to n (for the level of the growth rate) thus is given by $-h'/n^2 - [\text{ß}/(1-\text{ß})](1+a_1)$ which is negative; it would be ambiguous if we had considered a function $a = a_0 + a_1 n + a_2 n^2$; remember that $a_2 < 0$. Alternatively, we may use the approximation $\ln X = 1 - b'/X$; with b' chosen as a suitable positive parameter. Hence we would use the approximation term $1 - [b'/(n + a_0 + a_1 n + \delta)]$ for $\ln(n + a_0 + a_1 n + \delta)$, but the qualitative results will not change.

A higher growth rate of the population will not only affect the level of the growth rate through the standard capital deepening effect but also via the fall of the savings rate and the increase in the progress rate. The positive effect of n on the progress rate implies that per capita income in the very long run will be positively affected by population growth. By implication a fall of the growth rate of the population implies a one-off increase in the level of the growth path, but a fall of the growth rate of per capita income in the very long run. This is paradox since for OECD countries facing a transition to lower population growth rates the implication is that there will be a transitory increase in per capita income (the modified capital deepening effect) which many consumers and investors – and government authorities – might interpret as a signal for structural economic improvements while the contrary is true: Thus there is the danger that policy makers in ageing societies with falling population growth rates will not adopt timely reforms required to raise the progress rate. At the beginning of the 21st century the perspective for the EU and Japan is that a fall in population growth will lead to a fall of the progress rate and labor productivity– relative to previous long term trends.

An interesting question is how the result is affected by considering the role of embodied technological progress; STOLERU (1978, p. 373) has shown that a higher rate of technological progress in a vintage model amounts to a rising of the depreciation rate. His analysis leaves the broader implications unclear. Here we write $a = a_0 + h"\delta_1$ while taking into account that the rise of δ has reduced the level of the growth rate. As regards the increasing role of information and communication technology – that is the relatively rising role of software compared to hardware – one may argue that h" (a positive parameter) is higher in the age of modern ICT than in the 1960s or 1970s.

A further refinement could be the assumption that the government deficit ratio is a negative function of n so that a fall of n brings a rise of the structural deficit ratio. Denoting net exports as X' – and using the function X' = x'(q*) – and reinvested profits of foreign investors as D** we thus have the equilibrium condition in the goods market (with q*=:eP*/P; e is the nominal exchange rate, P the domestic price level, P* the foreign price level):

$$dK/dt + \delta K + x'(q*)X' = S + T\text{-}G + D**(q*) \qquad (A.XI)$$

Note that a permanent net import position of the country considered implies that foreigners will own a share of the capital stock b and obtain thus a share of profits. If we assume competition in goods and factor markets and that factors are rewarded in accordance with the respective marginal product, the share of gross domestic product accruing to foreigners is bß so that D**=b(q*)ßY. Following FROOT/STEIN (1991) we may assume that the desired share b(…) of foreign direct investment inflows depends on the real exchange rate q*. A rise of q* will bring higher net inflows in a world economy with imperfect capital markets and hence we also conclude that the desired share in the capital stock of country I – the home country – depends on q*. Foreign investors from country II will want to hold the highest share of K possible; the higher the share of K the easier it is to acquire assets in country I through international mergers and acquisitions. A real depreciation of country I currency will facilitate takeovers by firms from country II. Savings are now assumed to depend on national income which is Z=(1-bß)Y. Assuming that X=x(q*)Y and imports J=j(q*)Y and that real government expenditures (G) relative to AL – namely G/(AL) is a positive function of n – we get the following differential equation (where the government surplus ratio is denoted as τ"):

$$dk'/dt = \{s[1\text{-}\tau][1\text{-}hu][1\text{-}b(q*)ß]+ \tau"(n)\text{-} x'(q*) +b(q*)ß\}k'ß - \qquad (A.XVII)$$

$$(n+a+\delta)k'$$

This gives the following steady state solution (with j'=:-x' denoting the net import ratio):

$$k'\# = \{s[1-\tau][1-hu][1-b(q^*)\beta]+\tau''(n)+j'(q^*)+b(q^*)\beta\}/(n+a+\delta) \quad (A.XVIII)$$

In a country with a falling growth rate of the population – and in a setup with n not affecting the progress rate a - we thus can conclude: The level of the growth path is positively affected by the capital deepening effect (the rise of the denominator), but it is negatively affected by the fall of the government surplus ratio.

The net effect of foreign direct investment is an increase in the level of the growth path. One also may want to consider a setup in which the progress rate positively depends on b so that a=a$_0$ + a'b. Then foreign direct investment has an ambiguous effect on the level of growth as b is now both in the nominator and in the denominator. However, with a progress function a=a$_0$ + a'b (where a' is a positive parameter) the trend growth rate will be raised by foreign direct investment. A country with a short political horizon therefore will be hesitant to invest resources in attracting foreign direct investment – assuming that there are some sunk costs to be incurred to make the country truly attractive to foreign direct investment inflows. Only if the political time horizon is long enough (meaning that the long run improvement of trend growth through the presence of foreign investors is adequately considered), will there be political reforms conducive to foreign investment. Clearly, if the time horizon is sufficiently long policy makers will perceive a positive net welfare effect from foreign direct investment inflows, as the trend growth effect will finally dominate any negative effect on the level of the growth path.

Let us come back to the impact of population growth. The new growth theory is not really clear about the impact of population growth and ageing; and the empirical analysis is partly ambiguous although there seems to be clear evidence that falling population growth negatively affects growth dynamics (TEMPLE, 1999). The model mechanics in new growth approaches depend on the pattern of knowledge creation. In the new growth theory one basically explains the progress rate by certain efforts, e.g. the share of R&D personnel (L') in the overall workforce (L). One could also state that a = a''(L'/L) where a'' is a positive parameter. In such a setting the growth rate of A falls parallel to the growth rate of the population and the only way to stabilize the progress rate is through a continuously rising share of R&D personnel. In his theoretical and empirical analysis JONES (2002) argues that the long run growth rate of US labor productivity in the period 1950-93 can be explained through a permanent shift of factor inputs into knowledge activities – read R&D activities and human capital upgrading. The growth rate of educational attainment (human capital) was 0.63 % p.a. and that of the R&D labor force 4.8%. Without human capital upgrading and R&D intensification the US labor productivity growth would have been less than ½ percent.

From a theoretical perspective it is clear that one will have to consider both policy effects on the level of the growth path and the growth rate itself. In economic policy in OECD countries one hardly finds a broader discussion about these aspects – except in the European Commission and at the Council of Economic Advisors. While JONES estimates for the US the long run productivity multiplier (level effects after 50 years) to be 2.1% for a 1 percentage point increase of the physical investment share, the European Commission comes up with a similar estimate of 2.4%. An increase by one year in educational attainment brings a 7% increase in the JONES analysis, but a 12.8% increase in the analysis of the Commission. An increase by one percentage point of the R&D share brings a 16% increase in the JONES model, but 17.7% in the EU. A reduction of the working age population growth by 1 percentage point reduces the productivity growth in the US considerably (JONES' figures indicate a range of minus 2.5% to minus 16%); the estimate by the European Commission is -8.7% where the ECFIN analysis uses a slightly different approach than JONES. The overall EU analysis – the reader partly is referred to EUROPEAN COMMISSION (2003) - also shows a positive impact of openness and market size for the EU and positive effects of European deregulation.

A.7 Technological Progress and the Long Run Price Level

A.7.1 Process Innovations

In modern economies process innovations are an important element of economic development. It is surprising that the role of process innovations have not been considered much in medium term macro models. Only in long run growth models have process innovations played a role. However, the dominant neoclassical growth models are non-monetary models in the sense that money market equilibrium is not considered. Subsequently we will show that combining a growth model with a money market equilibrium condition is quite useful. The following analysis is not only relevant for Schumpeterian innovation dynamics in a monetary economy (and every modern economic system is a monetary economy), we also can state that the role of monetary policy cannot be fully assessed if we do not include the role of technology.

As regards the role of monetary policy it has been emphasized (BALL, 2001) that an income elasticity of the demand for money of less than unity has crucial implications for monetary policy, e.g. that the Friedman rule of monetary policy is not optimal and the growth rate of money should be below the growth rate of output in order to achieve price stability. Moreover, monetary aggregates are still important in the new era of inflation targeting (HAYO, 1999). Recent empirical work – based on co-integration analysis and error correction models - for broad money in Australia (VALANDKHANI, 2005), Germany (BEYER, 1998), the Euro zone (COENEN/VEGA, 2001) and the UK (ERICSSON), namely for narrow money, all have shown that the long-run income elasticity is rather close to unity which is consistent with the quantity theory of money (if the elasticity were 0.5 the implication is that the Baumol-Tobin transaction approach is applicable, if the elasticity is above unity money is a luxury good). As regards the growth of the demand for money relative to income LAMBSDORFF (2005) has presented empirical evidence for a cross-country approach. We will show that the income elasticity of the demand for money points to important long run implications in the context of technological progress.

Process innovations which amount to the cutting of costs typically are expected to lead to a fall of the price level. The expansion of the digital economy often is considered as a case where process innovations have played a strong role (AUDRETSCH/WELFENS, 2002; WELFENS, 2002). This is a typical perspective one might have in an economy in which all sectors are subject to process innovations. However, this apparently convincing insight from microeconomics has a pitfall, as we will show in a simple long run approach to the quantity theory of money. We will combine the money market equilibrium with the condition of profit maximization; namely that the real interest rate r should be equal to the marginal product of capital. We will prove that, in the case of the income elasticity of the demand for money being between 0 and 1, there will be an increase in the equilibrium price level.

Let us start the analysis with a standard microeconomic perspective of process innovations. Assume that there is a process innovation in market i (see in the following graph the downward shift of the marginal cost curve K'_i where i could represent the tradable sector) and an unchanged supply condition in market j. At first sight this will lead to a fall of price p_i and hence (with b denoting the share of income spent on good i) a decline of the aggregate price level $P = (p_i)^b p_j^{(1-b)}$. One may introduce some refinement in the argument, namely that a real income effect associated with the higher output in the i-market and the (potentially transitory) fall of p_i will shift the demand curve in the j-market upwards so that the price p_j will rise as a consequence of technological progress in sector i; thus the effect on the price level is ambiguous (see the following graph). However, we can prove within a macroeconomic approach that there is no ambiguity at all if the income elasticity of the demand for money is in the range between 0 and unity. If the income elasticity is above unity then the long run equilibrium price level will fall as a consequence of process innovations. The relevant mechanism partly includes the macroeconomic money market: the demand for money is affected by a rise of the technology level in two offsetting ways as we will see. In a consistent macro model with goods markets and a money market, the relevant mechanism is related to the demand for money and this in turn suggests that there must be a real balance effect in goods markets (or in the aggregate goods market).

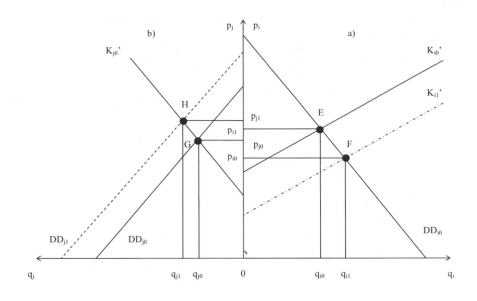

Fig. 10. Ambiguous Effect of Technological Progress on Price Level

A.7.2 The Model

A.7.2.1 True Long Run Equilibrium in the Money Market

Let us consider the long run money market equilibrium, namely, real money balances M/P equals the real demand for money m^d (Y,i) where M is the nominal money stock, Y aggregate output and i the nominal interest rate. As we will assume an expected inflation of zero, we will set i=r (real interest rate). Moreover, we will consider a Cobb-Douglas production function with a Harrod factor A

$$Y=K^{\text{ß}}(AL)^{1-\text{ß}} \tag{A.10a}$$

and impose the condition of profit maximization so that

$$r=Y_K=\text{ß}Y/K \tag{A.10b}$$

Here ß is the output elasticity of capital and Y_K the marginal product of K. In this approach the marginal product of capital determines the real interest rate. Thus we are not following the optimum growth model which leads to f'(k') = θ +n where k' is modified capital intensity K/[AL], f' the marginal product of capital, θ is the time preference and n the growth rate of the population (modified golden rule; alternatively the golden rule could be used f'(k')=n; see BLANCHARD/ FISCHER, 1989). For an optimum growth approach one would rather consider n to be endogenous here; one also could argue that the golden rule approach assumes that utility maximizing consumers dominate the capital market while our approach assumes that investors dominate capital markets (in reality both groups will have an influence so that r= b" θ + (1-b")f'(k'); b" represents that relative impact of consumers – we have a similar problem as with exchange rate determination in the presence of fundamentalist actors and speculators betting on present trends).

Next we follow the standard assumption that the real money demand m is a positive function of Y and a negative function of the nominal interest rate i. Money market equilibrium is defined by

$$M/P = m(Y,i) \tag{A.10c}$$

Taking a look at the long run money market equilibrium condition (defined by M/P=m and the equality of the real interest rate and the marginal product of capital) brings an important and surprising insight. It is convenient to define real money demand as

$$m= Y^\sigma \, \sigma'/i \tag{A.10d}$$

Let us point out that with a real money demand function $m= Y^\sigma \, \sigma'/i$ (or a similar specification; $\sigma>0$; $\sigma'>0$) and zero expected inflation (hence the nominal interest rate i=r), we get in an economy with profit maximization and a Cobb-Douglas production function $Y=K^\beta(AL)^{1-\beta}$ the somewhat surprising result that a once-and-for-all rise of the level of technology A could raise the price level P. This can be seen from the money market equilibrium condition $M/P= m^d(Y,i)$ which is solved here for the steady state price level P#:

$$P\#= M \, Y^{-\sigma} \, \beta[Y/K]/\sigma' =[\beta \, M \, Y^{1-\sigma}/K]/\sigma' \tag{A.10e}$$

It is obvious that a rise of M will raise the equilibrium price level while for a given real interest rate and hence a constant ratio Y/K a rise of output will reduce the price level. If the international law of one price is holding, namely P=eP*, the nominal exchange rate is given (assuming an exogenous P*) by P#/P.

Now let us consider the equation for the price level (true monetary long run equilibrium condition) in more detail:

$$P= (\beta/\sigma')M(AL)^{(1-\beta)(1-\sigma)} \, K^{\beta(1-\sigma)-1} \tag{A.10f}$$

We can see that a rise in the capital stock will reduce the price level which corresponds to standard results from a model with two markets (or one aggregate goods market) in which there has been an increase in production capacity.

$$\partial P/\partial K<0 \tag{A.10g}$$

Indeed, this condition obviously is fulfilled since ß is about 1/3 and σ close to unity. The multiplier for K is positive. Note that equation (A.10f) can be restated as $P= (\beta/\sigma')MA^{(1-\beta)(1-\sigma)}L^{(1-2\beta)(1-\sigma)+1}k$ so that one could display a P-k-line for money market equilibrium.

As regards the impact of process innovations (dA>0) (and similarly for dL) we find a rather paradoxical result (one should recall that the monetary approach to the balance of payments is also paradoxical as the Mundell-Johnson argument emphasizes that in a small open economy with a fixed exchange rate a rise of the foreign price level will raise through arbitrage the domestic price level and hence raise the demand for money; The excess demand for money translates into a current account surplus which leads to a rise of the money supply which is consistent with the initial rise of P). We indeed can see:

$$\partial P/\partial A > 0 \text{ if } 0 < \sigma < 1 \qquad (A.10h)$$

If the income elasticity of the demand for money is slightly below unity, a rise of the technology level (A) will raise the price level. If this elasticity were above unity, process innovations will lead to a lower price level. As is well known from the literature, there has been (at least since Milton Friedman's argument that money is a luxury good: hence the income elasticity should be above unity) a long debate about the income elasticity of money and the empirical evidence is not always conclusive as to whether the elasticity is below unity or above unity.

In our long run approach the level of technology has an impact both on real income and on the real interest rate: The reason for the interesting paradox presented is the role which the level of technology has on the marginal product of capital and hence on the interest rate; a rise of A amounts to raising the marginal product of capital and hence the interest rate so that the demand for money is reduced. Therefore money market equilibrium (at a given nominal money supply and a given capital stock) can only be restored if the price level is rising (this might be interpreted in a way that the real income effects of technological progress can overcompensate the direct price effect of falling marginal costs). If $\sigma = 1$, the price level would remain stable and the positive real output effect associated with the rise of A would generate exactly sufficient additional demand for money to restore the equilibrium. If $\sigma > 1$, the income-induced rise of the real demand for money would be so large that it would require a fall of the price level for equilibrium in the money market to be restored. Whatever the specification of the demand for money, there will always be a critical value of the income elasticity below which a rise of A has to be accompanied by a rise of the price level if a new equilibrium is to be achieved in the money market.

Basically, we have an interesting empirical question on the one hand and on the other hand the idea presented reinforces the natural skepticism one has when simple analogies from microeconomics are drawn to derive macroeconomic conclusions. Even parallel process innovation in both markets could ultimately lead to a rise of the price level, namely if the real income effect in both markets is strong enough to outweigh the productivity/cost effect related to process innovations.

A.7.2.2 Long Run Growth Perspective

Next we recall that $k' =: K/[AL]$. Let us rewrite the true long run monetary equilibrium condition in the following way, where we observe that in the following equation the elasticity of P with respect to AL apparently is negative (this seems to contradict the initial equation for true long run monetary equilibrium, however, one must take into account that the variable k' contains AL in the denominator!):

$$P = (\beta/\sigma')M(AL)^{-\sigma}k'^{\beta(1-\sigma)-1} \qquad (A.10i)$$

Assume that savings S=sY, reinvestment is proportionate to K (parameter δ) and that overall investment I=dK/dt+δK = S. From the standard neoclassical growth model we know that the equilibrium value k'# is expressed for the case of a given L and a given A by $k'\# = (s/\delta)^{1/1-\beta}$. Thus we get for the long run price level P#:

$$P\# = (\beta/\sigma')M(AL)^{-\sigma}[s/\delta]^{[\beta(1-\sigma)-1]/[1-\beta]} \qquad (A.10j)$$

One should note, however, that the assumption that there is profit maximization imposes a restriction on the parameter sets since we have $\beta k'^{\beta-1}=r$ and hence $k'\# = (\beta/r)^{1/1-\beta}$; and we have $k'\# = [s/\delta]^{1/[1-\beta]}$. This requires a specific savings rate, namely s=(β/r)δ which could be fulfilled by choice of a specific β; this effectively implises growth on a raizor's edge.

We can state that a rise of M raises the long run equilibrium price level while a rise of the savings rate will reduce it. An increase in the depreciation rate δ will raise the price level. In a stationary, non-growing economy inflation is always a monetary phenomenon.

Next we consider an economy with population growth and sustained progress so that (with e' denoting the Euler number, n the growth rate of population and a the growth rate of the technology level A) $L = L_oe'^{nt}$ and $A=A_oe'^{at}$. We therefore get the following equation which offers some non-monetarist insights about inflation:

$$P\#(t) = (\beta/\sigma') M [s/(a+n+\delta)]^{[\beta(1-\sigma)-1]/[1-\beta]} (L_oA_oe'^{(a+n)t})^{-\sigma} \qquad (A.10k)$$

Obviously in a growing economy there could be a sustained deflation, namely to the extent that a+n exceeds zero. A rise of the progress rate a will lead to both a rise of the level of P and of the deflation rate respectively (the expression β(1-σ)-1 is always negative, so that the impact for the level of P is unambiguous). For the case of a shrinking population (clearly a future problem of Japan and some other OECD countries) we also have to take into account the case n<0. Even if in a growing economy there is a potential case for a non-monetary inflation or deflation it is true that monetary authorities could achieve price stability, namely by adjusting the money supply accordingly. This will, however, affect seigniorage revenues for government.

We now return to the true long run monetary equilibrium condition. Let us briefly focus on the case of an open economy which suggests an additional potential paradox. A paradox in an open economy in which there is parallel technological progress in country I and country II (dA>0, dA*>0; and dA=dA*) will occur if the income elasticity of the demand for money is below unity (in the interval 0,1) in the home country and above unity in country II. The consequence of global technological progress is that the price level in country I will rise, while it will fall in country II; implicitly one has to assume downward wage flexibility if unemployment is to be avoided. If the nominal exchange rate is constant the effect is a real appreciation of the home country's currency and this has to be taken into account in the context of the interest parity which reads in the absence of inflation r=r* +dlnq*/dt where q* is defined as eP*/P (e is the nominal exchange rate); hence technological progress will affect capital flows through the logic of the interest parity. While some observers analyzing country I might argue that process innovations (or rises in labor productivity) lead to a real appreciation, the true story is that process innovations per se do not lead to this appreciation, rather it is a mechanism which is related to the money market. Our approach suggests that analyzing long run price level dynamics in open economies with technological progress should be done in a careful way and must include an analysis of the money market. The common analytical split between pure trade theory (never looking at the money market) and monetary theory of international economic relations is not adequate in certain cases.

If one considers the case of flexible nominal exchange rates and process innovations (again with σ in the interval 0,1 in country I and above unity in country II) one may assume that the nominal exchange rate is rising, so that there is a nominal depreciation of the currency. Speculators and scientists therefore should be interested in the size of the income elasticity of the demand for money. It seems likely that in poor countries the income elasticity of the demand for money is below unity while in countries with a high per capita income it is above unity as the demand for real balances and other wealth assets is rising more than proportionately as income is rising. Economic catching up of poor countries and thus international real income convergence could thus help to avoid the above paradox. To learn more about the role of this paradox from an empirical perspective, one should particularly study the link between progress and the price level in those countries where the income elasticity of the demand for money is below unity in a certain period and above unity in the following period.

Next we take a look at the real exchange rate eP^*/P while assuming that the above equilibrium equation holds in a similar way abroad:

$$P^*= (\text{\ss}^*/\sigma'^*)M^*(L^*_oA^*_oe'^{(a^*+n^*)t})^{-\sigma^*}[s^*/(a^*+n^*+\delta^*)]^{[\text{\ss}^*(1-\sigma^*)-1]/[1-\text{\ss}^*]} \qquad (A.10l)$$

Now we get a much better understanding about the long run real exchange rate which is given (denoting $s/(a+n+\delta)=: s''$, $L_oA_o=:Z'$ and $[\text{\ss}(1-\sigma)-1]/[1-\text{\ss}]=: \text{\ss}'$) by the following expression

$$q^*=e(\text{\ss}^*/\text{\ss})(\sigma'/\sigma'^*)(M^*/M)(Z'^*e'^{(a^*+n^*)t})^{-\sigma^*}[s''^*]^{\text{\ss}'^*}/(Z'e'^{(a+n)t})^{-\sigma}[s'']^{\text{\ss}'} \qquad (A.10m)$$

If $\text{\ss}'=\text{\ss}'^*$ we can state that a rise of the foreign savings rate relative to the domestic savings rate will raise the real long run equilibrium exchange rate; a relative rise of the domestic savings rate will bring about a real appreciation; as $-\sigma < 0$ we can add that a relative rise of the sum of the domestic progress rate and the population growth rate will also bring about a real appreciation (both a relative rise of the savings rate and a relative rise of the domestic progress rate are typical of economic-technological catching up (with Japan being a prominent example in the 1970s and 1980s). One should note that the world real income in terms of country I (home country) is $Y^W = Y+ q^*Y^*$.

If all goods are homogenous and indeed the array of goods produced in both countries are equal then we would have $q^*=1$, so that the nominal exchange rate can be inferred from the above equation. It is fairly clear that in a multi-product world economy with products a, b....z the relative import price eP^*/P will be determined by the weighted average of individual prices. If the range of goods a, b...z is in ascending order with respect to technology content and if one assumes that the Schumpeterian rent included in individual product prices is a positive function of the technological intensity of the product, a technologically leading country typically will produce more of the high-technology products x, y, z or be even the only producer, in which case the respective prices will contain a monopoly pricing element. Thus $q^*=1$ will hold only under the condition that there is both free trade and full international technological convergence; or an equivalent technological specialization in exports of both countries is considered.

Our findings for the case of a full employment growth model are consistent with a macroeconomic approach to the exchange rate and the current account, respectively. However, we will show later that the production function and the growth model also can be used in the presence of unemployment.

Let us get back to the standard literature: In the literature one often finds two contrasting views of explaining the real trade balance $X'=X-q^*J$ (where J is imports); one can argue that since export quantity $X=X(q^*,Y^*) - X$ is a positive function of q^* and Y^* and the import quantity $J=J(q^*,Y)$ the development of the trade balance depends for given Y and Y^* on the Marshall-Lerner condition or the Robinson condition; $X'=X'(q^*,Y,Y^*)$. Alternatively one can argue that since the goods market equilibrium condition in an underemployed economy can be written as $S(Y)=I(r) +\delta K +G-T + X-q^*J$ one can state (assuming for simplicity G=T) that net exports X' are a function of Y and r. Net exports will rise if savings rise relative to planned investment and for given Y, Y^*, P, P^* this obviously implies a nominal depreciation. We now also see this for the case of a full employment growth model. Again, as one may argue that the production function and the growth model respectively also work in an economy with a positive unemployment rate, we have shown a clear mechanism according to which the savings rate affects the exchange rate. However, it is clear that the net investment function in a full employment model cannot be I(r), rather we have $r=ßY/K$ and therefore we can state the equation $-dr + ß(dY/dt)/K = ß(Y/K^2)(dK/dt)$.

Moreover, to get a stationary real exchange rate we must either have all the goods being identical at home and abroad or that $(a+n)\sigma = (a^*+n^*)\sigma^*$; if $ß=ß^*$ and $\sigma=\sigma^*$ the growth rate of the population in the home country must exceed that of the foreign country by exactly the difference in the progress rate in favor of the foreign country.

Let us finally take a look at the basic form of the quantity theory of money, namely that $MV(Y,i) = PY$; we denote with g growth rates and with $E_{x,z}$ the elasticity of X with respect to Z. Thus we have:

$$g_M + E_{V,Y}g_Y + E_{V,i}g_i = g_P + g_Y \qquad (A.10n)$$

Therefore it follows (without loss of the validity of the basic argument) under the simplifying assumption $ß=1-ß$ (and taking into account that $r=ßY/K$) the following equation:

$$g_M = g_P + (1- E_{V,Y})[ßg_{KAL}] - E_{V,i}(ß-1)g_{(KAL)} \qquad (A.10o)$$

If the price level is to remain constant and hence $g_P=0$ the central bank must adopt a growth rate of the money supply which is equal to:

$$g_P = g_M - (1 - E_{V,Y})[\ßg_{KAL}] + E_{V,i}(\ß-1)g_{(KAL)} \qquad\qquad (A.10p)$$

The third term on the right-hand side of the equation has not been considered in standard analysis, rather one has implicitly considered the term through the interest rate. For long term analysis in open monetary economies it can be quite useful to adequately combine the real sphere and the monetary sphere. Even if short-term dynamics in some markets diverge from the long run equilibrium pattern (e.g. the case of Dornbusch overshooting in the exchange rate) one should study the long term equilibrium solution since that solution should guide expectations of rational actors in an economy in which one finds global stability (as regards the latter one always has to analyze the dynamics before one can consider long run equilibrium solutions as meaningful; provided that the adjustment process is stable).

The income elasticity of the real demand for money can change over time and might be related to both per capita income development and financial market innovations. Actually, we do not know very much about the determinants of the income elasticity of the demand for money. Transaction technologies clearly play a role but so do other factors.

A.7.3 Conclusions for Analysis of Process Innovations in a Monetary Economy

Process innovations are a standard phenomenon of the economic analysis. In a monetary economy one can, however, not neglect the impact of the money market on the price level. Since process innovations not only affect real output but also the marginal product of capital and therefore the real interest, one has a principal ambiguity with respect to the impact of technology on the price level. There is a critical size of the income elasticity below which a rise of the level of technology implies a rise of the price level; with an elasticity above the critical value, process innovations will bring about a fall of the price level. The impact of technology on the price level in turn will have an impact on capital flows since a change of the real interest rate is part of interest parity. Our analysis suggests that analyzing technological progress requires combining an analysis of the real sphere and of the monetary sphere of the economy. As we have shown, monetary policy could avoid inflation by an adequate choice of the growth rate of the money supply.

A.7.4 Solow Model and Role of Money for Growth

As regards growth dynamics in a broader sense, one may focus mainly on macroeconomic aspects or on the topic of the underlying structural change – with respect to the latter see BORBÉLY (2006) who presents for the case of Eastern Europe and EU eastern enlargement an innovative empirical analysis for explaining the dynamics of structural change, export specialization and export unit value dynamics for various sectors, including labor-intensive sectors and technology-intensive sectors. The macroeconomic analysis which is presented here is more mainstream and an analysis of structural change in open economies. However, it also is complex and it can be quite useful – as is argued here – in combining standard elements of traditional and modern growth analysis with some new thoughts about linking the real sphere of the economy and the monetary sphere. Moreover, in some fields macroeconomic analysis and the analysis of structural change can be combined fruitfully.

The Solow growth model is a very useful starting point for the analysis of economic growth, and it can be refined in many interesting ways. It determines the long run capital intensity k# (k=: K/L where K is capital and L is labor) and – in the context of technological progress – of k' (k'=: K/(AL)) through combining a production function and an equilibrium condition for the goods market. For the sake of simplicity, our analysis will at first consider the rather simple case of a Cobb-Douglas production function $Y=K^{\beta}(AL)^{1-\beta}$ where ß $(0<\beta<1)$ is the output elasticity of capital, Y is output and A is the level of labor-saving technology. As regards the level of technology, we assume that $A(t) = A_0\, e^{'at}$; a is the exogenous progress rate and A_0 the initial level of technology.

The basic Cobb Douglas function makes the following generalizations rather tractable. We are interested in discussing several generalizations which mainly refer to the savings function and the production function.

As a point of reference we assume – as in the original Solow model – that savings S is proportionate to real income Y so that S=sY; the population is $L=L_o e^{'nt}$ (n is the growth rate of the population). Imposing the equilibrium condition dK/dt=S (and hence [dK/dt]/[AL] = S/[AL]) and taking into account the definition of k', we get the fundamental differential equation:

$$dk'/dt = sy' - (n+a)k' = sk'^{\beta} - (n+a)k' \tag{a1}$$

This is a stable Bernoulli differential equation (See Appendix G 4) whose general solution is

$$k'(t) = [C_0\; e^{'-(n+a)(1-\beta)t} + (s/(a+n))]^{1/1-\beta} \tag{a2}$$

The initial conditions determine C_0. As long as the sum of the growth rate of the population and of the level of technology – that is (n+a) - is not negative the economy will converge to the steady state value $k'\#=[s/(a+n)]^{1/1-\beta}$ and as $y'=k'^{\beta}$ we get for the steady state per capita income:

$$y\# = [s/(a+n)]^{\beta/1-\beta}\, A_0\, e^{'at} \tag{a3}$$

This equation is our basic point of reference. It says that the steady state level of per capita income is a positive function of the savings rate s and a negative function of the progress rate a and the growth rate of the population n. The initial level of technology affects the level of per capita output. The long run growth rate is exogenous and is equal to a. Once the steady state capital intensity k# is achieved, output per capita y will grow at the constant rate a. Starting at k_0, the economy will experience a transitory economic catching up process characterized by the growth of k' over time (dk'/dt>0). The following figure shows the determination of the steady state through the intersection of the (n+a)k' line with the sy' line. Thus, we basically have a representation of the fundamental differential equation. We also can see the adjustment path in the sense of dk'/dt, and we see the adjustment path of lny' (y=:Y/L):.

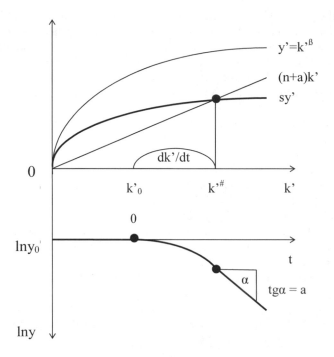

Fig. 11. Standard Neoclassical Growth Model and Adjustment Path

Where does the temporary growth rate of k' – and hence of y' – reach a maximum? In the fundamental differential equation, we take the derivative with respect to k' and set the result equal to zero (remember that $dlnk'/dt=:[dk'/dt]/k'$). Therefore

$$dlnk'/dt = ßsk'^{ß-1} – (n+a) \qquad (a4)$$

This implies a maximum growth rate $dlnk'/dt$ at the value $k'^{max} = (ßs/(a+n))^{1/1-ß}$ $= ß^{1/1-1/1-ß}k'\#$. The maximum growth is a positive function of ß (obviously taking logarithms gives $ln\,k'^{max} = (1/1-ß)(ln[ßs] - ln\,[a+n])$).

If we compare two countries (foreign variables are starred) it is clear that in a world economy with capital depreciation – the depreciation rate is δ in country I and δ* in country II – the relative per capita income position in the long run will be given (assuming ß=ß*) by:

$$y/y* = [(s/s*)(a*+n*+δ*)/(a+n+δ)\ (A_0/Ao*)\ ]e'^{(a-a*)t} \qquad (a5)$$

The term in square brackets determines the relative level of the growth path of the domestic economy. As long as the progress rates a and a* are exogenous, it is not possible to really discuss options for growth policies. If one further assumes that the income tax rate τ as well as the unemployment rate u negatively affect savings so that the savings function is S= sZ'(1-τ)(1-u)Y in country I and in a similar formulation $S^* = s'^*Z'^*(1-\tau^*)(1-u^*)\ Y^*$, we can modify the equation for relative income and obtain – after including the institutional variable Z':

$$y\#/y^*\# = \{(sZ'(1-\tau)(1-u)/Z'^*[s^*(1-\tau^*) \qquad (a6)$$

$$(1-u^*)])(a^*+n^*+\delta^*)/(a+n+\delta)(A_0/A_0^*)\}e'^{(a-a^*)t}$$

The main reason to assume that savings is negatively influenced by the unemployment rate is the fact that unemployed workers do not save, and indeed they often dissave for a certain time period. Economic catching up in the sense of narrowing the gap with respect to the level of the growth path of country II can now be achieved through various instruments – as viewed from country I:

- an improvement of the institutional setup (Z')
- a rise of the savings rate (s); this is in well-known contrast to the message of the standard short term Keynesian/Mundell Fleming model according to which a rise of the savings rate will reduce equilibrium income.
- a fall of the tax rate (τ)
- reduction of the unemployment rate (u)
- fall of the population growth rate (n)
- fall of the depreciation rate (δ); one should note that economic opening up of a country will bring about a once-and-for-all rise of the depreciation rate, as many firms will experience obsolescence of the capital stock once the economy is opened up to the world market. Hence economic opening up might bring about a fall of the level of the growth path unless economic opening up helps to upgrade the institutional setup factor Z' sufficiently.

If the government's planning horizon is short enough, a fall in the progress rate might be desirable since this will raise the level of the growth path in the short run while reducing the permanent growth rate in the long run. In an open economy, there are further long run constraints to be observed.

In an open economy setting – for simplicity considered under the constraint that there is no government budget disequilibrium, no unemployment, zero inflation, a zero current account and no capital flows – the implication clearly is that a poor country can catch up only if the parameters change in the long run in such a way that the same or at least a similar level of y is achieved as abroad (y*); and international economic convergence requires that the growth rate of technological progress of the initially poor country converge to that of the rich country. Hence if s=s*, a=a*, n=n* and ß=ß* – which is in line with the Heckscher-Ohlin assumption that technology is the same in country I (home country) and country II – both countries will converge towards the same long run per capita income, despite all initial differences in the initial per capita income positions.

A growth model which fits reality in a world economy with many different countries will naturally consider the empirically well established fact that very poor countries have a very small savings rate while countries with a medium per capita income (among the OECD countries) have a relatively higher savings rate. However, rather rich countries have a relatively low savings rate. We will suggest a rather simple way to deal with different savings rates in the course of economic catching up. How can we cover this phenomenon? We simply may assume a modified simple savings function (with z' denoting a positive parameter in the interval 0,1), namely

$$S= s(1+ z'dk'/dt)Y \tag{a7}$$

Alternatively, one can write $S/[AL]= s(1+ z'dk'/dt)y'$. A key argument why the savings rate should increase during a rise in k' is the fact that a rise in the ratio of capital to labor in efficiency units (AL) generates a desire of private households and entrepreneurial households to benefit from an expected increase in output growth related to positive external output effects of investment; the latter might be related to learning-by-doing effects. The modified fundamental differential equation therefore is

$$dk'/dt = s(1+ z'dk'/dt)k'^{\beta}- (n+a)k' \tag{a8}$$

$$(1-z'k'^{\beta})\, dk'/dt = sk'^{\beta}- (n+a)k' \tag{a9}$$

It is easy to see that the steady state solution for k'# is the same as in the above basic model (note that we assume $z'k'^{\beta} \neq 1$). However, the adjustment speed towards the steady state is now larger. Empirical research should tell whether or not the approach suggested is useful.

If country I (the relatively poor home economy) were to achieve in the long run the same per capita income as the rich foreign country II, a double convergence is required in the neoclassical growth model (for simplicity we assume zero population growth in both countries). The savings rate – effectively the investment output ratio – must converge to that of the foreign country, and the progress rate would have to be the same as abroad. Referring to the standard SOLOW model, one must therefore assume a mechanism which is reflected in a suitable equation such as (with z" standing for a positive parameter in the interval 0,1)

$$ds/dt = (s/s^*)(s^{*2}s^{z''-1} - s^{*1-z''}) \tag{a10}$$

This differential equation basically consists of the first term (s/s*) and a second term on the right hand side, which will bring about s=s* in the long term. As regards the savings income ratio, sound financial institutions – ultimately reflected in a relatively high level of real money balances per capita – may be expected to play an important role. If people have no confidence in the banking sector, the savings rate will naturally remain low. We emphasize here that the picture will have to be modified if we take into account foreign direct investment which requires making a distinction between gross domestic product and gross national product. One will have to raise – mostly ignored in the literature – the topic of how the savings function in the source country and the home country is to be modified adequately in a world with foreign direct investment.

For the moment, we will disregard the foreign investment issue. Turning to the above differential equation, it is rather unclear which forces will bring about such an international convergence of the savings rates. If one takes into account the possibility of permanent government deficits or surpluses, one may point to the role of government in the convergence of savings ratios. However, in few poor countries is the government known to maintain long term budget surpluses. Instead of looking for budget surpluses in poor countries, we may instead point out the role of permanent positive deficit-GDP ratios in rich countries which could contribute to international convergence of the savings rate.

Growth and the Role of Real Money Balances

Another element of generalization in the Solow model refers to the specification of the savings function in the sense that one might want to consider $S/(AL)=sy'^{\Omega}$. Moreover, we may consider the role of real money balances m (m is the ratio of the nominal stock of money M to the price level P) for savings and consumption, respectively. We assume that the higher m/(AL), the higher the desired savings, which effectively amounts to saying that a higher stock of m'=:m/(AL) will go along with a higher real capital stock relative to AL. We thus assume the parameter Ω" to be positive (Ω' is also assumed to be positive; in the Solow model it is zero). We therefore can specify:

$$S/(AL)=sy'^{\Omega'} m'^{\Omega''} \tag{a11}$$

We thus assume that savings per efficiency unity of labor has a positive effect on (relative) real income and (relative) real money balances.

Now let us assume – with i denoting the nominal interest rate; σ and σ' are positive parameters – that the real demand for money is given by

$$m^d/AL = y'^{\sigma}\sigma'/i \tag{a12}$$

With m/AL denoted as m', we can express money market equilibrium therefore as

$$m' = y'^{\sigma}\sigma'/i \tag{a13}$$

We insert this equilibrium condition in the savings function and obtain:

$$S/(AL)=sy'^{\Omega'} y'^{\Omega'} (\sigma'/i)^{\Omega''} \tag{a14}$$

If we assume profit maximization (real interest rate $r = \text{ß}y'/k' = \text{ß}k'^{\beta-1}$) and zero inflation and hence i= r, we obtain

$$S/(AL)= sk'^{\Omega'\text{ß} +\Omega''\beta''}(\sigma'/\text{ß})^{\Omega''}; \beta''=:[1+\beta(\sigma-1)] \tag{a15}$$

The fundamental differential equation for k' therefore reads:

$$dk'/dt = sk'^{\Omega'\text{ß}+\Omega''\beta''}(\sigma'/\text{ß})^{\Omega''}- (n+a)k' \tag{a16}$$

This equation – with C_0 to be determined by the initial condition $k(0)=k_0$ – has the solution

$$k'(t) = [C_0 e'^{-(n+a)(1-\Omega'\text{ß}-\Omega''\beta'')t} + s(\sigma'/\text{ß})^{\Omega''}/(a+n)]^{1/(1-\Omega'\text{ß}+\Omega'')} \tag{a17}$$

Assuming that n+a exceeds zero, this equation is stable if 1- Ω'ß - Ω"β''>0; Ω'>1 is a necessary condition that the transitory growth rate of this monetary Solow model exceeds that of the original model. Whether this condition is fulfilled is an

empirical question. Assuming the condition to hold, the steady state value for k'
is:

$$k'\# = [s(\sigma'/\text{ß})^{\Omega''}/(a+n)]^{1/(1-\Omega'\text{ß}+\Omega'')} \qquad (a18)$$

If $\sigma'>\beta$ and $\Omega''>1$ the steady state capital intensity in a monetary economy will
exceed that of a non monetary economy. As regards the empirical evidence on Ω''
the reader is referred to the final chapter.

Taking into account the modified savings function, the money market condition
and profit maximization thus implies the following (assuming that $\beta''>0$): The
long run equilibrium ratio of capital to labor in efficiency units

- positively depends on the savings rate and negatively on a and n (the standard
  results)
- positively on the interest responsiveness of the demand for money (σ')
- positively on the elasticity of savings with respect to real money balances (Ω')
- positively on the income elasticity of the demand for money (Ω'').

A similar reasoning holds with respect to the steady state value of y'. In addition, we can add the traditional result that the level of output relative to labor input
in efficiency units is a positive function of ß. However, the exponent for y' looks a
bit more complex than is traditionally the case; here it is $\text{ß}/(1-\Omega'\text{ß}+\Omega'')$ which is
identical with the traditional result $\text{ß}/1-\text{ß}$ if the income elasticity of savings is unity
and $\Omega''=0$. If the exponent $\text{ß}/(1-\Omega'\text{ß}+\Omega'')$ is equal to or greater than $\text{ß}/(1-\text{ß})$, we
may assume that the introduction of a monetary economy brings about a higher
capital intensity k' than the non-monetary SOLOW model, provided that $(\sigma'/\text{ß})^{\Omega''}$
exceeds unity.

A final remark shall refer to the progress rate. This rate can be endogenized in
principle, but it also could be considered as shaped by stable cyclical impulses.
For example, we may assume that $a(t)= a_0 + a_1\sin t$ ($a_0 + a_1$ are positive parameters). In this case, however, the solution of the fundamental differential equation
looks somewhat different as the progress rate a is no longer a constant parameter.
At the bottom line, one may consider the possibility that long term technology cycles overlap with short term cyclical forces. The latter could include variations of
the supply elasticity of input factors.

Money as a Positive External Effect in the Production Function

Another way to integrate the analysis of inflation in a long run growth model is to
assume that real money balances enter the production function in the form of a
positive external effect. The fact that households hold money and use it in market
transactions saves information and transaction costs not only for households but
also for firms selling in such markets. Assuming an output elasticity of real money
balances of ß', the production function may therefore be written as

$$y' = m'^{\text{ß}'} k'^{\text{ß}} \qquad (a19)$$

The savings function S=sY then leads to the fundamental differential equation

$$dk'/dt = s\, m'^{\beta'}\, k'^{\beta} - (n+a)k' \qquad (a20)$$

Obviously the variable m', which can be considered a policy variable in an open economy with flexible exchange rates, must not be ignored for determining the level of the growth path. The steady state solution for the capital stock relative to labor in efficiency units is:

$$k\# = [s\, m'^{\beta'}/(n+a)]^{1/(1-\beta)} \qquad (a21)$$

Again we could integrate the condition for money market equilibrium. In the production function, we have to replace m' by $y'^{\sigma} (\sigma'/i)$;

$$y' = y'^{\sigma\beta'} (\sigma'/i)'^{\beta'}\, k'^{\beta} \qquad (a22)$$

This implies

$$y' = (\sigma'/i)^{\beta'/(1-\sigma\beta')}\, k'^{\beta/(1-\sigma\beta')} \qquad (a23)$$

If we assume a relatively high inflation rate π we can replace i with $\pi\#$, which should be interpreted as the target inflation rate of the central bank. Interestingly, the apparent output elasticity of the capital stock is now lower than in a pure non-monetary growth model (we assume $0<\sigma\beta'<1$). By contrast, if we assume that the central bank's inflation target rate is zero, the nominal interest rate can be set equal to the real interest rate r. Now let us assume that firms are profit maximizers, so that $1/r = (1/\beta)k'^{1-\beta}$. We obtain

$$y' = (\sigma'/\beta')^{\beta'/(1-\sigma'/\beta')}k'^{\beta'/(1-\sigma'/\beta')+(1-\beta')\beta'/(1-\sigma'/\beta')} \qquad (a24)$$

We now have an apparent output elasticity of the capital stock in which the output elasticity of k' is determined by two elements: the elasticity of money balances m' and the income elasticity of the demand for money. With a standard savings function S=sY, we now get the fundamental differential equation

$$dk/dt = s(\sigma'/\beta')^{\beta'/(1-\sigma'/\beta')}k'^{\beta'/(1-\sigma'/\beta')+(1-\beta')\beta'/(1-\sigma'/\beta')} - (n+a)k' \qquad (a25)$$

This looks rather similar to the above case of a modified savings function – which includes a real balances effect – in combination with a production function which does not contain real money balances. Thus we have two good arguments to consider the role of real money balances in a long run growth analysis. The steady state solution is given by

$$k'\# = \{[s/(n+a)](\sigma'/\beta')^{\beta'/(1-\sigma'/\beta')}\}^{1/(\beta'(1-\sigma'/\beta'))} \qquad (a26)$$

The impact of money on the capital intensity is ambiguous.

Money, Transfers, Growth and Real Income

If one follows the basic TOBIN approach to monetary growth – we will recall this model in detail subsequently – who has argued that seigniorage should be taken into account in the government budget, one should expect the paradox result that equilibrium capital intensity and per capita output in long run equilibrium are smaller in a monetary growth model than in the traditional SOLOW model. However, we will show that under plausible assumptions – referring indeed to the core of defining a monetary economy (the production function) – we will not get TOBIN's result that introducing money in a neoclassical growth model will bring about a fall in both equilibrium capital intensity and per capita income y:=Y/L (L is population or labor).

Consider that the government budget equation $(\gamma''-\tau)Y = (dM/dt)/P$ can be written (with M nominal money stock, P price level, m''=: ratio of real money balances m to L; γ'' is government transfers relative to GDP, τ is the income tax rate and μ is the growth rate of money) as:

$$(\gamma''-\tau)y = \mu m'' \tag{i}$$

or (with m'= : m/[AL])

$$(\gamma''-\tau)y' = \mu m' \tag{ii}$$

Hence the income elasticity of money is unity; σ' is a parameter indicating the interest responsiveness of the demand for money and i is the nominal interest rate. As regards the production function, we assume that real money balances m' raise the productivity of firms so that we have a production function (with y'=: Y/AL; k'=K/AL and ß and ß' standing for positive elasticities):

$$y' = k'^{ß} m'^{ß'} \tag{iii}$$

The goods market equilibrium condition in a closed economy (with G denoting government expenditures as well as transfers, T real tax revenue) is given by $S + (T-G) = dK/dt + \delta K$. Thus we get

$$dk'/dt = s[y'(1-\tau)+\mu m'] - \mu m' - (n+\delta+a)k' \tag{iv}$$

Taking into account money market equilibrium (where i is the nominal interest rate and σ' a positive parameter indicating the responsiveness of the demand for money with respect to i), namely

$$m' = y'\sigma'/i \tag{v}$$

leads to the equation:

$$dk'/dt = s[y'(1-\tau)+(s-1)\mu y'\sigma'/i] - (n+\delta+a)k' \tag{v'}$$

Setting dk'/dt=0, we get the equilibrium value for k':

$$k'\# = \{sm'^{ß'}[(1-\tau) - \mu\sigma'(1-s)/i]/(n+\delta+a)\}^{1/1-ß} \tag{v''}$$

Here were have the TOBIN result that the steady state capital intensity in a monetary economy could be lower than in a non-monetary economy, however, per capita income could be higher according to our production function. Indeed, the steady state income Y/[AL]=: y' is given by:

$$y'\# = \{sm'^{ß'}[(1-\tau) - \mu\sigma'(1-s)/i]/(n+\delta+a)\}^{ß/(1-ß)} m'^{ß'} \tag{vi}$$

We can rewrite the equation as:

$$y'^{\#(1-\beta)/\beta} = \{s[(1-\tau) - \mu\sigma'(1-s)/i]/(n+\delta+a)\}\, m'^{\beta'/\beta} \tag{vii}$$

Necessary conditions for y' in a monetary economy to exceed y' in a non-monetary economy are that $(1-\tau) > \mu\sigma'(1-s)/i$ and $m'^{\beta'/\beta} > 1$.

We use the approximation that $\ln(1+z) \approx z$, which holds if z is close to zero. Taking logarithms thus gives

$$(1-\beta)/\beta\, \ln y' = \beta'/\beta\, \ln(m') + \ln s - \tau - \mu\sigma'(1-s)/i - \ln(n+\delta+a) \tag{viii}$$

It is obvious that in a monetary economy, y' in the steady state is higher than in a non-monetary economy if

$$\beta'/\beta\, \ln m' > \mu\sigma'(1-s)/i \tag{ix}$$

that is if

$$m' > \exp(\beta\mu\sigma'(1-s)/(i\beta')) \tag{x}$$

It is quite plausible that the introduction of money should raise the level of the growth path; otherwise evolutionary dynamics with open economies would not allow monetary economies to survive (moreover, standard microeconomic analysis suggests productivity-enhancing effects of using money in a market economy). Alternatively, one could argue that money makes the economy more effective in absorbing shocks at relatively low costs. Besides an impact of m' –and the inflation rate – on the level of the growth path, one should in principle also consider the effect of money on the progress rate; that is one should consider monetary endogenous growth models (For a specific approach in a quite different context see GRIES/SIEVERT/WIENEKE, 2004).

Note that if there is to be zero inflation, we must have the growth rate of the money supply $\mu = a+n$ so that the growth rate of the money supply is quasi-endogenous. We thus have an empirical question which refers to the relative size of β', s and τ where government has a choice of τ. Moreover, we have an interesting set of empirical issues where further analysis could drop, of course, the requirement $\beta=1-\beta$.

The more general question of monetary growth modelling refers to a situation with inflation – so that the inflation rate $\pi>0$ and $\mu = a+n+\pi$. Imposing the condition of profit maximization requires that the real interest rate $r=\beta k'^{\beta-1}m'^{\beta'}$. This aspect might be an additional element of analysis. The more interesting question concerns the impact of the inflation rate on the progress rate. Denoting the undistorted progress rate as a_0, we can write $a = a_0 - a_1\pi$ if we state the hypothesis that inflation diverts management's attention from the innovation process so that the progress rate is dampened by inflation. The impact of the inflation rate on the progress rate will dominate the impact of inflation on the level of the growth path in the long run. To the extent that inflation raises the level of the growth path in the short run, thereby reducing the progress rate, a short-sighted government will have a political preference in favour of inflation.

A.7.5 Monetary Growth Model and Tobin Paradox

The Solow growth model was modified by TOBIN (1965) in a way which allowed including money in a growth perspective which also is part of the debate about superneutrality of money. While the idea of the classics that money is neutral for the real economy has been discussed under the heading of neutrality the term superneutrality refers to the question whether a positive or negative growth rate of the nominal money supply will affect real variables.

In the model of TOBIN (1965) the main result of introducing money in a growth model is a reduction of the per capita capital intensity (k) and hence of per capita output (y) in the steady state. Moreover, a rise of the growth rate of the money supply was found to raise the inflation rate but also to possibly raise the level of the growth path in a simple model with an exogenous growth rate (n) of the population L. In such a model the long run growth rate of output is exogenous, namely n. Government can, however, affect the steady state value (denoted by #) of the capital intensity k=K/L (K is the capital stock) and hence the growth rate of output Y; in the simplest case output is described by a neoclassical production function Y(K,L).

In summarizing the TOBIN approach in a simple way we partly follow REITHER (1989). Money is introduced through the government budget constraint since the supply of money generates "seigniorage revenues" which consist of the real value of a rise of the nominal money supply. In an equilibrium approach one has to take into account that the nominal money supply M will have to be equal to the nominal money demand $M^d = Pm^d$ where P is the price level and m^d the real demand for money which positively depends on Y and negatively on the nominal interest rate i. The formal setup is as follows; first we consider the government budget constraint where G is real consumption of government, T real tax revenue and H real transfers.

$$(dM/dt)/P = G - T + H \qquad (1)$$

We define h" as transfers per capita (L) so that H=h"L which allows to write – with μ as growth rate of the nominal money supply M, m''=(M/P)/L and the definition of the government budget deficit ratio [G-T]/Y=: γ'' – the budget constraint in per capita terms as:

$$\mu\, m'' = \gamma''y + h'' \qquad (2)$$

We assume a per capita savings function (with z' denoting disposable per capita income and s a parameter in the interval 0,1), namely that savings S relative to L is given by:

$$S/L = sz' \qquad (3)$$

The disposable income is (with τ denoting the income tax rate):

$$z' = (1-\tau)y(k) + h'' \qquad (4)$$

Equilibrium in the goods market requires that the gross per capita savings S/L finance both per capita investment and the government deficit:

$$s \left[(1-\tau)y(k) + h" \right] = \left[dK/dt \right]/L + \gamma" y(k) + h" \tag{5}$$

If we assume that reinvestment is δK and that the growth rate of the population is n we get the following implicit expression for the steady state value of the capital intensity (k#):

$$\{ s[1-\tau] - \gamma" \} y(k^{\#}) = (n+\delta)k\# + (1-s)h" \tag{6}$$

With a standard Cobb-Douglas production function $y=k^{\beta}$ we get in the steady state:

$$\{ s[1-\tau] - \gamma" \} k^{\beta} = (n+\delta)k + (1-s)h" \tag{7}$$

The left hand side of the equation is portrayed as LHS in the subsequent graph, the right hand side as RHS. TOBIN (1965) assumes that the structural deficit ratio is zero so that h"=μm''. We can conclude from the graphical analysis that h">0 shifts the right-hand side curve upwards (RHS$_1$ instead of RHS$_0$) so that k# falls to k#$_1$. This is obvious since government must finance h" while savings per capita is raised only by sh" so that the equilibrium capital intensity is reduced.

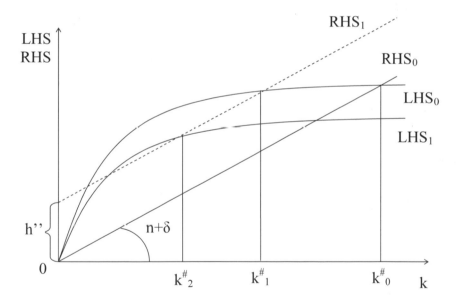

Fig. 12. Government Activity in the TOBIN Monetary Growth Model

If we had a structural deficit the LHS curve rotates downwards so that the intersection point shifts to the left: k# falls. If one assumes a positive growth rate of the money supply there could be inflation; the inflation rate is $\pi = \mu$-n (in an economy with technological progress rate a the steady state (long run) inflation rate is given by $\pi = \mu$-[a+n]).

Disregarding technological progress we can state: Printing money generates a "growth seigniorage revenue" nm and an inflation tax πm. As the money supply growth rate $\mu = \pi + n$ in the steady state we can write:

$$h" = [\pi\# + n]m''\# \tag{8}$$

If we require a zero structural budget deficit we get the steady state equilibrium condition:

$$s[1-\tau]y(k) - (1-s)nm''\# = (n+\delta)k\# + (1-s)\pi\#m''\# \tag{9}$$

With inflation we have to consider the impact of the inflation rate on the inflation tax – here we have to take into account money market equilibrium, too. That is real money supply per capita $(M/P)/L$ must equal real money demand per capita $m''^d(r+\pi, y)$ which one may specific for the sake of simplicity as $y^\sigma\sigma'/[r+\pi]$

$$s[1-\tau]y(k) - (1-s)nm''\# = (n+\delta)k\# + (1-s)\pi\#m''\# \tag{10}$$

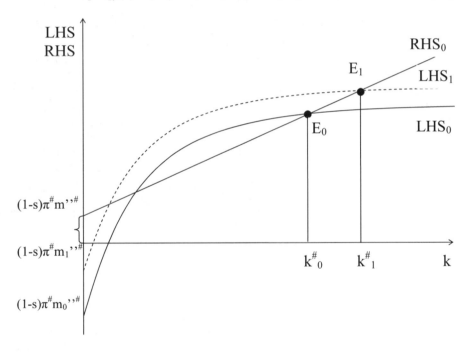

Fig. 13. Money Supply Dynamics and the Capital Intensity in the TOBIN Model

A rise of the inflation rate will reduce the per capita money supply so that the value of the starting point of LHS on the ordinate is shrinking. The effect is a rise of the steady state capital intensity: Higher inflation brings a rise from $k\#_0$ to $k\#_1$ (TOBIN effect). However, the growth seigniorage revenue effect is not the only effect to be considered. Depending on the interest elasticity of the demand for money we could get a rise of $\pi\#m\#$, no change in inflation tax or a fall of $\pi\#m\#$.

The latter case could lead to superneutrality of money which means that inflation would not affect the capital intensity.

Taking into account process innovations we will have to reconsider the results presented. The crucial question is whether and to which extent inflation negatively affects the progress rate. Since inflation is known to reduce the average maturity of bonds one may argue that inflation generally reduces the decision horizon of economic agents. Innovation projects which generate a high social rate of return in the long run could not be realized in an inflationary environment; at least not if the growth rate of the price level is beyond a critical inflation rate ($\pi'\#$).

A.7.6 Technological Progress Cycles

Let us briefly consider the logic of progress cycles in the neoclassical growth model. If we assume that savings $S = s(1-\tau)(1-u)Y$ where the income tax rate is τ and the unemployment rate is u, we get a simple steady state condition for per capita income $y' = Y/[AL]$ – that is output per efficiency units of labor. Note that the savings function presented assumes that savings is reduced by unemployment. Output Y is determined by a production function $Y = K^{\beta}(AL)^{1-\beta}$ – with $0 < \beta < 1$. At first the progress rate is exogenous in the sense that $d\ln A/dt =: a$; the growth rate of the population is given by the parameter n ($n = d\ln L/dt$). The unemployment rate is considered exogenous. In the case of a balanced government budget, the goods market equilibrium condition in a closed economy is given (with δ standing for the rate of capital depreciation) by

$$S = dK/dt + \delta K \tag{Ia}$$

We thus can state – with $k' =: K/[AL]$ - the differential equation for k':

$$dk'/dt = s(1-\tau)(1-u)k'^{\beta} - (n+a+\delta)k' \tag{Ib}$$

Solving this Bernoulli differential equation or simply setting $dk'/dt = 0$, we get the steady state (symbolized by #) for k', namely:

$$k'\# = \{s(1-\tau)(1-u)/(n+a+\delta)\}1/1-\beta \tag{Ic}$$

Thus y'# is is given by:

$$y'\# = \{s(1-\tau)(1-u)/(n+a+\delta)\}^{\beta/1-\beta} \tag{Id}$$

With e' denoting the Euler number we get for $y =: K/L$ the result

$$y\# = A_0 \{s(1-\tau)(1-u)/(n+a+\delta)\}^{1/1-\beta} e'^{at} \tag{Ie}$$

Thus output per capita is given an expression where the level of the growth path is negatively affected by the progress rate a, while a affects the growth rate positively – indeed $d\ln y/dt = a$. This has a straightforward implication if we assume that there is a long term normal progress rate a# while a can rise in certain periods. If we assume that in t_1 there is an increase in the progress rate, we will see a drop of the level of the growth path while the growth path itself becomes steeper (consider the reaction in stock markets: a fall of per capita income in t_1 could be interpreted by chartists – people with extrapolative expectations – as a signal that there will be a slowdown of the economy, but the opposite is true and after some time chartists will start noticing this favourable development, possibly after output per capita has increased after t_2 beyond the natural growth path). What happens if the progress rate falls back in t_3 to the normal level? The level of the growth path will rise and the growth rate will also be reduced (consider the potential incipient reaction in stock markets where market participants might anticipate that the one-off increase in output per capita is a signal for accelerated long run growth while in reality the growth rate has decreased).

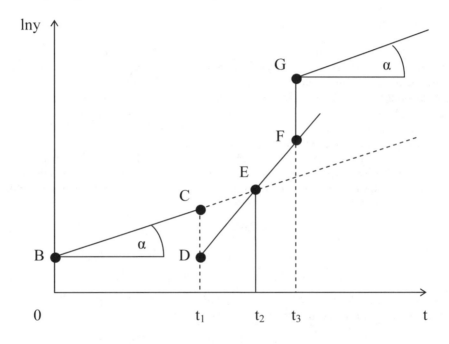

Fig. 14. Shifts in the Progress Function over Time

Semi-endogenous Progress

We can focus next on a semi-endogenized progress rate and thus consider aspects of population growth and the unemployment rate and hence implicitly of labor market dynamics. Let us assume that we have a progress function

$$a = a\# + a_1 n - a_2 u \qquad \qquad (If)$$

We thus assume the progress rate to positively depend on the growth rate of the population – hence a shrinking population brings a lower progress rate (which could be a major future problem of OECD countries) – and negatively on the unemployment rate. An argument for the latter is the common observation that workers in high unemployment countries are often resistant to outsourcing and rationalization investment so that technological progress is slowed down, obviously the result of workers' fears to be laid off during periods with a high progress rate. With countries such as Germany, Italy and France – as core countries of the Euro zone – facing a fall in population growth and even a negative long run n in combination with a high structural unemployment rate, the result will be a fall in the long run progress rate and hence in the trend growth rate. If a progress function with a negative impact of the unemployment rate exists, restoring full employment is enormously important since this will raise both the level of the growth path and increase the steady state growth rate itself.

A.7.7 Equilibrium and Terms of Trade Aspects in a Simple Open Economy Growth Model

In an open economy – without foreign direct investment/capital flows – an adequately specified growth model should take into account the fact that products exported become more sophisticated as capital intensity (capital K relative to labor in efficiency units AL) $k'=: K/[AL]$ rises. Assuming that more sophisticated products will fetch higher prices in world markets, we have to take into account a long term terms of trade effect, where the real exchange rate $eP^*/P=: q^*$ so that – with the assumption for the parameters $\alpha>0$ and $0<\alpha'\leq 1$ – we specify:

$$dq^*/dt = dk'/dt\,\alpha\,k'^{-\alpha'} \tag{I}$$

An investment boom goes along with a real depreciation, and the effect is stronger the lower capital intensity is. By integration we obtain (with C' as a constant to be determined from initial conditions) the equation:

$$q^*(t) = [\alpha/(1-\alpha')]k'^{-\alpha'+1} + C' \tag{II}$$

For simplicity we assume a balanced government budget and that neither exports X nor imports J depend on q^*. The result presented is rather robust as we shall subsequently see.

The goods market equilibrium condition requires that savings be equal to the sum of gross investment and net exports of goods and services. The quantity imported (J) has to multiplied by q^* in order to express imports in units of domestic output.

$$S = dK/dt + \delta K + [X - q^*J] \tag{III}$$

If we assume – with τ defined as the income tax rate – that imports $J=jY$ (hence $J/AL=jy'$), exports $X=x'Y$ (hence $X/AL=x'y'$), savings $S=sY[1-\tau]$, a constant growth rate of progress a ($a=:dlnA/dt$), a constant growth rate of the labor force n ($n=:dlnL/dt$) and output $Y=K^\beta (AL)^{1-\beta}$ – with $0<\beta<1$ –, we derive from the goods market equilibrium condition a differential equation in which we have inserted $q^*(t) = [\alpha/(1-\alpha')]k'^{-\alpha'+1} + C'$:

$$dk'/dt = s(1-\tau)k'^\beta + C'jk'^\beta - x'k'^\beta - (n+\delta+a)k' + j\alpha/(1-\alpha')k'^{\beta-\alpha'+1} \tag{IV}$$

Assuming that this equation is stable, we get the steady state solution by setting dk'/dt = 0. This equation cannot be solved analytically unless we make two assumptions, namely that $2 (s(1-\tau)+C'j-x')^{1/2} (j\alpha/(1-\alpha'))^{(\beta-\alpha'+1)/2}= (n+\delta+a)$ and that we have $(1-\alpha'+2\beta)/2 = 1$ – this implies $\beta>0.5$. In this case, we can express the condition that dk'/dt=0 as a quadratic equation:

$$0= [(s(1-\tau)+C'j-x')^{1/2} k'^{\beta/2} -(j\alpha)/(1-\alpha')^{1/2} k'^{(\beta-\alpha'+1)/2}]^2 \qquad (V)$$

We thus get the steady state solution as

$$k'\# = \{(s(1-\tau)+C'j-x)/[(j\alpha)/(1-\alpha')]\}^{1/(1-\alpha')} \qquad (VI)$$

The stronger the terms of trade improve (see the parameter α') as a consequence of a rising k' – the higher the fall of q* as a consequence of a higher capital intensity –, the higher the steady state capital intensity. Note that this implication is based on inspection of the exponent $1/(1-\alpha')$. We can thus argue that the stronger the impact of capital accumulation on the terms of trade, the higher the steady state capital intensity and hence the level of the long run growth path. In this context, the remarkable improvement of the US price of industrial products in the 1990s – relative to Germany – is crucial. A sustained improvement of the terms of trade has contributed to a series of rises in the level of the growth path. The growth rate of both per capita output y = Y/L and capital intensity k = K/L might be considered as exogenous. What looks like a rise in the US trend growth rate could thus in fact represent a combination of an increased trend growth rate and several increases in the level of the growth path associated with an improvement in the US terms of trade.

A.7.8 International Macroeconomics, FDI and Fiscal and Monetary Policy

A considerable part of modern macroeconomics is devoted to the question of how to optimally stabilize an open economy. The standard result in a Mundell Fleming model with perfect capital mobility is that monetary policy is ineffective under fixed exchange rates since an expansionary monetary policy will reduce the nominal interest in the short term, leading to massive capital outflows and an excess demand in the foreign exchange market. This excess demand forces the central bank to intervene and buy foreign exchange so that the domestic money supply will fall. In such a manner, monetary policy is not effective. By contrast, an expansionary fiscal policy is effective as the associated short term rise in the interest rate brings about an excess supply in the foreign exchange market – related to rising capital inflows – so that an expansionary fiscal policy indirectly causes an expansionary monetary policy.

Under floating exchange rates, the policy assessment is just the opposite. Monetary policy is effective, fiscal policy is not. Expansionary monetary policy causes a short-term fall in the interest rate and hence a real depreciation which will stimulate net exports of goods and services (provided the Marshall Lerner condition is met). An expansionary fiscal policy will cause a real appreciation, thereby reducing net exports of goods and services so that the expansionary effect is dampened.

Now let us include aspects of foreign direct investment where we focus on a small open economy which is a host country to FDI inflows but not a source country of FDI. If we integrate the argument of FROOT/STEIN (1991), namely that a real depreciation will cause higher foreign direct investment inflows – a rise of the real exchange rate $q^*=:eP^*/P$ will increase overall investment I and also net capital inflows Q –, we have to modify the standard model slightly. Additionally, we assume that output (or GDP) is produced with a Cobb Douglas function $Y=K^\beta L^{1-\beta}$ so that capital income is βY. Assuming the FDI capital stock to be a share b of the overall capital stock, K gross national income thus is $Z=Y[1-b(q^*)\beta]$; the desired b is a positive function of q^*, as a real depreciation will make it easier for foreign investors to acquire firms. We assume that consumption is proportionate to gross national income net of taxes (income tax is τ). The consumption function $C=cY(1-b(q^*)\beta)(1-\tau)$ so that we can write the consumption function as $C(q^*,Y,\tau)$; $\partial C/\partial q^*<0$. Overall investment I is composed of investment of domestic firms $I(r)$ and foreign direct investment inflows $I''(q^*)$. We thus have three medium term conditions for the goods market (X' is net exports), the money market – with m representing real money demand – and the foreign exchange market.

$$Y = C(q^*,Y,\tau) + I'(r)+ I''(q^*) + G + X'(Y,Y^*,q^*) \quad \text{(ISF curve)} \tag{1'}$$

$$M/P = m(i,q^*,Y) \quad \text{(LMF curve)} \tag{2'}$$

$$Q(i/i^*, q^*)= - X'(Y,Y^*,q^*) \quad \text{(BBF curve)} \tag{3'}$$

If we set $U = 1/D$
Where D is the system determinant:

$$D = -P/P^* ((1 - C_Y - X_Y)(Q_e m_i - Q_i m_e) + (C_e + I_e)(X_Y m_i - Q_i m_Y) + \tag{4'}$$

$$X_e m_i(1 - C_Y) + X_e m_Y(I_r - Q_i) + I_r(Q_e m_Y - X_Y m_e))$$

This expression has no unambiguous sign, but if we assume a negative sign we get the following results:

$$dY/dG = -UP/P^* (m_i(Q_e + X'_e) - m_e Q_r) \tag{5'}$$

which is positive if $X'_e < Q_e$
If we set

$$m_{q^*} = (P^*/P)m_e = 0, \text{ we get:} \tag{6'}$$

$$dY/dG = -UP/P^* m_i (Q_e + X'_e) \tag{7'}$$

which will still be positive if $X'_e < Q_e$

$$dY/dM = U/P^* (-I_r(Q_e + X'_e) + Q_r/i^*(C_e + I_e + X'_e)) \tag{8'}$$

which is negative if $X'_e < Q_e$ and $X'_e < -I_e -C_e$ and positive if $X'_e > Q_e$; and $X'_e > -I_e - C_e$. If we set $C_{q*} = (P*/P)C_e = 0$, we get:

$$dY/dM = U/P* (-I_r(Q_e + X'_e) + Q_r/i*(I_e + X'_e))$$ (9')

which is positive if $X'_e > Q_e$

Note that we have assumed a real money demand function which negatively depends on the nominal interest rate i and positively on gross national income $[Y(1-b(q*))ß]$ so that we can write $m(i,q*,Y)$; with $\partial m/\partial q* \leq 0$.

For simplicity, we assume in the subsequent medium term analysis that exchange rate expectations are static (otherwise such expectations would influence both FDI and net capital inflows). Under flexible exchange rates, an expansionary fiscal policy could now be even less expansionary in the medium term than in the traditional setup, since a real appreciation will reduce consumption through the fall in gross national income, as a higher share of firms is owned by foreign investors so that profit transfers flowing to the source country (II) increases. For a moment, let us disregard the impact of q* on I which basically means that all FDI is international mergers and acquisitions.

If foreign investment were mainly greenfield investment, the implication is that $\partial I/\partial q*$ (denoted subsequently as I_{q*}) is rather high so that a real depreciation will strongly influence investment demand – if $\partial I/\partial q*$ reaches a critical threshold, the net FDI effect on aggregate demand (the sum of the effect of FDI on consumption and investment) will be positive –; this is the standard case assumed subsequently. As regards net capital inflows, we have to take into account that a rise in the interest rate stimulates portfolio capital inflows directly but will indirectly dampen FDI inflows. As such, taking into account FDI implies that the excess supply in the foreign exchange market stemming from expansionary fiscal policy is smaller than without FDI. The consequence is that expansionary fiscal policy will cause a smaller real appreciation than without FDI so that net exports of goods and services are dampened less than in the standard setup of the Mundell Fleming model. If there is no shift in the money market equilibrium line, we can therefore state that an expansionary fiscal policy is less than expansionary in the presence of foreign investors if the combined effect on investment and consumption is not strongly negative. The presence of FDI dampens the traditionally negative indirect effect of expansionary fiscal policy on net exports. Moreover, we have assumed for simplicity's sake that a real appreciation will not cause a leftward shift of the money market equilibrium line LMF.

We may state that under certain conditions, expansionary fiscal policy is even less effective in a system of flexible exchange rates. The presence of foreign investors undermines the effectiveness of fiscal policy. There is also a serious caveat which concerns expected future tax rates. If one assumes that investment not only depends on the current income tax but on the future income tax rate as well, there could be a case in which expansionary fiscal policy causes such a high rise in medium term budget deficits that the expected future tax rate τ' will increase (a problem not considered in further detail here).

We have seen that foreign investment, including the ratio of greenfield investment to international mergers and acquisitions plays a crucial role for the effectiveness of fiscal policy. In a world economy in which FDI has become increasingly important, one should include FDI in a modified Mundell Fleming model.

Expansionary monetary policy will cause a real depreciation and hence increased net FDI inflows. Thus the relative advantage of monetary policy over fiscal policy in a system of flexible exchange rate might not really be affected by taking into account FDI within our asymmetric approach.

In an explicit two country model we could consider the simple case that investment in country 2 is given by $I^*(r,q^*) = I'^*(r^*) - I'(q^*)$ so that foreign investment flows accruing to country 1 imply a fully offsetting reduction of investment in country 2. Depending on the type of FDI one could consider a partial offset coefficient, namely an investment function $I^*(r,q^*) = I'^*(r^*) - \alpha I'(q^*)$ where α is in the interval 0,1.

If fiscal policy is less expansionary in the presence of FDI the political incentive for conducting expansionary fiscal policy is relatively weak. This could partially explain the success in the field of budget consolidation in countries with high cumulated FDI inflows.

Global Economy Perspective, FDI and International Policy Cooperation

The only closed economy in reality is the world economy. Therefore it must hold that the fiscal multiplier for the world economy is the same for a consolidated model with FDI as in a consolidated model without FDI. By implication, the finding that fiscal policy is less expansionary in the presence of inward FDI suggests that the benefits from coordinated fiscal policies (in a two-country setting) must be higher in the presence of FDI than in a model without FDI. If the open economy shows that fiscal policy is more expansionary in the presence of FDI than without FDI, the implication is that coordinated fiscal policies should be relatively less effective than the fiscal policy of the open economy.

Foreign Direct investment and Optimum Currency Areas

The role of foreign direct investment should be included in the analysis of optimum currency areas. Given that monetary union is a long term venture, one should not so much focus on medium term analysis, rather growth analysis is the appropriate framework. The basic issue is to what extent FDI (net) inflows increase the level of the equilibrium growth path and whether FDI affects the trend of growth rate in an endogenous growth model. If one considers this problem, one would have to ask how savings S is affected in the presence of FDI and how in a model with a production function $Y=K^{\beta}(AL)^{1-\beta}$ the growth rate of A (A is the level of technology) is affected by the presence of FDI. To the extent that FDI is associated with international technology transfer and that technology is a non-rival input in production functions, in a three country model with countries I, II and III – possibly all countries being both a source country of FDI and an FDI host country – one will have to ask which combination of countries I/II or I/III or II/III or I/II/III is an optimum currency union. If countries form a monetary union along the lines of traditional optimum currency area literature (Mundell-McKinnon-Kenen-approaches), where the monetary union then suffers from a reduced steady state growth rate or a lower level of the growth path, this negative effect would have to be considered against the advantages in terms of stabilization policy. Key aspects of the TOBIN monetary growth model also would have to be included in a consistent analysis – basically the issue is to which extent alternative exchange rate regimes or various groupings of countries in a monetary union will go along with a higher or a lower steady state inflation rate.

If policy makers in each country want to maximize per capita consumption and minimize the variance of consumption, one could combine aspects of optimum growth analysis with aspects of the traditional optimum currency area literature. If theoretical arguments or empirical findings should imply that a higher steady state growth rate is associated with a higher variance of real per capita income development and consumption, one would have further interesting aspects to consider.

A.7.9 Long Run Phillips Curve in a Growing Economy

There has been considerable debate about the link between the inflation rate π and the unemployment rate u. Most economists probably agree that in the short term there is a trade off between unemployment and inflation. In the long run there is no trade-off since one may assume that the inflation rate is fully anticipated in the long run. In his Nobel lecture, Milton Friedman argued that the natural rate of unemployment is that long run unemployment rate u# is determined by structural characteristics of labor markets and goods markets. He noted that the long run link between inflation and the unemployment rate could be positive. Here we want to add a straightforward aspect which is linked to the following question: How will long run unemployment and the long run inflation rate affect the output elasticity of capital? Put differently, we consider – with parameters ψ', ψ'', ω' and ω'' – the following modified Cobb-Douglas production function:

$$y' = k'^{\,\beta(1+\omega'u)(1+\psi'\pi)} \tag{a26}$$

A priori we have no clear idea with respect to the impact of the unemployment rate and the inflation rate on the output elasticity of capital. If high unemployment distorts the output responsiveness of the capital stocks (that is of firms) in the sense of reducing it, the output elasticity will fall – that is $\omega'<0$. A similar reasoning holds with respect to the inflation rate. Obviously, one cannot rule out a priori that in a situation of unemployment and inflation the output elasticity is that same as in an economy with full employment and zero inflation. This could indeed be the case if the parameters ω' and ψ' were of opposing value. Taking logarithms yields

$$\ln y' = \beta(1+\omega'u)(1+\psi'\pi)\ln k' \tag{a27}$$

Taking logarithms again while assuming that $\omega'u$ and $\psi'\pi$ are rather small in absolute terms – so that we can use the approximation $\ln(1+x) \approx x$ – we get an equation which can be estimated:

$$\ln \ln y' = \ln \beta + \omega' u + \psi' \pi + \ln \ln k' \tag{a28}$$

In a long term empirical analysis we should expect non-zero parameters for the impact of both the unemployment rate and of inflation. Such results imply a variable output elasticity of the capital stock variable.

One perspective useful with respect to this equation is to ask for the implication of the steady state. This requires the interpretation of u as the natural rate of unemployment (u#) and π as the steady state inflation target (π#) of the central bank. If the parameter signs for ω' and ψ' are equal, the result would be a negative slope of the long run inflation rate. If these two parameters carry opposite values, there will be a long run steady Phillips curve with a positive slope in the growing economy considered. In an open economy with flexible exchange rates we may consider both the natural unemployment rate and the inflation target as exogenous. We can now consider an additional aspect which implies a quasi-exogenous progress rate: Let us assume that the progress rate (a) is influenced by the inflation rate and the natural unemployment rate. One may assume that the impact of both variables on the progress rate is negative since a higher inflation rate implies that the management often will be absorbed with issues of optimally hedging against inflation risks. Moreover, workers in an economy with a relatively high long run unemployment rate will put pressure on firms to slow down the adoption rate of new labor-saving technologies. Hence we state the hypothesis (with parameters ω'', ψ''):

$$A(t) = A_0 e' \, ^{a(1-\omega''u)(1-\psi''\pi)\,t} \tag{a29}$$

Therefore we have an equation which says that under zero inflation and zero unemployment, we get the traditional SOLOW assumption. Otherwise the progress rate in the presence of unemployment and inflation is lower.

$$\ln A(t) = \ln A_0 + \{a(1-\omega''u)(1-\psi''\pi)\}t \tag{a30}$$

If we normalize $\ln A_0$ to unity we can write as an approximation (assuming $\{\ldots\}$ to be close to zero):

$$\ln \ln A(t) = [\ln a - \omega''u - \psi''\pi]t. \tag{a31}$$

Combining this hypothesis with the aforementioned idea, we can see that the unemployment rate can affect both the level of per capita income and the growth rate of per capita income. While the idea of suggesting that the output elasticity of capital intensity is not simply equal to β might look strange at first glance, one should indeed consider this conjecture as a challenge for empirical analysis. Moreover, we will show in a somewhat different setup again that the basic idea can be expressed in a different way.

A.7.10 Variable Output Elasticity of Capital

The standard Cobb-Douglas production function has several important implications, and in the case that one would like to diverge from one the implications –

considered to be unrealistic – one has to modify the production function accordingly. A more complex production function might be more realistic but often makes the analysis more complex. Let us consider a rather simple suggestion, namely that at the aggregate level of the economy output elasticity of capital is not governed by a Cobb-Douglas production function (consider $y=k^\beta$); the latter implies $(dy/dk)(k/y) = \beta$, so that the average product of capital is proportionate to the marginal product of capital. Instead we will assume at the macroeconomic level that

$$(k/y)\,(dy/dk) = \beta' + \theta k \tag{a32}$$

The parameter θ is assumed to be positive. Our assumption implies

$$dy/dk + [\theta - [\beta'/k]]\,y = 0 \tag{a33}$$

This is a linear-homogenous differential equation whose solution is (with C_0 determined from the initial conditions):

$$y(k) = C_0\,k^\beta\,e^{'\,\theta k} \tag{a34}$$

If θ is positive, we indeed have a modified case of ROMER (1986), where the output elasticity of capital at the aggregate level is higher than at the level of the individual firm (we may assume that from the individual perspective of the firm, output elasticity is β). Obviously a large economy should find it easier to achieve a high per capita income level since there are quasi-economies of scale at the level of the economy. Now let us assume that inflation rate π negatively affects output elasticity, which we may express as:

$$y(k) = C_0\,k^\beta\,e^{'\,\theta k - \theta'\pi} \tag{a35}$$

Per capita output indeed only depends on the capital intensity as becomes clear when we take into account a standard money market equilibrium condition. (For the sake of convenience, we use σ to denote the elasticity of per capita real money demand with respect to per capita income; this should not be confused with σ, denoted previously as the symbol of the elasticity of m'^d with respect to y').

$$(M/P)/L = y^\sigma\,\sigma'/i \tag{a36}$$

Here σ is the income elasticity of money and σ' a positive parameter which indicates the role of the interest rate as the opportunity cost of holding money. M is the nominal money supply, P is the price level and i the nominal interest rate. The real money balance will be denoted by m. To stay as simple as possible we will consider an economy with hyperinflation so that the real interest rate is neglected and i is set equal to the inflation rate π. We thus can rewrite money market equilibrium as:

$$m/L = k^{\beta\sigma}\,\sigma'/\pi \tag{a37}$$

Assuming for simplicity that $\beta\sigma=1$ and after replacing the inflation rate in the production function, we obtain:

$$y(k) = C_0 \, k^\beta \, e^{, \, \theta k - \theta' k(\sigma' m/L)} \tag{a38}$$

Indeed, per capita income only depends on the capital intensity; and on m/L which is considered to be a policy variable. It should be clear that we are not considering deflation here. An economy with deflation implies special problems which are not considered in this context. We also assume that the money market is stable as can easily be shown.

Denoting the growth rate of a variable by g we see that

$$g_y = \beta g_k + k(\theta - \theta'\sigma'm/L)g_k \tag{a39}$$

From this perspective, it is quite important to include the role of the money market in the analysis of economic growth.

A.8 Foreign Direct Investment and Innovation

A.8.1 Innovation Dynamics and Multinational Companies

The main long term drivers of economic development are captured in the macro-economic production function Y=Y(...). Gross domestic product typically is considered to be function of capital services – assumed to be proportionate to the respective stock K - , labor input L (one may distinguish between unskilled labor L' and skilled labor L"), technology A and some other input factors. The latter could include institutional aspects which indirectly refer to the fact that there is not only one firm producing but there are indeed many firms whose interaction is influenced by institutions which determine transaction costs and risks within the firm and in the market. Moreover, the institutional design also could affect the diffusion of knowledge and the size of knowledge spillovers. Hence government is important, namely in the design of the economic system. Moreover, government also is involved directly and indirectly in the provision of infrastructure. The diffusion of knowledge will be influenced by the size of the telecommunications network – and relative telecommunications prices – and the intensity of communications. As regards the latter, an empirical investigation for the Federal Republic of Germany by WELFENS/JUNGMITTAG (1995, 2002) have shown that output can be explained by a production function with capital, labor, technology (patents plus imported licences) as well as the intensity of telecommunications where the latter stands for a diffusion variable.

While it is true that there are many small innovative firms it is well established that large multinational companies are the main drivers of technological progress in OECD countries. However, the number of multinational companies is not constant, and the leading positions in the world economy are changing fast. In the 1950s and 1960s, it took 20 years to replace one-third of the Fortune 500. In the 1970s, it took ten years. In the 1980s, 1/3 of the Fortune 500 firms were replaced within five years, in the 1990s within about three years. Twelve per cent of the largest 50 US firms – as defined by stock market capitalization – had been created less than twenty years previously against only about 4% in the EU (SAPIR ET

AL., 2004; p. 43). From the pool of young dynamic SMEs, new firms have entered the Fortune 500; firms from the sector information communication technology play a particular role in this respect.

From a theoretical perspective technological advantages are a major basis of successful multinational activities, and in the evolving knowledge society the role of MNCs – and hence of foreign direct investment - is expected to grow. According to the OLI approach of DUNNING (1973), we should expect that firms with relatively strong ownership specific advantages – and those indeed are often technology advantages – will have conditions to successfully expand through foreign production in attractive host countries. This is a necessary condition for foreign direct investment (FDI) to be a superior alternative to service foreign markets, that is not to rely on exports or giving licenses to foreign firms. The sufficient condition for FDI outflows to emerge is that international intra-firm transaction costs are lower than international market transaction costs. A typical adjustment pattern in OECD countries could be to assume that for catching-up countries, one can assume that the marginal product of capital z is governed by the simple equation

$$dz/dt = (z-z^*)^2 = z^2 - 2zz^* + z^{*2} \qquad (Aa)$$

We consider z^* an exogenous benchmark. The solution of this RICATI differential equation is (with C_o determined by the initial conditions; consider a differential equation $dx/dt = P(t) + Q(t)x + R(t)x^2$, where parameter $P(t) = z^{*2}$, $Q(t) = -2z^*$, $R(t)=1$; as $x_1(t) = z^*$ is one solution of the initial equation, and since we can use the transformation $Z=x-x_1$, $dZ/dt = Z^2$ and the transformation $W=1/Z$ we then get $dW/dt = -1$. The latter has the solution $W(t) = -t+C_o$; hence $Z(t) = (C_o-t)$; $x(t) = (C_o-t)^{-1} + a$.

$$z(t) = (C_o-t) + z^* \qquad (Ab)$$

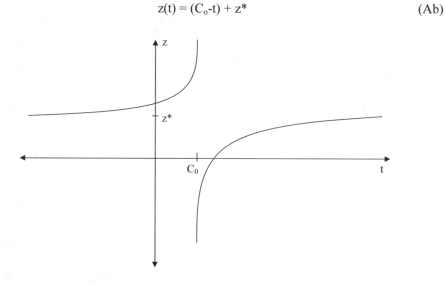

Fig. 15. Adjustment Path in the Differential Equation

The time path of z is such that it will approach z* from below (at point $t=C_o$), thereafter it will exceed z*. For a shift in global leadership in a simple world economy, this equation might be an adequate description. However, in a more complex world with many sectors there could be individual sectors which are characterized by some overtaking process while in the leading country new sectors emerge which restore the overall lead at the aggregate level. There also could be a particular relevance for diffusion. In the digital networked economy, diffusion of new knowledge has accelerated, while innovation cycles in some industries have shortened. Accelerated diffusion undermines innovation efforts to the extent that the period of obtaining a Schumpeterian rent in the market is squeezed. At the same time, faster diffusion could stimulate leading innovators to come up with innovations more frequently.

As regards the expanding information and communication technology, it is not really clear to which side the new technologies and expanding digital networks will tilt the balance. From this perspective, one may emphasize the firm's ability to accumulate information, to create new knowledge and to develop new products and services. In some sectors and for some production activities – read production of intermediate products and services – it seems that the move towards a digital economy implies a rise of international intra-firm activities. One should, however, not overlook that due to the internet one also can find sectors with increasing market activities, namely almost perfectly global markets with low transaction costs (e.g., see the example of eBay).

A key aspect of MNC activities is that production in the digital age might be shifted abroad rather easily. Research and development, however, are less footloose and typically concentrated in the headquarter country. This does not rule out that some research is conducted abroad (e.g., Opel in Germany for GM, or GE Germany/ GE Hungary in Europe for the US parent company and the respective local markets). However, the headquarters country will represent a disproportionate share in the overall R&D budget of the company (for the US see MARKUSEN, 2002). A crucial implication is that international mergers and acquisitions can change the geographical composition of R&D in the triad. For example, if a French firm takes over a German pharmaceutical company, one may expect that part of the German pharmaceutical company's R&D be shifted to the parent company, that is to France. Moreover, if European MNCs (US MNCs) acquire US firms (EU companies) the US research (EU research) activities might be reduced unless we have the case of asset-seeking foreign direct investment. The latter means that FDI indeed is motivated by obtaining better access to new technology – and within the OECD this could be a motive in some cases. Foreign subsidiaries account for 1/10 and 1/20 of all R&D expenditures in the computer and electronics industry and the US electrical equipment industry (NSF, 2004) in the US.

It seems that Swiss and EU firms strongly invested in the US in the 1980s and 1990s in order to better tap the technology pool of dynamics US innovators and of leading US universities. This case suggests a modified McDougall diagram (WELFENS, 1987). The initial allocation of capital – before economic opening up in country I and country II (foreign country) – is K_o and K_o^*, respectively. The traditional McDougall diagram says that with a given marginal product of capital schedule Y_{Ko} and $Y_{Ko}*$ (country II), the new equilibrium after economic opening up will be point E_o; the world income gain is equivalent to the triangle DE_oF. However, if the capital importing country I is a specialized in a way that generates international technology spillovers in favour of country II or if country I subsidiaries pick up superior technology, the marginal product schedule of country II will shift upwards. There will be an additional real income gain which corresponds to the area $A*E_oE_1B$. Such developments are particularly relevant in the context of asset-seeking foreign direct investment, and such FDI in turn is more likely in the triad if the ratios of R&D to GDP are rising in the EU, the US and Japan.

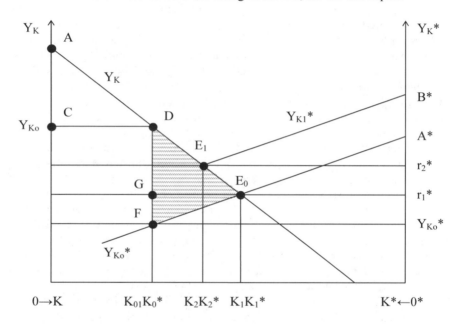

Fig. 16. Asset-Seeking FDI

In an explicit multi-sector model of two countries with high levels of technology, one could also expect two-way foreign direct investment which might be associated partly with increased global cooperation among firms in R&D-intensive sectors. In OECD countries there is indeed a long term tendency towards rising inter-firm R&D partnerships (HAGEDOORN, 2002); they allow international technology networking and often are useful for establishing global standards.

In many host countries, MNCs could set up local R&D facilities, and the higher the capital stock abroad and the larger the foreign market is, the more likely such offshore R&D activities (VEUGELERS ET AL., 2005). From this perspective, regional integration schemes could be useful to the extent that they raise per capita income and growth. At the same time, one may emphasize that oligopolistic interdependence among rivals from OECD countries is likely to play a considerable role in international FDI dynamics. If smaller MNCs follow the industry leader investing in a certain target country, the host country will receive more FDI inflows than is normally the case, and there indeed could be some temporary over-investment. The global expansion of the information and communication technology (ICT) – representing a general purpose technology useful in almost all sectors – is stimulating foreign direct investment directly, namely to the extent that the ICT sector is strongly technology intensive. In the perspective of the OLI approach, one should expect that the ICT sector is clearly shaped by MNCs. Indeed, NAVARETTI/VENABLES (2004) have found this sector to be second to the chemical industry. As regards one subsector, namely the telecommunications sector it is particularly true that the role of FDI has increased after EU opening up and after privatization in European countries and in many other countries as well. One also should note that the telecommunications sector was a leading sector in terms of patent applications in the 1990s. With increased patent dynamics, the incentive for capital accumulation in technology intensive industries will be reinforced, provided profit rates in such sectors are above average. Such a situation cannot persist under perfect competition. However, innovation dynamics imply that there is no perfect competition – there are market entry costs and risk where the latter naturally includes innovation risks. Investors are eager to benefit from excessive rates of return (in combination with modest risk), and this is a major reason why much capital flow became available for the US in the 1990s. US households which have benefited from high capital gains – be it in stock markets or in real estate markets – have reduced savings. At the same time, savings from ageing societies in Europe and Japan have partly been invested in the US which has benefited from high growth and favourable profit dynamics. In a closed economy the role of savings is less complex than in open economies. However, it is useful to take a closer look at the role of savings for growth in the context of a closed economy. The world economy is a closed economy, and the rather simple analytical setup facilitates the consideration of some useful modifications to the savings function.

The Role of Savings for Growth

An important variable in the neoclassical growth model is the savings rate s which, however, is difficult to measure for empirical purposes. Disregarding such measurement problems we can see that there are considerable differences among countries – with very poor countries having low savings ratios initially (but China stands for a very high savings ratio).

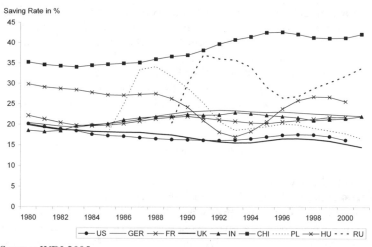

Source: WDI 2005

Fig. 17. Savings Rates in Selected Countries: USA, Germany, France, UK, India, China, Poland, Hungary, Russia

The development of the savings ratio is partly related to per capita income but there is certainly a broad set of influences which in the end come under the catch-all heading preferences and institutions. Religious forces as well as psychological aspects (e.g., trust in the stability of government/society and the banking system) play an important role here. Prudential supervision and monetary policy are also crucial. The role of financial markets is rarely considered in growth models; we will make a few suggestions going beyond traditional approaches. Since the ratio of narrow money to income and of broad money to income differs across countries, we should consider the influence of the degree of monetary development on savings behaviour. From a portfolio-theoretical perspective, there should be two aspects: A rise in opportunity costs of holding money will stimulate a shift in the demand for assets in favour of real capital. Moreover, a rise in the real money stock will increase the demand for complementary real capital whose risks are assumed to systematically diverge from financial assets. Investors eager to minimize risk and to maximize the rate of return of the portfolio will behave in such a way. Finally, a rise of m/Y could indicate an improvement in financial intermediation which stimulates savings. In the final chapter we will take closer look at Eastern Europe and new theoretical arguments.

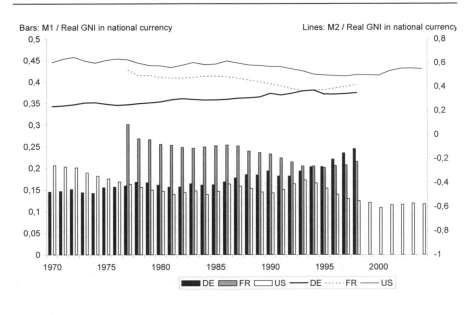

Source: IFS Database

Fig. 18. Ratio of M1/Nominal National Income and of Broad Money/Nominal National Income in Selected Countries (USA, Germany, France)

The anticipated inflation rate will affect the nominal interest rate which in turn will affect the demand for money. The role of real money balances is rather unclear in growth analysis. While one assumes in most textbooks that a standard macro model dealing with fiscal policy and monetary policy should include real balance effects in both the consumption function and the savings function, growth models largely ignore the role of real money balances, first by not considering it in the savings function and second by not considering a direct role in the production function. Traditional medium term analysis has in turn discussed the link between the inflation rate and the unemployment rate, but the long run growth analysis has not considered both phenomena in combination. Even if one would argue that in a long run steady state analysis one should not assume cyclical unemployment, there is a need to ask which role the natural rate of unemployment has. Moreover, taking a look at countries such as Germany, France or Italy in the second half of the century, we have countries which experienced high sustained unemployment rates over decades. This is also an argument to at least basically consider inflation and unemployment in the context of growth.

Table 3. Inflation Rates and Unemployment Rates in Selected Countries (moving centered three-year averages)

	Unemployment Rate				Inflation Rate			
	United States	Germany	France	Italy	United States	Germany	France	Italy
1981	8,1	5,5	7,0	8,0	10,0	6,3	13,0	18,5
1982	9,0	7,5	7,6	8,6	6,6	5,2	11,6	16,3
1983	8,9	9,1	8,4	9,3	4,6	3,2	9,7	14,0
1984	8,1	9,1	9,2	9,9	3,7	2,5	7,7	11,6
1985	7,2	9,3	9,9	10,5	3,2	2,0	5,3	8,6
1986	6,8	9,0	10,3	11,2	3,1	-0,1	3,9	6,6
1987	6,2	8,9	10,3	11,8	3,2	0,2	2,8	5,2
1988	5,7	8,7	10,1	12,1	4,2	1,2	3,2	5,4
1989	5,5	7,9	9,6	11,9	4,7	2,8	3,2	5,9
1990	5,9	7,2	9,2	11,5	4,8	2,6	3,4	6,3
1991	6,6	7,3	9,4	11,3	4,2	1,6	3,0	6,0
1992	7,1	8,5	10,0	10,9	3,4	5,1	2,6	5,3
1993	6,8	9,8	11,1	10,9	2,9	4,1	2,0	4,5
1994	6,2	10,6	11,7	10,8	2,8	3,0	1,9	4,6
1995	5,7	10,4	12,0	11,3	2,8	2,0	1,8	4,4
1996	5,3	11,5	12,0	11,5	2,7	1,7	1,7	3,8
1997	4,9	12,7	12,1	11,6	2,3	1,4	1,3	2,7
1998	4,5	12,3	11,9	11,5	2,0	1,1	0,8	1,9
1999	4,2	11,7	11,2	11,1	2,4	1,0	1,0	2,1
2000	4,3	10,7	10,2	10,4	2,8	1,3	1,3	2,3
2001	4,8	10,4	9,2	9,7	2,6	1,6	1,8	2,6
2002					2,2	1,5	1,9	2,6

Source: Ameco Database (1981-1993 West-Germany, Statistisches Bundesamt)

While the level of financial development and hence the stock of real money balances has been important for economic development for centuries, it seems that the technology factor has become increasingly important in the 1980s and 1990s as well as at the beginning of the 21st century: The European Commission and the European Council have adopted the Lisbon Agenda which is supposed to make the EU the most competitive knowledge-based economy by 2010, wonderful goals which apparently will not be reached (as emphasized in the Kock Report of 2004). This policy failure comes at no surprise since a solid theoretical analysis was missing prior to the policymakers' adoption of the ambitious goals.

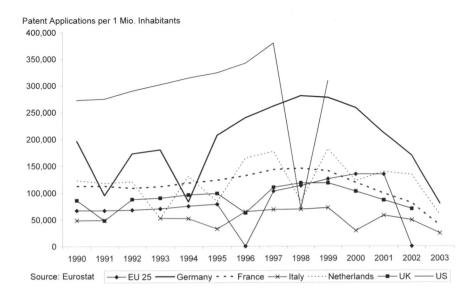

Source: Eurostat

Fig. 19. Patent Applications Per Capita of Selected Countries

Patent dynamics are different across countries, and we will learn more about this later. National patent applications are also misleading to some extent since many patent applications in Europe and Asia indeed reflect patents of US subsidiaries. As regards US patent applications, it also is obvious that a considerable part comes from subsidiaries from Europe and Japan. In the services sector, the picture is generally more opaque since few services qualify for patenting.

Table 4. Growth Rates of International Patents, 1990-1997

	1990	1991	1992	1993	1994	1995	1996	1997
EU 25	-8,10	3,29	3,76	9,93	6,75	10,23	2,25	-3,67
Germany	-10,54	5,18	3,20	9,06	10,53	12,89	0,96	2,70
France	-7,05	-7,60	2,89	10,38	1,92	10,71	1,09	-5,65
Italy	2,52	-12,91	8,91	-1,28	-1,56	12,02	4,42	-13,16
Netherlands	-3,91	7,99	-2,73	8,26	11,76	8,11	3,06	-5,14
UK	-13,82	4,40	3,50	7,99	3,85	5,07	-5,08	-2,51
US	-8,39	3,57	-0,71	5,45	8,89	6,38	8,20	-8,14

Source:Eurostat

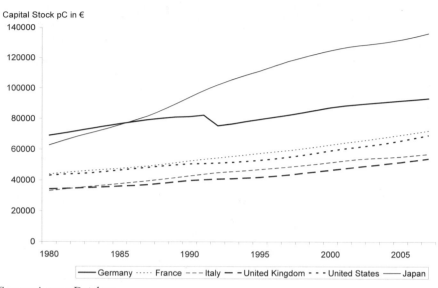

Source:Ameco Database

Fig. 20. Real Capital Stock per Capita in Selected Countries, 1980-2005 (figures are unadjusted for quality effect)

Capital stock accumulation has been a major driving force of economic growth in the 1980s and the 1990s as is apparent from the table above. However, one should not overlook the role of human capital formation which shows different rates of return across EU countries and also country-specific differentials – in some cases positive, in some cases negative – between the private rate of return and the social rate of return (DE LA FUENTE, 2003).

Growth accounting has become popular in explaining differences in growth performance of Europe and the US in the 1980s and 1990s. The role of information technology IT has also been important in the Euro zone as was shown by SAKELLARIS/VISELAAR (2005).

In a broader perspective, growth accounting is of particular interest with respect to Europe and the US. If one assumes a linear-homogenous production function and that factors are rewarded according to the respective marginal product, one can decompose Y(K,L,A) according to growth rate of output (Y) as the weighted sum of the growth rate of capital stock (K) growth and the growth rate of labor (L) – the weights are the respective income shares of capital and labor – plus the growth rate of total factor productivity (A). With respect to empirical analysis, data issues are important here. One may emphasize problems with an overall quality bias of equipment and software as well as embodied technological change (i.e., the role of the quality of capital which has been emphasized by SAKELLARIS/ VISELAAR, 2005). Their growth accounting for the Euro area indicates that quality-adjustment of capital goods implies a higher rate of output growth in the period from 1982 to 1990 than the unadjusted figures would indicate. In that period, one also finds – on the basis of quality-adjusted data – a rise of the growth rate of total factor productivity growth, namely of about 1/10. Quality-adjusted data also indicate a higher output growth in the 1990s but no change for total factor productivity growth. The growth accounting results reported indicate – on the basis of quality adjusted output and quality adjusted capital – that the Euro area has suffered a growth deceleration in the 1990s as compared to the 1980s while the US has reported an acceleration. The US lead amounted to 1.8 percentage points in the 1990s while it was only 0.6 percentage points in the 1980s. In the Euro area the long run growth of capital input – based on quality-adjusted data for the 1980s and 1990s – has been roughly twice the figure suggested by standard statistics.

Table 5. Growth Accounting: Comparison of Euro Area and US Developments

	1982-1990		1991-2000		Slowdown 1980s vs 1990s	
	Adj.	Unadj.	Adj.	Unadj.	Adj.	Unadj.
Output (i.e. GDP)	2.97	2.49	2.34	1.90	-0.63	-0.59
Capital growth source	0.90	0.57	0.96	0.51	0.06	-0.06
IT hardware	*0.11*	*0.07*	*0.11*	*0.08*	*0.00*	*0.00*
Software	*0.07*	*0.07*	*0.07*	*0.07*	*0.00*	*0.00*
Communication equipment	*0.08*	*0.05*	*0.12*	*0.05*	*0.04*	*0.00*
Other machinery and equipment	*0.43*	*0.17*	*0.45*	*0.17*	*0.02*	*0.00*
Transport equipment	*0.04*	*0.05*	*0.12*	*0.06*	*0.08*	*0.02*
Non residential construction	*0.16*	*0.16*	*0.09*	*0.08*	*-0.08*	*-0.08*
Labour growth source	-0.12	-0.12	-0.07	-0.07	0.05	0.05
TFP (i.e. disembodied technical progress)	2.20	2.04	1.45	1.46	-0.75	-0.58
Equipment and software	*0.59*		*0.63*		*0.04*	
Rest	*1.61*		*0.82*		*-0.79*	
Memo: embodied technological change	0.91		1.07		0.16	

Note: Slowdown is the difference between the 1982-1990 figures and the 1991-2000 figures, row by row

	1980s		1990s		Difference	
	EA	US	EA	US	1980s	1990s
Output	2.97	3.60	2.34	4.15	0.63	1.81
Contribution of capital	0.90	2.04	0.96	2.27	1.14	1.31
Quality of capital	*0.32*	*0.82*	*0.44*	*1.10*	*0.50*	*0.66*
Contribution of labour	-0.12	1.19	-0.07	1.22	1.31	1.29
TFP (incl. quality of labour)	2.20	0.35	1.45	0.66	-1.85	-0.79

Note: [a] euro area: this study; US: Cummins and Violante (2002)
[b] Output: average annual change;
Contributions: percentage points

Data Source: Sakellaris/Viselaar, 2005

Total factor productivity growth in the Euro area (this includes quality aspects of labor) has been higher in the Euro area than in the US, although this lead was lower in the 1990s than in the 1980s. The consistency of any growth accounting exercise depends on the theoretical approach used (i.e., essentially the production function used and assumptions made with respect to factor remuneration) and on the quality of the data.

As regards comparative growth accounting of (SAKELLARIS/VISELAAR, 2005; CUMMINS/VIOLANTE, 2002) the results can be summarized as follows: While the US had a positive contribution to labor in both decades the growth contribution of labor in the Euro area was negative. The latter is rather surprising since unemployment rates have increased in the Euro area. The contribution of capital has been close to 1 percentage point in both decades in the Euro zone, but more than twice as high in the US. Compared to the 1980s, the contribution of the quality of capital has been higher in the US and the Euro area in the 1990s.

The decline in the total factor productivity growth of the Euro area is difficult to interpret, since the 1990s were shaped by strong expansion of information and communication technology in both the US and the Euro area. This suggests an expansion of total factor productivity growth in the 1990s as compared to the 1980s. To some extent, a recent growth and ICT study (with a focus on Germany) of WELFENS/JUNGMITTAG/VOGELSANG (2006) sheds light on the issue, at least with respect to Germany which accounts for roughly 1/3 of the GDP of the Euro area. The results from data envelopment analysis – which is better suited to explain growth than traditional growth accounting which relies on the specific assumption of full employment – indicate a decline of the growth rate of total factor productivity growth in the second half of the 1990s. In particular, North-Rhine Westphalia, West Germany's largest state, and eastern Germany fell behind the technological frontier as marked by Hamburg closely followed by the state of Baden-Württemberg in southern Germany (thus, for regions with roughly 45% of the German population total factor productivity growth has declined!). Moreover, the analysis shows that the structure of labor demand partly explains the growth of total factor productivity: regions with a rising share of employment in high technology manufacturing and high technology services have recorded a relatively high increase in factor productivity growth.

Economic growth in industrialized countries is a complex phenomenon as is the topic of economic catching-up where recent empirical findings on economic catching-up dynamics for EU15 suggest a significant role of trade and the patterns of technological specialization (JUNGMITTAG, 2004; 2006). The growth decomposition analysis by JUNGMITTAG is summarized for in the following graph and shows a considerable positive impact of high technology specialization.

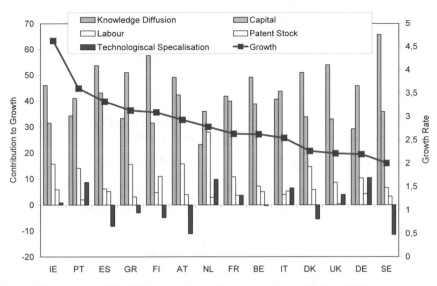

Source: Jungmittag, A. (2006), Internationale Innovationsdynamik, Spezialisierung und Wirtschaftswachstum in der EU, Berlin und Heidelberg.

Fig. 21. Decomposition of Average Growth Rates of GDP in Selected EU Countries, 1969-1998

A.8.2 Modified Multiplier in Macro Model with FDI Outflows

As foreign direct investment has become increasingly important in the modern world economy it is useful to refine standard macro models by taking into account FDI while assuming that factors are rewarded in accordance with the marginal product rule; hence profits are given by ßY. Let us assume that foreigners own a share b of the capital stock K in country I (home country) and that output Y is determined according to $Y=K^{\beta}L^{1-\beta}$. Moreover, imports J depend on national income Z which is the difference between gross domestic product Y and net profits transferred abroad b"bßY where b" is the share of MNC subsidiaries' profits transferred abroad (and b''' is the share of reinvested profits accruing to foreign investors):

$$J = j(q^*)[Y-b'\beta Y] \qquad (A.11)$$

Similarily we assume for exports while denoting the real exchange rate $q^*:=eP^*/P$ and $q=1/q^*$:

$$X = x(q^*)[Y^*-b'\beta Y/q^*] \qquad (A.12)$$

We assume that consumption is proportionate to national income and that investment consists of investment by domestic firms I(r) plus reinvested earnings of foreign investors: Reinvested earnings are proportionate to profits of foreign subsidiaries: b'''bßY; note that we implicitly take into account the argument of FROOT/STEIN (1991) which argue that FDI inflows – relative to Y – positively

depend on the real exchange rate $q^*=: eP^*/P$ so that a real depreciation will raise
FDI inflows. The FROOT/STEIN argument basically says that in a world of imperfect capital markets a real depreciation implies that foreign firms will have
higher equity capital expressed in terms of the potential target country which
raises the probability of a successful international merger & acquisition project.
Hence firms from country II – which faces a real appreciation – will find it easier
and more attractive to invest in country I.

According to our approach the short-term condition for the goods market equilibrium equation therefore reads in the FDI host country:

$$Y = cY[1-b'\text{ß}] + I(r) + b'''(q^*)b\text{ß}Y + G + x(q^*)[Y^*-b'\text{ß}Y/q^*]- \qquad (A.13)$$

$$j(q^*)[Y-b'\text{ß}Y]$$

Compared to traditional analysis we get a slope of the ISF curve which is flatter
for the FDI host country than in a model without FDI (with the traditional IS
curve). This effect implies an output expansion if the money demand schedule is
given in the conventional form, namely $M/P = m(i,Y)$ unless the LM curve – reflecting money market equilibrium – is vertical; i is the nominal interest rate, and
in the absence of inflation i coincides with the real interest rate r. A simple specification of the real money demand function m is $m=hY -h'i$: the parameter h is related to the transaction demand for money, while the parameter h' is related to the
speculative demand for money. If, however, the real money demand depends not
on GDP but on GNP the money market equilibrium condition is given by adequately refining the money market demand where we assume that subsidiaries of
multinational companies typically will use less domestic currency than domestic
firms; hence we have introduced the parameter a':

$$M/P = hY[1-a'b'\text{ß}] -h'i \qquad (A.14)$$

The effect of FDI on the money market is that the equilibrium schedule LMF is
flatter than the traditional LM curve so that the money market effect reinforces the
real expansion effect of FDI. To put it differently, as the transaction demand for
money is weaker in an economy with FDI a given real money supply will be absorbed for a given Y only if the interest rate is lower than before (read: in an
economy without FDI inflows). This, however, is rather implausible as FDI inflows typically will raise r and hence the nominal interest rate i. There is a caveat,
namely that a sufficient share of FDI inflows concerns banking and financial market services which then indeed might bring about a fall of the interest rate through
efficiency gains in financial intermediation. Moreover, one should consider that in
the presence of FDI the interest elasticity of the demand for money will increase
since the presence of foreign investors should lead to enhanced political stability
which in turn leads to financial market broadening: As a broader variety of liquid
bonds become available the interest elasticity of the demand for money should increase.

In the case of flexible exchange rates the foreign exchange market equilibrium
condition can be expressed as follows (with Q denoting real net capital inflows,

including FDI inflows which are assumed to positively depend on the relative market size Y/Y^*; * denotes foreign variables):

$$Q(q^*, Y/Y^*) = -x(q^*)[Y^*-b'\text{ß}Y/q^*]- j(q^*)[Y-b'\text{ß}Y] \qquad (A.15)$$

While the condition for the foreign exchange market equilibrium is identical for country II – the FDI source country – the equilibrium conditions for the goods market and the money market look as follows where we make the special assumption that profits earned in country I which are not reinvested in country I will be invested in country II:

$$Y^*=c^*Y^*+ c^*b'\text{ß}y/q^*+I^*(r^*) +[1-b'''(q^*)]b\text{ß}Yq^* + G^* - \qquad (A.16)$$

$$x(q^*)[Y^*-b'\text{ß}Y/q^*] + j(q^*)[Y-b'\text{ß}Y]$$

$$M^*/P^* = h^*Y^*[1-a'b'\text{ß}] -h'^*i^* \qquad (A.17)$$

The goods market equilibrium schedule ISF* is steeper than in the standard textbook case, the money market equilibrium schedule LMK* is steeper than in a world without FDI. However, the equilibrium output Y^* could well be higher than without FDI, namely due to the investment-enhancing effect of profits accruing from abroad. The results for a two country model are summarized subsequently.

Using the abbreviations:

$$k_1= \left\{ j_{q^*}[Y-b'\beta Y]-x_{q^*}Y^*-b'''_{q^*}b\beta Y+x(q^*)b'\beta Y/q^{*2} +x_{q^*}b'\beta Y/q^* \right\} P^*/P$$

$$k_2= \left\{ Q_{q^*}+x_{q^*}Y^*+j_{q^*}[Y-b'\beta Y]-x(q^*)b'\beta Y/q^{*2} -x_{q^*}b'\beta Y/q^* \right\} P^*/P$$

$$k_3 = \left\{ c^*b'\beta y/q^{*2}-j_{q^*}[Y-b'\beta Y]-b\beta Y+x(q^*)b'\beta Y/q^{*2} \right.$$
$$\left. +x_{q^*}b'\beta Y/q^*+b'''(q^*)b\beta Y+b'''_{q^*}b\beta Y \right\} P^*/P$$

$$k_4 = 1-c[1-b'\beta]-b'''(q^*)b\beta+x(q^*)b'\beta/q^*+j(q^*)[1-b'\beta]$$

$$k_5 = [1-b'''(q^*)]b\beta q^*+x(q^*)b'\beta/q^*+j(q^*)[1-b'\beta]$$

$$k_6 = Q_Y-x(q^*)b'\beta/q^*-j(q^*)b'\beta$$

and differentiating the equations (A.13), (A.14), (A.15), (A.16) and (A.17) we get the following system of equations:

$$\begin{pmatrix} k_4 & x(q^*) & k_1 & I_i & 0 \\ -h[1-a'b'\beta] & 0 & 0 & h' & 0 \\ k_6 & Q_{Y*}+x(q^*) & k_2 & 0 & 0 \\ k_5 & 1-c^*+x(q^*) & k_3 & 0 & I_{i*}^* \\ 0 & h^*[1-a'b'\beta] & 0 & 0 & h^* \end{pmatrix} \begin{pmatrix} dY \\ dY^* \\ de \\ di \\ di^* \end{pmatrix} = \begin{pmatrix} 1 & 0 & 0 & 0 \\ 0 & 0 & 1/P & 0 \\ 0 & 0 & 0 & 0 \\ 0 & 1 & 0 & 0 \\ 0 & 0 & 0 & 1/P^* \end{pmatrix} \begin{pmatrix} dG \\ dG^* \\ dM \\ dM^* \end{pmatrix}$$

We assume:

1. $k_1 > 0$
2. $k_2 < 0$
3. $k_3 > 0$
4. $k_4 < 0$
5. $k_5 < 0$
6. $k_6 > 0$
7. $k_1 k_6 < k_2 k_4$
8. $k_1 k_5 > k_3 k_4$
9. $1 - c^* + x(q^*) > 0$
10.1. $Q_{Y*} + x(q^*) > 0$

Furthermore we define:

$$\det(U) = \det \begin{pmatrix} k_4 & x(q^*) & k_1 & I_i & 0 \\ -h[1-a'b'\beta] & 0 & 0 & h' & 0 \\ k_6 & Q_{Y*}+x(q^*) & k_2 & 0 & 0 \\ k_5 & 1-c^*+x(q^*) & k_3 & 0 & I_{i*}^* \\ 0 & h^*[1-a'b'\beta] & 0 & 0 & h^* \end{pmatrix}$$

and $V =: 1/U$

This results in the following multipliers:

$dY/dG = -Vh'\Big(h^*\big(k_3\big(Q_{Y*}+x(q^*)\big)-k_2\big(1-c^*+x(q^*)\big)\big)+I_{i*}^*k_2h^*[1-a'b'\beta]\Big) > 0$

$dY/dG^* = Vh'h^*\big(x(q^*)k_2-k_1\big(Q_{Y*}+x(q^*)\big)\big) > 0$

$dY/dM = -VI_i\Big(h^*\big((Q_{Y*}+x(q^*))k_3-k_2\big(1-c^*+x(q^*)\big)\big)+h^*[1-a'b'\beta]k_2I_{i*}^*\Big)/P < 0$

$dY/dM^* = -Vh'I_{i*}^*\big(x(q^*)k_2-k_1\big(Q_{Y*}+x(q^*)\big)\big)/P^* > 0$

$de/dG = Vh'\Big(k_6\big((1-c^*+x(q^*))h^*-I_{i*}^*h^*[1-a'b'\beta]\big)-k_5h^*\big(Q_{Y*}+x(q^*)\big)\Big) < 0$

$de/dG^* = Vh^*\Big(I_ih[1-a'b'\beta]\big(Q_{Y*}+x(q^*)\big)+h'\big(k_4\big(Q_{Y*}+x(q^*)\big)-k_6x(q^*)\big)\Big) > 0$

$de/dM = -VI_i\Big(h^*\big(k_6\big(1-c^*+x(q^*)\big)-k_5\big(Q_{Y*}+x(q^*)\big)\big)-I_{i*}^*k_6h^*[1-a'b'\beta]\Big)/P < 0$

$de/dM^* = -VI_{i*}^*\Big(I_ih[1-a'b'\beta]\big(Q_{Y*}+x(q^*)\big)+h'\big(k_4\big(Q_{Y*}+x(q^*)\big)-k_6x(q^*)\big)\Big)/P^* > 0$

A.9 Output Dynamics: Interaction of the Demand Side and the Supply Side

In macroeconomics the short run Keynesian model reads for all intents and purposes as follows for the case of the closed non-inflationary economy (using simplified functions, namely consumption $C=cY$ and investment $I = b_0 - br$ while real money demand $m^d = hY - h'r$; Y is real output and r the real interest rate):

$$Y = cY + b_0 - br + G \text{ (goods market equilibrium condition)} \qquad (i)$$

$$M/P = hY - h'r \text{ (money market equilibrium condition)} \qquad (ii)$$

We get the familiar multipliers for fiscal and monetary policy, respectively: $dY/dG = - h'/[- sh' - bh] > 0$; $dY/d[M/P] = -b/[-sh'-bh] > 0$ unless h' approaches infinity.

According to these short-run multipliers both monetary and fiscal policy are effective in the closed economy within a short-run model. However, we will argue that a meaningful medium-term policy perspective comes up with rather different result which point to considerable needs for more empirical analysis. The approach suggested also allows to take into account both demand side impulses (Y^d is aggregate demand: the sum of planned consumption and investment plus exogenous government demand plus net exports) and long run supply side effects (the production potential Y^{pot} as proxied by a simple production function) since we basically will argue that in a medium term perspective actual output Y is determined according to

$$Y = (1 - \alpha)Y^d + \alpha Y^{pot}; \qquad (1a)$$

Note that α is a weighting parameter in the interval 0,1 and basically is determined by the dominant type of expectations which assign long run output potential Y^{pot} a certain weight α – under long run full employment equal to unity - and thus present demand conditions a weight $(1-\alpha)$.

Such a joint impact of Y^d and Y^{pot} indeed is obtained if we assume a special variant of the permanent income hypothesis, namely that consumption is determined by the weighted impact of current real income and expected long run income – this is dubbed a hybrid consumption function - which is assumed to coincide with the production potential (for simplicity we have no discounting here):

$$C = c(1-\alpha')Y + c \alpha'Y^{pot} = cY + c \alpha'[Y^{pot}-Y] \qquad (1b)$$

Thus consumption is proportionate to current real income; if consumers expect long run income to exceed current income – and hence anticipate real income to rise – current consumption is higher than cY. If α' is flexible variable (not a constant parameter) one may assume that a lasting gap between Y and Y^{pot} will lead to a decline of α'; and the combined impact of a rising gap and a falling α' could indeed imply a fall of consumption.

Assume that we have aggregate demand in an open economy given by the following simple equation which assumes that consumption C is determined according to a the hybrid consumption function and that investment I and imports J are proportionate to actual income while export X is proportionate to foreign output Y^* (γ is the exogenous ratio of government expenditures to output Y):

$$Y^d = c(1-\alpha')Y + c\alpha'Y^{pot} + b'Y + \gamma Y - jY + xY^* = [c(1-\alpha') + b' + \gamma - \quad (1c)$$
$$j]Y + c\alpha'Y^{pot} + xY^*$$

Inserting (1c) in (1a), namely $dY = (1-\alpha)dY^d + \alpha dY^{pot}$ we get:

$$dY = (1-\alpha)[c(1-\alpha') + b' + \gamma - j]dY + [(1-\alpha)c\alpha' + \alpha]dY^{pot} + (1-\alpha)xdY^* \quad (1d)$$

Let g denote growth rates; then we have (note that $Y^{pot}/Y =: u'$ which is the inverse of the degree of capacity utilization U') in a medium term perspective with a production function $Y^{pot} = K^{\beta}(AL)^{1-\beta}$ and defining $s' = 1-(1-\alpha)[c(1-\alpha') + b' + \gamma - j]$:

$$g_Y = [(1-\alpha)c\alpha' + \alpha][U'/s'][\beta g_K + (1-\beta)(g_A + g_L)] + (1-\alpha)[x/s'][Y^*/Y]g_{Y^*} \quad (1e)$$

Medium term output growth thus not only depends positively on the growth rate of capital accumulation g_K and the growth rate of labor input g_L and the rate of (Harrod-neutral) technological progress g_A and the growth rate of foreign output g_{Y^*} (the foreign growth rate will affect g_Y the more, the higher foreign output Y^* relative to Y is), but also on the import-GDP ratio j and the export-GDP ratio; this is in line with many empirical studies finding a significant impact of trade intensity on growth. Moreover, growth depends negatively on the term s'; this being said does, of course, not rule out that the savings rate s=1-c has a positive impact on the level of the long run growth path which is in accordance with long run growth theory. One should note that from a theoretical perspective the growth rate of labor saving technological progress might depend on the trade intensity x+j (or any suitable index reflecting the relative intensity of exports and imports); a more refined view might introduce specific weights for the impact of low, medium and high-technology trade intensity; one also should note in this context the empirical findings of JUNGMITTAG (2004) who finds that the degree of high-technology specialization Ω has a significant positive impact on economic growth of EU15 countries. If we assume that the growth rate of technological progress depends on the trend innovation input ratio (r'), namely weighted past R&D-expenditures relative to Y, and on the trend degree of high technology specialization (Ω') we can – using positive parameters f and f', respectively - replace gA by $f'r' + f'\Omega'$.

A.10 Growth Accounting Under Unemployment and Okun's Law

In economic growth, accounting is made under the implicit assumption of full employment. However, this restrictive constraint is, however, not necessary. Plausible assumptions about the link between unemployment and firms' factor input decisions shed even light on OKUN's Law which argues that there is a negative link between the unemployment rate and output growth.

Let us start with a brief look at the standard case. Standard analysis tells us for the case of a linear-homogenous production function: Assume for simplicity that $Y=Y(K,L)$ such that output

$$Y=Y_K K+Y_L L \qquad \text{(Ia)}$$

where Y_K and Y_L stand for the marginal product of capital K and labor L, respectively; we therefore also can write $g_Y=E_{Y,K}g_K + E_{Y,L}g_K$ (E denotes elasticities). If we assume competition in goods and labor markets and that production factors capital and labor are rewarded in accordance with the marginal product rule so that the real wage rate $w=Y_L$ and the real interest rate $r=Y_K$ we can write (with ß denoting the elasticity of output with respect to capital; g is growth rate):

$$Y = wL + rK \qquad \text{(Ib)}$$

$$g_Y=(1-ß)g_L + ßg_K \qquad \text{(Ic)}$$

Next we assume that there is a positive unemployment rate u. We will further assume that unemployment occurs in a way that workers with a relatively low productivity are laid off first and that trade unions and employer organizations agree to impose wages below the marginal product according to:

$$w(1+u)= Y_L \qquad \text{(Id)}$$

Alternatively, a more complex impact of the unemployment rate on the real wage rate may be considered by assuming that $w(1+u)^\chi = Y_L$ where χ is a parameter related to collective bargaining. However, we stay with our simple approach which basically says that firms in a situation with aggregate unemployment will pay a real wage which is below the marginal product of labor; as an argument for such a behaviour one might point to risk averse firms which consider demand uncertainty. In an economy with unemployment they are afraid that the situation might further become aggravated.

Moreover, we assume that the unemployment rate reduces the marginal product of capital as compared to full employment. The basic argument for this is that switching from full employment to unemployment typically goes along with situation in which part of the existing capital stock becomes obsolete. However, as firms assume with some probability that some of the idle machinery and equipment could be used during a future economic upswing more capital is employed than would be adequate if the firms strictly would follow the standard profit maximization condition $r=Y_K$. Hence we assume the following capital input condition to hold:

$$r(1-u)= Y_K \qquad \text{(Ie)}$$

The corresponding allocation of capital and labor in an economy with unemployment is shown in the following graph where L^d is labor demand and Y_K shows the marginal product of capital: Firms will hire only L_1 and pay w_2 (note that w_2 exceeds the full employment wage w_0). which is below w_1 and the marginal product of labor, respectively; moreover, firms will realize point E_2 (panel b) and employ K_2 – which exceeds K_1.

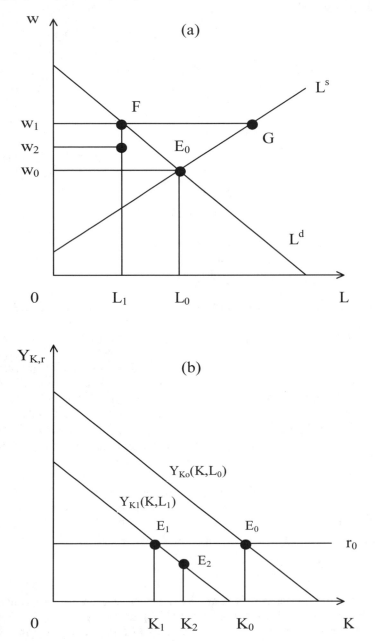

Fig. 22. Capital Input and Labor Input in an Economy with Unemployment

Inserting the modified factor input equations into the equation $Y= Y_K K + Y_L L$ we thus get:

$$Y = w(1+u)L + r(1-u)K \tag{If}$$

Under which condition is this equation identical with the full employment case of $Y=wL+rK$? This obviously is the case if $wL=rK$ since only then $wuL-ruK=0$; for the case of a Cobb-Douglas production function $Y= K^\beta L^{1-\beta}$ this would imply a parameter value of $\beta=0.5$. If it should turn out that the true factor market input conditions rather look like $w(1+u)^\chi = Y_L$ and $r(1-u)^{\chi^{"}} = Y_K$ a different value of β would be obtained. The relevance of the reflections presented here is that from an empirical point of view standard growth accounting can be useful even in an economy with unemployment. However, it also is true that in a situation of unemployment Data Envelopment Analysis might be more adequate.

In our simple modified growth accounting framework the implication is that the standard full employment production function $Y= K^\beta L^{1-\beta}$ can be rewritten – taking into account that there is idle capital in periods of unemployment – in a generalized way as

$$Y=(1-u)^{\chi^{"}} K^\beta L^{1-\beta} \tag{Ig}$$

To put it differently we get an implicit form of Okun's Law (OKUN, 1962); Okun's Law states – with a' denoting a positive parameter - that the difference between the current rate u and the natural rate $u^{natural} = a'[(Y^{pot}-Y)/Y]100)$: Taking logarithms while using the approximation that $\ln(1+x) \approx x$ we have

$$\ln Y = - \chi^{"}u + \beta \ln K(t) + (1-\beta)\ln L \tag{Ih}$$

$$g_Y = - \chi^{"}du/dt + \beta g_K + (1-\beta)g_L \tag{Ii}$$

Thus there is a negative link between the growth rate of output and the change in the unemployment rate; note that the existence of structural long run unemployment implies that one should not consider the actual unemployment rate but the difference between the actual rate and the respective national natural unemployment rate.

By implication a generalized Cobb-Douglas "output function" thus may be stated as follows (with e' as the Euler number):

$$Y=e^{'-\chi^{"}u} K^\beta L^{1-\beta} \tag{Ij}$$

In an empirical context on should not use u but the effective unemployment rate u': The variable u' is not the actual unemployment rate, rather it is the difference between actual unemployment rate and the natural (long run) unemployment rate. Additionally one might take into account technological progress as proxied by a time trend variable ($e^{'at}$).

$$Y= e^{'at}e^{'-\chi^{"}u'} K^\beta L^{1-\beta} \tag{Ik}$$

For the period from 1970 to 2004, the estimations of the output for the US, the UK, France, Germany and the Netherlands – with an additional time trend to capture technological progress – are shown in the subsequent table and the respective graphs which also show a hypothetical full employment line as well as actual output. Note that we have assumed a constant structural unemployment ratio of 4% in all countries so that the effective unemployment rate (u') is defined as actual unemployment rate minus 4%.

Finally one should note that the unemployment rate can, of course, be partly or fully related to aggregate demand dynamics. Thus the equations (Ig-k) – and indeed OKUN's Law – do not represent a pure supply-side perspective.

A.11 Innovation, Trade and Foreign Investment

From an economist's perspective rising trade should go along with rising specialization and efficiency gains in the medium term and – under certain circumstances – with higher innovation dynamics and an associated rise of firms' expenditures on research and development. Import competition can contribute to efficiency gains and process innovations, respectively; for such a link there is evidence for several sectors of manufacturing industry in the US – but not for Germany (MANN, 1998). As regards Germany, ZIMMERMANN (1987) found econometric evidence that import competition stimulates innovations in exporting firms and encouraged product innovations. FDI inflows as well as import competition and exports could stimulate innovation dynamics (LOFTS/LOUNDES, 2000) as domestic firms react with innovations to the external challenges. SCHERER/HUH (1992) find a negative impact of an increasing import competition on the R&D intensity of US firms. A possible explanation for the negative link between import competition and R&D intensity is a fall in profits which might be associated with a rising share of imports; with profits falling, firms in R&D intensive sectors will find it more difficult to finance innovations and hence, R&D intensity goes down. Note that a rising share of imports could also signal a parallel fall in exports, so that both falling market shares at home and abroad would translate into lower profits.

As regards FDI inflows, one may follow DUNNING (1977) who has emphasized that FDI will replace exports if the respective firm can profitably combine owner specific advantages – this typically means high innovation dynamics/a stock of patents – with locational advantages in the prospective home country; profitability is reinforced if intra-company transactions go along with internalization advantages: firm internal transaction costs are lower than costs for arms-length transactions through markets.

While there are many studies on the role of foreign competition and innovation in the manufacturing industry there are almost no studies in the field of the services industry. BLIND/JUNGMITTAG (2004) show in their pioneering study for Germany's service sector that import competition and also export activities and FDI inflows positively affect both product innovations and process innovations. Moreover, the size of the firm is found to have – up to a critical size – a positive impact on both product innovations and process innovations. If firms have the respective headquarter abroad the impact on innovations is negative. In a more general perspective and assuming that the findings for Germany apply to other OECD countries one may conclude: international mergers and acquisitions will reduce innovation activity in the host country unless this goes along with a minimum increase of exporting activities of the newly acquired subsidiary.

A familiar theoretical model about the link between foreign competition and innovations is the industrial economics approach of BERTSCHEK (1995) whose analytical framework is as follows: Suppose we have an imperfect competition so that total market volume consists of output (q_i) of firm i plus the quantity offered by other domestic firms (Q) or firms with foreign ownership (Q^{**}); and there can be imports J). Thus the price p_i can be written as the following function:

$$p_i = p_i (q_i, Q_i, Q_i^{**}, J_i, v_i) \tag{1}$$

Where a change in qi reflects a move along the demand curve; all other variables are shift parameters. The assumption here is that a rise of Q, Q^{**} or J will reduce the price. The output of firms under foreign ownership is assumed to be produced according to the stock of FDI of the previous period t-1. Marginal costs c_i depend on factor prices W_i, product innovations v_i and process innovations V_i; product innovations raise c_i, process innovations reduce marginal costs.

$$C_i = c_i (W_i, v_i, V_i) \tag{2}$$

Assuming fixed costs of process innovations C^V profits are thus given by:

$$\Pi_i = p_i (q_i, Q_i, Q_i^{**}, J_i, v_i) q_i - c_i (W_i, v_i, V_i) q_i - C^V. \tag{3}$$

In BERTSCHEK's model the domestic firm i is assumed to have the goal of maintaining profits so that the total differential of the above equation can be set zero. From this condition one obtains the following results (we drop the subscript i) with respect to process innovations:

$$dV/dQ^{**} > 0; \tag{4}$$

Hence, a rise of output of foreign subsidiaries will stimulate process innovations. Such innovations help to cut costs and thus counterbalance the negative effect of the expansion of Q^{**} with respect to profit. Note that $dV/dQ^{**}=dV/dQ$ if $p_Q=p_{Q^{**}}$ where we denote partial derivatives with a subscript, e.g $\partial p/\partial Q=: p_Q$. Moreover, one gets:

$$dV/dJ > 0 \tag{5}$$

Thus a rise of imports stimulates process innovations. A higher output of foreign subsidiaries as well as higher imports stimulate the firm engaged in process innovations. Moreover, and assuming that the marginal return of product innovations is higher than the associated rise of marginal costs, one gets:

$$dv/dQ^{**} > 0 \tag{6}$$

$$dv/dJ > 0 \tag{7}$$

Both additional import competition and higher output of foreign-owned firms stimulate the firm to come up with product innovations. Finally, the effect of the output of the domestic firm is given by:

$$dv/dq < 0; \qquad\qquad (8)$$

$$dV/dq < 0 \qquad\qquad (9)$$

At the bottom line, both the presence of FDI inflows and import competition should raise both process innovations and product innovations, while a rise of the output of the respective firm will reduce innovativeness. Not really satisfactory is the fact that in the particular case of $\partial p/\partial Q = \partial p/\partial Q^{**}$ a rise of output of other domestic firms should have the same effect on innovativeness as a rise of foreign subsidiaries.

As an interesting extension we suggest the following model in which the firm i is producing both for the domestic market and for export markets; the innovative firm is assumed to also export (e is the nominal exchange rate, p^*_i the world market price in foreign currency). We introduce a specific assumption here: the innovative firm can affect the foreign price by product innovations so that our model stands for the case of a small open economy with a major innovating company (e.g. Ericsson in Sweden, Nokia in Finland, Philips in the Netherlands or Samsung in Korea) – thus we are not subscribing to the traditional small open economy textbook model in which all firms are pricetakers in the world market. Moreover, our behavioural assumption is that we assume that the company has the goal to raise profit in line with export revenue; possibly because a rising export exposition is considered a risk by banks financing the firm which in turn, amounts to say that there is a required rate of export profitability (parameter n' which is in the interval 0, 1; in principle the firm can chose n' such that a critical overall profit/sales ratio is achieved). For sake of simplicity fixed costs are assumed to be zero. As regards exports we assume that part of higher output of foreign subsidiaries is exported so that with a given international demand exports of firm i will fall; other domestic firms are assumed not to be exporters. Finally, assuming that the export quantity positively depends on product innovations and on process innovations of firm i – with a given domestic demand a fall in marginal costs will allow larger exports at any given stock of factor inputs – we have the following profit equation

$$\Pi_i = p_i(q_i, Q_i, Q_i^{**}, J_i, v_i)\, q_i + e(v_i)p^*_i(v_i)X_i(Q^{**}, v_i, V_i) - \qquad (10)$$

$$c_i(W_i, v_i, V_i)[q_i + X_i(.)] = n'ep^*_i\, X_i(.)$$

A special assumption made here is that a rise of product innovations (v) can – if the firm considered is critically influential in the perspective of financial market actors – affect the nominal exchange rate e: A rise of v is assumed to bring about an expected appreciation in a flexible exchange rate system as market analysts anticipate a rising current account surplus in the future and hence, a fall of e; and the change in the expected exchange rate will bring about an actual fall of the nominal exchange rate. This assumption makes sense only if the firm considered is a large and dominant exporter (e.g. Nokia in Finland, less so Boeing in the case of the US).

The total differential thus reads as follows (we drop the subscript i again. Various alternatives with respect to interdependency of behaviour can be analyzed, for example $dq/dQ** < 0$ in the case of an oligopolistic setting - or $dq/dQ** = 0$ if the firm acts interdependently):

$$0 = [p_q dq + p_Q dQ + p_{Q**} dQ** + p_J dJ + p_v dv]q+ \tag{11}$$

$$+[1-n']ep*[X_{Q**}dQ** + X_v dv + X_V dV] + p*Xe_v dv + Xe\, p*_v dv + p(.)dq -$$

$$[c_W dW + c_v dv + c_V dV][q+X] - c(...)dq - c[X_v dv + X_V dV]$$

$$0 = \left[qp_q + p(.) - c\right]dq + qp_Q dQ + \left[qp_{Q**} + (1 - n')ep*X_{Q**}\right]dQ** + \tag{12}$$

$$+qp_J dJ + \left[qp_v + p*Xe_v + Xep_v^* - c_v(c + X) + ((1 - n')ep* - c)X_v\right]dv$$

$$+ \left[((1 - n')ep* - c)X_V - c_V(q + X)\right]dV - c_W(q + X)dW$$

A series of impact multipliers – process innovation multipliers and product innovation multipliers - can thus be derived, including different impacts of a rise of Q and Q**, respectively. Note that the behavioural assumption that the firm simply wants to maintain existing profits can be accommodated by setting n'=0.

$$\frac{dV}{dQ} = - \frac{1}{\left[((1 - n')ep* - c)X_V - c_V(q + X)\right]}\left(\left[qp_q + p(.) - c\right]\frac{dq}{dQ} + \right. \tag{13a}$$

$$\left[qp_{Q**} + (1 - n')ep*X_{Q**}\right]\frac{dQ**}{dQ} + qp_J\frac{dJ}{dQ} - c_W(q + X)\frac{dW}{dQ} +$$

$$\left.\left[qp_v + p*Xe_v + Xep_v^* - c_v(c + X) + ((1 - n')ep* - c)X_v\right]\frac{dv}{dQ} + qp_Q\right)$$

$$\frac{dV}{dQ**} = - \frac{1}{\left[((1 - n')ep* - c)X_V - c_V(q + X)\right]} \cdot \tag{13b}$$

$$\left(\left[qp_q + p(.) - c\right]\frac{dq}{dQ**} + qp_Q d\frac{dQ}{dQ**} + qp_J\frac{dJ}{dQ**} + \right.$$

$$\left[qp_v + p*Xe_v + Xep_v^* - c_v(c + X) + ((1 - n')ep* - c)X_v\right]\frac{dv}{dQ**} -$$

$$\left. c_W(q + X)\frac{dW}{dQ**} + \left[qp_{Q**} + (1 - n')ep*X_{Q**}\right]\right)$$

$$\frac{dV}{dJ} = -\frac{1}{\left[\left((1-n')ep^* - c\right)X_V - c_V(q+X)\right]}\left(\left[qp_q + p(.) - c\right]\frac{dq}{dJ} + \right.$$

$$qp_Q d\frac{dQ}{dJ} + \left[qp_{Q^{**}} + (1-n')ep^*X_{Q^{**}}\right]\frac{dQ^{**}}{dJ} +$$

$$\left[qp_v + p^*Xe_v + Xep_v^* - c_v(c+X) + \left((1-n')ep^* - c\right)X_v\right]\frac{dv}{dJ} -$$

$$\left. c_W(q+X)\frac{dW}{dJ} + qp_J\right)$$
(13c)

$$\frac{dV}{dW} = -\frac{1}{\left[\left((1-n')ep^* - c\right)X_V - c_V(q+X)\right]}\left(\left[qp_q + p(.) - c\right]\frac{dq}{dW} + \right.$$

$$qp_Q d\frac{dQ}{dW} + \left[qp_{Q^{**}} + (1-n')ep^*X_{Q^{**}}\right]\frac{dQ^{**}}{dW} + qp_J\frac{dJ}{dW} +$$

$$\left[qp_v + p^*Xe_v + Xep_v^* - c_v(c+X) + \left((1-n')ep^* - c\right)X_v\right]\frac{dv}{dW} -$$

$$\left. c_W(q+X)\right)$$
(13d)

Note that the impact of exports reinforces the effect of output from foreign-owned subsidiaries. If the process innovation multiplier is positive it is larger in an economy with exports in the respective sector. Note also: the impact of Q, Q** and J, respectively, could be negative with respect to process innovations if the term $[(1-n')ep^*-c]X_V$ is positive and exceeds the absolute value of qc_V; the expression is always positive in the case of $n'=0$ and if exports are profitable $(ep^*>c)$. The absolute size of X_V, that is the reaction of exports in the case of incipient excess capacities is important; the larger X_V is the more negative is the multiplier in absolute terms – if it is negative at all.

$$\frac{dv}{dQ} = -\frac{1}{\left[qp_v + p^*Xe_v + Xep_v^* - c_v(c+X) + \left((1-n')ep^*-c\right)X_v\right]} \cdot$$

$$\left(\left[qp_q + p(.) - c\right]\frac{dq}{dQ} + \right.$$

$$\left[qp_{Q^{**}} + (1-n')ep^*X_{Q^{**}}\right]\frac{dQ^{**}}{dQ} + qp_J\frac{dJ}{dQ} +$$

$$\left. \left[\left((1-n')ep^* - c\right)X_V - c_V(q+X)\right]\frac{dV}{dQ} - c_W(q+X)\frac{dW}{dQ} + qp_Q\right)$$
(13e)

$$\frac{dv}{dQ^{**}} = - \frac{1}{\left[qp_v + p^*Xe_v + Xep_v^* - c_v(c+X) + \left((1-n')ep^* - c\right)X_v \right]} \cdot$$

$$\left(\left[qp_q + p(.) - c\right]\frac{dq}{dQ^{**}} + qp_Q\frac{dQ}{dQ^{**}} + qp_J\frac{dJ}{dQ^{**}} + \right.$$

$$\left[\left((1-n')ep^* - c\right)X_V - c_v(q+X)\right]\frac{dV}{dQ^{**}} -$$

$$\left. c_W(q+X)\frac{dW}{dQ^{**}} + \left[qp_{Q^{**}} + (1-n')ep^*X_{Q^{**}} \right] \right)$$

(13f)

$$\frac{dv}{dJ} = - \frac{1}{\left[qp_v + p^*Xe_v + Xep_v^* - c_v(c+X) + \left((1-n')ep^* - c\right)X_v \right]} \cdot$$

$$\left(\left[qp_q + p(.) - c\right]\frac{dq}{dJ} + qp_Q\frac{dQ}{dJ} + \left[qp_{Q^{**}} + (1-n')ep^*X_{Q^{**}} \right]\frac{dQ^{**}}{dJ} \right.$$

$$\left. \left[\left((1-n')ep^* - c\right)X_V - c_v(q+X)\right]\frac{dV}{dJ} - c_W(q+X)\frac{dW}{dJ} + qp_J \right)$$

(13g)

$$\frac{dv}{dW} = - \frac{1}{\left[qp_v + p^*Xe_v + Xep_v^* - c_v(c+X) + \left((1-n')ep^* - c\right)X_v \right]} \cdot$$

$$\left(\left[qp_q + p(.) - c\right]\frac{dq}{dW} + qp_Q\frac{dQ}{dW} + \left[qp_{Q^{**}} + (1-n')ep^*X_{Q^{**}} \right]\frac{dQ^{**}}{dW} + \right.$$

$$\left. qp_J\frac{dJ}{dW} + \left[\left((1-n')ep^* - c\right)X_V - c_v(q+X)\right]\frac{dV}{dW} - c_W(q+X) \right)$$

(13h)

An interesting result is that export effects reinforce the multiplier for Q**; that is the more foreign subsidiaries are not only selling in the host country market but also in the global market, the stronger the incentive will be for product innovations. From the perspective of a two-country model the message is that two-way foreign direct investment – possibly concerning different sectors in country I and II – will stimulate global product innovativeness. Another interesting result is that if [(1-n')ep*-c] is negative – which requires n' to reach a critical threshold value – there is a positive link between higher output of other domestic firms or output from foreign subsidiaries only if the revenue-augmenting effect of product innovations reaches a critical value: The reaction of p,e and p* with respect to v is crucial here. From this perspective internationalization of the economy will lead to long term product upgrading only if product innovativeness really pays – and this is both a technological and an economic question; and, of course, an empirical issue.

The impact multipliers for product innovation and process innovation are crucial for policymakers since government is promoting R&D; government policies so far make no clear distinction between promotion of product innovations and process innovations. Moreover, there is only scant knowledge about the relative significance of external effects; and about the extent to which such effects are international external effects which naturally would raise issues about cooperation in innovation policies.

One finally may notice that one also could impose the behaviour of profit maximization as a long run requirement which technically requires to set $d\Pi/dv=0$ and $d\Pi/dV=0$ (and checking for additional constraints, including second-order conditions). These and other technical issues can be easily explored.

Our analysis of an industrial economics model with imports, exports and foreign direct investment raises some doubts about the adequacy of many standard macroeconomic models which so often assume that world market prices are given and which almost never consider product innovations or process innovations. This is all the more doubtful since the 20th century was characterized by an enormous rise of global innovation activities; and the 21st century is poised to be even more a Schumpeterian age than the century before. R&D expenditures relative to GDP (or firms' sales) are increasing in OECD countries and in newly industrialized countries; and the world-wide expansion of modern telecommunications and the Internet are accelerating the diffusion of new knowledge.

A.12 Conclusions

Essentially, one may draw several conclusions within the context of this analysis:

- Classification of exports and trade, respectively, is rather difficult
- The HOS model is a useful analytical tool for certain simple questions, but for the modern world economy with sustained innovation dynamics one should modify the model adequately
- The links between trade, foreign direct investment and growth are not fully understood.

For a consistent neoclassical analysis of trade and growth one has to assume that there are external effects of capital accumulation in the consumption goods sector on the investment goods sector. In principle one cannot rule out that the investment goods sector also has cross-sectoral spillover effects. Sectoral spillover effects can contribute to sustained growth in a closed economy. Sectoral spillovers could look more complex in an open economy since one might face in country I both sectoral spillovers from machinery and equipment in the consumption goods sector and from the production of investment goods – which is larger than net investment if there are net exports of capital goods. If positive externality comes only from the use of machinery and equipment a positive revealed comparative advantage (RCA) in machinery and equipment should not influence economic growth. Positive empirical evidence on a positive link between the overall capital stock of a country and the RCA of capital intensive industry would support the hypothesis of positive external effects of capital accumulation.If there are positive externalities stemming from actual and cumulated output in the investment goods sector it would be less important whether investment goods are sold at home or abroad – the latter aspects are, of course, always important with respect to capital formation as such.

We have seen that classification of sectors by capital intensity is difficult if there are cross-sectoral spillovers from the use of capital (or the production of investment goods). Hence the Leontief Paradox necessarily will occur if capital intensity of the foreign country's export sector is identified with the capital intensity of the import-competing industry; unless both countries are of roughly equal size in terms of the capital stock. The overall capital stock might be a more adequate measure for the size of a country than population.

Product innovations and process innovations are an important element of the world economy. The associated Schumpeterian dynamics should not be taken into account on the basis of the assumption of fully competitive markets. From a theoretical perspective technological catching up is a necessary condition for economic catching up if the world economy would consist of countries of equal size. However, if intersectoral spillovers and economies of scale in domestic markets play a role for international competitiveness the size of the economy matters. Small open economies effectively can enlarge their relevant economic geography by foreign direct investment outflows; to the extent that FDI outflows are linked to owner-specific technological advantages sufficient R&D activities – including international R&D in subsidiaries abroad – are crucial for catching-up of small open economies. Regional integration schemes which effectively enlarge the domestic market could help small open economies to offset some of the potential disadvantages which small economies might face.

Appendix A.1: Aggregation in a Two-Sector Growth Model: A Modified Solow Approach with Cobb-Douglas Production Functions

Economic growth represents crucial dynamics in market economies. New growth theory (ROMER 1990, GROSSMAN/HELPMAN, 1991; BRETSCHGER, 1997; SEGERSTROM, 1998) has highlighted some new aspects of economic growth, including the role of technological spillovers. Some models of the new growth theory also generate sustained endogenous growth, where the most interesting approaches are models which endogenize growth in the context of an innovation sector and R&D expenditures (e.g. JONES, 1995), respectively. The overall progress in recent growth theory is rather impressive (and emphasizing the role of R&D for technological progress) if one takes the book JONES (1998) as a useful point of reference. From a policy point of view one also finds increasing evidence on the role of technology, but also on the impact of entrepreneurship. The latter variable is only vaguely addressed in neoclassical growth models, namely in the form a SOLOW neutral technological progress.

While the many variants of the new growth theory represent important theoretical progress, some crucial questions of the older SOLOW-type growth theory (SOLOW, 1956) have not been solved. Here I will focus on a rather simple but important issue, namely two-sector modeling. The standard contribution to this field is UZAWA (1965). However, the results derived are cumbersome and rather ambiguous.

We will use the familiar SOLOW one-sector growth model as a benchmark for a two-sector model based on Cobb-Douglas production functions. As is well known, the SOLOW model is based on an exogenous rate of technological progress, the savings rate, and other parameters, including the growth rate of population n, and can only be modified to achieve a higher (or lower) equilibrium capital intensity and a fortiori per capita output in the steady state. The SOLOW model in its basic setup is based on a neoclassical production function with labor L and capital K, a standard savings function S =sY (with S and Y standing for savings and GDP, respectively) and the equilibrium condition investment I = sY. Here we disregard depreciation on capital. Together with the definition $d(K/L)/dt = dK/dt/L - nk$ one can derive the standard results of the model. If we use a Cobb Douglas function $Y = H\ K^{\beta}L^{1-\beta,}$ the important results concern capital intensity k=K/L and per capita output y in the steady state:

$$k = [s/(\alpha+n)]^{1-\beta} \tag{I}$$

$$y = Y/L = [s/(\alpha+n)]^{(1-\beta)/\beta} \tag{II}$$

The latter result is very straightforward for the case of ß=0.5. The steady state per capita output is directly proportionate to the savings rate. The more important the savings rate is for equilibrium capital intensity and per capita output, the more crucial are adequate reforms of the tax system and of the banking system, including the policy stance of the central bank. For any government aiming at raising long term per capita income the relative merits of measures affecting the savings rate and other relevant parameters are crucial. Moreover, with OECD economies ageing and savings rates falling in the long run, a full appraisal of the role of the savings rate for growth is indeed important. With this background in mind we turn in section 2 to the modeling of a two-sector economy in a setup with Cobb-Douglas production functions. In the final section we draw some policy conclusions and point out potentially important options for future refinements.

Two Sector Cobb-Douglas Model

Let us consider a small open economy with two sectors (sector 1= production of capital goods) which produce with labor L and capital K where we denote $k_1 = K_1/L_1$, $k_2 = K_2/L_2$, $k = K/L$, $\lambda = L_1/L$ and $q = P^C/P^I$. q is exogenous, that is it will be taken from the world market since firms are price takers. Assume that both sectors are characterized by a Cobb-Douglas production function

$$Y_1 = HK_1^{\beta_1} L_1^{(1-\beta_1)}; \ 0 < \beta_1 < 1 \tag{1}$$

$$Y_1/L = Hk_1^{\beta_1} \lambda \tag{1.1}$$

$$Y_2 = HK_2^{\beta_2} L_2^{(1-\beta_2)}; \ 0 < \beta_2 < 1 \tag{2}$$

$$Y_2/L = Hk_2^{\beta_2} (1-\lambda) \tag{2.1}$$

In a long term equilibrium approach requiring a balanced current account we have for an economy with zero government expenditures the following equilibrium requirement:

$$[I/L] + [C/L] = Y/L = y \tag{3}$$

We will use the definition of k=K/L, that is

$$k_2 = k + \lambda(k_2 - k_1) \tag{4}$$

$$H\lambda(k_1)^{\beta_1} + q \ Hk_2^{\beta_2} (1-\lambda) = y \tag{3.1}$$

Due to profit maximization, a condition not taken into account in the standard SOLOW model, we have

$$\beta_1 I/K_1 = r = \beta_2 C/K_2 = \beta_2 cY/K_2 \tag{3.2}$$

$$(\beta_1 I/L)/[(K_1/L)(L_1/L_1)] = \beta_2 (cY/L)/[(K_2/L)(L_2/L_2)] \tag{3.3}$$

$$\beta_1 (I/L)/[k_1\lambda] = (\beta_2 cY/L)/[k_2(1-\lambda)] \tag{3.4}$$

Assuming the equilibrium condition

$$I/L = sY/L \tag{3.5}$$

we have

$$\text{ß}_1 sy/(k_1\lambda) = \text{ß}_2(1-s)y/(k_2(1-\lambda)) \tag{3.6}$$

$$k_2 = (\text{ß}_2/\text{ß}_1)(1-s)\lambda/[(1-\lambda)s]k_1 \tag{3.7}$$

Using the definition of k in equation (4) we have:

$$\{(\text{ß}_2/\text{ß}_1)\lambda[(1-s)/s]\}k_1 = k - \lambda k_1 \tag{4.1}$$

$$k = \lambda\{1 + (\text{ß}_2/\text{ß}_1)[(1-s)/s]\}k1 \tag{4.2}$$

Assuming that $\text{ß}_2 = \text{ß}_1$, which is particular sensible when we turn to a comparison of our two-sector approach with the one sector SOLOW equation, we have:

$$k = (\lambda/s)k_1 \tag{4.3}$$

Inserting in 3.1 we get:

$$y = H\lambda\, k_1^{\text{ß}1} + (1-\lambda)qH\{(\text{ß}_2/\text{ß}_1)(1-s)\lambda/[(1-\lambda)s]\}^{\text{ß}2}\, k_1^{\text{ß}2} \tag{3.1'}$$

With $\text{ß}_2 = \text{ß}_1 = \text{ß}$ we have

$$y = H\, k1^{\text{ß}}\{\lambda + q(1-\lambda)[(1-s)\lambda/((1-\lambda)s)]^{\text{ß}}\} \tag{5}$$

Therefore

$$y = H\, k^{\text{ß}}\{s^{\text{ß}}\lambda^{1-\text{ß}} + q(1-\lambda)^{1-\text{ß}}(1-s)^{\text{ß}}\} \tag{6}$$

We now assume for ease of exposition that s=0.5. This assumption will not change our results in a qualitative way. We get

$$y = H\, k^{\text{ß}}\, s^{\text{ß}}\{(\lambda^{1-\text{ß}} + q(1-\lambda)^{1-\text{ß}}\} \tag{6'}$$

Note that profit maximization requires that the marginal value product of labor in each sector be equal to the uniform nominal wage rate W, that is

$$(1-\text{ß}_1)[Y_1/L_1]\, P^I = W = (1-\text{ß}_2)[Y_2/L_2]P^C \tag{7}$$

Using the definition $q = P^C/P^I$ and taking into account the assumption $\text{ß}1 = \text{ß}2$ we have

$$q = (Y_1/L_1)/(Y_2/L_2) = Hk_1^{\text{ß}}/ Hk_2^{\text{ß}} \tag{7'}$$

Taking into account (3.6) we have

$$q = \{(1-\lambda)s/[(1-s)\lambda]\}^{\text{ß}} \tag{8}$$

This gives us $q^{1/\text{ß}} = ((1-\lambda)/\lambda)(s/(1-s))$ or $q^{1/\text{ß}}(1-s)/s = (1/\lambda) - 1$ and therefore

$$\lambda = [1 + q^{1/\text{ß}}(1/s-1)]^{-1} \tag{9}$$

Replacing λ in (6') we obtain:

$$y = H\, k^{\text{ß}}\, s^{\text{ß}}\{([1+q^{1/\text{ß}}(1/s-1)]^{-1})^{1-\text{ß}} + q(1-[1+q^{1/\text{ß}}(1/s-1)]^{-1})^{1-\text{ß}}\} \tag{6''}$$

This finally results with s=0.5 in

$$y = Hk^{\beta}s^{\beta}\{(1+q^{1/(\beta-\beta^2)}) / (1+q^{1/\beta})\} \tag{6'''}$$

There is a „correction factor"{...} in the above equation which has implications for the neoclassical growth model when comparing this to the standard neoclassical one-sector model, which is $y = H k^{\beta}$.

In a model without depreciation and with an exogenous growth rate of technological progress of $dH/dt/H = \alpha$ (here we assume for simplicity $\alpha=0$), we have as the familiar equation for the steady state equilibrium - with equilibrium k denoted as k#:

$$s \, y = n \, k\# \tag{10}$$

$$s \, H \, k^{\beta} \{s^{\beta} \, ([1+q^{\beta}]^{\beta-1} + q)\} = n \, k\# \tag{11}$$

$$s^{1+\beta} \, H \, ([1+q^{\beta}]^{\beta-1} + q) = n \, k\#^{1-\beta} \tag{12}$$

The traditional formula for the one sector economy is $s = n \, k^{1-\beta}$. Thus our two-sector approach shows that the traditional SOLOW model overestimates (recall that $s<1$) the role of the savings rate for the equilibrium capital intensity and a fortiori for per capita income. The difference is not trivial. As an illustrative case take ß=0.5 which comes close to empirical estimates of the share of capital income in poor countries. Assume that s=1/4, which is the number entering into the standard Solow equation. However, here we have $s^{3/2}$ so that 1/8 is the number entering our two-sector equation.

Changes in the parameters, leaving α aside, will only affect the level of capital intensity and output per capita as is well known from the original SOLOW model.

Conclusions

The model has shown that the SOLOW one sector model overestimates the role of savings. On the one hand, the implication is that other variables are relatively underestimated. On the other hand, the secular fall of the savings rate in ageing OECD countries does not seem as dramatic with respect to long term growth as the original SOLOW model suggests.

As regards distinguishing different technologies in the two sectors, it should be pointed out that only for ease of exposition have we made the assumption of identical production functions in both sectors. Different sectoral capital intensities are naturally quite crucial in such a setup. In a more general model with different production function in both sectors or both countries the role of technology would receive more emphasis. A useful application a explicit two sector modeling is the analysis of the internet dynamics (WELFENS, 2001).

What is the impact of a rise in the exogenous variable q? According to (12) we can state: the higher the relative price P^C/P^I the higher will be the equilibrium capital intensity k#. According to the Samuelson-Stolper theorem the factor which is intensively used in the good which has become expensive will benefit from an increase in factor reward. If consumption is relatively capital intensive, then capital income should increase relative to labor income. However, this exactly is ruled out by using Cobb-Douglas production functions. This points to the necessity to consider even more complex modeling based on CES functions.

A final remark concerns the role of technology, somewhat neglected here. Ideally one could take into account the role of biased technological progress and product innovations. However, while innovations lead us more closely towards the real world, it will make analytics much more cumbersome. In a Schumpeterian setup it is not convincing to assume that technologies are identical in both countries. Moreover, a temporary technological edge will give firms the ability to profitably produce abroad. With foreign direct investment flows the setup becomes crucially different form the Heckscher-Ohlin world since with FDI one will have to distinguish between GDP and GNP, and this distinction is important for the issue of international per capita income convergence (WELFENS, 1996). These basic conclusions point to a rich field of refined future research, even without taking into account the new growth theory.

Appendix A.2: Two Sector Model (KHAN/BILGINSOY, 1994)

Nominal output is Q; we consider a two-sector economy with output I and H, respectively – prices are P' in the I-sector and P" in the H-sector.

$$Q = P'I + P''H \tag{1}$$

Consider the following two simple production functions (e' is the Euler number)

$$I = e'^{\psi t} f(K', L') \tag{2}$$

$$H = e'^{\xi t} h(K'', L'', I) \tag{3}$$

Competition and profit maximization gives (59)

$$f_K/h_K = f_L/h_L = P''/P' =: p \tag{4}$$

$$f_K/h_K = f_L/h_L = (1 + \delta')p \text{ in case of market power} \tag{5}$$

$$dQ/dt = HdP' + IdP'/dt + P''dH/dt + P'dI/dt \tag{6}$$

$$dI/dt = \psi I + f_K dK'/dt + f_L dL'/dt \tag{7}$$

Note that dK = dK' + dK"; and dL = dL'+dL". Substituting dH and dI from equations (7) and (9) and using equation (5) and equation (67 that is we use $f_k = (1+ \delta')$ [P"/P'] h_K and $f_L = (1+ \delta')$ [P"/P'] h_L

$$dH/dt = \xi H + h_K dK''/dt + h_L dL''/dt + h_I dI/dt \tag{8}$$

$$dQ = \psi P'I + \xi P''H + HdP'' + IdP' + h_K P''dK + h_L P''dL + h_I P''dI + \\ \delta'P''(h_K dK' + h_L dL') \tag{9}$$

Using (7) and (5) again we get:

$$dQ = \psi P'I + \xi P''H + HZdP'' + IdP' + hKP''dK + hLP''dL + hIP''dI \tag{10}$$

$$+ [\delta'/(1+\delta')]P'dI - [\delta'\psi/(1+\delta')]P'I$$

From equation (6)e have (11)P''dH = dY - (HdP''+IdP'+P'dI)

By chosing dH/dt as the dependent variable, we obtain from (9):

$$dH/dt = \xi H + h_K dK + h_L dL + h_I dI - [\delta'/(1+\delta')]pdI - [\delta'\psi/(1+\delta')]pI \tag{11}$$

With $\rho =: h_L \, L/H$ and $\Omega = h_I I/H$ – the elasticity of the sectoral externality - and s'=: P'I/P''H we get:

$$g_H = \xi + h_K \, [dK/dt]/H + \rho g_L + \Omega \, g_I - 1/(1+\delta')s' \, g_I + [\psi/(1+\delta')]s' \tag{12}$$

The output growth rate of H thus not only depends on the sectoral progress rate but also on the relative overall growth rate of the capital stock – the second term on the right hand side (using g for denoting growth rates) can be written als h_K $(g_K)/[H/K]$ – and the growth rate of the output of the other sector (with cross-sectoral spillovers) and the weighted technological progress rate of the I-Sector.

We may add that from (2) and (3) we directly obtain:

$$g_I = \psi + E_{f,K} \cdot g_{K'} + E_{f,L} \cdot g_{L'} \tag{2'}$$

$$g_H = \xi + E_{h,K''} g_{K''} + E_{h,L''} g_{L''} + E_{h,I} \, g_I \tag{3'}$$

Hence a general finding – ignoring profit maximization (note that $\Omega := E_{h,I}$) – is:

$$g_H = \xi + E_{h,K''} g_{K''} + E_{h,L''} g_{L''} + \Omega[\psi + E_{f,K} \cdot g_{K'} + E_{f,L} \cdot g_{L'}] \tag{3''}$$

However, the expression (12) is much more revealing. Returning to the result from (12) one may add that in a closed economy (and disregarding capital depreciation) dK/dt is equal to I so that the assumption I=sY and H=cY leads to

$$g_H = \xi + h_K \, s/c + \rho g_L + \Omega g_I - 1/(1+\delta')s'g_I + [\psi/(1+\delta')]s' \tag{13}$$

The growth rate of consumption output then is determined by the rate of technological progress plus – assuming that the real interest rate r is equal to h_K - the term r s/c plus the growth rate of labor plus the externality element (Ωg_I) from the production of investment goods plus the weighted progress rate of the other sector.

Appendix A.3: Labor Markets with Tradables and Nontradables

We present a simple model for the case of a small open economy. The model setup is with two labor markets, namely for skilled labor earning real wages w" and unskilled labor earning a real wage of w'. We assume that the nontradables sector employs only unskilled workers L'^N while the tradables sector employs both unskilled workers L'^T and skilled workers L". The demand for skilled workers is – denoting the real interest rate as r - assumed to be a negative function of w"/r, while the demand for unskilled workers is assumed to be a negative function of w'/r. We assumed that the supply of tradables depends on the input of skilled labor, unskilled labor and capital plus the import of intermediate products T** which is assumed to be a negative function of the real exchange rate $q*=eP^{T*}/P^T$ (e is the nominal exchange rate in price notation, P^T is the tradables price and * denotes foreign variables). Assuming that the domestic demand for tradable goods is proportionate to real wage income w"L"+w'L' the domestic quasi-equilibrium condition for the tradables sector is written as:

$$T^s(w"/r, w'/r, T**(q*)) = c"[w"L" + w'L'] \qquad (1)$$

Note that any excess supply in the tradables sector is equivalent to a current account surplus which will bring about a real appreciation, and a real appreciation in turn will raise the tradables output in turn.

We define a real wage index $w = z"w" + (1-z")w'$ – where z" is a proxy for the share of workers employed in the tradables sector; the w"-w' space the slope of the real wage rate line ww_o is negative. Using the definition of the real wage index we can easily write an equilibrium condition for the nontradables market where demand is assumed to be proportionate to real wage income wL (with L:=L'+L").

$$N^s(w'/r) = c'wL \qquad (2)$$

In the short run labor supply of unskilled workers and skilled workers is given, in the medium term on may assume that L' is a negative function of w"/w' while L" is a positive function of the relative wage ratio w"/w'.

In w"-w' space we can draw the LNN curve portraying equilibrium in the non-tradables sector and the LTT curve portraying equilibrium in the tradables sector. The intersection point E stands for full employment equilibrium and also for a simultaneous equilibrium in the N-market and the T-market. Above the LNN curve we have an excess demand (ED^{NN}), below there is an excess supply; and therefore also an excess supply of unskilled workers in the nontradables sector. An equilibrium in the unskilled labor market can be restored either be returning to point E or moving to a situation in which there is an excess demand for unskilled labor in the tradables market (one may assume that a parallel excess demand for skilled workers will be satisfied by training of unskilled workers which qualify as unskilled after a certain training time). Below the TT-curve there is an excess supply (ES^{TT}) in the tradables market.

Denoting the nominal money supply as M, the price level as P and assuming that the demand for money is proportionate to real output Y – and Y=wL+rK (where K is the capital stock) – and negatively depends on the interest rate money market equilibrium in a non-inflationary modelling setup is given by

$$M/P = n'(r)[wL+rK] = n'(r)[z"w"L + (1-z")w'L + rK] \qquad (3)$$

In w"-w' space the slope of the money market equilibrium line LMM is negative. A rise of M/P would shift the LMM curve temporarily to the right so that we get an excess supply in the money market so that the demand for bonds will rise which will bring about a rise of bond prices and a fall of the interest rate.

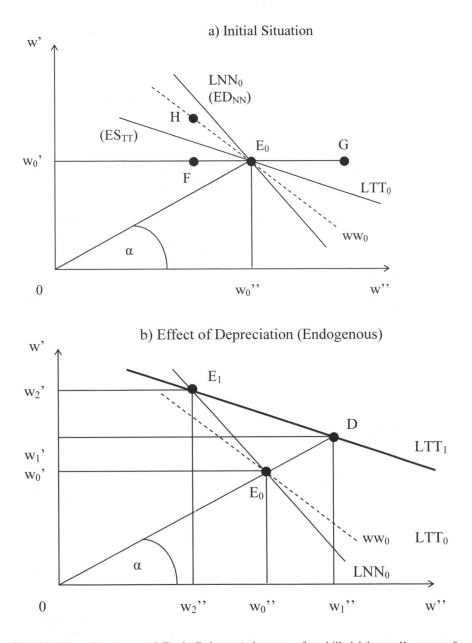

Fig. 23. Wage Structure and Trade Balance (w': wage of unskilled labor, w'': wage of skilled labor)

Equations (1), (2) and (3) determine jointly w", w' and r. The real exchange rate can change only temporarily since for a small country its medium term value is determined from the outside.

Appendix A.4: Product Innovations with Schumpeterian Intermediate Products: A Simple Formula

Product innovation dynamics in modern economies are internationalized in many respects. An important element concerns the fact that producers of innovative final products (say a good j) will rely on using imported intermediate novel products (say an intermediate goo i). One may state the hypotheses that the final goods producer can impose a higher top-up rate on the product – compared to a standard benchmark product (price p_j^*) in world markets – than the supplier of the intermediate product. What is the effective top-up rate compared to the benchmark final product? We will show that this question analytically is equivalent to the problem of the effective tariff rate in a world with tariff escalation (the tariff rate on the intermediate product is lower than for the final product); furthermore we will show that the well known formula for the effective tariff rate can be written in a simplified version which is quite useful.

Value-added of the standard product is $V_j^* = p_j^* - \alpha p_i^*$ Here α denotes the amount of the intermediate product i needed to produce 1 unit of the final product j. If we consider an innovative final product which uses an innovative intermediate product value-added is now: $v_j^* = (1 + \tau_j)p_j^* - \alpha(1+\tau_i)p_i^*$. By assumption the top-up ratio τ for the final product exceeds that for the intermediate product, that is $\tau_j > \tau_i$.(furthermore we will assume that intermediate producers from poor countries can obtain only smaller top-up rates than rich countries which produce the same intermediate product). The effective top-up rate (τ^{eff}) is defined as

$$\tau^{eff} = (v_j - V_j^*)/V^*_j = [\tau_j p_j^* - \alpha \tau_i p_i^*]/(p_j^* - \alpha p_i^*). \tag{A4.1}$$

We denote the share of the intermediate product in a €'s worth of the final standard product at free-trade prices by $\theta =: \alpha p_i^*/p_j^*$. Hence we can divide the equation for the effective top-up rate by p^*_j and get:

$$\tau^{eff} = (\tau_j - \theta \tau_i)/(1-\theta). \tag{A4.2}$$

The formula shows that the effective top-up rate is determined by the top up rate for the final product, the top up rate for the intermediate product and the share θ (we do not assume process innovations in combination with product innovations since this would imply that the innovative product would have α below the case of the standard/benchmark product). This formula exactly is the same as the well known formula for the effective rate of tariff protection.

We can go one step further and derive a modified new formula, namely by taking into account that $\tau_i = (1-\rho)\tau_j$ where ρ is a positive parameter in the interval 0,1 which indicates the percentage by which the top-up rate for intermediate products is below that of the final innovative product. We therefore can write:

$$\tau^{eff} = (\tau_j - \theta(1-\rho)\tau_j)/(1-\theta) \qquad (A4.3)$$

We assume that θ is rather small so that we can use the approximation $\ln(1+x) \approx x$. Taking logarithms results in:

$$\ln \tau^{eff} = \ln\tau_j + \theta\rho \qquad (A4.4)$$

This equation says that the logarithmized effective top-up rate – an indicator of profitability - obtained by innovative producers of final products is the larger the higher the (logarithmic) top-up rate for the final product and the higher the differential ρ between the two top-up rates and the higher the benchmark parameter θ. Taking into account the Amoroso-Robinson equation one might argue that the top up rate for the final product and the intermediate product, respectively, mainly will reflect the inverse of the absolute price elasticity (The result for the effective tariff rate is, of course, identical in the sense that the effective tariff rate τ^{eff} is the higher the higher the tariff rate on the final product, the higher the parameter θ – the more important intermediate products economically are - and the higher the differential ρ between the tariff for the final product and the intermediate product).

Final goods producers from Schumpeterian sectors thus have a massive interest in international outsourcing/offshoring to poor countries since this raises the effective profit ratio and the effective top up rate, respectively. There is, however, an economic mechanism which limits international outsourcing/offshoring: namely the fact that the higher θ the lower is the feasible τ_j. People will be willing to pay a premium – compared to standard cars – for a Porsche, Audi or Mercedes, Volvo or Jaguar provided that there is a considerable part of value-added which is undertaken in Germany, Sweden and the UK, respectively. Obviously, the feasible top-up ratio depends on a company-specific premium and a country-specific premium, otherwise final production stage of many premium cars would be relocated to developing countries or eastern Europe which has not been the case.

There is a clear conclusions to be drawn, namely that rich OECD countries will be characterized by considerable activities in final goods (and services) production. Economic catching-up in a multi-country model thus requires that poor countries are not only moving up the technology ladder by also grab an increasing share of final goods production in which relatively high Schumpeterian rents can be earned. From this perspective locational competition is particularly hard if international relocation of headquarters takes place since then the country/location will change where the final production stage is realized.

Appendix A.5: Medium-term Output and Wage Policies in an Open Economy

In countries with high unemployment rates, one often hears claims that output and employment could be raised through more aggressive wage policies. Higher real income would translate into higher aggregate demand which in turn raises output. We want to shed some light on this argument in a simple one-sector model, while ignoring that a major issue in reality is not just the size of the wage increase (or the wage level) but average wage increases on the one hand and cross-sectoral wage dispersion on the other. We also do not deal much with the issue of whether wage inequality and unemployment affect productivity growth. As regards this link ARNOLD (2006) has presented an interesting new model, namely a non-scale continuous-time overlapping-generation growth model which provides an explanation for why economies with relative wage rigidity record higher unemployment but not slower productivity growth than economies with more flexible wages. The result stems from two offsetting effects: (i) the compression of the wage distribution associated with relative wage rigidity slows down human capital accumulation due to negative incentive effects; (ii) high unemployment among the low-skilled workers reinforces the incentives to invest in human capital which stimulates growth. A knife-edge result for productivity growth thus is possible. The author refers to two strands of the literature: The link between innovation, growth and unemployment on the one hand and between innovation and human capital accumulation. As regards the latter the contribution by GROSSMAN/HELPMAN (1991) was crucial who rely on the approach of FINDLAY/KIERSZKOWSKI (1983) – looking at the link between human capital formation and research & development. YOUNG (1993) has analyzed a model with growth and human capital where skill acquisition via learning by doing is costless. EICHER (1996), GALOR/MOAV (2000) and GOULD ET AL. (2001) present approaches on the impact of growth on inter-group and intra-group wage inequality. As regards the link between growth and unemployment an important contribution of the literature concerns search models of the labor market (BEAN/PISSARIDES, 1993); AGHION/HOWITT (1994, 1998) have shown with a search framework how growth affects unemployment via a "capitalization effect" – higher growth raises profitability of offering vacancies – and a creative destruction effect (new products destroy jobs in the old industry). While this strand of the literature is quite interesting our focus is more modest and raises the question how wages in an open economy will affect output in a medium term framework.

Wage Policy in the Mundell-Fleming Model

Basically we wish to first consider a small open economy under flexible exchange rates, for which we assume that net exports of goods and services X' positively depend on exogenous world output Y* and the real exchange rate q*=: eP*/P (e is the nominal exchange rate) and negatively on real income Y and the ratio of domestic real wages w to foreign real wages w*. The price level is assumed to be sticky. The model determines e, Y and the real interest rate r in a short term approach. Moreover, we assume that consumption is proportionate to expected future wage income w'L' (w' is expected real wage, L' expected employment), current real wage income wL, where employment L is assumed to negatively depend on current real wage and the expected future wage rate w'. The current capital stock is given and underemployed so that it is not relevant for labor demand. Future employment is assumed to depend negatively on w' but positively on the future capital stock K'=K+I. Since we assume investment I to be a positive function of the expected profit rate z' and a function of w/r (with an ambiguous sign, as a higher w stimulates substitution of labor through capital but also could boost demand which would raise profitability of investment), we must assume L'(w', K, w/r, z'). We denote w/r as φ' and w/w* as φ''. To assume that the real wage rate is exogenous in the short run is justified on the basis of the assumption that the price level P is sticky. Real net capital inflows Q are assumed to positively depend on the ratio of the nominal interest rate i to the foreign rate i* and negatively on the expected nominal devaluation rate a'. As regards money market equilibrium, we assume that the real demand for money depends positively on Y, negatively on i and positively on the ratio of w/w# (denoted as φ'''), where w# is the equilibrium wage rate for the labor market. A rise of w/w# implies unemployment – for the case of w exceeding w# –, and a higher unemployment rate will increase the liquidity preference; the demand for money will therefore rise. The parameters c and c' are exogenous, as is government consumption G.

$$Y = cwL(w, w') + c'w'L'(w', K, w/r, z') + I(w/r, z') + G + \quad (1)$$

$$X(w/w^*, q^*, Y^*, Y) \quad \text{[IS curve]}$$

$$M/P = m(Y, i, w/w\#) \quad \text{[LM curve]} \quad (2)$$

$$Q(i/i^*, a') = X(\varphi', q^*, Y^*, Y) \quad \text{[ZZ curve]} \quad (3)$$

Assuming zero inflation and hence i=r, we get the following result from taking the total differential:

$$dY = cLdw + cwL_w dw + cwL_w \cdot dw' + c'w'L'_w \cdot dw' + c'w'L'_K dK + \quad (4)$$

$$c'w'L'_\varphi \cdot d\varphi' + c'w'L'_z \cdot dz' + I_z \cdot dz' + I_\varphi \cdot dw/r + dG + X_\varphi \cdot d\varphi'' + X_{q^*} dq^* +$$

$$X_{Y^*} dY^* + X_Y dY$$

$$dM/P = m_Y dY + m_i di + [m_{\varphi'''}/w\#] dw \quad (5)$$

$$Q_{i/i^*} dr/i^* + Q_a \cdot da' = X_\varphi \cdot d\varphi'' + X_{q^*} dq^* + X_{Y^*} dY^* + X_Y dY \quad (6)$$

We assume that aggregate demand determines output Y and that (with ψ denoting the degree of utilization of the capital stock) the supply side is determined according to Y=F(ψK,L) = ψrK + wL. Hence a rise in Y, which is not fully explained by a rise of w or L or r, must be explained by a rise in the degree of utilization of the capital stock. The case of a closed economy with c' assumed to be zero – to remain as simple as possible – leads to the following picture. Assuming that I_φ<0, a rise in the real wage rate will lead to a leftward shift of the IS curve if the labor demand elasticity with respect to labor exceeds unity or is equal to unity. In both an open and a closed economy, I_φ>0, and Iq exceeding a critical parameter would imply that a rise in w implies a rightward shift of the IS curve, which suggests that real income will increase and the real interest rate will rise for a given LM curve (that is with m $_{\varphi'''}$=0). Only if a rise in the real wage rate brings about a strong reaction on the side of entrepreneurs to raise investment can one expect a positive impact of the real wage rate on real equilibrium output. Even if the IS curve is shifted to the right through a rise in the real wage rate could the equilibrium income be stagnating, namely if there is a sufficient leftward shift in the LM curve as a consequence of a higher wage rate.

In an open economy under flexible exchange rates and perfect capital mobility – the ZZ equilibrium line horizontal in r-Y space –, a rise in the real wage rate will cause a real appreciation of the nominal exchange rate which in turn will cause a leftward shift of the IS curve so that any initial expansion of the wage rate will be undermined provided that the price level remains constant. A rise in the nominal wage rate (implying a rise in the real wage rate) could bring about a rise in price level, which in combination with the nominal depreciation could ultimately trigger a relatively strong rise in the price level and hence a medium term fall in the real wage rate. This would be a rather paradoxical output expansion path generated by an initial increase in both the nominal and real exchange rate. Note that a relatively strong rise in real output implies that the degree of capital utilization will increase.

The multipliers for the main cases of interest are shown subsequently where we assume that the system determinant is negative; this requires that the interest elasticity of investment is not exceeding a critical value and that the intertemporal substitution of labor is rather small (L'_r which refers to future labor input as a consequence of a change in the current factor price ratio). A rise of the wage rate will raise output in the short term only if the reaction of labor demand with respect to w is rather weak and if the reaction of net exports with respect to w is small. The multiplier expressions for r and M also are indicated. We have shown that a rise of the wage rate could be a way to overcome a recession only if both labor demand and net exports react only weakly with respect to a rise of the wage rate. The more the economy is specialized in high technology products and the higher the share of high technology exports in overall trade is the more likely is the case of a positive multiplier dY/dw. However, as only very few OECD countries indeed are specialized dominantly in high technology the standard case for OECD countries is dY/dw<0. Empirical analysis can shed more light on this issue. In an open economy there also is an important caveat, namely the reaction of other countries. It is clear that a reduction of wages in country I will not really improve the trade balance if wages abroad are also reduced. Moreover, in certain cases wage reductions could be an element of an undesirable beggar-my-neighbor policy.

$$dY/dw = (Q_r(cL + cwL_w + c'w'L_w/r + I_w/r + X'_w/w^*) - \tag{7}$$

$$(w/r^2 I_r + cw'L'_r w/r^2) X'_{w\#} i^*/w^*)/D$$

$$\text{where } D := (Qr(1 - X'_Y) + X'_Y i^*(w/r^2 I_r + cw'L'_r w/r^2)) \tag{8}$$

$$dr/dw = (X'_Y(cL + cwL_w + I_w/r + c'w'L_w/r) + w/w^*)/D \tag{9}$$

$$dM/dw = ((Q_r w^* m_w + X'_w i^* m_i w\#)(1 - X'_Y) - i^* (w/r^2 I_r + cw'L'_r w/r^2) \tag{10}$$

$$(X'_w m_Y w\# - X'_Y m_w w^*) - (cL + cwL_w + I_w/r + c'w'L_w/r +$$

$$X'_w/w^*)w\#w^*(Q_r m_Y - X'_Y i'm_i))/[w\# (Q_r(1-X'_Y) + X'_Y i^*(w/r^2 I_r +$$

$$cw'L'_r w/r^2))/Pw^*]$$

Flexible Exchange Rates

The situation is quite different under fixed exchange rates; endogenous variables are Y, r and the money supply M. Let us briefly consider the new setup.

An increase in the real wage rate will bring about a rise in the real interest rate, thereby causing a net capital inflow. This in turn translates into an excess supply in the foreign exchange market, which will bring with it – through intervention of the central bank – a rise in the nominal money supply. This rightward shift in the LM curve could finally bring about a rise in real output. From this perspective, one should not rule out that aggressive wage policies could be more common in a fixed exchange rate regime than in a system of flexible exchange rates. In a more long term perspective, one will have to raise the question as to whether a rise in the money supply will bring about a medium term increase in the price level so that the real wage rate might fall after a transitory increase. This also points to the issue of whether a system of fixed exchange rates is more inflationary than a system of flexible exchange rates. Taking into account the Mundell-Johnson monetary approach to the balance of payments, one could essentially argue that the monetary policy in combination with wage policies in the anchor country is the key to answering this question.

If we set $U = P^* / X'_e P(-m_Y Q_r/i^* - m_i + m_Y(w/r^2 I_r + cw'L'_r w/r^2))$. If $L'_r < 0$ then $U < 0$ then the multipliers for w are as follows:

$$dr/dw = -UX'_e P/P^* (m_w Q_r/(w\#i^*) + m_i X'_w/w^* - (cL + cwL_w + I_w/r \qquad (11)$$

$$+ c'w'L_w/r + X'_w/w^*)m_i - m_w wI_r/(w\#r^2) - cw'L'_r wm_w/(w\#r^2))$$

$$dY/dw = -UX'_e P/P^* (m_w/w\# + m_Y(cL + cwL_w + I_w/r + c'w'L_w/r)) \qquad (12)$$

$$> 0$$

$$de/dw = -U (Qrmww^* - Q_r X'_Y m_w w^* + X'_w i^* m_i w\# - (wI_r/r^2 + \qquad (13)$$

$$cw'L'_r w/r^2) (X'_w i^* m_Y w\# - X'_w i^* m_Y w\#) + (cL + cwL_w + I_w/r +$$

$$c'w'L_w/r + X'_w/w^*)(Q_r m_Y w\#w^* + X'_Y i^* m_i w\#w^*) -$$

$$X'_w X'_Y i^* m_i w\#)/i^* w\#w^*$$

$$dY/dG = m_i / (Q_r m_Y/i^* + m_i - m_Y(I_r w/r^2 + cw'L'_r w/r^2)) \qquad (14)$$

$$dr/dG = -m_Y / (Q_r m_Y/i^* + m_i - m_Y(I_r w/r^2 + cw'L'_r w/r^2)) \qquad (15)$$

$$de/dG = -(QrmY/i^* + m_iX_Y) / X'_e(Q_rm_Y/i^* + m_i - m_Y(I_rw/r^2 + \quad (16)$$

$$cw'L'_rw/r^2))$$

The fiscal policy multipliers for Y, r and e are positive provided that the system determinant – the denominator – is negative.

B. Savings, Investment and Growth: New Approaches for Macroeconomic Modelling

B.1 Introduction

In macroeconomics, there are two contrasting views to the role of the savings rate. In a short-term Keynesian perspective, a rise in the savings rate s reduces the equilibrium income. However, the long run neoclassical growth model suggests that a rise in the savings rate raises equilibrium real income. Short term macroeconomic analysis is rarely linked to long term dynamics and this can be misleading for policymakers. Moreover, it leaves policymakers, who would like to know under which conditions a rise in the savings ratio shows up in a contractionary or an expansionary impact, confused. The following analysis – for a non-inflationary world - is straightforward and first recalls the simple long run neoclassical growth model (SOLOW, 1956) and the short run Keynesian macro model before we merge both approaches within a new medium-term model. We present the multipliers for monetary policy, fiscal policy and supply side policy (rise in the savings rate s). Section 2 presents the model and the final section gives some policy conclusions. Several conclusions reached are in marked contrast to the standard Keynesian model and also go beyond the monetarist debate.

Analytical Starting Points

There have been various attempts at describing macroeconomic modernization in the literature. Real business cycle economists have emphasized the role of productivity shocks in models where the central bank has almost no options to influence employment and output (PRESCOTT, 1986; PLOSSER, 1989). New classical theorists have put the focus on the relevance of intertemporal optimization and rational expectations (LUCAS, 1981; LJUNGQVIST/SARGENT, 2000). Modern Keynesian economists have focussed on the effects of monopolistic competition, markups and costly price adjustment (MANKIW/ROMER, 1991; ROMER, 1993). The new neoclassical synthesis combines elements from both the Keynesian perspective and the classical approaches into a single framework where GOOD-FRIEND (2004) and GOODFRIEND/KING (1997/2001) have been particularly active – along with others (e.g. CLARIDA/GALI/GERTLER, 1999; WOOD-FORD (2003).

Combining short term economic perspectives with long term economic analysis is done here on the basis of a modified consumption function based on a variant of the permanent income hypothesis: It is assumed that at the macroeconomic level consumers' spending is a function of current income (Y_t) and the steady state value (Y#) where weights a' for discounted Y# and (1-a') for current income Y_t are used: $C_t = c(1-a')Y_t + ca'Y\#/(1+r)$. This consumption function may be interpreted as follows: one group of consumers is mainly influenced by current income, a second group mainly by long term expected steady state income; or each consumer considers both the current income and long term expected income.

Moreover, we consider a specific net investment function which implies – for a certain parameter set – that investment per capita demand is such that the capital accumulation dynamics are consistent with the capital-market driven capital supply accumulation implicit in the Solow growth model. Thus our medium term model is consistent with the transition dynamics of the capital stock. The investment function used states that net investment dK/dt is proportionate to the difference between the marginal product of capital Y_K - net of depreciation (depreciation rate δ) - and the real interest rate r; specifically we assume an adjustment parameter b'(K) where the adjustment speed is a positive function of the capital stock. The argument for the adjustment speed b to positively depend on K is that in a highly specialized interdependent economic system the adjustment speed for sectoral differentials in the net marginal product of capital and the real interest rate will be the higher the larger K is. A final goods producer relying on intermediate suppliers would want to avoid a diversion of suppliers from the profit maximization condition – ensuring efficient production. The more complex the supplier network is – in a larger economy (as proxied by K) - the supplier structure becomes more complex and hence the final goods producer faces high sunk costs (if suppliers are not efficient the economic viability of final goods producers is threatened). An alternative argument would be that with rising K the number of potential bidders willing to take over a company with unexploited opportunities for profits will increase – an increasing probability of takeovers will stimulate the management to rather quickly eliminate differences between the net marginal product of capital and the real interest rate. To put it differently: While from a microeconomic perspective each firm faces adjustment costs in investment projects we assume that each firm's adjustment speed is linked to the overall capital stock. The larger K the smaller the optimum adjustment speed chosen by the individual firm.

For simplicity we will consider the case that adjustment costs are determined by the function b'=bK. This case allows a straightforward solution of the investment function which then is a Bernoulli differential equation; as an alternative which is tractable we could consider b'=bK$^{1/2}$ which also results in a rather simple differential equation (the general case b(K) cannot be solved analytically). Assuming a specific numerical value of the output elasticity of capital allows a solution for b'= bK$^{1/2}$: we then still get an equation with k to the power ß. The basic differential equation is $dk/dt = bk^{1/2}$ [ßk$^{ß-1}$–[r+δ]k}. Thus dk/dt = b{ßk$^{ß-0.5}$ –[r+δ]k$^{0.5}$}; therefore [dk/dt]^2=bß^{2}k$^{2ß-1}$–2bß[r+δ]k^ß+b[r+δ]k; the equation can be rewritten as [dk/dt]^2 =2bß[r+δ]k^ß - bß^{2}k$^{2ß-1}$ - b[r+δ]k. If ß$\rightarrow$2ß-1 and thus ß$\rightarrow$1 we then can write -[dk/dt]^2 =bß{2[r+δ]- ß}k^ß - b[r+δ]k which implies a steady state value k#={ß[2(r+δ)- ß]/(r+δ)}$^{1/1-ß}$). We will not focus on the special case b'= bK$^{1/2}$ since ß is assumed to be in the interval 0,1; but the special case considered suggests that an adjustment function such as b'= bK$^{1/N}$ is generally admissible if we restrict N to fall in the interval 0.5, 1. Thus a broad range of adjustment costs functions could be considered in principle.

The model to be presented combines a sticky price short-term analysis (output is determined by aggregate demand) with an implicit long run flexible price model (Solow growth model); the mixture of Keynesain elements and the Solow growth model is not a contradiction as we will not consider a model with deflation or inflation. The price level is given because the Keynesian perspective implies a constant price level due to underutilization of production capacities in the short run; at the same time the Solow model is consistent with a constant price level as long as we are not considering process innovations (WELFENS, 2006b).

One should not easily dismiss that an alternative modelling strategy based on explicit microeconomic foundation and intertemporal maximization analysis for consumers and investors could be a useful alternative to the approach suggested. However, as we rely on the well established permanent income hypothesis and simply combine standard Keynesian analysis and well established results from long run growth analysis we are not relying on opaque ingredients for the medium term model. Moreover, the consumption function presented could indeed be derived from a rather simple two period model (with period 2 representing the long run, period 1 the short run); intertemporal optimization would bring out the role of subjective time preference. The only shortcoming which might be serious is that we are not considering delayed price adjustment which one could combine with monopolistic competition in a model with n product varieties – but one may emphasize that the simple model presented here already is highly complex in the multiplier analysis. Finally, for policy makers it will be quite useful to have a model which includes both parameters from consumption and investment demand as well as relevant supply-side parameters so that a broad range of options can be carefully considered.

B.2 A Medium-term Keynes-Solow Model

For the case of a production function is $Y = K^{\beta}L^{1-\beta}$, capital depreciation is δK (depreciation is proportionate to the capital stock K, $0<\beta<1$), savings S=sY and gross investment I=S the standard neoclassical growth model (assuming that the population L is constant) shows that long steady state equilibrium capital intensity k# and output Y#, respectively, is given by the expression

$$k\# = [s/\delta]^{1/1-\beta} \tag{1a}$$

$$Y\# = L[s/\delta]^{\beta/1-\beta} \tag{1b}$$

Here δ is the depreciation rate of capital, s is the savings rate.
Taking at first a look at the closed economy(with savings rate s, real interest rate r and output Y and government consumption G) one may at first state the IS curve for goods market equilibrium as Y= (1-s)Y - br + G. Using the hybrid consumption function suggested (with $L[s/\delta]^{\beta/1-\beta}$ representing the modified permanent income component) we get:

$$Y = (1-s)\{(1-\alpha')Y + [\alpha'/(1+r)] L(s/\delta)^{\beta/1-\beta} \} - br + G \tag{1c}$$

Taking into account the investment function suggested we are not using the investment demand in the form of b/r, rather – taking into account the production function, namely $Y_K=\text{ß}Y/K$ - gross investment is given by $\delta K + b[\text{ß}Y/K - \delta - r]K$ and thus the equilibrium condition for the goods market reads:

$$Y = (1\text{-}s)\{(1\text{-}\alpha')Y + [\alpha'/(1+r)]\, L(s/\delta)^{\text{ß}/1\text{-ß}}\} + b[\text{ß}Y/K - \delta - r]K + \delta K + G \qquad (1d)$$

Note here that for comparing the hybrid model with the standard Keynesian setup one should set K=1. What about the role of real government expenditure G? A rise of G will raise Y and hence consumption will increase – as in the standard case – but the effect on consumption and hence equilibrium medium term output is reduced through the factor $(1\text{-}\alpha')$. Moreover, the increase in Y implies an increase in the marginal product of capital (as long as K is constant) so that investment is raised. This is a quasi-accelerator effect, and the fiscal multiplier indeed is raised through the term bß. If one endogenizes r one will have to take into account a crowding out-effect both through lower consumption – see the modified permant income component – and lower investment. Note also that a rise of the savings rate s has an ambiguous effect since a rise of s reduces consumption with respect to current income (fall of marginal consumption expenditures) but stimulates consumption through the positive permanent income effect. Depending on the various parameters government might indeed consider to raise s as a medium term supply-side policy alternative to standard Keynesian policy options. Already from the inspection of the simple goods market equilibrium condition we see that a richer set of parameters is now determining multipliers: besides the standard Keynesian parameters we have supply side parameter such as ß, b, δ and the weighting factor α' for modified permanent income. One should note the advantage of the above approach in the sense that it easily allows to consider various crucial aspects at the same time; e.g. in an extended version (with production function $Y=K^{\text{ß}}(AL)^{1\text{-ß}}$; A denoting the level of Harrod-neutral technology) one may consider the role of process innovations easily as a standard vintage approach (STOLERU, 1978; p. 405) implies not only that A is rising at a certain rate but the depreciation rate δ, too. The multipliers for a setup with contant level of technology will be studied in more detail subsequently.

As the steady state value Y# is obtained from the differential equation for the change in the capital intensity k:=K/L, namely

$$dk/dt = s(Y/L) - \delta k = sk^{\text{ß}} - \delta k \qquad (1e)$$

long run output Y# is obtained by taking t→∞ or by setting dk/dt=0. Rational forward-looking individuals with infinite time horizons would thus expect Y to converge towards Y# in the long run. The simple neoclassical growth model has the well-known implication that the higher the savings rate, the higher equilibrium output. Hence in a long run perspective, a rise in the savings rate will lead to higher equilibrium output.

B.2.1 Capital Accumulation Dynamics and Profit Maximization

It is unclear how the neoclassical SOLOW growth model can be reconciled with profit maximization which suggests that dk/dt should depend on the difference between the net marginal product of capital $Y_K - \delta$ and the exogenous real interest rate r (note that we are considering an economy without inflation here). We briefly suggest a way to resolve the problem. One may interprete equation (1c) as the change in the supply of new capital per capita; this typically is represented by the supply of savings in capital markets. The change in the demand for new capital per capita can be written – as proposed here – as:

$$dk^D/dt = b(Y_K - \delta - r)k \qquad (1''a)$$

The equation - with b representing a positive parameter - says that net investment per capita is proportionate to

- the difference between the net marginal product of capital and the real interest rate
- the capital intensity k

Note that dk^D/dt will finally fall as the net marginal product of capital $Y_K - \delta$ is approaching the exogenous real interest rate; however, this effect is mitigated by the rise of k over time until finally $Y_K - \delta = r$ so that net investment demand per capita becomes zero.

The adjustment parameter b is exogenous at first glance. However, if the investment goods market is to be in equilibrium all the time, that is dk/dt=dk^D/dt, we must have $b[r+\delta]=\delta$ and s=bß. This follows from rewriting equation (1''a) as

$$dk^D/dt = b(ßk^{\beta-1} - r - \delta)k = bßk^\beta - [br+b\delta]k. \qquad (1''b)$$

Clearly the path for $k^D\#$ will coincide with the k# in equation (1') only if

$$bß= s; \qquad (1''d)$$

and

$$b[r+\delta]= \delta \qquad (1''e)$$

These two equations imply $[s/ß]\ [r+\delta]= \delta$ and therefore:

$$r = \delta[(ß/s)-1] \qquad (1''f)$$

By implication the real interest rate is positive only if ß>s. If (1''f) is fulfilled the supply of net investment per capita and the demand for net investment per capita coincide at any point of time. Note that the condition for the case of the golden rule (condition which maximizes per capita consumption) is fulfilled if $\delta=r$ and in the long run $r=Y_K$ if ß/s=2, that is s=ß/2. As ß is put for OECD countries typically at around 0.33 the optimal savings rate – maximizing long run per capita consumption – thus would be 16.5%. Note that for the case of a real money demand function m=hY-h'r (m is real money balances M/P where M and P stand for the nominal money stock and the price level, respectively; r is the real interest rate relevant in the present set-up with zero inflation) the implication is that the central bank must set long run [M/P] per capita such that we have $[m/L]\# = hk\#^{\beta} - h'k\#^{\beta-1}$ since $r = \beta Y/K = \beta k^{\beta-1}$.

The general solution to (1"b) is – with e' denoting the Euler number - given by the solution of the Bernoullian differential (see Appendix G.4) equation $dk^D/dt = b\beta k^{\beta} - b[r+\delta]k$; the solution for this is

$$k^D(t) = \{C_0 e^{,-(1-\beta)b(r+\delta)t} + \beta/[r+\delta]\}^{1/1-\beta} \qquad (1''g)$$

where C_0 is determined by initial conditions. The adjustment speed is the higher the higher b as well as the real interest rate and the lower ß. The adjustment speed for $k^D(t)$ is identical with that for k(t) if $(1-\beta)\delta = (1-\beta)b(r+\delta)$ which requires $(r+\delta) = \delta/b$ and this condition indeed is equal to equation (1"e). If adjustment speeds on the supply side and the demand side in the capital market are not coinciding we could have a picture as shown in the subsequent graph where during an initial time period the supply of net investment per capita is higher than the demand for investment per capita such that we will have unemployment while in a second period (after point F) we will have inflation as demand exceeds supply; in principle one also could have a first period of inflation followed by a second transition period of unemployment.

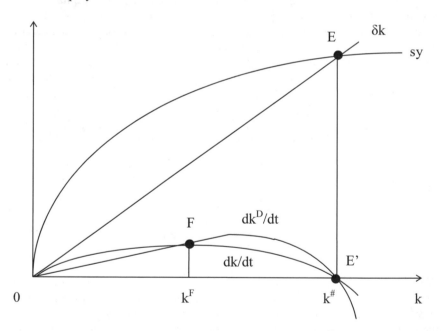

Fig. 24. Transitory Equilibrium (point F) and Steady-state Equilibrium ("time" 0F = unemployment, "time" FE' = inflation)

We thus may argue that the SOLOW growth model could indeed be consistent with profit maximization. Subsequently we will use the net investment function suggested in (1"a) in a medium term KEYNES-SOLOW model; the above specification is the only formulation which is consistent with the long run steady state value of the SOLOW model.

B.2.2 Chosing a Consistent Investment Function and a New Consumption Function

An investment function – for net investment – consistent with (1"a) thus is $I'= b(Y_K -r-\delta)K$ which will be used subsequently as the function describing investment demand. Whenever net investment is given by this equation we know that investment demand dynamics are potentially consistent with the SOLOW growth model. A possible modification of the case of unemployment (with the unemployment rate $u>0$) or inflation ($\pi>0$) could be formulated as $I'=b(Y_K -r-\delta)Ke'^{-\sigma'u-\sigma''\pi}$ where e' denotes the Euler number and σ' is a the semi-elasticity (in absolute terms) of net investment with respect to the unemployment rate (σ'' is the semi elasticity with respect to the inflation rate). Subsequently we will use the net investment function $I'=b(Y_K -\delta -r)K$.

Next we turn to a standard Keynesian model of a closed economy which implies that output is determined by aggregate demand consisting of consumption C, gross investment I and real government expenditures G. We denote reinvestment as I^R, net investment as $I'(r, Y_K, K)$, and we also consider a standard consumption function $C=cY^d$ (Y^d is aggregate demand). Hence output Y is given by

$$Y = cY^d + I^R + I'(r, Y_K, K) + G \qquad (2)$$

It is assumed that net investment $I'= b(Y_K-\delta-r)K$ so that total investment $I=: I^R + b(Y_K-\delta- r)K$ which implies for the goods market equilibrium

$$Y = cY^d + I^R + b(Y_K-\delta -r)K + G \qquad (3)$$

The capacity effect of investment is neglected in the standard Keynesian setup and thus the marginal product of capital is constant in the short run. Output Y is driven by aggregate demand and thus is given – with $s=: 1-c$ and $I^R - \delta K$ by the equation

$$Y^d = Y= [\delta K + G + b(Y_K-\delta-r)K]/s \qquad (4)$$

$$dY/ds= - [\delta K + G + b(Y_K-\delta-r)K]/s^2 <0 \qquad (5)$$

The conclusion is that the savings rate negatively affects the short term equilibrium real income: A rise in the savings rate (s'>s) implies that at any real income the desired savings $S=s'Y$ is higher than before; however, the condition I=S then implies a fall of equilibrium Y. This is in some contrast to the statement that savings from an individual perspective is useful and desirable as it is the basis for the accumulation of wealth. Note that the negative multiplier in (5) strongly differs –

according to (1b) - from the neoclassical long run multiplier which is given by
$dY\#/ds = \beta/(1-\beta)L[1/\delta]^{\beta/1-\beta}[s]^{-1/1-\beta} > 0$.

A straightforward hypothesis which combines the short run and the long run is to assume that output in the medium term is determined by weighted impacts from the demand side and the supply side (here the supply side is set equal to Y#):

$$Y = [1-a'(t)]Y^d + a'(t)Y\# \qquad (6)$$

The closer the economy is to full capacity utilization the higher a' is. In a situation of extreme capacity underutilization such as the Great Depression 1930-34 – with US output showing a cumulative fall of 27% (Germany 16%, France 11%) – a' is close to zero so that aggregate demand indeed determines output.

The idea of taking into account both impacts from the demand side and the supply side will be considered subsequently in a formal model whose approach is slightly different than the above equation, but the spirit is the same. Indeed, one may consider a medium term model which means taking into account that a rise in K will reduce the marginal product of capital (in contrast to the standard Keynesian analysis) and where we use the following modified consumption function, which is a simplified version of the permanent income hypothesis: The consumption function chosen emphasizes that consumption C is influenced not only by the present income but also by the long run expected income (here Y#); with a consumption function

$$C = ca''Y + ca'[1/(1+r)]Y\# \qquad (7)$$

we get the following equilibrium condition for the goods market in the medium term Keynes-Solow model:

$$Y = c\{a''Y + a'[1/(1+r)]L[s/\delta]^{\beta/1-\beta}\} + \delta K + b(\beta Y/K -\delta-r)K + G; \text{ with} \qquad (6')$$
$$a'' =: (1-a')$$

The consumption function suggested (for simplicity with a' independent of time) here states that $C = cY + ca'[Y\#-Y]$, and hence consumption will be higher than implied by the standard consumption function $C=cY$ whenever there is a positive expected difference between long run output Y# and present output Y. Approaching the steady state, we indeed will see that consumption C is converging towards $C_t = cY_t$. Expected future income – read steady state income Y# – is discounted by 1/(1+r); as an alternative, one might want to multiply it by a different discount factor which would also reflect the subjective probability that the economy will converge towards the hypothetical Y#. A more complex approach could take into account both demand and supply-side dynamics over many periods, but the approach presented here catches the basic idea of taking into account both present and future income.

In the above equation we have taken into account that the marginal product is equal to $\beta Y/K$. Assuming r to be exogenous we have medium term equilibrium output – based on our medium term approach – given by:

$$Y = \{ca'[1/(1+r)]L[s/\delta]^{\beta/(1-\beta)} + \delta K(1-b) - brK + G\}/[s + ca' - b\beta] \qquad (6'')$$

Note that the above equation determines Y through medium term aggregate demand where consumers are forward looking economic agents.

B.2.3 Multiplier Analysis

We now can take a look at the simple multiplier for the goods market (and later we turn to the broader picture with goods market, money market and the foreign exchange market). From (6") we get – while assuming that s+ca'> bß:

$$dY/dG = 1/[s + ca' - bß] > 0 \tag{7'}$$

In the medium term model fiscal policy is (ignoring at first the impact of ca') more effective than in the short run standard model since a rise of G raises output which translates not only into higher consumption but also into higher net investment since a rise of Y also implies a rise of the average product of capital. If by coincidence equation (1"d) is fulfilled so that bß=s the multiplier would be 1/(ca'); note that an economy which is close to the steady state value of output $Y^\#$ may be expected to have a' close to unity so that the fiscal multiplier is relatively small. If s + ca' approaches bß the multiplier will approach infinity. Whether such a case is of any practical relevance is an empirical question; note that one can dismiss the idea to artificially reduce the capital stock as a means to eliminate an excess supply in the capital market – followed by an expansionary fiscal policy whose multiplier thus is raised as the condition s = bß is fulfilled: An artificial reduction of the capital stock would, of course, reduce expected long run income.

Moreover, one should emphasize that approaching $Y^\#$ the equilibrium condition for the goods market will become $Y = cY^\# + \delta K^\# + G$ so that with Y approaching $Y^\#$ government consumption G is endogenous. By implication it is clear that a fiscal multiplier – and therefore fiscal policy - makes no sense if the economy is close to $Y^\#$ (the long run case). The following multiplier analysis thus is confined to a medium term policy perspective.

The medium term fiscal multiplier from (7') could be smaller or larger than the traditional short-run fiscal multiplier 1/s. If the transitory consumption demand effect as captured by ca' exceeds bß, we will have a smaller fiscal multiplier than the short-run Keynesian model suggests. The higher ß and b are, the higher is the fiscal multiplier. Thus fiscal policy becomes more effective if there is a change in technology which leads to a rise of ß and if the responsiveness of investors with respect to differences between the net marginal product of capital and the real interest rate has increased. The reason is straightforward since for a given interest rate a rise of G which translates into a rise of Y will have the higher an impact of the marginal (and average) product of capital and net investment the larger ß and b, respectively. The increasing role of information and communication technology (ICT) might have raised ß since increasing output is facilitated – at least in those sectors where supply is based on software and digital inputs. From this perspective ICT might have raised the effectiveness of fiscal policy. However, to the extent that expansion of ICT has translated into a rise of a' there is an offsetting effect, and only empirical analysis can tell whether the fiscal multiplier has increased or fallen in the digital economy.

In a period in which there is a high gap between present and long term income, a'' will be relatively high so that the fiscal multiplier is relatively low. From this perspective, emphasis on expansionary fiscal policy in a deep recession – such as the case during the Great Depression – is indeed useful, namely to the extent that deep recession is translated by economic actors as falling weight of future long run income. With massive underutilization of capacity, one could also argue that b – the reaction parameter in the net investment function – will be close to zero which also reinforces the statement that expansionary fiscal policy in a deep recession should be quite useful to raise real income. The fiscal multiplier effect should also be high if the time horizon of people is shortening, as is typically the case in periods of high business uncertainty or in war periods. If the output elasticity of capital is increased (ß goes up) – e.g., in the context of the unfolding of the New Economy –, the fiscal multiplier is reduced. It is also reduced if investors' responsiveness to a difference between the marginal product of capital and the real interest rate increases (e.g., the parameter b could be raised through reduced information costs about such differences). Again consider the impact of the new economy and information and communication technology which has raised market transparency with respect to investment opportunities in non-ICT fields while the ICT field itself – given its enormous technological dynamics – is rather opaque for outside investors.

As regards the multiplier for L it is obvious that a higher L raises the long run expected equilibrium real income – hence permanent income is raised - and therefore the multiplier is positive provided that s>ca'+bß. In an economy with a relatively small capital stock or with a very small responsiveness (sufficiently small b) of net investment with respect to the marginal product of capital, we have a positive multiplier.

$$dY/dL = \{ca'[1/(1+r)][s/\delta]^{\beta/(1-\beta)}\}/[s +ca' - b\beta] > 0 \qquad (9)$$

$$dY/ds = \{-(1+a')\{ca'[1/(1+r)]L[s/\delta]^{\beta/(1-\beta)} + (\delta - br)K + G\} + \qquad (10)$$

$$[(s + ca'-b\beta)ca'[1/(1+r)]L[\beta/(1-\beta)]s^{\beta(1-\beta)}]/ \delta^{\beta/(1-\beta)}\}/(s + ca'-b\beta)^2$$

A sufficient condition for dY/ds to be positive is given by: $s + ca' > b\beta$, $\beta > s$ and $ca'[1/(1+r)]L[s/\delta]^{\beta/(1-\beta)} + G < (br - \delta)K$ where there has to be $br > \delta$. These conditions – suggesting under the assumption that br>δ - that a rise of the savings rate raises output if the savings rate is and the impact (a') of the long run real income on consumption are relatively high - point to interesting empirical issues. Thus a society with a large positive gap between Y# and Y (and hence a high parameter a') is likely to benefit from government measures which stimulate the savings rate: medium term income will rise. To the extent than one interpretes ß as a distribution parameter one may conclude that in a country with a critically high ß – as might be observed in developing countries or in some transition economies – a rise of the savings rate might reduce medium term equilibrium output.

The real interest rate can, of course, be endogenized (assuming a zero inflation rate) by taking into account the money market equilibrium condition:

$$M/P = hY - h'r \tag{11}$$

$$r = [hY-M/P]/h' \tag{12}$$

If we endogenize the interest rate we get from inserting (12) into (6')

$$Y = c\{a''Y + a'[1/(1+[hY-M/P]/h')]L[s/\delta]^{\beta/1-\beta}\} + \delta K + b(\beta Y/K - [hY-M/P]/h')K] + G \tag{13}$$

Using Cramer's rule we can calculate the multipliers for monetary and fiscal policy from differentiating (6') and (11) and the respective equation written in matrix notation:

$$\begin{pmatrix} h & -h' \\ (s+ca'-b\beta) & bK - \dfrac{ca'L}{(1+r)^2}\left(\dfrac{s}{\delta}\right)^{\beta/(1-\beta)} \end{pmatrix}\begin{pmatrix} dY \\ dr \end{pmatrix} = \begin{pmatrix} 0 & 1 & 0 \\ 1 & 0 & \left(\dfrac{dY}{ds}\right)' \end{pmatrix}\begin{pmatrix} dG \\ d(M/P) \\ ds \end{pmatrix}$$

Where $\left(\dfrac{dY}{ds}\right)'$ denotes $(s+ca'-b\beta)\dfrac{dY}{ds}$ with the $\dfrac{dY}{ds}$ from equation (10)

And therefore $\left(\dfrac{dY}{ds}\right)' = \{-\{ca'[1/(1+r)]L[s/\delta]^{\beta/(1-\beta)} + (\delta - br)K + G\}$

$$+[(s+ca'-b\beta)ca'[1/(1+r)]L[\beta/(1-\beta)]s^{(2\beta-1)/(1-\beta)}]/\delta^{\beta/(1-\beta)}\}/(s+ca'-b\beta)$$

$$\det(A) = \det\begin{pmatrix} h & -h' \\ (s+ca'-b\beta) & bK - \dfrac{ca'L}{(1+r)^2}\left(\dfrac{s}{\delta}\right)^{\beta/(1-\beta)} \end{pmatrix} =$$

$$= \{([s+ca'-b\beta]h' + hbK)[1+r]^2\delta^{\beta/(1-\beta)} - ca'Lhs^{\beta/(1-\beta)}\}/[1+r]^2\delta^{\beta/(1-\beta)}$$

which implies:

$$\frac{1}{\det(A)} = \frac{(1+r)^2\,\delta^{\beta/(1-\beta)}}{((s+ca'-b\beta)h' + hbK)(1+r)^2\,\delta^{\beta/(1-\beta)} - ca'Lhs^{\beta/(1-\beta)}}$$

And therefore the Multipliers are:

$$\frac{dY}{dG} = \frac{h'(1+r)^2\,\delta^{\beta/(1-\beta)}}{((s+ca'-b\beta)h' + hbK)(1+r)^2\,\delta^{\beta/(1-\beta)} - ca'Lhs^{\beta/(1-\beta)}}$$

$$\left(s+ca'-b\beta\right)h'+hbK < 0 \quad \Rightarrow \quad \frac{dY}{dG} < 0$$

In a poor country – with very low s and low K – the condition for dY/dG is likely to be met so that fiscal policy is ineffective with respect to output. The condition stated implies that for dY/dG < 0; (s + ca' - bß) needs to be negative, but this is not sufficient as in equation (7). As well (s + ca' - bß) > 0 does not imply dY/dG > 0 but still is a necessary condition. Empirically, it will be interesting to study whether bß exceeds s + ca'. The multiplier dY/dG shows an ambiguous impact of the size of the country considered since a rise of L reduces any positive multiplier result; the same holds for K as long as s+ca'-bß is positive. The more strongly investors react to any difference between the net marginal product and r (parameter b) the lower is the fiscal multiplier.

The medium term fiscal multiplier is the larger (assuming that it is positive) the larger the interest elasticity of money and h', respectively, is. Comparing the above fiscal multiplier to the familiar short run Keynesian multiplier dY/dG = 1/(s + hb/h') – suggesting that the higher h' the larger the multiplier – we have a similar result. However, here we also see the impact of the effect of changes in aggregate demand on the average product of capital and investment, respectively; and we see the impact of reinvestment and of the technology parameter ß. The lower the depreciation rate the lower is the fiscal multiplier.

Compared to our simple fiscal multiplier we can see – as an impact from the money market –that a rise of a', namely the weight consumers attach to long run income has an ambiguous impact on the multiplier; the impact of ca' is positive if $h(1+r)^2\delta^{\,\beta/1-\beta}$ falls short of Lhs $^{\beta/1-\beta}$; a low real interest rate and a low income elasticity of the demand for money as well as a low capital depreciation rate make it more likely that the impact of ca' is positive. The impact of the savings rate is not as strong as the simple multiplier for the goods market suggests: the money demand effect is reducing the denominator. The higher the level of the real interest rate the smaller is the fiscal multiplier (assuming dY/dG>0) which points to a strategic advantage of countries with low real interest rates – this could e.g. reflect credibility of monetary policy or of fiscal policy. The US which is known to have the lower real interest rates among OECD countries – except for the special case of Switzerland – thus should have an advantage while the Euro zone has a disadvantage once that the conflicts about the non-fulfillment of the Stability and Growth Pact contribute to higher real interest rates. This points to an interesting paradox, namely that ministers of finance eager to loosen the stability pact in order to get a larger room for manoeuvre in fiscal policy matters ultimately will reduce the effectiveness of fiscal policy. The higher the depreciation rate the smaller is the fiscal multiplier provided that it is positive. This is an important message for developing countries eager to catch up with advanced industrialized countries: (i) in such countries repair management in firms often is relatively poor which implies a relatively high depreciation rate; (ii) choice of technology often is biased by government in favour of importing advanced capital equipment from OECD countries which, however, is not only likely to be inconsistent with international relative factor price differentials but also could force the country to pursue a modernization policy which tries to be in line with that in advanced countries; there is pressure to always introduce latest foreign technologies fast so that the effective depreciation rate could be high.

$$\frac{dY}{dM/P} = \frac{bK(1+r)^2 \delta^{\beta/(1-\beta)} - ca'Lhs^{\beta/(1-\beta)}}{\left((s+ca'-b\beta)h' + hbK\right)(1+r)^2 \delta^{\beta/(1-\beta)} - ca'Lhs^{\beta/(1-\beta)}}$$

$$\frac{dY}{ds} = \frac{h'(1+r)^2 \delta^{\beta/(1-\beta)}}{\left((s+ca'-b\beta)h' + hbK\right)(1+r)^2 \delta^{\beta/(1-\beta)} - ca'Lhs^{\beta/(1-\beta)}} \left(\frac{dY}{ds}\right)'$$

Obviously the multiplier for monetary policy is zero if bK $(1+r)^2\delta^{\beta/1-\beta}$ is equal to ca'Lhs $^{\beta/1-\beta}$. The multiplier for monetary policy will be infinte in absolute terms if ((s+ca'-bß)h' + hbK) $(1+r)^2\delta^{\beta/1-\beta}$ is approaching ca'Lhs $^{\beta/1-\beta}$. Note that for the special case that the depreciation rate is zero the multiplier is unity. Dividing the numerator and the denominator by bK$(1+r)^2\delta^{\beta/1-\beta}$ we can see that the multiplier is greater unity – provided that it is positive – if the condition holds that {[s+ca'-bß)h']/bK + h} is smaller than unity.

Comparing the above monetary policy multiplier to the familiar Keynesian short-run multiplier – dY/d(M/P) = 1 / ([sh'/b] + h)– we can see that there is no liquidity trap if s+ca' is equal to bß.

Monetary policy is the more effective, the higher b – assuming that the multiplier is positive. A supply-side policy, defined as a rise of s, can hav a positive or a negative impact where the sign for the multiplier dY/ds depends on a complex set of parameter conditions. The multiplier is zero if the interest elasticity of the demand for money is zero. The multiplier is the higher the higher the depreciation rate is and the higher the size of the capital stock is the lower the multiplier (assuming (dY/ds)' to be positive).

As regards the impact of real money balances one might want to consider a refined model in which real output is affected by real money balances so that Y=$(M/P)^{\beta'}K^{\beta}L^{1-\beta-\beta'}$; in addition one might want to modify the savings function by assuming S =sY[Y/(M/P + K)] so that savings per capita fall – assuming a given per capita income – as the ratio income to wealth increases.

Finally, one should note that from (6") we get the slope of the medium term goods market equilibrium schedule ISM as dr/dY = [s+(ca'-bß)]/[-ca'L(s/δ)$^{\beta/1-\beta}$ – b] which can be larger or smaller than the short-run schedule of the familiar IS curve with slope dr/dY=s/(-b). If we assume that (i) ca' =bß or (ii) ca'<bß while the numerator remains positive the slope of the ISM curve is definitively smaller in absolute terms than the standard IS curve. To put it different: An expansionary monetary policy will raise output in the medium term more strongly than in the short run (see appendix). However, we have a certain paradox of monetary policy since in the long run monetary policy is endogenous as we have emphasized. Any medium term monetary policy which reduces in a non-inflationary world the interest rate temporarily below the steady state equilibrium interest rate – the natural interest rate to use WICKSELL's term – must adopt in the long run a contractionary monetary policy which brings up the interest rate to the natural level. We thus

may conclude that expansionary monetary policy will have an effect on medium term output only if individuals discount future monetary policy strongly, or if the initial interest rate was above the natural rate.

Open Economy: Mundell Fleming Solow Model

For the case of an open economy we have to distinguish the case of fixed exchange rates versus the case of flexible exchange rates. The subsequent model is a hybrid Mundell-Fleming-Solow model (MFS) where – denoting real net capital imports as Q and q=eP*/P (e is the nominal exchange rate, P the price level, * denotes foreign variables) - we have added the following balance of payments equilibrium condition to equations (6') and (12):

$$Q (r,r^*, q^*) = q^* J(q^*, Y, Y\#) - X(Y^*, Y^*\#, q^*) \qquad (14)$$

In the context of an open economy we also have to modify the investment function I, which now includes – following the model of FROOT/STEIN (1991) who emphasize the role of imperfect capital markets – the real exchange rate variable, since a real depreciation of the currency of country I (home country) will stimulate the inflow of foreign direct investments: I= δK + b(βY/K $-\delta$ $-$r) + Hq*, where the parameter H is positive. Therefore net capital imports depend not only on the ratio of the domestic real interest rate r to the foreign interest rate variable, but also on the real exchange rate eP*/P. As consumption depends on both Y and Y# it is natural to state the hypothesis that imports also depend on both Y and Y#; and that real exports positively depend on both Y* and Y*#. Compared to traditional modelling, the impacts of q* and of Y# and Y*# are new in our statement of the balance of payments equilibrium condition; one may note that in principle one additionally might want to consider the impact of q*#/q* on capital inflows as well as trade, but for the sake of simplicity we will ignore this here. In a small open economy we can thus state the following equation system with e, Y and r as endogenous variables (case of flexible exchange rates). We can calculate the multipliers for three exogenous variables, namely for expansionary monetary policy (dM) or fiscal policy (dG) or a change of current foreign output (Y*) or a change of long run foreign output (dY*#) or a change of long run domestic output (dL) as well as the impact of a rise in the savings ratio (ds). In reality, a rise in the savings ratio could be linked to special incentives of government aimed at raising the savings rate and the investment ratio so that ds>0 can be interpreted as supply side policy. The medium term goods market equilibrium condition in an open economy with foreign direct investment reads:

$$Y=c\{a''Y+a'[1/(1+r)]L[s/\delta]^{\beta/1-\beta}\}+\delta K+b(\beta Y-eK)+ \qquad (15)$$

$$Hq^*+G+X(Y^*,Y^*\#,q^*)-q^* J(q^*, Y, Y\#)$$

Differentiating (15), (12) and (14) gives the following system of equations in matrix notation :

$$
\begin{pmatrix}
s+ca'-b\beta+q^*J_Y & bK-\dfrac{ca'L}{(1+r)^2}\left(\dfrac{s}{\delta}\right)^{\beta/(1-\beta)} & -H+J+q^*J_{q^*}-X_{q^*} \\[2ex]
h & -h' & 0 \\[2ex]
q^*J_Y+Q_{[M/P]/Y}\dfrac{[M/P]}{Y^2} & -Q_r & -Q_{q^*}+J+q^*J_{q^*}-X_{q^*}
\end{pmatrix}
\begin{pmatrix} dY \\ dr \\ dq^* \end{pmatrix}=
$$

$$
=\begin{pmatrix}
1 & 0 & -Ya''-\dfrac{a'L(s-\beta)}{(1+r)(1-\beta)\delta^{\beta/(1-\beta)}}s^{(2\beta-1)/(1-\beta)} & X_{Y'} & X_{Y'\#} & \dfrac{a'}{1+r}\left(\dfrac{s}{\delta}\right)^{\beta/1-\beta} \\[2ex]
0 & \dfrac{1}{P} & 0 & 0 & 0 & 0 \\[2ex]
0 & -\dfrac{Q_{[M/P]/Y}}{PY} & 0 & X_{Y'} & X_{Y'\#} & 0
\end{pmatrix}
\begin{pmatrix} dG \\ dM \\ ds \\ dY^* \\ dY^*\# \\ dL \end{pmatrix}
$$

This implies:

$$
\det(B)=\det\begin{pmatrix}
s+ca'-b\beta+q^*J_Y & bK-\dfrac{ca'L}{(1+r)^2}\left(\dfrac{s}{\delta}\right)^{\beta/(1-\beta)} & -H+J+q^*J_{q^*}-X_{q^*} \\[2ex]
h & -h' & 0 \\[2ex]
q^*J_Y+Q_{[M/P]/Y}\dfrac{[M/P]}{Y^2} & -Q_r & -Q_{q^*}+J+q^*J_{q^*}-X_{q^*}
\end{pmatrix}
$$

=(- H - X$_{q^*}$ + J + q*J$_{q^*}$)(-Q$_{q^*}$h + h'(q*J$_Y$ + Q$_{[M/P]/Y}$ [M/P]/Y^2)) + (- Q$_{q^*}$ - X$_{q^*}$ + J + q*J$_{q^*}$)[-h'(s + ca' - b\beta + q*J$_Y$) - h(bK - ca'L[s/\delta]$^{\beta/1-\beta}$/(1 + r)^2)]

Furthermore we will define:

  U = 1/det(B)

The multipliers for a change in G, M, s and other variables are as follows:

  dY/dG = -Uh'(-Q$_{q^*}$ + J + q*J$_{q^*}$ - X$_{q^*}$)

$$
dY/dM= -U/P\left\{\left(bK-\frac{ca'L}{(1+r)^2}\left(\frac{s}{\delta}\right)^{\beta/(1-\beta)}\right)\right.
$$

$$
\times\left(-Q_{q^*}+J+q^*J_{q^*}-X_{q^*}\right)+Q_r\left(-H+J+q^*J_{q^*}-X_{q^*}\right)\bigg\}
$$

  -Uh'Q$_{[M/P]/Y}$[1/P]/Y(-H-X$_{q^*}$+J+q*J$_{q^*}$)

$$
dY/ds = Uh'\left(Ya''+\frac{a'L(s-\beta)}{(1+r)(1-\beta)\delta^{\beta/(1-\beta)}}s^{(2\beta-1)/(1-\beta)}\right)(-Q_{q^*}+J+q^*J_{q^*}-X_{q^*})
$$

$dr/dG = -Uh(-Q_{q*} + J + q*J_{q*} - X_{q*})$

$dr/dM = U/P \left\{ \left(s+ca'-b\beta+q*J_Y -X_Y \right)\left(-Q_{q*} +J+q*J_{q*} -X_{q*} \right) \right.$

$$\left. -\left(q*J_Y +Q_{[M/P]/Y}[M/P]/Y^2 \right)\left(-H+J+q*J_{q*} -X_{q*} \right)\right\}$$

$\quad - UhQ_{[M/P]/Y}[1/P]/Y (- H - X_{q*} + J + q*J_{q*})$

$dr/ds = Uh (-Q_{q*} + J + q*J_{q*} - X_{q*})$

$$\times \left(Ya''+ \frac{a'L\left(s-\beta\right)}{\left(1+r\right)\left(1-\beta\right)\delta^{\beta/(1-\beta)}} s^{(2\beta-1)/(1-\beta)} \right)$$

$dY/dY* = -Uh'X_{Y*}(H - Q_{q*})$

$dY/dY*\# = -Uh'X_{Y*\#}(H - Q_{q*})$

$$dY/dL = -U\frac{a'}{1+r}\left(\frac{s}{\delta}\right)^{\beta/1-\beta} h'(- Q_{q*} - X_{q*} + J + q*J_{q*})$$

$dr/dY* = -Uh X_{Y*}(H - Q_{q*})$

$dr/dY*\# = -UhX_{Y*\#}(H - Q_{q*})$

$$dr/dL = -U\frac{a'}{1+r}\left(\frac{s}{\delta}\right)^{\beta/1-\beta} h(- Q_{q*} - X_{q*} + J + q*J_{q*})$$

$dq*/dY* = U X_{Y*}(-hQ_r + h'(q*J_Y + Q_{[M/P]/Y}[M/P]/Y^2))+[-h'(s + ca' - b\beta + q*J_Y)$
$- h(bK - ca'L[s/\delta]^{\beta/1-\beta}/(1 + r)^2)])$

$dq*/dY*\# = U X_{Y*\#} (-hQ_r + h'(q*J_Y +Q_{[M/P]/Y}[M/P]/Y^2) +[-h'(s + ca' - b\beta +$
$q*J_Y) - h(bK - ca'L[s/\delta]^{\beta/1-\beta}/(1 + r)^2))$

$$dq*/dL = U\frac{a'}{1+r}\left(\frac{s}{\delta}\right)^{\beta/1-\beta} [-hQ_r + h'(q*J_Y +Q_{[M/P]/Y}[M/P]/Y^2)]$$

One can see that U is negative if the following conditions are met:

$$s + ca' > b\beta \tag{I}$$

$$q*J_Y > X_Y \tag{II}$$

$$(1+r)^2bK > ca'L(s/\delta)^{\beta/(1-\beta)} \tag{III}$$

$$J > Q_{q*}+X_{q*}-q*J_{q*} \tag{IV}$$

As well as:

$$J > H+X_{q*}-q*J_{q*} \tag{V}$$

$$Q_{q*}h > h'q*J_Y \tag{VI}$$

Or alternatively

$$J < H+X_{q*}-q*J_{q*} \text{ which is equivalent to } H > Q_{q*} \tag{V'}$$

$$Q_{q*}h < h'q*J_Y \tag{VI'}$$

If one set of conditions is met, then we can draw the following conclusions about the multipliers:

$dY/ds > 0$ if $s < ß$

$dY/dG > 0$

$dY/dM > 0$ if V. is met

dY/dY^* depends on the sign of X_{Y*} and if V. or V'. is met

$dY/dY^*\#$ depends on the sign of $X_{Y*\#}$ and if V. or V'. is met

$dY/dL < 0$

Note that if $s=ß/2$ – which implies fulfilment of the golden rule – the multiplier for dY/ds indeed is positive. The medium term model suggests that fiscal policy can be effective. Monetary policy – under certain conditions – also is effective; namely if imports are relatively high in comparison to the impact of the real exchange rate on foreign direct investment inflows and the net exports of goods and services, respectively. An important aspect concerns supply-side policy: If the savings rate is smaller than ß a rise of s will raise medium term output. The impact of a rise of Y^* and $Y^*\#$, respectively, can differ in the respective sign which suggest that international policy coordination is more complex than the standard macro model suggests. Governments with emphasis on long run output – hence governments with a more long run time horizon – thus could favour different policy options than short-run oriented political actors. The assignment debate thus is affected. An explicit two country model could offer more refined results. The multipliers for the exchange rate also are interesting:

$dr/dG > 0$

$dr/dM < 0$ if V'. is met

$dr/ds < 0$

dr/dY^* depends on the sign of X_{Y*} and if V. or V'. is met

$dr/dY^*\#$ depends on the sign of $X_{Y*\#}$ and if V. or V'. is met

$dr/dL < 0$

A rise of government consumption raises the interest rate which is in line with the standard model. Expansionary monetary policy will reduce the interest rate under certain conditions while a rise of the savings rate will reduce the interest rate. The impact of Y^* and $Y^*\#$ on the interest rate might differ in sign. A rise of long run employment will reduce the medium term interest rate.

B.3 Conclusions and Possible Extensions

The results show a more differentiated picture than the familiar debate on Keynesianism versus monetarism. The analysis suggested here is a useful medium term analysis bridging in a consistent way short run standard macroeconomic analysis and long term growth analysis. Many refinements and modifications are possible, and there is a broad set of empirical issues which emerges in the model suggested. The relative size of s, ß, δ and b are of particular importance. Changes of the technological regime – such as the switch to the New Digital Economy – could alter ß, δ and b.

The model presented suggests that policymakers should not only consider monetary and fiscal policy but also policies stimulating the savings ratio (and the investment ratio) as well. The more consumption is influenced by long run expected steady state income, the more attractive supply-side policies are. Countries with a stable political system should be able to exploit the impact of policy measures designed to raise long run output. However, in countries with political instability or with politicians without much reputation government will naturally have a bias in the field of supply-side policy; instead of raising the savings rate, government will be inclined to follow the logic of the short-run Keynesian model and try to raise short run output by reducing the savings ratio. With only temporary increases in output and a growing stock of public debt, there is a considerable risk that the debt-GDP ratio will increase and hence the anticipated future tax rate τ'. Indeed in a two-period approach, it must hold that real government consumption as well as real interest rate payment on the stock of public debt (B) and discounted future government expenditures $G^{\#}$ be equal to current tax revenue and discounted future tax revenue:

$$G + rB + G\#/(1+r) = \tau Y + \tau' Y\#/(1+r). \tag{16}$$

In a more elaborate MFS model, taking into account that the current tax rate and the future tax rate will negatively affect present consumption and investment, one could endogenize τ' while assuming, for example, that $G = G\#$. Risk-averse taxpayers will calculate τ' not simply from (16), rather with $G = G\#$ they will calculate it as:

$$\cdot \tau' = (1+r)\{\tau Y - [G + rB + G\#/(1+r)]/Y\# + \Omega^{T} \tag{17}$$

The variable Ω^{T} indicates the credibility of government tax policies, or alternatively, its history in political cheating. If past governments have always kept their promises in the field of taxation and borrowing, Ω^{T} is zero. The more often taxes or deficit-GDP ratios were raised in violation of election promises (or international treaties such as the Stability and Growth Pact in the Euro zone) the higher Ω^T will be. Thus, Ω^T can be considered within a broader approach an endogenous variable which could be explained in the framework of a New Political Economy approach. At the bottom line, a loss in government reputation will therefore reduce present consumption and investment. Moreover, it might reduce net foreign direct investment inflows and hence net capital inflows.

The new approach presented can be extended in various ways (WELFENS, 2005) and allows to combine short run macroeconomic analysis with many of the standard results of modern growth theory – as e.g. summarized in JONES (1998). The model presented also raises many new issues for the debate about the efficiency of fiscal policy and monetary policy.

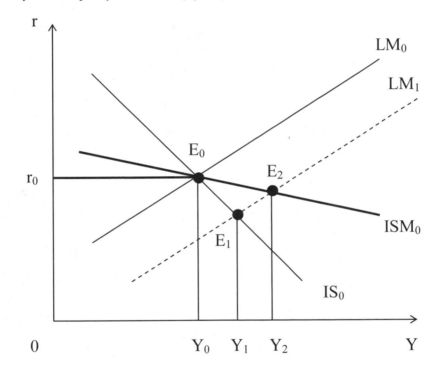

Fig. 25. Standard IS-LM Model versus Keynes-Solow Model

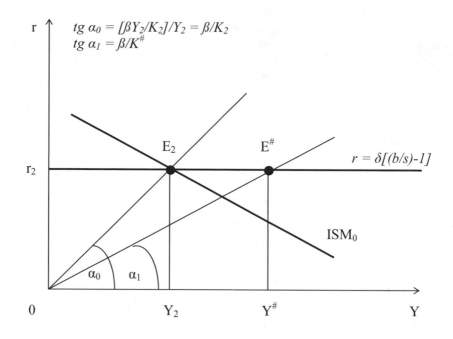

Fig. 26. Medium Term and Long Run Equilibrium

As regards the money market: note that – with m =: M/P – in the long run the condition must hold: $(m/L)^{\#} = hk^{\#\beta} - h'\beta k^{\#\beta-1}$

C. Economic Integration, Technological Progress and Growth

C.1 Rich Countries vs. Poor Countries and Economic Integration

The world economy consists of many poor countries and a few dozen relatively rich countries. Per capita income differentials across countries were fairly large at the beginning of the 21st century. Asian countries did relatively well in catching-up with leading OECD countries in the 1970s and 1980s. As respect to the 1990s, several transforming countries from eastern Europe have also achieved relatively high per capita income ratios, and there is some optimism that EU accession countries could catch up relatively quickly with EU-15. BEN-DAVID (1996) has empirically shown that economic integration has contributed to economic convergence, SACHS/WARNER (1995) have presented evidence on the positive links between trade liberalization and economic growth. LEVINE/RENELT (1992) have also found that economic openness is closely related to growth. MANKIW/ ROMER/WEIL (1992) have emphasized the role of human capital for growth and economic convergence; however, below we do not look into the human capital issues – but capital K could be adequately defined to include human capital and thus we include some such aspects, at least implicitly. Various alternative approaches to growth modelling in open economies and the issue of international real convergence have been discussed in the literature (OBSTFELD/ROGOFF, 1996), but no convincing general approach has emerged.

Much of the convergence optimism in the context of EU eastern enlargement is related to the Heckscher-Ohlin-Samuelson (HOS) theorem which shows for the case of identical linear-homogeneous production functions in a 2country-2goods-2factor model that moving from autarchy to free trade will bring about relative price equalization that will go along with relative factor price equalization. The ratio of real wage w to the real interest rate r in the home country will become equal to the foreign relative factor price ratio w*/r*.

While there are many trade modelling variations in modern Economics – partly taking into account economic integration – (eg BRETSCHGER, 2002; SLAUGHTER, 1997), there is no doubt that many economists would emphasize convergence optimism in the context of the HOS model. This holds despite that fact that DEARDORFF (1986) has shown that small deviations in the underlying modelling assumptions can undermine the convergence results of the HOS approach – there could be convergence of relative prices while relative factor prices are diverging.

The traditional HOS-modelling – based on free trade, absence of international factor mobility and identical technologies in both countries of the model – implies medium term economic convergence. As national income in real terms is Y=wL +rK, for countries I (home country) and II, K/L is denoted as k, Y/L as y and * is used for foreign variables:

$$y=w+rk \tag{1}$$

$$y^* =w^* + r^*k^* \tag{2}$$

Hence if the factor price ratio w/r is converging towards w*/r*, free trade will bring about partial convergence at given k and k*, respectively. Moreover in the medium term, profit maximization will drive k towards k* since capital intensity is a function of the factor price ratio. Hence trade can bring about full international economic convergence. However, the HOS model is silent on the accumulation dynamics. By contrast, the neoclassical growth model has explicit accumulation dynamics, but does not consider the role of trade – although both trade and capital accumulation must be considered when analysing the issue of convergence vs. divergence.

Theoretical analysis shows (GRIES/JUNGBLUT, 1997) that growth models can be built in which there will be a permanent income differential between two countries. The GRIES/JUNGBLUT model is based on a three sector approach in which a traditional sector, an industrial sector and a research sector interact. This model already raises some scepticism about the prospects for full economic convergence across countries.

As regards empirical evidence for international economic convergence, BARRO/SALA-I-MARTIN (1992; 1995) and BAUMOL (1986) – among others – have presented evidence on international economic convergence. ROMER (1986) and DE LONG (1988) have suggested considerable criticism on the Baumol interpretation since there is a sample selection bias problem which leads to overstating the case for convergence. DURLAUF/QUAH (1998) offer new empirical evidence, as it seems that there are certain regional convergence clubs, but one can hardly argue that the world economy has witnessed global convergence.

When discussing problems of globalisation or aspects of economic integration, part of economists' convergence optimism is based on the neoclassical growth model which predicts that relatively poor countries – that is with a per capita capital stock k=K/L which is much below the steady state value – will experience relatively faster catching-up in the growth of k than medium income countries which in turn might catch-up vis-à-vis the leading country (USA in a global context or Denmark in the EU).

Integrating trade theory and growth theory has been rather difficult in Economics, and two sector growth models indeed are not easy to handle. WELFENS (2002b) has argued that the neoclassical growth model within a two-sector approach suggests that the original Solow-model overemphasizes the role of the savings rate.

In the following analysis we want to look at a two-country model where country I, the home country, is small and relatively poor, while country II is large and has a high per capita income and an exogenous growth rate of Harrod-neutral technological progress a*=[dA*/dt]/A*. We will focus on a one sector growth model but nevertheless integrate important elements from the HOS-model, namely the hypothesis that trade will stimulate economic catching-up.

To the extent that the two countries considered are engaged in a regional integration scheme – such as EU-15 and the 8 east European accession countries –, one might point out that the parameters of the model have to be calibrated adequately. Analytical understanding of convergence potentials could indeed become quite interesting for both EU enlargement and for expansion of ASEAN or NAFTA.

As is well known, the rate of technological progress plays a role both for the level and the long term growth rate in the neoclassical model with (exogenous) technological progress. The neoclassical growth model is relatively mechanistic and does not take into account profit maximization. This is much in contrast with Heckscher-Ohlin-Samuelson models in which profit-maximizing firms in each country will specialize according to the given respective relative factor endowment. The subsequent modifications suggested the desire to reconcile growth theory and trade theory but also the desire to avoid excluding crucial problems from the beginning.

We will not consider a third potential avenue of determining the growth rate, namely Ramsey-Cass-Koopmans models, which assume that infinitely-lived households maximize discounted utility $\int U(C/L)e^{-\zeta t}dt$ subject to $Y/L = w+rK/L$ where e' is the Euler number, ζ is the discount rate, C is consumption, L and K stand for labor and capital, respectively; w and r denote the real wage rate and the real interest rate, respectively. This leads to optimum growth $g_{C/L}$ (with g denoting the growth rate) of per capita consumption which is equal to $[r-\zeta]/\upsilon$ where υ is the inter-temporal rate of substitution: $\upsilon = -U"(C/L) [C/L]/U'(C/L)$. This way the optimisation of per capita consumption easily determines long-term growth rates of C/L and, of course, of K/L, where some modification can be built into the approach by opening up the economy so that temporary current account imbalances could affect consumption and capital accumulation, respectively. The country with the lowest time preference would accumulate the fastest and run correspondingly temporary current account deficits – with the output of this country finally exceeding that of its trading partner. In such a set-up real economic convergence in the sense of equal growth rates can be obtained only in a rather artificial way, namely that the time preference rates and the inter-temporal elasticities of substitution at home and abroad would have to adjust endogenously.

A first step to go beyond the neoclassical growth model – determining the steady state level of capital intensity k=K/L and k'=K/(AL), respectively – will be to state a hypothesis with respect to the technological catching-up process. We will at first describe this process with a differential equation in which trade intensity on the one hand and government per capita R&D expenditure on the other hand will play a crucial role. In a subsequent modification of the technological progress function we will assume that foreign direct investment will also affect international technological catching-up. Hence we will present a model in the spirit of the New Growth Theory, but we will use part of the neoclassical model in our approach. In a quasi-neoclassical growth model, we want to determine the capital intensity on the basis of a modified Solow model that thus – at first glance – is inconsistent with HOS. However, we want to show a way to integrate profit-maximization in a model which is asymptotically consistent with (new) growth theory, respectively. The model developed is asymmetric in the sense that we have a small poor open economy (country I) and a large rich country (II) with an exogenous rate of technological progress. In this set-up we can analyse the conditions for technological catching up and economic convergence. The main results derived are as follows:

- trade stimulates economic catching-up;
- R&D-expenditures per capita (v) also play a crucial role for technological progress and catching up; moreover, in our model they make the tax rate an endogenous variable so that v indeed is the only government variable with which government has an influence on the convergence process.
- We can determine an optimum government R&D-GDP ratio (v^{opt}) in the sense that v^{opt} will maximize consumption per capita.
- Finally, we demonstrate how foreign direct investment will affect the analysis where we point out that the share of foreign direct investment in the capital stock of the host country has an ambiguous effect on convergence.

Combining trade analysis and growth analysis should be quite useful for policymakers in all countries with slow growth which consider changes in trade or FDI or innovation policy.

C.2 Set-up of the Model

At first we recall the basic neoclassical growth model – here with a Cobb-Douglas production function $Y=K^{\beta}(AL)^{1-\beta}$, a depreciation rate δ, savings rate s, income tax rate τ and growth rate of population n. The technological progress rate AL is dubbed Harrod-neutral, that is labor-saving – a problem with the simple Cobb-Douglas function is that Harrod neutrality cannot be distinguished from Hicks neutrality and Solow neutrality, but as we are not looking into the empirical issues here this issue is neglected here. We assume that savings S are proportionate to disposable national income, so that $S = s(1-\tau)Y$. The standard model is summarized in a basic set of equations (see appendix) and the following Bernoulli differential equation for $k'=K/(AL)$:

$$dk'/dt = s(1-\tau)k'^{\beta} - (n+a+\delta)k' \tag{3}$$

$$k'(t) = \{C_o e^{-(n+a+\delta)(1-\beta)t} + [s/(n+a+\delta)]\}^{1/1-\beta} \tag{3'}$$

The steady state value for k' is

$$k'^{\#} = [s(1-\tau)/(n+a+\delta)]^{1/1-\beta} \tag{4}$$

Hence the steady state value for y' is

$$y'\# = k'^{\beta} = [s(1-\tau)/(n+a+\delta)]^{\beta/1-\beta} \tag{5}$$

Abroad we have – assuming a Cobb-Douglas function $Y^*=K^{*\beta}(A^*L^*)^{1-\beta}$ – a similar equation for the steady state variable:

$$y'^*\# = k'^*\#^\beta = [s^*(1-\tau^*)/(n^*+a^*+\delta^*)]^{\beta/1-\beta} \qquad (5')$$

Hence output per capita in country I and country II is (denoting the Euler number as e') given by (6) and (6'):

$$y = [s(1-\tau)/(n+a+\delta)]^{\beta/1-\beta}A_oe'^{at}; \qquad (6)$$

$$y^* = [s^*(1-\tau^*)/(n^*+a^*+\delta^*)]^{\beta/1-\beta}A^*_oe'^{a^*t}; \qquad (6')$$

In the subsequent analysis, we will consider a model in which technological progress is endogenous in country I, but for simplicity we assume that it is exogenous in country II. Indeed, we will consider various technological catching-up regimes ranging from the simple HOS assumption that technology is the same at home and abroad to progress functions in which the progress rate is linked to trade intensity and R&D per capita expenditures or to these variables plus FDI. As is well known changes in s, τ, n and δ will affect the level of the growth path, while a change of the progress rate a will affect both the level and long-term growth rate (see. Fig. 1): A rise in t_1 of the level of the growth path means that the originial curve AA' is shifted upwards as shown by BB' while an additional rise of the growth rate is displayed as BB".

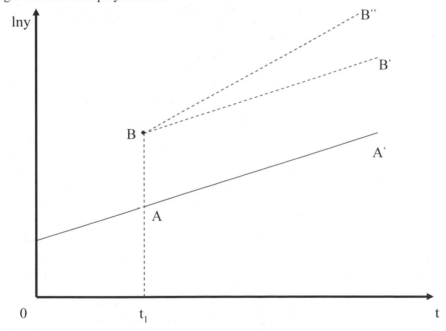

Fig. 27. Level vs. Growth Effect

At the end of this section we notice that monetary aspects – actually financial market institutions – might be taken into consideration in a simple way. As the efficiency of the banking system, or more generally, of the intermediation process is important for the savings process, one may take into account international differences in the efficiency of the intermediation process through a parameter λ which would be quasi-augmenting for the savings rate.

$$y\# = \{s(1-\tau)[1+\lambda]/[n+\delta+a(t)]\}^{\beta/(1-\beta)} \tag{7}$$

In this way one could consider the effects of financial market integration and thus combine trade analysis and financial market analysis. Poor countries often suffer from unstable financial institutions and inadequate prudential supervision, which implies that efficiency parameter λ is low. However, in the following analysis we will disregard financial market aspects.

C.2.1 Convergence in a Hybrid Growth Model with Trade and R&D

We will now consider a modified model that follows the spirit of the approach by WELFENS (2002) in which trade intensity has an impact on the growth rate of technological progress. A balanced government budget and a balanced current account are imposed for the long-term analysis by the hybrid growth-trade model. Trade intensity is measured by import-GDP ratios at home (j) and abroad (j*). Moreover, we assume that R&D expenditures per capita (v) have a positive impact upon the speed of technological catching up. The hypothesis stated here is that a rise in the growth rate of technological progress (a) is more difficult the higher the level of a already achieved; however, da/dt is a positive function of the ratio of a*/a. We will use a simple function to express our catching up hypothesis - parameter b, σ, ψ, ε are assumed to be positive - where we assume that technological catching-up is a positive function of the technology gap a*/a (we will not look into the potentially interesting case that k' enters the parameter for a*/a):

$$da/dt = -ba + (jj^*)^{\sigma}v^{\psi}(a^*/a)^{\varepsilon} \tag{8}$$

Defining h' $=(jj^*)^{\sigma}v^{\psi}$ we have:

$$da/dt = (h'a^{*\varepsilon})a^{-\varepsilon} - ba \tag{9}$$

The solution of this equation is:

$$a(t) = \{C_o'e^{-b(1+\varepsilon)t} + (h'a^{*\varepsilon})/b\}^{1/(1+\varepsilon)} \tag{10}$$

The rate of technological progress will converge with t$\rightarrow\infty$ towards a*$^{\varepsilon/(1+\varepsilon)}$ (h'/b)$^{1/(1+\varepsilon)}$, where the Steady state of a# depends positively on a* and on h'$=(jj^*)^{\sigma}v^{\psi}$: the higher the import-GDP ratios j and j* are and the larger government R&D promotion per capita, the higher will be the long term equilibrium value a#. The parameters b and $(1+\varepsilon)$ determine the adjustment speed.

Regional integration will raise j and j*, respectively – and regional integration might indeed raise the import ratio of two countries forming a customs union more than it would in a three-country model of global free trade. This conclusion could emerge in the context of a homogenous 3 country setup of countries with equal population size but rather different per capita incomes; and the two relatively rich countries joining in a customs union. The elasticities σ and ψ also could be affected through integration. It is unclear whether the deceleration impact of the parameter b will be affected by regional integration. However, we may assume that regional integration stimulates competititon on the one hand, on the other hand it could create more technological opportunities for applying innovations; and this would reduce the parameter b.

The steady state value of a(t) is given by

$$a\# = a*^{\,\varepsilon/(1+\varepsilon)} (h/b)^{1/\varepsilon} \tag{11}$$

We note that regional integration and R&D promotion stimulate the long-term growth rate of technological progress. Once a is stable, the neoclassical growth equation can be used in a traditional way, namely to determine the convergence of per capita income:

$$y\# = \left[s(1-\tau)/\left(n + a*^{\varepsilon/(1+\varepsilon)} (h/b)^{1/\varepsilon} + \delta \right) \right]^{1/1-\beta} A_0 e^{,\, a*^{\left[\varepsilon/(1+\varepsilon)\right]}(h/b)^{[1/\varepsilon]}_t} \tag{6'''}$$

The level of the growth rate of per capita income y is negatively affected by technological progress, but the exponential term with technological progress clearly implies that the overall impact of technological progress on y is positive. Note that the government budget constraint $vL = \tau Y$ implies that the tax rate is endogenous once that v is set by the authorities.

Finally, we may note that we can derive a modified golden role for maximization of per capita consumption (C/L). Denoting output as Y=Y(K,AL) we can state that the marginal product of capital z in the optimum – in steady state - must be equal to

$$z(k\#) = n + \delta + a*^{\,\varepsilon/(1+\varepsilon)} (h/b)^{1/\varepsilon} \tag{12}$$

If it would hold additionally – as suggested later – that $z=r=r*$ in the steady state we have:

$$r* = n + \delta + a*^{\,\varepsilon/(1+\varepsilon)} (h/b)^{1/\varepsilon} \tag{12'}$$

The intersection point of the S/L curve with the I/Y curve must occur in the golden age at the point where the slope of the y-curve is equal to $(n+a+\delta)$. Government can indeed influence the intersection point by adquate choice of the tax rate or by directly influencing the savings rate. However, one must not overlook that the government can chose only the tax rate or v to be an exogenous variable, and for government it is rational to strive for a golden rule at the highest possible growth rate of technological progress. Thus the optimization problem for the golden rule is more complex than in the standard approach.

If from a golden rule perspective $s[1-\tau]$ is too high (low) government could reduce (raise) the tax rate accordingly so that the intersection point between the per capita savings curve and the per capita investment curve is shifted to fulfill equation (12). If one would integrate cyclical output movements into the long-term analysis, it may be suggested that a situation marked by recession in which $s > s^{\text{opt}}$ will not pose any problem for stabilization and growth policy, respectively. Keynesian logic would suggest reducing the savings rate in order to stimulate demand and output; the golden rule logic also argues in favor of a reduction of s. A serious problem would occur, of course, if $s<s^{opt}$ since stabilization policy and growth policies would want to move in opposite directions.

The two country perspective raises the problem that the golden rule for the two countries will not be identical under profit maximization conditions that imply $r=z=r^*=z^*$, however, unless in the case of $a+\delta=a^*+\delta^*$ there is indeed full convergence of a towards a*.

Full technological convergence a#=a* will be observed under a specific parameter constellation:

$$(h/b)^{(1/\varepsilon)[1-(\varepsilon/(1+\varepsilon)]} = a^* .\tag{11'}$$

If ε is in the range between zero and unity, the exponent of h/z exceeds $1/\varepsilon$. It may be worth noting that economic integration is likely to raise both ε and h. A priori it is unclear whether integration policy and government policies are sufficient to achieve a sustained progress rate that could bring convergence. However, it is clear that government can influence h through the innovation policy variable v. Full convergene of per capita income will occur – taking into account (6) and (6') – if in addition to (11') which brings about technological convergence (a#=a*) we have:

$$[s(1-\tau)/(a+n+\delta)]^{1/1-\beta} A_o = A^*_o[s^*(1-\tau^*)/(a^*+n^*+\delta^*)]^{1/1-\beta}\tag{13}$$

It is clear that (6) and (6') are the result of an inhomogeneous differential equation with constant coefficients. However, if a=a#=a* - and if relative convergence speed of a(t) is sufficiently high - we can asymtotically treat a as a constant coefficient so that the steady results are as presented in (5). The adjustment path of y' towards the steady state can be analyzed on the basis of simulations.

Equation (13) suggests a crucial role for the savings rate and the tax rate, respectively. Note that the budget constraint vL=τY effectively leaves government only one instrument beyond trade policy (economic integration policies). It is interesting that the convergence of a(t) towards a* - or any other steady state value a# - implies a twin convergence role for a since a(t) will affect both the level of the growth path and the growth rate. This suggests that the process of closing the international technology gap is most crucial for real economic convergence. Moreover, all variables entering the technology gap function must be carefully studied. The model developed here suggests that trade – in the spirit of the HOS-model – and Schumpeterian innovation policies play an important role for catching-up.

However, our model set-up is not a full HOS-framework since we have not assumed identical technologies in both (or in all) countries. Reality indeed reveals an obvious truth about technological heterogeneity, with the US having a share of roughly 40% of all international patents. The number of international (or US patents) per capita of EU countries also differs significantly, with Germany and Sweden as EU leaders – upon closer inspection these figures would have to possibly be corrected by the effect of patenting of US subsidiaries in Germany and Sweden; in Belgium, US subsidiaries account for about 40% of all patents granted. In a global perspective technological heterogeneity is likely to increase as the share of R&D expenditures relative to GDP increases over time and the role of multinational activities grows. MNCs ability to successfully produce abroad is – according to DUNNING – based on ownership specific advantages – read technological advantages.

C.2.2 Profit Maximization in the Hybrid Growth Model

A strange problem in traditional economics is that the HOS-model assumes profit maximization – and emphasizes trade as an engine of economic convergence – while the neoclassical growth model does not consider profit maximization. The only exception is that the golden rule, namely marginal product of capital $z=n=g_Y$ in the basic fundamental model, is often interpreted so that real interest rate r must be equal to the growth rate – but the adjustment of the marginal product of capital and r is opaque.

For a consistent link between trade theory, growth modelling and profit maximization we suggest here a simple approach: The hypothesis is that the marginal product of capital z is governed by an adjustment process according to

$$z_t = \alpha (z^*-z) + z_{t-1} \tag{14}$$

Equation (14) states that domestic investors want to achieve the same return on investment as firms in the foreign benchmark country. Here, α is the speed of adjustment. With continuous time we have:

$$dz/dt = \alpha(z^*-z) \tag{14'}$$

If a and z* are constant, (14') is an inhomogenous differential equation with constant coefficients whose steady state solution is z#=z*=r*. In our approach we will see the HOS result that r=z=z*=r* through the indirect mechanism r=z and r*=z*, where convergence of z to z* will bring about r=r*=z*. In the foreign country we can assume that r*=z* remains constant.

Equation (14) implies with domestic profit maximization that $z=ßk'^{ß-1}$, suggesting a corresponding adjustment of k(t) which can be considered the implicit demand for real capital per capita. The idea to reconcile trade and growth theory is that the adjustment speed α be not constant, but that the relative divergence between the steady state value of capital intensity k'# from the hybrid growth model and actual capital intensity k' matters for the adjustment speed; k'# is interpreted here as the implicit capital supply per capita (in efficiency units) offered by those willing to save. We assume

$$\alpha = [k'\#-k']/k'\# \tag{15}$$

Hence the investors act according to:

$$dz/dt == \{[k'\#-k']/k'\#\}(z^*-z) \tag{16}$$

The mechanics of the hybrid neoclassical model makes sure that with t→∞ we have:

$$k'=k'\#. \tag{17}$$

Asymptotically, we will thus also have z=z*=r*, which is consistent with profit maximization. If free trade asymptotically brings about the convergence of factor price ratios (w/r=w*/r*), we also have r=r*.

$$r=r^*=z=z^* \tag{18}$$

This results occurs without international capital mobility. The steady state solution will thus bring about a result in which the supply of capital is equal to the profit-maximizing demand for capital. Both sides of the implicit capital stock market try to anticipate some elements from the other side: S=I can be interpreted in such a way that the supply side wants to offer savings in line with actual investment; the dynamic equation (16) indicates that investors take the logic of capital accumulation resulting from planned savings into account.

From an empirical point-of-view, it would be quite interesting to analyze whether the adjustment speed in rich countries and poor countries is different. Such differences could indeed explain part of the observed nonconvergence or conditional convergence observed in reality. Moreover, the various elasticities in the hybrid growth model are also quite interesting; it goes without saying that the impact of trade and innovation could be modelled in various ways so that our model is one of several straightforward approaches.

C.3 Asymmetric Foreign Direct Investment in a Two-Country Growth Model

Next we consider an asymmetric 2-country-model with given populations ($L=L_o$, $L^*=L^*_o$) where the home country (I) attracts foreign direct investment flows, but country I is not investing abroad. Foreign investors make a once-and-for-all choice to hold a certain share of φ as the capital stock in country I (a more complex modelling approach could make φ for each period dependent on instantaneous profit maximization). Both countries produce according to Cobb-Douglas functions $Y=K^{\beta}(AL)^{1-\beta}$ and $Y^*=K^{*\beta}(A^*L^*)^{1-\beta}$. Moreover, we assume profit maximization in competitive markets so that profit income accruing for foreign investors is $\varphi\beta Y$, and consequently we have to distinguish between gross domestic product Y and gross national product $Z=Y(1-\varphi\beta)$ in country I. Similarly, national income in country II is now $Z^*=Y^*+ \varphi\beta Y =Y^*+ \varphi\beta Y^*(Y/Y^*)$. If investors from a country are not repatriating all profits, one should interpret parameter φ as the product of the share of foreign investors in the domestic capital stock times the share of MNC subsidiaries' profits repatriated in the analysis of the said country.

Consequently, assuming that savings depends on disposable national income savings per capita, efficiency units in country I and country II is now given by equations (19) and (20), respectively.

$$S/(AL)= s(1-\tau)(1- \varphi\beta)y' \tag{19}$$

$$S^*/(AL^*) = s^*(1-\tau^*)(y'^*+ \varphi\beta y^*'[k'^\beta L_o/k'^{*\beta}L_o^*]) \tag{20}$$

$$k'^{\#} = \left[s(1-\tau)(1-\varphi\beta)y'/(\delta+a)\right]^{1/1-\beta} \tag{19.1}$$

$$k'^{*\#} = \left[s^*(1-\tau^*)\left[1+(L_0/L^*_0)\varphi\beta(k'/k'^*)^\beta\right]/(\delta^*+a^*)\right]^{1/1-\beta} \tag{20.1}$$

At first we consider an exogenous technological progress rate a and a*, respectively. Hence the steady-state solutions for country I and II are:

$$k'^{\#} = \left[s(1-\tau)(1-\varphi\beta)y'/(\delta+a)\right]^{\beta/1-\beta} \tag{19.2}$$

$$k'^{*\#} = \left[s^*(1-\tau^*)\left[1+(L_0/L^*_0)\varphi\beta(k'/k'^*)^\beta\right]/(\delta^*+a^*)\right]^{\beta/1-\beta} \tag{20.2}$$

The steady-state per capita income for country I is reduced by foreign direct investment according to (19.1), while that in country II is raised (see 20.1). However, the implausible result of a negative impact of FDI on country I will no longer hold after the next analytical step. We will use a modified technological progress function as we assume that foreign direct investment contributes to technological catching-up, hence for the poor country I, we have:

$$da/dt = -ba + (jj)^\sigma v^\psi \varphi^\theta [a^*/a]^\varepsilon \tag{21}$$

Note that the presence of FDI could bring about an increase of the parameters σ and ψ. However, the size of j will be smaller since a balanced current account requires that $jY^*-jY-\beta$ $\varphi Y=0$. Now the steady state value of a(t) is given – with $h'=(jj)^\sigma v^\psi \varphi^\theta$ by definition - by

$$a\# = a^{* \ \varepsilon/(1+\varepsilon)} (h'/b)^{1/\varepsilon} \tag{22}$$

Since FDI raises the steady state value of the growth rate of technological progress, one may assume that FDI indeed contributes to improving convergence prospects for the initially poor country where the dynamics of per capita steady state income is determined in country I according to:

$$y\# = A_0 e'^{at} \{s(1-\tau)(1- \varphi\beta)/(a+\delta)\}^{\beta/1-\beta} \tag{19.3}$$

The fact that φ might negatively affect the level of the growth path – which is influenced by $a\#(\varphi, ...)$ – while φ also increases long-term technological progress raises the issue of how long-term the time horizon of policymakers actually is. As the following figure shows GNP per capita will fall once the country opens up to FDI inflows, however, long-term growth rate of the economy will increase as a result of FDI inflows.

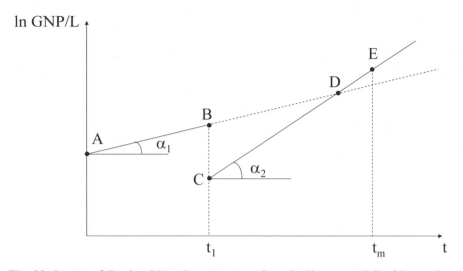

Fig. 28. Impact of Foreign Direct Investment on Growth (Short-term Fall of Per-capita-GNP Level and Rise of Growth Rate as a Consequence of FDI Inflows)

Since country II is the source of foreign direct investment and thus obviously has a technological advantage over country II, it is not adequate to assume that technological catching-up will be only positively influenced by φ. Rather we have to consider there will be a systematic gap that has to be reflected in a modified equation (19) such as:

$$da/dt = -ba + (jj)^\sigma\, v^\psi\, (1-\varphi)^\eta \varphi^\theta\, [a*/a]^\varepsilon \qquad (21')$$

Clearly, FDI inflows as modelled here will not affect short-term gross domestic product, rather it will influence the level of GNP per capita and the growth rate of GNP per capita, respectively. Politicians can be expected to be more interested in GNP per capita than in GDP per capita since high GNP per capita is a natural interest of voters. The difference between GNP and GDP can be rather high if the share of cumulated FDI inflows in overall capital stock is large as is the case in Ireland for example.

Such long-term progress effects might be heavily discounted in political reality so that the potentially negative impact of FDI inflows on the level of the growth path could encourage politicians to be hesitant in accepting FDI.

C.4 Policy Conclusions

The theoretical analysis has shown that one can integrate trade analysis and new growth theory in a rather simple way. Thus, endogenous growth theory is quite useful and should play a larger role in the policy arena. This holds particularly for relatively poor countries, but also for those OECD countries that have suffered from slow growth for many years.

There are at least four policy conclusions to be drawn:

- Governments should promote R&D in order to stimulate long-term growth (and regional integration might reinforce the potential for positive technology spillovers)
- Regional integration could be useful in accelerating technological catching up; both the role of regional and of global integration for technological progress should be carefully analysed.
- Effects of FDI inflows on economic catching up will be positive if the share of FDI in the capital stock of the host country strongly contributes to economic catching up.
- One can calculate a new golden rule in which endogenous technological progress plays a crucial role. In this context growth policy and stabilization policy are interesting as a simultaneous challenge; if the savings rate s is below the optimum savings rate in a recession, both growth policies and demand-side stabilization policies would suggest the same policy direction, namely to reduce the savings rate. The situation is quite different in a situation when s exceeds the golden rule savings rate since demand-side stabilization policies would entail negative welfare effects associated with the fall of per capita consumption below the optimum level. One would have to distinguish between temporary and permanent deviations from the golden rule.

Obviously in our modelling exercise we deliberately have not considered that the role of the terms of trade which might be affected – according to the Balassa-Samuelson argument – by relative economic catching up. Here we have one further interesting area of future research. Another interesting question is whether the interaction of trade, FDI and capital accumulation within a fully developed two-country model will raise per capita income in both countries. Another possible extension concerns a monetary growth model in which real money balances would directly enter the production function. Finally, one might want to analyse the role of public capital formation – and of public consumption - which would not only affect the production function but also the budget constraint.

Appendix C.1: Basic Neoclassical Model

The following is a standard approach (see e.g. JONES, 1998)

$$Y = K^{\beta}(AL)^{1-\beta} \tag{23}$$

Cobb-Douglas function with capital K, labor L, $0<\beta<1$

$$L = L_o e^{\prime nt} \tag{24}$$

(e' is the Euler number);

$$S = s(1-\tau)Y; \text{ savings function, where } \tau \text{ is the tax rate} \tag{25}$$

$$I = s(1-\tau)Y; \tag{26}$$

goods market equilibrium reflecting I=S

$$I = dK/dt + \delta K; \tag{27}$$

gross investment is net investment plus depreciations

$$A(t) = A_o e^{\prime at} \tag{28}$$

Harrod-neutral technological progress

$$dk'/dt = (dK/dt)/[AL] - (n+a)k'; \tag{29}$$

$$dk'/dt = s(1-\tau)k'^{\beta} - (n+a+\delta)k'; \tag{30}$$

Bernoulli-type differential equation in k'

$$k'(t) = \{C_o e^{-(n+a+\delta)(1-\beta)t} + [s/(n+a+\delta)]\}^{1/1-\beta} \tag{31}$$

$$k\#' = (Y/AL) = [s(1-\tau)/(a+n+\delta)]^{1/1-\beta} \text{ steady state for k'} \tag{32}$$

$$y\# = Y/L = A_o e^{\prime at}[s(1-\tau)/(a+n+\delta)]^{\beta/1-\beta} \text{ steady state for y} \tag{33}$$

The most fundamental and simple set-up is with a=0 and δ=0.

Appendix C.2: General Approach and Simulations

In the model presented we have the differential equations

$$dk/dt = sk^{\beta} - [n+\delta+a(t)]k; \text{ capital stock accumulation} \tag{34}$$

$$da/dt = (ha^{*\varepsilon})a^{-\varepsilon} - ba; \text{ technological progress function} \tag{35}$$

The solution of equation (IIa) is:

$$a(t) = \{C_o'e^{\prime -b(1+\varepsilon)t} + (ha^{*\varepsilon})/b\}^{1/(1+\varepsilon)} \tag{36}$$

Hence the general equation for capital accumulation is given by

$$dk/dt = sk^{\beta} - [n + \delta + \{C_o'e^{-b(1+\varepsilon)t} + (ha^{*\varepsilon})/b\}^{1/(1+\varepsilon)}]k; \tag{37}$$

Profit maximization requires $\beta k\#'^{\beta-1} = z = r$ and hence $k'\# = (r/\beta)^{1/(\beta-1)}$. This determines the real interest rate r and requires for the steady state that $= (r\#/\beta)^{1/(\beta-1)} = [s(1-\tau)/(n+a+\delta)]^{1/(1-\beta)}$; therefore.

$$r\# = \beta(n+a+\delta)/[s(1-\tau)] \tag{38}$$

Opening up the economy in the context of an asymmetric two country model - the home country being small - brings the problem that profit maximization in the sense of $z=r$ cannot hold instanteneously, rather domestic capital accumulation will be driven by an equation in which the technological progress function and the impact of a* on a are playing a role. We could, however, assume that asympto-cially the profit maximization condition $z=r^*$ will be fullfilled. However, the implication is powerful, namely that $k'\#=k'^*\#$. However, it remains unclear how the savings rate s could adjust in a way which is consistent with this implication.

Simulation

The following simulation is run for the general solution

$$k(t) = \left(\left(k_0^{1-\beta} - \frac{s}{n+\delta+a(t)}\right)e^{in+\delta+a(t)(1-\beta)t} + \frac{s}{n+\delta+a(t)}\right)^{\frac{1}{1-\beta}} \tag{39}$$

We can show a parameter constellation which does not lead to convergence and simulations where convergence will hold. The parameters assumed are as follows.

We can consider a simulation on the basis of $\beta = 0.33$, $n = 0.02$, $\delta = 0.1$, $C_o = -0.8$, $h = 0.4$, $a^* = 0.03$, $\varepsilon = 1/2$:

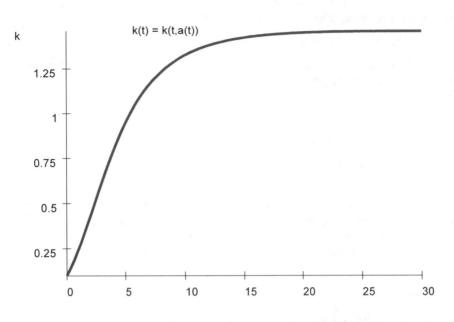

Fig. 29. Capital Formation Under Endogenous Technological Progress

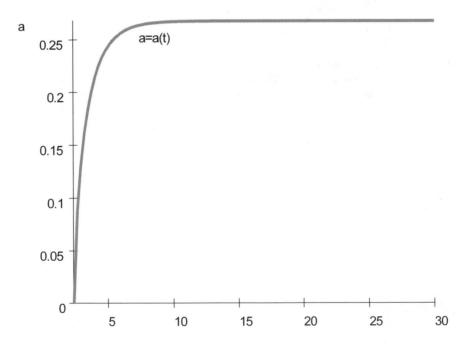

Fig. 30. Endogenous Technological Progress

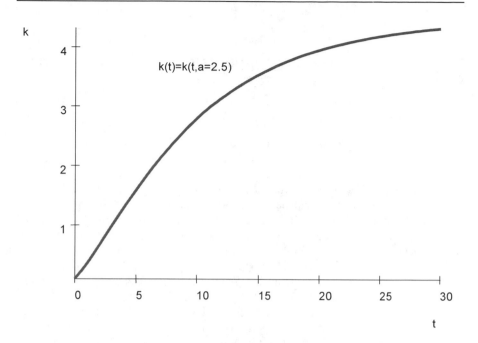

Fig. 31. Capital Formation Constant Technological Progress (progress for 2.5 periods)

D. Impact of the Real Exchange Rate on Trade, Structural Change and Growth

D.1 Introduction

As regards economic transition countries as well as EU accession countries, one can observe that they have recorded a long term real appreciation vis-à-vis the Euro and other currencies. Long term appreciation does not exclude considerable short term real exchange rate dynamics where stages of temporary nominal and real currency depreciation can be an element of a long term real appreciation process. One thus has to ask which role volatility – including potential overshooting – plays on the one hand. On the other hand, the focus is on the impact of the real exchange rate trend on economic development.

The real exchange rate q is defined here as $eP*/P$ (e is the nominal exchange rate in price notation, P the price level, * denotes foreign variables) while the relative price of nontradables (N goods; T is tradables), is denoted as $\varphi=P^N/P^T$. It is clear that the international law of one price will not hold strictly for tradables if we take into account transportation costs, tariffs and other trade impediments. However, even without these physical and political impediments, the law of one price does not hold universally across countries. Subsequently, we will take a closer look at potential explanations and the implications.

From a theoretical perspective, the real exchange rate affects trade, structural change and economic growth in an interdependent way. In the medium term the real exchange rate will affect the trade volume, the product mix of exports and imports plus the current account position. Moreover, the structure of output will be affected; this will partly be linked to sectoral productivity growth. In the medium term and in the long run, there will be direct and indirect effects on national income and per capita income. Those changes will in turn affect structural change and trade. In an open economy, the picture would be incomplete if one did not consider the effects of exchange rate dynamics on capital inflows as well as the stock market. To the extent that there is an increase of capital inflows and in particular foreign direct investment inflows, there will be effects on the production potential and productivity growth (see Fig. 1). From a policy perspective one must ask whether and which impulses are coming from regional integration and economic globalization. Moreover, the question arises as to which EU policy impulses are relevant and which national policy measures could be adopted to spur growth and a stable economic development.

Subsequently, we take a closer look at alternative explanations for real exchange rate changes (section 2). Moreover, we consider macroeconomic effects of real exchange rate changes. This concerns the link between the real exchange rate and economic development (section 3.1), selected links between real exchange rate dynamics and structural change (section 3.2), and the links between the real exchange rate and economic growth (section 3.3). In the final section, we present some basic policy conclusions. The appendix presents some innovative modelling related to the topic of exchange rate dynamics and macroeconomic analysis (including smooth linking of supply-side effects and demand-side impulses). Moreover, we emphasize product upgrading and product innovations in a macroeconomic context which includes an approach of an extended open economy model: the Mundell-Fleming-Schumpeter-model, which gives new insights for policy options in a broader macroeconomic perspective. A major element of the analysis presented is that we do not assume the law of one price to hold all the time.

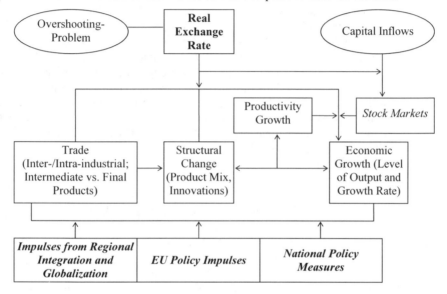

Fig. 32. Exchange Rate Dynamics, Trade, Structural Change and Growth

D.2 Reputation, Market Size and Relative Price Effects: A Quasi-Balassa-Samuelson Effect

In reality the law of one price does not always hold on the one hand, while the real exchange rate can change considerably over time on the other. In order to focus more closely on the theoretical problems we first define the price level as

$$P=(P^T)^{a'}(P^N)^{(1-a')} \text{ in country I and} \tag{1}$$

$$P^*= (P^{T*})^{a'^*}(P^{N*})^{(1-a'^*)} \text{ in country II.} \tag{2}$$

We assume – with $0<h<\infty$ – that there is a premium factor h(…) which implies that the law of one price for tradables does not hold universally.

$$P^T=heP^{T*} \tag{3}$$

Thus, the real exchange rate is given by:

$$P/(eP^*) = h(\ldots)[\varphi]^{(1-a')}/[\varphi^*]^{(1-a'^*)} \qquad (4)$$

The parameter h is an indicator which reflects forces that render the law of one price internationally invalid. If country I is a relatively poor and small open economy, h will be less than unity since the firms' standing in international markets – especially if said firms are relatively young and unknown – will be weaker than that of firms from country II. Identical products of firms from country I and II will fetch different prices. Alternatively, a situation with h smaller than unity could reflect a gap in product innovativeness in country I (In this case, we enter a world economy with monopolistic competition and truly heterogeneous goods where country II, for example, is producing more varieties than country I).

According to equation (4), a rise of the real exchange rate – an appreciation – is consistent with a rise of the relative price of nontradables compared to the respective price ratio abroad. However, it is also clear that the parameter h could rise over time. One may assume that the size of the domestic market (Y vs Y*), and the relative share of high-income people (y** is the critical high income here which for simplicity is assumed to be equal to y*) affects product reputation positively so that we can write:

$$h = h(Y/Y^*; L'/L^*) \qquad (5)$$

Here we have assumed that L' is the number of people with at least y*-income in country I and that all people in country II have income y* so that the share of high income people in country I relative to that of country II is L'/L (In country I, overall population L=L'+L" where L" is the number of people with income below y*). Denoting L'/L as γ' and per capita income as y in country I and y* in country II, we can rewrite the equation for the case of a linear homogenous function as

$$h' = h'(y/[\gamma'y^*], 1) \qquad (6)$$

According to the approach presented here one indeed would expect that the real exchange rate is a positive function of relative international per capita income y/y*. This would be in the spirit of the BALASSA-SAMUELSON effect, but the mechanism suggested here is distinctly different. One may note that the reputation of firms in country I might benefit from foreign direct investment since a foreign investor brings reputation to the newly acquired firms, and adequate international branding might then help to fetch higher tradable prices abroad. The h' function could be specified in such a way that with y approaching y*, the value of h' converges towards unity.

According to the traditional BALASSA-SAMUELSON effect (BALASSA 1965), the relative price of nontradables will increase along with real per capita income. Writing this relative price as P^N/P^T, it is clear that in principle such a shift can be brought about by a combination of a rise of P^N and a stable P^T or a stable P^N and a fall of P^T, which in turn – assuming an exogenous international tradables price P^T* – can be brought about only by a nominal appreciation, a fall of e. From this perspective, flexible exchange rates are preferable for catching-up countries which aim at a stable overall price level. The combination of a rise of the nontradables with an absolute fall of the tradable price is quite useful here.

Let us take a closer look at q=P/(eP*). If the relative price of nontradables in country I rises relative to country II, the implication is that at a given world market price P* either P will rise or the nominal exchange rate will fall. In a system of flexible exchange rates, the nominal exchange rate of country I might indeed fall or the price level P could increase – indeed P will rise if the relative price of nontradables rises while the price of tradables is constant. However, if the law of one price holds for tradables, the nominal appreciation in combination with a constant world market price implies a fall in the absolute level of the tradable price.

For simplicity we assume that a'=a'*; thus we can rewrite (4) as

$$P/(eP^*) = h''(y/y^*)[\varphi]^{(1-a')}/[\varphi^*]^{(1-a')} = h''(y/y^*)\{[P^N/P^{N*}][P^{T*}/P^T]\}^{(1-a')} \qquad (7)$$

The real exchange rate q=:P/(eP*) will increase according to the traditional Balassa-Samuelson effect, because the ratio of the relative price of nontradables increases along with a rising per capita income. Here we have shown a new additional element for a real appreciation along with a rise of relative per capita income – the h'' function ultimately reflects the impact of relative market size and of the size of relatively affluent people in society. Hence as the country's economic size and the development of income distribution enter the picture, the relative size of an economy catching-up will increase and income distribution will change in the course of economic catching up (note that a change of γ' will imply a new h'' function).

It is easy to see that there will be a real appreciation if:

- (i) the premium factor h'' and y/y* (or the share of relatively rich people as expressed in the parameter γ') both increase.
- (ii) P^N/P^{N*} should rise more strongly than P^{T*}/P^T falls; such a development could occur, for example, if there is a relatively strong demand shift in favour of the nontradables sector in country I while there is a strong productivity increase in the tradables sector of country II (the latter implies a fall of P^{T*}/P^T; the law of one price is not necessarily assumed to hold for tradables).
- (iii) P^N/P^{N*} should fall less than P^{T*}/P^T rises (e.g., because the relative productivity growth of the nontradables sector could be strong in country I while relative productivity growth in the tradables sector is high compared to country II. The latter means that the relative price of tradables will fall and hence P^{T*}/P^T will rise);
- (iv) if both P^N/P^{N*} and P^{T*}/P^T are rising, but the relative increase of the nontradables price is larger than that of the tradables price ratio. This could occur, for instance, if the demand for nontradables in country I rises relatively strongly (or if the relative productivity growth in the nontradables sector abroad is relatively high) while the relative productivity growth in the tradables sector is relatively high.

For EU accession countries, situation (ii) and (iii) should be quite characteristic. We expect particularly strong productivity growth if there are high foreign direct investments and if competition has been reinforced.

A long run real appreciation as measured by official statistics is to a considerable extent an overstatement if there is sustained upgrading in the quality of exports of the appreciating country. With respect to eastern European accession countries, there is indeed evidence of quality upgrading in exports, in particular in Hungary and the Czech Republic (BORBÉLY, 2004).

D.3 Real Exchange Rate Dynamics and Economic Effects

D.3.1 Real Exchange Rate and Trade

The rise of the real exchange rate has effects in transition countries. It affects:

- the volume of imports whose growth is reinforced as import goods become cheaper;
- the volume of exports whose dynamics are dampened – this does not exclude high export growth to the extent that domestic firms show a rising export orientation or that subsidiaries of foreign multinationals increase exports;
- with standard price elasticity assumptions there will be a deterioration of the trade balance which could be reinforced by relatively high growth over time; as one can write net exports (X') of goods and services as a function of the real exchange rate (with $\partial X'/\partial q<0$), domestic demand Y (with $\partial X'/\partial Y<0$), foreign demand Y* (with $\partial X'/\partial Y^*>0$), the domestic production potential Y' (with $\partial X'/\partial Y'>0$) and the foreign production potential Y*' (with $\partial X'/\partial Y^*'<0$), it is clear that demand side effects as well as supply side effects have to be taken into account;
- there is an incentive to upgrade export products in terms of quality and technological sophistication which is a strategy to offset the upward price pressure from the appreciation of the currency.

Real appreciation will reduce the influx of foreign direct investment which implies a long term deterioration of the current account since the increase of the production potential will slow down.

D.3.2 Real Exchange Rate and Structural Change

A rise of the real exchange rate will stimulate product upgrading in the export sector and thus contribute to rising national income. This is particularly true if Schumpeterian rents that can be fetched in world markets are a positive function of the level of technological sophistication of products. Assume that we can order all sectors by technology intensity, starting with A as that sector with the lowest intensity (the sector is assumed to have perfect competition and employ only unskilled labour at the nominal wage rate W'), B the second-lowest intensity...Z the highest technology intensity. Assuming that the markup factor which can be realized in international markets depends on the level of technology intensity, we can calculate value-added in a three-sector economy – producing products A, B and Z – on the basis of labour inputs L_1, L_2 and L_3 (with W as the wage of unskilled workers paid in sector A and W" paid to skilled workers which are employed in B and Z; foreign capital is only used for Z-output) as follows:

$$Y^{nominal} = L_1 W' + L_2 W''(1+B'(q, L'')) + [L_3 W'' + r*K**(q)P^K][1+ \qquad (8)$$

$$Z'(q, K**(q))]$$

Note that $K**$ is the stock of foreign capital in country I, P^K is the price of capital – this may be approximated by the stock market price index – and B' and Z' are parameters for the markup ratio in sector B and Z; B' and Z' are assumed to positively depend on the real exchange rate. That is, an appreciation of the currency, which brings the prospect of losing market share in existing markets abroad, will encourage firms to move towards higher quality ranges where one can fetch higher profit rates. Note also that sector B's markup ratio is assumed to benefit from network effects among skilled workers and therefore B' positively depends on the number of skilled workers L". Thus sector A is (unskilled) labor intensive and might be identified with the nontradables sector, B is skilled-labor intensive and Z is intensively using foreign direct investment and hence international technology; here both B and Z stand for tradable goods. Real income is given by

$$Y = w'L_1 + w''L_2(1+B'(q, L'') + [L_3 w'' + r*K**(q)P^K][1+Z'(K**(q),q)] \qquad (9)$$

The average real wage rate is w= $[L_1/L]$w' + w"$[1-L_1]/L$, where we naturally assume w">w'. Real output and real income will increase if:

- training helps to transform unskilled workers into skilled workers;
- skilled workers move from a sector of medium technology and a low mark-up factor to a high technology sector with a higher markup factor (Z'>B')
- there is real appreciation which stimulates firms in the medium technology sector and in the high technology sector to upgrade product quality which in turn goes along with a higher mark-up factor (B' and Z' will rise along with q); however, in the high technology Z-sector, q has an ambiguous effect on the mark-up ratio Z' since a rise of q stimulates product upgrading while reducing the optimum stock of foreign direct investment inflows.
- the mark-up factor can be raised by attracting foreign direct investment (FDI as well as cumulated FDI =$K**$); real appreciation reduces FDI inflows, while real depreciation raises FDI inflows relative to GDP (FROOT/STEIN, 1991).

The extent to which unskilled workers can be transformed into skilled workers depends on many aspects, including economic incentives for skill upgrading for both unskilled workers and firms in medium technology and high technology sectors. We thus have pointed out some key aspects of structural change in an open economy:

- An excess of unskilled labor in the A sector will translate fully into long term unemployment unless there is upgrading of both unskilled workers and unemployed people; this is the implication of our assumption that the tradables sector employs only skilled workers.
- One may emphasize that any excess supply of skilled labour in sector B (or Z) can be absorbed by Z (or B) if the country considered is a small open economy. However, there one serious caveat which is normally not considered in the standard model of a small open economy. If one sector produces and exports high-technology goods, one may not assume that the international demand for such products is infinitely elastic; this standard assumption would fully contradict the idea of a high technology product (e.g., advanced computers or medical drugs) which face a limited international demand well known to all – the few – producers in the world.

If there is real appreciation, technological and economic catching-up might be facilitated not least through a rising import of cheaper sophisticated intermediate imports. At the bottom line, it is clear that the structural perspective of economic dynamics described here is in marked contrast to the broader approaches in growth theory and growth analysis.

D.3.3 Real Exchange Rate and Growth

D.3.3.1 Growth and FDI in a Modified Neoclassical Framework

If accession countries are characterized by a long term real appreciation associated with a nominal appreciation, the implication for capital flows is that there will be higher net capital imports than otherwise. We can write interest rate parity prior to EU membership in the following form where the domestic economy is the accession area/country (where i stands for the nominal interest rate, z^E for the expected depreciation rate and R' for the risk premium, * for foreign variables):

$$i = i^* + z^E + R' \tag{10}$$

Prior to EU membership there will be a positive politico-economic risk premium for every accession country. Assuming that the nominal interest rate reflects inflationary expectations, we obtain for the case of expectations coinciding with actual inflation rates (π in accession country and π^* in the EU-15 countries) the equation

$$r = r^* + [z + \pi^* - \pi] + R'' \tag{11}$$

If there is real appreciation, the bracket term for the change of the real exchange rate (with z denoting the actual depreciation rate) is negative so that the cost of capital in accession countries is reduced; profit maximization will drive firms to realize equality of r and the marginal product of capital. The risk premium after EU accession, R'', is certainly much smaller than prior to accession. As one may assume that prudential supervision and the ability of firms to survive recessions and phases of temporary strong appreciation (including overshooting phenomena) in accession countries is smaller than in EU-15 and the Euro zone, one may assume that R" is positive. If the risk premium were zero, the real interest rate in accession countries would be smaller than in EU-15, which in turn would stimulate both investment and growth. At the bottom line, the real exchange rate appreciation of catching-up countries implies a rise in the level of the growth path. However, as the real exchange rate appreciation z^r can be assumed to be a positive function of relative per capita income y/y^*, the pace of real appreciation will decline over time, and indeed becomes zero if $y=y^*$.

Growth Model with Foreign Direct Investment

In an open economy, it is important to understand the role of foreign direct investment for production and per capita income. Subsequently we consider a simple model of an open economy which receives foreign direct investment inflows – those depend on the real exchange rate (FROOT/STEIN, 1991) – and produces based upon a Cobb-Douglas function. To understand basic growth dynamics, consider country I and country II which – with K, L and A denoting capital, labor and a Harrod-neutral progress factor, respectively, – both produce according to a Cobb-Douglas function

$$Y=K^{ß}(AL)^{1-ß} \text{ and} \qquad (12a)$$

$$Y^*=K^{*ß^*}(A^*L^*)^{1-ß^*}. \qquad (12b)$$

We will subsequently consider an asymmetric world economy – or integration zone – where one country is a single source of foreign direct investment outflows. The home country is the accession area where we will assume for simplicity that a part b of the capital stock is owned by foreign investors; b could be determined through a gradual process of foreign direct investment inflows or through a set of initial transactions in the course of privatization of a post-socialist economy involving foreign investors as bidders. We denote the real exchange rate as q and assume that $b=b(q)$ which – with $\partial b/\partial q<0$ – is in the spirit of FROOT/STEIN (1991). If technology is identical in both countries, we have $A=A^*$ and $ß=ß^*$. If factor reward is according to the marginal product rule, we have national income at home

$$Z=Y-bßY; \qquad (13a)$$

ßY is profit and b reflects the share of the capital stock owned by foreign companies. Abroad – in the source country of foreign direct investments – we have

$$Z^*=Y^*+[bßY/q^*]. \qquad (13b)$$

It is easy to recognize that asymmetric FDI will lead to sustained differences in per capita income across countries (WELFENS, 1997). In the presence of FDI, it is certainly necessary to carefully distinguish between GDP and GNP. We will assume that savings

$$S = s(\ldots)Z \tag{14}$$

$$S^* = s^*(\ldots)Z^*. \tag{15}$$

Let us at first modify standard neoclassical growth theory – assuming a as the rate of exogenous labour-augmenting technological progress, n as the growth rate of L and denoting k'=K/[AL]) – by considering a savings rate which positively depends on the real interest rate r. Imposing the conditions of a long term balanced government budget and that investment I (I= dK/dt + δK) is equal to savings S of domestic residents plus foreign investment from part (exogenous parameter b") of profits (b"ßY):

$$S+b"ßY = I \tag{16}$$

$$S^* - b"ßY/q^* = I^*. \tag{17}$$

The differential equation for the home country (country I) is given by:

$$dK/dt + δK = s[1-b(q)ß]Y + b"ßY \tag{18}$$

Taking into account the definition k'=K/[AL] and the respective expression for dk'/dt = [dK/dt]/AL – [n+a]k' and the production function, we obtain from equation (18) after dividing by AL:

$$dk'/dt = [s[1-b(q)ß] +b"ß]k'^{ß} – [n+a+δ]k' \tag{19}$$

This is a Bernoullian equation (we assume a constant q and hence constant b) whose steady state solution – with r=r* – is:

$$k'\# = \{\{s(r^*)[1-b(q)ß] + b"ß]\}/[n+a+δ]\}^{1/[1-ß]} \tag{20}$$

The steady state value k'# can be smaller or larger than in a closed economy. It is larger if ß[b"-sb] is positive, that is if b">sb or if

$$s < b"/b(q). \tag{21}$$

If government is considering foreign direct investment (FDI) as a means of raising gross domestic product, it will have to influence the savings rate or b"/b; as regards the latter, government might have to influence the real exchange rate adequately – indeed, one may assume that not just b is a function of q but that b"/b is a function of the real exchange. Fulfilling (21) is rather likely, especially if b" is close to b so that b"/b is close to unity. However, a country which loses the confidence of foreign investors might face b"/b<s so that gross domestic product would be smaller than in a closed economy. If we assume that imports positively depend on gross domestic product, the fulfilment of condition (21) implies that from a source country perspective, FDI outflows and rising trade rise in parallel. While on a sectoral basis FDI outflows are likely to replace sectors exports, the aggregate effect of FDI inflows in the host country has an offsetting and possibly dominating effect.

Equation (20) and (21) basically point to the fact that reinvested earnings of foreign investors contribute to capital accumulation and a higher GDP while profits transferred abroad reduce gross national product. We will still have to consider under which conditions in the steady state real national income will be higher than in a closed economy.

As a simple step to endogenize the growth rate of output, we assume that the growth rate a is composed of the basic growth rate a" as well as an endogenous element b'b (with parameter b'>0). The share of the foreign direct investment in the overall capital stock b thus has a positive impact upon the growth rate.

$$a = a'' + b'b \tag{22}$$

Output per capita (or GDP per capita) in the steady state (y#) is given – denoting the Euler number by e' – by the following equation:

$$y\# = e'^{at} A_o \{\{s(r^*)[1-b(q)\beta+b''\beta]/[n+ a''+ b'b(q)+ \delta]\}^{\beta/[1-\beta]} \tag{23}$$

Note that the adjustment dynamics for k' is affected by the expression $[n+a+\delta]$ and $[1-\beta]$. The higher both expressions are, the faster the adjustment towards the steady state will be. Hence, part of the benefit of foreign direct investment occurs in the form of faster adjustment towards the steady state. As regards the steady state we can see from (20) that the higher q is, the lower b is and therefore the lower k'# is as well. From this perspective, the early initial real depreciation occurring in countries opening up suggests that the level of the long term growth path is raised through an exchange rate effect which, however, will fade out in the course of the medium and long term appreciation. Nevertheless, b has a positive long term impact upon per capita income since the slope of the lny(t) line is raised by b (see the following figure where b jumps – e.g., in the course of privatization involving foreign investors – from zero to the new equilibrium value in t_1). Depending on s relative to b/b", this will lower or raise the level of the growth path (see point E versus point C). This does not rule out a long term equilibrium growth gap, namely if a<a*. Compared to existing literature, the proposed model differs since it takes into account both a change in the level of the growth path as well as a rise of the permanent growth rate. The familiar model by BARRO/MANKIW/ SALA-I-MARTIN (1995) takes into account international borrowing, where this approach affects the adjustment speed towards the steady state which itself is not affected by capital flows.

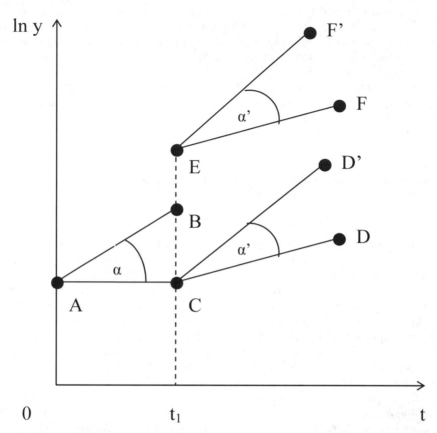

Fig. 33. Effect of FDI on the Level of Per Capita Income and the Growth Rate

The ability to generate a higher growth rate in the presence of foreign investors is likely to be reinforced if government expenditures on research and development is relatively high; the R&D policy variable is denoted as Ω and one may assume $a(b,\Omega)$. Hence the degree of supply-side government fiscal policy matters (the higher the share of Ω relative to output or to overall government expenditures, the higher the degree of supply-orientation in government fiscal policy).

Steady state national income (Y') per capita is given by:

$$(Y'/L)\# = [1\text{-}b(q)\text{ß}]y\# = [1\text{-}b(q)\text{ß}]\{s[1\text{-}b(q^*)\text{ß}]+b"\text{ß}\}e^{\text{'}a(b(q))t}A_o\{s(r^*) \qquad (24)$$

$$/[n+a(b(q))+\delta]\}^{\text{ß}/[1\text{-}\text{ß}]}$$

Whether GNP per capita is larger than in a closed economy depends (ignoring the question whether opening up changes the real interest rate) on

$$[1\text{-}b(q^*)\text{ß}]\{s[1\text{-}b(q)\text{ß}]+b"\text{ß}\}>s \qquad (25)$$

$$s[1-b(q)\beta]^2 + b"\beta > s \qquad (26)$$

Dividing by s gives

$$[1-b(q^*)\beta]^2 > 1-b"\beta/s \qquad (27)$$

Assuming that bβ and b"β/s are both close to zero, we can use the approximation that $\ln(1-x) \approx -x$ and thus obtain – quite interesting also for empirical analysis – as a critical condition for GNP per capita to be larger than in a closed economy:

$$s > b"/2b(q) \qquad (28)$$

More empirical analysis needs to be done. From equation (28), we can only conclude that a rise of q which reduces b makes it less likely that s exceeds the right-hand side of the equation. A government of an open economy interested in raising the level of the growth path of per capita GNP should encourage savings as we can see from equation (28).

One should also note that real appreciation reduces the burden of foreign debt, which often is considerable in poor countries. Thus long term real appreciation is welcome by many poor countries.

D.3.3.2 Negative International Spillovers?

It is interesting to take a look at appreciation dynamics within the context of a three-country perspective: Country I is a poor country while country II is a high income country. Both country I and II are part of a regional customs union. We assume that the catching-up country (I) records a gradual long term real appreciation of the currency. At the same time, we assume that productivity growth in the tradables sector is higher than the appreciation rate so that the price of exported goods falls from the perspective of the (net) importing country II. We now have to distinguish two cases in the context of a three-country perspective:

1. Country II imports intermediate products built into products exported to third country markets. Here, country II could ultimately benefit from rising net exports, higher profits and higher employment.
2. Country II imports final products which puts strong downward pressure on the price of tradables (much more than in the case of cheaper intermediate products) and hence implies downward inflation pressure. The welfare effect will be ambiguous since lower prices of final consumer goods will benefit consumers. At the same time lower prices of tradables imply lower profits in the tradables sector – and in case of wage rigidity also lower employment. Unemployment problems will be reinforced if the implied rise in the real interest rate in country II reduces the equilibrium capital intensity and hence investment.

From an EU-15 perspective, the implication thus is the following with respect to rising imports from EU accession countries: The mix of imported products is quite crucial – namely intermediate products versus final products – as is the relative productivity effect in accession countries. If the productivity growth effect is so strong that the relative price of imported tradables falls in EU-15, further analysis will have to focus on the above-made distinction. To identify such patterns is quite difficult since product upgrading in Eastern Europe makes price measurement rather cumbersome.

D.4 Real Effective Exchange Rate (p/ep*) Dynamics in Selected EU Countries

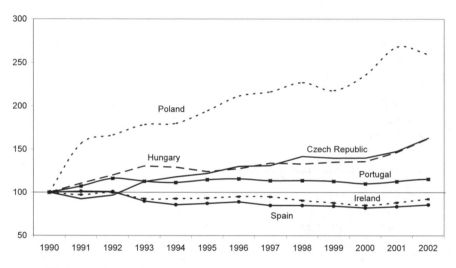

Source: World Development Indicators 2004.

Fig. 34. Real Effective Exchange Rate (p/ep*) Dynamics in Selected EU Countries: Poland, Hungary, Czech Republic, Portugal, Spain, Ireland, 1990-2002

D.5 Wages, Prices and the Real Exchange Rate

Assuming that accession countries face long term real appreciation pressure – eP*/P falls over time – the implication is that relative wage costs increase over time. The latter is an implication of the assumption that prices are determined through a mark-up J on wage costs so that

$$P^* = J^* W^* \text{ and} \tag{29}$$

$$P = JW; \tag{30}$$

With a constant mark-up ratio a and a*, respectively, a real exchange rate appreciation will always go along with a relative rise of domestic wage:

$$[1/e][P/P^*] = [1/e][J/J^*][W/W^*] \tag{31}$$

We assume that the nominal wage W and W* will both be determined by expected price dynamics (P^E and P^E* represent the expected price level at home and abroad) and labor productivity growth, which is in line with profit maximization on the part of firms. They all are assumed to use a Cobb-Douglas production technology $Y=AK^\beta L^{1-\beta}$ and $Y*=A*K*^{\beta*}L*^{1-\beta*}$

$$W:= P^E w = P^E (1-\text{ß})A[Y/L] \tag{32}$$

$$W*=P*^E w* = P*^E (1-\text{ß}*)A*[Y*/L*] \tag{33}$$

Hence for the relative wage ratio we get:

$$W/W*= [P^E /P*^E] \{(1-\text{ß})[A/A*][Y/L]/[1-\text{ß}*] [Y*/L*]\} \tag{34}$$

$$[1/e][P/P*] = [1/e][J/J*][P^E /P*^E] \{(1-\text{ß})[A/A*][Y/L]/[1-\text{ß}*] [Y*/L*]\} \tag{35}$$

From this perspective a real exchange rate depreciation – assuming a constant nominal exchange rate – will occur if there is

- a relative increase in the mark-up ratio (a/a*),
- a rise of the relative expected price level,
- a rise of the foreign relative output elasticity of capital (ß*/ß),
- a rise of relative labor productivity.

In countries of a customs union area which have opened up towards free regional trade and foreign direct investment, one can expect high growth in investment, output and per-capita-income. This holds all the more the more politically stable the country under considered is. Structural change will go along with a rise of relative labor productivity while in a context of rational expectations, the expected relative price increase is largely linked to relative money supply.

D.6 Towards an Integrated Macroeconomic Approach

We will emphasize that for certain analytical purposes it is useful to take a look at the macroeconomic impact of both supply-side and demand-side impulses. In every economy, output dynamics can be understood to be a mixture of the impact of the supply side – its macroeconomic equivalence is the production potential $Y^{pot} =K^\beta L^{1-\beta}$ (K is capital and L is labor) – and of aggregate demand Y^d. In transition countries, both supply-side dynamics and the demand side are important with some sectors being dominated by supply-side developments while others are shaped by demand side dynamics. If one were to include labor saving technological progress (stock of knowledge is A), the production function $Y^{pot} =K^\beta(AL)^{1-\beta}$ would be used.

Taking into account both the impact of the supply side and the demand side, a hybrid equilibrium approach for the goods market can be written as follows:

$$Y = \alpha Y^{pot} + (1-\alpha) Y^d \tag{36}$$

An important question is what determines α (in the interval 0,1), the size of the relative supply-side impact parameter. It reflects various forces, including expectations. The most simple way to think about α is to consider it as identical with 1-u (with u denoting the unemployment rate). In a full employment economy, u is zero and hence only the supply side dynamics – that is the accumulation of input factors – will determine actual gross domestic product. If u were rather high, it would be clear that supply-side dynamics would hardly influence actual output while the demand side would have a strong impact on Y. A more refined way would be to replace a with u^{χ}, where the parameter χ is assumed to be positive. In a small open economy – which asymptotically faces a totally elastic world demand curve – the impact of the supply-side should be relatively high.

It is obvious that for the case of a closed economy the fiscal multiplier for the case of standard specification of the demand side is smaller than the standard textbook case of 1/s; with α =1-u the fiscal multiplier is

$$dY/dG= 1/[1-uc] \tag{37}$$

An exogenous increase in the production potential raises actual output by

$$dY/dY^{pot} = (1-u) + u\partial Y^d/\partial Y^{pot} >0. \tag{38}$$

For the special case of an increase of the production potential through one unit of net investment and assuming an exogenous real interest rate, we have $\partial Y^d/\partial Y^{pot}= r$ and hence

$$dY = [(1-u)K^{\beta-1}L^{1-\beta} +ur]dK \tag{39}$$

If one simply assumes that the impact of aggregate demand reduces over time while that of aggregate supply increases in the long run, one might restate equation (36) as follows (with e' denoting the Euler number):

$$Y = [1-e'^{-bt}] Y^{pot} + e'^{-bt}Y^d \tag{36'}$$

Output and Wage Pressure in a Hybrid Supply & Demand Macro Model

One also should note that the hybrid approach suggests an interesting answer to the question of how a rise of the real wage rate will affect both output and employment. Consider a small open economy which can raise exports in accordance with the growth the potential output – here we assume that all output is tradable. We can rewrite equation (36) as follows if one assumes that consumption C=cY – with Y=wL+rK# (assuming that factors labor L and capital K are rewarded in accordance with their respective marginal product; K# is the equilibrium capital stock, r the real interest rate, w the real wage rate); investment I=I(r) and government consumption G is exogenous, net exports X' are a negative function of the international real wage ratio (* denotes foreign variables), a negative function of the real exchange rate q=P/(eP*), whereby P is the price level, e the nominal exchange rate, W the nominal wage rate and the real wage rate is defined as w=W/P.

$$Y = \alpha \, Y^{pot}(W/P) + [1-\alpha]\{c[wL+rK^{\#}] + I(r) + G + X'(W/eW^{*}, \, q) \tag{37}$$

We assume that the real interest rate r and the exchange rate e are exogenous; denoting eW* as W'* and W/W'* as φ we obtain from differentiation:

$$dY/dW = \alpha \, \partial Y^{pot}/\partial W + [1-\alpha]\{c[L+ r\partial K^{\#}/\partial W] + \partial X'/\partial \phi" dW/W'^{*} \tag{38}$$

By assumption, the partial derivative $\partial X'/\partial \phi"$ is negative. Given P, the rise of the nominal wage rate is, of course, equivalent to a real wage increase. The impact of a higher wage rate on consumption is positive, namely $c[L+ r\partial K^{opt}/\partial W]$; the overall sign for dY/dW is thus unclear. In a small open economy the net export effect may be expected to outweigh the domestic consumption effect (and also the effect $\partial Y^{pot}/\partial W$ if it should be negative). Moreover, if α=1-u and u=u(w/[Y/L]) the total differential for (1''') yields even a somewhat more complex result for dY/dW (if dY/dW is negative, the sign for du/dW should be positive). The ambiguity of dY/dW remains, but we can learn from the approach presented that the risk of adopting an excessive wage rate is higher the less open the economy is.

One should, however, not rule out that net exports could be a positive function of W/W'*, namely if the quality and innovativeness of the export base is a positive function of the relative wage ratio. Such a function implicitly assumes that the country considered can sufficiently move up the quality ladder in line with the rise of the international wage ratio. Analytically, we thus enter a world of imperfect competition, where the export price P** might well diverge from domestic price P for the same good. Assume that export quantity X=X(Ω'), that is X negatively depends on the ratio of the wage rate W to marginal market revenue per worker P**ßY/L – relative to the respective foreign indicator. We thus consider a relative cost pressure indicator

$$\Omega' = \{[W/P^{**}]/[\beta Y/L]\} / \{[W^{*}/P^{*}]/[\beta^{*}Y^{*}/L^{*}]\}; \tag{39}$$

Note that real exports are XP**/P while real imports, expressed in domestic quantity, are q*J, where J is the quantity of imports. Now let us assume that we have the following pricing rule (with v as a quality index or novelty index; σ" is a positive parameter):

$$P^{**} = W(1-\text{ß}) + \sigma'v \tag{40}$$

We furthermore assume (with parameter σ'>0) that the quality index realized by exporters is a positive function of the international nominal wage ratio because a relative rise of wage costs stimulates firms to move up the technology and quality ladder (an argument which, however, might be doubtful in the case of technologically leading countries where R&D expenditures as well as global product innovations are quite important).

$$v = \sigma"W/[eW^{*}] \tag{41}$$

Hence

$$P^{**} = W(1-\text{ß}) + \sigma'\sigma"W/[eW^{*}] = W[(1-\text{ß}) + \sigma'\sigma"/[eW^{*}]] \tag{42}$$

For the foreign country, we have (implying a specific effective relative international price P**/eP*):

$$P^* = W^*(1-\text{\ss})+ \sigma'^*\sigma''^*W^*/[e^*W\,] = W^*[(1-\text{\ss}^*) + \sigma'^*\sigma''^*/[e^*W]] \qquad (43)$$

Thus we can write

$$\Omega'= (1+ \sigma'^*\sigma''^*e/W)[\text{\ss}^*Y^*/L^*]/(1+ \sigma'\sigma''/eW^*)[\text{\ss}Y/L] \qquad (44)$$

Real imports are qJ and J is assumed – with W/W'* denoted as φ" – to be a function of J(q, φ", Y)

With respect to J, all three partial derivatives J_q , $J_{\varphi''}$ and J_Y are positive; J_q reflects a demand shift effect since the quantity of imports will reduce when their price is raised relative to domestically-sold goods; $J_{\varphi''}$ reflects the relative importance of wage income in overall income. J_Y is the familiar increase of imports resulting from higher aggregate income.

Hence, we paradoxically find that the ratio of real exports to real imports [XP**/P]/[qJ] could be positively influenced by the international nominal wage price ratio. A critical assumption here is that the price of exports indeed can be raised which is possible only under imperfect competition in international goods markets and if the firms of the countries considered sufficiently move up the quality ladder. Quality here includes product innovativeness.

A simplified case in which we assume the quantity of imports not to be reacting to Y and q* (q*=1/q) – more or less the case in a country whose imports are dominated by natural resources (as is the case of Japan and a few other countries). We assume that the quantity exported is X=X(φ"), where X is a negative function of φ" and a positive function of process innovations v"; the quantity imported J is a positive function of φ". Net real exports X' are given by

$$X' = [P^{**}(\varphi'',v'')X(\varphi'')/P] - eP^*J(\varphi'')/P \qquad (45)$$

Denoting E as an elasticity we get:

$$dX'/d\varphi'' = [X/P][P^{**}/\varphi'']E_{P^{**},\varphi''} + P^{**}\partial X/\partial\varphi''/P - q^*\partial J/\partial\varphi''. \qquad (46)$$

The expression dX'/dφ" (note that the elasticity φ might fall in absolute terms if φ" is increased again and again, which implies that there is an optimum wage pressure!) is positive only if the elasticity exceeds a critical value:

$$E_{p^*,e''} >-[\varphi''/X]\,\partial X/\partial\varphi''+[P/P^{**}]q^*\partial J/\partial\varphi''. \qquad (47)$$

Whether this inequality is fulfilled is an empirical question. One may assume that this will only be the case if the firms of the respective country have strong performance in product innovations (OECD countries – or some of them). Even if dX'/dφ" is positive, it is clear that there will be a positive link between Y and φ" only if a rise of φ" has no critical negative effect on domestic absorption (e.g., a rise of φ" could cause unemployment in the nontradables sectors). Assume that the unemployment rate negatively depends on process innovations A and positively on wage pressure as captured by φ". Denoting absorption by H'(u, φ") – where u is the unemployment rate and for simplicity we may assume $u=u(\varphi",A)$, with $\partial u/\partial\varphi">0$, $\partial u/\partial A<0$ – we have in a "Schumpeterian demand-oriented approach":

$$Y = H'(u(\varphi",A), \varphi", r) + [P^{**}(\varphi", A)X(\varphi")/P] – eP^*J(\varphi")/P \qquad (48)$$

This equation is a quasi-equilibrium condition for the goods market. Denoting with lower case suffix a partial derivative, we get:

$$dY=H'_rdr+ H'_uu_AdA + H'\varphi"+H'_uu_{\varphi"}+ X/P\ P^{**}_AdA \qquad (49)$$

$$+\{[X/P][P^{**}/\varphi"]E_{P^{**},\varphi"}+P^{**}X_{\varphi"}/P–q^*J_{\varphi"}\}\}d\varphi"$$

Within a simple framework, one may set $dr=0$ and $dA=0$ and then solve for $dY/d\varphi"$. This expression in a nutshell suggests that there is an optimum wage pressure in countries catching-up: set $dY/d\varphi"=0$ which yields the output-maximizing wage rate (where we assume that the second derivative is negative). Note also that in the case that $\partial P^{**}/\partial\varphi"=0$ – so that $E_{P^{**},\varphi}= 0$ – net real exports are always negatively affected by wage pressure. Taking into account a simple real money demand equation $m(Y,i,u)$ – where we assume $m_u>0$ (as a rise of the un-employment rate signals higher uncertainty and hence a rising real demand for liquidity: see ARTUS, 1989) – and stating the money market equilibrium condition, we have:

$$M/P= m(Y,i,u) \qquad (50)$$

As prices are sticky, we have assumed that process innovations will not reduce the domestic price level in the short run. For a constant domestic price level we get after differentiation:

$$dM/P = m_YdY + m_idi + m_udu \qquad (51)$$

Assuming zero inflation – in line with the assumption of a stable domestic price level P – and hence real interest rate r = nominal interest rate I, we obtain

$$dr = [1/m_i]dM/P – [m_Y/m_i]dY – [m_u/m_i]du \qquad (52)$$

Inserting this finding from the money market equilibrium in the goods market quasi-equilibrium condition, we get

$$dY= [H'_r/m_i]dM/P– H'_r[m_Y/m_i]dY – H'_r[m_u/m_i][u_{\varphi"}d\varphi"+u_AdA] \qquad (53)$$

$$+[H'_uu_A+X_AX/P]dA +\{H'\varphi"+H'_uu_{\varphi"}$$

$$+\{[X/P][P^{**}/\varphi"]E_{P^{**},\varphi"}+P^{**}X_{\varphi"}/P–q^*J_{\varphi"}\}\}d\varphi"$$

Ignoring for the moment any impact from the foreign exchange market, we can thus see some of the impact on Y. It is an empirical question of whether process innovations have a positive impact on Y, that is whether $dY/dA>0$.

It is straightforward to determine the endogenous variables r, q and Y on the basis of the equilibrium conditions for the goods market, the money market and the foreign exchange market. The latter is given (using Q to denote real net capital imports which are assumed to positively depend on r/r* and q) by

$$Q(r/r^*,q) = qJ - P^{**}X'(\ldots)/P \qquad (54)$$

In a short term model, one would use the equilibrium condition as stated in (48); in the context of a medium term approach one would replace (48) by (36) and in a long term perspective (36') which converges towards the traditional neo-classical model. One should note that in the medium term framework and in the long term analysis we have to consider the impact of technological progress (A) on both the demand side and the supply side. The model would look more complex if one would relax the assumption of a small open economy which faces no restrictions in exports to the world market. We thus have a fairly general macro-economic approach which can accommodate different time horizons in a consistent way.

A serious problem could be that the optimum wage pressure is not necessarily consistent with full employment. However, government can be assumed to be able to also influence P^{**}, namely by R&D promotion measures designed to stimulate product innovations in the tradables sector. With the goal of full employment it certainly is important to avoid excessive wage pressure (ex ante) and rather raise the marginal value-added in the tradables sector through adequate R&D promotion. Wages will then adjust ex post to the rising marginal value-added.

Finally it is interesting that a change of the real exchange rate q will affect net exports and investment in different ways. In a period of a fall in the real exchange rate – due to a relatively slow increase of the domestic price level – one will have a rise of net exports. At the same time, there will be a dampening effect on inflation, which drives up the real interest rate. In countries which are catching up economically, the real exchange rate is likely to temporarily increase so that net exports are dampened while domestic investment increases. This development should not be interpreted as simply a loss of international competitiveness since a major driver behind this development is, according to the Balassa-Samuelson effect, the natural adjustment of relative prices within a long term economic adjustment process. For small open economies acting in a system of flexible exchange rates there will be the long term policy option to adopt a restrictive monetary policy so that domestic absorption will be reduced through rising real interest rates; at the same time net exports will increase.

Economic catching-up (associated with both supply-side effects and demand dynamics) is subsequently understood as moving up the technology ladder of products (i.e., the adoption of more sophisticated quality products over time). Product innovation rates will largely be considered as exogenous so that we leave open the explanation as to why and at what time firms in the respective countries will upgrade product assortments (e.g., this may be linked to foreign direct investment inflows or to a rise in the ratio of government expenditures on research and development relative to GDP). The analytical focus will be on a one sector model or a two sector approach with tradables and nontradables. Moving up the technology ladder thus means that the share of high quality products in overall exports or total output is increased in the respective transition country. An interesting theoretical challenge is to consider both product and process innovations which we will undertake in one simple model – a more refined approach includes endogenous process innovation (and possibly endogenous product innovations).

While political reforms in transition countries affect opportunities for economic growth, there are naturally favourable prospects of economic catching up in the context of economic opening up. Once those countries have opened up for trade and capital flows they can benefit from:

- competitive pressure from world markets stimulating efficiency-enhancing economic restructuring;
- productivity-stimulating effects from OECD imports of intermediate products used for the production of final goods, including export goods;
- import of investment goods with embodied technological progress;
- exploitation of scale economies in the context of rising exports in scale-intensive industries;
- inflows of foreign direct investment (FDI) which raise the capital stock in the case of greenfield investment and raise factor productivity in the context of international mergers and acquisitions.

For economic analysis, it is rather useful to make a distinction between the non-tradableses (N-) and the tradables (T-)sector.

- Rising trade will naturally only affect the tradables sector, however the tradables sector will typically be the main impulse for structural change.
- FDI inflows can be in both the T-sector and the N-sector. A major effect of FDI inflows should be productivity growth. The structure of FDI inflows will thus partly determine the relative price of tradables, namely to the extent that productivity determines the relative price. If FDI affects both sectors in a parallel way with respect to productivity growth, we should expect a smaller rise in the relative price of nontradables compared to the case that FDI inflows are concentrated in the tradables sector.

D.7 Medium Term Approach to Product Innovations, Output and the Exchange Rate

As countries catch up, the export-GDP and the import-GDP ratio will grow while the share of intra-industrial trade increase. Moreover, foreign direct investment inflows will rise and in the long run there will typically be two-way FDI flows. Firms will become more innovative and will emphasize product innovations; the rate of product innovations will be denoted as v. Note that the term product innovation is understood here in the sense that the respective product is new from the perspective of the respective catching-up country (from the perspective of a global technology leader country this looks like product imitation). The term v may be understood as the country's product innovations relative to that of foreign countries: v is a stock variable, that is the share of product innovations given the overall number of products n_0. In the following analysis we will raise the issue of how product innovations will affect output, the interest rate and the exchange rate. The following macroeconomic model set up is a "Schumpeter-Keynes" approach in the sense that product innovations are integrated into the familiar Mundell-Fleming model. Hence the price level at home and abroad is given.

As regards the goods market our basic assumption is that investment I is a function of the real interest rate at home I and abroad (r*), the real exchange rate q*(that is eP*/P) – following the FROOT/STEIN argument – and the product innovation rate v, which is exogenous in the model. Hence we implicitly assume a model with foreign direct investment inflows. Moreover, we basically assume that new products can be produced only with new equipment so that investment is a positive function of v. Consumption is also assumed to be a positive function of v; and a positive function of disposable income Y(1-τ) and of real money balances M/P so that we have a real balance effect in the consumption function. Net exports X' are assumed to be a positive function of Y*, q* and v, but a negative function of Y. As regards the money market we assume that the real demand for money m depends positively on Y and v – the latter as a higher rate of product innovations suggests that the marginal utility of holding liquidity increases for consumers looking for shopping opportunities of innovative goods; m depends negatively on the nominal interest rate I which is equal to r plus the expected inflation rate (assumed here to be zero).

The foreign exchange rate market equilibrium requires here that net capital imports Q(i/i*, v, q*) – with positive partial derivatives of Q with respect to both i/i*, q* and to v – plus net exports of goods and services are equal to zero. Net capital imports react positively to a real depreciation in line with the FROOT/STEIN argument. Net capital imports are assumed to depend positively on v because a higher rate of product innovations will stimulate FDI inflows. Foreign investors become more active as they anticipate higher profit opportunities. Linearizing the consumption function as

$$C= c(1-\tau)Y +c'(M/P) + c''v \tag{55a}$$

and using a simple investment function for an open economy (with foreign direct investment inflows so that investment depends both on the domestic real interest rate and the foreign interest rate and the real exchange rate in line with the FROOT-STEIN argument)

$$I= -hr - h'r* + h''v + h'''q* \tag{55b}$$

and a net export function

$$X'= xq* + x'Y*/Y +x''v \tag{55c}$$

we have the following three equations (56, 57, 58) as the equilibrium condition in the goods market, the money market and the foreign exchange market, respectively (G is real government expenditures):

$$Y= c(1-\tau)Y+c'(M/P) +c''v + G -hr - h'r* + h''v + h'''q* + xq* + \tag{56}$$
$$x'Y*/Y +x''v \qquad\qquad\qquad\qquad\qquad \text{[IS]}$$

$$M/P=m(Y,r,v) \hspace{3cm} [LM] \hspace{1cm} (57)$$

$$Q(i/i^*, v, q^*) + xq^* + x'Y^*/Y + x''v = 0 \hspace{2cm} [ZZ] \hspace{1cm} (58)$$

Product innovations shift the IS curve to the right, the LM curve to the left and the ZZ curve downwards. The latter holds since net exports of goods and services increases as a consequence of a higher v. An initial negative trade balance will thus be reduced so that required net capital imports fall. If one assumes that foreign direct investment inflows and hence Q depends positively on Y/Y^* – that is the relative size of the market –, the implication is that the balance of payments equilibrium curve (ZZ) can have a zero slope even if $\partial Q/\partial (i/i^*)$ is not infinite in absolute terms, and hence the domestic interest rate could diverge from the foreign interest rate.

If m_v is zero, the LM curve is not directly affected by a change of v so that product innovations clearly raise both equilibrium output and the interest rate. Under flexible exchange rates, there will be an appreciation of the currency in point E_1 – as this point is above the ZZ line – so that the IS_1 curve (driven by reduced net exports of goods and services) shifts a little to the left (IS_2) while the ZZ_1 curve shifts upwards (ZZ_2). It remains true that product innovations raise the output level and the real interest rate and contribute to a current account surplus. This situation could continue until a new intersection point in the initial equilibrium E_o (note that in a system of fixed exchange rates, point E_1 implies higher net capital inflows and an excess supply in the foreign exchange market) is observed. The stock of money M will increase, and the LM-curve and the IS-curve – the latter due to higher consumption – will shift to the right).

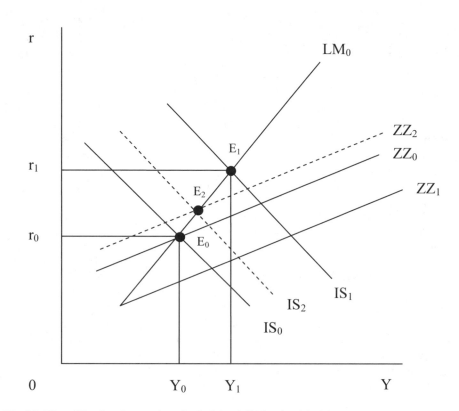

Fig. 35. Rise of Product Innovations in the Mundell-Fleming Model

This, however, does not mean that government promotion of policy innovation is inefficient since in a medium term perspective, the capital stock K will increase as the consequence of net investment – actually increased net investment in the context of product innovations. Indeed, a modified simple medium term model could consider that consumption $C= c(1-\tau)Y+c'[(M/P)+(P'/P)K] +c''v$ where the term $c'[...]$ is a broader real wealth effect on consumption, namely including the real value of capital stock; P'/P is the ratio of the stock market price index P' to the output price index P. A consistent medium term export function would read $X= xq* + x'Y*/Y +x''v + x'''K$ where the term $x'''K$ (with $x'''>0$) is a supply shift variable in the export sector. This term will then shift both the IS curve to the right and the ZZ curve downwards as K is raised. Thus the general equilibrium point in our diagram will shift to the right over time where we assume that monetary policy raises the money supply in parallel with the capital stock K so that medium term money supply equilibrium is given for the case of an income elasticity of output of unity by the simple equation $(M/P)/K = [Y/K]m'(i,v)$. In a non-inflationary economy it is equal to the real interest rate r which under profit maximization and a Cobb-Douglas production function $Y=K^\beta AL^{1-\beta}$ (with L standing for labor and A for Harrod-neutral technological progress) is equal to $\beta Y/K$ so that Y/K=r/ß. Hence a monetary policy strategy which aims at a constant ratio [M/P]/K is then consistent with a constant money demand $\{[r/ß]m'(i,v)\}$ – assuming that v, i and r are constant; they have reached an equilibrium value. An interesting long term question concerns the relation between product innovations v and the process innovations A. If A is a positive function of v – since new products can often be produced only with new equipment (and the innovation system may be assumed to be responsive to the higher demand for A) – an exogenous rate of product innovations dv/dt>0 would indeed generate a continuous growth process. A more realistic picture would emerge if we would also consider a quasi-depreciation rate of the stock of product innovations or a vintage type approach to product innovations so that in each period the oldest product generation is removed from the shelf and production.

As endogenous variables we have Y, r and e (changes in e stand for a real exchange rate change as long as P or P* do not change). So we are interested in the medium term multipliers for Y, r and e with respect to v, the product innovation rate. Using Kramer's rule we obtain (with $\zeta = i/i^*$) after differentiation of (II), (III), (IV):

$$dY/dv > 0 \text{ (sufficient condition is } m_v=0) \tag{59a}$$

$$dr/dv > 0 \text{ (sufficient condition is } m_v=0) \tag{59b}$$

de/dv <0 if (see appendix; the system determinant is negative; the following expression reveals that the nominator expression of the multiplier de/dv) Q_φ and m_r are sufficiently small so that (59c)

$$\left\{\left(1-c'(1-\tau)+\frac{x'Y^*}{Y^2}\right)m_r\left(Q_{q^*}+x\right)-hm_Y\left(Q_{q^*}+x\right)\right\} \tag{60}$$
$$>\left\{\left(h'''+x\right)\left(m_Y Q_\zeta - m_r\frac{x'Y^*}{Y^2}\right)\right\}$$

and Y^* exceeding Y_0^* (home country is relatively small). Product innovations will bring about a real appreciation; one may also note that it raises equilibrium output. This is much in line with the original reflections of Schumpeter who argued that firms facing the pressure of economic recession will launch new products in order to generate more sales. From a policy perspective, our analysis suggests that government could stimulate product innovations in recessions in order to raise output; indeed one may split government expenditures G into government consumption G' plus government R&D support (G") for product innovations. Such an approach is certainly rather appropriate in countries catching-up, as for them a higher rate of product innovations largely means to accelerate the speed of international imitations of foreign product innovations. As regards advanced countries it is questionable whether higher government R&D subsidies could strongly stimulate product innovations in the short term so as to easily overcome a recession. At the bottom line, the model presented clearly suggests that the structural breakdown of government expenditures is crucial. Since the ratio of R&D expenditures to GDP has increased over the long run in OECD countries, it is obvious that innovation issues have become more important while standard macroeconomic modelling largely ignores innovation issues.

Total Multiplier Effect

The distinction between different types of government expenditures is crucial as we will subsequently show and is totally ignored in the traditional macro models. Real government expenditure G is split here into government consumption G' and expenditures G" on the promotion of product innovations:

$$G = G' + G" \tag{61}$$

Expenditures on the promotion of product innovations mean in the case of leading OECD countries that development of true product innovations is stimulated and no short-run results can be expected. However, for catching-up countries this could mainly refer to the acceleration of imitation of foreign product innovations which in many cases should be possible within one or two years. We subsequently assume that there is a link between government expenditures on research & development – with a focus on product innovations – that can be described by

$$v = \Omega G" \tag{62}$$

Hence we have a link between two exogenous variables. As regards multipliers for G" they clearly differ from that for G' since a change in G" will not only affect aggregate demand (direct impact) but also the product innovation rate v (indirect impact) so that the overall multiplier for any endogenous variable Z_i (=Y, r, e) can be written as

$$dZ_i/dG" = [dZ_i/dG] + \Omega dZ_i/dv \tag{63}$$

is the same for dG=dG' and dG=dG", but the second term is relevant only with respect to a change of G". The output multiplier dY/dG" for a rise of G" is clearly larger than that for a rise of government consumption G'.

There is another link between exogenous variables in the context of product innovations which imply an effective fall of the price level P – a problem which theoretically comes under the heading of hedonic price measurement. Using a simple approach – with the hedonic parameter H (H>0) – we can thus write

$$dP = -Hdv \tag{64}$$

Product innovations are indeed a non-monetary aspect of the price level. At the bottom line the complete multiplier analysis for the impact of a rise of G" is given by

$$dZ_i/dG" = [dZ_i/dG] + \Omega dZ_i/dv - HdZ_i/dP \tag{65}$$

The following graphical analysis shows both the direct effect of a rise in government expenditures promoting product innovations and the indirect effects of this policy which consists of a double rightward shift of the IS curve related to the impact of G" on v and of v on P and M/P, respectively; the effective rise of M/P amounts to a hedonic real balance effect. Moreover, there is a rightward shift of the LM curve which is to say that product innovations are equivalent to a rise of M/P unless there is a dominant money demand effect.

In a more general perspective, it is true that the impact of v on P must be considered with respect to all multipliers dZ_i/dv so that these multipliers are composed of a direct effect and an indirect effect related to a change of the price level. Thus a consistent analysis of the multipliers for Y, r and e is achieved. As regards the change in the "hedonically-adjusted" real exchange rate, one has to take into account that $d(eP^*/P)$ is given for a constant foreign price level P^*, normalized to unity by $(1/P)de/dv- (e/P^2)dP/dv$. Our analysis offers a new and broader analytical picture of important policy issues.

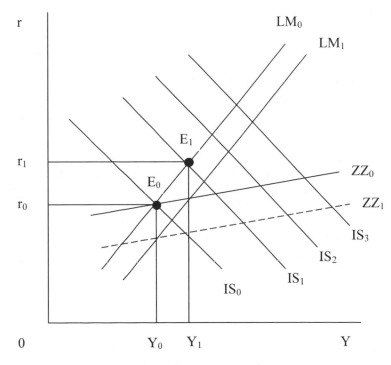

Fig. 36. Direct and Indirect Effects of Product Innovation

D.8 Economic Catching-up and Long Term Real Exchange Rate Dynamics

From a theoretical perspective, we expect a long-term real appreciation of the currency of accession countries which are assumed to catch up in economic and technological terms with EU-15. Thus, the Balassa-Samuelson effect would work. However, how will this effect indeed be realized? One may ask whether it is mainly a nominal appreciation which brings about the BS effect, thereby requiring flexible exchange rates or whether it is a rise in price level relative to the foreign price level (in a setting with a constant or stable nominal exchange rate). A rise in the domestic price level could bring problems with respect to the inflation convergence criterion and the interest rate convergence criterion of European Economic and Monetary Union. From this perspective, it is clear that countries eager to join the monetary union quickly might prefer an extended period of flexible exchange rates and enter the Euro zone only after a transition period of several years.

A Simple Long-Term Approach

In the following approach, we assume that net exports X' positively influence the real exchange rate $q=:[P/(eP*]$ (parameter $b>0$) and that it is a negative function of the relative innovation differential a*". On the link between the real exchange rate and the current account, consistent models are available. A relative rise of innovativeness abroad (country II) – we focus here mainly on product innovations – will lead to relatively lower export prices of country I. The prospects for technological catching-up depend on technology policy and education policy, and both can be expected to negatively depend on the share of the natural resource sector in the overall economy. As regards the link between q and a*", one may also note that net capital exports will be larger the higher our a*" is (i.e., a technological progress differential in favor of the foreign country). Here we assume a*" to be an exogenous variable. Hence we find the following:

$$dq/dt = bX' - a*"q \tag{66}$$

We furthermore assume that net exports negatively depend on q where the elasticity η is negative. Hence, we have:

$$X' = q^{\eta}(\text{with } \eta \leq 0) \tag{67}$$

This leads to the following Bernoullian differential equation for q(t):

$$dq/dt = bq^{\eta} - a*"q \tag{68}$$

In the subsequent graph, we have drawn the first right hand side expression as the BB line and the second expression as the AA line. For given parameters, there will be a monotonous real appreciation (see the QQ-line). With C_o determined from initial conditions and e' denoting the Euler number, the solution of the differential equation is:

$$q(t) = \{C_o e^{,-a^*(1-\eta)t} + b/a^{*"}\}^{1/(1-\eta)} \qquad (69)$$

This equation is convergent for q. Hence we have an equation for the long-term real exchange rate with q converging and thus has the steady state value (for t approaching infinity) q#:

$$q\# = (b/a^{*"})^{1/(1-\eta)} \qquad (70)$$

For a small, open – non-innovative (!) – economy facing an infinite price elasticity in export markets, the equilibrium real exchange rate is clearly unity (see equation 70). If the export demand elasticity is zero, thereby reflecting the extreme case of a country exporting a very large share of high technology goods, we find that:

$$q\# = b/a^{"}* \text{ (case of high technology dominance in exports)} \qquad (71)$$

If the absolute value of η is unity, we would get as the steady state value $q\#=(b/a^{"}*)^{1/2}$. Clearly, technological catching-up with $a^{*'}$ being reduced will lead to downward rotation of the AA curve (AA$_1$ in Fig. 7b). Technological upgrading could also go along with a fall in the absolute value of the price elasticity. Both elements could occur simultaneously.

Take E_o as the starting point. If there is only a fall in price elasticity (in absolute terms), the rotation of the hyperbola indicates that there will be a real depreciation effect. Next we take a look at the fall of $a^{*"}$. Taking E_0 as the starting point, we observe a real appreciation in point E_{01}. Catching-up of the home country is also associated with a rise in the share of technology intensive goods. Should catching-up go along with a higher share of (medium-) technology intensive goods (e.g., due to foreign investors increasingly producing product cycle goods in modern plants for exports to world markets), we find a rotation of the BB curve, since the price elasticity – in absolute terms – of exports is falling (BB$_1$). This elasticity effect will dampen the real appreciation so that E_1 is the final equilibrium point. If, however, the reduction of the technology gap is relatively strong (intersection point of AA is to the right of point F), the reduction of the absolute price elasticity will reinforce the real appreciation effect. Note that there may be cases when $a^{*"}$ rise and the price elasticity falls in absolute terms.

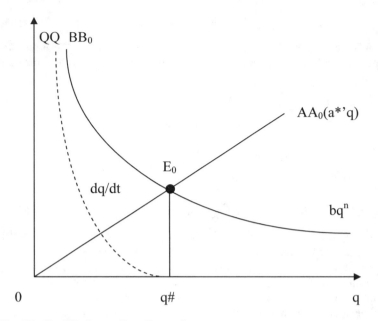

Fig. 37a. Real Exchange Rate Dynamics

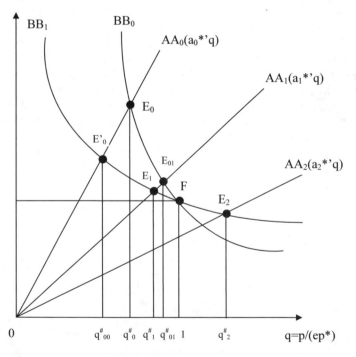

Fig. 37b. Model of the Long Term Real Exchange Rate ($dq/dt = bq^n - a^{*'}q$)

From an empirical perspective, we may expect that countries opening up will liberalize trade and adopt internal modernization measures which help to raise per capita income in the medium term. This would help to stimulate capital inflows (in particular FDI inflows) so that per capita output will further increase. (Per capita GNP might increase more slowly than per capita GDP, however, since rising FDI inflows could raise the share of profit transfers relative to GDP.) As per capita income y rises, the share of intra-industrial trade should increase, accompanied by intensified competition. The latter, in turn, should stimulate static efficiency gains as well as innovation, and government policy may then stimulate innovation through subsidies for research and development.

As a possible further analytical step, consider the following modifications. We restate our basic equation by focusing on x' which is per capita net exports and assuming that b is a function of the capital intensity k' – where k'=K/(AL) which is capital per efficiency unit of labor (A standing for Harrod neutral technological progress) because net exports will contribute to an appreciation the higher the capital intensity for a given net export x' is. We thus have

$$dq/dt = b(k')[x'] - a''*q \qquad (66')$$

We specify

$$b(k')= b'k'^{\Omega} \qquad (66'')$$

Moreover, we state a modified neoclassical accumulation dynamic which includes foreign direct investment inflows F' per unit of labor in efficiency unit which we assume to be proportionate to y'=-Y/(AL) in the following way:

$$F/(AL)= f(q)y'= q^{\lambda}y' \qquad (67')$$

The parameter λ is – in line with the FROOT-STEIN argument – negative. Assuming a simple savings function S (where the real exchange rate affects savings but we make no a priori assumption about the partial derivative; with a net foreign debt position, a rise in q reduces the burden of the debt and thus might raise the ability to save, with an international net creditor position a rise in q could reduce the savings rate – ultimately, all this is an empirical issue) we have

$$S = sq^{\sigma}Y \qquad (68')$$

The modified neoclassical equilibrium condition is therefore:

$$\delta K + (dK/dt) = sq^{\sigma}Y + F' \qquad (69')$$

Dividing by AL and taking into account (II') and using a Cobb-Douglas production function y'=k'^{ß} (this production function might include – as a kind of positive external effect of household's money holdings – real money balances M/P if M/P=1) yields

$$dk'/dt +[n+a+\delta]k = sq^{\sigma}k'^{\,ß}+ q^{\lambda}k'^{\,ß} \qquad (70')$$

Note that using the equilibrium condition equation (III') implies that investment is linked to output and the real exchange rate, but one should note that this equilibrium perspective is also fully compatibly with an investment function I(Y,q) in a disequilibrium approach. We define x' as net exports per efficiency unit of labor and now assume that x'= q^η. The accumulation dynamics for the capital stock are governed by:

$$dk'/dt = [sq^\sigma + q^\lambda]k'^\beta - [n + \delta + a]k' \qquad (71')$$

An analytical solution of this pair of differential equations is quite complex. If a steady state for k,q exists, then we can solve this by setting dk'/dt =0 and dq/dt=0:

$$q\# = [b'k'^\Omega / a''*]^{1/(1-\eta)} \qquad (72)$$

A solution of (VI') is rather easy if we take a look at the special case $\sigma = \lambda$:

$$k'\# = \{[(s+1)q^\sigma]/[n + \delta + a]\}^{1/1-\sigma\beta} \qquad (73)$$

$$k'\# = \{[(s+1)(b'k'^\Omega / a''*)^{\eta'\sigma}]/[n + \delta + a]\}^{1/1-\sigma\beta}; \text{ we define } 1/(1-\eta)=\eta' \qquad (74)$$

From this we have

$$k'\#^{\sigma\Omega\eta'/(1-\sigma\beta)} = \{[(s+1)(b'/a''*)^{\eta'\sigma}]/[n+\delta+a]\}^{1/1-\sigma\beta} \qquad (75)$$

There is a problem with the interpretation of output Y (or Y/AL) when we have product innovations. However, one may assume that true output Y" – a hedonically-deflated nominal output variable – can be written as Yq^μ, since q is strictly a negative function of a''* (the parameter μ is positive).

A potential variant of this model would be to endogenize the rate of product innovations (e.g., by making it dependent on the per capita income and the real exchange rate). This would be a new line of research in endogenous growth modelling. Moreover, the model can be linked to endogenous growth theory based on endogenous process innovations (e.g. WELFENS, 2003).

D.9 Policy Implications

Policy conclusions can be drawn on the basis of theoretical analysis and empirical analysis. As regards the latter, WELFENS/BORBÉLY (2004) have pointed out links between the foreign exchange market and the stock market. From this perspective both overshooting phenomena in foreign exchange markets and in stock markets can cause considerable temporary volatility. Moreover, it has been shown (JUNGMITTAG, 2004) that poor countries such as Spain and Ireland have been able to catch up technologically over time, while Portugal and Greece stand for a much more modest catching-up record in the EU-15. From this perspective, it is obvious that there is no easy path toward sustained technological and economic catching-up in Europe.

According to the approach presented here, the size of markets/countries and the share of relatively rich households in overall households is important for quasi-Balassa-Samuelson effects. Hence the price of tradables in poor countries will not show a uniform pace of convergence towards the price of tradables across leading EU or OECD countries.

Government should stimulate and encourage the upgrading of human capital and cross-sectoral labor mobility as well as foreign direct investment inflows. The upgrading of export products could take place not only through the presence of multinational companies and R&D promotion – of national or supranational poli-cymakers – but also through a rising share of sophisticated intermediate imports (in this respect, EU-15 offers broad opportunities for EU accession countries in eastern Europe).

Theoretical analysis has shown that a real appreciation of the currency – in a country catching up economically – can have several major effects (see Fig. 19):

- it reduces the costs of capital;
- it reduces foreign direct investment inflows, but it has an ambiguous effect on output per capita;
- it stimulates product upgrading in the tradables sectors. However, it is unrealis-tic to assume that firms can quickly upgrade export products in terms of quality or product innovativeness. The adjustment time or learning phase required typi-cally depends on the general ability of firms to adjust, the level of technological sophistication already acquired (and hence the presence of foreign investors) and the share of skilled workers available. A sudden strong real appreciation should be avoided, as the supply-side responsiveness of firms can cope only with limited exchange rate pressure. Moreover, as real appreciation tends to re-duce foreign direct investment inflows, phases of sudden and strong real appre-ciation could become a problem for an accession country (and this all the more the higher initial trade balance deficit is);
- it raises net imports of goods and services in the medium term – after the initial negative J-curve effect;.
- it could reduce the inflation rate (a topic not much dealt with here)
- it reduces net foreign debt.

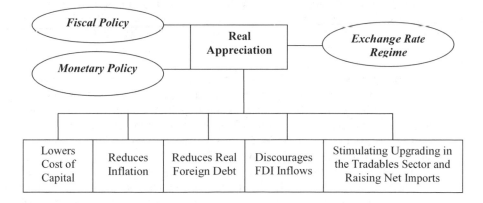

Fig. 38. Effects of a Real Appreciation

E. Macroeconomic Aspects of Opening up, Unemployment, Growth and Transition

E.1 Introduction

Economic opening up has been a natural element of systemic transformation in the former Soviet Union and the smaller post socialist countries of Eastern Europe. Anticipating EU eastern enlargement, eastern European transition countries have reoriented the regional focus of trade towards the EU-15 countries. The change in regional orientation coincided with changes in the structure of output and trade. As regards structural change of exports, several countries underwent rapid structural change and achieved gradually improved RCAs (revealed comparative advantage) in non-labor intensive sectors (BORBÉLY, 2004).

After high inflation rates and a massive transformational recession in the early transition stage – reflecting obsolescence of part of the capital stock and adjustment costs in the course of restructuring – in the first transition stage, most transition countries have achieved considerable economic growth. Countries with relatively low per capita income, a well educated labor force and a functioning banking system should indeed be able to record considerable economic growth if stable and efficient institutions, competitive pressure and opening up are combined in a sustained manner. It is not easy for transition countries with a young democracy to come up with the right combination of constitutional foundations and efficiency enhancing political learning, in particular since governments eager to generate quick improvement in some fields might favour short-term political action over long term growth strategies.

The analysis will focus on economic catching-up in the sense that we consider economies which become open for trade, foreign direct investment flows and technology transfer. Attracting rising FDI inflows – those often are associated with international technology transfer – has been not only a major element of EU eastern enlargement but of southern EU enlargement as well. FDI inflows have two major effects for the host country: It raises capital intensity and thus – according to the Rybczynski theorem - implies that the production of capital intensive goods should increase. If such sectors dominate wage bargaining, the parallel increase in labor productivity should lead to high general wage increases which in turn could lead to unemployment outside of capital intensive sectors. From an EU-15 perspective, high FDI outflows towards the transition countries imply a continuous outsourcing of manufacturing value-added in tradables sectors T_i (i=1, 2...n) towards EU accession countries (as well as Ukraine and Russia). This vertical FDI outflow from Western Europe is likely to improve global international competitiveness of firms from EU15 countries. Thus one may anticipate that revealed comparative advantages (RCAs) of EU15 countries in transatlantic trade are positively correlated with those fields n, n', n" in which accession countries have a positive RCA in trade with EU15. At the same time, growing vertical FDI could lead to a convergence of sectoral export specialization – a process which is likely to be reinforced by economic catching-up in eastern Europe and the associated relative rise of intra-industrial trade. The relative rise of the nontradables price in accession countries will, however, raise the relative share of nontradables production so that the development of production specialization in eastern Europe could diverge from export specialization.

We assume that the first stage of economic opening up is accompanied by a rise of price elasticities, however, in a second transition stage during which firms increasingly specialize in more technology intensive (and less price sensitive) products, requiring a higher share of sunk costs in investment, labor demand elasticity will be assumed to fall. As regards innovations we will focus partly on process innovations, but more important here are product innovations in countries catching-up. Product innovations are new for the respective poor country but not new to the world economy so that from the perspective of a leading global economy we focus on international diffusion phenomena. The following analysis presents certain analytical building blocs but not an integrated model, although one may combine the various blocs to a consistent meta model. Moreover, there will be no microeconomic foundations of behaviour at the macroeconomic level; this certainly is possible but as we will consider only minor – but powerful – modifications of well-known models we are not so much interested in the aspects of microeconomic foundations.

We will not deal much with the issue of international economic convergence – that is convergence of per capita national income across countries - except for an important observation: Since GDP (Y) is equal to real wage income wL (w is the real wage rate, L is employment, K is capital, $k=: K/L$ and * denotes foreign variables) it holds for per capita income $y=:Y/L$ and y^*, respectively that

$$y = w + rk \qquad (1)$$

$$y^* = w^* + r^*k^* \qquad (2)$$

Assume that country I (home country which is assumed to have a relatively low per capita income) and country II product according to a Cobb-Douglas production function, then we will have

$$y = k^\beta \qquad (3)$$

$$y^* = k^{*\beta^*}. \qquad (4)$$

The only explanation for temporary international differences in per capita income is a difference in capital intensity. If we consider an open economy with free trade and free flows of technological knowledge such that $\beta=\beta^*$ (a mysterious implication of the Heckscher-Ohlin-Samuelson [HOS] approach which assumes that there is no factor mobility), we will have – according to the HOS approach - convergence of relative factor rewards which in combination with the assumption of profit maximization leads to $w=Y_L$ (Y_L is marginal product of labor; Y_K is the marginal product of capital) and $r=Y_K$ and $w^*=Y_L^*=w$ and $r^*=Y_K^*=r$. Since the optimum capital intensity k depends on w/r (abroad: k* depends on w*/r*), it is clear that – in line with neoclassical growth theory – there will be a convergence of capital intensities across countries. Which adjustment mechanism will bring about this result? We suggest that the mechanism is the Balassa-Samuelson effect which says that the relatively poor country – with the relatively low capital intensity – will witness a real appreciation in the course of economic catching-up, and the real appreciation in turn is linked to changes in the relative price of nontradables (the nontradables price relative to the tradables price in a poor country is lower than in a rich country: as relative per capita income rises the relative price of nontradables will rise, too). The real exchange rate eP*/P will fall over time, which in a system of flexible exchange rates could mean that there is a fall of the nominal exchange rate (e) of country I while the foreign level (P*) and the domestic price level (P) are constant; alternatively both e, P* and P could change adequately. From the perspective of country II which is capital abundant (initially k*>k), the profit rate Ω' for an investment in country II and in I are in the case of constant price levels:

$$r^* = Y_K^* = \Omega' \tag{5}$$

$$\{[de^*/dt]/e^*\}P/P^* + Y_K = \Omega'^* \tag{6}$$

Profit maximization in a model with both capital mobility and foreign direct investment implies $\Omega'^* = \Omega'$. The real depreciation of the country II currency – the rise of e* - implies that investment of firms from country II in country I will generate a higher profit rate than for domestic investors from country I. As long as the real depreciation of the country II currency continues as long will there be a special incentive for foreigners to invest in country I. Until finally y approaches y* and hence $Y_K = Y_K^* = r^* = r$. From this perspective, a new open economy model with trade in investment goods and asymmetric foreign direct investment lets one expect that convergence will take place faster than without foreign direct investment (in the HOS model the convergence of relative and absolute factor rewards can occur even if the two tradable goods considered are consumption goods).

As regards the links between trade and growth, the HOS model might be misleading to the extent that the real world is characterized by high mobility of capital, namely foreign direct investment. Moreover, part of the changes in eastern Europe and Russia take place in a period of a strong rise of oil and gas prices – those prices increased strongly after 2000. According to the Samuelson Stolper theorem the price of capital – which we assume to be the factor intensively used in the oil and gas sector – will increase in Europe. This in turn could stimulate investment in the long run.

E.2 Growth, Trade and Innovation

E.2.1 New Production Function for Open Economies

Economic growth in open economies is only partly understood, and modelling it in a consistent way is not easy. Consistent modelling is, however, crucial if one is to understand the dynamics of international economic catching-up. The standard neoclassical growth theory is a consistent analytical tool for simple growth analysis in closed economies, however, is unsatisfactory with respect to the role of trade and some other key aspects. A straightforward way to improve growth modelling - for the case of a country catching-up - and to combine the supply side with the international demand side may be suggested as follows:

- Consider the fact that import competition in many countries contributes to competitive pressure which in turn stimulates specialization as well as efficiency gains. Hence output should be a function not only of capital and labor inputs but of the ratio of imports J to national income Y. We assume that J= V(q*)Y where q* is the real exchange rate eP*/P. Specifically we can specify J= jq*$^{\lambda"}$Y where $\lambda"\leq0$. Subsequently we will use for simplicity J=jY, and j$^{\chi'}$ indicates the impact of import competition on output
- Take into account that the higher the share of exports X in national income Y the higher competitive pressure from global markets will be. This implies that we will use a production function in which not only capital K and labor L enter but also x:=X/Y. We will assume as a simple export function that X= q*$^{\lambda}$Y*$^{\chi}$ so that X/Y = q*$^{\lambda}$Y*$^{\Omega}$/Y
- Take into account that the use of telecommunications stimulates the diffusion of knowledge so that telecommunications density T' (a proxy variable for the use of telecommunications) – the number of access lines per capita – has a positive impact on national output Y
- Consider the impact of (cumulated) R&D expenditures F'. For the sake of simplicity, we will ignore the problem of accumulation of R&D expenditures. Moreover, to stay as simple as possible, we will assume that F' is an exogenous variable chosen by government – effectively we have government R&D promotion here.

Thus we can state as (assuming Harrod-neutral technological progress A(t) and f as a parameter to indicate the impact of F on output) the macroeconomic production function where we assume ß"=1-ß':

$$Y = F'^f K^{\beta'} T'^{\sigma} [AL]^{\beta"} x^{\chi} j^{\chi'} \tag{7}$$

Hence

$$Y^{[1+\chi]} = F'^f K^{\beta'} T'^{\sigma} [AL]^{\beta"} X^{\chi} j^{\chi'} \tag{8}$$

$$Y^{[1+\chi]} = F'^f K^{\beta'} T'^{\sigma} [AL]^{\beta"} X^{\chi} j^{\chi'} \tag{9}$$

We denote ß'/[1+χ] =:ß, f/[1+χ]=:f', χ/[1+χ]=: χ', χ"/[1+χ]=: χ"',σ/[1+χ] = :σ', λ/[1+χ] = :λ'.

$$Y = F'^{f} K^{\beta} T'^{\sigma'} [AL]^{1-\beta}[q*^{\lambda'}Y*^{\chi''} j^{\chi'''}] \qquad (10)$$

Thus we have a production function which looks like a Cobb-Douglas function with both a Harrod-neutral progress A and a Hicks-neutral technological progress ; the relevant "parameter" for the latter is $[F'^{f} T'^{\sigma'} q*^{\lambda'}Y*^{\chi''} j^{\chi'''}]$. Note that per capita income y=:Y/L is (with k=:K/L) given by

$$y = F'^{f} k^{\beta} T'^{\sigma'} [A]^{1-\beta}[q*^{\lambda'}Y*^{\chi''} j^{\chi'''}] \qquad (11)$$

As one can see, the import-GDP ratio j will only affect the level of per capita output y, but not the growth rate - unless one would specify that A=A(j,...); note, however, that the balance of payments equilibrium constraints implicity suggests that trade positively affects both the level of output and the growth rate. Output per efficiency unit of labor (y':=: Y/[AL]; and k':=: K/[AL]) is given by

$$y' = F'^{f} k'^{\beta} T'^{\sigma'} [q*^{\lambda'}Y*^{\chi''} j^{\chi'''}] \qquad (12)$$

Assuming a constant growth rate of A(t), namely dlnA/dt= a, per capita income grows (with e' denoting the Euler number) according to :

$$y=A_{o}e'^{at} F'^{f} k'^{\beta} T'^{\sigma} `[q*^{\lambda'}Y*^{\chi''} j^{\chi'''}] \qquad (13)$$

Assuming a constant import-GDP ratio j this equation implies for the growth rate (g) of per capita income y=:Y/L (the exogenous growth rate of L is denoted as n):

$$g_{y} = a + f'g_{F}' + \sigma'g_{T'} + \beta g_{K} - \beta n + \lambda'gq* + \chi''g_{Y*} \qquad (14)$$

We assume profit maximization so that the marginal product of capital Y_{K} – under Cobb-Douglas it is equal to ßY/K – is equal to the real interest rate, or:

$$r=\beta Y/K \qquad (15)$$

Since we can rewrite [dK/dt]/K as [[dK/dt]/Y][Y/K] and since we assume that savings S are proportionate to national income Y – that is S=sY– and that S equals gross investment dK/dt+δK (δ is the depreciation rate of capital) we have:

$$g_{y} = a + f'g_{F}' + \sigma'g_{T'} + \beta[sr/\beta - \delta - n] + \lambda'gq* + \chi''g_{Y*} \qquad (16)$$

If one assumes that the savings rate depends on the real interest rate r and on the ratio of real money balances per capita to real income per capita so that s=s(r, m/Y) - namely that s is rising until a critical ratio m/Y is achieved, beyond this point s is a negative function of m/Y – we can state:

$$g_{y} = a + f'g_{F}' + \sigma'g_{T'} + s(r, m/y)r - \beta\delta - \beta n + \lambda'gq* + \chi''g_{Y*} \qquad (17)$$

Note that since the real demand for money balances m is assumed to depend on the nominal interest rate i which in turn is the sum r and the anticipated inflation rate π' – assume the inflation rate to be zero here - we can restate the above equation as:

$$g_{y} = a + f'g_{F}' + \sigma'g_{T'} + s'(r,y) r - \beta\delta - \beta n + \lambda'gq* + \chi''g_{Y*} \qquad (18)$$

A simple specification for the function s' is

$$s'=s''(r)/y \qquad (19)$$

and hence we have

$$g_y = a + f'g_F' + \sigma'g_T + s'(r) \, r/y - \beta\delta - \beta n + \lambda'gq^* + \chi''g_{Y*} \qquad (20)$$

In a small open economy with free capital flows, r will be equal to r*. The above equation is a differential equation in y.

$$dy/dt - [a + f'g_F' + \sigma'g_{T'} - \beta\delta - \beta n + + \lambda'gq^* + \chi''g_{Y*}]y = s''(r^*)r^* \qquad (21)$$

Hence we have (with C' denoting a constant to be obtained from initial conditions) :

$$y(t) = C'e'^{[a + f'gF' + \sigma'gT' - \beta\delta - \beta n + \lambda'gq^* + \chi''gY^*]t} - s''(r^*)r/[a + f'g_F' + \sigma'g_{T'} - \beta\delta - \qquad (22)$$
$$\beta n + \lambda'gq^* + \chi''g_{Y*}]$$

The growth rate of per capita income is higher the higher parameter a is, the higher the growth rate of R&D expenditures is, the higher the growth rate of telecommunication density is, the higher foreign output growth is and the higher the real depreciation rate is. Note that according to the Balassa-Samuelson effect, there will be a continuous real appreciation in an open economy with tradables and nontradables, which would therefore slow down economic growth.

There will be permanent growth of per capita income if

$$[a + f'g_F' + \sigma'g_{T'} + \lambda'gq^* + \chi''g_{Y*}] > \beta[\delta + n] \qquad (23)$$

Besides empirical issues, the only major theoretical issue is to endogenize parameter a. However, it is obvious that government has an impact on economic growth, in particular through the growth rate of real R&D expenditures and the growth rate of telecommunications services, which will depend not least on government policies with respect to the allocation of scarce spectrum for mobile telephony.

As regards the initial condition we have in t=0:

$$y_o = C' - s''(r^*)r/[a + f'g_F' + \sigma'g_{T'} - \beta\delta + \lambda'gq^* + \chi''g_{Y*}] \qquad (24)$$

Hence

$$C' = \{y_o + s''(r^*)r/[a + f'g_F' + \sigma'g_{T'} - \beta\delta + \lambda'gq^* + \chi''g_{Y*}]\} \qquad (25)$$

Thus the savings rate s'' positively affects the level of the growth path so that we have a familiar element of standard neoclassical growth theory.

E.2.2 Towards an Integrated Macroeconomic Approach

We will emphasize that for certain analytical purposes it is useful to take a look at the macroeconomic impact of both supply-side and demand-side impulses. In every economy output dynamics can be understood to be a mixture of the impact of the supply side – its macroeconomic equivalence is the production potential $Y^{pot} = K^\beta L^{1-\beta}$ (K is capital and L is labor) - and of aggregate demand Y^d. In transi-

tion countries both supply-side dynamics and the demand side will be important –
with some sectors being dominated by supply-side developments while others are
shaped by demand side dynamics. If one is to include labor saving technological
progress (stock of knowledge is A) one would use the production function Y^{pot}
$=K^{\beta}(AL)^{1-\beta}$

Taking into account both the impact of the supply side and the demand side a
hybrid equilibrium approach for the goods market can be written as follows:

$$Y = \alpha \, Y^{pot} + (1-\alpha) \, Y^d \qquad (26a)$$

An important question is what determines α (in the interval 0,1): the size of the
relative supply-side impact parameter. It will reflect various forces, including expectations; the most simple form to think about α is to consider it at identical with
1-u (with u denoting the unemployment rate). In a full employment economy u is
zero and hence only the supply side dynamics, that is the accumulation of input
factors, will determine actual gross domestic product. If u would be rather high it
is clear that supply-side dynamics would hardly influence actual output while the
demand side will have a strong impact on Y. A more refined way would be to replace a with u^{χ} where the parameter χ is assumed to be positive. In a small open
economy – which asymptotically is facing a totally elastic world demand curve -
the impact of the supply-side should be relatively high.

It is obvious that for the case of a closed economy the fiscal multiplier for the
case of standard specification of the demand side is smaller than the standard textbook case of 1/s; with $\alpha =1-u$ the fiscal multiplier is

$$dY/dG= 1/[1-uc] \qquad (26b)$$

(see appendix).
An exogenous increase in the production potential raises actual output by

$$dY/dY^{pot} = (1-u) + u\partial Y^d/\partial Y^{pot} >0. \qquad (26c)$$

For the special case of an increase of the production potential through one unit
of net investment and assuming an exogenous real interest rate we have
$\partial Y^d/\partial Y^{pot}= r$ and hence

$$dY = [(1-u)K^{\beta-1}L^{1-\beta} +ur]dK \qquad (26d)$$

If one simply assumes that the impact of aggregate demand reduces over time
while that of aggregate supply increases in the long run, one might restate equation (26a) as follows (with e' denoting the Euler number):

$$Y = [1-e'^{-bt}] Y^{pot} + e'^{-bt}Y^d \qquad (26a')$$

Output and Wage Pressure in a Hybrid Supply and Demand Macro Model

One also should note that the hybrid approach suggests an interesting answer to
the question how a rise of the real wage rate will affect output and employment,

respectively. Consider a small open economy which can raise exports in accordance with the growth the potential output - here we assume that all output is tradable. We can rewrite equation (1a) as follows if one assumes that consumption C=cY – with Y=wL+rK# (assuming that factors labor L and capital K are rewarded in accordance with their respective marginal product; K# is the equilibrium capital stock, r the real interest rate, w the real wage rate); investment I=I(r), government consumption G is exogenous, net exports X' are a negative function of the international real wage ratio (* denotes foreign variables) and a negative function of the real exchange rate q=P/(eP*) – P is the price level, e the nominal exchange rate, W the nominal wage rate and the real wage rate is defined as w=W/P.

$$Y = \alpha\, Y^{pot}(W/P) + [1-\alpha]\{c[wL+rK^{\#}] + I(r) + G + X'(W/eW^*, q)\} \qquad (26e)$$

We assume that the real interest rate r and the exchange rate e are exogenous; denoting eW* as W'* and W/W'* as φ" we obtain from differentiation:

$$dY/dW = \alpha\, \partial Y^{pot}/\partial W + [1-\alpha]\{c[L+ r\partial K^{\#}/\partial W] + \partial X'/\partial\varphi"dW/W'* \qquad (26f)$$

By assumption the partial derivative $\partial X'/\partial\varphi$" is negative; with P given the rise of the nominal wage rate is, of course, equivalent to a real wage increase. The impact of a higher wage rate on consumption is positive, namely $c[L+ r\partial K^{opt}/\partial W]$; the overall sign for dY/dW thus is unclear. In a small open economy the net export effect may be expected to outweigh the domestic consumption effect (and also the effect $\partial Y^{pot}/\partial W$ if it should be negative). Moreover, if $\alpha=1-u$ and $u=u(w/[Y/L])$ the total differential for (26e) yields even a somewhat more complex result for dY/dW (if dY/dW is negative, the sign for du/dW should be positive). The ambiguity of dY/dW remains, but we can learn from the approach presented that the risk to adopt an excessive wage rate is the higher the less open the economy is.

One should, however, not rule out that net exports could be a positive function of W/W'*, namely if the quality and innovativeness of the export basked is a positive function of the relative wage ratio. Such a function implicitly assumes that the country considered can sufficiently move up the quality ladder in line with the rise of the international wage ratio – analytically we thus enter a world of imperfect competition where the export price P** might well diverge from domestic price P for the same good. Assume that export quantity X=X(Ω'), that is X negatively depends on the ratio of the wage rate W to marginal market revenue per worker P**[1-ß]Y/L – relative to the respective foreign indicator: We thus consider a relative cost pressure indicator (denoting 1-ß as ß' and 1-ß* as ß'*)

$$\Omega'=\{[W/P^{**}]/[ß'Y/L]\}/\{[W^*/P^*]/[ß'^*Y^*/L^*]\}; \qquad (26g)$$

Note that real exports are XP**/P while real imports, expressed in domestic quantity, are q*J, where J is the quantity of imports. Now let us assume that we have the following pricing rule (with v as a qualityindex or novelty index; σ" is a positive parameter):

$$P^{**} = W(1-ß) + \sigma'v \qquad (26h)$$

We furthermore assume (with parameter σ'>0) that the quality index realized by exporters is a positive function of the international nominal wage ratio because a relative rise of wage costs stimulates firms to move up the technology and quality ladder (an argument which, however, might be doubtful in the case of technologically leading countries, where both R&D expenditures and global product innovations are quite important).

$$v = \sigma''W/[eW^*] \tag{26i}$$

Hence

$$P^{**} = W(1-\text{ß}) + \sigma'\sigma''W/[eW^*] = W[(1-\text{ß}) + \sigma'\sigma''/[eW^*]] \tag{26j}$$

For the foreign country, we have (implying a specific effective relative international price P^{**}/eP^*):

$$P^* = W^*(1-\text{ß}) + \sigma'^*\sigma''^*W^*/[e^*W] = W^*[(1-\text{ß}^*) + \sigma'^*\sigma''^*/[e^*W]] \tag{26k}$$

Thus we can write

$$\Omega' = (1 + \sigma'^*\sigma''^*e/W)[\text{ß}'^*Y^*/L^*]/(1 + \sigma'\sigma''/eW^*)[\text{ß}'Y/L] \tag{26l}$$

Real imports are qJ and J is assumed – with W/W'* denoted as φ" - to be a function

$$J(q, \varphi'', Y) \tag{26l'}$$

With respect to J, all three partial derivatives J_q , $J_{\varphi''}$ and J_Y are positive; J_q reflects a demand shift effect since the quantity of imports will reduce when their price is raised relative to domestically sold goods; $J_{\varphi''}$ reflects the relative importance of wage income in overall income. J_Y is the familiar increase of imports resulting from higher aggregate income.

Hence we paradoxically find that the ratio of real exports to real imports $[XP^{**}/P]/[qJ]$ could be positively influenced by the international nominal wage price ratio. A critical assumption here is that the price of exports can indeed be raised, which is possible only under imperfect competition in international goods markets and if the firms of the countries considered sufficiently move up the quality ladder. Quality here includes product innovativeness.

A simplified case in which we assume the quantity of imports not to be reacting to Y and q^* ($q^*=1/q$) is more or less the case of a country whose imports are dominated by natural resources (as is the case of Japan and a few other countries). We assume that the quantity exported is $X=X(\varphi'')$, where X is a negative function of φ" and a positive function of process innovations v"; the quantity imported J is a positive function of φ". Net real exports X' are given by

$$X' = [P^{**}(\varphi'', v'')X(\varphi'')/P] - eP^*J(\varphi'')/P \tag{26m}$$

Denoting E as an elasticity we get:

$$dX'/d\varphi'' = [X/P][P^{**}/\varphi'']E_{P^{**}, \varphi''} + P^{**}\partial X/\partial\varphi''/P - q^*\partial J/\partial\varphi''. \tag{26n}$$

The expression $dX'/d\varphi$" (not that the elasticity φ might fall in absolute terms if φ" is increased again and again which implies that there is an optimum wage pressure!) is positive only if the elasticity exceeds a critical value:

$$E_{p^*,e^*} > -[\,\varphi"/X]\,\partial X/\partial\varphi" + [P/P^{**}]q^*\partial J/\partial\varphi". \qquad (26o)$$

Whether this inequality is fulfilled is an empirical question. One may assume that this will only be the case if the firms of the respective country have strong performance in product innovations (OECD countries – or some of them). Even if $dX'/d\varphi$" is positive, it is clear that there will be a positive link between Y and φ", only if a rise of φ" has no critical negative effect on domestic absorption (e.g., a rise of φ" could cause unemployment in the nontradables sectors). Assume that the unemployment rate negatively depends on process innovations A and positively on wage pressure as captured by φ". Denoting absorption by H'(u, φ") – where u is the unemployment rate and for simplicity we may assume u=u(φ",A) – with $\partial u/\partial\varphi$">0, $\partial u/\partial A$<0 - we have in a "Schumpeterian demand-oriented approach" :

$$Y = H'(u(\varphi",A), \varphi", r) + [P^{**}(\varphi", A)X(\varphi")/P] - eP^*J(\varphi")/P \qquad (26p)$$

This equation is a quasi-equilibrium condition for the goods market. Denoting with lower case suffix a partial derivative, we get:

$$dY=H'_r dr + H'_u u_A dA + H'\varphi" + H'_u u_{\varphi"} + X/P\,P^{**}_A dA \qquad (26q)$$

$$+\{[X/P][P^{**}/\varphi"]E_{P^{**},\varphi"} + P^{**}X_{\varphi"}/P - q^* J_{\varphi"}\}\}d\varphi"$$

Within a simple framework one may set dr=0 and dA=0 and then solve for $dY/d\varphi$". This expression in a nutshell suggests that there is an optimum wage pressure in countries catching-up: set $dY/d\varphi$"=0, which yields the output-maximizing wage rate (where we assume that the second derivative is negative). Note also that in the case that $\partial P^{**}/\partial\varphi$"=0 – so that $E_{P^{**},\varphi} = 0$ – net real exports always is negatively affected by wage pressure. Taking into account a simple real money demand equation m(Y,i,u) – where we assume m_u>0 (as a rise of the unemployment rate signals higher uncertainty and hence a rising real demand for liquidity: see ARTUS, 1989) – and stating the money market equilibrium condition, we have:

$$M/P = m(Y,i,u) \qquad (26r)$$

We have assumed that process innovations will not reduce the domestic price level in the short run as prices are sticky. For a constant domestic price level we get after differentiation:

$$dM/P = m_Y dY + m_i di + m_u du \qquad (26s)$$

Assuming zero inflation – in line with the assumption of a stable domestic price level P – and hence real interest rate r = nominal interest rate I, we obtain

$$dr = [1/m_i]dM/P - [m_Y/m_i]dY - [m_u/m_i]du \qquad (26t)$$

Inserting this result from the money market equilibrium in the goods market quasi-equilibrium condition, we get

$$dY = [H'_r/m_i]dM/P - H'_r[m_Y/m_i]dY - \qquad\qquad (26u)$$

$$H'_r[m_u/m_i][u_{\varphi''}d\varphi'' + u_A dA] + [H'_u u_A + X_A X/P]dA +$$

$$\{H'\varphi'' + H'_u u_{\varphi''} + \{[X/P][P^{**}/\varphi'']E_{P^{**},\varphi''} + P^{**}X_{\varphi''}/P - q^*J_{\varphi''}\}\}d\varphi''$$

Ignoring for the moment any impact from the foreign exchange market, we thus can see some of the impact on Y. It is an empirical question whether process innovations have a positive impact on Y, that is whether $dY/dA > 0$.

Determining the endogenous variables r, q and Y on the basis of the equilibrium conditions for the goods market, the money market and the foreign exchange market is straightforward. The latter is given (using Q to denote real net capital imports which are assumed to positively depend on r/r^* and q) by

$$Q(r/r^*, q) = qJ - P^{**}X'(\ldots)/P \qquad\qquad (26v)$$

In a short term model, one would use the equilibrium condition as stated in (26p). In the context of a medium term approach, one would replace (26p) by (26a) and in a long term perspective (26a') which converges towards the traditional neoclassical model. One should note that in the medium term framework and in the long term analysis, we have to consider the impact of technological progress (A) on both the demand side and the supply side. The model would look more complex if one would relax the assumption of a small open economy which faces no restrictions in exports to the world market. We thus have a fairly general macroeconomic approach which can accommodate different time horizons in a consistent way.

A serious problem could be that the optimum wage pressure is not necessarily consistent with full employment. However, government can be assumed to be able to also influence P**, namely by R&D promotion measures designed to stimulate product innovations in the tradables sector. With the goal of full employment, it certainly is important to avoid excessive wage pressure (ex ante) and rather raise the marginal value-added in the tradables sector through adequate R&D promotion. Wages will then adjust ex post to the rising marginal value added.

Finally, it is interesting that a change of the real exchange rate q will affect net exports and investment in different ways. In a period of a fall in the real exchange rate – due to a relatively slow increase of the domestic price level –, one will have a rise of net exports. At the same time, there will be a dampening effect on the inflation, which drives up the real interest rate. In countries which are catching up economically, the real exchange rate is likely to increase temporarily so that net exports are dampened while domestic investment increases. This development should not simply be interpreted as a loss of international competitiveness since a major driver behind this development is, according to the Balassa-Samuelson effect, the natural adjustment of relative prices within a long term economic adjustment process. For small open economies acting in a system of flexible exchange rates, there will be the long term policy option to adopt a restrictive monetary policy so that domestic absorption will be reduced through rising real interest rates; at the same time, net exports will increase.

Economic catching-up (associated with both supply-side effects and demand dynamics) is subsequently understood as moving up the technology ladder of products, ie. the adoption of more sophisticated quality products over time. Product innovation rates will largely be considered as exogenous so that we leave open the explanation as to why and at what time firms in the respective countries will upgrade product assortments (e.g. this may be linked to foreign direct investment inflows or to a rise in the ratio of government expenditures on research and development relative to GDP). The analytical focus will be on a one sector model or a two sector approach with tradables and nontradables. Moving up the technology ladder thus means that the share of high quality products in overall exports or total output is increased in the respective transition country. An interesting theoretical challenge is to consider both product and process innovations which we will undertake in one simple model – a more refined approach includes endogenous process innovation (and possibly endogenous product innovations).

While the political reforms in transition countries will affect opportunities for economic growth there are naturally favourable prospects of economic catching up in the context of economic opening up. Once those countries have opened up for trade and capital flows they can benefit from:

- competitive pressure from world markets stimulating efficiency-enhancing economic restructuring;
- productivity stimulating effects from OECD imports of intermediate products used for production of final goods, including export goods;
- import of investment goods with embodied technological progress;
- exploitation of scale economies in the context of rising exports in scale intensive industries;
- inflows of foreign direct investment (FDI) which raise the capital stock in the case of greenfield investment and raise factor productivity in the context of international mergers and acquisitions.

For economic analysis it is rather useful to make a distinction between the nontradables (N-) and the tradables (T-)sector.

- Rising trade will naturally only affect the tradables sector, however the tradables sector will typically be the main impulse for structural change.
- FDI inflows can be in both the T-sector and the N-sector. A major effect of FDI inflows should be productivity growth. The structure of FDI inflows will thus partly determine the relative price of tradables, namely to the extent that productivity determines the relative price. If FDI is affecting both sectors in a parallel way with respect to productivity growth, we should expect a smaller rise in the relative price of nontradables compared to the case that FDI inflows are concentrated in the tradables sector.

Foreign Direct Investment

It is an interesting question as to whether asymmetric FDI inflows – e.g. a dominance of FDI in the tradables sector – will cause any problems for the economy. More generally put, to what extent large differences in productivity growth could be a problem for balanced growth and full employment? Furthermore, to what extent will the production elasticity of domestic capital affect the long term ratio of domestic capital to foreign capital (K**) employed? We consider the production potential to be given. We take up the latter question first and assume that output is determined on the basis of domestic capital input K and the stock of foreign capital K** (production function and gross domestic product, respectively, is $K^\beta K^{**1-\beta}$) while demand consists of domestic investment – assumed to be proportionate to national income - and net exports X' which we assumed to be proportionate (proportionality factor z") to cumulated foreign direct investment inflows K** in country I: the higher the stock of cumulated FDI inflows the better the access to the world market will be – to provide just one simple reasoning for the proposed specification.

$$\beta\, K^\beta K^{**1-\beta} = z"\, K^\beta K^{**1-\beta} + z'K^{**} \tag{27a}$$

Here we have assumed that both domestic capital K and foreign capital K** are rewarded in accordance with the marginal product rule so that national income is ß times gross domestic product.

$$(1-z")\beta K^\beta K^{**-\beta} = z' \tag{27b}$$

Hence it holds:

$$[K/K^{**}] = \{z'/[1-z"]\beta\}^{1/\beta} \tag{27c}$$

The ratio of domestic to foreign capital employed in the country is therefore positively correlated with z'/(1-z") and negatively correlated with the output elasticity of domestic capital ß.

One should emphasize that a combination of trade and FDI liberalization – observed in the reality of catching-up economies - takes us outside of the familiar Heckscher Ohlin model, and we clearly have a lack of modelling when it comes to taking into account both trade and FDI effects. There are also other potential problems associated with economic opening up, in particular there could be the problem of:

- high current account imbalances; indeed high deficit-GDP ratios can be a problem as foreign indebtedness is rising – however, a large sustained current account surplus also can be a problem since it will go along with "unnatural" net capital exports and a strong temporary boom which could raise the price of nontrables relative to tradables strongly;
- volatile short term inflows which raise the exposure of the respective country in the sense that high outflows might follow in the future: an exceptional period is represented by election years as these may be associated with political instability and large ideological swings in the case of a change in power.

- Transition countries differ in many ways including the size of the respective country and factor endowment. Russia, Romania and Kazachstan are resource rich countries while other transition countries are relatively richly endowed with labor (and in some cases capital – taking into account countries which have attracted high FDI inflows). Countries which are relatively abundant in natural resources should clearly benefit from economic expansion in periods in which the relative price of resources is high – as was the case in the late 1990s.

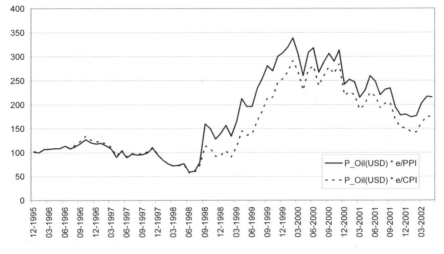

Source: www.recep.org

Fig. 39. Relative Price of Oil

One should not overlook that many resource abundant countries have a tendency for artificially low prices – for instance oil and gas prices in countries with rich oil or gas sites. If prices were raised to the world market price level then income levels from the natural resources sector would be high, however a fast price convergence would undermine the viability of energy-intensive firms and could raise unemployment. Countries rich in oil and gas also tend to have high nontradables prices and strong Balassa-Samuelson effects in the sense of a relative rise of nontradables prices. The latter may, however, not so much reflect technological economic catching-up but rather a pure natural resources boom effect. As regards the impact of a relative rise of energy prices on employment the effect will be negative in the non-energy sector and positive in the oil and gas sector. Assume that the energy sector uses only capital K' and labor L' while the non-energy sector (NE) uses factor inputs capital K and labor L, namely according to $Y^{NE}=K^{\beta}E^{\beta'}L^{1-\beta-\beta'}$. In the short term we can assume a constant capital stock and obtain from profit maximization and assuming competition in goods and labor markets so that factors are rewarded according to the marginal product rule (we denote the energy price as P'', output price in the non-energy sector as P):

$$w=[1-\text{ß}-\text{ß"}][K/L]^{\text{ß}/1-\text{ß'}} \ (\text{ß'}/[P\text{"}/P])^{\text{ß'}/1-\text{ß'}} \tag{28}$$

Hence, labor demand in the non-energy sector is a positive function of capital intensity and a negative function of the real energy price $P\text{"}/P$. However, in the energy sector – with output $E=K\text{"}^{\text{ß"}}L\text{"}^{1-\text{ß"}}$ - we will have (defining $W/P\text{"}=w\text{"}$)

$$w\text{"}= [1-\text{ß"}][K\text{"}/L\text{"}]^{1/\text{ß"}} \tag{29}$$

Overall labor demand is $L'=L\text{"}+L$. For countries which are richly endowed with natural resources a rise of the oil price could indeed raise overall labor demand and overall real income which is, expressed in terms of the non-energy good: $Y\text{"}=(P\text{"}/P)E+Y^{NE}$. The option is all the more attractive if the country considered enjoys alone or with other countries together – as in the case of OPEC – some international market power (then profit maximization leads to a slightly modified labor demand schedule).

Transition and Unemployment

As regards the dynamics of unemployment in transformation countries the unemployment rate is high in many transition countries (e.g. in Poland it has risen continuously in the first twelve years of transformation reaching a specific unemployment rate of close to 30% in 2004). In the following table, countries are ranked according to the degree of economic openness: It seems that small open economies face less problems in the field of unemployment than large economies – except for Russia which has benefited after the 1998 crisis from strong economic growth, stimulated strongly by high real oil prices.

Table 6. Openness (Trade/GDP), Growth and Unemployment in Transition Countries

	2000			2001			2002		
	Openness	GDP growth	Un-empl. Rate	Openness	GDP growth	Un-empl Rate	Openess	GDP growth	Unempl Rate
	(% of GDP)	(%)	(%)	(%of GDP)	(%)	(%)	(%of GDP)	(%)	(%)
Estonia	172.2	6.4	14.8	182.5	6.5	12.6	177,7	6,0	NA
Slovak Republic	149.6	2.2	18.9	156.5	3.3	NA	152,7	4,4	NA
Czech Republic	146.6	2.9	8.8	144.2	3.1	NA	132,7	2,0	NA
Belarus	137.2	5.8	NA	137.1	4.7	NA	143,4	4,7	NA
Hungary	129.2	5.2	6.5	150.2	3.8	5.7	131,1	3,3	5,8
Bulgaria	122.5	5.8	16.3	118.7	4.1	NA	112,9	4,8	NA
Slovenia	121.8	4.6	7.5	116.5	2.9	5.9	114,4	3,0	13,8
Latvia	100.1	6.6	8.4	100.0	7.9	7.7	101,5	6,1	NA
Lithuania	96.7	3.9	11.1	107.3	6.5	12.9	113,9	6,7	NA
Romania	73.9	1.6	10.8	74.4	5.3	NA	76,7	4,3	NA
Russian Federation	70.7	8.3	11.4	59.8	5.0	NA	58,7	4,3	NA
Poland	61.8	4.0	16.7	59.8	1.0	16.2	59,5	1,4	17,8

Source: WDI 2002, WDI Online (Openness and GDP Growth 2001, 2002), IFS (Unemployment Rate 2001, 2002).

A typical phenomenon of transition countries is that the specific unemployment rate of unskilled labor is rather high, although labor markets seem to be quite flexible in most of these countries. This has to be explained, and our analysis will present a simple model which is mainly related to the interaction of the tradables and nontradables sectors.

Another element of transition and economic catching up is that firms will upgrade in terms of technology and specialize according to comparative advantages – here analysis shows that revealed comparative advantage is changing relatively quickly in countries with high foreign direct investment inflows. Shifts in revealed comparative advantages of different types of industries, ordered in accordance with technology intensity, are observed (BORBÉLY, 2004). In the course of technological upgrading and specialization one may expect that factor demand becomes more inelastic; which consequences this might have for labor has to be analyzed. Unemployment also has other effects crucial for macroeconomic analysis, as will be shown subsequently.

Patterns of economic catching up are difficult to reconcile with Heckscher-Ohlin-Samuelson (HOS) modelling. Successful catching-up seems to be comprised of two elements where one indeed is HOS-compatible. A typical pattern of economic catching up in the context of EU southern and EU eastern enlargement (EU eastern enlargement effectively started with the EU association treaties with postsocialist countries of eastern Europe) is that poor countries specialize in labor intensive products which is consistent with the Heckscher-Ohlin-Samuelson approach. Poor countries are relatively labor abundant and thus should specialize in labor intensive products – economic opening up will raise the share of labor intensive production and exports will concern labor intensive products. Indeed countries such as Spain, Portugal, the Czech Republic, Poland and Hungary show a revealed comparative advantage (RCA) and high export unit values in part of labor intensive production: This combination of a high RCA and high export unit values in labor intensive production represents profitable exports in this field.

However, there is a second element of successful catching up, namely a gradual rise of the RCA in science-intensive and human-capital intensive products: if in such sectors a high and rising export unit value can be obtained this will stimulate long term expansion of these sectors (narrowly defined) and related sectors into which firms might move in the course of product differentiation (broadly defined) and catching-up. Such developments are associated with product innovation dynamics where a product innovation in a poor country typically will stand for diffusion when defined from the perspective of a leading OECD country. It is unclear whether the ability to achieve positive RCA in technology-intensive and science-intensive goods and differentiated goods (largely electronics) depends mainly on domestic human capital formation or mainly on foreign direct investment. A quick product upgrading and hence rising RCAs can hardly be expected without foreign direct investment inflows in those sectors unless there is considerable domestic research and development; and it requires active human capital formation policies and government support for research and development. Such traits are not only found in catching-up dynamics of Spain and Portugal in the 1980s and Hungary, Poland and the Czech Republic in the 1990s but also in Asian Newly Industrializing Countries in the 1970s and 1980s. One may argue that this second element of catching-up - it may be dubbed the DUNNING-SCHULTZ-SCHUMPETER element - is of general importance for product innovation and technological upgrading: Once labor intensive profitable production contributes to reducing unemployment and rising technology-intensive plus human-capital-intensive production contributes to growth of net exports of goods and services there is a broad potential for future structural change and shifts towards high-value added sectors. This amounts to favourable prospects for sustained long term economic growth. A crucial sustainability test for economic catching up is the phase of continuous real appreciation which will stimulate firms to upgrade product quality and to move towards industries which are more technology intensive and hence less price sensitive.

Taking simply a look at the output structure of countries in eastern Europe or Asia can be misleading, particularly if there is a high share of technology intensive production and positive RCAs in this field (positive RCA means that it should exceed unity if it is defined as sector export-import balance relative to the national export-import balance or exceed zero if one uses the natural logarithm of this variable). There is a caveat which concerns vertical multinational investment: e.g. even if computers were manufactured in Hungary or Poland one must analyze whether production statistics showing computer manufacturing are not hiding the fact that high tech components are imported and that value-added is mainly from "screw-driving factories" so that ultimately there is labor intensive production taking place. Production and export of intermediate inputs can, however, lead to more complex long term production and upgrading: e.g. Portugal initially developed intermediate product assembly for the automotive industry abroad, but later was able to attract final assembly in the automotive sector – not least because it had developed a competitive supplier industry. From this perspective technological upgrading does not only mean to switch to more advanced products but also to shift more into final product assembly. Another example is Toyota in Japan which started out decades ago as a producer of textile machinery before it became a very innovative and profitable automotive firm. We leave open here how upgrading in production takes place – in subsequent modelling the idea is basically that it is associated with foreign direct investors and that international technology transfer occurs (for simplicity) at zero marginal costs.

In the following analysis we want to highlight selected macroeconomic problems of transition and economic opening up. In particular, we are interested in innovation issues. We suggest new ideas in three different fields of transformation:
1. we state the hypothesis that there is a link between the Balassa-Samuelson effect and unemployment of unskilled labor;
2. we argue that product innovations are crucial in the course of economic catching up and opening up – and we show how product innovations can be integrated into the Mundell Fleming model;
3. it is shown in a simple dynamic model how the current account and relative innovation performance affect the long term real equilibrium exchange rate.

In addition our analysis recalls standard sceptical approaches to high output growth in resource-rich countries when they based growth largely on depletion of non-renewable natural resources. As regards policy conclusions, government promotion of product innovation seems to be rather important in transition countries and NICs.

E.3 Growth, Resource Dynamics, Balassa-Samuelson Effects and Unemployment

E.3.1 Growth, Natural Resources and Economic Welfare

Before we take a closer look at innovation aspects of catching-up we briefly look into the issue of countries which are abundant with natural resources. In transition countries aggregate output can typically be described by a standard production function which for simplicity can have the arguments capital K, labor L, technology A – assumed to be labor augmenting - and natural resources dR/dt where R is the stock of natural resources. In the case of a Cobb-Douglas production function we can write:

$$Y = K^{\beta} R'^{\beta'} (AL)^{1-\beta'-\beta} \tag{30}$$

Hence output growth is – with g denoting growth rate and R'=dR/dt - given by

$$g_Y = \beta g_K + \beta' g_{R'} + (1-\beta'-\beta'')[g_L + g_A] \tag{31}$$

As we have a homogenous production function we also can write

$$Y = Y_K K + Y_{AL}(AL) + Y_R |dR/dt| \tag{32}$$

If factors are rewarded according to the marginal product rule we have

$$Y = rK + w[AL] + [P^R/P] |dR/dt| \tag{33}$$

If resources are non-renewable resources an adequate measure of welfare – or of "modified net national product" - would be (assuming that capital depreciation is proportionate to K) the following term Z':

$$Z' = Y - \delta K - A'' |dR/dt| \tag{34}$$

A" is a real shadow price variable which reflects the value of resource depletion in terms of consumption goods; a should be determined on the basis of a sustainable growth model – at a given level of technology (not discussed here).

In a broad perspective this concept corresponds to the logic of net value added. One has to deduct capital depreciations and resource depletion if one wants to focus on value added along with maintaining the stock of capital and natural resources, respectively.

The term adR/dt catches the depletion of natural resources which are considered as a natural asset here. Combining equations (33) and (34) yields

$$Z' = rK + w[AL] + \{[P^R/P] |dR/dt| - A'' |dR/dt|\} - \delta K \tag{35}$$

If the relative price of natural resources were identical to the parameter a, an adequate welfare measure would be simply the sum of capital income and labor income. The analysis is rather complex in reality since the first element in the term $\{[P^R/P] |dR/dt| - A'' |dR/dt|\}$ refers to the physical use of resources while the second term dR/dt should effectively be corrected by a factor (1-b"), where b" is a technological progress parameter allowing a better exploitation of existing stocks of resources. As b" can be assumed to be relatively large in transition countries one should not overemphasize the problem of natural resources depletion in the medium term. However, in the long run this aspect is clearly important.

$$Z' = rK + w[AL] + \{[P^R/P]|\ dR/dt|- A''(1-b'')|\ dR/dt|\} - \delta K \qquad (35')$$

If the relative price of oil is increasing (as was the case in the late 1990s) we can expect a rise of Z'.

In any case we may emphasize that resource rich countries are well advised to take into account the problem that early growth dynamics can only be sustained if there is long term industrial diversification in production and exports. This view does, of course, not rule out that proceeds from the export of natural resources can be quite useful to finance the import of machinery and equipment as well as technology useful for the expansion of manufacturing exports in the long run. There is also a risk that strong wage growth from the resource sector – in periods of high international resource prices – spills over to other sectors and thus could raise unemployment. Russia, Kazakhstan, Azerbaijan and Romania are crucial countries in this respect.

E.3.2 The Balassa-Samuelson Effect, Unemployment and Exports

The catching-up process of poor countries will be accompanied by relatively high growth rates which in turn will raise the relative price of nontradable (N) goods. The relative price of nontradables – including rents - will increase in the course of rising real per capita income; this is the Balassa-Samuelson (1964) effect which we assume to work in transition countries. The price index is $P=(P^N)^b\ (P^T)^{(1-b)}$. If we assume a fixed exchange rate and an exogenous and constant world market price of tradables the domestic price of tradables is exogenous – the price level is determined by the Balassa-Samuelson (BS) effect and the rise of the nontradables price. The assumption of a constant exchange rate might be inadequate in resource abundant countries, which in a regime of flexible exchange rates will face considerable appreciation pressure in periods of a rise of the world market price of natural resources. Rather, one would expect long term appreciation – bringing about a rise of the nontradables price in the context of stable nontradables prices and a fall of the domestic price of tradables (due to strong appreciation) - in combination with high volatility of the exchange rate.

Now let us take a look at the labor market for unskilled workers. A first issue concerns the size of the true unemployment rate; if state-owned firms have a policy of not laying off excessive workers such firms stand for hidden unemployment. Other distortions also could be important: In poor countries government and state-owned firms, respectively, tend to distort international trade by buying – often for pure prestige reasons - the latest technology in OECD countries while a private company often would have preferred instead to buy older vintages of machinery and equipment because this is cheaper and represents a higher labor intensity (with labor abundance it makes no economic sense to buy the latest technology which is developed in capital intensive countries) than ultra-modern equipment. From this perspective one should not be surprised if empirical analysis of international specialization would not exactly find Hecker-Ohlin dynamics in poor countries.

Tradables and Nontradables

Next we turn to the role of tradable goods versus nontradable goods. Assuming that consuming nontrables is a basic necessity for survival – think for instance of housing – one may argue that the reservation wage (the beginning of the labor supply curve) is determined by the absolute price of nontradables. Hence the Balassa-Samuelson (BS) effect will shift up the labor supply curve over time. At the same time we may assume that there is labor saving technological progress in both the tradables and the nontradables sector. We have sectoral neoclassical production functions for T (sector 2) and N (sector 1) with the inputs unskilled labor L, capital K and labor augmenting technological progress A; in addition we assume that skilled labor H is employed in the T sector (an alternative would be to assume that only skilled labor is employed in the T sector, then full employment in the presence of any excess supply of L in the nontradables sector can be only eliminated through retraining efforts and skill-upgrading which is costly)

$$T^s = T(L^T, H, K^T, A^T) \tag{36}$$

$$N^s = N(L^N, K^N, A^N) \tag{37}$$

where A^N is assumed to be governed by positive spillover effects from A^T because the tradables sector typically is the more dynamic sector and indeed often has technology spillover effects. Let L^{Ns} denote the short-term labor supply of unskilled labor in the N-sector which is supposed to depend positively on the sectoral nominal wage rate W^N and negatively on the price level and the nontradables price P^N. We will consider a rise in the price of nontradables which implies a leftward shift of the labor supply curve in W^N, L^N space. Assume a constant capital stock K^N in the nontradables sector, then the – exogenous or endogenous (for instance determined by the level of international trade relative to output in the tradables sector) - spillover effect from technological progress in the T-sector: labor-saving progress in the T-sector, A^T, is assumed to have a positive spillover to A^N, that is to trigger labor-saving progress in the N-sector, and this rise of A^T implies a leftward shift of the labor demand curve in the N-sector. In the subsequent diagram we assume this leftward shift to dominate the rightward shift associated with a rise of the nontradables price. The effect is a reduction in employment in the N sector and to the extent that in the short run labor is immobile across sectors (or regions in the case that N and T are located in different regions), we will have quasi-unemployment, namely the difference between initial employment L^N_0 and L^N_1. Strictly speaking we have voluntary unemployment but those losing their job will certainly register as unemployed although they do not want to work at the going wage rate in the official economy. They might, however, be interested in working in the unofficial economy provided that the official economy is subject to considerable burdens in terms of income taxes and social security contributions. If there is full labor mobility across sectors one might argue that unemployed workers from the N-sector could find a job in the T-sector. However, this argument is not very convincing if physical capital and human capital are strongly complementary – hence the expansion of the tradables sector is accompanied with only a modest increase in the demand for unskilled labor.

The result could be that there is economic growth and poverty at the same time, and indeed a high share of the population may suffer from malnutrition. The rise of the relative price of non-tradables will not only be a problem for unemployed people but also for pensioners who cannot expect to automatically get annual increases of benefits in line with inflation.

As regards medium term labor dynamics, labor is assumed to be mobile across sectors, and in the long run a certain fraction of unskilled workers can be transformed through training and education into skilled workers. Retraining efforts require investment in human capital, however, it is unclear whether there are financial resources available for this. If there are low mobility costs and excess unskilled labor from the N-sector can easily move towards the T-sector, unskilled labor unemployment should decline over time. There is, however, a problem if production in the T-sector is using skilled labor intensively and if government is unable or unwilling to subsidize training and human capital upgrading adequately.

Moreover, if there are barriers to mobility, e.g. excess demand in regional housing markets or administrative barriers, this will make unemployment of unskilled labor a sustained problem. Moreover, to the extent that structural change, stimulated by economic opening up and FDI inflows, favors expansion of sectors with a relatively high demand for skilled labor, the excess unskilled labor from the N-sector will find it difficult to get a new job. The real adjustment dynamics in poor countries opening up in a world with trade and FDI flows indeed does not often show a general expansion of labor intensive production which would absorb unskilled labor. Rather we see some expansion and positive revealed comparative advantage in labor intensive sectors, while sectors with high FDI inflows are often sectors which are technology-intensive or skill-intensive. In a nutshell these problems are found in many transition countries and certainly also in many Newly Industrializing Countries and in developing countries.

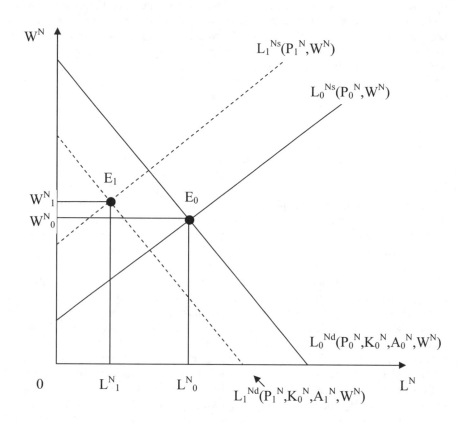

Fig. 40. Balassa-Samuelson Effect, Technological Progress and Quasi Unemployment

E.3.3 Wage Bargaining as Inherent Source of Unemployment?

The reasons for long term high unemployment in transition countries are not well understood, and it is unclear how economic and institutional developments in the course of catching-up will affect employment and unemployment, respectively. Keynesian models suggest that a lack of effective demand is a major reason for high unemployment as neoclassical models emphasize a lack of investment and problems in labor markets. The following analysis emphasizes problems of wage bargaining and argues that it might be rather difficult to implement a policy framework which gives incentives to trade unions to target full employment. An important point of departure is that trade unions represent both employed and unemployed workers where for an individual trade union organization (O_i in sector i) an unemployed member might be more important in terms of membership fees than a member with a job who will change with a certain probability from sector I to sector j and thus leave the initial trade union organization O_i and join O_j instead.

It is clear that unemployed members pay a lower membership fee to the trade union since membership fees typically are proportionate to income.

It is often argued that trade unions have a tendency – in particular in large countries – to lobby for excessively high wage rates. If wage bargaining leads to a wage rate w_1 above the market-clearing wage rate w^E, we have a situation in which workers obtain wages $w(1-\tau)L$ – with the tax rate τ partly or fully determined by the costs of unemployment and unemployment benefits paid; in addition unemployed workers will obtain unemployment benefits which are proportionate to their former income (see the shaded area in the following graph). As regards unemployed workers, an alternative assumption considered subsequently is to assume for simplicity that unemployment benefits are proportionate to the wage rate fixed in the bargaining process, and indeed this simplifying assumption will not change the basic results as long as labor supply is inelastic. While we will not consider an explicit model with tradables and nontradables, this assumption can be defended on the grounds that with wages fixed above the market-clearing rate the (overall wage) income is higher than under market-clearing which in turn leads to higher nontradables prices, eg housing prices and rents, than under market-clearing so that government and parliament will have a natural incentive to consider a rule under which unemployment benefits are implicitly proportionate to the going wage rate.

The incentive for trade unions to strive in wage bargaining for a wage rate above the equilibrium wage rate will increase over time if technological upgrading and specialization makes labor demand less elastic. The graphical analysis in panel a) shows that in the case of labor demand curve L^d_0 switching from a market-clearing wage rate to a higher real wage rate w_1 has two effects: It reduces labor income due to the fall in employment, namely by the area $GE_0L_0L_1$, but labor income will be raised in line with the rise of the wage rate (area $FGw^E_0w_1$). The net effect of the fall in employment and the rise in the real wage rate is ambiguous, however, if the labor demand becomes more elastic the income-enhancing effect from the rise in the real wage will become more important (the theory of efficiency-wage bargaining suggests that firms also may have a tendency to support strong wage pressure – we will, however, no t consider these effects here).

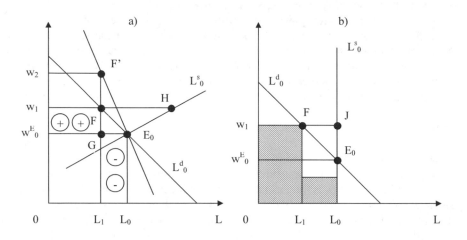

Fig. 41. Wage Rate Fixing above the Market-Clearing Rate

Economic caching-up of the transition countries is associated with increasing specialization of firms – partly reflecting the very impact of opening up and international competition - the demand for labor becomes less elastic and hence the risk is rising that wage bargaining will lead to excessive wage rates and unemployment. Part of the problem is, of course, related to the degree of wage centralization and the strength of trade unions and employer organizations. The problem considered might effectively be rather negligible in small open economies where fixing wage rates above marginal labor productivity will lead to large visible losses in world market shares which renders part of the capital stock obsolete and thus shifts the labor demand curve to the left: Labor income and national income will reduce in parallel. However, in a large economy the trade-GDP ratio is much below that in small open economies which implies – along with a home bias of consumers with respect to tradables goods – that a period of excessive wage fixing will not be followed by as quick a fall of overall market shares of firms in the tradables sector as in a small economy. Since incentives in a large economy to fix the wage rate at the equilibrium level are weaker than in a small economy the risk of neoclassical unemployment is rather strong in large transition economies.. This holds except for large countries in which wage bargaining is rather decentralized and in which trade unions are relatively weak (see for instance the US). A priori it is unclear, in transition countries, whether the influence of trade unions will rise over time and how their behaviour will develop.

The Model

Taking a closer look at a simple model of wage bargaining can shed some light on the issues raised. In the following analysis we assume that firms are profit-maximizing and the economy is characterized by a Cobb-Douglas production function $Y = K^{\beta} L^{1-\beta}$ where Y is output and capital K and labor L, respectively. Labor demand L is derived from profit maximization of the firm. Those unemployed (L' which is equal to labor supply minus labor demand) get unemployment benefits which are proportionate to the average gross real wage paid (w); unemployment benefits are assumed to be $w(1-z)[L_o-L]$ where L_o is the exogenous labor supply and $0 < z < 1$. Unemployment benefits are financed by taxes on labor income where the tax rate is τ. We will assume that the tax rate depends on w – alternatively wL might be considered – where the partial derivative is positive.

$$\tau = \tau (w) \tag{38}$$

With a Cobb-Douglas production function profit-maximization leads to labor demand L given by

$$L = [(1-\beta)/w]^{\beta} K \tag{39}$$

The elasticity of labor demand with respect to the real wage rate is $-\beta$ which in absolute terms is below unity. Pure gross wage income is $wL == [1-\beta)]^{\beta} K w^{1-\beta}$ so that the elasticity of pure labor income – income earned in the market – is below unity. Trade unions are assumed to aim at maximizing the sum Z of net wage income $w(1-\tau)L$ and the quasi-income of unemployed which is defined as $w(1-z)(L_o-L)$; however, as trade unions are averse to unemployment we will use a slightly modified expression, namely $\alpha w(1-z)(L_o-L)$. The parameter α indicates how strongly the trade union weighs the unemployment benefits and unemployment. If this parameter were zero or the effective replacement ratio $(1-z)=z'$ zero, the trade union would disregard the income accruing to unemployed workers. Trade unions are thus assumed to maximize (see also appendix):

$$Z = w[1-\tau(w)]L + \alpha w(1-z)(L_o-L) \tag{40}$$

The solution for maximizing Z is shown in the appendix. This solution has to be compared to the full employment wage rate so that one can draw conclusions with respect to an adequate replacement parameter $z'=(1-z)$ – the parameter has to be fixed by the political system - which would lead to full employment. To the extent that the full-employment enhancing z' is very low and imply an income of unemployed below a critical minimum, government may want to consider giving unemployed workers a fixed per capita unemployment benefit – regardless of the previous income of those who lost their job. There are also other ways of providing an incentive compatible labor market regime: eg those regions and sectors which exhibit unemployment rates below average would have lower contribution rates to the unemployment insurance system than regions and sectors with unemployment rates – or job loss rates – above the national average; or some other benchmark figure.

Unemployment and Current Account Position

Economic catching-up is associated with growing exports and imports, where poor countries typically record net imports for an extended period – later a current account surplus emerges as firms in the tradable sector become more competitive. However, we will argue that macroeconomic developments play a role for the current account, too.

We assume that there is a move from full-employment to a situation with a high unemployment rate. How does this affect the current account? An answer to this question should help us to understand changes in current account positions. In particular we will see in a simple model – with all goods assumed to be tradable - that a high current account surplus is not always an indicator of high competitiveness of countries. The basic point can be shown in four equations: Assume that consumption C and Investment I are proportionate to real income Y and are negatively affected by the number of unemployed L' (the unemployment rate u is defined as the ratio of unemployed L' to those employed L).

Furthermore real government expenditures G are written as

$$G= \gamma Y+n'L' \tag{38a}$$

Hence

$$G/L= \gamma[Y/L]+n'u \tag{38b}$$

where n' is the replacement ratio paid by the unemployment insurance system to the unemployed. Hence we have two behavioural equations for real consumption C and real investment I plus the equilibrium condition for the goods market where X' denotes net exports of goods and services, Y^{pot} is the production potential, while actual output supplied is assumed to be $(1- \omega u)Y^{pot}$ which implies that with a positive unemployment rate u (u is defined as unemployed L' over employed L) there will also be underutilization of capital and labor in firms – this is quite a realistic assumption. Our approach – with parameter $\omega>0$ and $\omega u<1$- implies that output supply will be equal to the production potential once u converges towards zero. Moreover, the proposed specification allows the building of models that represent medium term approaches for a situation with unemployment and looking in a consistent manner at long term growth. The term $(1- \omega u)$ affects the level of output but not growth as e.g. the fall of the number of unemployed must be equal to the rise in the number of new jobs (du is zero!). Our simple consumption function and the investment function are as follows:

$$C= cY -fL'; f>0 \tag{38c}$$

$$I= b'Y - a'L' ; a'>0 \tag{38d}$$

Note that one might introduce the assumption that a=a(r,q) so that the investment function to some extent becomes more similar to the traditional investment function in Mundell Fleming models; and to take into account the impact of FDI inflows along the lines suggested by (FROOT/STEIN, 1991). Moreover, in an open economy with FDI inflows and outflows it would be adequate to assume that investment depends on the ratio of the marginal product of capital at home to that abroad which implies – relying on the case of a Cobb-Douglas production function which has proportionality of marginal product and average product of input factors – that $I=I([Y/K]/[Y^*/K^*]$ so that $I=I(q,Y,Y^*...)$: This would imply a net export function $X(q,Y,Y^*)$ with familiar partial derivatives! In Addition to the goods market one might, following (ARTUS, 1989, p.45), consider the money market equilibrium and assume a money demand function where the demand for real money balances m depends on output, the interest rate and the unemployment rate; the partial derivative for the unemployment rate is positive since higher unemployment raises the demand for liquidity: higher u means higher uncertainty. Thus a modified Mundell Fleming model in r-u-space could be drawn where a fall in u implies a rise of Y. The approach proposed also easily lends itself to combining a goods market quasi-equilibrium condition with Phillips-curve analysis; moreover, the capacity effect of investment could be incorporated as well, however, these possible extensions are not pursued here. We state our basic idea for output supplied as follows:

$$Y^s = (1-\omega u)Y^{pot} \tag{38e}$$

Equation (40) states that output supplied is proportionate to the production potential but also is negatively affected by the unemployment rate u; if there is a positive unemployment rate firms will realize some labor hoarding for various reasons so that output is less than the number of employed people normally would suggest. Potential output is defined as follows:

$$Y^{pot}=K^\beta L^{1-\beta} \tag{38f}$$

The quasi-equilibrium condition– output is not at the full employment level - for the goods market can be written as follows:

$$(1-\omega u)Y^{pot} = (b'+c+\gamma)Y -(f+a'-n')L' + X' \tag{38g}$$

Dividing equation (38g) by L and taking into account the production function – and denoting K/L as k - we get for net exports per worker:

$$X'/L = (1-\omega u)[1-c-b'- \gamma]k^\beta + (a'+f-n')u \tag{38h}$$

Hence net exports per capita are – for a given capital intensity – a positive function of the unemployment rate if $(a'+f-n') >\omega$ $[1-c- b'- \gamma]k^\beta$. Therefore a rise of net exports per worker thus must not simply be interpreted as a rise of competitiveness. It simply may reflect a rise of the unemployment rate and the associated fall in domestic absorption – corrected for supply effects related to changes in the unemployment rate. This case of a positive impact of the unemployment rate on net exports per worker is shown in the subsequent graph.

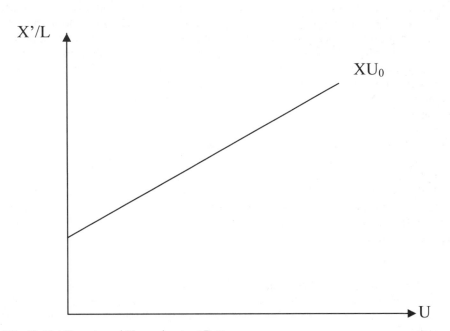

Fig. 42. Net Exports and Unemployment Rate

E.4 Product Innovation and Macroeconomic Developments: Schumpeter and the Mundell-Fleming Model

E.4.1 The Role of Risk and Innovation

An important aspect of innovation dynamics concerns risk. As a simple way to take into account risk and innovation one may proceed as follows. We consider a consumption function C where consumption depends on income on the one hand and on wealth A' on the other hand. The expected rate of return on innovation is μ, the variance is σ. There are only two assets considered, namely real capital K and real money balances m (m=M/P). We chose deliberately a specification where K/AL and [M/P]/AL (denoted as m') both enter the consumption function as a variable to the power ß since otherwise the mathematical calculation would become very intricate. All exponents are assumed to be positive. Hence a higher variance of innovation (and investment) yield imply a higher consumption since saving obviously brings relatively uncertain rewards; a higher expected yield on innovation reduces consumption and indeed stimulates savings as the reward for those saving is increased.

$$C/[AL]= cy' + c'[\sigma/\mu]^{\varepsilon} [k'^{ß} + m'^{ß}] \qquad (60)$$

As regards the term $[k'^{\beta} + m'^{\beta}]$ this formulation is rather unusual at first sight; an ideal specification would indeed use $[k'^{\beta} + m'^{\beta}]^2$ but for ease of exposition we will drop the square. Our basic reflection in this context will focus on a special case where $A=A_o=4$ and $L=L_o=1$. Assume that $\beta=1/2$ and the production function contains real money balances M/P as a positive external spillover effect, where real balances factor in as $(M/P)^{\beta}$; hence we have output as $Y=K^{\beta}(M/P)^{\beta}L_o^{\beta}$. One may then indeed state a simple consumption function as

$$C/[AL] = cy' + c'\,(K^{0.5} + m^{0.5})^2 = cy' + c'[K + 2K^{0.5}m^{0.5} + m] \tag{61}$$

$$= c''y' + c'[K+m].$$

We will use the Cobb-Douglas output function to replace k'^{β} by y' and a simple CAGAN-type real money demand equation to replace m', namely (with the Euler number written as e' and the semielasticity of the nominal yield on investment denoted as ψ and the expected inflation rate denoted as π'):

$$m'^d = e'\ ^{-\psi'[\mu+\pi']}\,y \tag{62}$$

Let us assume that both σ and μ are positive functions of the product innovation variable v. The corresponding savings function is therefore as follows:

$$S/[AL] = \{1-c - c'[\sigma(v)/\mu(v)]^{\varepsilon}\,[1+e'^{\psi'[\mu(v)+\pi']}]\}y' \tag{63}$$

We assume that the partial derivative of the expected rate of return with respect to v is higher than that for the reaction of the variance with respect to changes in v. This assumption is sufficient to bring about a rise of savings if v is increased. If we insert this equation in the familiar neoclassical growth model we will get the following steady state result for $k'\#$ (note we we use v/v*' instead of a'*):

$$k'\#^{\,\sigma\Omega\eta'/(1-\sigma\beta)} = (\{1-c - c'[\sigma(v)/\mu(v)]^{\varepsilon}\,[1+e'^{\psi'[\mu(v)+\pi']}]\}+1) \tag{64}$$

$$\cdot (b'/[v/v*])^{\,\eta'\sigma}]/[n+\delta+a]\}^{1/1-\sigma\beta}$$

This result includes both process innovations and product innovations and represents a much richer approach than traditional models. Domestic product innovations clearly raise the optimum capital intensity and output per efficiency unit of labor.

E.4.2 Endogenous Product Innovations in Countries with Similar Development Levels

Which research perspective is useful for countries which are of similar sophistication in product innovations? Let us consider two open economies of a similar technological level which are exporting goods and importing goods. Households consume domestic and foreign goods, including new products launched at home and abroad; in addition there is a kind of consumption technology which allows households to develop novel consumption patterns which depend on the interaction of v and v* in the market. The stock of product innovations abroad is v*, in the home country it is v. We assume that there are network effects (in commercial novelties) N' in country I which can be described as follows:

$$N' = (v+v^*+2vv^*)^\alpha \tag{65}$$

The rights hand side term says that the stock of novelties available depends on domestic product innovations (v), foreign product innovations (v*) and a third term which represents the interaction of both terms. We can rewrite the above equation as

$$N' = (v+v^*)^{2\alpha} \tag{66}$$

Abroad we may assume a similar network effect $N'^* = (v+v^*+2vv^*)^{\alpha^*}$. The next question to be raised is how v and v*, respectively, can be explained. Research expenditures H is obviously one relevant variable.

How can we define true quality-adjusted output? One useful definition would be:

$$Y'' = YN'^{\alpha'} \tag{67}$$

If the term a' is unity (and abroad a'* is unity) we can calculate relative quality-adjusted output as

$$Y''/Y''^* = [Y/Y^*]N'/N'^* \tag{68}$$

There are indeed considerable differences across countries when it comes to the willingness of households to use new products as was shown.

E.5 Conclusions and Policy Implications

We have analyzed some key issues of transition countries from a theoretical point. From an analytical perspective it is clear that the familiar Heckscher-Ohlin Samuelson framework has to be refined if the challenges of opening up and transition are to be understood. Transformation is not a quick process where a country can jump from the distortions of the old system towards a new full employment market economy. First, it is important to take into account that transition countries differ in important aspects, e.g. the degree of natural resource abundance. Second, there has been high unemployment in many transition countries over decades, particularly high amongst unskilled workers. The analysis presented argues that economic and technological catching-up – accompanied by increasing specialization – will make labor demand less inelastic. This in turn reinforces the problem that wage negotiations may lead to a wage rate above the market-clearing rate where we suggest that government should fix unemployment benefits in a way which effectively leads to full employment. Unemployment in a small open economy (by assumption it can export the excess supply of the tradables sector) in turn is likely to raise net exports so that an improvement in the current account is not necessarily related to an improvement of technological competitiveness. Misinterpretation of the net export position by government and international organizations can have very serious consequences.

As regards medium term modelling of output development in transition countries we focus on the role of product innovations within a Schumpeter-Mundell-Fleming model (product innovations effectively means – from the perspective of leading OECD innovators – diffusion). We argue that the law of one price will not hold in such a model and show that product innovations raise output and bring about a real appreciation. To the extent that government innovation policy (with a focus on promotion product innovations and diffusion, respectively) can stimulate product innovations there is an important policy variable beyond traditional fiscal policy and monetary policy. It would be interesting to have empirical analysis for various countries which shows how important the share of product innovations in overall (net) exports is and how strongly government R&D promotion affects the product innovation rate. As regards policy conclusions government promotion of product innovation seems to be rather important in transition countries and NICs.

Finally, we take a look at real exchange rate dynamics in a setup in which the current account position and the relative rate of product innovation is affecting the real exchange rate. The approach presented argues that catching-up means a reduction of the price elasticity of net exports and a fall of the foreign relative innovation rate. Both effects contribute to a real appreciation of the currency.

The contribution has presented analytical building blocs relevant for transition countries. It is beyond the scope of our analysis to integrate those blocs into one coherent model. However, we have raised several crucial issues relevant for economic catching-up and transition countries. There certainly is need for further research which should help to reconcile real world dynamics with standard economic wisdom.

Appendix E.1: Maximization of Total Quasi-Income of Workers through Trade Unions (labor supply L_o is exogenous, parameter $0 \leq \alpha \leq 1$)

$$Z = w\left[1 - \tau(w)\right]L + w(1-z)\alpha\left[L_0 - L\right] \text{ mit z' = 1 - z} \tag{69}$$

$$= wL - w\tau(w)L + wz'\alpha L_0 - z'\alpha L \tag{70}$$

$$= (1-\beta)^{\beta} w^{1-\beta} K\left(1 - \tau(w) - z'\alpha\right) + wz'\alpha L_0 \tag{71}$$

$$\frac{dZ}{dw} = \left[(1-\beta)(1-\beta)^{\beta} w^{-\beta} K\left(1 - \tau(w) - z'\alpha\right)\right] - \tau_w(1-\beta)^{\beta} w^{1-\beta} K - z'\alpha \tag{72}$$

$$\left[(1-\beta)(1-\beta)^{\beta} w^{-\beta} K\left(1 - \tau(w) - z'\alpha\right)\right] - \tau(w)\varepsilon_{\tau,w}(1-\beta)^{\beta} w^{-\beta} K = z'\iota \tag{73}$$

$$= K\left[(1-\beta)^{1+\beta}\left(1 - \tau(w) - z'\alpha\right) - \tau(w)\varepsilon_{\tau,w}(1-\beta)^{\beta}\right] \Big/ z'\alpha L_0 = w^{\beta} \tag{74}$$

$$w^{\beta} = K(1-\beta)^{\beta}[(1-\beta)(1-\tau(w) - z'K) - \tau(w)\varepsilon_{\tau,w}]/z'\alpha L_0 \tag{75}$$

$$w^{\beta} = K(1\text{-}\beta)^{\beta}[(1\text{-}\beta)(1\text{-}\tau(w)\text{-}z'\,\alpha)\text{-}\tau(w)\varepsilon_{\tau,w}]/z'\alpha\,L_o \tag{76}$$

The optimum w# is obviously a negative function of ß.

(note that ßln=lnK + ß(-ß)[-ß - τ(w) -z'-α –t(w)εт,w) – ln (z' α L₀). The larger ß (the lower 1-ß), the lower the optimum wage set by trade unions will be. Note, the term [(1-ß)(1- τ(w) -z'- α –t(w)εт,w]) is assumed to be positive – otherwise the real wage rate would be negative. The wage rate set by trade unions depends negatively on the tax rate, labor supply, the parameter α and z' (w# depends positively on z!): A rise of α which indicates that trade unions weigh the unemployment element in the target function relatively higher implies a lower wage rate; and indeed higher employment. Government can induce trade unions to attach a higher weight to unemployment if government assigns funds to trade unions, for instance, earmarked for training programs, that should be a negative function of the unemployment rate. Compare (76) to profit maximization and full employment, respectively, namely the equation

$$L_o = [(1\text{-}\beta)/w]^{\beta} K; \text{or } w = (1\text{-}\beta)(K/L_o)^{1/\beta} \tag{77}$$

Comparing (76) and (77) equation (76) will coincide with (77) only if

$$[(1\text{-}\beta)(1\text{-}\tau(w)\text{-}z'\,\alpha)\text{-}\tau\varepsilon_{\tau,w}]/z'\,\alpha = 1 \tag{78}$$

$$[(1\text{-}ß)\,(1\text{-}\tau(w)) - \tau(w)\varepsilon_{\tau,w}]/z'\,\alpha\,-1+ß = 1 \tag{79}$$

$$[(1\text{-}ß)\,(1\text{-}\tau(w) - \tau(w)\varepsilon_{\tau,w}]/z'\,\alpha = 2\text{-}ß \tag{80}$$

Taking logarithms we have – assuming ß and $\tau(w)(1+ \tau(w)\varepsilon_{\tau,w})$ and z to be close to zero - we have the following approximation:

$$-ß(\tau(w)\,\text{-}1) - \tau(w)(1+ \tau(w)\varepsilon_{\tau,w}) = \text{-}z + \ln\alpha + \ln(2\text{-}ß) \tag{81}$$

Hence government policy should set z according to:

$$z = \tau(w)(1+ \tau(w)\varepsilon_{\tau,w}) + \ln\alpha + ß(\tau(w)\,\text{-}1) +\ln(2\text{-}ß) \tag{82}$$

The larger α, the larger should government choose z in order to obtain full employment. So if trade unions attach a high weight to unemployment benefits, government should counterbalance this by reducing unemployment benefits. Unemployment benefits should be the smaller (hence z would rise) the larger the tax rate and the elasticity $\varepsilon_{\tau,w}$. If z would be so small that the survival of unemployed would be difficult one may consider a system which basically gives a fixed per capita payment to all the unemployed. Finally, note that maximization of Z requires conditions to be considered that guarantee that the second derivative of Z with respect to w is negative. However, we rather will focus on a refined approach in the next section and then look at both the necessary and sufficient condition for a maximum.

Rational Trade Unions

Next note that the government budget constraint is as in equation (69'), and we assume that trade unions take this also into account – this is most likely in small open economies in which there are transparent macroeconomic feedback effects on wage setting. The budget constraint is:

$$\tau(w)wL = w[1\text{-}z][L_o\text{-}L] \tag{69'}$$

where on the left hand side we have tax payments (read: contributions to the unemployment insurance system), on the right hand side we have expenditures on the unemployed. We rewrite the above equation

$$\{\tau(w) +[1\text{-}z]\}L = (1\text{-}z)L_o \tag{69.1'}$$

Denote 1-z=z', divide the equation by L and separate $\tau(w)$:

$$\tau(w) = z'\,(L_0/L - 1) \tag{69.2'}$$

Trade unions maximize the following equation (83) while taking into account (69) and profit maximizing labor demand – see (70'):

$$L = [(1-\beta)/w]^{\beta}K \tag{70'}$$

Trade unions now maximize the equation while taking into account (69') and (70'):

$$Z = w[1 - \tau(w)]L + w(z') \alpha[L_0 - L]; \text{ we replace the tax rate by (69.2'):} \qquad (83)$$

$$Z = w[1 - z' (L_0/L - 1)] L + wz' \alpha (L_0 - L) \qquad (83')$$

$$= w[L - z'(L_0 - L)] + wz' \alpha (L_0 - L) \qquad (83'')$$

$$Z = wL [1 + (1 - \alpha)z'] - (1 - \alpha)wz'L_0; \text{ we next insert L from (70'):} \qquad (84)$$

$$Z = (1 - \beta)^{\beta} K \left[1 + (1 - \alpha)z'\right] w^{1-\beta} - (1 - \alpha)z'L_0 w \qquad (85)$$

Next we take a closer look at dZ/dw=0 to obtain the optimum w#:

$$\frac{dZ}{dw} = (1 - \beta)^{1+\beta} K \left[1 + (1 - \alpha)z'\right] w^{-\beta} - (1 - \alpha)z'L_0 = 0, \qquad (86)$$

$$w\# = \left(\frac{(1 - \beta)^{1+\beta} K \left[1 - (1 - \alpha)z'\right]}{(1 - \alpha)z'L_0}\right)^{1/\beta}. \qquad (87)$$

The larger ß is, the higher will be the optimum w#. The smaller a (that is the higher 1-a), the smaller w# which is rather paradox: The less the trade union cares about income accruing to the unemployed the less it will push for a high real wage rate. The larger z' – that is the smaller z – the lower the desired wage rate w#. This also is rather paradox since it suggests that governments with a generous unemployment system (that is wage replacement regime) will face less the risk of excessive wage pressure. There is, of course, a caveat here since we do have inelastic labor supply and thus are not analyzing how the unemployment insurance system will affect effective labor supply.

Compare (87) to profit maximization and full employment, respectively, namely the equation

$$L_0 = [(1 - ß)/w]^{ß} K \text{ or } w = (1 - ß)(K/L_0)^{1/ß} \qquad (88)$$

Hence (87) is consistent with this only if $\{(1-ß)^{1+ß}[1-(1- \alpha)z']/[(1- \alpha)z']=1$; w# will exceed the full employment wage rate if $(1-ß)^{1+ß}[1-(1- \alpha)z']/[(1- \alpha)z']>1$. From (87) in combination with (70') we can derive the z'# which government should chose. If z'# is politically not feasible there will be no full employment.

$$(1-ß)^{1+ß}[1-(1- \alpha)z'] = [1- \alpha]z' \qquad (87.1)$$

We now assume that ß and $-(1- \alpha)z'$ and α are rather small so that we can use the approximation ln $(1+x) \approx x$.

$$-(1+ß)(-ß) -(1- \alpha)z' = - \alpha + z' \qquad (87.2)$$

$$\alpha +(1+\beta)\beta = z'[\, 2- \alpha] \tag{87.3}$$

Hence we obtain the full-employment preserving z# as:

$$z\#=1-[\alpha +(1+\beta)\beta]/[2- \alpha] \tag{87.4}$$

There is only a certain range of parameters under which z falls in the interval 0,1. If ß is rising and hence (1-ß) is falling z should fall. However, it is unclear whether government will be able to impose a corresponding z#.

The second order condition for a maximum of Z is negative:

$$\frac{d^2 Z}{dw^2} = -\beta(1-\beta)^{1+\beta} K\left[1+(1-\alpha)z'\right]w^{-(1+\beta)} < 0. \tag{88}$$

Appendix E.2: Mathematical Appendix

$$dY=c'(1-\tau)dY+c'd(M/P)+c''dv-hdr+c''m_r dr+h'dv+h''de+xde-\frac{x'Y^*}{Y^2}dY+x'dv \tag{89}$$

$$(1-c'(1-\tau)+\frac{x'Y^*}{Y^2})dY + (h-c'm_r)dr - (h'''+x)de = c'd(\frac{M}{P})+(c''+h''+x'')dv \tag{90}$$

$$d(\frac{M}{P}) = m_Y dY + m_r dr + m_v dv \tag{91a}$$

$$m_Y dY + m_r dr = d(\frac{M}{P}) - m_v dv \tag{91b}$$

$$Q_\varphi dr + Q_v dv + Q_{q*} de + xde + \frac{x'Y^*}{Y^2}dY + x''dv = 0 \tag{92a}$$

$$\frac{x'Y^*}{Y^2}dY + Q_\varphi dr + (Q_{q*} + x)de = -(Q_v + x'')dv \tag{92b}$$

The equation system in matrix notation is:

$$\begin{pmatrix} k_1 & h-c'm_r & -(h'''+x) \\ m_Y & m_r & 0 \\ \dfrac{x'Y*}{Y^2} & Q_\varphi & Q_{q^*}+x \end{pmatrix} \begin{pmatrix} dY \\ dr \\ de \end{pmatrix} = \begin{pmatrix} c' & c''+h''+x'' \\ 1 & -m_v \\ 0 & -(Q_v+x'') \end{pmatrix} \begin{pmatrix} d(\dfrac{M}{P}) \\ dv \end{pmatrix} \tag{93}$$

$$k_1 = 1 - c'(1-\tau) + \frac{x'Y*}{Y^2}$$

Define $a = 1 - c'(1-\tau) + \dfrac{x'Y*}{Y^2}$, then we have the system determinant:

$$|A| = \{am_r(Q_{q^*}+x) - (h-c'm_r)m_Y(Q_{q^*}+x)\} + [-(h'''+x)(m_YQ_\varphi - m_r\frac{x'Y*}{Y^2})]\,\mathrm{I}$$

f $\{...\}$ exceeds $[...]$: $|A|<0$; if Q_φ and $|m_r|$ are sufficiently small, then $|A|<0$.

$$\frac{de}{dv} = \frac{1}{|A|} \begin{vmatrix} a & h-c'm_r & c''+h''+x'' \\ m_Y & m_r & -m_v \\ \dfrac{x''Y*}{Y^2} & Q_\varphi & -(Q_v+x'') \end{vmatrix} = \tag{94}$$

$$\frac{1}{|A|}\left\{ a\left[m_r(-Q_v-x'')+m_vQ_\varphi \right] - (h-c'm_r)m_Y\left[-m_Y(Q_v+x'')+\frac{x'Y*}{Y^2}m_v \right] \right. \tag{95}$$

$$\left. +b'(m_YQ_\varphi - m_r\frac{x'Y*}{Y^2}) \right\} < 0$$

Whereas $b' = c'' + h'' + x''$.
For Y* > critical Y_0* (home country is relatively small), second term in squared brackets then is positive.

$$\frac{dY}{dv} = \frac{1}{|A|} \begin{vmatrix} c''+h''+x'' & h-c'm_r & -(h'''+x) \\ -m_v & m_r & 0 \\ -(Q_v+x'') & Q_\varphi & Q_{q^*}+x \end{vmatrix} \tag{96}$$

$$= \frac{1}{|A|}((c''+h''+x'')m_r(Q_{q^*}+x) + hm_v(Q_{q^*}+x)$$

$$+ (h'''+x)(m_vQ_\varphi - m_r(Q_v+x'')))$$

Sufficient condition for $\dfrac{dY}{dv} > 0$ is that $\left| m_r Q_v - m_v Q_\varphi \right| > \left| m_r x^{''} \right|$.

$$(97)$$

$$\frac{dr}{dv} = \frac{1}{|A|} \begin{vmatrix} a & c^{''} + h^{''} + x^{''} & -(h^{'''} + x) \\ m_y & -m_v & 0 \\ \dfrac{x'y*}{y^2} & -Q_v - x^{''} & Q_{q*} + x \end{vmatrix}$$

$$= [-am_v(Q_{q^*} + x) - bm_Y(Q_{q*} + x) + (h^{'''} + x)[m_Y(Q_v + x^{''})$$

$$- m_v(x^{''} + \frac{x'Y*}{Y^2})]$$

Appendix E.3: Reflections on EU Eastern Enlargement

Eight transition countries will join the EU in 2004: On May 1, 2004 there will be an EU Eastern enlargement, and this will be the largest EU expansion to date. The population of the EU will increase by 1/5, national income of the EU by some 5% (of EU-15 GDP) at face value and by about 10% if purchasing power standards, which take into account the fact that the prices of nontradables are still relatively lower in accession countries compared to EU-15, are used. The accession countries have benefited from pre-accession EU transfers and also from asymmetric trade liberalization in Europe. The Commission has estimated that the growth rates of the accession countries will be in the range of 4.5% to 6% in the period from 2005 to 2009, which is clearly above the estimated 3% growth projected in a simulation without accession (SOLBES, 2004). EU accession countries will benefit from adopting the EU legal system – the acquis communautaire – which makes investment less risky but some business ventures also more complex to organize. EU accession countries of Eastern Europe are former socialist countries which adopted a very broad range of new institutions and policy patterns in the transformation decade of the 1990s when they also opened up to the world economy and reoriented trade strongly towards Western Europe. Accession countries will benefit from EU transfers for decades which go particularly to regions with per capita income below 75% of EU average (at purchasing power parity), with the average per capita income level of accession countries of Eastern Europe in 2004 close to 45%.

With eastern enlargement, there will be ten new countries in the EU – eight from Eastern Europe – plus Malta and Cyprus, whereby the latter is a Mediterranean island divided between a Greek population in the West and a majority of Turkish people in the East. Cyprus is difficult political turf, but it also is the home of Russia's largest expatriate banking community. The 1990s were a period of massive capital flight from Russia and the echo effect particularly found root in the dynamic banking scene in Cyprus and massive "Cyprian" (read: Russian) foreign direct investment in Russia. EU eastern enlargement also brings major changes for the Community and Russia as the latter will suffer from trade diversion. Russia's exports of industrial goods – disregarding oil and gas – will decline, in particular due to the protective nature of EU standards. Moreover, the people of the new Russia face exclusion in the sense that almost all European countries are no longer accessible for Russians without a visa. The situation will become worse after Bulgaria and Romania join the Community in 2007. Russia also feels threatened by Nato enlargement which is organized on the side of Western Europe and the US with utter disregard for Russian interests, creating a feeling of alienation in the new Russia. Nato enlargement is also an eastern enlargement, but while Brussels is the center of gravitation of EU eastern enlargement, it is Washington which is steering Nato enlargement. The Bush administration obviously wants to get Nato involved in many new hot spots, including Iraq where some new Nato members from Eastern Europe are already active. Poland, whose president obviously expected to gain in prestige and political clout from following the Bush administration into Iraq, is one example. Foreign adventure to compensate for social tensions at home is not a new motive in politics. The borrowed prestige is in stark contrast to the weak economy in Poland. EU accession countries might, however, be tempted to follow the US in military adventures in more regions, and this brings Europe back to Africa and Asia in a second wave of quasi-colonial activities, this time under the US umbrella. Germany has so far been hesitant to follow the US, but there is little doubt that a future conservative government might close ranks with the US again.

The enlarged Community is a new mixture of advanced OECD countries and relatively poor countries which are characterized by wage rates that are roughly 1/9 of that in Germany. Certainly, productivity of firms in Germany is higher than those in EU accession countries, but it is clear that there will be a new international division of labor in EU-25. Labor-intensive production and partly capital intensive production as well will be relocated to accession countries which therefore naturally become important markets for German exports of investment goods. As EU enlargement goes along with heavy investment in upgrading infrastructure in accession countries, both eastern European supplier firms and exporters will find faster and cheaper access to EU-15 markets in the future. From an EU-15 perspective, it holds that import competition from EU accession countries will therefore grow. At the same time, firms in high wage countries such as Germany, France, Austria or Sweden will have to specialize more on goods using technology and human capital intensively.

The EU enlargement of 2004 means that the Community population will increase by some 70 million inhabitants, whereby Poland is the largest country with 39 million people. In 2002, per capita income relative to EU-15 was 73.7% for the leading country, Slovenia, followed by 59.8% for the Czech Republic and Hungary with 55.9%. At the bottom level were Poland, Lithuania and Latvia which stood at 39.4%, 39.1% and 35.2%, respectively. Figures for Bulgaria, Romania and Turkey were 24.7, 24.5 and 22.9%, respectively; for 2006 the forecast figures (EUROPEAN COMMISSION, 2003) are 28%, 27.6% and 24.5%, respectively. Except for Slovenia and Hungary with inflation rates of 7.5% and 5.3% in 2002, inflation rates were low in accession countries in 2002 and are expected to remain low in 2006 with the relevant range between 0% and 3%. In line with relatively low per capita income, the consumer price level in Eastern European accession countries in 2002 was around ½ of EU-15, except for Slovenia and Poland where the price level stood at 70 and 61, respectively. The unemployment rate was very high in Poland in 2002/03, namely close to 20%; in the Slovak Republic and in Lithuania it reached about 18% and 14%, respectively. At the same time, Poland had the highest participation rate, namely 76%.

Current account imbalances are not a major problem for accession countries, except for Estonia and Poland. If Poland's current account deficit should grow over time, the country might face a major depreciation and a confidence crisis associated with sudden capital outflows and hence rising interest rates. One-third of Poland's government debt is foreign debt. If Poland should face a major crisis in the future, both Germany and the Euroland will have to find an answer to the question addressing the extent to which a problem of a major neighbouring country is considered a common interest worth solving. If such a problem should emerge, neither the German government nor the ECB is likely to be very forthcoming with financial and political support to stabilize the country; there is no pretext with respect to this. However, as much as the US has always helped its neighbouring country, Mexico, through a financial crisis, there are good reasons why Germany and the EU should not treat Polish problems with a benign neglect attitude.

From the perspective of EU-15 countries and Germany, current account deficits in accession countries are rather welcome if they remain manageable for the respective countries; the mirror position of EU-15 countries are net exports of goods and services which stimulate the rise of national output. If EU accession countries' import growth would mainly reflect higher imports of investment goods, a current account deficit would be only a temporary problem since one may assume that rising production potential will contribute to higher production and exports in the future.

The EU will face quickly massive internal problems if serious financial market problems in accession countries should emerge in a period of slow growth in EU-15 core countries. Germany together with Italy is the weak core of the EU in the first decade of the 21st century. Both countries are aging rapidly and both countries have serious problems in their political systems for adopting adequate political reforms. What the North-South divide is for Italy is more or less the East-West divide of Germany. Moreover, the fact that Germany's per capita income (at figures based on purchasing power parity) fell below the EU average in 2003 is shocking news for the largest EU economy. The longer slow growth continues, the more EU partner countries in Western and Eastern Europe will suffer from this.

Table 7. Selected Macroeconomic Indicators for EU Accession Countries and Turkey

Consumer price inflation (annual % change)	2002	2006
Cyprus	2,8	2,0
Czech Rep.	1,8	2,5
Estonia	3,6	3,2
Hungary	5,3	3,0
Latvia	1,9	3,0
Lithuania	0,3	2,6
Malta	2,2	2,0
Poland	1,9	2,9
Slovak Rep.	3,3	3,0
Slovenia	7,5	3,7
Bulgaria	5,8	3,9
Romania	22,5	6,0
Turkey	45,0	6,2
EU	2,1	:

Gross domestic product	average annual real growth rate		GDP/head (PPS, in % of EU average)	
	1998-2002	2003-2006	2002	2006
Cyprus	4,2	3,8	72,3	77,3
Czech Rep.	1,5	3,0	59,8	62,0
Estonia	4,7	5,5	41,7	47,6
Hungary	4,3	4,0	55,9	60,2
Latvia	5,7	6,2	35,2	41,2
Lithuania	4,5	6,4	39,1	46,1
Malta	2,8	2,7	na	na
Poland	5,4	4,7	39,4	43,5
Slovak Rep.	3,0	4,3	47,3	51,6
Slovenia	3,9	3,9	73,7	79,0
Bulgaria	4,1	5,3	24,7	28,0
Romania	1,4	5,2	24,5	27,6
Turkey	1,2	5,2	22,9	24,5
EU	2,4		100,0	100,0

* without demographic effects; candidate countries growth rates 2003-06: PEPs; EU Growth rates 2003-04: Spring 2003 COM forecast; EU growth rates 2005-06: 2,4%

Current account balance (% of GDP)	2002	2006
Cyprus	-5,3	-1,4
Czech Rep.	-6,5	-6,2
Estonia	-12,3	-9,0
Hungary	-4,0	-5,0
Latvia	-7,8	-7,6
Lithuania	-5,3	-5,6
Malta	-4,7	-4,4
Poland	-3,5	-5,1
Slovak Rep.	-8,2	-3,3
Slovenia	1,7	1,1
Bulgaria	-4,4	-3,8
Romania	-3,4	-4,6
Turkey	-0,8	-1,2
EU	-0,2	

Consumer price levels (in % of EU-15)	2002	2006
Cyprus	90	92
Czech Rep.	47	47
Estonia	52	54
Hungary	50	55
Latvia	52	54
Lithuania	51	51
Malta	n/a	n/a
Poland	61	61
Slovak Rep.	42	50
Slovenia	70	77
Bulgaria	41	43
Romania	49	67
Turkey	71	a)
EU	100	100

Inflation rates : PEPs; EU: 2%; const. Nominal exchange rates a) not meaningful

General government debt				Labour markets					
	(% of GDP)		foreign debt (% of total debt, 2002)		Unemploy-ment rate[1]		Participation rate[2]		
	2002	2006			2002	2006	2002	2006	
Cyprus	59,7	56,1	22,9	Cyprus	3,2	3,0	70,0	70,0	
Czech Rep.	26,9	39,4	2,3	Czech Rep.	7,3	7,5	71,1	70,9	
Estonia	5,8	4,6	93,0	Estonia	10,3	9,2	62,3	62,5	
Hungary	56,3	54,0	n/a	Hungary	5,8	5,8	59,7	61,5	
Latvia	14,6	17,4	61,5 [1]	Latvia	12,0	10,1	68,8	68,8	
Lithuania	22,7	23,3	69,9 [1]	Lithuania	14,0	10,2	69,3	70,5	
Malta	66,6	68,4		Malta	5,2	4,9	56,8	58,0	
Poland	41,8	49,1	33,1 [1]	Poland	19,7	n/a[4]	76,4	76,1	
Slovak Rep.	44,3	48,5		Slovak Rep.	18,5	16,1	70,0	70,3	
Slovenia	27,8	25,9	41,1	Slovenia	6,4	5,0	67,8	68,3	
Bulgaria	56,2	39,0	88,4	Bulgaria	17,8	14,0	53,3	54,4	
Romania	22,7	25,1	55,0	Romania	8,4	6,8	47,1	46,4	
Turkey	102,5	83,2	47,0	Turkey	10,3	9,6	49,6	50,8	
EU	63,1			EU	8,2	:	:	:	
1: central governement				1: ILO definition 2: Age 15-64 3: Population aged 15 years and over 4: rates based on registered unemployed: 2002: 18,1%;					

Source: European Commission, 2003 Pre-Accession Economic Programme of the Acceding and Other Candidate Countries: Overview and Assessment

Poland is the largest accession country with close to 40 million people. However, the country is weak in economic terms with its unemployment rate reaching 20% in 2004. This is not intended to overshadow the considerable growth rate of 3-4% p.a. in recent years. However, for a poor country which reaches less than 50% of EU-15 per capita income, one should indeed expect high growth rates in the context of economic and technological catching-up. The Polish economy made enormous progress after a bold comprehensive transformation in the early 1990s. Successive governments have been slow to modernize infrastructure, however, where for instance building a highway between Warsaw and Berlin is moving forward at a snail's pace. On the positive side, one should emphasize that the inflation rate is very low and the trade balance deficit does not present a serious problem. Rather Poland has recorded a surplus vis-à-vis Germany in 2003 for the first time in a decade. At the same time it is true that Poland is facing rising social tensions as its society is divided in young dynamic strata with rising real incomes and a large number of poor – and often – unemployed people. The creation of more firms is of utmost importance for Poland, but indigenous entrepreneurial dynamics are likely to suffer in the context of EU accession as regulations will become more complex and costly. In addition, access to bank loans could become more difficult as Polish banks will have to obey the stricter rules of Basel II principles of prudential supervision. Warsaw is a very dynamic city with many students in private and public universities with many foreign students, including a minority from Arab countries (and it has been stated that for years Palestinian students attended Polish universities, in most cases studying seriously, however in certain cases students came simply to recover from "action" in the Middle East). On both sides of the German-Polish border, unemployment rates are very high, namely close to 20%.

It is not only Poland which is having problems stimulating growth and employment. There are indeed similar problems in eastern Germany where productivity levels in 1991 stood at 1/3 of western Germany, but at 2/3 in 1999. Since then the productivity gap has not closed. There has been some industrial revival in 2003/04 in eastern Germany, but East Germany suffers from a lack of entrepreneurs, a declining population – there is continuing East-West migration within Germany – and insufficient government spending on public investment and promotion of innovation. At the same time, East Germany is spending too much on civil servants, as there is overstaffing in parts of the government bureaucracy.

EU accession countries have adopted very low corporate tax rates (e.g. 15% in the Slovak Republic) which in turn forced Austria to reduce its corporate tax rate to 20% in 2003. A major weakness of EU eastern enlargement is that the EU-15 has not imposed a minimum corporate tax rate which would be binding for all accession countries after a transition period. Indeed, it is strange that German taxpayers contribute heavily to the EU budget which in effect means that accession countries – getting EU structural funds of up to 4% of gross domestic product – use German taxes to artificially reduce corporate tax rates. As a consequence, there will be accelerated relocation of industry from EU-15 to accession countries. With corporate tax rates effectively reduced to below 20% in the Community, the implication is that mainly workers of EU-15 countries finance tax reductions for corporations with their tax payments. Worse yet, strange tax competition in the EU leads to a weakening of growth and employment in EU-15 which must not be the ultimate goal of EU enlargement. If the strange tax competition would allow accession countries - representing roughly 1/10 of EU GDP – to raise output growth by one percentage point while the growth rate in EU-15 would be reduced by 1/5 of a percentage point the net effect for the community would clearly be negative. To avoid any misunderstanding: countries which are not obtaining major EU transfers should be free to have low corporate tax rates, but it is inappropriate for countries obtaining massive transfers to adopt low rates.

Germany and other EU countries – including those of Eastern Europe – could benefit from a certain growth acceleration effect associated with the expansion of information and communication technology (WELFENS, 2003; VAN ARK/PIAT-KOWSKI, 2004). In Germany, the government has adopted several initiatives including a private public partnership project (D21) which has stimulated reforms. It is noteworthy that the head of the advisory committee, Chancellor Schröder, has participated in all sessions of the committee which is a clear signal the he takes this field quite seriously. At the bottom line, Germany has adopted many new reforms, but only a few of them really meet the challenges ahead – setting adequate priorities has not been a hallmark of government. EU eastern enlargement will bring new pressure to accelerate reforms. However, short-sighted politicians are not very likely to adopt those reforms which are most necessary. Germany is unlikely to record high growth in the coming years unless the government adopts a more professional and consistent set of policy elements.

If Germany should continue to face rising unemployment and slow growth over many years as well as the prospect of EU membership for Turkey, one should not rule out the possibility of debate about a reunited Germany leaving the enlarged community. One can only warn against illusory policy as supported by EU Commissioner Verheugen, who would support Turkey's quick accession into the Community. Neither Germany, the EU-25 nor Turkey are in good shape, and international politics have become quite complicated not least of which is due to the problems of terrorism. Responsible policymakers interested in preserving a stable and dynamic Community should first successfully digest EU eastern enlargement before embarking upon new enlargement dreams. The enlargement of the Federal Republic of Germany, that is German unification, has shown everybody how difficult the merger of two very different countries really is. With Turkey the situation is even much more difficult, not least because the Turkish population is growing by about 1 million p.a.; the country will have some 120 million inhabitants by 2050. Germany alone can be expected to attract some 5 million Turkish immigrants in the period 2020-2050 (assuming that Turkey were to become a full EU member by 2020). Mr. Verheugen's view that full EU membership of Turkey could be combined with restrictions on labor mobility in the EU is illusory since the European Court of Justice has stated in its rulings that restrictions on labor mobility can only be temporary for EU member countries.

Appendix E.4: Fiscal Multiplier in a Hybrid Approach

A hybrid approach can be written as follows: Output is a weighted sum of the production potential and aggregate demand.

$$Y = \alpha Y^{pot} + (1-\alpha) Y^d \tag{98}$$

To see the implication of a medium term analysis – with $\alpha = 1-u$ – one may consider the case of closed economy with consumption $C = cY$, investment $I(r)$ and exogenous government consumption G; and production potential $Y^{pot} = K^\beta L^{1-\beta}$ (K is capital, L is labor, $0 < \beta < 1$). Hence we can rewrite equation (1) as follows

$$Y = [1-u] K^\beta L^{1-\beta} + u \{cY + I(r)+G\} \tag{98'}$$

$$dY/dG = 1/[1-uc] \tag{98''}$$

Only if the unemployment rate approaches unit we get the familiar Keynesian multiplier $dY/dG = 1/[1-c]$. For any positive unemployment rate below unity the multiplier for fiscal policy is smaller than the standard textbook result.

Appendix E.5: Reconsidering Aggregate Output in a Two-Sector Approach

Assume that aggregate demand consists of tradables demand T and nontradables demand N, the relative price between tradables and nontradables is φ. We can thus state, as an equilibrium condition for the goods market (with Y^{pot} denoting potential aggregate output) in a fully employed economy:

$$Y^{pot} = N + \varphi T \tag{99a}$$

Instead – and assuming for simplicity $\varphi=1$ - we may state:

$$[Y^{pot}]^{\sigma'(N,T)} = N^{\sigma'(N,T)} T^{1-\sigma'(N,T)} \tag{99b}$$

The elasticity σ' depends on N and T in a way which is not clear here (more on this subsequently). We can thus state

$$\sigma'(N,T) \ln Y^{pot} = \sigma'(N,T) \ln N + [1- \sigma'(N,T)]\ln T \tag{99b'}$$

Thus the elasticity of potential output with respect to N-demand is unity and with respect to tradables demand is $(1-\sigma)/\sigma$. This elasticity should not be confused with the pure output elasticity for the case of a production function (say $Y^{pot}=K^{\beta}L^{1-\beta}$ where K and L are respectively, capital input and labor input). Why can we state equation Ib? Note simply that for any two variables A and B ($A\neq 0$; $B\neq 0$) the following equation holds – with a specific exponent α:

$$[A+B]^{\alpha} = A^{\alpha} B^{\alpha} \tag{99c}$$

Taking logarithms results in:

$$\alpha\{\ln[A+B] - \ln A + \ln B\} = \ln B \tag{99d}$$

Hence the above equation (99d) holds for

$$\alpha = \{[\ln[A+B]/\ln B] - [\ln A/\ln B] + 1\}^{-1} \tag{99e}$$

A useful approximation is $\ln[A+B] - \ln A \approx \ln B - n'\ln A$.

$$\alpha = \{2 - [[1-n]\ln A/\ln B]\}^{-1} \tag{99e'}$$

Moreover, for the special case that A+B are normalized to unity α is even simpler:

$$\alpha = \{[\ln A/\ln B] + 1\}^{-1} \tag{99f}$$

An interesting application of this theorem in mathematics – with many useful applications in Economics - is the familiar goods market equilibrium condition in macroeconomic analysis (C is consumption, I investment, Y real income):

$$Y = C + I \tag{99g}$$

Without loss of generality we can state instead

$$Y^{\alpha} = C^{\alpha} + I^{1-\alpha} \tag{99h}$$

Hence

$$\ln Y = \ln C + \{[1/[1/\alpha] - 1\}\ln I \tag{99i}$$

If we assume a consumption function C=cY we can state:

$$\ln Y = \ln c + \ln Y - \{[2- [1-n][(\ln c + \ln Y)/\ln I]\ln I \tag{99j}$$

Hence we can easily calculate the elasticity of Y with respect to a change in exogenous investment I.

Alternatively one can consider an investment function (with e' denoting the Euler number) $I = e^{-\mu'r}$.

Basically the equilibrium line for the goods market can be drawn in lnY-r space.

F. Productivity Shocks, Innovations, Stock Market Dynamics and Growth

F.1 Introduction

The banking business in the late 20th century has undergone profound changes. A first aspect is that the speed of adjustment in financial markets has increased in the course of digitization, computer expansion and the internet revolution, at the same time bringing down heavily prices of transactions in financial markets and thus contributing to the internationalization of financial markets and banking. A second key aspect is economic globalization with the result that for many financial products there exists a global market in which only a few large banks compete. A third element is that prudential supervision has started to emphasize risk-based equity requirements – indeed, Basel II rules will bring about broader spreads across different classes of loan risk. A fourth element is the increasing role of investment banking and the role of international mergers & acquisitions which accounted for roughly 3/5 of foreign direct investment in the 1990s. This in turn reinforces the role of stock markets on whose dynamics our analysis will focus. Moreover, in the presence of imperfect capital markets there is a renewed interest in the development of the real exchange rate since it will affect foreign direct investment: FROOT/STEIN (1991) have emphasized that a real depreciation of the currency of the host country implies that equity capital of foreign bidders – expressed in terms of the currency of the host country - is increased so that a successful leveraged international M&A will become more likely; FDI inflows will increase. Defining the real exchange rate of country I (home country) as $q=P/eP*$ or $q*= eP*/P$ where e is the nominal exchange rate and P the price level (*denotes foreign variables) it is clear that both nominal exchange rate dynamics and changes in the sticky price level at home and abroad will affect the real exchange rate. Our analytical focus will be partly on short term stock market dynamics in open economies which we define as having trade and foreign direct investment inflows. We will present a new short term model which models the interaction of money market, stock market and foreign exchange rate. Moreover, a medium term model based on the capital asset pricing model will be presented and finally we will plug the stock market into a modified growth model. Indeed, we will emphasize the role of stock markets for short-term and long term dynamics.

As regards the potential relevance of research on stock markets – and related wealth effects – it is clear that the impact of changes in the real wealth of stocks is rather small in many countries. E.g. as regards the impact of changes in stock market prices empirical analysis points to only a minor impact on consumption in cross-country analysis. However, observing individual countries could reveal a different story; a priori one would expect a relatively large impact on consumption and savings, if the share of stocks in overall wealth is relatively large and if a sizable share of the population owns stocks: This is for instance the case in the US, the UK and Sweden. One may, however, also raise the issue as to why theoretical and empirical analysis finds investment dependent on stock market dynamics – in a simple equilibrium growth model this implies that savings must also be affected by the stock market. E.g. a simple approach is to assume that savings depends on the real interest rate r and the ratio of (exogenous) target wealth A'^T to actual wealth A' which for simplicity one may consider as to be comprised of real money balances M/P and the real value of stocks P'K/P where P' is the stock market price level, K is the capital stock – equal to the number of stocks – and P is the output price level. A sustained increase in P'/P should translate into a fall of savings as the gap between the wealth target and actual wealth has fallen. Since stock markets are very volatile it is clear that people will discount stock market prices strongly. Another caveat to the relevance of the stock market is that when considering wealth, real estate is more important than stock market dynamics for macroeconomic development. In many OECD countries real estate is somewhat higher than the value of stock market capitalization. While it is true that real estate is an important variable, in particular in countries with a high share of owner-occupied housing (e.g. US, UK, France, Spain), one should not overlook the fact that stock market capitalization relative to GDP has increased considerably in the 1990s. Taking a look at the Great Depression also reveals a strong impact of stock markets, although one should emphasize that the respective dynamics could be covered adequately in a disequilibrium model.

Stock markets have strongly shaped economic growth in the 1990s as real stock prices and real GDP growth increased in most OECD countries and emerging markets; and when stock market prices collapsed in 2001/02 there was also a considerable fall in output growth. As regards international links among stock market developments, empirical analysis suggests that the US stock market dominates EU stock market developments. From this perspective any overshooting or bubble phenomenon on the US stock market translates into similar movements in other OECD countries. However, it is not fully understood why we observe such international correlations. Within a simple medium term model we will suggest a simple transmission channel which is linked to product innovations and network effects. The model we present is for an innovative small open economy with full capital mobility in the sense that foreign direct investment inflows are allowed.

A special aim of the analysis presented concerns economic catching up on the one hand, on the other hand we want to better understand the links between stock market and exchange rate dynamics with real economic development in leading OECD countries and follower countries. Our analysis presents a model for combining stock market dynamics, the real exchange and capital accumulation dynamics plus product innovations. The paper thus looks into some unchartered waters of modern Economics. As regards policy options we emphasize that governments should try to avoid overshooting in stock markets and foreign exchange markets. Cooperation among leading OECD countries in the field of stock market regulation could be useful. The real exchange rate in catching-up countries typically is expected to increase in the long term (BALASSA-SAMUELSON effect), however, it is unclear how short-term dynamics will affect exchange rate development.

In this context one must bear in mind the implications of the DORNBUSCH model which emphasizes that in a system of flexible exchange rates there can be overshooting stemming from the interaction of sticky prices and fast adjusting exchange rates.

There is a link between the real exchange rate and the burden of the debt. A real depreciation is particularly important for a country with foreign debt since it raises the burden of foreign debt; this effect offsets the stimulating effect of a depreciation of the currency on net exports of goods and services. The literature on pricing to market has undermined previous elasticity optimism – at least in a more short term view. Pricing to market implies that an exchange rate change will not go along with a full exchange rate pass-through. With respect to potential overshooting the problems associated could be more likely than with full pass-through.

There is also a link between the real exchange rate and capital flows, in particular foreign direct investment. A real appreciation, namely a fall of eP^*/P, implies that home firms will find it easier to acquire foreign assets. In imperfect capital markets (FROOT/STEIN, 1991), a fall of eP^*/P implies that at a given relative price of stocks (ratio of stock market price P' to output price level P) both home and abroad, foreign firms (in country II) can be acquired more easily after an appreciation; firms from country I can put up more equity capital as expressed in terms of the foreign currency. Hence they will be able to obtain more loans in the target country than previously so that there is a higher likelihood to outbid rival firms in the target country. A rarely considered implication – not considered by FROOT/STEIN - is that in open economies investment depends on the real exchange rate.

With respect to short-term analysis, with P and P* considered as sticky variables, nominal exchange rate changes are equivalent to real exchange rate changes. Over a long-term perspective price levels are flexible, however, so that discussing the real exchange rate requires us to take a look at both the nominal exchange rate as well as the price level at home and abroad. In a world with tradable (T) goods and (N) nontradable goods, the internal exchange rate is defined as P^T/P^N. It can be shown – we pick up on this point subsequently – that the real exchange rate, q, is related to both the internal exchange rate and relative international sectoral productivity differentials. Economic opening up and economic growth are associated with considerable sectoral changes and hence productivity shifts. Not all countries which have opened up to the world economy have achieved both high productivity growth and real income growth. It will be interesting to focus on this issue and to raise some issues related particularly to productivity growth and the nominal and real exchange rate.

While arbitrage in a two country model with homogeneous traded goods implies that $P^T = eP^T*$ the analysis looks different in a setup with product innovations and heterogeneous goods: It will hold $P^T = V'eP^T*$ where $V' \neq 1$ in equilibrium. In our analysis we are interested in looking into a world with Schumpeterian product innovations. Firms and countries differ in terms of product innovations. In certain countries the size of the market and consumer preferences might be particularly appealing for launching new products, and the large market with high per capita incomes in the US is therefore often an important lead market; this is all the more true since many US multinational companies have a strong record in product innovations and since in new niche markets innovative young firms can often be found. As regards Western Europe there are clearly differences across countries when it comes to per capita income and patenting per capita; and one may distinguish between large and small countries. However, there are also considerable differences in terms of response time to innovative products: time-to-takeoff in years (average time between product introduction on the national market and sales takeoff) was found to be around four years in Denmark, Norway and Sweden, around five years in Finland, Ireland, Belgium, Switzerland and the Netherlands, about six years for Austria and Germany, seven years for Italy, Spain and France and roughly nine years for the UK, Greece and Portugal (TELLIS/STREMERSCH/ YIN, 2003).

Finland and Sweden also are among the leaders in the EU's European Innovation Scorebord (EUROPEAN COMMISSION, 2003, p. 27) when it comes to questions such as:

1. What is the percentage of "new to market products" of all turnover in manufacturing and of all turnover in services, respectively? In the 2003 scoreboard the EU-15 average (with missing data in the case of Ireland, Luxembourg and Netherlands) was 10.5 in manufacturing, while it was 27.2 for the top-leader Finland followed by Italy, Portugal and Denmark with 18.7, 16.0 and 14.3, respectively. In the field of services the EU-15 average was 7.4 (with missing data in the case of Ireland, Netherlands and the UK), while the leaders were Greece, Spain, Finland and Italy with 17.9, 13.7, 12.2 and 11.6, respectively. In the leader countries the price of tradables – in the field of manufacturing and services – should be higher than the EU average to the extent that novel products can fetch higher prices in the market. The data must be interpreted with caution since many products are newly introduced in the national market while this product does not necessarily stand for a global product innovation. If we concentrate on manufacturing products – typically all tradable - in high income countries where products new to the market should normally also mean new to the world market, Denmark has a clear lead, trailed by France and the UK with 9.5 for both countries, followed by Austria and Germany with 8.4 and 7.1, respectively. As a general hypothesis we expect that an increase in the share of new products to the market – relative to the EU average - will go along with a relative rise of the tradables price in the respective country. From a Schumpeterian perspective it is thus not adequate to assume the law of one price to hold strictly.

2. What is the percentage of "new to the firm but not new to the market products", namely as a percentage of all turnover in manufacturing and of all turnover in services, respectively? In manufacturing, the EU-15 average (data missing for Ireland) was 28.6, while leaders were Germany, Sweden, Finland and Italy with 40.3, 32.1, 31.1 and 30.1, respectively, they are followed by Spain, Denmark and the Netherlands (25.8, 24.2 and 23.8, respectively). In services the EU-15 average (data missing for Ireland) was 18.8, while leaders were Greece, Spain, Sweden and Belgium scoring 37.1, 26.4, 23.7 and 23.5, respectively. Leading

countries here indicate a high ability for imitation. It is, however, not ruled out that relatively poor countries have a relatively high score in the imitation index simply because they are catching up. As regards relatively poor countries one should not underestimate the role of diffusion in economic catching up. In the context of EU eastern enlargement this implies that firms in accession countries should perform well in imitation in the medium term. Over the longer term, the role of true innovations should gain importance, and this should become visible in international patent statistics.

In the literature the traditional analysis of the link between catching-up and relative price changes is the Balassa-Samuelson effect. This effect – narrowly defined - suggests that the relative price of nontradables will increase along with a rise in per capita income (BALASSA, 1964; SAMUELSON, 1964). Basically, the reason could be that income elasticity for nontradables is higher than for tradables or that during economic catching-up productivity growth in the tradables sector is higher than in the nontradables sector. An alternative definition of the Balassa-Samuelson effect –broadly defined – is that the real exchange rate will rise along with the growth of per capita income. As is well known the two types of Balassa-Samuelson effect are linked to each other, and we will pick up on this later.

Under flexible exchange rates the foreign exchange market determines – as part of an interdependent system of macro markets – the nominal equilibrium exchange rate. The short-term exchange rate is consistent with a long-term fundamental equilibrium exchange rate only if all other macro markets (including the goods market and the labor market) are also in equilibrium. Hence there are different analytical time horizons with respect to exchange rate analysis. Moreover, if we look at a given economy, it is important to consider the goods market and the labor market first; if these markets are in equilibrium and the exchange rate clears in a situation of a roughly balanced current account, we have an equilibrium real exchange rate.

Very short term models are based on the analysis of financial markets, where the Branson model is a standard approach. A well-known medium-term analytical framework is the Mundell-Flemming model for an economy with unemployment. A simple full employment model is the model from MUNDELL (1968), who emphasized the distinction between tradable goods and nontradable goods. More recent contributions to the literature with a particular focus on the Balassa-Samuelson effect, are from DE GREGORIO/WOLF (1994), HALPERN/ WYPLOSZ (1997), CHIN/JOHNSTON (1997), MALISZEWSKA (1997), KRAJNYAK/ZETTELMEYER (1998), CANZONERI/CUMBY/DIBA (1999), GRAFE/WYPLOSZ (1999), CIPRIANI (2000), ROTHER (2000), SZAPARY (2000). It is worth mentioning that the real exchange rate can increase relatively quickly during economic catching up, e.g., the case of Spain in the European Monetary System by 25% between 1986 und 1993. Several eastern European EU accession countries have also recorded phases of high real appreciation in the late 1990s. Many accession countries have also recorded a rise of the relative price of nontradables.

There are, however, no models considering the long-term link between growth/technology and the real exchange rate. As such, we will present the first such model. At the same time there is also no model dealing with very short-term financial market analysis and economic catching up which marks – along the time axis – the other extreme. Short-term exchange rate developments can have considerable effects, possibly including foreign debt problems if there is a strong short depreciation such as overshooting effects in a country with high foreign debt. Thus we will present both a very short-term financial market model (namely an augmented BRANSON model) and a long-term model of the real exchange rate. Additionally we will present some new ideas on the role between economic catching up and the exchange rate in the context of a modified perspective on Balassa-Samuelson effects related to the rise of the real exchange rate and the relative price of nontradables in the context of economic catching-up. We will first present the very short term financial market analysis, followed by a refined medium term model for Balassa-Samuelson effects in the context of product innovation; moreover, we suggest a basic approach for analysing the long term real exchange rate, where relative innovativeness also plays a key role. As a medium term approach we consider a modified Mundell Fleming model: we integrate product innovations into the model. We model innovativeness as changes in total factor productivity, product innovations and capital productivity changes. In the very short term model the focus is on productivity shocks, while the medium term and long term analysis put the focus, respectively, on product and process innovations.

The analysis suggests that relative international innovativeness is a crucial determinant for both the short term exchange rate, the medium term rate and the long term rate. As the medium term model suggests that the equilibrium nominal exchange rate could rise or fall as a consequence of a relative rise in per capita income (y/y^*; with y standing for per capita income) there are some doubts about a system of fixed exchange rates – in particular for countries catching up. As the ratio of research and development expenditures to GDP is increasing in OECD countries and Newly Industrializing Countries so that innovation dynamics intensify globally, one may indeed argue that in a world with stronger Schumpeterian innovation dynamics there are arguments for adopting more flexible exchange rate systems. As regards the 1980s und 1990s it is noteworthy that relative innovativeness – as proxied by patent applications per capita and other variables – has witnessed considerable shifts in Europe and across OECD countries (JUNGMITTAG, 2003, 2003a).

F.2 Traditional and New Approaches to the Exchange Rate and Stock Market Dynamics

F.2.1 Stylized Facts of Exchange Rates and Stock Market Prices

Let us first take a closer look at the links between the exchange rate e and stock market price at home P' and abroad P'*. As regards nominal exchange rate dynamics and stock market fluctuations it is not surprising that the growth rate of the exchange rate is strongly positively correlated to the growth rate of the price of the stock market – such linkage reflects a kind of interest parity in the sense that international arbitrage requires that the growth rate of the stock market price at home should be equal to the expected sum of the growth rate of the stock price index abroad plus the anticipated relative change of the exchange rate (WELFENS, 2001): Due to such arbitrage it will hold (g denotes growth rate):

$$g_{P'} = g_e + g_{P'}* \tag{1}$$

There is empirical evidence (WELFENS, 2001)– including a nice out-of-sample forecast – that a simple model of the euro-dollar exchange rate based on the independent variables nominal interest rate at home and abroad plus the change of stock prices at home and abroad can explain exchange rate development; and the modelling brings indeed a nice out-of-sample forecast.

According to (1') it must be true that for a given percent change of the foreign stock price index there must be a parallel movement of the domestic stock market price and the exchange rate e. Indeed, if foreign (read US) stock market price dynamics strongly influence domestic (read: eg European) stock market price dynamics – eg for simplicity gP'=(1-x)gP'* where x is between 0 and 1 – it is clear that the depreciation rate must run rather parallel to the stock market price changes. The US and Japan seem to indicate such a link while German dynamics are more difficult to interpret. What we can also see is that the stock market volatility on the basis of three-months-moving averages of monthly average figures is greater than the exchange rate variability. What is, of course, interesting is the covariance of the exchange rate and the stock price index.

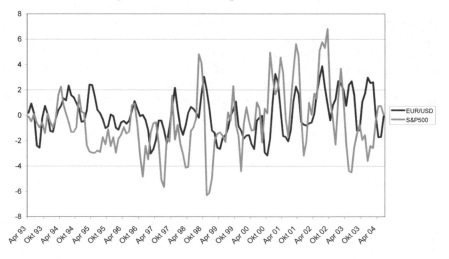

Fig. 43. Exchange Rate and Stock Market Dynamics in the US (3-months moving average)

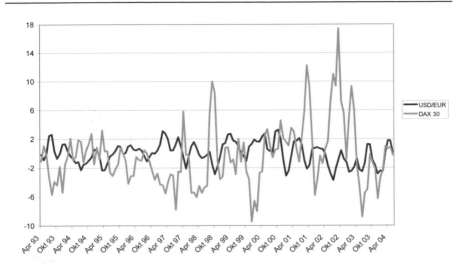

Fig. 44. Exchange Rate and Stock Market Dynamics in Germany (3-months moving average)

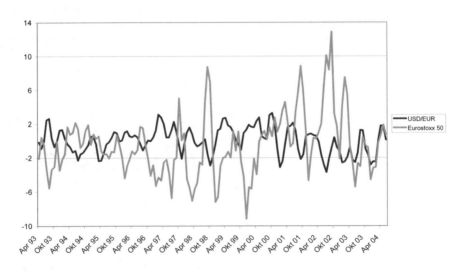

Fig. 45. Exchange Rate and Stock Market Dynamics in Europe (3-months moving average)

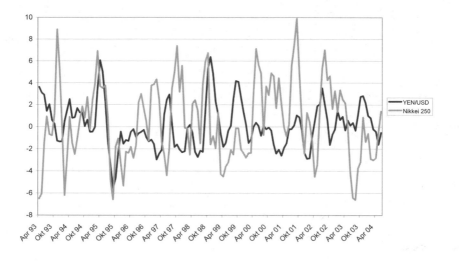

Fig. 46. Exchange Rate and Stock Market Dynamics in Japan (3-months moving average)

Taking a closer look at Eastern European countries and Newly Industrializing Countries one also finds a high volatility of stock market prices, while the volatility of the exchange rate is rather limited: this is probably due to the fact that central banks have adopted some implicit pegging of the exchange rate.

As regards levels of the stock market indices of various countries it is obvious that the US dominates many foreign stock markets.

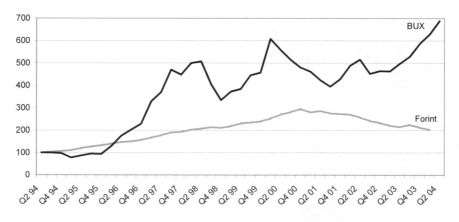

Fig. 47. Exchange Rate and Stock Market Dynamics in Hungary (annual data)

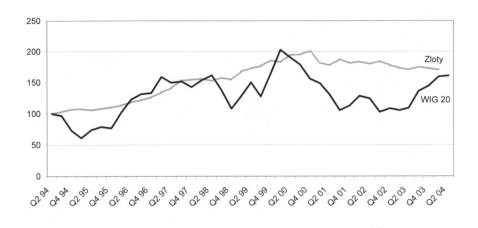

Fig. 48. Exchange Rate and Stock Market Dynamics in Poland (annual data)

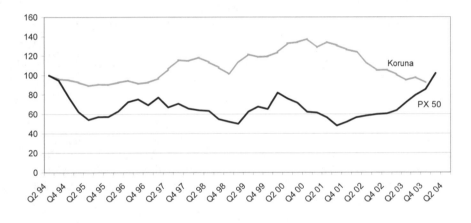

Fig. 49. Exchange Rate and Stock Market Dynamics in the Czech Republic (annual data)

A traditional approach to exchange rate dynamics is the DORNBUSCH-model – which assumes sticky prices and instantaneous exchange rate movements in a system of flexible exchange rates - in which overshooting plays a crucial role. In our modified DORNBUSCH model which assumes that the price of stocks (P') has a positive impact on the demand for money can be summarized by a set of equations which represents the Phillips curve (1a), aggregate demand – in a logarithmic approximation – (1b), money market equilibrium (1c), capital market equation (1d: full capital mobility and full substitution of domestic and foreign bonds, that is interest parity will hold where E is the expectation operator) and expectation formation (1e). We will assume that the foreign stock market dominates P' so that in the money demand equation for simplicity one may replace P' through the foreign stock market price index P'* times e: the condition $eP'* = \xi'P'$ could also be read as a kind of arbitrage condition – with $E(eP'*) = E(e)E(P'*) + Cov(e,P'*) = E(e)E(P'*) + \sigma_e \sigma_{P'*} \rho(e,P'*)$ and variance VAR $(eP'*) \approx [E(e)]^2 VAR(e) + [E(P'*)]^2 VAR(P'*) + 2E(e)E(P'*)Cov(e,P'*)$ - for stock markets of open economies with a similar level of technology and hence profitability of firms; for simplicity we set $\xi' = 1$ ($P^{*'}$ could itself be subject to overshooting; moreover, one may note that a priori the sign of the correlation $\rho(e,P'*)$ is unclear; policy makers could restrict the covariance by declaring a maximum acceptable variance of the exchange rate). We will use the following simple (with Y# denoting full employment output) :

$$dlnP/dt = f'(lnY^d - lnY\#) \tag{1a}$$

$$lnY^d = \delta'(lne - lnP) + \varphi'lnY + lnG \tag{1b}$$

$$lnM = lnP + \mu'lnY - \sigma'i + \omega'[ln\ e + lnP^{*'}] \tag{1c}$$

$$i = i^* + E(dlne/dt) \tag{1d}$$

$$E(dlne/dt) = \theta'(lne\# - lne) \tag{1e}$$

An alternative to adaptive expectations as stated in (1e) would be perfect foresight (we will disregard this for the moment):

$$E(dlne/dt) = dlne/dt \tag{1f}$$

Note that all parameters are positive and that e# and Y# denote, respectively, the equilibrium exchange rate and full employment output. Combining (1c), (1d) and (1f) gives an equation for the monetary sector (M'M' line) showing an inverse relationship between lnP and lne. The economy will be characterized by this M'M' line at any moment of time since adjustments in the fast variables i and e will keep the system on the M'M' line.

$$lnP = lnM - \mu'lnY + \sigma'i^* - \omega'lnP'^* + \sigma'\ \theta'\ (lne\# - lne) - \omega'lne \tag{1g}$$

The slope in lnP-lne-space is determined by $-\sigma'\ \theta' - \omega'$ which is negative: the absolute interest rate elasticity of the demand for money and the "learning" parameter θ' (in the expectation equation) are crucial which indicates how quickly the actual exchange rate adjusts towards the equilibrium value e#. The smaller both parameters are, the flatter the negatively sloped M'M' curve - and the smaller the learning parameter is the closer is the location towards the origin. The flatter the M'M' curve is, the higher is the overshooting phenomenon; a low value for ω' reinforces the overshooting problem. Conversely, the higher the learning speed and the higher in absolute terms the interest rate of the interest elasticity (the steeper M'M'), the smaller is exchange rate overshooting; and the higher ω' the smaller is the overshooting problem. This points to potential stabilizing properties of stock market transaction (one may state the hypothesis that the larger the long term stock market capitalization is the higher is ω'). Government can influence the interest elasticity of the demand for money by encouraging the development of an efficient financial sector offering a broad variety of financial market instruments: The larger the range of liquid short term investment alternatives in the market, the higher (in absolute terms) the interest elasticity in the demand for money.

Note that overshooting is critical for developing countries with high foreign debt since it will bring the risk that excessive transitory (overshooting) devaluation will raise the foreign debt level to a critical value: To the extent that investors will not agree on the relevance of overshooting a potential liquidity problem then might translate into a solvency problem – the country is considered to have such a high foreign debt that default is expected in the near future.

Combining (1a) and (1b) gives – with $d\ln P/dt=0$ – a medium term equilibrium condition for the real sector of the economy (I'S' curve which has slope unity in $\ln P$-$\ln e$ space):

$$\ln e\# = \ln P\# + [1/\delta']\ln G - [(1- \varphi')/\delta']\ln Y \tag{1h}$$

Expansionary monetary policy leads to overshooting (see the following figure) in the sense that the exchange rate will jump from e_0 to e_{01} immediately, while the long run equilibrium value of the exchange rate is e_1. The long run depreciation is smaller than the medium term depreciation of the currency.

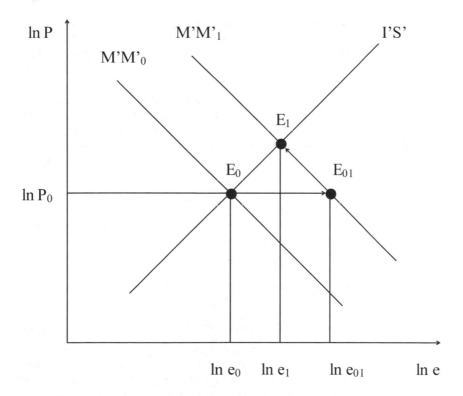

Fig. 50. Financial Market Equilibrium (M'M') and Real Economy (I'S')

An increase in the foreign stock market price – reflecting for instance intensi-fied innovation dynamics and hence higher expected profits and higher stock market prices – will shift the M'M' curve upwards. Hence there will be a strong short term depreciation and a more modest long term depreciation. If foreign stock markets are characterized by a series of upward price increases we can expect to see a zig-zag exchange rate movement which will reflect the overshooting phenomenon. One might include additionally on the demand side in the goods market the variable P'/P – Tobin's q (denoted here as Q'): This means introducing a real "Tobin Q' demand effect" in the goods market equilibrium by adding a term $\delta"P'/P$ in 1b) which would mean that the overshooting effect is reinforced since the I'S'curve will shift to the left if the stock market price P' and P'*, goes up: The long term depreciation effect is reduced – assuming that there is a depreciation at all – and in this sense the relative overshooting has increased. If the "Tobin Q' demand effect" were very strong, there could even be the case that short term depreciation will be accompanied with long term appreciation; here we touch upon an empirical issue where one may anticipate a priori only rather limited relevance of such a case.

The long term equilibrium solution is obtained by inserting (1h) in (1g) to re-place lnP (which is equal to lnP') and by setting lne=lne#:

$$\ln e\#(1+\omega') = \ln M + \sigma' i^* + \omega' \ln P'^* + [1/\delta'] \ln G - \{\mu' + [(1- \varphi')/\delta']\} \ln Y \qquad (1i)$$

Clearly, this equation can be estimated empirically. Note that a rise of the for-eign stock market price will bring about a nominal depreciation. If the stock market price index abroad is positively influenced by product innovations v – and as-sociated improved profitability of firms – the effect of product innovations abroad is a nominal long term depreciation. Moreover, in the long run the elasticity of e with respect to P is unity. An expansionary monetary policy will shift the M'M' curve to the right; and the nominal exchange rate will react immediately and jump – as a short term reaction (only the M'M' curve is binding) to a higher nominal exchange rate; in the short run dlne/dlnM will exceed unity so that there is over-shooting. If we replace the adaptive expectation process by perfect foresight, that is

$$E(dlne/dt)=dlne/dt \qquad (1f)$$

we will get a differential equation from combining (1c), (1d) and (1f) which reads:

$$dlne/dt = [1/\sigma']/[1+ \omega'] [\ln P + \mu' \ln Y -\ln M] - 1/[1+ \omega'] i^* + \qquad (1j)$$
$$\omega'/[1+\omega'] \ln P'^*$$

Note that (1a) and (1b) can be combined to the following differential equation for the dynamics:

$$dlnP/dt = [-f'\delta'] \ln P + [f'\delta'] dlne/dt + f' [\ln G-(1- \varphi') \ln Y] \qquad (1k)$$

The phase diagram for the system of two equations (1j) and (1k) – the curves EE (for 1j) and PP (for 1k) - shows that there is a saddle path so that there is only one unique trajectory (the M'M' line) to the equilibrium point. Again it is true that shifts in exogenous variables will lead to an overshooting of the nominal exchange rate so that the long term equilibrium exchange rate differs from the short term exchange rate. Imperfect capital mobility could reduce, but not necessarily eliminate, the phenomenon of overshooting.

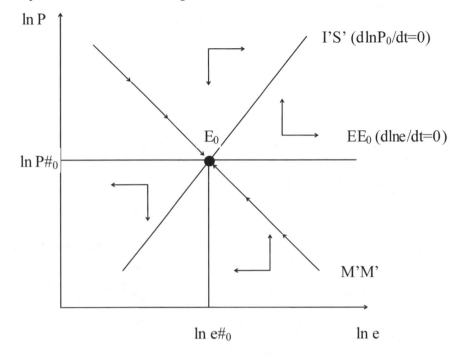

Fig. 51. Saddle Point Stability in a Perfect Foresight Model

F.2.2 A Short-Term Analysis of Financial Market Dynamics and Technology Shocks

A look at the effective real exchange rate of several countries shows that the real exchange rates show a long term rise – parallel to output per capita. This is true both for Asian NICs (until 1997, the year of the Asian crisis) and selected EU accession countries in the 1990s as is shown in the subsequent graph. Such a long term appreciation trend does, however, not rule out that there can be considerable short term depreciation periods; e.g. in the context of expansionary monetary policy and falling interest rates or as a consequence of investors' fears with respect to the sustainability of government debt policy. In addition to this, oil price shocks could affect short term nominal and real exchange rate development.

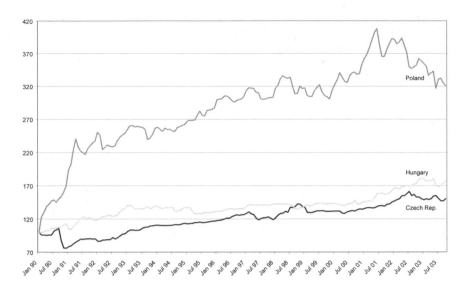

Fig. 52. Real Effective Exchange Rates for Selected EU Accession Countries in the 1990s, Jan 1990=100

Now let us turn to some modelling analysis. Over the short-term, all stock variables – such as the capital stock K – and the price level P are given. There can however be productivity shocks, namely changes in the marginal or average capital productivity. As for a Cobb-Douglas production function, the marginal productivity is proportionate to the average productivity. Interesting cases to consider are changes in expectations and in productivity growth and in the price level, capital stock and the stock of money, where the latter is a policy variable.

New Open Economy Approach: Augmented Branson Model

A well known model of financial markets in open economies is the BRANSON model, which focuses on the money market as well as the short term domestic bonds market and the short term foreign bonds market, with foreign bonds being denoted as F* (in foreign currency). Essentially, the model allows for the simultaneous determination of the exchange rate and the nominal interest rate in a setting with a domestic bonds market (BB line), a foreign bonds market (FF line) and the money market (MM line). This model determines the nominal exchange rate e and the nominal interest rate i.

Subsequently we will modify the approach by dropping the domestic bonds market and adding the stock market. This allows for a convenient graphical exposition. The more complex augmented BRANSON model, which includes the original three markets of the seminal model and the stock market, could be discussed analytically.

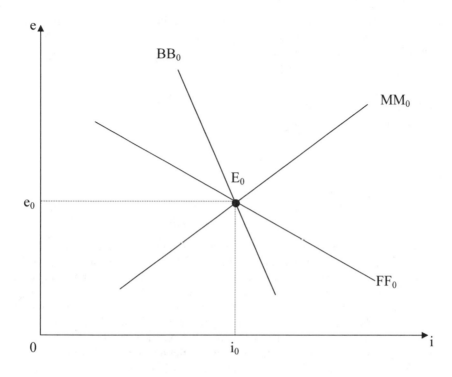

Fig. 53. Portfolio Equilibrium in the Simple Basic Branson Model

The simple augmented BRANSON model, with i^* representing the foreign interest rate and a^E the exogenous expected exchange rate change, can be written as follows (with V representing the marginal utility of money, z capital productivity, ψ expected growth rate of the stock market price; M is the nominal money stock, K the capital stock, P' the stock market price and $A'=[M/P] + [eF^*/P] + P'K/P$ is overall real wealth):

$$A' = (M/P) + (eF^*/P) + P'K/P \text{[budget constraint]} \tag{2a}$$

$$M/P = n(V, i^*+a^E, z, \psi)A'; \ n_1>0, n_2<0, n_3<0, n_4<0 \text{[MM curve]} \tag{2b}$$

$$eF^*/P = f(V, i^*+a^E, z, \psi)A'; \ f_1<0, f_2>0, f_3<0, f_4<0 \text{[F*F* curve]} \tag{2c}$$

$$P'K/P = h(V, i^*+a^E, z, \psi)A'; \ h_1<0, h_2<0, h_3>0, h_4>0 \text{[KK curve]} \tag{2d}$$

We have dropped the domestic bonds market for convenience; in principle there is no problem in also taking into account the domestic bonds market.

The system for equations (2c) and (2d) can be written in matrix form (remember that only two of the three equations (2b)-(2d) are independent as n+f+k=1) and determine – using Kramer's rule and taking into account the budget constraint equation (2a) – the multipliers for e and P'; while e and P' are endogenous variables, the other variables are exogenous. Thus we differentiate the system and look at interesting multipliers such as:

- $de/dz > 0$
- $de/d\psi \Leftrightarrow 0$
- $de/dK = 0$
- $de/dM > 0$
- $de/di* > 0$
- $dP'/dz > 0$
- $dP'/d\psi > 0$
- $dP'/dK < 0$
- $dP'/dM > 0$
- $dP'/di* \Leftrightarrow 0$

A rise of capital productivity will raise the stock market price level, and it – under certain parameter constellations – brings about a nominal depreciation. In such a case we cannot easily infer whether the domestic stock price has increased P' relative to the price of foreign stocks (eP'*). Only if the percentage rise of P' exceeds that of the nominal exchange rate would this be the case. One may dub such a case as an improvement in the international terms of capital where the latter is defined as P'/(eP'*); in an open economy with two-way foreign direct investment and portfolio investment in stocks, a rise of the terms of capital implies that the amount of foreign real capital per unit of domestic real capital has increased. Such a perspective implicitly goes one step beyond the existing model in the sense that we would have to also consider foreign stocks – at a given price of stocks abroad – so that domestic investors can trade domestic stocks for foreign stocks.

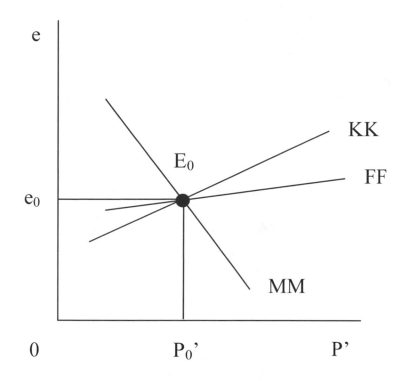

Fig. 54. Foreign Bonds Market, Stock Market and Money Market

In an e-P' diagram, we can display the equilibrium line (MM) for the money market, which has a negative slope since a rise in e (increase in the demand for money) must be combined with an adequate fall of the stock market price if money market equilibrium is to be maintained. The equilibrium line for the stock market (KK) has a positive slope, as a rise in P' (its impact is a net supply effect) must be combined with a rise in e, namely an increase in the demand for stocks if stock market equilibrium is to be maintained. The slope of the equilibrium curve for the foreign bonds market is also positive and smaller than that of the KK curve. A rise of e causes a net supply effect – indeed an excess supply – in the foreign bonds market. This excess supply is eliminated if the stock market price and hence the real value of wealth is adequately increased.

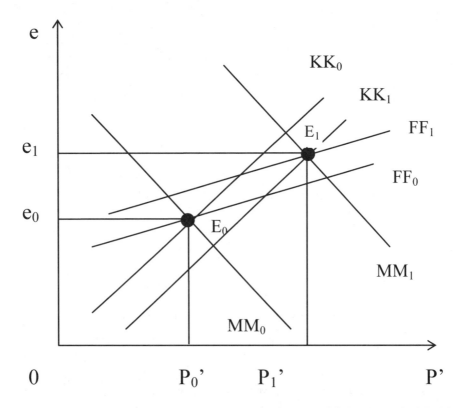

Fig. 55. Effects of an Increase in Capital Productivity in the Modified Branson Model with Stock Market

An expansionary monetary policy implies an upward shift of the MM curve so that we observe depreciation and a rise in the stock market price. Net investment (i.e., a rise in K) will shift the KK curve upwards so that we can learn from the new intersection point with the MM curve that the nominal exchange rate will increase and the stock market price will fall in the short run. A rise in capital productivity (as occurs in the course of both structural change and economic catching-up) implies a downward (upward) shift of the KK (FF) curve and a rightward shift of the MM curve. From our multiplier analysis one may derive some ideas with respect to the correlation coefficient $\rho(e, P'^*)$.

The short-term result of an expansionary monetary policy is nominal depreciation and a rising stock market price. In the medium-term, however, one must take into account that for foreign investors from country II, depreciation in country I is equivalent to an appreciation of the currency of country I, allowing the purchase of assets more cheaply. This, however, does not hold for either stocks (or real capital) if the percentage increase in stock prices is higher than the depreciation rate of the currency in country I. Based on this perspective, a modified Branson model suggests that foreign direct investment could fall over the medium-term. In the long run, the situation is different if one assumes that a relative rise of the stock market price will stimulate emission both of new stocks and net investment. The KK curve will shift upwards, thereby dampening the medium-term increase in stock market prices. This, in turn, will stimulate FDI inflows over the long run.

F.3 Hybrid Model: Combining Interest Parity and Augmented Money Market Equilibrium

A simple approach to exchange rate modelling is to combine "interest parity" with money market equilibrium; we will augment traditional approaches not least by assuming that the demand for money is not only a function of output and the nominal interest rate but also of the stock market price index P' – assuming that the higher P' the higher the transactions financed in stock markets. According to open interest parity we should have (with e as the nominal exchange rate, i as the nominal interest rate, * to denote foreign variables and R' as the risk premium)

$$\left[Ee_{t+1} - e_t \right] / e_t = i - i^* - R_t' \tag{3a}$$

$$\left[Ee_{t+1} / e_t \right] = 1 + (i - i^*) - R_t' \tag{4a}$$

Assuming that $(i - i^*) - R_t'$ is relatively small we can use the approximation $\ln(1 + x) = x$ and write:

$$\ln Ee_{t+1} - \ln e_t = (i - i^*) - R' \tag{5a}$$

$$\ln e_t = \ln Ee_{t+1} + (i^* - i) + R' \tag{6a}$$

We will assume that the risk premium R depends on the sustainability of fiscal policy as proxied by the debt-GDP ratio d'.

$$\ln e_t = \ln Ee_{t+1} + (i^* - i) + R'(d') \tag{7a}$$

The expected exchange rate is supposed to be determined according to another part of the book:

$$\ln Ee_{t+1} = \ln e_{t-1} + \beta(\ln Y - \ln Y^*) + \beta'(\ln e\Diamond_t - \ln e_t) + \beta''(\ln e_t - \ln e_{t-1}) = \tag{8a}$$
$$-\beta(\ln Y^* - \ln Y) + (1 - \beta'') \ln e_{t-1} + \beta' \ln e\Diamond - (\beta' - \beta'') \ln e_t$$

This equation – where we assume $0 < \beta'' < 1, (\beta' - \beta'') \leq 1$ – states that the expected exchange rate is based on the past spot exchange rate plus three factors, namely the current account impact related net exports of goods and services and hence the differential $\ln Y / Y^*$, the difference between the hypothetical long term (read purchasing power: PPP) equilibrium exchange rate $e\Diamond$ and the actual exchange rate; and the difference between the present exchange rate and the ex-

change rate of the previous period. This learning pattern may reflect pragmatic
learning in the sense that economic agents consider the present exchange rate with
a certain probability as an equilibrium exchange rate (perfectly rational if the equilibrium exchange rate were characterized by a random walk), but also consider the
relevance of the rational component $e\Diamond$; and $e\Diamond$ is based on purchasing power
parity. Inserting (8) into (7) gives

$$\ln e_t[1+(\beta'-\beta")] = -\beta(\ln Y *-\ln Y)+(1-\beta")\ln e_{t-1} \qquad (7'a)$$
$$+ \beta'\ln e\Diamond+(i*-i)+R_t'(d') $$

As regards the hypothetical equilibrium exchange rate – according to PPP – we
follow the monetary approach to exchange rate determination in a modified form.
The modification concerns the role of the stock market price index P' which is assumed to positively affect real money demand as transactions on stock markets
will rise along with P'. The expected exchange rate is assumed to depend on relative money supply. Hence we assume the law of one price (in its weak form, that
is $V'\neq 1$), that is purchasing power parity, and hence

$$P_t = V'e\Diamond_t P_t * \qquad (9a)$$

$$\ln P_t = \ln V'+ \ln e\Diamond_t + \ln P_t * \qquad (9'a)$$

We assume money market equilibrium at home and abroad; and we denote real
money demand $m = m(Y,i,P')$ and $m* = m*(Y*,i,P')$ abroad. P' is the
stock market price index (real income is denoted as Y, the income elasticity of
money demand denoted as α and the semi-interest elasticity denoted as α' and
the elasticity with respect to the stock market price index as α''). The real money
supply is M/P in the home country and $M/P*$ in the foreign country so that the
equilibrium conditions read as follows (with e' denoting the Euler number):

$$M_t / P_t = Y_t^\alpha P_t'^{\alpha"} e'^{-\alpha'i_t} \qquad (10a)$$

$$M_t * / P_t* = Y_t *^{\alpha*} P_t'^{*\alpha"*} e'^{-\alpha'*i*_t} \qquad (11a)$$

$$\ln M_t - \ln P_t = \alpha \ln Y_t - \alpha'i_t +\alpha"\ln P_t' \qquad (10'a)$$

$$\ln M_t *- \ln P_t* = \alpha * \ln Y_t *-\alpha'* i_t *+\alpha"*\ln P_t'* \qquad (11'a)$$

Inserting from (8') and (9') P and $P*$ into the equation for purchasing power
parity (7') we have:

$$\ln e\Diamond_t = -\ln V'+\ln M_t - \ln M_t *+\alpha *\ln Y_t *-\alpha'*i_t *+\alpha"*\ln P_t'* \qquad (12a)$$
$$-\alpha \ln Y_t +\alpha'i_t -\alpha"\ln P_t'$$

Inserting (12a) in (7a) we get:

$$[1+(\beta'-\beta'')]\ln e_t = -\beta \ln Y / Y^* +(1-\beta'')\ln e_{t-1} - \beta'\ln V' \quad\quad (13a)$$
$$+\beta'\ln M_t - \beta'\ln M_t^* +\alpha^*\beta'\ln Y_t^*$$
$$-\alpha\beta'\ln Y_t +(1-\alpha^*\beta')i_t^* -(1-\alpha'\beta')i_t$$
$$+\beta'\alpha^*{''}\ln P_t'^* -\beta'\alpha''\ln P_t'+R_t'$$

Defining $[1+(\beta'-\beta'')]$ as b we obtain:

$$\ln e_t = (1-\beta'')/b \ln e_{t-1} - \beta'/b\ln V'+ \beta'/b\ln M_t - \beta'/b\ln M_t^* \quad\quad (14)$$
$$+[(\alpha^*\beta'+\beta)/b]\ln Y_t^* -[(\beta+\alpha\beta')/b]\ln Y_t$$
$$+\{[1/b][1-\alpha^*\beta']i_t^* -[1/b][1-\alpha'\beta']i_t\}$$
$$+[\beta'/b]\alpha^*{''}\ln P_t'^* -(\beta'/b)\alpha''\ln P_t'+(1/b)R_t'$$

If we assume that the semi-interest elasticity for the demand for money is the same at home and abroad we can replace the expression $\{...\}$ by the interest differential i^*-i. Equation (14) is a testable hypothesis, which takes into account both short term dynamics from the capital account and more long term dynamics related to the current account and purchasing power parity, respectively. For an empirical analysis with respect to transition countries see WELFENS/BORBÉLY (2004) who find positive empirical evidence for equation (12).

F.4 Capital Asset Pricing Model and Product Innovations

The capital asset pricing model (CAPM) focuses on the behavior or risk-averse investors who have a choice between bonds and stocks here understood as a promise for paying out future profits of the respective firms. The contemporaneous yield of stocks consists of the dividend yield plus the percentage change in the stock market price P'. What is the minimum rate of return s^E an investor in stocks will require? The CAPM is straightforward in that it considers the risk free bond interest rate i, the expected variance of stock market prices $E\sigma^2_{t+1}$ and the market price of risk λ'_{t+1} which reflects the degree of risk aversion of investors.

$$s^E = i + \lambda'_{t+1} \, E\sigma^2_{t+1} \quad\quad (15)$$

Investors in the stock market will raise the required yield if there is a rise in

- the opportunity rate of return (i): Here the Growth and Stability Pact of the EU – assuming that it enjoys creditability - contributes to low interest rates as does the very size of the Euro area which allows more easily economies of scale in the issuing of debt instruments.
- the degree of risk aversion λ': The degree of risk aversion is likely to rise with the median age of the population – in the long run the age level is rising considerably in the EU and Japan, but hardly in the US.

- or stock market volatility σ^2: The variance of stock prices is affected by the variance of the underlying fundamentals, including eg innovation dynamics and the price of energy.

If we additionally take into account that the real money balances M/P will affect the demand for stocks as well as the role of Tobin's Q' (P'/P: the ratio of the stock price – reflecting the existing capital stock – to the price of investment goods/the price of newly produced goods) and the FROOT-STEIN argument relevant in an open economy we get a simple long term demand function for stocks Z:

$$Z^d = Z^d(i, M/P, E\sigma^2_{t+1}, v, \lambda', Q', q^*) \tag{16}$$

The partial derivatives (denoted $a_0, a_1, \ldots a_6$) of the first and third variable, the degree of risk aversion and of Q' are negative, while M/P and q^* will positively affect the stock demand. From the perspective of a small open economy the volatility is determined by the US stock market dynamics. The degree of product innovativeness v will positively affect the demand for stocks since product innovation will allow firms to fetch higher prices in goods markets and thus to raise profitability. In the medium term the market price of risk can be assumed to be exogenous. The nominal interest rate is affected by – domestic and foreign – bonds markets while M/P is a policy variable to the extent that the nominal money supply is concerned. P is a predetermined variable to the extent that medium term dynamics of national output Y are governed by the existing stocks of factor inputs (for a given trajectory of M and Y we can implicitly determine P). The real exchange rate is endogenous under flexible exchange rates, but exogenous in a fixed exchange rate system; in a medium term perspective we might even consider the exchange rate as pre-determined if purchasing power parity is remains steady, which will be done here.

As regards the supply of stocks Z^s we will use the following simple function (partial derivatives denoted as $b_1, b_2, \ldots b_6$) which assumes that supply is determined by the interest rate and K^{opt} (the profit maximizing capital stock; if actual K falls short of this optimum investment I will stimulate the supply of new stocks) the rate of product innovation v – the higher the innovation rate the higher anticipated profits -, the corporate income tax rate τ, Tobin's Q and the real exchange rate q^*. The partial derivative of i, K^{opt}, v, Q' and q^* are positive where a rise of q^* is assumed to translate into higher export profits. The tax rate will negatively affect the supply of stocks.

$$Z^s = Z^s(i, K^{opt}, v, \tau, Q', q^*) \tag{17}$$

Using a linearized function for the demand and the supply side in the stock market, medium term equilibrium $Z^d = Z^s$ in stock markets is therefore given by a rather simple equation (where we replace domestic volatility by foreign volatility):

$$P'/P[b_5 - a_5] = (a_0 - b_0)i + a_1 E\sigma^{*2} + a_2(M/P) + (a_3 - b_3)v \tag{18}$$

$$+ a_4\lambda' - b_2[K_{t-1} + I^{opt}] - b_4\tau + (a_6 - b_6)q^*$$

Note that a similar equation will hold abroad. Indeed the equation is an implicit two-country model for a small open innovative economy. The term $[b_5-a_5]$ is positive, the term (a_0-b_0) is negative and (a_6-b_6) is positive. We can thus state that a rise of the interest rate negatively affects the real stock market price (read Tobin's Q'). There is also a negative impact of volatility, risk aversion, the capital stock and the tax rate. The real exchange rate has a positive impact on the real price of stocks. With sticky output prices it holds that a rise of the nominal exchange rate e will raise the stock market price P', which is consistent with our basic short term financial market model. As regards the impact of right-hand side variables on the real stock price one should note: The only unclear sign is for v, namely $[a_3-b_3]/[b_5-a_5]$. Before we look closer into the innovation variable one may emphasize the role of structural similarities of countries considered here. If the home country and the foreign country are of equal size and composed of equal firms the law of one price must hold for stock prices:

$$P'=\xi'eP'* \tag{19}$$

or (assuming constant ξ' with g for growth rate) $g_{P'} = g_e + g_{P'*}$ which reads that the expected capital gains rate on domestic stocks must equal the expected capital gains rate on foreign stocks plus the expected currency depreciation rate, that is:

$$[E(P'_1)/P'_o] -1 = [E(e_1)/e_o -1]+[E(P'*_1)/P'*_o] -1 \tag{19'}$$

In a setting characterized by (19) and a given real exchange rate the endogenous variable in the above equation is investment, which no longer can be determined by autonomous domestic firms, rather investment follows immediately from the law of one price for the stock market. The law of one price for the stock market will hold in the long run only for countries with a similar technology basis and across which knowledge flows rather freely. This amounts to saying that there must be some factor mobility (and the internet creating broad transparency). In the subsequent analysis we will not consider this special case of stock market price arbitrage. Finally, note that with given K and sticky output prices equation (18) can be rearranged and solved for e, namely for the case of a small open economy whose stock market price dynamics are determined by the foreign stock market price according to $P'=\xi'eP'*$: The real and nominal exchange rate thus would be a positive function of i, a positive function of the variance of stocks and of the risk premium as well as a negative function of real money balances and a positive function of the capital stock and the price of (foreign) stocks relative to the price level; the impact sign of the product innovation variable is unclear.

With a focus on equation (18) we turn to the innovation variable: If the innovation variable affects the demand side more strongly than the supply side, namely $[a_3>b_3]$, we will have a positive impact of v on Q'. There could be periods of irrational exuberance when investors anticipate a wave of exogenous product innovations – see the internet bubble or a potential future bubble centered on nanotechnologies – to strongly stimulate future profitability and thus raise the demand for stocks (for this case we assume $a_3>b_3$). A simplifying assumption is that such a wave of product innovations will not affect volatility in the market.

One should note that the interdependency of financial markets suggests that the nominal exchange rate and the stock market price should be determined simultaneously. WELFENS (2002) has argued that the real demand for money should be specified in a way which includes the contemporaneous stock market price: The demand for money m does not only reflect transactions in goods markets but also transactions in stock markets so that m=m(Y,i, P') for country I and m*(Y*,i*,P'*) for country II; the partial derivative of m with respect to the stock market price P' is expected to be positive. Using purchasing power parity e=P/P* and replacing P and P* from an explicit money demand function at home and abroad one should expect the nominal exchange rate to depend on Y,Y*, i, i*, P' and P'* - note, that in a case of global dominance of the US stock market (that is the US S&P 500 development determines P') the elasticity of P' would be the same as that for P'*; and this seems to be relevant for both countries in Western Europe and Eastern Europe. A two stage least-square estimation (WELFENS/ BORBÉLY, 2004) for Hungary has shown domestic and foreign stock market price indices to be significant variables for the nominal dollar exchange rate; for Poland the domestic stock market price was a significant variable, the foreign stock market price index was only weakly significant. Adequate Durbin-Watson statistics and a high R squared underline that the approach chosen is useful.

A more extensive modelling could endogenize v, eg by assuming that some path dependency in innovation in accordance with $dv/dt = \Sigma f(..)v_{t-n} + B'E(P')$ where $f(...)$ is a density function for past innovations (B' is a positive parameter); moreover, a rise in v may be assumed to be associated with a rise of volatility. Here we are not so much interested in such extensions, rather we want to consider another impact, namely that domestic innovations and foreign innovations are interacting through network effects: We assume that the effective domestic rate of product innovations v' (v' replaces thus v in the demand side function and the supply side function) is determined by interaction of product innovations launched by domestic firms (v) and by foreign firms (v*) where we have positive efficiency parameters λ", λ"* and a simple multiplicative term included which makes sure that there are positive marginal cross fertilization effects from innovations.

$$v' = \lambda"v + \lambda"*v* + 2\ \lambda"\lambda"\ *vv* = [\lambda"v + \lambda"*v*]^2 \qquad (20)$$

We thus have a real Schumpeterian channel which implies a positive cross country correlation of stock market prices (note we define $[b_5-a_5]=b$"):

$$P'/P = (a_0-b_0)/b"i + a_1/b"E\sigma*^2 + a_2/b"(M/P) + a_3/b"\lambda' - b_2/b"[K] - b_4/b"\tau + \qquad (21)$$

$$(a_6-b_6)/b"q* + b_3/b"\ [\lambda"v + \lambda"*v*]^2$$

Equation (VII) seems to be adequate for the US but an estimation for any other country would have to add a term $b_7P'*^{US}/P*^{US}$ which reflect the global dominance of the real US stock market index $(b_7P'*^{US}/P*^{US})$; the sign of b7 should be positive for OECD countries and any other country where the structure of the stock market index reflects a set of industries similar to that in the S&P500 index of the US. If one were to estimate the dynamics of the stock market and the exchange rate simultaneously the implication for any non-US country is an ambiguous sign for the impact of the foreign stock market variable.

From an industrial economics perspective it would be interesting to consider countries where both goods markets are shaped through international oligopolistic interdepence in technology intensive innovative industries. A term such as that associated with b_3 should then be highly relevant.

F.5 Consumption, Volatility and Growth

In the following analysis we will turn towards the problem of modified neoclassical growth modelling with labor augmenting technological progress A(t). This approach implies that dK/dt is now determined by a goods market equilibrium condition for an open economy. We are mainly interested to understand how volatility will affect respectively output and growth. To simplify matters we impose the long term interest parity condition in the form i=i*; as we will not consider inflation we indeed have real interest rate parity in the form r=r*. There is one modification which must be additionally considered, namely that instead of M/P and K we will use (M/P)/(AL)=:m' and K/(AL)=:k', respectively. We do so as we want to focus on an economy with process innovations in the production function $Y=K^\beta$ (AL)$^{1-\beta}$, that is a=[dA/dt]/A>0 and population whose exogenous growth rate is n.

$$P'/P=(a_0-b_0)/b"i+a_1/b"E\sigma*^2 +a_2/b"m'-b_2/b"k'+a_3/b"\lambda'-b_4/b"\tau+(a_6-b_6) \qquad (21')$$
$$/b"q* + b_3/b" [\lambda v"+\lambda*"v*]^2$$

Now consider the following consumption function which basically states that consumption per efficiency units of labor C/[AL] is proportionate to income per efficiency unit of labor (y'), the real stock price and real wealth which we deliberately write in a somewhat unusual form. A standard model derived from utility maximization would be to assume that consumption is proportionate to income and proportionate to real wealth where the expected rate of return and the variance of yields play a role for the real wealth variable (DIXIT, 1998). Here we use a modified approach: Real wealth per efficiency unit of labor consists of real money balances per efficiency units of labor m' and the stock of real capital per efficiency units of labor k'. The consumption function assumes in particular that volatility of investment returns has a positive impact on consumption – a higher volatility is discouraging savings – and that a higher expected yield has a negative impact on consumption. A rise of Tobin's Q' is assumed to have a positive impact on consumption, where Q' can be inserted from (21).

$$C/[AL]= cy' + \{c'(r*)[\sigma/\mu]^\varepsilon [k'^\beta + m'^\beta] Q'^{\varphi'} \} \qquad (22)$$

Assume that all investment is in innovative projects associated with product upgrading. The expected rate of return on innovation is μ, the variance is σ. There are only two assets considered, namely real capital K and real money balances m (m=M/P). We chose deliberately a special specification where K/AL and [M/P]/AL (denoted as m') both enter the consumption function as a variable to the power ß since otherwise the mathematical processes would become very intricate (ß also is the supply elasticity of capital here). All exponents are assumed to be positive.

As regards the term $[k'^{ß} + m'^{ß}]$ this formulation is rather unusual at first sight; an ideal specification would – as we will show - indeed use $[k'^{ß} + m'^{ß}]^2$ but for ease of exposition we will drop the square. Our basic reflection in this context – with setting Q' unity for simplicity (and Q*'=Q') - will focus on a specific case where $A=A_o=4$ and $L=L_o=1$. Assume that ß=1/2 and the production function contains household's real money balances M/P as a positive external spillover effect, where real balances factor in as $(M/P)^{ß}$; hence we have output as $Y=K^{ß}(M/P)^{ß}L_o{}^{ß}$. One may then indeed state a simple consumption function as follows, namely $C/[AL] = cy' + c'(K^{0.5} + m^{0.5})^2 = cy' + c'[K + 2K^{0.5}m^{0.5} + m] = C'y' + c'[K+m]$. Here C'=c+2c'.

We will use a somewhat different Cobb-Douglas output function to replace $k'^{ß}$ by y' and a simple CAGAN-type real money demand equation to replace m', namely (with the Euler number written as e' and the semielasticity of the demand for money with respect to the nominal interest rate denoted as ψ' - defined as negative - and the expected inflation rate denoted as π'):

$$m'^{d} = e'{}^{\ \psi'[\mu+\pi']}\, y' \tag{23}$$

Let us assume that both σ and μ are positive functions of the product innovation variable v:

The corresponding savings function is therefore as follows:

$$S/[AL] =\{1-c - c'[\sigma(v)/\mu(v)]^{\varepsilon}\, Q^{\,\varphi'}\, [1+e'^{\psi'[\mu(v)+\pi']}]\}y' \tag{24}$$

In the presence of FDI inflows F' the modified neoclassical equilibrium condition is (with S denoting savings and depreciation rate on capital δ).

$$\delta K + (dK/dt) = S + F' \tag{25}$$

Dividing by AL and taking into account that we assume that FDI inflows F' are proportionate to output – we assume $F'/[AL]= q^{\lambda}k'^{ß}$ while depending on q (in accordance with FROOT/STEIN we assume that the higher q the lower FDI inflows so that λ<0) and using a Cobb-Douglas production function $y'=k'^{ß}$ (this production function might include – as a kind of positive external effect of household's money holdings - real money balances M/P where M/P is normalized to unity) gives

$$dk'/dt +[n+a+\delta]k = sk'^{ß}+ q^{\lambda}k'^{ß} \tag{26}$$

The accumulation dynamics for the capital stock are governed by:

$$dk'/dt = [s+q^{\lambda}]k'^{ß} - [n+ \delta+a]k' \tag{27}$$

We assume that the real exchange rate reaches a steady state value q# relatively quickly so that we can treat q# asymptocially as a constant in the above Bernoullian equation. The steady state value for k' (denoted k'#) is:

$$k\# = \{[s+q^{\lambda}]/[n+ \delta+a]\}^{1/(1-ß)} \tag{28}$$

The openness of the economy – as far as associated with FDI inflows and captured in the term q – allows reaching a higher steady state level of growth, however, the higher q#, the lower is the positive effect on the level of the growth rate. We emphasize that s need not to be a constant. One may assume that the partial derivative of the expected rate of return with respect to v is lower – ultimately, this is of course, an empirical question - than that for the reaction of the variance with respect to changes in v: This assumption is sufficient to bring about a rise of the savings rate and S, respectively, if v is increased; note that we must take into account that $s=:[1-c - c'[\sigma(v)/\mu(v)]^{\varepsilon} Q'^{\varphi'} [1+e'^{\psi'[\mu(v)+\pi']}]\}$. Thus we have both process innovations and product innovations as well as stock market dynamics. The long term real exchange rate $q=1/q^*$ can be determined within a simple analytical approach (WELFENS, 2004a); it also should be noted that the growth rate of technological progress can be endogenized (WELFENS, 2004b). It certainly would be useful to have more empirical research along the lines suggested by our modelling approach.

F.6 Policy Issues and Conclusions

A first policy issue is overshooting, respectively, in stock markets and the foreign exchange market. It would be useful to avoid strong overshooting effects, most importantly in the case of countries with relatively high foreign debt. For a country with a high foreign indebtedness – relative to GDP – there is a risk that what might at first glance be considered as temporarily excessive devaluation become a systemic risk once a critical level of foreign debt has become relevant. If the respective country is close to a critical limit in foreign debt, overshooting can translate liquidity problems into serious solvency problems. It will not help the country much if an expert would state publicly that the massive devaluation which has occurred was only a transitory problem on the way towards a mild long term devaluation. Hence there is critical interest on the part of heavily indebted countries to avoid overshooting problems. Slowing down the adjustment speed of financial markets or raising the speed of goods and factor markets principally are potential policy options. The adjustment speed in financial markets could fall endogenously, eg as there is a graduation towards a higher average maturity in the bonds market which in turn could be stimulated by reducing inflation rates.

An interesting problem are international spillovers which on the one hand can occur both through network effects in product innovations; on the other hand there could also be international external effects in the sense that the foreign variance of stock market yields enter the equation for the domestic economy. This is not a major problem as long as regulation in the dominant country(ies) makes sure that there is no bias in stock market dynamics; eg as fraudulent investment bankers in the US publicly recommended certain stocks of firms in the ICT (information and communication technology) sector in the 1990s – while privately saying that one should simply sell such stocks as they had attained non-sustainable levels - this did not only amount to US stock market manipulation, rather it also affected other OECD countries as the US stock market bubble influenced other stock markets abroad. The considerable covariance of stock market dynamics and exchange rate changes also raises the issue as to whether or not stock market bubbles tend to contribute to market instability in foreign exchange markets.

It would be interesting to consider policy options that help to avoid excessive short term fluctuations of stock market prices and exchange rates. A useful policy option would be to impose – for both private and corporate customers (so far some OECD countries have such rules only for private households which is the smaller part of the market) – "time-progressive" yield taxation. The longer customer X holds a certain stock, the lower will be the tax rate applied to earnings. If owners of firms are not to be favored unfairly, one should consider imposing a minimum corporate tax rate as well.

There are some key links between the monetary/financial sector of the economy and the real economy. Stock market dynamics will feed into the consumption market – obviously the higher the stock market capitalization is relative to national income.

There is a lot of empirical research to be done; and simulations to be run. It is not really understood how strong exchange rate dynamics and exchange rate chances are intertwined. Moreover, it is unclear whether a kind of stock market parity holds over the long run, namely $eP'^*=P'$. The analysis – based on an ADF test – suggests that there has been, in some countries, non-stationarity of the term eP'^*/P' over the decade following 1992. One can, however, not rule out that adjustment needs more than a decade when it comes to international stock market comparisons. There finally is the issue of causality, namely to what extent exchange market dynamics dominate the stock markets; or vice versa. Hence there is a broad research agenda for open economies with capital mobility and innovation under flexible exchange rates.

Appendix F.1: Slope of Equilibrium Lines

$$\frac{M}{P} = n\left(V, i^* + a^E, z, \psi\right)\left(\frac{M}{P} + \frac{eF^*}{P} + \frac{P'K}{P}\right)$$

$$-n\left(V, i^* + a^E, z, \psi\right)\frac{eF^*}{P} = n\left(V, i^* + a^E, z, \psi\right)\left(\frac{M}{P} + \frac{P'K}{P}\right) - \frac{M}{P}$$

$$n\left(V, i^* + a^E, z, \psi\right)eF^* = -n\left(V, i^* + a^E, z, \psi\right)\left(M + P'K\right) + M$$

$$eF^* = -\left(M + P'K\right) + \frac{M}{n\left(V, i^* + a^E, z, \psi\right)}$$

$$e = -\frac{K}{F^*}P' + \left(\frac{M}{F^* n\left(V, i^* + a^E, z, \psi\right)} - \frac{M}{F^*}\right)$$

$$\frac{de}{dP'} = -\frac{K}{F^*}$$

$$\frac{eF^*}{P} = f\left(V, i^* + a^E, z, \psi\right)\left(\frac{M}{P} + \frac{eF^*}{P} + \frac{P'K}{P}\right)$$

$$\frac{eF^*}{P} - f\left(V, i^* + a^E, z, \psi\right)\frac{eF^*}{P} = f\left(V, i^* + a^E, z, \psi\right)\left(\frac{M}{P} + \frac{P'K}{P}\right)$$

$$\frac{eF^*}{P}\left(1 - f\left(V, i^* + a^E, z, \psi\right)\right) = f\left(V, i^* + a^E, z, \psi\right)\left(\frac{M}{P} + \frac{P'K}{P}\right)$$

$$eF^*\left(1 - f\left(V, i^* \mid a^E, z, \psi\right)\right) = f\left(V, i^* + a^E, z, \psi\right)\left(M + P'K\right)$$

$$e = \frac{M f\left(V, i^* + a^E, z, \psi\right)}{F^*\left(1 - f\left(V, i^* + a^E, z, \psi\right)\right)} + \frac{K f\left(V, i^* + a^E, z, \psi\right)}{F^*\left(1 - f\left(V, i^* + a^E, z, \psi\right)\right)}P'$$

$$\frac{de}{dP'} = \frac{K f\left(V, i^* + a^E, z, \psi\right)}{F^*\left(1 - f\left(V, i^* + a^E, z, \psi\right)\right)}$$

<u>KK-Kurve:</u>   (31)

$$\frac{P'K}{P} = h\left(V, i^* + a^E, z, \psi\right)\left(\frac{M}{P} + \frac{eF^*}{P} + \frac{P'K}{P}\right)$$

$$P'K = h\left(V, i^* + a^E, z, \psi\right)\left(M + eF^* + P'K\right)$$

$$- eF^*h\left(V, i^* + a^E, z, \psi\right) = h\left(V, i^* + a^E, z, \psi\right)\left(M + P'K\right) - P'K$$

$$e = \frac{-h\left(V, i^* + a^E, z, \psi\right)\left(M + P'K\right) + P'K}{F^*h\left(V, i^* + a^E, z, \psi\right)} = -\frac{M}{F^*} - \frac{P'K}{F^*}$$

$$+ \frac{P'K}{F^*h\left(V, i^* + a^E, z, \psi\right)}$$

$$\frac{de}{dP'} = -\frac{K}{F^*} + \frac{K}{F^*h\left(V, i^* + a^E, z, \psi\right)} = \frac{K - Kh\left(V, i^* + a^E, z, \psi\right)}{F^*h\left(V, i^* + a^E, z, \psi\right)} =$$

$$= \frac{K\left(1 - h\left(V, i^* + a^E, z, \psi\right)\right)}{F^*h\left(V, i^* + a^E, z, \psi\right)}$$

Appendix F.2: International Bonds Market Integration, Interest Rates and Stock Market Volatility

In the last quarter of the 20th century financial market integration has made enormous progress as capital flows have been liberalized and privatization and lifting restrictions to foreign direct investment inflows have created new opportunities for cross-border capital flows. Changes in exchange rate regimes also have affected international financial market integration, but we will ignore this aspect here. The issue we are interested in is simply the following: How will an increase in international bonds market integration affect stock market prices and interest rates – and in particular we would like to know how changes in the capital stock will affect the model. The model is simple and consists of the domestic bonds market, the domestic money market, the foreign bonds market and the domestic stock market.

With respect to the impact of asset yields we assume that all assets are gross substitutes. Money has a yield of v (marginal utility of money – this is exogenous here), short-term domestic bonds carry interest rate i, foreign bonds F the foreign interest rate i*. The nominal exchange rate is e. B is the stock of domestic bonds, M the stock of money, K the stock of capital, P is the price level of goods, P' is the stock market price index. The marginal product of capital is z', and the demand for stocks is a positive function of z', a negative function of the two interest rates and of v. The desired shares of assets in total wealth are denoted by n', b, f and h; namely for money, domestic bonds, foreign bonds and stocks, respectively. Moreover, we assume that demand for each asset is proportionate to real wealth $A' = M/P + B/P + eF^*/P + P'K(1-\delta)/P$; thus it holds that $n'+b+f+h=1$. We assume for simplicity an instantenous capital depreciation whose rate is δ. Only three equations out of the four equilibrium conditions for the four asset markets are independent. We will consider only the two bonds markets (BB line for domestic bonds market equilibrium, FF line for equilibrium for foreign bonds) and the stock market (KK line). For simplicity we assume that expected stock market price changes are zero and expectations are static. The endogenous variables in this implicit two country model – with flexible exchange rates - are the domestic interest rate i, the exchange rate and the domestic stock market price index P'. We will assume that foreign direct investment flows are the only type of capital flows existing.

As it is interesting to consider the role of foreign direct investment inflows D in the home country (country I) – where we only focus on international mergers & acquisitions; according to FROOT/STEIN (1991) D is a positive function of the real exchange rate $q^*=: eP^*/P$ as in imperfect capital markets a real depreciation of the exchange rate raises the amount of potential foreign investors' equity capital expressed in terms of country I currency. Additionally we assume that foreign investors taking over a publicly quoted stock company will transform it into a limited liability company which is the typical pattern observed in OECD countries. Moreover, we assume that any excess supply of stocks will result in higher foreign direct investment inflows (the home country is small relative to the world real capital market). Hence the real value of stocks – with the number of real capital units initially being equal to the number of stocks – is reduced in accordance with D. Note that we have assumed that there is instantaneous capital depreciation where the depreciation rate is δ.

The equilibrium conditions for the four markets are given (with the left-hand side denoting the supply side) by:

$$M/P = n'(v,i,i^*,z')A' \tag{1}$$

$$B/P = b(v,i,i^*,z')A' \tag{2}$$

$$eF^*/P = f(v,i,i^*,z')A' \tag{3}$$

$$P'K[1-\delta]/P - D(q^*, \text{excess supply in stock market}) = h(v,i,i^*,z')A' \tag{4}$$

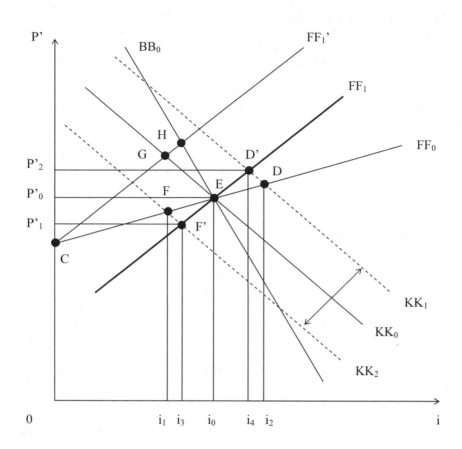

Fig. 56. International Bonds Market Integration, Stock Market Volatility and Interest Rate Volatility

$$dP'/di = n_i/K(1 - \delta) + 1/K(1 - \delta) ((1/n_i - 1)dM/di - dB/di - deF^*/di \qquad (1)$$
$$- A'P(n_v \, dv/di + n_{i*}di^*/di + n_{z'} \, dz'/di))$$

$$dP'/di = b_i/K(1 - \delta) + 1/K(1 - \delta) ((1/b_i - 1)dM/di - dB/di - deF^*/di \qquad (2)$$
$$- A'P(b_v \, dv/di + b_{i*}di^*/di + b_{z'} \, dz'/di))$$

$$dP'/di = f_i/K(1 - \delta) + 1/K(1 - \delta) ((1/f_i - 1)dM/di - dB/di - deF^*/di \qquad (3)$$
$$- A'P(f_v \, dv/di + f_{i*}di^*/di + f_{z'} \, dz'/di))$$

The system determinant is:

$$U = F^*K(1 - \delta)(b_i n - n_i b)/P^2 < 0 \qquad (4)$$

This leads to the multiplier:

$$de/dM = - (b_i f - fib) / F^*(b_i n - n_i b) < 0 \qquad (5)$$

The slope of the KK curve in P'-i-space is negative as is the slope of the BB curve. The slope of the FF curve is positive. Concerning cyclical aspects we assume that during unanticipated recessions the deprecation rate will increase while during booms it will fall. This implies that in P'-i-space a boom is indicated by an upward shift of the KK-line – from KK_0 to KK_1; in a recession there is a downward shift from KK_0 to KK_2. A rising degree of international financial market integration in the sense of domestic bonds becoming closer substitutes to foreign bonds implies that the absolute value of the partial derivative $\partial f/\partial i$ has increased. Hence the FF curve becomes steeper – and indeed the FF_0 curve is rotating upwards in point C which will cause a rise of the stock market price and a fall of the interest rate: The instantaneous intersection point is G; however, as G stands for an excess supply in stock market which will translate in higher foreign direct investment inflows so that the KK curve shifts to the right (not shown in the graphic): Point H is the final intersection point; the effect of a higher foreign direct investment inflow is a rise of stock market price and a slight increase in the interest rate – but the interest rate still is lower than initially. Note that a rise of FDI inflows might have occurred endogenously through a nominal and real exchange rate depreciation (this will cause a rise of the real supply of foreign bonds).

Thus increasing financial market integration reduces the nominal interest rate; and it raises the stock market price and foreign direct investment inflows. If inflation remains constant the real interest rate also will fall. From an EU perspective the creation of the Euro has contributed to raising the substitutability between \$ denominated bonds and Euro denominated bonds – the size of the Euro zone is closer to that of the USA than the previously relevant pair DM zone compared to the USA. In the perspective of the simple model presented the impact of greater substitutability of domestic bonds and foreign bonds is a fall of the interest rate and a rise of the stock market price index.

However, we also are interested to understand the pure effect of the FF curve becoming steeper so that we draw the new FF curve through the initial intersection point of all three curves. This initial equilibrium point determines P'_0 and i_0. It is interesting to consider the case that monetary authorities will embark upon an expansionary open market operation (leaving real wealth unaffected).

If one compares the impact of cyclical movements in the KK curve for the case of FF_0 and FF_1 the conclusion is clear:

- international bonds market integration will increase stock market volatility (compare points D' and F' with F and D)
- international bonds market integration will reduce interest rate volatility.

This raises the question what the impact of greater stock market volatility and lower interest volatility will be. One should note an important caveat here, namely that monetary policy might change its strategy once it has noted the increased international bonds market integration.

G. Innovation Dynamics and Optimum Growth

G.1 Introduction

Standard and New Growth Theory

In all industrialized countries, achieving sustained economic growth in the sense of a long run increase of output or output per capita is a crucial goal. From a neo-classical perspective, the basic growth models of SOLOW (1970) emphasize the role of the production function – and the respective input factors capital and labor - and the savings rate, respectively. Growth is modeled as a steady state equilibrium phenomenon which is characterized by accumulation dynamics for capital and certain parameters of the utility function (DIXIT, 1976). Modern growth theory to some extent has added emphasis on the role of human capital formation (LUCAS, 1979), but the mechanics of the basic neoclassical growth model can be retained if one interprets capital as human capital or skilled labor.

Standard growth theory suggests that accumulation dynamics of capital determine long run equilibrium output per capita. The simplest model is based on the assumption that savings $S=sY$ (with Y standing for real income) and that the growth rate of the population L is n while per capita output $y=f(k)$; k is capital intensity K/L (K is the capital stock) and the production function is well-behaved, that meets Inada-conditions. Imposing the equilibrium condition that investment $I=S$ we can summarize the accumulation dynamics in such an economy as follows:

$$dk/dt = sf(k) - nk \tag{1a}$$

If we assume that $f(k)=k^\beta$ – so that output is determined by a Cobb-Douglas production function (with $0<\beta<1$) – we can easily solve for the steady state solution by setting $dk/dt=0$:

$$sk^\beta = nk \tag{1b}$$

Hence the steady state solution for k is given by

$$k\# = [s/n]^{1/1-\beta} \tag{1c}$$

$$y\# = [s/n]^{\beta/1-\beta} \tag{1d}$$

As population dynamics (with e' denoting the Euler number) are given by $L(t)= L_o e'^{nt}$ we have equilibrium output determined by

$$Y(t)= L_o e'^{nt} [s/n]^{\beta/1-\beta} \tag{1e}$$

In the long run – in the steady state - output Y grows with the exogenous growth rate n; the level of the growth path is higher, the higher s and the lower n are.

Technological Progress

If one assumes that savings S= sY, a stationary population and that savings S equals investment I = dK/dt while there is labor-augmenting Harrod-neutral progress in the production function so that output $Y = K^{\beta}[AL]^{(1-\beta)}$, one obtains – with a denoting the exogenous growth rate of A(t) - a slightly modified equation for the accumulation dynamics of k'=: K/[AL] where k' is dubbed capital per efficiency unit of labor:

$$dk'/dt = sk'^{\beta} - ak' \tag{1f}$$

We might further refine this equation by introducing population growth (growth rate n) which leads to [a+n]k' as the second right-hand side term in the equation for the accumulation dynamics;

$$dk'/dt = sk'^{\beta} - [a+n]k' \tag{1f'}$$

The solution of this Bernoullian differential equation is (with C_o to be determined from the initial conditions and e' denoting the Euler number; see appendix):

$$k'(t) = \{C_o e'^{-[a+n](1-\beta)t} + [s/[a+n]]\}^{1/1-\beta} \tag{1f''}$$

Clearly, there is a convergence for k' as long as ß<1; and one should add: as long as the growth rate n is not critically negative, that is the shrinkage speed of the population must not exceed a – obviously a problem which a priori cannot be dismissed for the case of ageing societies with declining population.
The steady state value for k' is

$$k'\# = [s/[a+n]]\}^{1/1-\beta} \tag{1g}$$

Per capita consumption in the steady state is given by the difference of per capita output and investment per capita (I/L), that is C/[AL]= f(k') – [I/L]#; as [I/L]# is equal to (n+a)k maximizing per capita consumption requires – with c'=: C/[AL] as a necessary condition:

$$dc'/dk' = f'(k') - (n+a) = 0; \tag{1g'}$$

$$f'(k'\#) = n+a \tag{1g''}$$

Let us point out one important aspect: In the case of a Cobb-Douglas production function, the marginal product of capital is given by $f'(k') = \beta k'^{\beta-1}$. If one assumes that firms also maximize profits and hence f'(k')=r the optimum growth policy is defined by the condition:

$$r = \beta k'^{\beta-1} = a+n \tag{1g'}$$

Therefore

$$k'^{opt} = \{\beta/[a+n]\}^{1/1-\beta} \tag{1g''}$$

Obviously this coincides with (1g) only if s=ß. Since ß in industrialized countries roughly is 1/3 and since savings ratios in most OECD countries are only around 20% it seems that the major challenge for a government interested in maximizing long run per capita consumption is to indeed raise the national savings rate. From an empirical perspective it is, however, unclear to which extent ß is changing in the course of technological development; as regards the expansion of the digital "New Economy" one may anticipate that the ß, the production elasticity of capital, will increase.

We also could add capital depreciation at rate δ so that the second right-hand term in the above equation becomes $[a+n+\delta]k'$; this will not affect the mechanics of the model in a critical way. All this is in the framework of standard textbook growth analysis (see e.g. JONES, 1998), and it is indeed a good starting point for some theoretical progress and certain refinements and theoretical innovations. Before we take a look at those it is useful to briefly recall some key insights from the optimum growth theory in the traditional sense, namely of neoclassical growth models that have been used to derive optimum growth policies (PHELPS, 1961; WEIZSÄCKER, 1962): In those models, government can achieve maximum per capita consumption if the savings rate is manipulated in a certain way; in an economy with a constant growth rate of the population (n), profit-maximizing firms, no technological progress and zero capital depreciation the optimum growth policy is characterized by the equality of n and the real interest rate r. Since output growth in the steady state is equal to n the implication is that the growth rate of output is equal to r. GROSSMAN/HELPMAN (1991) have presented broad analytical progress in growth modeling, however, the issue of optimum growth was not picked up. AGHION/HOWITT (1998) presented new ideas about endogenous (New) growth; in particular they have emphasized the role of innovation.

The result in a model in which consumers discount utility – thus going beyond the traditional approach - is not much different since maximizing the welfare function F (with U denoting Utility relevant for an integral from 0 to infinity, per capita consumption c', e' the Euler number and ρ the rate of time preference) to be maximized is $F = \int U(c't) e'-\rho t \, dt$ subject to $dk'/dt = f(k') - c' - (n+a)k'$ which gives – with denoting the current-value shadow price - the Hamiltonian: $H = \int U(c't) e'-\rho t \, dt + \lambda[f(k') - c' - (n+a)k']$. The optimality conditions ($\partial H/\partial c' = 0$ and $\partial H/\partial k' = - d\lambda/dt$) give the Ramsey rule: $r = -d\ln U'(c')/dt + \rho + n + a$. In the steady state – were c' is constant and hence the growth rate of the marginal utility U' is zero – we thus get $r = \rho + n + a$.

As we are not so much interested in the role of the time preference, we will not rely on the complex Hamiltonian approach. Rather a simple graphical model is sufficient to bring out the main critical results. The reader interested in the role of time preference can replace in the relevant steady state condition n through n+ρ if he wants to highlight the role of ρ. One may also note that adjusting the utility function in a way which contains both c' and k' – or more generally wealth - gives only a minor modification. The optimum steady state k# is rises in comparison with traditional optimum growth approaches.

In the subsequent analysis, we at first are interested in endogeneizing technological progress. The following section takes a closer look at some key issues of endogenous growth and proceeds with combining optimum growth approaches and endogenous growth modeling; we also will consider the role of long run relative price changes in the context of technological progress. The analysis presented then leads to several interesting policy conclusions related to growth policy and innovation policy, respectively. The main conclusions clearly go beyond the standard analysis in the literature and basically suggest considerable changes in economic policy in both advanced and catching-up countries.

G.2 Endogenous Growth, Innovation and Maximum Consumption per Capita

G.2.1 Optimum Endogenous Growth

The standard optimum growth literature of PHELPS (1961) and WEIZSÄCKER (1962) has established for the case of a closed economy that within a neoclassical growth model the optimum growth – defined by maximization of steady state per capita consumption C/L – is determined by the condition that in the absence of technological progress, the growth rate of the population n is equal to the marginal product of capital Y_K; moreover, in a world of implicit profit maximization and zero capital depreciation this also implies the real interest rate $r=F'(k)=n$, where $F'(k)$ is the marginal product of capital (alternatively we denote the marginal product of capital as Y_K); the function $y=F(k)$ is linear homogenous, $y=Y/L$ is per capita output and $k=: K/L$ capital intensity. From an optimum growth perspective, a government's growth policy should aim to manipulate the savings rate s - establishing indeed a new adequate savings rate s' - in a way such that the intersection point of the curve nk with $sF(k)$ is such that for the respective $k\#$ the slope of the $F(k)$ curve is equal to n. Similarily, if there is Harrod-neutral technological progress we have a production function $Y/[AL] = f(k')$ where $k'=K/[AL]$; graphically the steady state value $k'\#$ is determined by the intersection of $[n+a]k'$ and the curve $sf(k')$ as shown in point E_0. In the steady state output, Y will grow at the rate n+a. Again, government could consider the topic of optimum growth, namely maximizing consumption per capita in the steady state. As $y=C/[AL] + I/[AL]$ it is clear that point k'^{opt} is the optimum (DE_1 is parallel to the curve $[n+a]k'$), and it will be achieved - see the subsequent figure - if government reduces the savings rate to s'. In the implicit case of profit maximization the optimum is characterized by the equality of r and the marginal product of capital $f'(k')$ and hence by $r=f'(k')=a+n$. Note that in the model profit maximization is introduced here in an ex post fashion, there is no endogenous mechanism which drives the economy towards k'^{opt}.

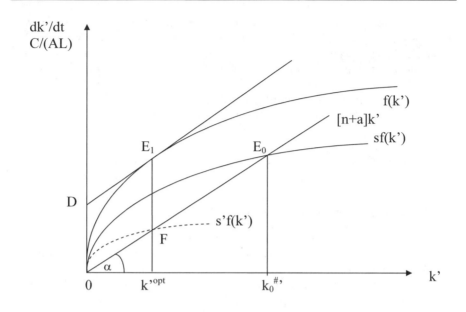

Fig. 57. Optimum Growth in the Standard Model

The standard optimum growth approach takes the population growth rate n as given and suggests that government should adjust the aggregate savings rate s; indeed government could do so by adjusting the government budget deficit-GDP ratio in an appropriate way.

G.2.1.1 Role of Government Consumption

In the case of a constant Harrod neutral progress rate a the mechanics of the neoclassical growth model remain the same as in the basic model. An interesting refinement suggested here is to analyze the role of government consumption G under the simple assumption that $G=\gamma Y$ and that private consumption and government consumption are full substitutes while γ negatively affects the progress rate as we assume $a=a_1(1-b'\gamma)$ where a_1 is the progress rate which would hold without government consumption and b' is a positive parameter in the interval 0,1. Progress is still exogenous here as γ is exogenous. Ruling out government deficits and therefore taking into account that $\gamma=\tau$ (where τ is the income tax rate) the accumulation dynamics now are given by:

$$dk'/dt = s[1-\gamma]k'^{\beta} -[a_1(1-b'\gamma)]k' \tag{1m}$$

The effect of government consumption on long run growth and technological progress is negative. However, the effect of γ on the level of the growth path is ambiguous since the steady state solution is given by

$$k'\# = \{s[1-\gamma]/[a_1(1-b'\gamma)]\}^{1/1-\beta} \tag{1n}$$

The numerator in the above expression is reduced by rising government consumption so that the $s[1-\gamma]k'^{\beta}$ curve – in dk'/dt-k' space - is bending the more downward the higher γ is. However, the ray OF (for $\gamma=0$) showing $[a_1(1-b'\gamma)]k'$ is also rotating downward (see OF' for a certain γ in the interval 0,1) so that k'# could rise or fall as the consequence of relatively higher government consumption. Our analysis thus raises some interesting questions about the role of government in a neoclassical growth model. Politically optimal growth obviously can diverge considerably from what is optimal from a situation in which perfectly informed rational economic agents are interacting. If government in an economy with profit maximization wants to maximize long run per capita consumption while ignoring the link between γ and the progress rate the optimum k' is given by the condition:

$$r = [a_1(1-b'\gamma)] \tag{1n'}$$

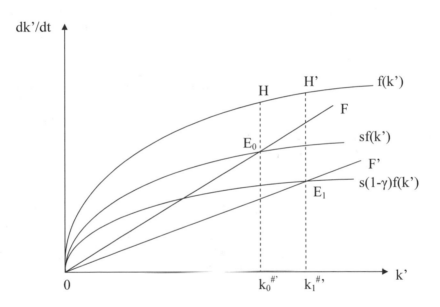

Fig. 58. Government Consumption and the Steady State in a Neoclassical Growth Model

G.2.1.2 New Political Economy

From the perspective of New Political Economy, the case of a rise of the level of the growth path is particularly interesting. Under a myopic government or in the presence of myopic voters, one could not rule out that government will adopt a kind of short-run maximization of consumption (either pure consumption of households or the sum of private and public consumption), taking into account effects of γ on the level of the growth path and on long run growth rate itself: Gov-

ernment would adopt a policy – based on raising the ratio of government consumption to GDP - which raises the level of the growth path while lowering the
long run growth rate; the initial per capita output path VJ would be given up in
point t' in order to switch to the new path V'J'. If voters are sufficiently myopic
and thus consider the increase in output as sufficiently attractive government will
be reelected through a policy which dampens long run growth. There is some
critical time horizon of voters marked by t''' beyond which the trajectory with the
low long run growth path certainly would look inferior to voters when compared
to VJ (the starting point here). A government aiming to realize V'J' would hope
that for ordinary voters and even experts the overlap of changes in the level of the
growth path and in the long run growth rate is opaque on the one hand and on the
other hand that the time horizon of voters is sufficiently short. Periods of war are
particularly known to be characterized by a shortening of time horizon of indi-
viduals/voters so that indeed the strategy described is particularly likely to be realized during war times (there is well-known positive historical evidence on this);
and the existence of ratchet effects would then suffice to make the rise of γ a permanent phenomenon for a considerable time – until new generations of voters increasingly gain influence and start to look more critically at the choices at hand.
The mechanism described would amount to an endogenous rise of γ and thus
could be an explanation for the size of government in a growing economy. Note
that if V'J' is the initial trajectory the adoption of a policy that raises the progress
rate would – with effects realized after time t' – lead to a transitory fall of the level
of y which is followed by a higher y after time t'' (remember that in the standard
growth model with exogenous progress and population growth the steady state
value of per capita income is $y\# = A_0 e^{'at} (s/[a+n])^{\beta/1-\beta}$).

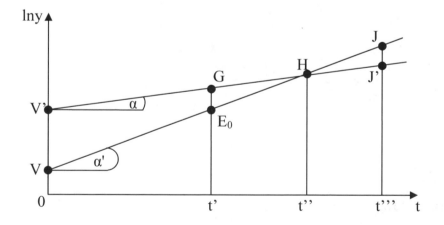

Fig. 59. Change of the Level of Growth Path vs. Growth Rate

Within the strategy described here politicians thus could exploit the bounded
rationality of voters and economic actors, respectively. Since ROOS (2005) has
provided empirical evidence that private households to a large extent disregard the

opinion of experts on macroeconomic forecasting, it also is plausible that voters will widely ignore the message from empirical growth analysis that a high share of government consumption in GDP is undermining long run growth. However, one may assume that in an economy with an increasing share of well-educated people the information costs about processing the information of experts will fall so that the resistance against an excessive government size will rise along with human capital. From this perspective, there might be a two-pronged impact of human capital formation on growth:

- The efficiency of production increases or the growth rate of technological progress rises;
- The increase in the share of skilled workers reinforces the resistance against high government consumption, and the fall of government consumption – relative to output – will then translate into higher long run growth.

The second point should be expected to be relevant in democratic societies, not in countries with an authoritarian regime. From this perspective, the switch from autocracy to a democratic society, combined with increased human capital formation, could raise long run growth.

G.2.1.3 High Population Growth vs. Ageing Societies

Let us consider the role of the growth rate of the population in a quasi-endogenous growth model (here government variables can affect the progress rate). We assume that the growth rate of the population will reduce the savings rate since in industrialized countries with a rising growth rate of the population governments tend to adopt a pay-as-you-go public pension scheme so that private savings is reduced. Thus we get a modified equation for the accumulation dynamics in which the factor $[1-\alpha n]$ indicates the impact of population growth on the savings rate (with s_0 denoting the savings rate in a society with zero growth of the population). Moreover, we assume that the growth rate of Harrod-neutral technological progress is affected by the growth rate of the population – it is likely to negatively affect the progress rate since a higher n means a greater abundance of labor and thus less incentives for research and development with a focus on labor-saving progress. At the same time, we assume that (modest) tax pressure stimulates innovation since firms will try to evade labor intensive sectors in which high social security contributions are part of production costs. Denoting the progress rate at zero population growth with a_0, we can describe the progress rate as $a = a_0 - a_1 n + a_2 \tau$ (a_1 and a_2 are positive parameters). The accumulation dynamics is now given by:

$$dk'/dt = s[1-\alpha n][1-\tau]f(k') - [n + a_0 - a_1 n + a_2 \tau] \tag{1o}$$

In the case of a Cobb-Douglas function $y' = k'^\beta$ we get as the steady state value k'#:

$$k'\# = \{s[1-\alpha n][1-\tau]/[n(1-a_1) + a_0 + a_2\tau]\}^{1/1-\beta} \tag{1p}$$

The $s[1-\tau][1-\alpha n]$ curve is the more bending downward the higher n and a are; and the higher the tax rate τ – necessary to financing social security benefits - is.

At the same time, the denominator in the above expression is reduced through the term a_1n but raised through the tax pressure effect so that the effect of population growth on the long run capital intensity and the progress rate – and hence growth - is ambiguous. Only careful empirical investigation can clarify the issues raised here. Countries with ageing societies and declining population growth, respectively, are facing two key problems:

- n becomes negative
- the tax rate (social security contribution rate) for financing public pensions systems rises

The level of the growth path is thus reduced, but the progress rate could increase. The net effect of both influences on the level of the growth path and the growth rate itself has to be analyzed also in empirical studies.

Assuming that government is myopic and thus neglecting the impact of its policy on the progress rate a quasi-optimum growth policy thus is defined by the condition:

$$r = [n(1-a_1) + a_0 + a_2\tau] \qquad (1p')$$

Government can use tax policy to achieve this. A rise of the real interest rate thus would have to be accompanied by a rise of the tax rate. If government takes into account the short term cyclical dynamics of the economy and the likely negative effects of such a policy mix – read restrictive monetary policy and restrictive fiscal policy – government will fail to adopt the suggested long term strategy. It is indeed an interesting finding that there is a potential trade off between short term cyclical strategies and long run growth policy options of government.

G.2.1.4 Unemployment and Growth

Finally we take a look at basic unemployment aspects within a growth model. We assume that unemployed people are not saving or even dissaving so that aggregate savings S is given by $S= s(1-u'u)Y$ where u is the unemployment rate – defined as unemployed L' relative to all workers L - and u' a positive parameter. The unemployment rate is determined by collective bargaining decisions which are exogenous here. As there is an unemployment insurance there also must be taxes to finance benefits for the unemployed. The benefits are assumed to be proportionate to the per capita income Y/L; u" (falling in the interval 0,1) is a positive parameter. Government expenditures thus are given by uLu"Y/L; and these are the only government expenditures considered here. Denoting tax revenues as T the accumulation dynamics are now determined by

$$S+T = dK/dt + uLu''(Y/L) \qquad (1q)$$

Assuming that tax revenue $T=\tau y$ and dividing by AL gives:

$$(1r) S/[AL] + \tau Y/[AL] = [dK/dt]/[AL] + uu''(Y/[AL]) \qquad (1r)$$

Hence the accumulation dynamics read for the case of zero population growth and an exogenous unemployment rate u and a negative link – reflecting increased workers' resistance against technological progress in a society with unemployment - between the progress rate a and u (expressed as $a = a_0 - U'u$ where the parameter U' falls in the interval 0,1; a_0 is the progress rate at full employment).

$$dk'/dt = s(1-\tau)k'^{\beta} + \tau k'^{\beta} - uu''k'^{\beta} - [a_0 - U'u]k' \qquad (1s)$$

Note here that we have used $Y = K^{\beta} [(1-u)L]^{1-\beta}$ so that $y = k^{\beta}(1-u)^{1-\beta}$ and thus $S = sk^{\beta}(1-u)^{1-\beta}$. The steady state for k'# is now given by:

$$k'\# = \{[s(1-\tau) + \tau - uu''] (1-u)^{1-\beta}/[a_0 - U'u]\}^{1/1-\beta} \qquad (1t)$$

If the unemployment rate would not affect the progress rate the implication simply would be that that the unemployment rate reduces the steady state k' and hence the level of the growth path of the per capita income y. However, here we focus on the progress function $a = a_0 - U'u$. As regards the impact of the unemployment rate on steady state capital intensity the result is clear: There will be an upward rotation of the per capita investment curve and hence the nominator in the above expression is raised. At the same time the denominator is reduced. From a welfare economic perspective the unemployment rate has, however, two negative effects: Unemployment itself is undesirable from the perspective of workers – and even of those who are employed as they interpret positive unemployment rates as a risk of losing the job in the future; moreover, the unemployment rate reduces the progress rate and hence long run growth.

In an economy with unemployment, it is difficult to define an optimum growth policy. Only as a second-best policy one may consider that government adopts a policy which is characterized by the equation:

$$r = [s(1-\tau) + \tau - uu''] (1-u)^{1-\beta} = [s + \tau(1-s) - uu''] (1-u)^{1-\beta} \qquad (1t')$$

Government can respond to a change in the long run real interest rate by adequate changes in the tax rate: A rise of r must go along with a rise of the tax rate, however, this policy mix is likely to undermine cyclical growth and hence government might instead prefer to reduce unemployment benefits (parameter u").

G.2.2 Optimum Growth and Endogenous Growth Modeling in Open and Closed Economies

The traditional optimum growth model assumes a given rate of population growth, a given relative price of capital goods and is assuming that the aggregate savings rate should be manipulated by government intervention, namely for the sake of maximizing long run per capita consumption. Subsequently we will at first assume that the savings rate of private households indeed is the result of individual optimization approaches and that the government budget is fully determined by government expenditures on research and development (R&D); thus there is no room for manipulation of the savings rate. Moreover, as we will assume endogenous growth in the sense that the progress rate is explained by certain variables, including government policy, we can develop a new concept of an optimum growth model. One variant presented will also relax the assumption of a constant relative price of capital goods.

In an extension of the traditional model – and using for simplicity the Cobb Douglas production function $Y = K^{\beta}[AL]^{(1-\beta)}$ and δ as the capital depreciation rate - we can introduce (endogenous) Harrod-neutral progress and capital depreciation so that the dynamic equation now is:

$$dk'/dt = sk'^{\beta} - (a+\delta+n)k' \tag{1}$$

Optimum growth is achieved if the condition holds that

$$(a+\delta+n) = Y_K \tag{2}$$

As profit maximization requires

$$r+\delta = Y_K \tag{3}$$

we obtain from both equations the condition relevant for optimum growth:

$$a + n = r \tag{4}$$

Aspects of Taxation

If government imposes an income tax rate τ, profit maximization in a closed economy requires

$$r = [Y_K - \delta][1-\tau] \tag{3'}$$

Note that in an open economy we would have instead $r = [Y_K - \delta][1 - \psi'\tau]$ where ψ' reflects the degree of capital mobility; ψ' approaches zero under infinite capital mobility, but in a closed economy it is equal to unity ($0 \leq \psi' \leq 1$).

Assuming that τ is small so that $1/[1 - \psi'\tau] \approx [1 + \psi'\tau]$ we get

$$r[1 + \psi'\tau] + \delta = Y_K \tag{3''}$$

Opening up the economy will reduce the parameter ψ' and thereby stimulate a transitory expansion of the economy, as the marginal product will tend to fall and hence k' tend to rise. This might hold even more if (with * denoting foreign variables; E is the expectation operator and e the exchange rate) interest parity holds in the form $r = r^* + d\ln E(e)/dt$ where the home country faces a nominal and real appreciation so that $d\ln E(e)/dt < 0$.

As Y_K is a negative function of k' it is clear that imposing a tax on capital income implies that the profit maximizing k' is lower than without taxation. The condition relevant for optimum growth is

$$a = r(1 + \psi'\tau) - n \tag{4'}$$

The problem looks, however, somewhat different if the progress rate is positively affected by the tax rate since either tax rate pressure stimulates – below a critical threshold τ' – innovativeness or as government uses tax receipts to promote research and development. Denoting the neutral progress rate as a_0 - this is the progress rate in the absence of taxation - we get:

$$a_0(1+ a'\psi'\tau) = [r(1+\tau)-n] \qquad (4'')$$

Here the impact of the tax rate now is not much different from the world without government, so that the income tax rate here is rather neutral.

Finally, we may have to consider that opening up – both in the form of trade and in the form of capital mobility - affects the progress rate positively; this case (with a" and a"' representing positive parameters and x and j standing for the export-GDP ratio and the import-GDP ratio, respectively) may be expressed for an initial situation of $0< \psi'<1$ as:

$$a_0(1+ a'''[x+j]+ a''/(1-\psi') + a'\psi'\tau) = [r(1+\tau)-n] \qquad (4''')$$

Impact of Capital Intensity on the Progress Rate

We return to the situation of a closed economy. For simplicity let us assume here that the progress rate a depends on k' and on the cumulated ratio (R) of research and development expenditures to national output, namely over the past from a distant point T' to the present t=0:

$$a = T'R+a''k'; \qquad (5)$$

This is a simple progress function which has an exogenous part in the form of the first term where government determines once and for all R; and an endogenous part which is a"k.

A potentially interesting modification of this progress function could be to assume that the progress rate a depends negatively on the growth rate of the population: a=T'R+a"k'-a"'n. This variant – not further emphasized subsequently - implies that ageing societies will face a long run decline of the progress rate unless government R&D promotion is raised adequately. With respect to open economies one also could include a technology gap element (a* is the progress rate abroad) in the sense that the progress function becomes

$$a=T'R + a''k' - a'''n + a''''(a*-a). \qquad (6)$$

Let us now turn back to the simple approach a=T'R + a"k'. For simplicity we assume that all R&D expenditures are indeed government expenditures. Thus then we have to replace s in the basic differential equation for k' through s(1-τ) where τ is the average tax ratio on income; our specific assumption that real government expenditure (G) consist only of R&D expenditures indeed implies that S=I is consistent with the condition that the sum of savings plus tax payments (T), namely S+T= I + G. Note that the budget constraint for each period is:

$$\tau = R \qquad (7)$$

The optimum growth condition reads is now difficult to determine since the growth rate is no longer constant; a is a function of k'; however, we know that in the steady state

$$T'R + a''k'\# + n = r \tag{8}$$

Policy Perspective

This implicit condition for the optimum endogenous growth requires government to chose R in such a way that this condition is fulfilled. As ageing societies in Japan and the EU will face a medium term decline of n (see eg McMORROW/RÖGER, 2004). Since the long run world nominal interest rate i* may be considered as exogenous from the perspective of the EU and Japan, respectively, the Euro zone and Japan face a specific real interest rate r*** consistent with nominal interest rate parity i=i*+ g_e, where g_e, is the long run depreciation rate of the Euro and the Yen, respectively (this rate could be considered as exogenous or related to differences in national savings rates). The real interest rate then is derived by subtracting the inflation rate from i.

We may recommend to Japan and the Euro zone – both facing a long run fall of n - to raise the progress rate through adequate long run R&D promotion; deregulation and stricter competition policies as well as government support for venture capital also might be useful in this respect. From the perspective of the Euro zone the challenge would be for individual member countries to realize an optimum progress rate in the respective country (a special problem also is that national inflation rates differ considerably in the Euro zone so that a constant nominal global interest rate i not automatically will imply a uniform real interest rate for each member country). Given the findings of JUNGMITTAG (2004), who demonstrates that innovation dynamics are not generally converging across countries of the EU/the Euro zone, one could indeed consider a stronger emphasis on national innovation policies as useful from the perspective of an optimum growth policy in the Euro zone and the EU, respectively.

To the extent global or regional competition bring about sustained pressure on governments to reduce the tax rate, there could be a critical divergence from the optimum growth policy; this then would give a rationale for cooperation in tax policies. From this perspective, the growth-enhancing strategy of the EU's Lisbon Agenda neglects the issue of a common tax policy. There is a critical caveat: Greater cooperation in tax policies could, however, lead in reality not so much to higher R&D-GDP ratios but to higher expenditures on social security expenditures - relative to GDP - in ageing OECD countries. Another caveat concerns the challenge of integrating monetary aspects in the optimum growth model (see appendix).

If one takes an illustrative look at the period 1960-2000, we have some interesting observations in the OECD. The implied optimum progress rate a^{opt} – calculated on the basis of long term real interest (r) rate minus population growth rate (n) – was low in has the 1960s in the technologically-leading US, but it fell then in the 1970s under rather irregular circumstances, namely two oil price shocks and the inflationary policy of the FED (partly reflecting the impact of the Vietnam War). As regards the 1970s, a similar finding holds for the EU15, while the implied optimum progress rate in Japan was positive (1%). In the 1980s the optimum progress rate reached rather high levels of slightly above 3% in the US and Japan and even 3.6% in the EU15. In the 1990s, the optimum growth rate fell by almost a full percentage point in the EU15, as the growth rate of the population increased while the real interest rate fell slightly. In the US, where the real interest rate fell a full percentage point as compared to the 1980s, the optimum growth rate fell to 2%. With the growth rate of the population in Japan reaching only 0.26% p.a. – a quarter of the figure in the 1960s and 1970s – and a fall of the real interest rate to slightly below 2%, the optimum progress rate fell to 1.7%. As regards the optimum progress rate, the differences across EU15-USA-Japan were modest in the 1980s but much higher in the 1990s, which could imply considerable policy conflicts among OECD countries and within the TRIAD. As regards the actual rate of technological progress, there is a broad range of estimates of factor productivity growth. Here we rely on those of the European Commission which shows progress rates for the US of around 1% in all four decades of the period 1960-2000. The EU15 performed better than the US in the 1980s, but it was slightly weaker in the 1990s. Japan had a very low progress rate in the 1990s. If the actual progress rate exceeds the optimum rate the implication is that profit maximization leads to a capital intensity below the social optimum; if the actual progress rate is smaller than the optimum progress rate profit maximization will lead to an excessive capital intensity (which is the case for the US in the 1970s and 1980s). The figures presented suggest that the growth rate of progress was close to the optimum in the US in the 1990s – but there was a large gap in the 1970s and 1980s; and as regards the EU it witnessed a relatively small gap in the 1990s – but the gap still was 1.6 percentage points. Japan was relatively close to the optimum in the 1970s and 1990s. This suggests that economic policy could generate considerable benefits in OECD countries if the concept of optimum growth would be taken seriously. Judging by the figures for the 1990s the US and Japan should raise the progress rate and thus should increase public R&D support. The EU15 had every reason to further stimulate the progress rate. If one would assume that the first decade of the 21st century will be similar to the 1990s it is obvious that the strong emphasis of the EU' Lisbon Agenda on technological progress seems adequate despite the fact that the growth rate of the population is expected to slightly decline (as compared to the 1980s and the 1970s the 1990s show a slight improvement for the EU, but the EU shows a large gap with respect to the optimum progress rate when compared to the case of the US and Japan in the 1990s).

Table 8. Real Interest Rates*, Population Growth Rates and Progress Rates in Selected OECD Countries (annual average growth rates)

	EU15			USA			Japan		
	r	n	a^{opt}	r	n	a^{opt}	r	n	a^{opt}
1960-70	Na	0.82		1.54	1.34	0.20	na	1.12	
1970-80	-0.42	0.51	-0.93	-0.50	1.11	-1.61	0.18	1.18	1.00
1980-90	3.90	0.28	3.62	4.02	0.98	3.04	3.69	0.56	3.13
1990-00	3.67	0.81	2.68	3.02	1.01	2.01	1.92	0.26	1.66

Source: German Council of Economic Experts and AMECO databank (European Commission), own calculations
*Long term nominal interest rate minus growth rate of GDP deflator; $a^{opt} = r-n$

Table 9. Actual versus Optimal Total Factor Productivity Growth in Selected OECD Countries

TFP Growth Rates	EU15			USA			Japan		
	a	a^{opt}	$a-a^{opt}$	a	a^{opt}	$a-a^{opt}$	A	a^{opt}	$a-a^{opt}$
1960 – 70	3.10	-	-	1.79	0.20	+1.59	6.91	-	-
1970 – 80	1.63	-0.93	-2.56	0.72	-1.61	-2.33	1.98	1.00	+0.98
1980 – 90	1.09	3.62	-2.53	0.83	3.04	-2.21	1.67	3.13	-1.46
1990 – 00	1.05	2.68	-1.63	1.14	2.01	-0.97	0.35	1.66	-1.31

Source: AMECO Database, own calculations

G.2.3 Biased Technological Progress and Optimum Growth

The New Economy – with digital products and ever-cheaper computers – has been characterized by an enormous long run fall of relative prices of computer equipment and more generally of capital goods (disregarding real estate and land). From this perspective it is interesting to consider the impact of biased technological progress which is defined here by its impact on the relative price of capital goods: Assume that the Harrod-neutral progress rate will lead to a relative fall of the price of capital goods $p= P^K/P$ (P^K is the price of capital goods and P the price of newly produced output which in a two sector economy will consist of a sub-price index for consumption goods and a sub-price index for investment goods). We subsequently assume that the change in the relative price is given by:

$$dlnp/dt=-a_o a; \text{ where } 0 \leq a_o < 1. \tag{9}$$

Profit maximization requires that

$$Y_K = r+\delta -d\ln p/dt \qquad (10)$$

As the change of the relative price is (using a positive parameter a'_0 in the interval 0,1) governed by $d\ln p/dt= -a'_0 a$, we get

$$Y_K = r + \delta +a'_0 a \qquad (10')$$

$$(a+\delta+n) = Y_K \qquad (11)$$

Optimum growth requires that

$$a[1-a'_0] + n = r \qquad (12)$$

The optimum progress rate now is given by

$$a^{opt} = [r-n]/[1-a'_0] \qquad (13)$$

As an illustrative initial example, assume that the long run real interest rate r is 3%, long run population growth 1% and $a'_0 =0.5$, then the optimum growth rate of technological progress is 4%. If, however, a'_0 is 2/3 the optimum progress rate would be 6%. Thus - and adopting a normative perspective - the switch to a New Economy in the 1990s (AUDRETSCH/WELFENS, 2002; BARFIELD/HEIDUK/ WELFENS, 2003) which brought a rise of the impact of a on the relative price change (a'_0 increased to a''_0) - should go along with a rise of the optimum progress rate. To date, governments have not responded to the relative fall in capital goods prices in the 20 years after 1985.

If the population growth rate falls to -1% the optimum progress rate – with a'_0 assumed to be 0.5 – is increasing: 8% is now the optimum growth rate of techno-logical progress. This points to the need that governments in ageing societies (with n falling in the long run) should strongly reinforce R&D promotion. No such pol-icy strategy has been adopted thus far in OECD countries, except for the EU's Lisbon Agenda perhaps, which aims to stimulate innovation dynamics by lifting the Community's R&D-GDP ratio to 3% (the EU approach has, however, never made any reference to optimum growth approaches).

G.3 Policy Implications

If the business community brings about a socially optimum progress rate by itself there is, of course, no need for government intervention. This holds particularly because government intervention itself typically entails certain costs to society, including rent-seeking activities. If, however, the business community does not bring about an optimum progress rate, government should carefully consider effi-cient ways to promote research and development/technological progress, respec-tively. In an open economy with a low per capita income this typically will also include incentives for diffusion and foreign direct investment, respectively (JUNGMITTAG/WELFENS, 2003). In addition, trade liberalization might con-tribute to efficiency gains. Enhancing trade could stimulate competition and thus can enhance international diffusion of new technology so that the level of technology A(t) in the relatively poor country will catch up more quickly with the level of technology A*(t) of the leading economy. Foreign direct investment is also known to be an important route for international technology transfer.

Governments in ageing societies should reinforce promotion of innovation dynamics where measures could include impulses for broader and better human capital formation and higher R&D expenditures as well as better exploitation of global technological progress through raising inward foreign direct investment and outward foreign direct investment – the latter in leading industrialized countries, as only in those countries does the sourcing of advanced technologies through subsidiaries seem to be relevant.

Growth policy should be adequately redefined in OECD countries, namely within the framework of optimum growth models under endogenous technological progress. This would be a major step forward to making the traditional and the new growth theory more fruitful for policymakers. Within a G-8 framework, it is rather obvious that there will be considerable differences in preferred strategies since the optimum progress rates implied for individual countries differ. As regards the role of international organizations such as the the World Bank or the IMF – or the EU and the EBRD in a regional (European) context – it would be wise to place emphasis on aspects of optimum growth policies.

The benefits of optimum growth policies could be considerable not only in OECD countries but in newly industrializing countries as well. As the goal of optimum growth policy is to raise consumption per capita – in many poor countries implying a higher survival rate and hence endogenous growth of the population – there should be clear benefits in catching-up countries. However, there are three caveats as regards the role of optimum growth policy:

- politicians interested in optimum growth policy should adopt a long time horizon, and it is unclear whether such a long time horizon can realistically be expected;
- policymakers in many countries will be tempted to translate a stronger emphasis on innovation policy in expansion of protectionist industrial policy which favors selected sectors – possibly including decline ones – and impairs free trade and a level playing field of foreign investors; due to growing economic inefficiencies such a policy is likely to impair growth and maximum long run per capita consumption;
- there will be serious problems with data forecasting over a long time period relevant for growth policy; within an optimum growth policy one will have to rely on solid empirical data and modeling. Here policymakers should invest more in empirical analysis.

As regards the EU the SAPIR Report (SAPIR ET AL., 2004) has made useful proposals on how to enhance European economic growth and innovation, respectively: Stronger promotion of R&D, opening up of markets and deregulation as well as reforms of the EU budget were key aspects discussed in that report. The analysis presented here adds new elements to the options for growth-promoting economic policy - both in Europe and elsewhere. Our analysis suggests that governments which adopt an optimum growth approach will realize major benefits for consumers and voters, respectively. The paper also has raised interesting empirical issues, including the question about the progress function. Here, the aspect of declining population growth is of particular interest.

Appendix G.1: Optimum Quantity of Money

Traditionally, growth models have rarely been linked to monetary policy issues, although PATINKIN on the one hand and TOBIN and JOHNSON on the other introduced money in growth models from the supply-side and the demand side, respectively (survey: SIJBEN, 1977). Monetary policy has been discussed mostly in the context of cyclical issues in the literature. The role of inflation in growth models was first considered by SIDRAUSKI (1967), SINAI/STOKES (1972) emphasized the role of money in the production function and fiscal policy issues in a growing monetary economy were introduced in the literature by STEIN/INFANTE (1980). Our perspective is different since our starting point is a model with technological progress and since we focus on linking money and growth through the optimum growth condition, which requires in the simple form that the real interest rate $r = a+n$. Hence we raise the question of how long run monetary policy must be conducted to be consistent with optimum growth in a closed economy.

If we assume that real money demand per efficiency unit of labor $(m'^d =:[M^d/P]/[AL]$ where M is the nominal stock of money and P the price level; i is the nominal interest rate) is given by $m'^d = [y']^\sigma /[\sigma'i]-$ with σ and σ' (both parameters >0) denoting the income elasticity of the demand for money and a parameter related to the interest elasticity of money $(E_{m,i}= -m'[y']^\sigma/[\sigma'i])$, respectively, we can focus on equilibrium in the money market:

$$m' = [y']^\sigma/[\sigma'i] \tag{a.1}$$

We assume that the central bank wants to achieve an inflation rate of zero, so that $i=r$. Taking into account that under profit maximization $r= ßk'^{ß-1}$, we can write:

$$m' = [k'^ß]^\sigma/[\sigma'ßk'^{ß-1}] = \sigma'ßk'^{1+ß\sigma-ß} \tag{a.2}$$

Replacing k' through the steady state value $k'=[s/(a+n)]^{1/1-ß}$, the optimum money stock therefore is given by:

$$m'\#^{opt} = \sigma'ß[s/(a+n)]^{1+ß\sigma-ß/(1-ß)} \tag{a.3}$$

Hence in the steady state it holds that

$$M(t)/P = \sigma'ß[s/(a+n)]^{(1+ß\sigma-ß)/(1-ß)} L(0)e'^{nt} A(0)e'^{at} \tag{a.4}$$

We assume that $1+ß(\sigma-1)>0$ since empirical evidence is known to suggest an income elasticity of the demand for money around unity, indeed exceeding unity if one follows the hypothesis that money is a luxury good. Note that the parameter σ' is the lower the higher the absolute value of the elasticity of the demand for money $(E_{m,i}= -[y']^\sigma/[m'\sigma'i])$. Hence the level of real money supply in the steady state is higher

- the higher the interest elasticity of the demand for money (the lower σ'),
- the higher the savings rate,
- the higher the income elasticity of the demand for money,

- the lower the progress rate,
- and the lower the population growth rate.

One may point out that financial innovation and regional economic/financial integration could bring about changes in the interest elasticity. In a larger integrated market there will be more liquid financial assets which are good substitutes for holding money, and thus a rise of the interest elasticity of the demand for money would once-and-for-all require the reduction of the real money stock. The optimum growth perspective therefore presents a challenge for both the monetary and fiscal policy.

The growth rate of the nominal money supply should be equal to the sum of a and n. We thus have a new perspective on the old topic of the optimum quantity of money. Here it is that money stock brings about the golden rule of capital accumulation and maximum growth of per capita consumption. The concept proposed here is clearly different from that of FRIEDMAN (1969), and given the specification of the money demand chosen here we indeed cannot apply the FRIEDMAN condition that the inflation rate (π) be set equal to $-r$ so that $i=0$. We finally note that introducing money in a growth model with government clearly requires stating the government budget constraint in an adequate way, namely: $\gamma y' = \tau y' + \pi m'$. We measure the inflation we obtain for the equilibrium money $[k'^\beta]^\sigma / [\sigma'(\pi + \beta k'^{\beta-1})]$ so that $(\gamma - \tau) = \pi k'^\sigma / [\sigma'(\pi + \beta k'^{\beta-1})]$: The long run budget deficit ratio outside the golden rule age then is a function $F(k, \pi)$, whereby the function allows us to determine a revenue-maximizing inflation rate, including the potential modification to assume that k' is a function of the inflation rate and other variables. From this perspective, one could extend the research perspective suggested here in many ways.

Appendix G.2: Specialization, Technological Progress and Factor Price Ratios

In a closed two-sector economy with labor mobility we can characterize the economy in a straightforward manner if we assume that there is one sector producing consumption goods and the other is producing investment goods. Both sectors produce with labor L and capital K, namely according to Cobb-Douglas functions: Investment output is given by

$$Y^I = [K^I]^{\beta'} [L^I]^{1-\beta'} \tag{A.I}$$

and consumption output by

$$Y^C = [K^C]^{\beta''} [L^I]^{1-\beta''} \tag{A.II}$$

Aggregate GDP – expressed in units of the consumption good - is given by the sum of output of the consumption goods sector (C) plus output of the investment goods sector where $Y = C + pI$ where $p = P^I/P^C$; and per capita income $y = y^C + py^I$. Goods market equilibrium in the standard sense requires $S = sYP = P^I Y^I$. As $P = [P^I]^v [P^C]^{1-v}$ we can write

$$Ip^{1-v} = sY \qquad\qquad (A.III)$$

It is assumed that the capital intensity of the consumption goods sector exceeds that of the investment goods sector which is a necessary condition for stability of the model. With linear-homogeneous production function we can (see for a summary JUNGMITTAG (2005)) write (with v':=1-v; ω=:W/r which is the ratio of the nominal wage to the real interest rate r):

$$y^l =: I/L = sy/p^{v'} = sf'_1(k_I(\omega))(k+\omega) \qquad\qquad (A.IV)$$

and

$$dlnk/dt = sf'_1(k_I(\omega))[(k+\omega)/k] - [n+\delta] \qquad\qquad (A.V)$$

The long run steady state – in analogy to the one sector model – is given by:

$$sf'_1(k_I(\omega))[(k+\omega)/k] = [n+\delta] \qquad\qquad (A.IV)$$

With respect to the short-run it can be shown that $d\omega/ds>0$ and that $dy^l/d\omega>0$ so that an increase of the relative factor price ratio raises the share of investment per capita output.

Appendix G.3: Endogenous Progress in the Capital Goods Sector

In a one sector economy - with a given level of technology - we have to consider y=y(k) and y'=w + rk (y is per capita income, k the capita intensity; the factor price ratio is w/r; w is the ratio of nominal W to price level P). Graphically we have a production function in which the distance OA indicates for the production y(k) where OA indicates w and the distance OB is equal to w/r. If the real interest rate is equal to tgα the line BA determines the optimum capital intensity k_2 (see point E_0). If the factor price ratio falls – and the income line shifts towards the origin – we get a new equilibrium point E_1, the optimum capital intensity has fallen (k_1): Transitorily firms will drop reinvestment plans in order to achieve the lower capital intensity k_1 so that there will be transitory unemployment and an excess supply in the goods market, respectively.

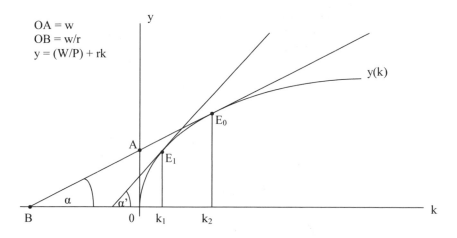

OA = w
OB = w/r
y = (W/P) + rk

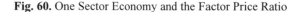

Fig. 60. One Sector Economy and the Factor Price Ratio

Next we turn to a two sector economy where capital and labor is mobile across sectors so that we have a uniform factor price ratio. Graphically we have two production functions for sectors C and I where equilibrium output is determined by the line BA (slope α) which is tangent to both production functions, namely in E_0 and in E_1; the capital intensity (k_{II}) of the consumption goods sector is higher than that of the investment goods sector (k_{I0}); L' and L" will denote labor employed in the C-sector and the I-sector, respectively. Note that y_0 is I/L and y_1 is C/L (see the following graph). Denoting the initial Hicks-neutral progress factor as A'_0 and using a simple Cobb-Douglas function $I=A'_0[K'/L']^{\beta'}$ and $C=[K''/L'']^{\beta''}$ while defining overall (exogenous) labor supply $L =L'+L''$ we can write – setting $A'_0=1$: $C/L=[1-\alpha'](K''/L'')^{\beta''}$ and $I/L= \alpha'(K'/L')^{\beta'}$ where $\alpha'=L'/L$. What happens if the factor price ratio falls (see the new income line starting in point B')? It is clear that the new optimum would be characterized by lower capital intensity in both sectors so that an adjustment process towards the lower capital intensities will have to be brought about – possibly by dropping previously planned reinvestment. This is not what the investment goods producing sector will want since any excess supply of capital will reduce the price of investment goods and hence the profitability and hence the share price of firms producing investment goods. What is the alternative for profit-maximizing firms in the investment goods sector? For that sector in particular it makes sense to try to achieve some technological progress which amounts to raising the level of technology from A'_0 to A'_1 such that the production function in the investment goods industry becomes steeper (an alternative could be to raise ß', the output elasticity of capital in the I-sector). The new equilibrium point shown in the graph – see point E_2 – requires only a modest fall of the sectoral capital intensity; point E_2 is in marked contrast to the solution suggested by traditional adjustment patterns, namely point E_{01} (with a given level of technology). To the extent that economic globalization reduces the factor price ratio there will be a strong incentive for firms in OECD countries to become more innovative in the investment goods sector, and as almost all machines are customer-taylored anyway it is indeed plausible to expect that producers of investment goods – facing changing factor price ratios - will explore new technologies in the production process

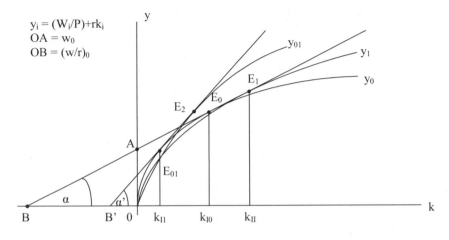

Fig. 61. Two Sector Economy

One may also consider besides the Harrod-neutral technological progress A(t) in the I-sector a progress rate in the I-sector, too (dlnB(t)/dt). In this case we can express output relative to efficiency units of labor.

Appendix G.4: Simple Differential Equation and Bernoulli Differential Equation

Let us consider for X(t) the following simple differential equation with constant coefficients a and b, written in the „elementary form":

$$dX/dt + aX = b \qquad (A.I)$$

The solution of this equation is (with e' for Euler number; C_o determined by the initial condition X(0)):

$$X(t) = C_o \, e^{,-at} + b/a \qquad (A.I')$$

If a>0 there is long term convergence to X#, that is with t→∞ we get the long run value ("steady state value") X#=b/a. From t=0 the value for C_0 is easily obtained: X(0)=X_o, so that: [X_o –(b/a)]=C_o. This elementary form of a differential equation will be used subsequently to solve a more complex equation, namely the Bernoulli differential equation:

Let us write the Bernoulli differential equation in a specific way so that we can recognize a simple similarity with the above differential equation:

$$dX/dt = bX^{\beta} - aX \qquad \text{(A.II)}$$

Dividing by X^{β} gives:

$$X^{-\beta}dX/dt + aX^{1-\beta} = b \qquad \text{(A.II$'$)}$$

We make the substitution: $X^{1-\beta}=V$ so that $dV/dt = (1-\beta)X^{-\beta}dX/dt$ and hence we can restate the above equation as follows:

$$(1/(1-\beta))dV/dt + aV = b \qquad \text{(A.II$''$)}$$

Dividing by $(1/(1-\beta))$ results in

$$dV/dt + [a(1-\beta)]V = b(1-\beta) \qquad \text{(A.II$'''$)}$$

With respect to the variable $V(t)$ this is exactly the simple differential equation in the elementary form so that the solution is:

$$V(t) = C_o e^{,-a(1-\beta)t} + b/a \qquad \text{(A.III)}$$

As $X^{1-\beta}=V$ we finally get as the solution of the differential equation:

$$X(t) =[C_o e^{,-a(1-\beta)t} + b/a]^{1/1-\beta} \qquad \text{(A.IV)}$$

If a is positive and $\beta<1$ we have convergence of $X(t)$ towards the steady state value

$$X\# = (b/a)^{1/1-\beta} \qquad \text{(A.V)}$$

C_o is determined from the initial equation as:

$$X_o = [C_o + b/a]^{1/1-\beta}$$
$$X_o^{1-\beta} = C_o + b/a$$
$$C_o = X_o^{1-\beta} - b/a$$

H. Trade, Structural Change and Growth in an Open Monetary Economy

H.1. Introduction

As regards structural change in Eastern Europe, it is clear that one should expect considerable structural change in the initial transition stage and possibly also once high foreign direct investment inflows occur. This occurred early on in Hungary, and the Slovak Republic, but only with a considerable delay in Poland. The various subsequent indicators show different intensities of structural change, and the intensity of change is not equal across the various indices. On theoretical grounds (see appendix) one should focus mainly on the Lilien index and the modified Lilien index. As the feature of those two indicators consider the sectors' relative weights, and also meet other standard requirements. As we can see in the subsequent table, the various indicators which summarize the intensity of structural change in the period from 1993 to 2001/02, the statistics point to rather strong structural change in several accession countries. Ideally, workers move out of sectors with low productivity growth towards sectors with high productivity growth, the latter often being found in sectors with high foreign direct investment inflows (FDI). FDI and investment of domestic firms will increase capital intensity and this, along with improved technology, will raise productivity. A positive gap between the growth rate of the wage rate and sectoral productivity growth will reinforce sectoral profit rates which in turn should stimulate sectoral FDI inflows. To the extent that economic catching-up and modernization is associated with high cumulated FDI inflows, one should expect that a considerable part of trade is shaped by FDI. Intra-company trade accounts for roughly 1/3 of trade in OECD countries.

By contrast, the degree of structural change in Germany was rather low, though this might be an artefact related to rather rough sectoral decomposition. For example, if international outsourcing to Eastern Europe takes place this can be associated with considerable structural change although at the two-digital level one would not note that less automotive parts are produced in Germany in the early 21st century than a decade ago.

Table 10. Various Indicators Measuring Structural Change Based on Production Data at the NACE 2-digit level (LI=Lilien Index; MLI= modified LI)

		NaV	EuN	SRD	IG	GRP	LI	MLI
Deutschland	93-02	0,1727	0,076	4,0043	0,0434	0,0731	0,1097	0,0327
Griechenland	95-02	0,2181	0,0737	5,742	0,0529	0,0912	0,1222	0,0318
Ungarn	93-01	0,5903	0,1967	20,7673	0,4593	0,2248	0,4124	0,0814
Polen	93-01	0,2601	0,0656	9,5737	0,0756	0,1146	0,1427	0,0282
Portugal	95-01	0,1503	0,0409	4,5519	0,0246	0,064	0,082	0,0177
Slowak Rep.	93-99	0,2749	0,1119	8,7107	0,1933	0,0994	0,2766	0,0442
USA	93-01	0,0825	0,0222	2,6044	0,0097	0,0364	0,0497	0,0096

Source: OECD STAN Database, own calculations

As regards structural change this is partly related to technologies, while also partly to other factors – including real exchange rate changes. There are two alternative definitions of the real exchange rate q=P/(eP*) – with * denoting a foreign variable and P and e representing the price level and the nominal exchange rate, respectively; P represents a basket of goods which is composed of tradables and nontradables. An alternative for defining the real exchange rate is $\lambda'= P^T/(eP^T*)$ where T stands for tradables. A rise in q or a rise in λ' can be identified with a real appreciation.

Subsequently, we take a closer look at alternative explanations for real exchange rate changes which must include an analysis of the links between nominal exchange rate dynamics and the real exchange rate (section 2). We demonstrate within a monetary growth model that the real money demand does not depend on the real interest rate unless the savings rate is a function of the real interest rate. Moreover, it is shown that the real interest rate will affect both the level of the growth rate and the growth rate itself. We use a rather simple growth model with trade, endogenous innovation and foreign direct investment. In section 3, we highlight an alternative approach to generating a Balassa-Samuelson effect which is linked to income distribution at home and abroad. Section 4 is on the real exchange rate and economic development, trade, structural change and growth where we also focus on a new structural model with product and process innovations but also on some aspects of the more complex HANSEN-RÖGER model. Our analysis also takes a look at the links between the real exchange rate and economic growth, including aspects of optimum economic growth. In the final section, we present some basic policy conclusions. The appendix presents some innovative modelling related to the topic of exchange rate dynamics and macroeconomic analysis (including smooth linking of supply-side effects and demand-side impulses). At the bottom line, there is strong emphasis on the fact that the dynamics of exchange rate development and growth should simultaneously consider trade and foreign direct investment (FDI). With reference to both the OECD countries in general as well as to Eastern Europe and Asian countries in specific, a considerable share of trade is intra-company trade. The perspective adopted here is a mixture of Schumpeter and Dunning, namely in the sense that innovation and FDI are emphasized.

Both trade and FDI depend on the real exchange rate, however, as the FDI stock contributes to the overall capital stock in the host country the net trade position – more precisely the current account – depends on cumulated FDI: The difference between output produced and domestic absorption (sum of consumption, government consumption and investment, including FDI inflows) is equal to net exports. There also is a geographical coincidence in the sense that the gravity equation for FDI and trade typically shows similar patterns. This applies to Eastern Europe for which Western Europe represents the main export markets and also the main source of FDI inflows. Such inflows contribute to product upgrading over time.

The analytical focus has various time horizons and brings some new insights, including the fact that in a non-inflationary economy the demand for money does not depend on the (long term) real interest rate. Indeed ambiguous results from empirical analysis in this field are well known. We also develop a rather convenient graphical model to focus on the issues of structural change and competitiveness and we propose new ways of how to include the optimum growth literature in the analysis of Schumpeterian economic dynamics. From a policy perspective, it becomes clear that analyzing macroeconomic topics can hardly be done adequately without taking into account structural change and innovation dynamics. While innovation and structural adjustment are a natural element of EU eastern enlargement both in western Europe and eastern Europe (or in a North-South perspective), not much is known about the adjustment costs of firms and countries when moving up the technology ladder.

H.2. Exchange Rate Dynamics, Relative Prices, Employment and Growth

H.2.1 Nominal Exchange Rate, Real Exchange Rate and True Long Run Money Market Equilibrium

Naturally, there is a link between the nominal exchange rate and the real exchange rate q^*. It holds that $E(\ln e) + E(\ln P^*) = E(\ln P)$. As regards the variance VAR it holds that $VAR(\ln e + \ln P^*) = VAR(\ln e) + VAR(\ln P^*) + 2 cov \ln e, \ln P^* = VAR \ln P$. If one were to assume that $VAR \ln P = VAR \ln P^*$, it is clear that for any variance of $\ln e$ and of $\ln P^*$, there must be negative $cov \ln e, \ln P^*$. It indeed is plausible that a depreciation of country I's currency will go along with a fall in country II's price level as goods imported from country I will become cheaper in country II.

From the perspective of a small open economy, the short term nominal exchange rate e is determined by the interest rate parity $i = i^* + a^E$ where a^E denotes the expected depreciation rate and i the nominal interest rate. In the long run the interest rate at home and abroad is given by $i = r + \pi$ (sum of the real interest rate r and the inflation rate π) and $i^* = r^* + \pi^*$ which implies with profit maximization r=

Y_K and $r^* = Y^*_K$, respectively: $(r-r^*) + (\pi - \pi^*) = a^E$. If there is free capital mobility and domestic and foreign bonds are perfect substitutes – but no free movement of foreign direct investment – it holds that $r = r^*$ which makes the interest parity fully consistent with long run purchasing power parity $P = eP^*$ if there is no (systematic) difference between expected and actual devaluation rate. The real exchange rate $q^* =: eP^*/P$ is determined in the short run by nominal exchange rate dynamics, in the long run P and P^* plays a role as well. Overshooting phenomena of the short term nominal exchange rate thus will affect the real exchange rate temporarily.

If domestic and foreign bonds are not perfect substitutes while we have full mobility of foreign direct investment, the marginal products at home and abroad will be equal in the long run: $Y_K = Y^*_K$. Hence profit maximization in both countries will indirectly bring about the condition $r = r^*$ in the long run. However, there is not really a long run in a strict sense if one does not consider a growth model and some other aspects. A specific aspect will refer to the fact that foreign direct investment flows will be a function of the real exchange rate as argued by FROOT/STEIN (1991). We will turn to this later and at first focus on the issue of a long run equilibrium real exchange rate.

If we are to make a prediction about the domestic price level we could use a model that predicts the nominal exchange rate (WELFENS/BORBÉLY, 2004) and combine this with a model which explains the foreign price level P^*. As regards the latter one may consider a rather simple approach based on four elements:

- money market equilibrium: This must be considered in long run growth modelling of a monetary economy;
- profit maximization: In the long run the real rate of interest must be equal to the marginal product of capital (with a standard Cobb-Douglas production function $Y = K^\beta(AL)^{1-\beta}$ the marginal product of capital $Y_K = \beta Y/K$ where K is capital, L is labor and A the level of labor-saving technology);
- a simple growth model: In a neoclassical growth model – with a growth rate $d\ln A/dt =: a$, a Cobb-Douglas production function (as above) and a savings function $S = sY$ – the steady state solution for per capita output $y\# = A_o e^{'at} (s/n)^{\beta/1-\beta}$; here e' denotes the Euler number. Hence the level of the growth path of y is a positive function of the initial level of technology A_o and the savings rate s, and the growth rate a. We will show that in an open economy with trade and foreign direct investment – and monetary transactions – the equilibrium solution looks more complicated and suggests new empirical approaches;
- an assumption with respect to the strategy of monetary policy.

At first we are interested in the level of P^* which is not really exogenous here. One can show – as an innovative feature of the model – that the long run demand for money is independent of the real interest rate unless the savings rate depends on the real interest rate.

Money market equilibrium requires that real supply (M/P; M is the nominal money stock) equals real money demand $m^*(\ldots)$:

$$M^*/P^* = m^*(Y^*, i^*) \tag{H.1}$$

The equilibrium condition for the money market is fairly general as we will see. Indeed, it is reasonable both for a narrow definition of the money supply (M_1) and for a broad money supply (M_3). If we consider M_1, cash balances plus deposits, one should expect a close medium term link with the price level. In an underemployed economy a rise in the money supply will raise output Y, and as the capacity utilization rate is increased, the price level P will increase with a certain delay. If one wants to express (A.1) in a kind of a quantity-theoretical framework we can simply write: $M_1 = V'(i,Y)PY$, with V' denoting the inverse of the income velocity of money. While it often is claimed that M_3 (M_1 plus term deposits plus savings deposits) is linked with the price level, there are no serious arguments why a rise in broad money M_3 should raise the price level unless one argues that there is a strong real balance effect. A serious argument would look different: A rise in M'_2 – here defined as M_3 minus M_1 – would increase within a portfolio-theoretical approach with the demand for stocks as real capital being complementary to money balances. Combining a higher stock of M'_2 with a higher value of stocks P'K (P' is the stock market price level and K the capital stock) reduces the portfolio risk. To the extent that P' is positively correlated with P, one may expect that empirical investigations on the long term demand for money come up with positive evidence for a link between M_3 and P. This point is easily understood if we assume that the fundamental value of stocks reflects discounted future profits which are – in a very simple two-period perspective (with Ω denoting unit labor costs and E the expectations operator) – given by the straightforward expression: $(P_t-\Omega_t)Y_t + (E(P_{t+1})-E(\Omega_{t+1}))Y_{t+1}/(1+i)= P'$. Assuming for simplicity that market participants expect $E(Yt+1)=Yt$, that unit labor costs are constant, that output Y= KlnL (we will, however, later switch to Cobb-Douglas) and that firms finance all investment through the stock market, we can state the following equation: $M'_2= V''(i,Y)P'K$ and – assuming that $\Omega=P\omega$ – thus $M'_2=V''(i,Y) (P(1-\omega))(1+ (1+i)^{-1})$ Y/lnL. We can then add M_1 and M'_2 and state – with $\omega'=:1-\omega$ – the long term money market condition:

$$M_3=V'(i,Y)PY+V''(i,Y)(P\omega'(1+(1+i)^{-1})Y/lnL=PY(V'(..)+ \qquad (H.1')$$

$$V''(..)\omega'(1+ (1+i)^{-1})\ Y/lnL.$$

This now looks more or less like the quantity theory of money $MV(Y,i) = \psi PY$. We therefore can indeed return to (H.1) while specifying for country II a specific money demand function:

$$M*/P* = Y*^{\sigma*}\ \sigma*'/i* \qquad (H.1'')$$

Thus the real money demand m* is specified as $Y*^{\sigma*}\ \sigma*'/i*$ where Y* is foreign real output and i* the foreign nominal interest rate which in turn is the sum of the expected inflation rate plus the real interest rate r. The parameters σ and σ' stand for the apparent income elasticity of the demand for money and the implicit interest responsiveness of the demand for money, respectively. However, we will show that in a long term perspective that $\sigma*$ is not really the income elasticity of the demand for money and the domestic real interest rate, respectively. Assuming (with K*, A*, and L* denoting capital, the level of technology and labor input) a Cobb-Douglas production function abroad, we have

$$Y^* = K^{*\beta^*}(A^*L^*)^{1-\beta^*} \tag{H.2}$$

Moreover as we assume that factors are rewarded in accordance with the marginal product rule, it holds that:

$$r^* = \beta^* Y^* / K^* \tag{H.3}$$

In the absence of inflation/deflation, we can thus write that the money market equilibrium for country II is as follows:

$$M^*/P^* = = Y^{*\sigma^*}\sigma^{*'}/(\beta^* Y^*/K^*) = K^* Y^{*\sigma^*-1}\sigma^{*'}/\beta^* \tag{H.4}$$

Here we have taken into consideration that i=r and that under profit maximization r=ßY/K. Taking logarithms we get:

$$\ln P^* = \ln M^* - (\sigma^*-1)\ln Y^* + (\ln\beta^*/\sigma^{*'}) - \ln K \tag{H.5}$$

As is obvious that the long run income elasticity of the demand for money is not σ*, rather it is σ*-1. We can rewrite the equation in per capita terms (actually in efficiency labor units AL) on the right-hand side, and this will be dubbed true long run money market equilibrium:

$$\ln P^* = \ln(M^*/A^*L^*) - (\sigma^*-1)\ln(Y^*/A^*L^*) + (\ln\beta^*/\sigma^{*'}) - \ln(K^*/A^*L^*) - \tag{H.6}$$
$$(\sigma^*-1)\ln(A^*L^*).$$

Note that in the case of flexible exchange rates, the nominal money supply is exogenous, and this is the main case we want to consider subsequently. The problem looks different under fixed exchange rates (in the case of eastern European accession countries this largely corresponds to the situation of moving to the European Exchange Rate Mechanism II).

If we assume that savings S=sY, no population growth, a zero rate of capital depreciation and that technological progress rate (dA/dt)/A=a is exogenous, we get – with y'=:Y/(AL) and k'=:K/(AL) and # for steady state – the standard neoclassical steady state solution, namely y'# = (s/a) $^{\beta/1-\beta}$ and K/(AL)=k'# = (s/a) $^{1/1-\beta}$. Thus it is obvious that in the long run demand for money, the savings rate and the progress rate will enter into play. The interest elasticity of money should be zero. If empirical analysis on the long run money demand finds a significant impact of r, it effectively confuses r* and r, that is the condition r=r*! (In an inflationary world one may, of course, have to consider the inflation rate as an additional variable determining the demand for money). Only in the case that one assumes that the savings rate depends on the interest rate would the long run money market equilibrium depend on the interest rate.

For the case that monetary policy maintains a constant m"#(with m"*=: M*/(A*L*)), we get:

$$\ln P^* = \ln m''^* \# - \{[1 + (\sigma^*-1)\beta]/(1-\beta)\}\ln(s^*/a^*) + (\ln\beta^*/\sigma^{*'}) \tag{H.7}$$
$$- (\sigma^*-1)\ln(A^*L^*).$$

   The long run equilibrium therefore is a positive function of the central bank's target money stock m'. Assuming that the apparent income elasticity of the demand for money (σ) is smaller than unity, the price level is a negative function of the level of technology and of the size of the labor force. Moreover, it is a negative function of the ratio of the savings rate to the progress rate provided that $((1+ (\sigma*-1)\beta*)/(1-\beta*))$ is positive. Note that the price level is stationary only if labor input declines with the same growth rate as the level of technology rises or if the apparent income elasticity of the demand for money is unity. The long run expected price level depends only on exogenous parameters, in particular the savings rate and the progress rate.

   In an open economy we may assume – now considering the world from a country I perspective – that savings $S=s(Y+ q*r* F^{n}**/P*)$, where $F^{n}*$ is nominal net claims on the rest of the world. Hence $q*r* F^{n}**/P*$ is interest income accruing in terms of domestic goods. We assume that net real foreign assets $q*F^{n}**/P*$ expressed in domestic goods - are proportionate to Y. Defining $f**':= q*F^{n}**/P*AL= q*F^{r}**/AL$, assuming that $f**'=vy'$ and assuming a constant progress rate in country I, namely a, and a production function

$$Y=K^{\beta}(AL)^{1-\beta} \tag{H.8}$$

we get a steady state value

$$y'\# = (s(1+ r*v)/a)^{\beta/1-\beta} \tag{H.9}$$

If we define $Fr**/AL=v'$ and assume that households consider v' as a target ratio we can write:

$$y'\# = (s(1+ r*q*v')/a)^{\beta/1-\beta} \tag{H.9'}$$

Per capita income therefore is – denoting with e' the Euler number - given by

$$y\# = A_o e'^{at} s(1+ r*q*v')/a)^{\beta/1-\beta} \tag{H.9''}$$

   Hence the long run steady state value of y'# depends on the real exchange rate. Moreover, long run money market equilibrium will also depend on the real exchange rate as is obvious if we plug in (H.9) into (H.6'); equation (H.6') is the corresponding equation for the domestic economy:

$$\ln P= \ln m'' - (\sigma-1)\ln y' + \ln(\beta/\sigma') – \ln k' - (\sigma-1)\ln(AL) \tag{H.6'}$$

$$\ln P=\ln m''- \{[1+(\sigma-1)\beta]/(1-\beta)\}\ln(s(1+ r*q*v')/a)+(\ln\beta/\sigma')- (\sigma-1)\ln(AL). \tag{H.6''}$$

   If we assume for simplicity that $r*q*v'/a$ is close to zero, we may use the approximation that $\ln (1+ r*q*v')/a) \approx r*q*v'/a$. A rise in the real exchange rate – hence a real depreciation – will increase the price level if $(1+(\sigma-1)\beta) <0$. This now points to an empirical issue.

H.2.2 Real Exchange Rate, Growth Path and Steady State

Let us get back to (H.9'). A real depreciation will raise the level of the growth path. This implication is, however, not robust if we assume that the progress rate depends negatively on q^*, for example, if we assume that imported licences or technology intensive intermediate products play an important role for the country considered. Then we may state the hypothesis (with a_1 denoting the progress rate in a closed economy).

$$a = a_1 - B"q^*; \text{assumption: } a_1 \neq B"q^* \text{ where } B" \text{ is a positive parameter re-} \quad (H.10)$$
$$\text{lated to } v'$$

We now also get an ambiguous result with respect to the impact of q^* on the price level (see H.6"). It still holds that the level of the growth path is positively influenced by q^* (see H.9'). However, the growth rate is negatively influenced and the sum of both effects on real per capita income will become negative after some critical time $t=t'$. We have a quasi-endogenization of growth and the progress rate, respectively, since from a traditional small country perspective, the real exchange rate – in a world in which only tradables exist – is exogenous. This, however, is no longer true if there are nontradables and differentiated tradables. For every product variety sold in the world market, increasing exports will correspond to a fall in the price of the respective product; this problem will be neglected for now. Rather we turn to the accumulation dynamics of foreign assets where an important aspect to consider is that $dF^n**/dt = r^* \, F^n** + PX/e - P^*J$ so that

$$(dF^n**/dt)/P^* = r^* \, F^r** + X/q^* - J = r^* \, F^r** + xY/q^* - jY \quad (H.11)$$

$$(dF^r**/dt)/F^r** = r^* + x(Y/q^*)/F^r** - jY/F^r** = r + x/v - jq^*/v \quad (H.12)$$

In the next section we take a closer look at the real exchange rate from a medium term perspective, where the link between the real exchange rate and investment will be considered. Before we turn to this aspect let us briefly consider the case of an open economy with foreign direct investment inflows and a production function where real money balances and the ratio of per capita imports $j'=J/(AL)$ and export intensity $x'=X/(AL)$ enter the production function

$$Y = K^{\beta}(AL)^{1-\beta}(J/AL)^{\beta'}(X/AL)^{\beta"}(m/AL)^{\beta"'} \quad (H.13)$$

The specific assumption here is that the output effect of imported intermediates/imported machinery and equipment – only those should be included in J here – is diluted if there are more workers in efficiency units. This mechanism could be associated with learning-by-doing in the sense that importing, say machinery, brings a one-off productivity increase for workers dealing with the sophisticated imports. If one assumes that imported machinery and equipment is employed with a lag of one period, the current import J would also show up in a higher K. A similar reasoning holds with respect to X/(AL) to the extent that one assumes that X/AL is a measure of the exposure of workers to world market dynamics. It is debatable whether or not m or $m'=:m/(AL)$ – or m/L – should enter the production function; only empirical analysis can solve the issue. Here we use m', as one may argue that liquidity on a per capita basis is relevant for saving transaction costs and actually contributing to labor productivity. Finally, note that in a model with both inward and outward foreign direct investment, one might also have to include the stock of outward FDI, namely to the extent that there is considerable asset-seeking investment which implies international transfer of technology from the subsidiaries to the parent company. Firms in technology-intensive industries which invest abroad – namely in technologically-leading countries so that new technologies can be picked up rather easily – will benefit from a company wide technology transfer which is not just from the company headquarters to the subsidiary but also from the subsidiary back to the parent company.

Instead of using J/AL=:j' and X/AL=x' in the production function, one might chose a production function with 1+j' and 1+x' in the production function so that zero imports and zero exports imply a consistent output for the case of the closed economy. However, we use j' in the production function on the basis of the assumption that the country considered has become so specialized that it requires indispensable foreign inputs (in empirical investigations only the import of intermediate products and capital goods should be considered). For the sake of simplicity, we also use x' and not (1+x').

One may assume that real money balances enter the production function through a positive external effect of households using money in all transactions in the goods market. Therefore

$$y' = k'^{\beta} j'^{\beta'} x'^{\beta''} m'^{\beta'''} \tag{H.14}$$

The accumulation dynamics is given by

$$dk'/dt = s(1-b\beta)k'^{\beta} j'^{\beta'} x'^{\beta''} m'^{\beta'''} - ak' \tag{H.15}$$

Here we have assumed that foreign investors have a share b of the capital stock; and as capital income is βY, the national income is GDP minus $b\beta Y$. Savings S is proportionate to national income and therefore we have $S = sY(1-b\beta) = s'Y$. As we assume $J/AL = j(q^*)Y/AL$ and $X/AL = x'(q^*)Y^*/AL$ or more conveniently $X/AL = x'(q^*)y'^* A^*L^*/AL$ so that we get

$$y'\# = s(1-b\beta) j'^{\beta'} y'^{\beta} x'^{\beta''} y'^{*\beta''} (A^*L^*/AL)^{\beta''} m'^{\beta'''} /(n+\delta+a))^{\beta/1-\beta} \tag{H.16}$$

If one were to impose a strict long run trade balance requirement one might want to impose in (H.15) the long term equilibrium condition that $X = q^*J$ so that $x' = q^*j'$ which, however, is not done here.

Taking into account the money market equilibrium condition (H.6') in an appropriate way, namely $m' = y'^{1/\beta + (\sigma-1)} (AL)^{\sigma-1} \sigma/\beta$ we obtain with $\Omega' =: (A^*L^*/AL)$:

$$y'\# = s(1-b\beta) j'^{\beta'} y'^{\beta'} x'^{\beta''} y'^{*\beta''} \Omega'^{\beta''} y'^{(1/\beta+(\sigma-1))\beta'''} (AL)^{(\sigma-1)\beta'''} (\sigma/\beta)^{\beta'''} \tag{H.17}$$

$$/(n+\delta+a))^{\beta/1-\beta}$$

The implicit solution for the steady state output therefore is:

$$y\#^{,\,1-(1/\beta+(\sigma-1))\beta'''-\,\beta''} = s(1-b\beta)j^{,\,\beta'}x^{,\,\beta''}y^{,\,*\beta''}\Omega^{,\,\beta''}(AL)^{(\sigma-1)\beta'''}(\sigma/\beta)^{\,\beta'''} \qquad (H.18)$$
$$/(n+\delta+a))^{\beta/1-\beta}$$

$$y\#' = \{s(1-b\beta)j^{,\,\beta'}x^{,\,\beta''}y^{,\,*\beta''}\Omega^{,\,\beta''}(AL)^{(\sigma-1)\beta'''} \qquad (H.19)$$
$$(\sigma/\beta)^{\,\beta'''}/(n+\delta+a))^{\beta/1-\beta}\}^{1/1-(1/\beta+(\sigma-1))\beta'''-\,\beta''}$$

We will assume that bß is close to zero so that ln (1-bß)≈bß. If we take logarithms and define ß#:= 1/(ß/(1-ß))(1-(1/ß)+(σ-1))ß'''-ß'') we have a testable production function, namely for per capita income y=:Y/L

$$\ln y = \beta\#\ln s - \beta\#b\beta + \beta\#\beta'\ln j + \beta\#\beta''\ln x + \beta\#\beta''\ln y'^* + \beta\#\beta'''\ln(A^*L^*) \qquad (H.20)$$
$$+\beta\#((\sigma-1)\beta'''-\beta'')\ln(AL) +\beta\#\beta'''\ln(\sigma/\beta) - \beta\#(n+\delta+a) + at$$

Taking a look at (H.19) we can see that the level of the growth path positively depends on the effective savings rate s', x', y'* and the relative technology level (A*L*/AL); note that the y'* variable effectively reflects the impact of exports. The steady state equilibrium output per capita – in efficiency units – therefore is a positive function of the income elasticity of the demand for money provided that σ<0. As regards the impact of q* one has to consider b(q*), x'(q*) and j'(q*), which is not unambiguous. Only empirical research can give a clear answer. The growth rate of per capita income y=Y/L is a, and one could consider how foreign direct investment, government expenditures (consumption vs. R&D promotion) and trade will affect the progress rate which raises many new interesting issues. We will pick up the issue of government expenditures and discuss the impact on the level of growth and growth itself.

An interesting refinement is to assume that S=sY(1-bß)(1-u)(1-τ) where u is the structural unemployment rate and τ the income tax rate. The we get for y' in the steady state:

$$y\#' = \{s(1-b\beta)(1-u)(1-\tau)j^{,\,\beta'}x^{,\,\beta''}y^{,\,*\beta''}\Omega^{,\,\beta''}(AL)^{(\sigma-1)\beta'''} \qquad (H.21)$$
$$(\sigma/\beta)^{\,\beta'''}/(n+\delta+a))^{\beta/1-\beta}\}^{1/1-(1/\beta+(\sigma-1))\beta'''-\,\beta''}$$

We thus could consider the impact of unemployment and the income tax rate – both a higher tax rate and a higher unemployment rate will reduce the level of the growth path - as well as that of j' and x' on the level of the growth path. Moreover, we can also discuss the effects of the unemployment rate and the tax rate – making specific assumptions how tax revenues are used (public consumption vs. R&D financing) – on the growth rate.

Finally, we should take into account the requirement that in the long run the current account must be balanced. For the simple case of no foreign direct investment we have

$$XP = eP^*J \qquad (H.22)$$

We will assume that

$$X=j^*(q^*)Y^* \tag{H.23}$$

$$J=j(q^*)Y \tag{H.24}$$

Therefore we get – while multiplying the left hand side of (H.22) by $A^*L^*/[A^*L^*]$ and the right hand side by $AL/[AL]$ – the equation $XP=eP^*J$ or

$$j^*Y^*P = eP^*jY \tag{H.22'}$$

Thus we obtain:

$$[A^*L^*]j^*Y^*P/[A^*L^*] = ALeP^*jY/[AL] \tag{H.22''}$$

$$[A^*L^*]/[AL]= q^*jy'/j^*y^* \tag{H.23}$$

Note that there is a relation between j' and j since $J/(AL) =:j'= jy'$; this applies in a similar way to the foreign country, namely $j'^*=:x'=j^*y'^*$.

Replacing in (H.17) the expression $\Omega'=: A^*L^*/AL$ from (H.23) we get

$$y'\#= s(1-b\beta) \, j^{\beta'} y'^{2\beta'} x'^{\beta''} y^*\,^{\beta''}[q^*jy'/j^*y^*]^{\beta''} y'^{(1/\beta +(\sigma-1))\beta'''} (AL)^{(\sigma-1)\beta'''} \, e'^{\beta'''\sigma/\beta} \quad (H.17')$$
$$/(n+\delta+a))^{\beta/1-\beta}$$

Therefore we can write

$$y'\#= s(1-b\beta) \, j'^{\beta'} y'^{\beta'+\beta''} x'^{\beta''} y^*\,^{2\beta''}[q^*j/j^*]^{\beta''} y'^{(1/\beta +(\sigma-1))\beta'''} (AL)^{(\sigma-1)\beta'''} \quad (H.17'')$$
$$e'^{\beta'''\sigma/\beta} /(n+\delta+a))^{\beta/1-\beta}$$

We thus could derive a similar equation to (A.21) where the elasticity ψ' of y' with respect to the modified expression {…} is higher than in (A.21); note that we make the assumption that y'* actually is foreign steady state per capita income in efficiency units. Moreover, one can see that the elasticity of y'# with respect to the real exchange rate also will have to consider the expression $[q^*j(q^*)/j^*(q^*)]^{\beta''}$ which reflects a modified Marshall Lerner impact. The overall effect of q* on y' can, however, not be assessed without considering that b, j' and j' also are a function of q*. At the bottom line one may consider to allow a permanent trade balance surplus in our model with asymmetric foreign direct investment and this leads to a minor modification:

$$j^*Y^*P = eP^*jY + b\beta YP \tag{H.22'}$$

On the right hand side we have nominal imports plus nominal dividends accruing to the foreign parent companies. Obviously we can write:

$$j^*Y^* = [q^*j +b\beta]Y \tag{H.24}$$

It also is debatable whether or not an adequate import function should not read $J=jZ$ (with national income $Z=:Y- b\beta Y$); and an adequate export function $X=jZ^* = jY^*+b\beta Y/q^*$.

H.2.3 Investment, Real Exchange Rate and Employment

As is well known the real exchange rate ($q^*=eP^*/P$) has an impact upon the trade balance, however, the real exchange rate also will affect foreign direct investment as was emphasized for the case of imperfect capital market by FROOT/STEIN (1991). Foreign investment inflows in the recipient country – say an EU accession country or a newly industrializing economy – can be expressed as a share ψ in overall investment where $\psi(q^*)$; the partial derivative of ψ with respect to q^* is positive since a depreciation of the host country currency effectively makes it easier for foreign investors to be successful in mergers and acquisitions. We thus assume that the overall investment output ratio I/Y is a positive function of the real exchange rate (in empirical analysis a positive correlation between I/Y also will catch the impact of improving net export expectations on the side of investors). Assuming profit maximization in an open economy in the form that the marginal product of capital Y_K is equal to the foreign real interest rate r^* we can write for the growth rate of real output

$$g_Y = (I/Y)r^* \tag{I}$$

Denoting the investment output ratio as $z=z(q^*)$ and recalling Verdoorn's Law, namely that the growth rate (g) of labor productivity Y/L is a positive function of the growth rate of output (V and V' are positive parameters) we have:

$$g_{Y/L} = Q' + Q''g_Y; \tag{II}$$

According to Verdoorn's Law the growth rate of employment will be a positive function of output growth

$$g_L = - Q' + [1-Q'']g_Y; \tag{III}$$

hence

$$g_L = - Q' + [1-Q'']z(q^*) \, r^* \tag{IV}$$

If we assume that the parameter Q' is a positive function of the productivity-wage lag – meaning the time it takes for the real wage to fully catch up with marginal labor productivity Y_L (the long run equilibrium values are denoted by #) – we have in the case that the marginal product is proportionate (1-ß is a parameter in the interval 0,1) to the average labor productivity ($Y_L=(1-\text{ß})y$; ß is the output elasticity of capital):

$$g_L = - Q' + Q''([y\#/w\#]/[y/w]) \, z(q^*) \, r^* \tag{V}$$

The parameter Q'''=:1-Q'' thus depends positively on the steady state productivity-wage ratio relative to the current productivity wage ratio. Hence outside the steady state – according to which (1-ß)y would be equal to the real wage rate w – the growth rate of labor demand will be a negative function of the current real wage rate and a positive function of per capita income y. An interesting case is to assume that Q''' – we have assumed Q'' to be smaller than unity – follows an inverted logistical adjustment path as y/w approaches y#/w#.

The following figures show the growth rate of employment and the annual change of investment/ GDP ratio for the EU 15 countries, Germany, Hungary, Poland, and the Czech Republic.

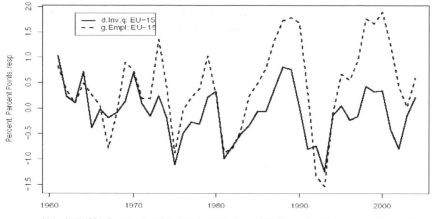

Note: Until 1991: Growth rates of Western Germany, since 1992: Unified Germany, also in E–15–Aggregates

Fig. 62. EU 15: Growth Rate of Employment and Annual Change of Investment / GDP Ratio

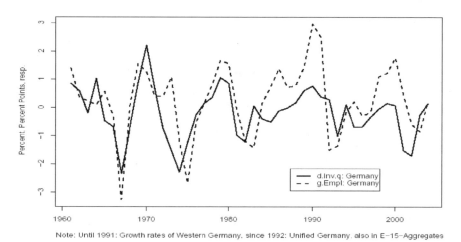

Note: Until 1991: Growth rates of Western Germany, since 1992: Unified Germany, also in E–15–Aggregates

Fig. 63. Germany: Growth Rate of Employment and Annual Change of Investment / Ratio

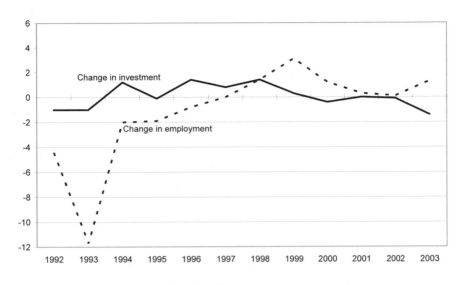

Source: Transition Report, EBRD, various issues

Fig. 64. Hungary: Growth Rate of Employment and Annual Change of Investment / GDP Ratio

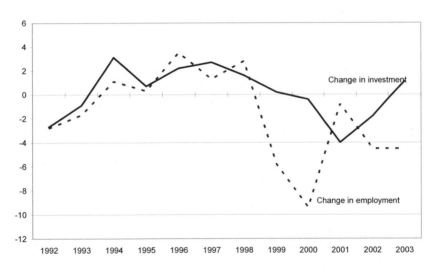

Source: Transition Report, EBRD, various issues

Fig. 65. Poland: Growth Rate of Employment and Annual Change of Investment / GDP Ratio

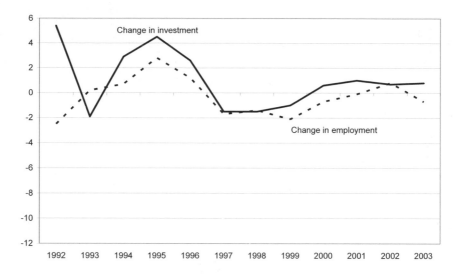

Source: Transition Report, EBRD, various issues

Fig. 66. Czech Republic: Growth Rate of Employment and Annual Change of Investment / GDP Ratio

H.2.4 Technology, Exchange Rate Changes and the Relative Tradable Price

In the following analysis, we will take a closer look at the role of technological progress - while sectoral capital stocks are assumed to be given in the short run - which for simplicity we assume to only occur in the tradables sector (T). Tradables and nontradables are gross substitutes on the demand side and the supply side. There is a technology shift parameter in the tradables market, namely A. In addition, the demand for tradables is assumed to negatively depend on the relative price of nontradables ($P^N/P^T=:\varphi$) and positively on the real money balances M/P – a proxy for wealth. M denotes the nominal money supply and P the price level. We assume that the quality of N-goods is given and does not change, but the quality index Q of tradables could change through product innovations in the tradables sector. Hence the hedonic price index is given by $P=P^{N\ \alpha}\ P^{T\ 1-\alpha}/Q=\varphi^{1-\alpha}\ P^T/Q$; the parameter α is in the interval 0,1. Due to arbitrage, we have $P^T=e\lambda'P^{T}*$ where e is the nominal exchange rate, λ' is a parameter reflecting trading costs (before full regional integration $\lambda'>1$, full integration $\lambda'=1$). Supply in both sectors depends on φ and labor as well as on capital stocks.

We can state a straightforward equilibrium condition for the tradables sector, namely tradables supply T=T' where T' denotes tradables demand. Any excess supply in the tradables sector is equivalent to a current account surplus since we are considering a small open economy. Equilibrium in the nontradables market is given by the equality of nontrables supply N' and nontradables demand

N'= N"(...) +G where N"(φ, τ, M/P) is the private sector demand for nontradables and G government consumption of nontradables; τ denotes the tax rate. Note that the nominal exchange rate e enters the demand for both goods since M/P can be written as $M/(\varphi^{1-\alpha}e\lambda'P^{T*}/Q)$. The initial equilibrium is determined by the intersection of the NN curve - which portrays equilibrium in the nontradables markets - and the TT curve which portrays equilibrium in the tradables sector – as well as a balanced current account. Technological progress in the tradables sector, that is a rise in the supply parameter A, will shift the TT-curve upwards (TT_1) so that there is a rise in the relative nontradables price and a nominal depreciation. The price level remains constant if the nominal appreciation rate $-g_e = (1-\alpha)g_\varphi$ where g denotes growth rates. A given price level P_o is here indicated simply by the curve $\varphi=(QP_o/P^T*e)^{1/(1-a)}$.; the PP_o line indicates a given price level in φ-e space. Thus it depends on the slope of the NN curve whether or not technological progress in the T-sector brings about a fall in the price level or a rise in the price level. If the nominal wage is inflexible, a falling price level will bring about classical unemployment which in the context of empirical analysis should not be misinterpreted as technological unemployment! If there is no downward wage flexibility points below the PP line, an excess supply in the labor market is indicated. If the composition of tradables is increasingly characterized by product innovations, the tradables supply will become less price elastic as a higher share of product innovations typically will require more specialization and indeed higher sunk costs on the tradables supply side. Moreover, the demand for tradables becomes less price elastic; that is $\partial T'/\partial\varphi$ will fall and the slope of the TT curve will rise. Hence a depreciation will bring about a higher current account than previously. This is somewhat surprising as one might think that a lower relative price elasticity makes the trade balance (or the current account) less price sensitive. However, one has to take into account that a rise in the relative price level of nontradables will cause less supply-switching on the supply side of the economy.

An expansionary fiscal policy in the sense of raising G would shift the NN curve to the right and hence bring about a higher relative nontradables price and a depreciation of the currency. A fall in trading costs will shift the NN curve upwards and the TT curve downwards which in any case will bring about a nominal depreciation while the effect on the relative price of nontradables is unclear. An expansionary fiscal policy in the form of a cut in the tax rate τ will bring about a rightward shift of TT and an upward shift of NN. In the lower part (b) of the following graph we have drawn – for an exogenous expected exchange rate $E(e_1)$ - the interest parity line according to $i=i^*+E(e_1)-e/e$. The short term impact of an expansionary monetary policy would be a fall in the nominal interest rate and hence a nominal and real depreciation. As prices are assumed to be sticky, there would be a price reaction only in the medium term. An expansionary monetary policy therefore moves the economy (see panel a)) from point E_o to point F' so that we have an excess supply in the tradables market – with a temporary current account improvement - and an excess supply in the N market. The rise in the real money stock shifts the NN curve and the TT curve to the right and finally also will raise the price level (which implies that the long run rightward shift of NN and TT will be smaller than in the medium term). Hence we will get a new real equilibrium point which might be between E_o and F'. Assuming that money market equilibrium can be written as M= V'(i)PK, a rise in M will shift the PP-line upwards; a rise in i dampens the shift.

The approach is more complex if we consider the HANSEN/RÖGER (2000) model. In the HANSEN/RÖGER model, the real exchange rate is determined through the intersection point of the domestic equilibrium line and the foreign equilibrium line. In that model, consumption is assumed to depend positively on real income Y and negatively on the gap between the desired stock of wealth (F) and actual real financial wealth f. It also depends negatively on the real interest rate r relative to the long run equilibrium level r# (in a small open economy equal to r*). Interest parity together with the domestic equilibrium condition gives a differential equation in q, while the current account equilibrium equation is given by df/dt = CA = rf + TB (with CA and TB denoting current account an trade balance, respectively). Setting dq/dt=0 and df/dt=0 gives two equilibrium lines (qq and ff) which jointly determine general equilibrium. We will pick up some aspects of this model subsequently.

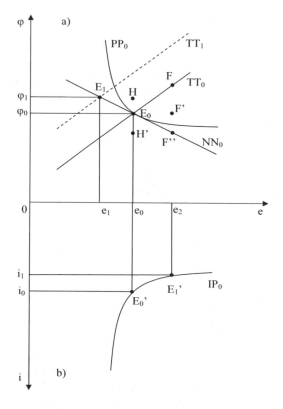

Fig. 67. Equilibrium in the (a) Tradables Market (TT) and Nontradables Market (NN) and Interest Parity (b); Model Can Track Fiscal and Monetary Policy & Supply Shocks

Tradables supply is T, demand T'; $T(\varphi, A, K^T) = T'(\varphi, \tau, M/P)$; with $P^N/P^T = : \varphi$; $M=PV(i)K$; $P=\varphi^{1-\alpha}P^T/Q$; nontradables equilibrium : $N(\varphi, K^N)=N''(\varphi, \tau, M/P)+ G$; arbitrage: $P^T=e\lambda P^{T*}$; interest parity $i= i^* +E_1(e)-e/e$.

There is one particular instability area in part a) of the figure, namely between the PP curve and the NN curve (starting in point E_o: the area where NN_o is written). We observe in this area both an excess supply in both goods market and an upward real wage pressure – at a given nominal wage – so that the risk of unemployment is quite high unless workers who lost their job in the N-sector easily find a new job in the T-sector which in turn would have to generate a rather high trade balance surplus. If there is product innovation in the tradables sector both the TT curve and the NN curve will become steeper.

H.3 Real Exchange Rate Dynamics and Economic Effects

Among the policy implications, we find that government in poor countries – such as EU accession countries – should stimulate savings and encourage foreign direct investment. It also would be wise to avoid early fixing of the nominal exchange rate, since the normal rise in the relative price of nontadables can no longer be achieved through nominal and real appreciation but only through an increase of the nontradables price which must be stronger than the price increase of the tradables price. That is, combining low inflation rates and the long term increase of nontradables prices is difficult to achieve unless one has flexible exchange rates. There is, however, some risk that flexible exchange rate regimes could be associated with temporary overshooting. Since the exchange rate is an international relative price, the reason for overshooting dynamics could be internal or external. Strong and sudden real appreciations should be avoided. If the real appreciation comes not through a fall in the nominal exchange rate but through a very low inflation rate, this could create serious problems in an economy with insufficient downward wage flexibility. Moreover, the relative rise in the nontradables price to normally be expected along with a process of economic catching-up requires a fall in the nontradables price which could be difficult to achieve. While foreign direct investment inflows are basically a welcome ingredient for economic catching up, governments in host countries should be careful to avoid unnecessary concentration tendencies which could undermine the flexibility and innovativeness needed in an open economy exposed to temporary or permanent real appreciation of its currency.

The EU Eastern enlargement will bring a medium term real appreciation for the accession countries, which will affect foreign direct investment, trade and the current account. From a EU-15 perspective, Eastern Europe generates pressure for structural change and international outsourcing on the one hand, while driving high wage countries to increasingly specialize in technology-intensive goods on the other. For the governments of EU-15 countries, this could encourage promotion of technological progress through R&D subsidies. From an optimum growth perspective, both national governments and supranational EU policy should consider opportunities to bring about optimum growth. There clearly is a special challenge for the Euro zone due to uniform interest rates The long term dynamics of the current account, FDI growth and structural change require further analysis. It is not easy to design a consistent economic policy which stimulates the overall growth of EU-25 while maintaining economic stability.

The EU would be well advised to seriously consider the implications of endogenous growth theory and of the optimum growth theory. National governments in leading EU countries could indeed try to influence the progress rate, and in the Euro zone achieving optimum growth could be a challenge for the cooperation between national governments of the Euro zone's member countries – adjusting R&D promotion policy adequately – ad the ECB with its opportunities to adjust the interest rate. Eastern European accession countries also should carefully study the options of an optimum growth policy.

A major challenge for EU25 is that an efficient modernization and innovation process requires that the adjustment in EU15 – especially in high wage countries – should be structural change towards skill-upgrading and product innovations which normally go along with a relative rise in export unit values ("relative" means in comparison to the USA, which is the leading OECD country). In a triangular economic perspective, rising EU15 outsourcing towards EU accession countries in eastern Europe should strengthen global competitiveness so that EU15 RCAs in the global market should improve in particular in sectors in which EU15 countries have rising imports from accession countries. Whether the overall development of EU25 terms of trade will be positive in the medium term is unclear. As regards Germany, it is remarkable that the weighted average export unit value for industrial products stayed flat in the 1990s while that of the US strongly increased. Hence, the relative German export unit value has fallen considerably.

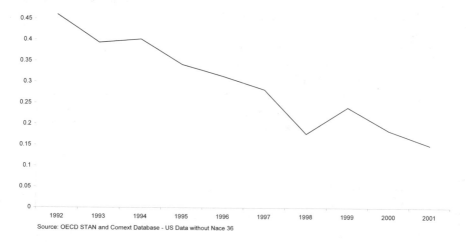

Source: OECD STAN and Comext Database - US Data without Nace 36

Fig. 68. Relative Export Unit Value of German Industry (Germany Relative to US, Weighted)

The developments in Germany suggest that it is facing declining profit rates in world markets and might therefore face an intensified struggle for income (i.e., social conflicts between workers and capital owners). If Germany is forced by the interplay of domestic dynamics and global structure change to move more towards less profitable sectors, the German current account balance might improve if import demand is sufficiently elastic. It will in any case be important to conduct further research on European and global economic dynamics in the future.

Appendix H.1: Statistical Measures of Structural Change

According to STAMER (1999), the degree of structural change between the time points or time periods, 1 and 2, can be measured by the following indicators (for output X) if we distinguish sectors i = 1 ... n,

$$\sum_{i=1}^{n} X_i = X \tag{1}$$

and $x_i = \dfrac{X_i}{X}$

$$\sum_{i=1}^{n} x_i = 1 \tag{2}$$

1. Norm of absolute values (*NAV*):

$$NAV_{1,2} = \sum_{i=1}^{n} \left| x_{i2} - x_{i1} \right| \tag{3}$$

2. Euclidean norm (*EuN*):

$$EuN_{1,2} = \sqrt{\sum_{i=1}^{n} \left(x_{i2} - x_{i1} \right)^2} \tag{4}$$

3. Sum of relative differences' absolute values (*SRD*):

$$SRD_{1,2} = \sum_{i=1}^{n} \left| \frac{x_{i2} - x_{i1}}{x_{i1}} \right|, \quad x_{i1} > 0 \tag{5}$$

4. Information gain (*IG*):

$$IG_{1,2} = \sum_{i=1}^{n} x_{i2} \, \mathrm{ld} \left| \frac{x_{i2}}{x_{i1}} \right|, \quad x_{i1} > 0, \quad x_{i2} > 0 \tag{6}$$

5. Growth rate parameter (*GRP*):

$$GRP_{1,2} = \sum_{i=1}^{n} x_{i1} |g_{i2} - g_2|,$$ (7)

that is with $g_{i2} = \ln X_{i2} - \ln X_{i1}, \quad g_2 = \ln X_2 - \ln X_1$

$$GRP_{1,2} = \sum_{i=1}^{n} x_{i1} \left| \ln \frac{x_{i2}}{x_{i1}} \right|, \quad x_{i1} > 0, \quad x_{i2} > 0.$$

6.LILIEN Index (*LI*) (see LILIEN, 1982a, b):

$$LI_{1,2} = \sqrt{\sum_{I=1}^{n} x_{i2} \left(\ln \frac{x_{i2}}{x_{i1}} \right)^2}, \quad x_{i1} > 0, \quad x_{i2} > 0.$$ (8)

7. The modified LILIEN Index (*MLI*) (see STAMER, 1999, p. 42-44):

$$MLI_{1,2} = \sqrt{\sum_{I=1}^{n} x_{i1} x_{i2} \left(\ln \frac{x_{i2}}{x_{i1}} \right)^2}, \quad x_{i1} > 0, \quad x_{i2} > 0.$$ (9)

Some important features of these indicators of structural change are summarized in Table 1. Note that the first three properties are necessary (and sufficient) conditions for an indicator to be a metric space.

Table 11. Features of Structural Change Indicators

	Zero distance in case of identity	Symmetry in respect of time direction	Fulfillment of triangular inequality	Measure of dispersion	Consideration of sector's weights
Norm of absolute values	yes	Yes	Yes	no	yes
Euclidean norm	yes	Yes	Yes	no	yes
Sum of relative differences' absolute values	yes	No	No	yes	no
Information gain	yes	No	No	no	yes
Growth rate parameter	yes	No	No	yes	yes
LILIEN Index	yes	No	No	yes	yes
Modified LILIEN Index	yes	yes	Yes	yes	yes

Source: STAMER (1999), p. 53

All indicators mentioned above have advantages and drawbacks. The choice of an indicator has to be made on the basis of the goals of the respective research. For many purposes, the norm of absolute values and/or the Euclidean norm are frequently used measures. A useful indicator as a measure of diversification is the index proposed by LILIEN (1982a). Some drawbacks of this indicator are remedied by the Modified LILIEN Index of STAMER (1999). This, however, comes at the cost of a more complex interpretation.

Appendix H.2: Indicators Measuring Structural Change

Table 12. Various Indicators Measuring Structural Change Based on Export Data to the EU 15 at the NACE 2-Digit Level (Difference Between Indicators in the Time Periods 1998-2003 and 1993-1998

	Div NaV	Div EuN	Div SRD	Div IG	Div GRP	Div LI	Div MLI
Austria	0.0282	0.0070	-17.4023	0.0568	0.0236	0.0482	0.0023
Belgium & Luxembourg	0.0649	0.0380	-1.7611	0.0068	0.0352	-0.0016	0.0165
Bulgaria	-0.0957	-0.0584	2.1720	-0.0652	-0.0692	-0.0350	-0.0241
Croatia	0.1755	0.0605	25.0527	0.3429	0.0209	0.3068	0.0217
Cyprus	-0.2069	-0.1975	-10.8361	-0.4727	-0.0511	-0.2426	-0.0754
Czech Republic	-0.0921	-0.0071	3.2848	0.0815	-0.0639	0.0978	-0.0075
Denmark	-0.1066	-0.0607	-2.4890	-0.0621	-0.0344	-0.0915	-0.0260
Estonia	-0.4466	-0.1878	-1108.0745	-1.8960	-0.0219	-1.1023	-0.0680
Finland	0.2072	0.0843	-4.3084	0.1243	0.1531	0.0365	0.0351
France	0.0696	0.0404	1.0470	0.0288	0.0342	0.0387	0.0174
Germany	0.0202	0.0050	1.2968	0.0100	0.0086	0.0192	0.0021
Greece	0.2293	0.0914	7.0727	0.2469	0.1065	0.1867	0.0368
Hungary	-0.5494	-0.1816	-20.5246	-0.8139	-0.1937	-0.4597	-0.0670
Ireland	-0.0376	0.0209	-1.1866	-0.0090	-0.0222	-0.0057	0.0089
Italy	0.0090	0.0020	2.0360	0.0121	0.0085	0.0135	0.0008
Latvia	-0.6174	-0.3150	-1095985614.4010	-0.7041	-0.1577	-0.3684	-0.1372
Lithuania	-0.6986	-0.3804	-120.0675	-0.9331	-0.4341	-0.3363	-0.1342
Malta	0.1057	0.0405	1.4643	0.2840	0.2601	0.0441	-0.0094
Netherlands	-0.1648	-0.0787	-0.8003	-0.0468	-0.0472	-0.0777	-0.0352
Poland	0.0589	0.0602	-2.6743	0.0225	0.0260	0.0051	0.0256
Portugal	0.0851	0.0184	44.1747	0.1498	0.0161	0.1505	0.0059
Romania	0.0188	-0.0055	9.3168	0.0527	0.0127	0.0518	-0.0030
Russia	0.0496	0.0131	11.8606	0.0730	0.0515	0.0336	0.0022
Slovak Republic	-0.3409	-0.1297	-36.6218	-0.6989	-0.0743	-0.4170	-0.0386
Slovenia	-0.0613	-0.0314	-52.7684	0.0738	-0.0343	0.0955	-0.0158
Spain	0.0764	0.0380	-5.9234	0.0157	0.0362	0.0274	0.0165
Sweden	0.0107	-0.0043	-14.2139	-0.0239	0.0231	-0.0422	-0.0015
Turkey	-0.0547	-0.0298	-6.2853	-0.0181	-0.0300	-0.0068	-0.0148
UK	-0.0016	-0.0013	0.8464	-0.0016	-0.0019	-0.0006	-0.0005

I. Innovations in the Digital Economy: Promotion of R&D and Growth in Open Economies

I.1 Introduction

Starting in the 1980s, a new wave of economic globalization has brought about a relative increase of foreign direct investment and hence a rising role of multinational companies (MNCs). MNCs are crucial for the diffusion of new knowledge, and those firms are also key actors in research and development. With China and a new Russia – plus the smaller former socialist CMEA countries of Eastern Europe – opening up to the world economy, new players have entered global markets and competition has intensified. The end of the Cold War has intensified the global innovation race for civilian products as the share of military R&D expenditures in the US, France and the UK has fallen to close or less than 50%.

There is a long-term upward trend in the ratio of expenditures on research and development (R&D) to national income. While the ratio of R&D to GDP was close to 1% in OECD countries in the 1960s, it reached about 2% in the 1980s and is moving towards 3% at the beginning of the 21st century. Technological competition has increased since expenditures on research and development have grown relative to GDP. While process innovations have reduced production costs, product innovations stand for novel goods for which consumers (or investors) show a higher willingness to pay than for standard products. Product innovations also tend to raise profitability of firms and hence stimulate investment. While innovations in industry are often reflected in patents, innovations in services are more difficult to protect through intellectual property rights. A special case is software which enjoys copyright protection and more recently patent protection in the US. Technological competition also increased in the 1990s and the early 21st Century, because global diffusion of new knowledge accelerated due to the expansion of the internet.

With the expansion of the digital economy, there is an increasing role of innovative services whose significance is rather difficult to assess since patenting is relatively rare. Moreover, while a rise of export unit values (corrected for inflation) is, to some extent, a useful indicator for assessing the novelty of a product, a similar analytical category for services is not available. First, many tradable services are intra-company services for which transfer prices are applied which might reflect the tax considerations of multinational companies rather than the novelty of the service provided. Second, many services are nontradable, thereby bringing identification problems in the context of the Balassa-Samuelson effect, which suggests that the relative price of nontradables will increase parallel to the rise of per capita income. (There is also the more general problem that the effects of process innovations which reduce costs and product innovations – which raise the willingness to pay – often overlap in reality). This structural relative price effect makes it difficult to relate price increases in services to the degree of innovativeness in the provision of services. Thirdly, productivity measurement in services is more difficult than in industry, which makes the distinction between product innovations and process innovations cumbersome. Finally, many services are provided by government which has a particularly weak record in measuring productivity growth and in developing innovations. In a modern services society, it is hardly conceivable to fully exploit technological dynamics without carefully nurturing and stimulating innovativeness in the services sector, a point which has largely been overlooked in the Lisbon agenda of the EU aimed at making the union the most competitive economy in the world by 2010.

As regards technologically-leading countries, the US saw an acceleration in both economic growth and patenting in the 1990s. With respect to the EU, growth was slower than in the US in the 1990s, but the combination of the single market and EU enlargement in 2004 should allow higher growth in the EU-25. According to the Lisbon summit, the EU is to become the most competitive knowledge-based economy by 2010, a goal which includes the aim of raising employment rates considerably. The Lisbon goal cannot be achieved if EU member countries do not see improvements in the growth of output and employment. Germany, France, Italy and the UK play a key role here. The smaller open economies achieved a solid performance in the late 1990s with higher growth, higher employment and reduced budget deficits or even surpluses bring achieved. (The latter holds true even for Finland, which had a record high 18% unemployment rate in 1993 yet only 9% in 2004).

While the UK achieved full employment and sustained growth in the 1990s, the three core countries of the Euro zone still have to make progress. High unemployment rates in France, Italy and Germany are key problems with close to 30% unemployment in Southern Italy and Eastern Germany. A wide range of policy reforms in Germany in 2003/2004 (Hartz reforms) is likely to yield positive effects in terms of both lower unemployment and higher employment ratios within a medium-term adjustment period. However, restoring sustained growth is a different issue, as is overcoming the economic West-East divide in Germany.

The German government has declared that raising expenditures on R&D promotion relative to GDP is a medium term policy priority. It is unclear whether the German states, which account for roughly ½ of government R&D expenditures, will contribute significantly to this goal. Both national and regional governments face the constraints of the Stability and Growth Pact, with Germany having exceeded the 3% deficit ratio in 2002, 2003, and 2004 (the latter year judging by the deficit ratio of the first half of 2004). Hence, Germany – and other EU countries with similar problems – will face serious dilemmas in raising R&D expenditures.

EU enlargement and economic globalization mean a changing international division of labour. The new international division of labour at the beginning of the 21st century is characterized by economic catching-up processes in newly industrializing countries of Asia – including China – and in Eastern Europe and Russia. Asian NICs are richly endowed with labour and have achieved rising capital intensity due to domestic investment and foreign direct investment. Former socialist countries in Eastern Europe and Russia are richly endowed with unskilled labour and human capital. Western Europe's high wage countries must increasingly specialize in technology intensive and knowledge intensive products. Focusing on the ratio of R&D-expenditures to GDP, Sweden as the OECD leader reached 4% at the beginning of the 21st century. As regards the ratio of expenditures on higher education to GDP, Sweden is No. 2 behind the USA. As regards R&D expenditures, Germany achieved 2.4% of GDP in 2003, slightly higher than in the years before but much lower than the 2.9% of 1989. Germany's problems with the 3% deficit ceiling impair efforts to raise expenditures on R&D and education, and similar problems can be found in Italy and France. While the US spends about 2.5% of GDP and Sweden (and Finland) about 1.7% of GDP on higher education, Germany spends only 1% of its GDP in this field for which German states are almost exclusively responsible. The latter also contribute to roughly 50% of public R&D expenditures. Skilled labour is largely complementary to R&D (and R&D requires skilled labour inputs itself). As regards skilled labour, this category is not only represented by university graduates, rather skilled labour is also related to training activities in firms. With workers' tenure falling gradually in large firms in Europe, the incentive for firms to invest in training and retraining is falling. The New Growth Theory has emphasized the role of R&D, skills and differentiated products.

Economic globalization forces firms to relocate production more often on an international scale, and the risk to train workers for domestic and foreign competitors also fails to encourage firms to reinforce training activities. To the extent that globalization places stronger pressure on capital markets to come up with a high return on investment in the short term, this could also undermine firms' long-term activities to invest in human capital. This could be a particular problem for Germany and Austria (as well as Switzerland) whose firms have a long record of investment in training and retraining. As international competitiveness always reflects relative competitive advantages, it is also noteworthy that many countries in the EU have caught up with the Federal Republic of Germany in terms of infrastructure capital, R&D expenditures and education expenditures (relative to GDP). EU eastern enlargement has opened up new opportunities for the relocation of industry, and often supplier firms – they are expected to deliver on-time innovative high quality inputs ("complex subsystems") – follow the foreign investment of large companies, thereby accelerating the international transfer of know-how and knowledge. Moreover, the internet reinforces the international diffusion of knowledge so that first mover advantages could fade away more quickly.

These developments as well as the long record of high unemployment raise many questions in terms of raising innovativeness, accelerating structural change and launching adequate policy reforms for high wage countries. The careful exploitation of opportunities to raise productivity in the information and communication technology (ICT) could be a new and important policy element (BARFIELD/HEIDUK/WELFENS, 2002). Raising labour productivity has been an important element of high growth in the US and several EU countries in the 1990s. While there is no debate about the productivity-enhancing role of ICT production, it is less clear that the use of ICT – linked to ICT capital accumulation – strongly contributes to higher growth of output and productivity. (A strange case is productivity measurement in the US retail sector where a firm with 10 employees selling 10 standard PCs in 1999, but 10 more modern PCs in 2000– worth 5 times as much, according to hedonic price measurement, as a 1999 PC – shows up as a productivity growth of 500%!) Production of computers or telecommunication equipment seems to be crucial for growth.

Given the increasingly important role of innovation dynamics for international markets, the promotion of research and development becomes a crucial part of economic policy. The traditional argument in favour of R&D promotion is the existence of positive external effects which imply that marginal social benefit exceeds marginal private benefits of R&D expenditures. However, some new developments in innovation dynamics have to be taken into account when raising the issue as to which role government should assume in the promotion of innovation and skills.

I.2 Innovations and New Economic Structures in the Digital Economy

I.2.1 Selected Innovation Traits in OECD Countries

Product innovations allow for the increase in product prices in world markets and hence the earning of high incomes (wages and profit). Process innovations are equivalent to cost reductions and allow firms to fetch higher market shares and high incomes, in particular if price elasticity is larger than unity or if increased market share also allows for the exploitation of dynamic scale economies (e.g., learning by doing effects). Innovation dynamics can be assessed in different ways:

- Innovation expenditures, usually scaled by sales ("R&D intensity"); this in an R&D input indicator
- Patents per capita (R&D output indicator)
- Product innovation rate (new products to the market in % of sales, survey data, innovation output indicator)
- Diffusion rate (new-to-the-firm products, figures are from surveys)

Taking a closer look at selected EU countries as well as the US and Japan, one finds that Sweden, Germany and Finland were leading in R&D intensity in manufacturing (6.4, 4.7 and 3.9, respectively, in 2003; EU average 3.45). France and the Netherlands achieved 3.1, the UK 3.0. Germany's R&D intensity in the services sector was much weaker, namely 1.6 compared to the EU average of 1.8. Sweden was a clear leader in this field. France and the UK recorded 1.6 and 1.4, respectively. It is interesting to observe that in the field of product innovations in manufacturing, Germany was below the EU average despite its leading position in R&D intensity. Finland, Sweden and France were leading countries in the field of product innovations. This suggests that the German innovation system might have considerable efficiency problems. A similar picture is found in production innovation in the services market. As regards diffusion indicators, Germany is a leading EU country. Moreover, Sweden and Germany recorded a high ratio of New-to-firm to New-to-market in the manufacturing industry, which points to relatively fast diffusion (this could reflect strong competition).

Table 13. European Innovation Scoreboard, 2003

European Innovation Scoreboard 2003 – Selected
Member States

	EU15	DE	FR	NL	AT	FI	SE	UK
Innov exp manuf	3.4	4.7	3.0	3.0	2.8	3.9	6.4	2.9
Innov exp serv	1.8	1.6	1.5	0.7	0.9	0.9	19.1	1.3
New-to-mark prods manuf	10.5	7.1	9.5	-	8.4	27.2	3.5	9.5
New-to-mark prods serv	7.4	3.7	5.5	-	4.3	12.2	9.3	-
New-to-firm prods manuf	28.6	40.3	17.5	23.8	23.1	31.1	32.1	-
New-to-firm prods serv	18.8	16.4	17.1	13.9	12.8	18.8	23.7	-
New-to-firm/New-to-mark prods manuf	2.7	5.7	1.8	-	2.8	1.1	9.2	-
New-to-firm/New-to mark prods serv	2.5	4.4	3.1	-	3.0	1.5	2.5	-

Source: European Commission (2003), Staff Working Papers, European Innovation Scoreboard 2003, page 27, Brussels and own calculations (DE = Germany, FR= France,
NL=Netherlands, AT= Austria; FI= Finland; SE = Sweden; UK = United Kingdom).

Against such apparent innovation weakness, one might consider it surprising
that Germany has such a high current account surplus, e.g. 5% of GDP in 2002.
However, 90 billion net exports recorded in 2002 would quickly melt away if full
employment could be restored; investment would increase by about 10% or by
about Euro 20 bill., consumption also by about 5% or 60 bill., which would leave
net exports down at Euro 10 bill. The assumption here is that consumption is a
positive function of disposable income and a negative function of the expected unemployment rate u^E. Investment is assumed to depend negatively on the real interest rate and the expected unemployment rate. To put it differently, a high net export position of a country with a high unemployment rate cannot simply be
considered an indicator of high international competitiveness. Rather, it largely reflects weak domestic demand. The reduction of net exports in the case of rising
employment and hence a falling expected and actual unemployment rate will hold
even if one takes into account the expansionary impact of higher employment on
the supply side. This perspective is, of course, not to deny that in a situation of
high net exports (and also in the case of net imports: see the US in the 1990s), certain sectors are positively successfully-specialized in production and export of
technology intensive or innovative products.

International competitiveness in specific sectors can be assessed on the basis of revealed comparative advantage indicators (RCA: sectoral export-import balance relative to overall export-import balance in the EU15 single market with an indicator above 1 indicating a positive sectoral competitive advantage) or with respect to export unit values. Higher RCAs and higher export unit values in certain sectors are likely to contribute quite strongly to output growth in the long run. Scale intensive sectors and science intensive sectors are obviously two potentially relevant sectors. In a high wage economy, emphasis on science-based products can strengthen competitiveness through product innovations which will temporarily lead to rising export unit values and hence higher profitability. This is a Schumpeterian perspective which leads away from perfect competition. Scale intensive products also imply that the perfect competition model does not hold. In some cases, scale intensive products exhibit both static and dynamic scale economies so that high production volumes could be combined with first mover advantages.

As regards export unit values and the change of export unit values over time, one should also take a look at weighted export unit values so that the relative economic significance of certain sectors can be understood. As regards Germany, it is well-known that the country has a positive RCA – read RCA above unity – in both the automotive industry and in other transport equipment (NACE 34 and 35). Taking a closer look at German industry, one can see that specialization in terms of RCA changed slightly in the decade after 1993. There is a high RCA in the manufacturing of fabricated metal products (NACE 28, notincluding machinery and equipment). It is also noteworthy that the export unit value has increased over time for this product group. In the field of office machinery and computers (NACE 30) – a sector which (together with NACE 32: telecommunications equipment) is considered highly relevant for productivity growth –, Germany has a negative RCA. Worse yet, the export unit value in this sector has declined. NACE 32 has improved over time. The overall picture with respect to the long term development of export unit values in German industrial export reveals that export unit values – average revenue per quantity unit (e.g. kilogram of steel etc.) – showed few changes over the period from 1993 to 2001. Which sectors are most important for economic dynamics: In a narrow sense those sectors which show a positive RCA and a high weighted export unit export value; this at least is the concept presented here. As regards the economic significance of export unit values it is indeed useful to take a closer look at weighted unit values where sectoral shares in overall manufacturing exports are taken as weights: considering only weighted indicators reaching at least 0.75 (hence export unit value must be high or the share of the respective sector in overall export of manufacturing) – see the bold figures in the respective tables - we see that 29, 30, 32, 33, 34 and 35 are crucial sectors for Germany; 32, 33, 34 (33 and 34 stand for the automotive sector; 32 is medical, precision and optical instruments, watches and clocks) are important sectors in each of the three countries considered, 35 and 29 only in Germany and the UK, 31 only in Hungary. Note that the change in the weighted export unit value of 32, 33 and 34 was positive in Germany, the UK and Hungary over the period 1992-2001; and this should translate into relatively rising wages for skilled workers as we may assume that these sectors are using skilled labor intensively. Interestingly, 18 (wearing apparel) which stands for labor intensive production is important in both the UK and in Hungary. Moreover, 18 stands indeed for a positive RCA both in the UK and in Hungary (figures underlined in the subsequent tables). As regards Germany 29, 33, 34 and 35 stand for an economically significant positive RCA, in the UK we have 29, 34 and 35 (note that 29 and 34 both stood for a positive RCA in the UK and Germany in 2000/01); as regards Hungary we find 18, 30, 31, 32, 34 as positive RCA: 34 is an overlap with the UK and Germany. The fact that Hungary could improve the weighted export unit value strongly in 34, the automotive sector, points to a strong catching-up process in the Hungarian automotive sector. To the extent that this finding is representative for accession countries in eastern Europe Germany's automotive firms acting in the lower quality segments of the market might face profitability problems in their German plants. The new international division of labor in Europe suggests that mass production of standard cars will be largely relocated to Eastern Europe's low wage countries. Hence the respective regions will face serious labor reallocation challenges in the early 21st century.

In sector 18 there is an overlap of Hungary with the UK, 30, 31 and 32 indicate successful Hungarian specialization. However, note that 31 and 32 - differentiated goods (this also includes 29) – stand for relative footloose industries: the manufacturing of office machinery and computers (30) and of electrical machinery and apparatus n.e.c. (31) could internationally be relocated relatively quickly. As regards Germany it is important to not that the country – in contrast to the UK (whose labor productivity has reached about 80% of the German level in the 1980s and 1990s) has no positive RCA in labor intensive industries - and this is surprising in a country which has more than four million unemployed; most of which are unskilled workers. One may consider this finding as an indicator for insufficient wage differentiation in Germany.

Obviously in all three countries medium technology fields are important for export dynamics and RCAs, respectively. One should point out that RCAs typically follow relative sectoral patent positions. A rising share in global patents in the respective sector translates with a time lag of 3-4 years into an improved sectoral RCA. Hence expenditures on research & development and innovation policies are important.

Compared to the apparently stable German industrial specialization pattern, Hungary has launched a rather impressive catching-up process since reinforcing the RCAs in some technology intensive sectors and was also able to fetch higher export unit values – a proxy for its ability to extract high prices in competitive EU market – in EU-15 markets. The British industry, whose relative size has declined over decades, still has certain fields in which it shows considerable strength. Interestingly, RCA and export unit values in labour intensive production increased in the period between 1993 and 2001, which obviously is consistent with the improved employment record of the UK. At the same time, the UK has also improved its position in science intensive products. Particularly important is NACE 30 (office equipment and computers), where the export unit value has improved over time while the RCA remained fairly stable below unity. The UK has shown a strong weighted improvement of the export unit value in NACE 32, the manufacturing of radio, television and communication equipment. With respect to the UK, considerable employment growth in the overall economy must, however, be explained largely by the expansion of the services sector. To some extent, it seems surprising that the UK has a positive RCA (exceeding unity) in only a few sectors. Moreover, where RCA is above unity, it is only weakly so. By contrast, Germany's industry shows some clear fields of comparative advantage as does Hungary, an interesting case of new economic dynamics in an EU accession country. It is quite noteworthy that Hungary achieved higher export unit values in several sectors. The table shows that weighted improvements of export unit values were strong in 30, 32 and 34, essentially electronic products which represent scale-intensive goods, science-based goods and differentiated goods (Classification of Industries follows OECD; (See BORBÉLY, 2006) RCA is modified RCA).

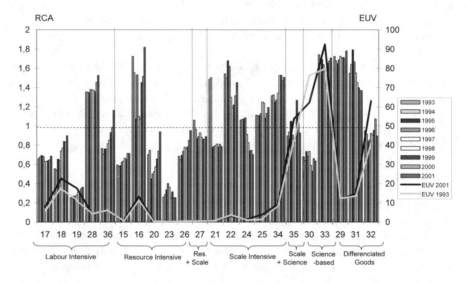

Fig. 69. Germany – RCA and Export Unit Values

Table 14. Germany – RCA, EUV, EUV Weighted with the Sectoral Export Shares of Manufacturing

NACE rev.1 (2-digit)	RCA 2000/01	EUV 2001	EUV 1993	EUV 2001 Weighted (exp. share)	EUV 1993 weighted (exp. share)	dEUV weighted (exp. share)	EUV 2001 weighted (GDP share)	EUV 1993 weighted (GDP share)	dEUV weighted (GDP share)
15	0.71	0.62	0.52	0.03	0.03	0.01	8,55	2,93	5,62
16	1,67	13.25	10,82	0.07	0.05	0.01	8,37	4,00	4,37
17	0.67	7,82	6.12	0.13	0.10	0.03	20,67	11,22	9,44
18	0.86	22.60	17.51	0.33	0.26	0.07	25,94	13,86	12,08
19	0.35	17.65	11,39	0.08	0.05	0.03	0,89	4,96	-4,07
20	0.84	0.38	0.40	0.00	0.00	0.00	0,43	0,15	0,28
21	0.80	0.85	0.73	0.02	0.02	0.00	3,58	1,56	2,02
22	1,38	3.11	3,83	0.03	0.04	-0.01	5,21	2,81	2,40
23	0.25	0.26	0.18	0.00	0.00	0.00	0,64	0,10	0,55
24	0.72	1,43	1.01	0.16	0.11	0.05	28,49	11,78	16,71
25	1,16	3,92	1,38	0.13	0.05	0.09	21,49	9,50	12,00
26	0.90	0.43	0.44	0.01	0.01	0.00	1,17	0,60	0,57
27	0.88	0.66	0.51	0.04	0.03	0.01	6,50	2,10	4,40
28	1,49	4,22	4,18	0.14	0.14	0.00	21,27	9,46	11,81
29	1,74	12.02	12,20	1,50	1,52	-0.02	197,6	96,45	101,1
30	0.65	62.26	76.05	4,29	5,24	-0.95	799,7	208,0	591,6
31	1,37	14.70	13.64	0.69	0.64	0.05	101,1	35,49	65,68
32	0.99	63.06	40.44	3,54	2,27	1,27	561,7	113,0	448,6
33	1,69	92.49	80.01	3,16	2,73	0.43	217,7	114,9	102,8
34	1,49	9,27	8,80	1,94	1,84	0.10	307,5	107,2	200,2
35	1.03	53.74	42.32	2,53	2.00	0.54	341,7	163,2	178,4
36	1.07	5,92	6,28	0.12	0.12	-0.01	19,83	8,25	11,58

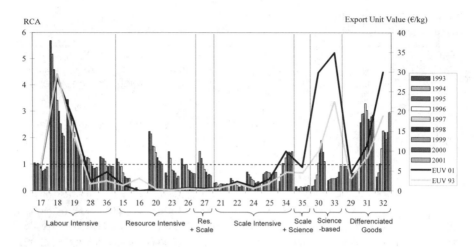

Fig. 70. Hungary – RCA and Export Unit Values

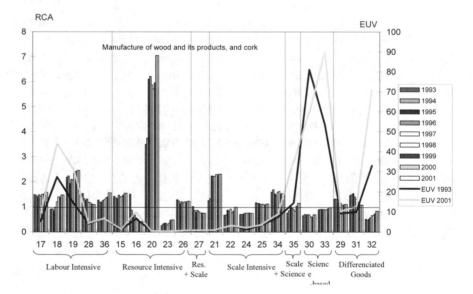

Fig. 71. UK – RCA and Export Unit Value

Table 15 Hungary – RCA, EUV, EUV Weighted with the Sectoral Export Shares of Manufacturing.

NACE rev.1 (2-digit)	RCA 2000/01	EUV 2001	EUV 1993	EUV 2001 weighted (exp. share)	EUV 1993 weighted (exp. share)	dEUV weighted (exp. share)	EUV 2001 weighted (GDP share)	EUV 1993 weighted (GDP share)	dEUV weighted (GDP share)
15	0,46	1,45	1,27	0,05	0,04	0,01	19,29	16,37	2,92
16	0,00	0,00	3,19	0,00	0,00	0,00	0,00	0,00	0,00
17	0,85	5,72	6,29	0,11	0,12	-0,01	48,85	26,15	22,70
18	2,11	28,39	29,41	1,05	1,09	-0,04	494,8	438,1	56,65
19	1,42	17,21	13,31	0,28	0,21	0,06	118,3	70,66	47,72
20	1,05	0,37	0,38	0,00	0,00	0,00	1,62	0,63	0,99
21	0,25	0,84	0,75	0,01	0,01	0,00	2,72	0,50	2,22
22	0,19	2,32	1,89	0,00	0,00	0,00	1,69	0,83	0,87
23	0,51	0,27	0,18	0,00	0,00	0,00	1,59	0,29	1,30
24	0,31	1,09	0,56	0,04	0,02	0,02	22,93	5,09	17,85
25	0,70	3,04	1,93	0,07	0,04	0,02	27,75	4,43	23,32
26	0,65	0,73	0,53	0,01	0,01	0,00	2,89	1,46	1,44
27	0,60	0,56	0,29	0,02	0,01	0,01	8,56	1,76	6,80
28	0,87	2,40	1,69	0,05	0,04	0,02	21,86	6,41	15,45
29	0,73	4,51	3,16	0,29	0,20	0,09	113,7	26,54	87,21
30	1,28	29,81	9,74	3,59	1,17	2,42	2503	9,06	2494
31	2,83	11,36	8,32	1,10	0,81	0,29	489,9	74,79	415,1
32	2,59	29,91	18,76	5,06	3,17	1,89	1624	35,17	1589
33	0,82	34,83	22,37	0,80	0,51	0,29	198,1	20,40	177,7
34	1,46	9,93	4,68	2,35	1,11	1,24	941,1	20,94	920,1
35	0,18	5,96	4,54	0,05	0,03	0,01	6,85	2,63	4,23
36	0,92	4,69	2,50	0,09	0,05	0,04	37,21	8,30	28,91

Table 16. United Kingdom – RCA, EUV, EUV Weighted with the Sectoral Export Shares of Manufacturing and of GDP

NACE rev.1 (2-digit)	RCA 2000/01	EUV 2001	EUV 1993	EUV 2001 weighted (exp. share)	EUV 1993 weighted (exp. share)	dEUV weighted (exp. share)	EUV 2001 weighted (GDP share)	EUV 1993 weighted (GDP share)	dEUV weighted (GDP share)
15	1,54	1,42	1.09	0.10	0.08	0.02	10,51	8,35	2,15
16	0.41	9,48	6,53	0.01	0.01	0.00	5,47	0,62	4,85
17	1,57	9,72	5,33	0.22	0.12	0.10	14,20	10,73	3,47
18	1,47	43.62	27.33	0.75	0.47	0.28	50,97	32,08	18,89
19	2,45	31.73	14.65	0.39	0.18	0.21	9,44	6,13	3,31
20	7.05	0.52	0.37	0.01	0.00	0.00	0,14	0,08	0,06
21	2,30	0.91	0.82	0.03	0.03	0.00	1,79	1,24	0,55
22	0.99	3,31	3,33	0.03	0.03	0.00	9,62	6,64	2,98
23	0.48	0.28	0.13	0.00	0.00	0.00	1,27	0,58	0,69
24	0.74	2.02	1,25	0.22	0.14	0.08	33,81	17,26	16,55
25	1.11	3,72	3,44	0.10	0.09	0.01	10,91	6,70	4,21
26	1,22	0.68	0.48	0.01	0.01	0.00	0,98	0,61	0,37
27	0.74	0.88	0.75	0.03	0.03	0.01	4,67	2,41	2,26
28	1.09	4,37	4.05	0.09	0.09	0.01	8,67	4,09	4,58
29	1.10	10.12	9,26	0.81	0.74	0.07	55,21	45,32	9,88
30	0.68	59.74	81.05	9.10	12,35	-3.25	1.637	395,7	1.242
31	1.07	12,73	9,98	0.43	0.33	0.09	52,73	21,90	30,82
32	0.83	71.05	32.98	5,88	2,73	3,15	984,8	134,2	850,5
33	0.96	89.80	53.50	2.05	1,22	0.83	175,4	108,4	66,95
34	1,53	9.10	7,36	1,51	1,22	0.29	98,09	47,35	50,74
35	1,15	35.19	14.48	1,16	0.48	0.68	169,5	63,42	106,0
36	1,56	6,82	6,72	0.15	0.15	0.00	14,48	8,24	6,23

Table 17. France – RCA, EUV, EUV Weighted with the Sectoral Export Shares of Manufacturing and of GDP

NACE rev.1 (2-digit)	RCA			EUV 2001	EUV 1993	dEUV	EUV 2001	EUV 1993	dEUV
	2000/ 01	EUV 2001	EUV 1993	weigh ted (exp. share)	weigh ted (exp. share)	weigh ted (exp. share)	weigh ted (GDP share)	weigh ted (GDP share)	weigh ted (GDP share)
15	1,19	0,99	1,07	0,09	0,16	-0,07	13,09	11,13	1,96
16	0,27	7,03	4,75	0,01	0,00	0,01	1,28	0,32	0,97
17	0,92	4,20	5,84	0,09	0,20	-0,12	12,59	12,83	-0,24
18	0,78	13,40	33,46	0,19	0,72	-0,54	27,65	47,64	-19,98
19	0,45	11,10	13,97	0,06	0,12	-0,06	8,73	7,73	0,99
20	0,74	0,37	0,32	0,00	0,00	0,00	0,36	0,17	0,19
21	0,78	0,81	0,69	0,02	0,02	0,00	2,87	1,33	1,54
22	0,85	3,14	4,48	0,02	0,03	0,00	3,48	2,56	0,92
23	0,75	0,34	0,17	0,01	0,00	0,00	0,84	0,18	0,66
24	0,97	1,46	1,02	0,21	0,17	0,04	30,50	11,16	19,34
25	1,07	3,45	3,72	0,11	0,14	-0,03	16,61	10,57	6,04
26	0,95	0,56	0,49	0,01	0,01	0,00	1,19	0,76	0,43
27	1,12	0,56	0,47	0,03	0,03	0,00	5,07	2,38	2,68
28	0,81	2,78	2,79	0,06	0,07	-0,01	8,31	4,68	3,63
29	0,83	6,91	7,08	0,49	0,50	-0,01	72,10	38,88	33,23
30	0,68	36,65	82,90	2,70	4,11	-1,41	398,1	285,9	112,1
31	1,06	6,92	8,29	0,25	0,29	-0,04	36,60	21,68	14,92
32	0,88	31,66	29,68	1,59	1,11	0,48	234,8	74,82	159,9
33	0,80	23,99	49,62	0,47	1,12	-0,65	69,53	70,81	-1,28
34	1,34	7,27	7,24	1,56	1,13	0,43	229,6	91,59	138,0
35	1,72	86,05	72,65	5,62	4,83	0,80	829,9	347,0	482,8
36	0,74	5,18	2,52	0,08	0,10	-0,02	11,61	3,03	8,58

Table 18. Italy – RCA, EUV, EUV Weighted with the Sectoral Export Shares of Manufacturing and of GDP

NACE rev.1 (2-digit)	RCA 2000/01	EUV 2001	EUV 1993	EUV 2001 weighted (exp. share)	EUV 1993 weighted (exp. share)	dEUV weighted (exp. share)	EUV 2001 weighted (GDP share)	EUV 1993 weighted (GDP share)	dEUV weighted (GDP share)
15	0,84	1,07	1,04	0,07	0,07	0,00	7,93	4,70	3,23
16	0,01	0,70	0,75	0,00	0,00	0,00	0,01	0,00	0,00
17	2,79	9,53	10,83	0,59	0,96	-0,37	69,33	65,67	3,67
18	1,85	15,80	29,77	0,52	1,36	-0,83	61,52	92,67	-31,14
19	3,76	17,62	11,43	0,78	0,68	0,11	92,16	46,23	45,93
20	0,62	1,30	1,49	0,01	0,01	0,00	0,84	0,53	0,31
21	0,68	1,12	0,99	0,02	0,02	0,01	2,72	1,24	1,48
22	0,89	2,69	2,88	0,02	0,02	0,00	2,51	1,48	1,02
23	0,49	0,28	0,15	0,00	0,00	0,00	0,36	0,11	0,25
24	0,65	1,79	1,30	0,17	0,10	0,07	19,81	7,00	12,82
25	1,46	2,95	2,90	0,13	0,13	0,00	15,50	8,73	6,77
26	2,00	0,59	0,65	0,02	0,02	-0,01	2,10	1,70	0,39
27	0,92	0,71	0,57	0,04	0,02	0,01	4,23	1,71	2,52
28	1,72	2,58	2,57	0,11	0,10	0,01	13,07	6,92	6,14
29	1,99	6,19	6,35	1,04	0,96	0,08	122,2	65,92	56,40
30	0,29	56,58	89,47	1,81	4,88	-3,06	212,8	333,2	120,3
31	1,10	6,54	5,67	0,24	0,19	0,05	28,73	13,04	15,69
32	0,45	24,50	19,24	0,63	0,42	0,21	73,63	28,80	44,83
33	0,72	20,28	24,72	0,36	0,43	-0,08	41,91	29,62	12,29
34	0,77	6,32	5,81	0,78	0,48	0,30	91,19	32,51	58,68
35	0,95	24,99	21,79	0,90	0,82	0,09	105,9	55,71	50,25
36	2,39	3,89	5,20	0,19	0,29	-0,10	22,38	19,76	2,62

Table 19. USA – RCA, EUV, EUV Weighted with the Sectoral Export Shares of Manufacturing and of GDP

NACE rev.1 (2-digit)	RCA 2000/01	EUV 2001	EUV 1993	EU V 2001 weighted (exp. share)	EU V 1993 weighted (exp. share)	dE UV weighted (exp. share)	EU V 2001 weighted (GDP share)	EU V 1993 weighted (GDP share)	dE UV weighted (GDP share)
15	0,24	0,40	0,26	0,01	0,01	0,00	0,16	0,11	0,06
16	0,07	2,04	1,64	0,00	0,00	0,00	0,02	0,01	0,00
17	0,28	6,85	5,28	0,04	0,06	-0,02	0,95	0,67	0,28
18	0,11	28,16	17,75	0,06	0,11	-0,05	1,25	1,23	0,02
19	0,16	9,17	11,17	0,02	0,04	-0,03	0,39	0,48	-0,09
20	0,79	1,37	0,82	0,01	0,01	0,00	0,21	0,14	0,08
21	0,50	0,84	0,50	0,01	0,01	0,00	0,29	0,12	0,16
22	1,10	14,21	9,48	0,14	0,11	0,03	3,07	1,20	1,87
23	0,29	0,11	0,09	0,00	0,00	0,00	0,02	0,01	0,00
24	0,91	3,95	2,25	0,52	0,32	0,20	11,56	3,50	8,06
25	0,57	8,00	6,13	0,14	0,13	0,00	3,09	1,49	1,61
26	0,49	3,91	2,66	0,03	0,02	0,01	0,65	0,24	0,41
27	0,53	7,35	4,33	0,21	0,14	0,07	4,75	1,54	3,21
28	0,56	12,57	8,64	0,18	0,13	0,05	3,90	1,43	2,48
29	1,24	20,61	14,22	2,16	1,57	0,59	48,12	17,43	30,70
30	1,40	144,8	117,8	22,11	20,29	1,82	492,2	225,1	267,0
31	1,31	35,90	25,52	1,60	1,01	0,58	35,52	11,22	24,29
32	1,93	252,7	125,4	27,94	8,35	19,59	622,0	92,67	529,3
33	3,64	150,7	84,41	13,41	7,53	5,88	298,5	83,58	214,9
34	0,20	9,73	6,96	0,32	0,22	0,10	7,06	2,43	4,63
35	4,73	299,9	76,10	53,81	10,36	43,45	1197	114,9	1082
36	0,97	22,27	12,45	0,44	0,23	0,22	9,89	2,50	7,39

I.2.2 Innovation System and Innovation Record

From a microeconomic perspective, the innovation process is clearly affected by incentives for the firm and the interdependency within the market. Key drivers of the innovation process are:

- adequate governance of the firm which is a crucial challenge particularly in large companies and in small companies growing fast;
- the expected rate of profit which is partly determined by first mover advantages, patenting performance and R&D subsidies;
- the intensity of competition and the growth of the overall market – intensive competition will typically stimulate innovations, and such innovations are easier to finance if the overall market is growing;
- technological dynamics – the 1990s witnessed an acceleration of patents of several countries in the US, above all of the US itself;
- locational advantages which include the availability of skilled labor and the associated tacit knowledge (codified knowledge is easily transferable, while tacit knowledge is immobile to the extent that skilled workers cannot be easily moved abroad).

As regards immobility of industries, one should point out that few technology intensive industries are really immobile, namely those where R&D activities and production activities cannot easily be separated geographically. This is typically the case in the air & space industry (high technology intensive which is a typical trait of the US industry and of part of the French industry) and in the production of specialized machinery and capital equipment (medium technology intensive which is a typical trait of German industry). High technology production is not generally immobile as the case of the chip industry clearly illustrates (e.g., one can develop the blueprint for a new generation of chips in California or Bavaria or Scotland, but after the first innovation stage, the production can be relocated to countries with low wage costs in Eastern Europe or Asia.)

Countries have different innovation systems as the interaction of government institutions, firms, universities and research labs has evolved within different countries in various ways. Innovation dynamics is not only a matter of specialization and human capital formation. In the case of integrated countries – e.g., in the case of the EU, ASEAN or NAFTA –, it is important to launch novel final products tailored to regional and global markets. What also matters at the level of the firm is the ability to adequately use the knowledge of specialized suppliers whose ability to develop novel subsystems is a crucial asset in the automotive industry of many countries. Moreover, using novel intermediate products imported from countries with successfully innovative firms is also an element of competitiveness in open economies. What matters more in the long run is the dynamics of the overall innovation system, which not only includes firms and their innovative suppliers but also specialized R&D firms, the innovative potential of researchers and labs at universities and the availability of modern infrastructure (roads, railways, airports, telecommunications). The incentives for innovation are partly intrinsic, partly in the form of expected rewards for which intellectual property rights and R&D promotion by government are important. Moreover, innovation is associated with a certain degree of risk, so that sustained high innovation dynamics require favourable access to equity capital including venture capital.

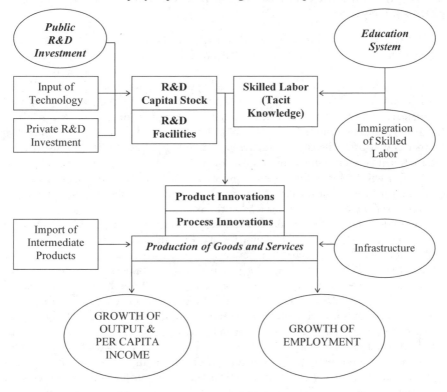

Fig. 72. Actors and Institutions in the Innovation System

   Continental EU countries have traditionally relied much on the banking system which, in turn, financed most investments and innovation projects on the basis of collateral. In a modern digital service economy, the availability of collateral, however, becomes a problem since knowledge and software play an increasing role for existing and new innovative firms. Compared to the continental banking system, Anglo-Saxon capital markets – with a strong tradition in venture capital financing – are easier sources of financing innovative projects in the services sector. This could undermine the dynamics of modern industry in continental EU countries to the extent that innovative services are crucial inputs for manufacturing products or a key element for optimum after-sale service. To the extent that US multinational services companies invest in Europe or Asia, innovative services might become available despite weaknesses of the respective domestic services sector. However, high profits earned in innovative service firms will then accrue in the US which, in turn, could thereby strengthen digital US growth. In high wage countries of the

EU, it seems to be quite important that nurturing innovative services not be neglected.

I.2.3 High Technology, ICT Growth and Modernization of the Economic System

The EU has adopted a strong focus on ICT in the 6th framework programme. The Community has thereby stimulated cross-border ICT research in the EU. However, it is unclear that the Community adequately emphasizes the ICT sector and that the interplay between national R&D policies and supranational R&D policy is optimal. R&D policy is optimal if positive external effects are internalized efficiently. National external effects can be internalized mainly at the national level, international external effects could be internalized through R&D policy in partner countries or through adequate supranational policy. If there is insufficient international cooperation (within the EU or within the OECD) the level of innovation policy will be lower than optimal. From the perspective of the respective government it is clear that positive growth effects and the associated additional tax revenues provide an incentive for R&D promotion.

R&D intensities in the EU do not seem to converge across countries – only for a subgroup of early leading EU countries and Finland there is convergence, at the same time one finds empirical evidence for a convergence of trade structure among EU15 (JUNGMITTAG, 2006). It is, however, unclear what convergence really means here: One may state the hypothesis that through increasing vertical trade – within industries – there is some structural convergence in the EU (or in the world economy). If convergence should mean that intermediate products with low profit rates are more and more concentrated in Spain and Portugal while final goods production is in Germany, France, the UK and the Benelux group plus Scandinavian countries plus Ireland one would not really expect economic convergence in terms of per capita income. The main reason for non-convergence or divergence is that final goods producers in technology-intensive industries will appropriate a Schumpeterian rent in their respective profit rates. In a Heckscher-Ohlin approach to international trade technologies are the same across countries and Schumpeterian profit differentials across countries therefore cannot play a role. In reality Schumpeterian profits indeed play a crucial role; this holds not only for countries with high patent intensities but also for countries with a specialization in sectors shaped by high progress rates. ICT is such a sector; the OECD (2001) has emphasized that it is one of the most important fields of innovation dynamics in the US and some other OECD countries.

From a theoretical perspective international network effects are of particular relevance in ICT innovations in certain fields; network effects are positive demand-side externalities which are rather unusual. ICT R&D is likely to have positive cross-sector spillover effects and one also may anticipate considerable international spillovers; either in the ICT sector itself or through increasing use of ICT capital in other sectors. One should, however, carefully distinguish sub-sectors of ICT; e.g. chip production is scale intensive and knowledge intensive (referring to the overall product not the rather simple chip production as such) as is software.

However, many digital services have to be very customer specific so that economies of scale play a limited role; to some extent economies of scale can be exploited for the basic product – say the core algorithm – while customization requires specific adjustment involving the employment of skilled labor.

While ICT facilitates international outsourcing it is not true that leading OECD countries are natural losers from outsourcing; BAILEY/LAWRENCE (2004) have shown that the US software sector has outsourced some 100 000 jobs in the period 2000-03, however, the overall number of software personnel in the US has increased in that period; mainly rather simple programming jobs were outsourced; often to Asian countries. This suggests that international outsourcing of standardized services will allow advanced countries with relative abundance of skilled workers to specialize increasingly on advanced services. The EU15 also should benefit in a similar way as leading software firms become globally more competitive by outsourcing to Eastern Europe or Asia.

At the beginning of the 21st century OECD countries are shaped by intensified innovation dynamics and the need for flexible adjustment in a world economy with a high rate of technological progress and in which Newly Industrialized Countries – including China and India – are becoming increasingly important players in international markets; China particularly has become a major host country for foreign investment and FDI indeed has stimulated modernization and economic opening up of the Chinese economy (GRAHAM, 2004). Both Asian countries benefit technologically mainly by imitating foreign technologies, however, they can combine incipient innovation with strong imitation dynamics and economies of scale in many sectors which should help to achieve considerable economic growth.

As regards links between the US, the EU and Japan one should emphasize the role of international R&D alliances which have become rather important in the 1980s and 1990s in OECD countries – not only in ICT. As regards international alliances the emphasis is more on EU15 countries than on EU accession countries. Strategic R&D alliances played an increasing role in the EU in the late 1980s as globalization and the run-up to the single market programme as well as higher EU funds for cooperative R&D projects stimulated the internationalization of European R&D (NARULA, 1999); the IT sector and biotechnology played a particular role. Moreover, there also have been renewed dynamics in R&D in the form of both asset-exploiting and asset-seeking FDI in the EU and the US (CRISCUOLO/ /NARULA/VERSPAGEN, 2005) argue that R&D facility's capacity to exploit technological competences is a function not just of its own resources, but the efficiency with which it can utilise complementary resources associated with the relevant local innovation system; the empirical analysis indicates that both EU (US) affiliates in the US (EU) rely strongly on home region knowledge sources, although they appear to exploit the host knowledge base as well. The crucial emphasis on home knowledge suggests doubts about a potential R&D strategy of the EU which would neglect the EU countries as prime locations for leading edge R&D in technologically dynamics sectors, in particular the ICT sector. One also must raise the issue to which extent the expansion of ICT requires reforms of the innovation system and in particular a stronger role of virtual research networks and "Digital

Universities"; optimal linkages between R&D facilities and firms in technology-intensive sectors are crucial which naturally will include foreign investors.

Both the US and the EU belong to the group of major source countries and host countries while Japan is mainly a source country of FDI – at least if one is to believe Japanese statistics (note: according to US FDI outflow statistics Japan should have high US FDI inflows). In the US and the EU innovation plays a crucial role for economic growth. The US and several EU countries have achieved rather high growth rates of per capita income and total factor productivity in the 1990s, and the expansion of information and communication technologies (ICT) has played a particular role. From a theoretical perspective one may emphasize the endogenous growth model of ZON/MUYSKEN (2005) who have highlighted in a refined LUCAS-model the role of ICT in a modern growth model where the ICT capital intensity has a positive impact on the knowledge accumulation process; ICT is important both in final goods production and in knowledge accumulation. The expansion of knowledge and the rise of ICT capital intensity contribute to higher steady state growth of output. Knowledge accumulation thus plays an important role for economic growth. The implication is that the long run increase of ICT capital intensity in OECD countries and NICs – fuelled by falling relative prices of ICT capital goods – will reinforce the role of knowledge in production. As regards long term dynamics one should, however, not overlook the problems of information markets themselves which suffer from market imperfections. The special aspects of ICT and growth will not be analyzed here as many special aspects would have to be emphasized, including the considerable role of intangible assets, network effects as a dynamic demand side-effect and static as well as dynamic economies of scale in several subsectors. ICT seems to facilitate the outsourcing of services as it supports virtual mobility of the supply-side and the demand side. With the role of digital services increasing in modern economies one might find at the aggregate level that the macroeconomic production function is characterized by economies of scale. However, there is no clear evidence about this.

The EU has adopted the Lisbon Agenda in 2000 which has emphasized the need for higher innovation, higher growth and higher employment so that the EU should become the most dynamic knowledge based economy by 2010; interim results are rather sobering according to the KOK (2004) report. With EU eastern enlargement the EU is facing additional challenges. The EU is increasingly moving towards a digitally networked high technology knowledge society. Western Europe's high-wage countries are particularly facing the need to adjust to globalization and EU eastern enlargement in a way which requires increasingly the use of information and communication technology (ICT). ICT is one of the most dynamic fields in terms of technological progress in OECD countries and therefore it is of prime importance for economic growth, productivity increases and employment. ICT markets in Europe and worldwide are growing at a pace which exceeds regional and global economic growth, respectively.

The ICT sector also has become a major driver of the innovation process and of productivity growth. High Schumpeterian dynamics are not only observed in ICT production but also in the use of ICT. Hence ICT investment relative to overall investment may be expected to grow continuously, not least because falling relative prices of software and hardware stimulate ICT investment. With digital (broadband and narrowband) networks expanding in Europe, North America, Asia and in other regions of the world economy one may anticipate a further acceleration in digital knowledge creation and information as well as e-commerce – often also associated with favourable network effects. With so many changes shaped by ICT the question arises whether traditional economic systems, historically shaped by industry, should adjust in order to optimally support - digital - economic growth. Liberalization of EU telecommunications in 1998 (UK already in 1984) has stimulated product innovations and possibly innovations in the overall telecommunications sector. The picture for telecommunication network operators is inconclusive as one finds some firms with rising R&D-sales ratios and other with falling R&D-sales ratios. One can, however, not overlook that the R&D-sales ratio of the equipment industry has increased which suggests that in the course of restructuring of telecommunications network operators – in the post-1998 period – R&D activities were effectively shifted to a considerable extent to the equipment industry which is both knowledge-intensive and scale-intensive. The more competition drives e-communication towards global technological standards the higher will be the pressure in the equipment industry to consolidate. It is noteworthy that R&D-sales ratios of telecommunications operators are lower than in the continental EU where the liberalization of the telecommunications sector occurred only 14 years after the market opening up in the US.

Taking a broader look at R&D expenditure in ICT – relative to overall business R&D expenditure – one can considerable differences across countries: Ireland and the Scandinavian EU countries were leaders at the beginning of the 21st century. The three top OECD countries Ireland, Finland and Korea have spent 70, 64 and 50% of total business R&D expenditures on ICT in 2003. Kanada, the Netherlands, the US and Japan followed with an ICT share of about 35%; France had 31%, the UK 24 and Germany, Italy and Spain about 22%. Ireland, the UK, Norway, Denmark, Australia, Spain and the Czech Republic had a relatively high share of R&D ICT expenditures in the service sector. The ranking in terms of ICT patents looks rather similar to that in ICT R&D expenditures. The top countries are Singapore, Finland, Israel, Korea, Netherlands and Japan, Ireland the US, Canda and Sweden which recorded an ICT patent share – based on figures at the European Patent Office - of close to or above 40% (top scorers Singapore and Finland close to 60%); follower countries are the UK, Chinese Taipei, China, Australia, Hungary France, EU, Russia, Germany, Norway, Switzerland, Denmark, New Zealand, South Africa, Belgium Spain, Austria, Italy, India and Brazil. It is clear that the ICT patent position of US firms – with subsidiaries in many of the top countries – is much stronger than that of the US as a country. Moreover, taking a look at US figures shows a clear lead of the US even if one assumes that there is a home bias (in the US in favour of US firms, in the EU in favour of EU firms). As regards ICT goods Japan is very strong in global markets; this also becomes apparent from the fact that the share of Japan in EPO patents was very close to the share of the US – see the subsequent figures.

Table 20. R&D Expenditures for PTO's (USD millions)

PTO	R&D expenditure (1997)	R&D as a percentage of total revenue (1997)	R&D expenditure (1999)	R&D as a percentage of total revenue (1999)	R&D expenditure (2001)	R&D as a percentage of total revenue (2001)	R&D expenditure (2003)	R&D as a percentage of total revenue (2003)
NTT	2 388	3.1	3 140	3.4	3216.0	3.3	3061.0	3.2
Deutsche Telekom	692	1.8	697	2.0	804.0	1.9	1011.0	1.6
BT	502	2.0	556	1.6	525.0	1.7	548.0	1.8
France Telecom	918	3.5	632	2.2	506.0	1.3	507.0	1.0
AT&T	829	1.6	550	0.9	325.0	0.6	277.0	0.8
Korea Telecom	113	2.2	258	2.6	293.0	2.4	195.0	2.0
Telefonica[1]	153	0.8	96	0.4	153.0	0.6	494.0	1.6
Telia	202	3.3	190	3.0	126.0	2.3	:	:
Telecom Italia	:	:	352	1.2	123.0	0.4	166.0	0.5
SK Telecom	41	1.7	89	2.4	119.0	1.8	232.0	2.9
Vodafone	55	1.4	74	0.6	104.0	0.3	280.0	0.51
Telenor	113	3.1	68	1.6	102.0	2.0	65.0	0.9
Sonera[2]	52	3.5	64	3.5	73.0	3.7	:	:
KPN Telecom	60	0.8	59	0.6	41.0	0.4	26.0	0.2
Elisa	:	:	16	1.4	32.0	2.5	27.0	1.6
Telekom Austria	:	:	20	0.6	19	0.5	48	1.08
Hanaro Telecom	:	:	6	28.4	10.0	1.6	8.0	0.7
Dacom	3	0.6	8	1.0	4.0	0.5	:	:
Telecom New Zealand	4	0.2	5	0.1	3.4	0.1	5.8	0.2
Qwest	:	:	36	0.9	:	:	:	:
Telstra	43	0.3	19	0.1	:	:	17	0.12
OTE	:	:	11	0.3	:	:	3	0.1
Belgacom	18	0.4	7	0.1	:	:	:	:
KDDI							115	0.5
TPSA							15	0.3
Portugal Telecom							30	0.5
MMO2							16	0.2
Cable & Wireless	169	1.2	18	0.1	:	:	:	:
Total/average of above	6 355	1.7	6 970	2.5	6 578	1.5	7 147	1.0

1. Telefonica used a different methodology to calculate R&D prior to 2001.
2. Following Telia and Sonera's merger, the new entity does not report R&D as a separate line item.

StatLink: http://dx.doi.org/10.1787/114880223717

Source: OECD Communications Outlook 2005

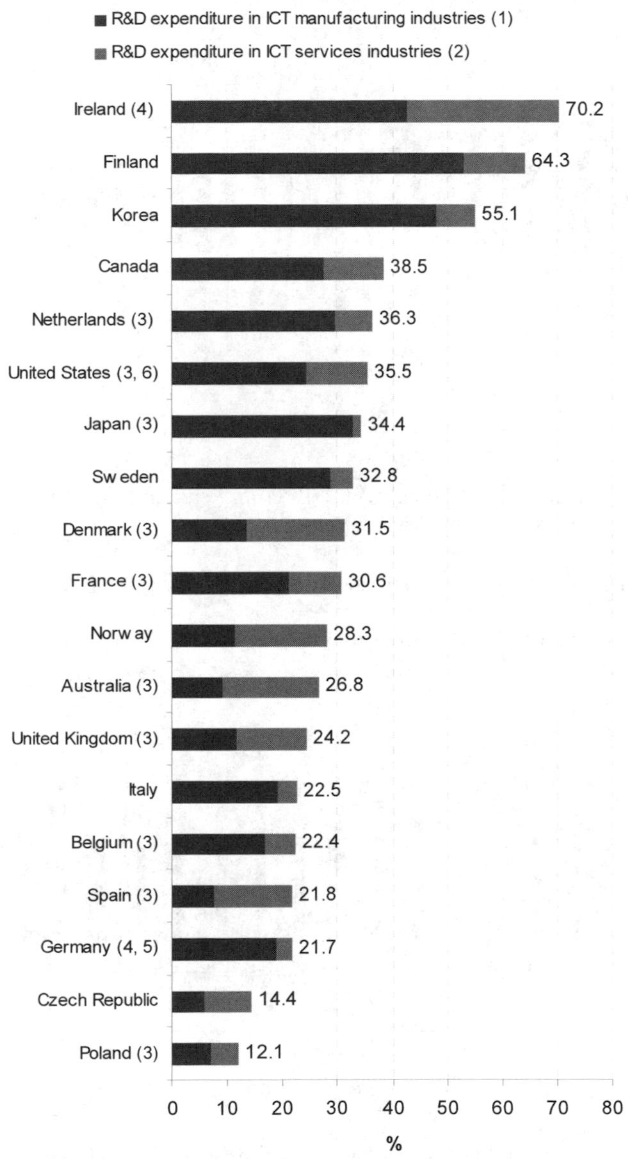

- ■ R&D expenditure in ICT manufacturing industries (1)
- ■ R&D expenditure in ICT services industries (2)

Country	Value
Ireland (4)	70.2
Finland	64.3
Korea	55.1
Canada	38.5
Netherlands (3)	36.3
United States (3, 6)	35.5
Japan (3)	34.4
Sweden	32.8
Denmark (3)	31.5
France (3)	30.6
Norway	28.3
Australia (3)	26.8
United Kingdom (3)	24.2
Italy	22.5
Belgium (3)	22.4
Spain (3)	21.8
Germany (4, 5)	21.7
Czech Republic	14.4
Poland (3)	12.1

%

Source: OECD, ANBERD database, March 2005

Fig. 73. R&D Expenditure in Selected ICT Industries, 2003 or Latest Year Available as a Percentage of Business Enterprise Sector R&D Expenditure

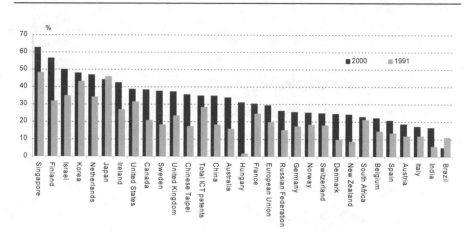

Source: OECD, Patent Database, September 2004.

Fig. 74. ICT Patents[1] as a Percentage of National Total (EPO) in Selected Countries[2]. According to the Residence of the Inventors, by Priority Year.

1. The provisional definition of ICT patents is presented in Annex B of the OECD compendium
2. Cut-off point: countries with more than 100 EPO applications in 2000

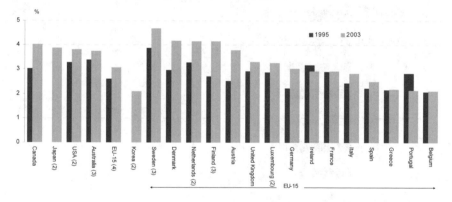

Source: OECD Information Technology Outlook 2004

Fig. 75. ICT Employment Across the Economy- Share of ICT-Related Occupations in the Total Economy in Selected Countries, 1995 and 2003, Narrow Definition (1).

Based on methodology developed in chapter 6 of the Information Technology Outlook 2004. See also van Welsum, D., and G. Vickery (2004), New perspectives on ICT skills and employment, Information Economy Working Paper DSTI/ICCP/IE(2004)10, OECD.
2. 2002 instead of 2003
3. 1997 instead of 1995.
4. Estimates.

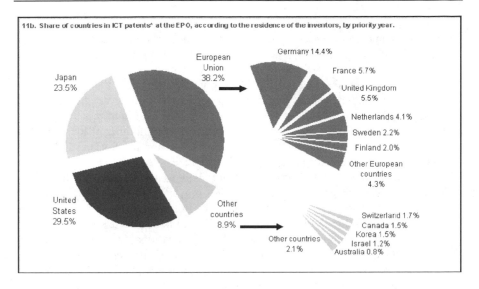

11b. Share of countries in ICT patents' at the EPO, according to the residence of the inventors, by priority year.

Source: OECD, Patent Database, September 2004

Fig. 76. Share of Countries in ICT Patents' at the EPO, According to the Residence of the Inventors, by Priority Year

(The provisional definition of ICT patents is presented in Annex B of the Compendium of patent statistics 2004.)

As regards ICT employment – narrowly defined – it has increased in most OECD countries in the period 1995-2003; Ireland is a negative example. The share of ICT-related occupations in the total economy was in a range of 3-5%; Sweden was the OECD leader in 2003; the US was ahead of the EU by almost 1 percentage point. This finding points to a transatlantic lead of the US which is well ahead of the EU in terms of patenting, R&D-sales ratio and employment. Given the relatively small employment shares it is impressive to see how important ICT patents are in comparison with other sectors. As regards EU innovation dynamics one might want to consider a broader coordinated R&D effort in the ICT sector, in particular some form of coordinated international R&D program; the latter should not mean that all EU countries or very many are embarking upon coordinated projects under the heading of EU programmes. Rather it would be desirable that several countries team up under the heading of a multi-country ICT R&D programme of excellence. The typical EU R&D programme which effectively requires involving countries/partners from Western Europe, Eastern Europe and the Cohesion countries makes ICT project unnecessarily complex and often undermines efficiency. The EU might well want to subsidize employment of R&D researchers from relatively poor countries in leading EU R&D countries. There could be a particular role for EU-funded R&D projects but overemphasizing EU projects is damaging for European innovation dynamics. Political control of EU R&D policy is rather weak which implies inefficiency risks. The EU might want to consider a special role for the supranational policy level in stimulating diffusion and in financing R&D centers of excellence in the Community. Finally, there is a major inconsistency in the EU R&D projects which typically require 50% co-financing.

As regards university research institutes one should expect that national government or special R&D funds with partial government funding would provide the co-financing for successful bidders. This is not the case and indeed is adequate for industrial R&D consortia. However, only a rather limited number of R&D projects are dominated by the business community, namely in applied R&D. Fundamental R&D should be financed mainly by government; in Germany and several other EU countries – including EU accession countries in eastern Germany – there is no adequate co-financing from government for projects in fundamental research. Moreover, the broad lack of private universities in most EU countries means that there is insufficient funding of higher education and insufficient R&D activities at the same time (e.g. Germany spends only 1% of its national income on university funding and has very few private universities – which all are very small).

The ICT sector has a special feature which makes adequate financing of innovation projects difficult in the continental EU countries. Many sub-sectors of ICT are characterized by a high share of intangible assets which undermines bank financing – the typical bank will always want collateral and neither intangible assets (e.g. software) nor computer equipment whose price is absolutely falling over time can serve as collateral for bank financing. This implies for many Eurozone countries that one has enormous problems with financing innovative young ICT firms. Interestingly, there are some big companies, including e.g. Siemens, SAP and Deutsche Telekom, which have set up special venture capital funds. However, the general conclusion is that the Euro zone countries should move more towards a capital market system and thus become more Anglo-Saxon in terms of the financial market system. Financial markets are important for growth and structural change (WELFENS/WOLF, 1997). *Mutatis mutandis* this also holds for university financing where continental EU countries have underdeveloped banking markets for students; part of EU underfunding of the university system actually is a lack of private universities on the one hand and of adequate university study financing on the other hand. As one may argue – from a theoretical perspective – that adequate financial market deepening will contribute to a higher level of growth and potentially to a higher trend growth rate (namely to the extent that the structure of financial markets influences R&D intensity and human capital formation and hence contributes to endogenous growth dynamics) one should make serious efforts in the new EU knowledge society to develop financial institutions that are up to the challenges and opportunities of the digital age. These arguments do not imply that one should underestimate the risks from volatile stock markets.

Slow growth in the Eurozone over many years – in particular in Germany and Italy- should be a wake-up call for many continental EU countries to modernize the innovation system and to put more emphasis on R&D funding which at the same time should become more efficient. Conditional tax credits should play a larger role than traditional subsidies which effectively favour large firms which can afford to spend much money on active lobbying. R&D tax credits would be less distorting in the sense that large countries and SMEs are acting in a more level playing field. Since innovative SMEs are so important in R&D in the ICT sector – and since Germany/the Eurozone is lagging behind the US – one should seriously consider the reform proposals made here.

I.3 Theory of Innovation Policy

I.3.1 The Standard Case

Why should government support R&D? This is obvious when it has a particular individual interest in innovations as is the case in the field of defence. Besides this special sector, it is only in case of positive intersectoral or intrasectoral effects that R&D subsidies are adequate. Assume that the demand for an innovative product is given by the demand curve AZ (DD_0) – expressing private benefits – while social benefits are reflected by the demand schedule A'Z' (DD_{01}). As there are positive external effects of using the innovative product (or service), the optimum quantity will not be brought about by private markets themselves. The market would bring q_0 while the optimum quantity is q_1; the latter would be produced if government reduces marginal costs by a fraction, b, so that there should be R&D subsidies. The price would fall to p_1 instead of p_0 in the simple market equilibrium. However, R&D subsidies would then amount to the area HGFD, which can only be financed through (income) taxes, in turn shifting the AZ curve downward. Taxation in turn will impose deadweight losses – that is, reduce economic welfare – unless the tax is on activities with a negative external effect. Since the latter case can be assumed to be relatively rare, the optimum R&D subsidy is slightly smaller than indicated by the subsidy rate, b. Moreover, subsidization of R&D makes sense only if the increase in net welfare is higher than the costs of subsidization. These costs could ultimately include the costs of other sectors calling for equal treatment: read subsidization (while not showing positive external effects). In addition, there is a risk that government combines R&D subsidies with interference in the business sector which can cause efficiency losses. As a practical issue, one also has to look into the issue of granting subsidy payments or offering tax credits for R&D intensive firms. Subsidy payments appeal to the lobbying and rent-seeking efforts, particularly of large firms. Tax credits are a superior instrument to the extent that R&D intensive small and medium-sized firms can also benefit from this relatively easily.

Government also plays a role in the field of intellectual property rights. In the digital economy, intellectual property rights have come under pressure because the violation of copyrights is rather easy (see e.g., the Napster trial).

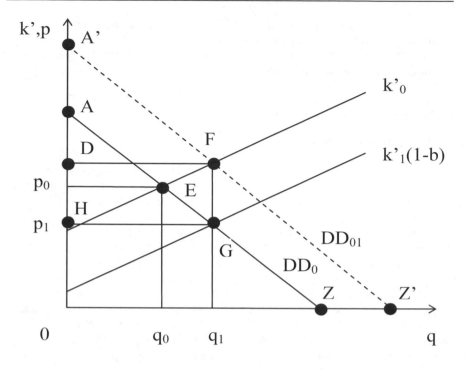

Fig. 77. Product Innovation with Positive External Effects and R&D Promotion

Making profits by selling digital contents is not easy. There are technical reasons for this problem, but there also is a lack of adequate legislation in some countries. Germany has introduced national legislation that is supposed to implement the EU e-commerce directive. As regards copyrights, Germany's new laws clearly weaken the copyrights of authors, thereby reducing the incentive to develop quality contents for traditional and digital publications.

In an open economy, it is important to understand that subsidies can influence trade (Fig. 6). If the world market price is $p*_0$, the initial situation without R&D subsidies implies net imports of AB. If country I (home country) subsidizes R&D so that the marginal costs schedule shifts downwards, we would have net exports equivalent to the distance BC. If country II ("the rest of the world") also introduced subsidies – pointing to the positive external effects of R&D –, the world supply curve would shift downwards so that country I would be a net importer again. The quantity imported would thereby be equivalent to the distance DF. The problem with R&D subsidies and trade is that such subsidies are adequate to the extent that the subsidy rate reflects positive external effects (at home and abroad). Since the size of external effects of innovation is very difficult to assess, subsidization in technology-intensive tradables sectors naturally presents a potential field of controversy.

Country I – assuming it to be a globally leading country in the respective sector – might argue that R&D subsidies in this sector abroad are adequate since positive external effects in other countries should be relatively small. Yet country I might argue that other countries aim at catching market shares by way of unfair subsidization. If the sector concerned has dynamic scale economies in the long run or is characterized by an international oligopoly, there are additional aspects to be considered. International rent-shifting opportunities will particularly accrue to first movers and large aggressive firms which, in turn, should enjoy particular opportunities if the home market is large and characterized by high per capita income. In a large home market, it is fairly easy to exploit static- and dynamic-scale economies. Countries such as the US, Japan, the EU – and in the future, China or India – offer special opportunities in this respect. Thus, it would not be surprising if trade conflicts emerge between these large economies.

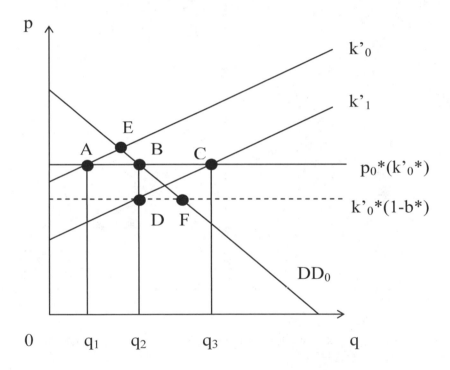

Fig. 78. R&D Promotion, Production and Trade

I.3.1.1 Intermediate Traded Products, R&D Subsidies and Rent-Shifting

Another neglected field of R&D promotion in open economies concerns the case of an intermediate technology-intensive product produced in country I and exported as an intermediate input to country II. We will subsequently consider the case of traded intermediate product innovations whose use in country II raises the marginal willingness in the market for the final product. Assume that the government in country I offers R&D subsidies, largely reflecting thereby the positive external effects in country II, so that q_1 of the intermediate product is produced in country I instead of the natural market solution, q_0. R&D subsidization allows for the production of a higher quality of the intermediate product so that the demand curve for the final product shifts outward in country II. As intermediate products are obtained at subsidized costs from producers in country I, we have a downward shift of the k* curve abroad (see panel b). The positive welfare effect accruing for country II is given by the area A*B*C*F*G*D*. However, the costs of R&D subsidies in country I are equivalent to the area FGHI.

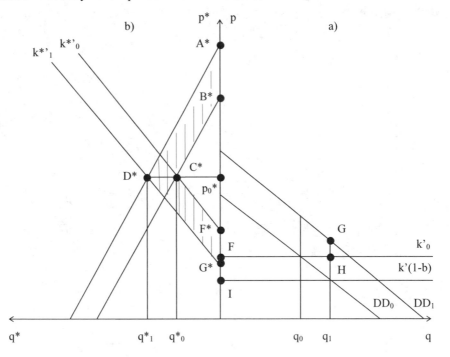

Fig. 79. International External Effects of Domestic R&D Promotion (Technology-intensive Inputs for Tradable Products)

Under which conditions would country I be interested in providing an R&D subsidy for an intermediate product when the main welfare effect is observed abroad (as shown in our simple partial equilibrium model in the above figure)?

1. If country II could offer country I an adequate share in income taxes as a compensation for the R&D costs.
2. If the firms in country II are largely owned by residents of country I – at least with respect to higher profits in country II (sent to country I as profit remit-

tances), there is effective taxation in country I; the profit increase in country II is equivalent to the area, C*F*G*D*.
3. If a large share of demand abroad effectively represents users from country I (e.g., in the case of tourism or in the case of mobile internet services).
4. If there are positive effects not only for country II but also for other sectors in country I so that part of the shift from DD_0 to DD_1 represents domestic positive external effects. The latter could explain why Korea subsidizes R&D in Boeing, intermediate inputs manufactured in Korea.

In the EU-25 single market where technology-intensive intermediate inputs are partly produced in EU countries catching-up, there are indeed arguments that rich countries which dominate the final assembly of technology intensive products should transfer an adequate share of income taxes to those countries which deliver intermediate products developed on the basis of R&D subsidies in the respective country. Since one may assume that this typically concerns cases in industry and that the main producers of technology intensive final products are Germany, France, Sweden, Finland and the Netherlands, we have a new argument that these countries contribute over-proportionately to the EU budget. It is, however, unclear that countries producing much technology intensive intermediate inputs really obtain an adequate share of EU transfers. So far, the EU transfer scheme does not consider the case of technology-intensive intermediate products.

In a more general sense, the existence of the single EU market and the ongoing globalization imply that there could be an increasing role of the internationalization of R&D, including the production of innovative intermediate products. This internationalization of R&D and the associated positive international external effects could imply that all governments spend less on R&D than would be optimal. The simple reason for this is that an international tax revenue sharing scheme has not yet been developed by the OECD. (As the basis for such a scheme, one would have to analyze the size and direction of technology spillovers, which could be quite cumbersome).

Network Effects

In the digital economy, there are more fields with network effects than in the traditional industrial economy. Network effects can be understood as an endogenous outward rotation of the demand curve (alternatively, as a rightward shift of the demand curve) in the process of network expansion. For example, the marginal utility of having access to the telephone network will increase for the initial users if more users – read potential communication partners – are switched on the network, at least as long there are no additional congestion costs. This is also the case for advanced software and novel internet services. A monopolistic supplier facing the demand curve DD_0 would impose under the standard Cournot monopoly solution the monopoly price p_2 which goes along with output q_0. For simplicity, we assume that a conservative monopoly firm would neither be willing nor able to exploit network effects, that is, to anticipate that the dynamic demand curve – including network effects – is DD_2 and not DD_1. If government offered a one-off

R&D subsidy for process innovations (shifting the marginal costs curve from k'_0 to k'_1) to several firms under the condition that network effects be jointly exploited, the conditional competitive solution would be point G. The positive welfare effect from the network effect is the area AEF plus the effect seen by cost cutting, namely EFGH. An additional welfare benefit – not related to network effects – would come in the form of the area p_0EHp_1. Thus, network effects represent a neglected and interesting field of R&D subsidies (for a broader partial equilibrium analysis, also see appendix 2).

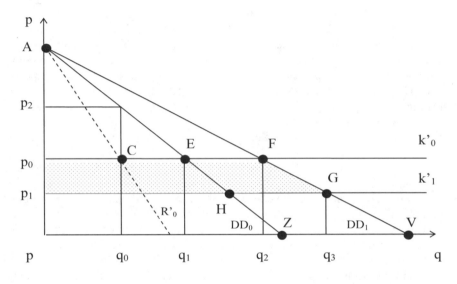

Fig. 80. Network Effects and Cost-Saving Progress

I.3.1.2 Macroeconomic Approach: A Schumpeter-Mundell-Flemming Model

The familiar Mundell Fleming model suggests that fiscal policy is effective under fixed exchange rates, while monetary policy is ineffective. Under flexible exchange rates, it is monetary policy which is effective while fiscal policy is relatively ineffective. In the following analysis, we suggest that supply-side oriented fiscal policy – namely raising R&D expenditures in order to promote product innovations – can have positive effects on output and employment within the framework of an extended model. The basic arguments have been presented in WELFENS (2004), where a key idea is that consumption C, investment I and (net) exports X positively depend on product innovations v. In reality, a higher export unit value could be obtained due to product innovations, and the quantity shipped abroad might increase as well. The larger the tradables sector affected relative to the overall economy, the larger the effect on net exports of goods and services.

Through an innovation-promoting fiscal policy – with a focus on product innovations –, we basically get a rightward initial shift of the IS curve since government R&D expenditures and hence aggregate demand increase. In the medium term, we get more product innovations v so that investment and consumption increase; net exports also increase. While the ensuing real appreciation of the currency dampens the net export effect (the IS curve shifts back to the left, while the balance of payments equilibrium curve ZZ shifts upwards), the overall effect on output and employment is favourable as is shown in the following graph. A minor complication in a model with product innovation is that in applying the logic of hedonic pricing, we implicitly get a fall of the price level, thereby shifting the LM curve to the right (not shown in the graph). There also is the potential problem of considerable time lags. Higher R&D promotion could translate into more product innovations only after several years. However, as investors will anticipate this effect, improved profit expectations should already stimulate output after a short period. From a policy perspective, there could also be a problem stemming from strategic R&D behaviour of firms which cut R&D expenditures more strongly in recessions with the hope that government R&D support will effectively allow for the substitution of company funds through governmental subsidies. Government could cope with this problem by using an adequate base year.

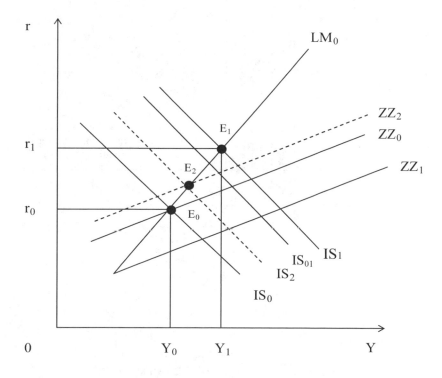

Fig. 81. Expansionary Fiscal Policy Promoting Product Innovations

If government raises R&D expenditures in order to promote process innovations, we get a less favourable result to the extent that technological progress is labor-saving. Labor in efficiency units is AL and the production function is Y (K,AL), where Y is output, L is labor, and K is capital. Depending on the strength of the upward shift of the production function, labor-saving technological progress might indeed lead to a new equilibrium in which the demand for workers is lower than initially the case. There are less jobs available than in the initial equilibrium ($L_3 < L_0$: see graph).

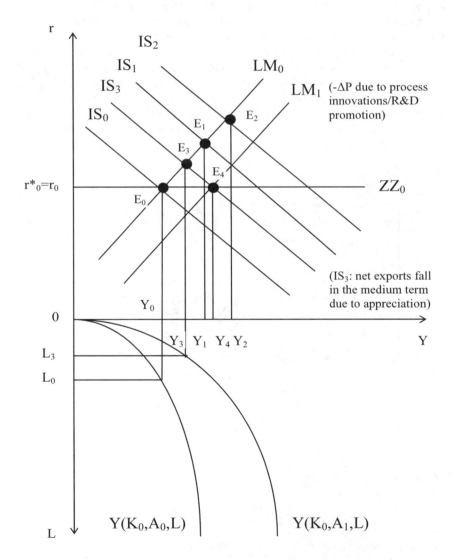

Fig. 82. Expansionary Fiscal Policy with a Focus on Promoting Process Innovations

In the above model setting, we have assumed that net capital imports Q=Q(i,i*,v,q*), where v is the rate of product innovations, raises profitability and hence foreign direct investment inflows. The impact of the domestic and foreign interest rate i and i*, respectively, requires no further comment. Not so apparent is the positive impact of q*=eP*/P (e is the nominal exchange rate, P and P* the domestic and foreign price level, respectively). The link is explained by the FROOT-STEIN argument, which emphasizes the role of imperfect capital markets for foreign direct investment inflows. The ZZ line has a slope of zero if the interest elasticity of capital flows ($\partial Q/\partial i$) is infinite.

Note that the balance of payments equilibrium line (ZZ) does not only have a slope of zero when the interest elasticity of capital inflows is infinite; it could also have a slope of zero if we assume – a realistic case in view of empirically significant gravity equations of foreign direct investment – a net capital import function Q(i,i*,v,Y,Y*), where the partial derivative $\partial Q/\partial Y$ is positive and $\partial Q/\partial Y*$ is negative. Both $\partial Q/\partial Y$ and $\partial Q/\partial Y*$ reflect the impact of domestic and foreign output on net foreign direct investment inflows on net foreign direct investment inflows. If$\partial Q/\partial Y$ is equal to $\partial J/\partial Y$ – with $\partial J/\partial Y$ denoting the marginal propensity to import goods –, the slope of the ZZ curve is zero, even if the interest elasticity of capital mobility is low. In the case of poor countries opening up to trade and foreign direct investment – e.g., in the case of Newly Industrializing Countries or post-socialist transition countries – the marginal propensity to import will at first increase. After some time, $\partial Q/\partial Y$ will increase and the special case $\partial Q/\partial Y = \partial J/\partial Y$ could occur and hold for some time, thus leading to an interesting empirical question.

I.3.1.3 Empirical Insights from the Analysis of Innovation, Growth and Structural Change

Recent empirical analysis (JUNGMITTAG, 2004) shows that a macroeconomic production function is useful in which not only labor, capital and technology enter into play, but also the degree of economic specialization in high technology products. An alternative specification in which specialization as such – Smithian specialization – matters did not yield significant results for the production function. We assume that the pressure to specialize more strongly in technology intensive products is reinforced if there is increasing import competition of countries which are catching up technologically (e.g. as measured by R&D input indicators or R&D export indicators). According to this line of reasoning, measures to liberalize trade could have long term benefits in terms of both higher per capita income and higher growth rates.

In the context of EU Eastern enlargement, it was shown (BORBÉLY, 2004) that accession countries have specialized in different ways while also recording specific performance with respect to the development of export unit values. Hungary and the Czech Republic recorded positive RCA dynamics in both medium technology intensive products and in selected high technology sectors. Moreover, in some sectors, improvements in export unit values were recorded in the decade after the early transition recession. This ability to move up the technology ladder and to obtain higher prices in world markets might be strongly related to foreign direct investment inflows.

I.4 Policy Conclusions

I.4.1 General Policy Conclusions for Innovation Policy in Open Economies

In open economies, there is some risk that R&D promotion is smaller than would be optimal under global welfare considerations. If there are symmetric international R&D spillover effects, one would have little reason to wonder about optimum R&D support. However, reality is likely to show asymmetric positive international external effects since countries trading with each other have different technology levels and since the degree of openness and trade in intermediate technology intensive products differs across countries. Obviously, it would be useful for countries with high technology-intensive tradables output to cooperate in R&D policies which might include international tax revenue sharing. Assuming that the difference between private and social benefits of innovation is even larger at the level of the world economy than at the national level, one may raise the question of whether the internationalization of business has not brought about an increased divergence between existing and optimum R&D subsidies. (While the EU might be considered a supranational player in R&D promotion, one must point out that the share of R&D promotion in the budget is very small and that the current transfer system is not rewarding countries which support R&D in firms which produce technology intensive intermediate products.)

Innovation systems differ across countries. However, some key ingredients can be identified: There are public R&D funds and there are private R&D funds, whereby the latter typically has a focus on applied R&D while the former emphasizes basic research. Funds have to be partly invested in R&D facilities. At the same time, hiring highly skilled workers and dynamic researchers is crucial for high innovation performance. Skilled workers represent tacit knowledge, which often make international relocation of R&D intensive production difficult. In addition to this, a modern education system as well as the import of technology intensive imports and government R&D promotion must be considered. This should then result in sustained innovation dynamics and growth of output and employment.

Countries have specialized in certain technology intensive fields which typically show a positive RCA over time. Facing economic globalization and intensified global competition, it makes sense for governments to focus their R&D support within internationally-competitive sectors. This seems to be even more the case the larger the backward linkages and forward linkages are and the larger the respective sector is itself. Such a strategy of supporting existing fields of comparative advantage and also fields of rising export unit value would, however, leave open the question to which extent relatively new sectors – such as nanotechnology or biotechnology or information & communication technology – should be supported. Obviously, it is useful to support such sectors to the extent that the respective country is richly endowed with complementary human capital and that the capital markets encourage creation of technology-intensive innovative start-up companies. (In the field of digital services, Germany faces particular problems since the dominance of banks and the relative weakness of venture capital funds impairs the creation and expansion of firms which offer little collateral.)

I.4.2 Specific Policy Conclusions for Germany

I.4.2.1 R&D Promotion for Medium Technologies and High-tech Industry

Germany's traditional strength is in medium intensive technologies such as automobiles, machinery and equipment. The government should continue to encourage R&D in medium intensive technologies, provided there are good arguments in favour of positive external effects. There are long established cooperations between universities and firms in the automotive industry and in the capital goods sector. However, one might want to broaden cooperation across borders and also internationalize the German university system in a way that teaching and conducting research abroad would be a normal element of a long term strategy of achieving excellence in research and teaching and of creating networks allowing for the finance of innovative projects in both teaching and research. As regards international activities of German universities, there are only a few exceptions. State-owned universities would find all kind of bureaucratic barriers if they wanted to expand internationally. Thus, privatizing several universities and giving more autonomy to universities would be highly desirable, but in the political arena no such initiatives have been adopted.

Given the medium term technological catching-up of EU accession countries in Eastern Europe and of Asian and some Latin American countries, the high wage economy of Germany would be well-advised to increasingly specialize in knowledge intensive and technology intensive sectors; this should include high technology sectors. Germany must move up the technology ladder and undertake serious efforts to modernize the education system accordingly. There have been very few efforts in the field of modernizing the education system. The PISA shock which saw bad results for Germany has encouraged some reforms in basic schooling. However, there are few efforts to really modernize the education system on a broader basis. Such commitment could be visible with the creation of new universities, tax incentives for the creation of private universities and tax incentives for adults to engage in advanced training and retraining. Such measures have not been undertaken thus far in Germany. One should also note that Germany, with its ageing society, could face a long term decline in output growth unless the rate of technological progress and the quality of human capital formation are improved in a sustained way. Short-sighted politicians are also sometimes inclined to impair innovativeness simply to get additional short term revenues. (A prime example in this respect involves the Ministry of Health, which forced leading pharmaceutical companies to pay an extra lump sum tax as a contribution aimed at alleviating the funding problems of the health care system. Such a policy is a wonderful starter for gradually killing the once globally leading German pharmaceutical firms. At the bottom line, the government obtained a few hundred million Euros yet thereby undermined innovation dynamics worth billions of Euros.

I.4.2.2 Skill Upgrading and Reform of the Education System

Facing economic and technological catching-up in Eastern Europe, Russia, Asia and Latin America (plus a few countries in Africa), the German economy will have to increasingly emphasize the production of technology-intensive and skill-intensive or knowledge-intensive products. More training and retraining as well as the modernization of the basic education system are major challenges for Germany. As regards incentives for firms and employers to engage more in training and retraining/skill-upgrading, the government could introduce adequate conditional tax benefits. Given Germany's budget problems, higher expenditures or reductions in tax revenues are only acceptable if new sources of tax revenue become available. Since Germany has a very low VAT rate among EU countries, one could consider raising the VAT rate as a means to finance incentives for the training, retraining and modernization of the education system.

As regards the university system, it would be useful to not only step up competition among universities but also to encourage foreign universities to set up satellite centers in Germany. A broader and more international supply side in the academic system would be quite useful not only for Germany but for other EU countries as well. A major weakness of the German university system is the low share of female graduates in engineering and informatics. The low share of female graduate in informatics (abut 15% at the beginning of the 21st century) is a serious disadvantage for a country which is facing an ageing of its society in the long run and modest economic growth in the short term. The US and many countries in the EU have been relatively successful in raising the share of female graduates and in encouraging a high share of female entrepreneurship. Germany has a long way to go in this respect.

I.4.2.3 Problems with Immigration of Unskilled Labour

The specific unemployment rate of unskilled workers was roughly twice the national average. Among immigrant workers, the specific unemployment rate is even higher. This poor result is partly due to the weakness of the German schooling system at successfully integrating foreigners. Since foreign workers have below average skills, it is not surprising that they become unemployed more often than workers born in Germany. The situation in Sweden (and some other EU countries) is different. Sweden in particular has emphasized and facilitated the immigration of skilled workers.

The free movement of labour has been restricted in the enlarged EU-25 until 2011 (at the latest). Germany is likely to attract a high degree of unskilled labour after 2011, since youth unemployment and overall unemployment rates in many accession countries of Eastern Europe are high. Economic geography – Germany's proximity to the accession countries – and economic incentives, namely high German wage rates and low social integration costs due to a large stock of foreigners (from eastern Europe) from previous immigration waves, make Germany a natural target country for those wishing to emigrate from eastern Europe. Such immigration will include citizens from Bulgaria and Romania, where relative per capita income (at purchasing power parity relative to EU-15) was only about 22% in 2003.

If the EU were to seriously consider Turkish membership, one would have to anticipate a large wave of additional Turkish immigrants in the future. The population in Turkey is growing at a pace of about 1 million per year, with the population growing from roughly 70 million in 2004 to 120 million by 2050. The high wage economy of Germany would thus face millions of Turkish immigrants once Turkey – with a per capita income of about 20% of EU-15 average in 2003 – enjoys full membership. Immigrants from Turkey would be largely unskilled workers which would reinforce unemployment problems in Germany. Against this background, it is doubtful that German politicians would quickly embrace EU membership for Turkey. If EU leaders were to quickly move towards EU membership, this might signal an integration overstretch, which could even result in a future German government leaving the EU under the heading "we want control of immigration, want to save funds used inefficiently by the EU and prefer having the D-Mark again." One should remember that the very purpose of creating the EU in 1957 was to firmly anchor the Federal Republic of Germany in Western Europe, and it would be historically tragic if enlargement to include Turkey drove Germany out of the Community (in the accession year 2004, the EU is hardly able to work effectively since there are so many new politicians and inexperienced bureaucrats in Brussels).

I.4.2.4 Improving Knowledge Transfer from University to the Business Community

Traditionally, there have been close links between firms and universities in Germany. However, universities have been relatively reluctant to promote early entrepreneurship of graduates. Moreover, many public universities are highly inflexible, bureaucratic and reluctant with respect to innovation and internationalization. Incentives to improve knowledge transfer from the university system to the business community would be much stronger if half of the universities were private universities which were more competitive in acquiring research funds from industry and public institutions. Privatizing a considerable number of universities and attracting foreign private universities could be interesting policy options to accelerate knowledge transfer.

The existing transfer institutions are rather bureaucratic and slow, the incentives from the slow marketing of patents obtained by professors at the universities are weak. While the three leading US universities had revenues of about 15% from patents and licensing at the beginning of the 21st century, the leading German universities had a revenue share in this category of not more than 2%.

While the links between the university and large MNCs in Germany are well established, such networking hardly exists with respect to most SMEs. Here, the internet offers new platforms and opportunities. However, local telecommunications is relatively expensive in Germany, not least due to the quasi-monopoly which the Deutsche Telekom AG (still largely government-owned) has maintained in traditional fixed-line telecommunications. Moreover, the German government allowed Deutsche Telekom AG to establish a dominant market position in the DSL market with the market share of the state-owned firm having been close to 90% in 2003. Germany cannot really deliver an optimum contribution to the Lisbon process if government does not strongly promote competition in both fixed-line telecommunications and the DSL market. DSL competition in France is much stronger than in Germany, and consequently France has overtaken Germany in terms of the absolute number of DSL lines in late 2004 when France reached a level of about 5 million lines. The share of households with broadband internet connection was close to 30% in Belgium, Denmark and the Netherlands (largely due to cable TV) in early 2004. In Sweden, Finland and Austria, it was in the range of 15-20%. Spain, France and Portugal had close to 15%, while Italy, the UK and Germany had only 12-13%. From this perspective, neither Italy, the UK nor Germany currently have an ideal starting point for developing and marketing innovative digital services. However, large countries always enjoy the benefit of a large home market.

I.4.2.5 Keeping Skilled Workers and Innovation Leadership in the Region

Facing the new international division of labour in Europe and worldwide, it is obvious that a high wage country such as Germany should specialize more on producing knowledge intensive and technology intensive goods and services. Advanced services seem to be particularly underrepresented in Germany with part of the problem being a lack of competition in retail banking, telecommunications and energy. These sectors have been sheltered from international competition for many years, and productivity growth has been relatively slow except for the post-1998 period in fixed-line telecommunications. Universities should be encouraged to focus more on these potentially dynamic liberalized sectors.

At the same time, regional government or national government could provide tax incentives for venture capital funds set up by large companies in these sectors (and other sectors). A rising share of venture capital funds should go to young firms created by university graduates. Regional government could provide R&D facilities and modern infrastructure for young technology oriented firms centred around a business park. Regional governments would be wise to promote existing clusters of excellence as well as new dynamic fields with growing long-term demand and a high rate of technological progress. Regional government can try to keep potentially mobile innovative companies in the respective region by offering generously modern facilities for innovators. Promoting innovative supplier clusters is also an option to reduce the mobility of innovators. An important ingredient in gluing innovative companies to a region is a network of highly innovative and flexible universities and R&D labs. Germany faces major financial problems in university and public research funding, and this could become a serious impediment for implementing adequate policy priorities.

I.4.2.6 A European Policy Perspective

Germany would be wise to embrace the best-practice approaches of other EU countries. Among the interesting new developments are open innovation systems such as the R&D park in Eindhoven where Philips is the leader in a large network of innovative firms. Cross-licensing is a typical element of networking in this R&D park. A major strategic goal of Philips is to nurture international R&D networking in a way that helps to set global standards quickly. Revenues from international licences increasingly contributed to Philips' revenue in the 1990s and in the beginning of the 21st century.

As industry becomes increasingly mobile in the EU-25 and as accession countries catch up over time, it is natural that research activities also become more footloose. In a dynamic open economy, nobody should expect to easily earn high income in traditional fields of specialization. Rather, it will be necessary to react relatively flexibly and to move into new markets and niches. For firms, the challenge is to develop flexible, efficient and innovative-enhancing structures. For national policymakers and the EU, the medium-term challenge is to shift the focus of R&D policy more towards success-promising new fields. Both the national and the supranational policy level should become more efficient and effective in R&D promotion. Moreover, at both the national and the supranational level, a strong emphasis on competition and open markets is essential. While better digital intellectual property rights seem to be necessary in general, the special case of software patenting raises serious doubts. In a sector in which network effects automatically become an endogenous barrier for market entry, software patents are quite doubtful. It is true that the software market is not homogenous, but easy patenting of software should certainly be avoided if the policy goal is to encourage digital innovations in the long run.

One should take the Lisbon process seriously in all EU member countries, in particular in large Eurozone countries such as Germany, France and Italy. There is little doubt that Germany and Italy have underestimated the challenges of achieving sustained growth for many years. The heated public debate of 2003/04 between politicians and researchers in France – the latter pointing out a massive funding gap for top R&D institutions and projects – shows that not only Germany (or Italy) has serious problems in allocating sufficient funding to promoting innovations. Regular monitoring of national and regional R&D policies could be quite useful in generating more pressure on member states to adopt efficient R&D policies and to increase spending on innovation and human capital formation.

Appendix I.1: Optimum Product Innovation under Uncertainty

As regards innovation efforts, firms can undertake R&D at fixed costs H, where one may assume that the probability to obtain a (temporary) monopoly depends on H. Let us assume that without product innovations we have a linear demand function p=a-bq; we assume that R&D costs H reflect efforts in product innovations which raise the willingness to pay, so that denoting α as the parameter to indicate the rise in the willingness to pay for innovative products and α as the probability of successful innovation, the expected demand function in the case of a product innovation is:

$$p = a + \alpha(H) - bq \tag{1a}$$

Here α is the probability to successfully launch a product innovation and thus also the probability to obtain a monopoly provided that competitors are expected to remain passive as is assumed here. Production costs are assumed to be proportionate to q and to include R&D costs which are fixed costs H (an alternative would be to assume that R&D costs for product innovations are equal to H +[n/q]):

$$Z = hq + H. \tag{1b}$$

Under standard competition, the market is characterized with p=h and q=(a-h)/b; standard monopoly theory suggests a monopoly quantity $q^M=(a-h)/2b$ and monopoly price $p^M = (h+a)/2$.

Denoting α as the probability of a successful product innovation, r' as the revenue under monopoly, R^C under competition, R^E as expected revenue and Q as profit we assume that the firms wants to maximize the profit function:

$$Q = R^E - Z = \{\alpha(H)r' + [1-\alpha(H)R^c]\} - [hq + H] \tag{2}$$

Expected revenue in our approach is:

$$R^E = \alpha(H)[aq + \alpha(H)q - bq^2] + [(1- \alpha(H)][aq-bq^2] = [aq-bq^2] + \{\alpha^2(H)q\} \tag{3}$$

The term {…} makes the difference to the standard approach in profit maximization. The monopolist will equal marginal production costs k'(q) and marginal expected revenue $R^{E'}$ which is

$$R^{E'} = a - 2bq + 2\alpha(H) \tag{4}$$

Optimum output is given by $h = R^{E'}$ and therefore:

$$q\# = [a-h + 2\alpha(H)]/2b \tag{5}$$

The corresponding price is – enforceable in the case of successful product innovation is:

$$p\# = a + \alpha(H) - b[a-h + 2\alpha(H)]/2b \tag{6}$$

Compared to standard monopoly theory, the approach presented shows a marginal revenue which is higher so that optimum output in a Schumpeterian economy will indeed be higher in every market with product innovations than in a non-innovative economy. The optimum H can be determined from dV/dH=0, which yields:

$$Q= [aq-bq^2]+ \{\alpha^2(H)q\} - [hq + H] \tag{7}$$

$$\partial Q/\partial H= 0 \tag{8}$$

$$2\alpha(H)\alpha_H\, q =1 \tag{9}$$

Inserting optimum q implies:

$$2\, \alpha\,(H)\, \alpha_H\, [a\text{-}h +2\alpha(H)]/2b= 1 \tag{10}$$

Denoting the elasticity of α with respect to H as $E_{\alpha,H}$ we can write

$$2(1/H)\, E_{\alpha,H}\, [a\text{-}h +2\alpha(H)]/2b= 1 \tag{11}$$

Implicitly from this function, the optimum H can be derived. Note that the optimum H – which is a fixed cost here – must be below the expected profit from product innovation, because the firm is otherwise squeezed out from the market. One should also note that the market will be characterized by excess capacity if the product innovation cannot be launched successfully. The reason for a tendency to overcapacity in the market is that the firm will decide about optimum q in advance. If the product innovation cannot be launched successfully, the firm can still cut back production – and hence avoid marginal costs of initially-planned production – in a way that excess production in the market is avoided. Finally, it should be noted that in innovative sectors temporary excess capacity should not be identified with signs of a recession since it simply is a by-product of product innovation under uncertainty. If a rise of per capita income goes along with a rising degree of product differentiation and hence a stronger tendency towards product innovation the problem of apparent excess capacity in the overall economy could gradually become more important during certain periods. If government promotes product innovation, an unwelcome by-product could be temporary excess capacity in some sectors. Moreover, government measures to promote growth (raising per capita income) could indirectly stimulate product innovations and hence bring about the problem of temporarily idle capacities. In an open economy, such excess capacity might lead to unplanned net exports in the respective sector. If the exporting country is large, this will entail a temporary reduction of world market prices.

Appendix I.2: Product Innovations and Network Effects in a Simple Model

Assume that willingness to pay depends on the degree of product innovation V, which in turn is proportionate to innovation efforts H, while production costs positively depend both on the quantity produced q and the innovation efforts H. In the following simple model, we will look at some interesting aspects of product innovations in sectors with network effects. We will consider the behaviour of an experienced innovator who is certain that innovation expenditures on product innovation will translate into a temporary monopoly position. For simplicity, we assume V=H and that the demand function is $q= H^{\alpha'}a/p$ (where a and α' are positive parameters; and by assumption α'>0. Note $E_{y,x}$ will denote the elasticity of variable y with respect to variable x). Note that such a demand function implies that revenue is constant since $R =pq = H^{\alpha'}a$.

Thus for the profit maximizing firm undertaking product innovations, we the following expressions for the demand function function and for profit Q, respectively:

$$q= H^{\alpha'}a/p \tag{1}$$

$$Q = p(H)q - k(q,H) \tag{2}$$

Maximization of this function requires in a competitive framework:

$$dQ/dq = p - k'(q,H) = 0 \tag{3}$$

Hence

$$p=k'(q,H) \tag{3'}$$

under competition (a minor problem occurs with maximization due to the constancy of revenue for any given H!)

$$R'(q,H)=k'(q,H) \tag{3''}$$

under monopoly; with revenue R=p(q.H)q
and

$$dQ/dH = \partial p/\partial H\, q - \partial k/\partial H = 0 \tag{4}$$

Inserting the demand function we have:

$$\partial p/\partial H\, H^{\alpha'}a/p = \partial k/\partial H \tag{5}$$

$$E_{p,H}\, H^{\alpha'-1}a = \partial k/\partial H \tag{6}$$

Hence the optimum product innovation effort H# is given by the necessary condition

$$H\# = \{[\partial k/\partial H]/aE_{p,H}\}^{1/1-\alpha'} \tag{7}$$

After choice of H#, the firm can choose output q in a way that the condition marginal revenue equals marginal costs is fulfilled. According to the above equation, the product innovation effort will be the higher the lower the marginal costs of innovation $\partial k/\partial H$ and the lower the elasticity $E_{p,H}$ of the price with respect to innovation (efforts) and the lower the basic willingness to pay as expressed by a is.

How will network effects affect the elasticity of p with respect to H? If the market is characterized by network effects, we may assume that the elasticity of p with respect to product innovation effort H is lower than in a normal market (this effect could be estimated empirically), because network effects stimulate competition which in turn drives down the market price. Hence the optimum product innovation effort would be higher – every round of product innovation is a new starting point to escape the move towards low competitive prices. At the same time, there could be scale effects whose exploitation is facilitated in the presence of network effects. If there is only one firm, it should be easy to anticipate the positive network effect. However, the firm will charge not only a temporary monopoly price – which is a natural side-effect of the product innovation itself – but it will charge a monopolistic price even in the long run; it also will adopt a lower rate of product innovation. With many firms in the market, the firm which launches a product innovation only has a temporary monopoly. As soon as there is broad imitation, the innovating firm can no longer fetch a monopoly price in the market. It must accept a price which is equal to long-term marginal costs (assumed to be constant in the subsequent graph where we show an initial monopoly price plus a situation with a product innovation in the context of monopoly pricing as an analytical starting point).

If there are quasi-scale economies in the sector considered, the marginal costs of product innovation will be negatively influenced by the size of the market, which in turn is positively affected by network effects. The latter thus bring about a positive external costs effect for all competitors. The assumption that network effects reduce the marginal costs of innovation can be justified only if the size of the market is a positive signal for attracting more researchers to R&D activities in which learning by doing or intra-sector spillovers plays a role. Note that under monopoly, we have price p^N for the product innovation both in the short term and in the long term, but under competition, it would be the lower price p_1 in the long run. Hence government should encourage competition and help high barriers to entry from occurring.

Endogenous barriers resulting from strong network effects in industry (e.g., in the software sector) could also be a problem which would not always justify standard patent protection.

Our line of reasoning can also be seen form the following graph where we show an initial marginal costs curve k'_0 and a new marginal cost curve k'_1 which is relevant in the context of the product innovation. The initial equilibrium point under monopoly and the initial demand schedule DD_0 is point C and hence output is q_1 and the monopoly price p_M. Now we turn to product innovation. There will be a rise of the cost curve stemming from product innovation efforts, and this reduces consumer welfare. At the same time, there will be an upward rotation of the demand curve (see DD_1) reflecting the increased willingness to pay for the novel product; the latter effect is associated with higher consumer welfare. A positive network effect is reflected in the graph as a rightward shift of the demand curve (see DD_2). If there are quasi-scale effects, there will also be a downward shift of the k' curve. For simplicity, we can assume that this shift effect fully offsets the initial shift from k'_0 to k'_1: Hence taking into account quasi-scale effects associated indirectly with network effects results in k'_0 so that the long-term competitive equilibrium is point H, output q_5 and price p_0 (without scale effects output would be q_2). Transitorily, there could be a monopoly situation with a monopoly price p_o and output q_6.

There are cases when industry itself is able to exploit network effects fully (e.g., when leading firms in the sector agree on a new standard in the context of a product innovation). Setting standards in an environment of open interfaces of equipment allows for the exploitation of both network effects and scale effects. Modern electronics offers many examples of successful standard setting through industry itself. There are, however, well known examples of competing proprietary standards as well, as was the case with video recorders.

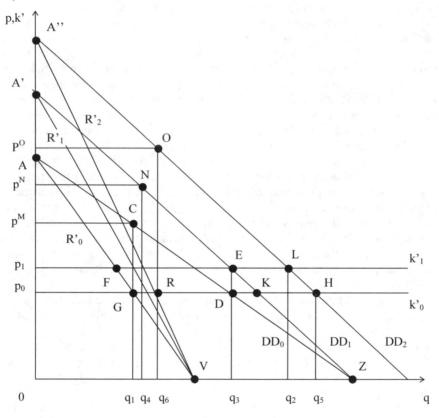

Fig. 83. Product Innovation and Network Effects

Appendix I.3: NACE (EU classification) rev. 1.1 Classification at the 2-digit level (in parts)

D Manufacturing
- 15 Manufacture of food products and beverages
- 16 Manufacture of tobacco products
- 17 Manufacture of textiles
- 18 Manufacture of wearing apparel; dressing and dyeing of fur
- 19 Tanning and dressing of leather, manufacture of luggage, handbags, saddlery, harness and footwear
- 20 Manufacture of wood and of products of wood and cork, except furniture;
- 21 Manufacture of pulp, paper and paper products
- 22 Publishing, printing and reproduction of recorded media
- 23 Manufacture of coke, refined petroleum products and nuclear fuel
- 24 Manufacture of chemicals and chemical products
- 25 Manufacture of rubber and plastic products
- 26 Manufacture of other non-metallic mineral products
- 27 Manufacture of basic metals
- 28 Manufacture of fabricated metal products, except machinery and equipment
- 29 Manufacture of machinery and equipment n.e.c.
- 30 Manufacture of office machinery and computers
- 31 Manufacture of electrical machinery and apparatus n.e.c.
- 32 Manufacture of radio, television and communication equipment and apparatus
- 33 Manufacture of medical, precision and optical instruments, watches and clocks
- 34 Manufacture of motor vehicles, trailers and semi-trailers
- 35 Manufacture of other transport equipment
- 36 Manufacture of furniture, manufacturing n.e.c.
- 37 Recycling

Appendix I.4: Model for Digital Innovation

The following model (VOGELSANG, 2006) puts the focus on the role of R&D in intermediate production and uses a Dixit-Stiglitz utility function where we quote from WELFENS/VOGELSANG, 2006, p. 120-123: Consider "a general equilibrium model with two sectors and simultaneous Cournot and Betrand-Competition which follows the approach of GROSSMAN/HELPMAN (1991). The main point of the model is described by the following characteristics:

- The aspatial character of digital companies is stressed. They are located in the 'rest of the world'. The model describes their decision of entering a (new) market of a small, open economy.

- The expected profits are crucial for the internationalisation strategy.
- The revenues are influenced by the quality of the products.
- In the model the marginal costs of producing digital goods become irrelevant.
- Only one input factor: labour. This stresses the low capital intensity of digital goods production functions.

First the framework of a closed economy is developed. For a representative household a standard CES-utility function is assumed:

$$U = \left(\sum_{j=1}^{n} x_j^{\rho} \right)^{1/\rho} \tag{a}$$

with elasticity of substitution

$$\sigma = \frac{1}{1-\rho} > 1 \tag{b}$$

In the model each of the n different industries produce a final product x. The final products are imperfect substitutes which mean that monopolistic competition is predominant in the final goods markets. The budget constraint reads

$$E = x_j \, p_j = w_H \, L_H + w_I \, L_I \tag{c}$$

with L_H and L_I for the labour employed in the sectors sales/marketing H and intermediates production I respectively, w_H and w_I for real wage rate in the sectors, p_j for the prices of the n different final products x.
With regard to the standard assumptions of monopolistic competition (free-entry, Cournot-Competition) it results in mark-up λ so that the prices for the final products xj exceeds their marginal costs by

$$\lambda = 1/\rho \tag{d}$$

Variable costs of assembling the final goods x_j out of intermediates q and fixed costs for marketing add up to the total Cost function C:

$$C_j = Hw_H + v\pi_j x_j \tag{e}$$

with H for fixed sales and marketing costs, π for the price of the intermediates. The input factor v results from the production function for the final products

$$x_j = \sum_{i=1}^{v_j} \frac{1}{v} z_{j,i} \, (q_{j,i}) \tag{f}$$

with assuming $v_j = v = \bar{v}$. For mathematical convenience and without loss of generality the input factor $1/v$ balances the number of v different intermediate products z so that for the production of x units of final product j, exactly z units of the intermediates are used. $q_{j,i}$ indicates the quality of intermediate product z_{ji}

Following GROSSMAN/HELPMAN (1991) a quality ladder like in the graph below represents the enhancements achieved by producing the intermediates.

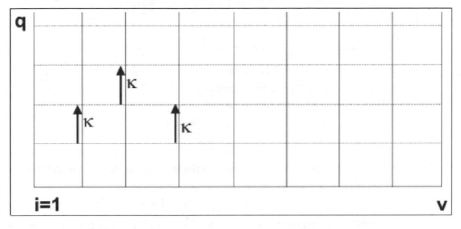

Source: GROSSMAN/HELPMAN (1991)

Fig. 84. Quality Ladder for Industry j

The horizontal axis represents the intermediate producers of industry j indexed by i. The quality level q of the intermediates is shown on the vertical axis. Improving quality means to develop a next generation version of an intermediate. By assumption, a next generation intermediate provides exactly κ times as much quality (or services) as the product of the generation before it. $\kappa > 1$ is constant and exogenous.

The production function to produce the intermediates z has a fixed component α and variable component with a fixed input factor β :

$$z_{j,i} = \alpha + \beta L^{\text{var}}{}_{j,i} \tag{g}$$

Bertrand competition in the market of intermediates for industry j leads to the result that only the company offering the best quality adjusted price will survive: Consider two companies A and B which both offer intermediate i for industry j. They produce intermediates of quality $q_{j,i,A}$ and $q_{j,i,B}$ respectively. Quality adjusted prices Q are

$$Q_{j,i} = \frac{\pi_{j,i}}{q_{j,i}} \tag{h}$$

The intermediates i for industry j are perfect substitutes. The quality adjusted price is the only criterion for the final goods producer to decide which company should supply the intermediates. With equal quality adjusted prices it chooses the higher quality product for convenience. Therefore results $z_{j,i,k}$ with $k \in B, C, D, ..$

when $Q_{j,i,A} < Q_{j,i,k}$ for every k. So company A sells all $z_{j,i}$ at price $Q_{j,i,B} = \kappa\, Q_{j,i,A}$, which reflects Bertrand competition in this market segment.

Introducing marginal cost pricing for company B, which yields βw_I with w_I for the real wage in the intermediates producing sector according to (16) the price which has to be paid by the final good producer of industry j to company A, yields marginal costs of B times the factor κ:

$$\pi_{j,i} = Q_{j,i,B} q_{j,i,A} = \kappa \beta w_I \tag{i}$$

For determining a general solution some symmetry assumptions are introduced now:

1.) $\beta_{j,i} = \beta$, 2.) $w_{I,j,i} = w_I$ and 3.) $\kappa_{j,i} = \kappa$ for all j,i.

The quality of an intermediate depends on the amount invested in Research & Development which is measured by α. To agree on producing $z_{j,i}$ company A has to achieve a non negative profit $\prod_A \geq 0$:

$$\prod_A = z_{j,i}\left[\pi_{j,i} - \frac{\alpha}{z_{j,i}} - \beta \right] = z_{j,i}\left[\kappa w_I \beta - \frac{\alpha}{z_{j,i}} - \beta \right] = z_{j,i}\left[(\kappa-1)\beta \right] - \alpha \tag{j}$$

The equilibrium conditions for the labour market complete the description of the closed economy:

$$L = L_H + L_I \tag{k}$$

$$L_H = n H \tag{l}$$

$$L_I = \sum_{j=1}^{n} \sum_{i=1}^{v_j} \left(\frac{z}{\beta} + \alpha \right) \tag{m}$$

The next step is to transform equation (j) so that profit can be expressed with the exogenous variables of the closed economy only. Then the expected profit function of potential new intermediate suppliers can be examined when the closed economy is opened. First the cost-function is amended by the industry's j pricing model. The expenditure per industry is calculated which gives solutions for x and

z. Assuming symmetry of all n v industries a general cost function can then be determined.

Total costs of producing and selling final products x_j are:

$$C_j = Hw_H + v\, p_j\, x_j = Hw_H + v\, \beta\, w_I\, \kappa\, x_j \tag{n}$$

Marginal costs account to:

$$\frac{\partial C_j}{\partial x_j} = v\, \beta\, \kappa\, w_I \tag{o}$$

In equilibrium the price of the final product equals the marginal costs times the mark-up λ:

$$p_j = \lambda\, v\, \beta\, \kappa\, w_I \tag{p}$$

Choosing the price index $P_{Index} = 1$ as numeraire the spending account for industry j yields:

$$x_j = \frac{E}{p_j}\, \frac{1}{P_{Index}} = \frac{E}{\lambda\, v\, \beta\, \kappa\, w_I} \tag{q}$$

With (e) holds for all i:

$$x_j = \frac{E}{\lambda\, v\, \beta\, \kappa\, w_I} = z_{j,i} \tag{r}$$

so that assuming labour flexibility between all sectors $w_H = w_I = w$ leads to

$$z_{j,i} = \frac{wL}{\lambda\, v\, \beta\, \kappa\, w_I} \tag{s}$$

The profit function then reads:

$$\Pi_A = \frac{wL\,(\kappa-1)\beta}{\lambda\, v\, \beta\, \kappa\, w} - \alpha = \frac{L\,(\kappa-1)}{\lambda\, v\, \kappa} - \alpha = \frac{L}{\lambda v} - \frac{L}{\lambda\, v\, \kappa} - \alpha \tag{t}$$

This equation expresses the expected profit Π in terms of exogenous variables. The special model specification leads to the result that the marginal costs β are irrelevant which reproduces a main characteristic of a digital economy. The interpretation of equation (t) is intuitive:

- A positive profit can be expected when the additional revenues resulting from quality leadership are greater than the fixed costs α which may be needed for Research and Development.
- Marginal costs β are irrelevant in the intermediate sector: this reproduces a main characteristic of a digital economy and is a result of the Bertrand price-quality competition.
- Wage w is irrelevant in a closed economy with labour as single input factor and full employment
- Technological leadership affects profits positively.

$$\frac{\partial \Pi_A}{\partial \kappa} > 0$$

- The higher the number of intermediate goods producers in an industry, the lower the profit.

$$\frac{\partial \Pi_A}{\partial \upsilon} < 0$$

- Total market size matters. Big markets raise expected profitability.

$$\frac{\partial \Pi_A}{\partial L} > 0$$

- Fixed costs, e.g. expenditures for Research & Development diminish profits directly, which should be true in a one-period-model especially.

$$\frac{\partial \Pi_A}{\partial \alpha} = -1$$

Opening the economy changes the perspective to consider a single company F outside this country, whose headquarters is located 'somewhere' in the rest of world (or is aspatial in this sense). The production function of F corresponds to (g), moreover μ denotes the additional marketing and sales costs for market entry in the closed economy and ψ describes the probability of having success, which means to become the quality-price-leader. The Bertrand-Competition game compares the possible strategies of market entry:[1]

- 1. Strategy 1: F enters the market and offers its own digital products as intermediates. Transport costs are neglected because of the special characteristics of digital goods. Assuming that the product is developed already, which means the fixed costs α are not relevant for the decision on market entry, the profit function then yields:

---

[11] For convenience it is assumed that the company F is the only potential competitor and that F is 'small' in the sense that possible disequilibria in the balance of payments can be neglected.

$$\Pi_{foreign} = \psi \left[\frac{L(\kappa-1)}{\lambda v \kappa} \right] - \mu \qquad (u)$$

- 2. Strategy 2: The foreign company F buys domestic company A. K is the price of the acquisition and ρ the discount factor for the next period's profits

$$\Pi_{foreign} = K - \sum_{t=1}^{\infty} \left[(1-\psi) \frac{L(\kappa-1)}{\lambda v \kappa} - \alpha \right] \rho^{-t} \qquad (v)$$

- 3. Strategy 3: Do nothing

$$\Pi_{foreign} = 0 \qquad (w)$$

Despite the anecdotic evidence equations (30) to (32) predict the internationalisation strategies of digital goods producers:

- The larger L, κ and the smaller λ, v and μ the company would rather choose strategy 1 (trading) despite a low ψ.
- Strategy 2 (acquisition) is chosen, when technological leadership of the domestic price-quality leadership is dominant and sustainable and the risk of not achieving the leader position oneself is high.
- Internationalisation from a macroeconomic point of view means that countries with a high L and a low λ are preferred.

The price-quality competition is pivotal in this model."

The model is quite useful when trying to understand competition in digital goods markets where marginal costs in intermediate products play no crucial role. One may emphasize that long run digital dynamics in the world economy will be increasingly shaped by market size, R&D and different types of monopolistic competition.

J. EU Innovation Policy: Analysis and Critique

J.1 Introduction

Economic globalization has accelerated the innovation race among leading OECD countries as foreign direct investment in Newly Industrializing Countries (NICs) plus China and India have created a new international divison of labor. Indeed, globalization went along with a more intensive innovation race (JUNGMITTAG/ MEYER-KRAHMER/REGER, 1999). Moreover, in the 1990s increased R&D expenditures in China and many NICs as well as Russia have reinforced the ability of economic and technological catching-up. There is a certain minimum R&D expenditure requirement – relative to GDP – if countries are to be able to effectively adopt foreign technologies. Both innovation and fast diffusion can contribute critically to international innovativeness. Improving the international competitiveness of the overall EU-15 has been an explicit goal of the EU Lisbon summit of 2000. This summit has proclaimed the goal to make the EU the most competitive economy by 2010; exploitation of the digital information society is to play a crucial role in this respect as the Heads of State and Government of European Union endorsed the idea of a European Research Area (ERA) and declared the creation of a European knowledge-based society a crucial element of the political strategy.

With the expansion of digital networks and the internet, respectively, there are also new global channels for technology diffusion on the one hand, on the other hand modern digital networking also facilitates cooperation among researchers and engineers which enhances the effectiveness of the innovation process in leading OECD countries; this also applies to the EU-15 which has emphasized building a European Information Society early on.

The European Commission has considered some broad reforms in EU innovation policy in the document "Towards a European Research Area (ERA)" (EUROPEAN COMMISSION, 2000b). The European Parliament has supported the project in a Resolution adopted on May 18, 2000. The new strategy accepts that national innovation policy is crucial but it seeks a well-defined complementary role of supranational innovation policy. Key elements of the new strategy are:

- better and more flexible co-ordination of national innovation policies;
- creating Networks of Excellence (NoE) which aim at reinforcing excellence on a research topic by creating large networks of R&D actors with a common focus on a joint programme of activities;
- establishing Integrated Projects (IP) which stand for multi-partner ventures which aim at bringing together a critical mass of resources to reach a specific research objective – with a strong focus on combining new knowledge for launching product innovations and process innovations.

According to the EU the Networks of Excellence and Integrated Projects, respectively, should reflect the following idea (Extract from the Decision No.

1513/002/Ec. of the European Parliament and of the Council of 27 June 2002 as quoted in CARACOSTAS, 2003, p.39):

"The purpose of Networks of Excellence is to strenghten and develop Community scientific and technological excellence by means of the integration, at European level, of research capacities currently existing or emerging at both national and regional level. Each Network will also aim at advancing knowledge in a particular area by assembling a critical mass of expertise. They will foster co-operation between capacities of excellence in universities, research centers, enterprises, including SMEs, and science and technology organizations. The activities will be generally targeted towards long-term, multidisciplinary objectives, rather than predefined results in terms of products, processes or services..."

"Integrated Projects are designed to give increased impetus to the Community's competitiveness or to address major societal needs by mobilizing a critical mass of research and technological development resources and competencies. Each Integrated Project should be assigned clearly defined scientific and technological objectives and should be directed at obtaining specific results applicable in terms of, for instance, products, processes or services. (...) Subject to conditions to be specified in the specific programs and in the rules for participation, the Integrated Projects will have a high level of management autonomy including, where appropriate, the possibility to adapt the partnership and the content of the project. They will be carried out on the basis of overall financing plans preferably involving significant mobilization of public and private sector funding, including funding or collaboration schemes such as EUREKA, EIB and EIF."

Taking into account the principle of subsidiarity it is clear that EU R&D programmes must have extra EU-value-added, e.g. positive mutual – uniltaral or reciprocal - spillover effects in a joint innovation project.

To some extent the idea of creating networks of excellence certainly is adequate in the sense that in a single EU market there should be international R&D joint ventures organized within the framework of top R&D groups from several countries; this typically would bridge various national systems of innovations and also various languages in the Community. To some extent it also could bring useful cross-country R&D spillover effects, in particular for relatively backward countries which under different circumstances would find it more difficult to catch-up in terms of innovativeness. To the extent that successful R&D consortia applying for EU funds have integrated partners from EU countries with a relatively low per capita income – e.g. cohesion countries – one may anticipate accelerated diffusion of new technology in the community. It remains, however, an open question whether partners from low income countries can make considerable contributions to top R&D performance. Whether or not this is the case clearly will depend on stable networking and hence sufficient learning and cumulation effects. Establishing integrated projects also is a useful approach to the extent that university R&D (or similar external R&D centers) and R&D centers of firms cooperate smoothly.

J.2 Innovation Policy in the EU

In the EU innovation policy is mainly a policy task faced at the national level. National innovation policies of EU member countries must take into account the "national innovation system" which is defined as the respective set of institutions, agencies and cultures relevant for the innovation process (LUNDVALL, 1992; HOLLINGSWORTH/BOYER, 1997). The EU has two elements of innovation policy at the level above national government:

- There are Framework Programmes (FP 1-FP 6) which aim at stimulating joint research efforts. The first FP of 1984 has emphasized industrial technologies, information technology, telecommunications and biotechnology. Subsequent framework programmes have broadened with respect to the scope of research topics and technologies.
- Outside the Framework Programmes the Commission has launched a range of regional innovation policy initiatives. E.g. in 1993 a special initiative termed Regional Technology Plans (RTP) was started, where the idea was to nurture regional innovation and growth in disadvantaged regions. Such pilot programmes can help to stimulate growth. The Commission is mainly playing a mentor role in RTP, the regions which finally were selected to enter with their projects the experimental stage are mainly responsible for the success of the respective programme.

In addition, there are transnational programmes such as COST and EUREKA. The latter, starting in 1985, includes not only the EU countries but countries from Eastern Europe and Russia as well. These programmes are intergovernmental initiatives which are mainly bottom-up programmes and emphasize international networking in R&D.

All this does not mean that the EU has a strong comprehensive innovation policy. Major problems in this respect refer to:

- Availability of rather limited funds at the level of the EU: Supranational funds have not reached more than roughly 4% of expenditures at the national level.
- Conflicting interests among high income countries with a high share of medium and high technology in manufacturing output as compared to low income countries with a high share of low and medium technology in manufacturing output. Low income countries anticipate that they will get a disproportionate share of EU R&D funds which implies considerable resistance against raising the relative share of supranational R&D expenditures in the overall EU budget. With EU eastern enlargement this problem might be reinforced.
- Problems in creating an integrated innovation system.

Despite all these problems one should not overlook the impact of the single market dynamics which include emergence of a large integrated capital market in the Euro area.

J.3 Innovation Dynamics in OECD Countries

J.3.1 Innovation, Specialization and Growth: Empirical Analysis for EU-15 and USA

Comparing economic development in the US and the EU and individual EU countries, respectively, there are various differences which might explain the relatively high dynamics of the US and the more modest growth in the EU in the 1990s. Superior US innovation dyanmics is only one aspect, a relatively high rate of population growth of the US is a second factor; and the growth of information and communication technology (ICT) is a third element where the US has benefitted both from increasing production of ICT goods and increasing use of ICT – based on the accumulation of ICT capital. It is well known that the expansion of ICT production has strongly contributed to technological progress in the US; it seems that most of the rise of total factor productivity in the 1990s indeed is attributable to ICT production (JORGENSEN, 2003). The issue of spillover effects and a more detailed analysis of total factor productivity growth thus remains on the agenda.

Taking a closer look at the EU requires to focus on individual countries and their respective catching-up and innovation dynamics. From an analytical perspective an augmented production function is useful in which capital, labor, technology and telecommunications play a role (WELFENS/JUNGMIITAG, 2002). Moreover, there is an additional growth bonus from specialization itself which can be divided into general specialization effects and high technology specializion effects. As regards technological catching-up dynamics within the EU there is clear empirical evidence that specilization effects matter, in particular in high technology (JUNGMITTAG, 2004). Moreover, there is evidence that some EU countries have made considerable progress in technological catching-up in the period 1970-95, this holds in particular for Finland and Ireland, but there is also some modest catching up of Spain. The following figure shows some of the relevant catching-up dynamics in the EU where we leave open to which extent diffusion, enhanced human capital formation and gross fixed capital formation plus innovation – strictly defined (and partly linked to foreign direct investment inflows) have contributed to convergence.

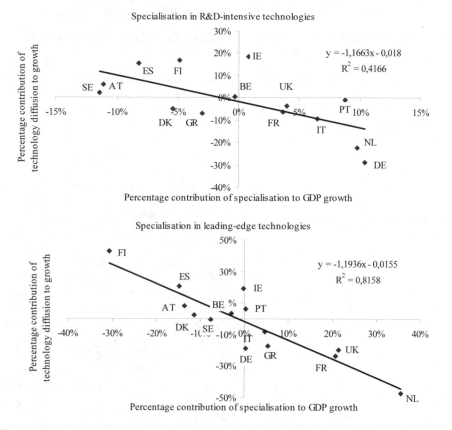

Source: Jungmittag (2004), Innovations, Technological Specialisation and Economic Growth in the EU, Brussels.

Fig. 85. Correlations Between Contributions of Transferable Technical Knowledge and Technological Specialisation to GDP Growth

J.3.2 Comparative Innovation Dynamics

Innovation dynamics can be measured in various ways. There are two key figures to be considered crucially:

- As regards input in the R&D process one is interested in R&D expenditures relative to GDP or R&D expenditures per capita. If one is interested in a refined analysis one may take a look at expenditure figures on the basis of purchasing power parity which mainly reflects differences in the absolute price of nontradables across countries (e.g. construction prices in Spain are lower than in Germany or France or Scandinavia so that building a new research lab is relatively cheap in Spain – and other low income countries).

- As regards innovation output there is a natural interest in patent applications – and patents granted – on a per capita basis. Not all patents are equal so that there is particular interest in medium technology and high technology patents; and in those patent classes which show the highest growth rate. High growth rates reflect strong innovation dynamics. Not all innovations can, of course, be patented; in the case of innovative services and software trade marks and copyrights are important to some extent; alternatively, one might want to take a look at the share of new products in overall sales. As regards patenting one might have to consider two special problems: There seems to be an international tendency of leading firms to generally seek more patents where patent applications to some extent are used as a strategic means to deter rivals in the innovation race. In some high technology fields patenting might not be attractive as innovation cycles are so short that patenting does not give effective protection. Finally, there can be a rise in patent applications due to the fact that one patent at time t goes along with more "follower patents" in t+1 than in previous periods.

Comparing the EU with the US and Japan we find that the share of EU-15 in overall patent applications at the European Patent Office has gradually declined in the 1990s. By contrast the share of the US has increased considerably. If the trend would continue for another twenty years the natural home bias – read: home lead – of EU countries would no longer exist.

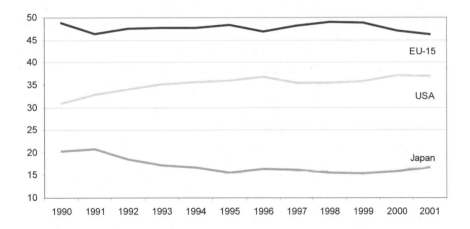

Fig. 86. Percentage Shares of Patent Applications at the European Patent Office

As regards the number of patent applications at the EPO per one million inhabitants the US and Japan were ahead of the EU-15 at the beginning of the 21st century. This also points to a certain weakness of EU innovation dynamics. From this figures it is fairly clear that the EU will be unable to reach the Lisbon target and become the world's leading economy in terms of competitiveness.

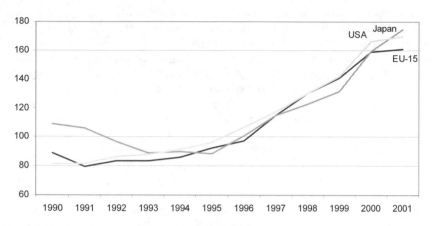

Fig. 87. EU-15, Japan and USA: Number of Patent Applications Per One Million Inhabitants at EPO

A particular problem is Germany where the stock of national patents has been declining in the 1990s. While taking a look at patent applications relative to applications of other countries means to consider marginal patenting dynamics the focus on the stock of patent gives a much broader picture. If we assume that the stock of knowledge enters the production function and if we approximate that variable by the stock of patents it is obvious that a declining stock of patents indicates a dampening vintage effect in the field of technology; moreover, if Schumpeterian rents are proportionate to the stock of patents – we assume that products made on the basis of patented technology can fetch relatively high prices in world markets – a decline in the stock of patents should indeed go along with reduced income growth.

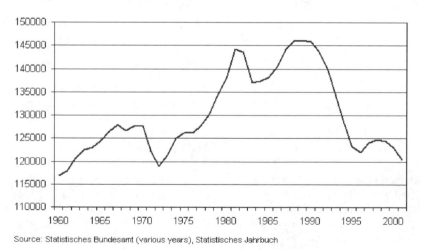

Source: Statistisches Bundesamt (various years), Statistisches Jahrbuch

Fig. 88. Stock of Patents at the German Patent and Trade Mark Office (1960 – 2001)

As regards per capita patent applications at the EPO several small EU countries were quite successful in terms of raising the respective figure, however, Germany, France and Italy have only a modest record.

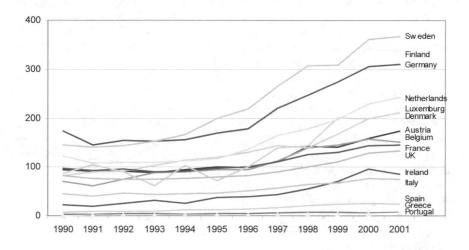

Fig. 89. EU 15: Number of Patent Applications Per One Million Inhabitants at the EPO

As regards EU accession countries patenting dynamics are relatively low, however, this is not surprising since they still have low per capita income and still modest ratios of R&D expenditures relative to GDP.

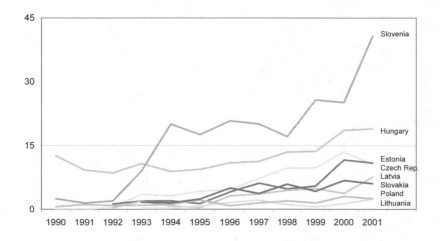

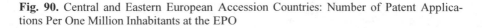

Fig. 90. Central and Eastern European Accession Countries: Number of Patent Applications Per One Million Inhabitants at the EPO

There are, however, good prospects that continuing growth and foreign direct investment inflows in combination with rising public R&D expenditures – plus EU support – will raise patenting performance. For the accession countries there is still need to emphasize to some extent diffusion of new technologies and adoption of advanced technology. Generating higher innovation dynamics and technological upgrading is a necessary element of the medium term adjustment and growth process. There are indeed new empirical findings which show that Hungary, the Czech Republic and Poland (BORBÉLY, 2004) have embarked upon a process of structural change and economic and political catching-up. The analysis of trade between the EU-15 and selected accession countries by means of a modified Revealed Comparative Advantage Index in the context of R&D expenditure shows, that Poland mainly specializes in the exportation of low and medium R&D intensive sectors, whereas the Czech Republic has clusters both in medium and high R&D intensive sectors, and Hungary specialises mostly in high technology products already. Although R&D expenditure ratios are still much lower in eastern European countries than in the current EU member states, the sectoral distribution of R&D expenditures is, however, similar.

As regards R&D expdenditure per capita Japan and the US have shown a considerable growth in the 1990s while EU-15 has achieved only modest growth at the end of the decade.

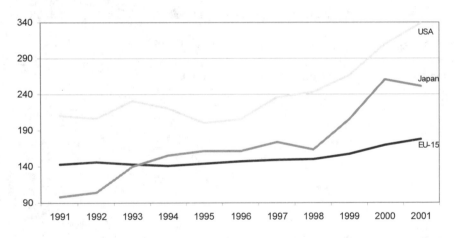

Fig. 91. R&D Expenditure Per Capita in EU-15, Japan and the USA (EUR, Current Prices)

As regards R&D expenditure in percent of GDP in the EU-15, Japan and the USA, it is obvious that Japan and the US have a clear lead compared to the EU, and the gap has not really narrowed in the 1990s.

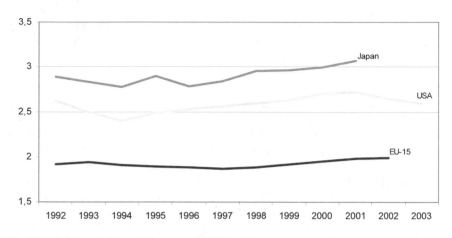

Fig. 92. R&D Expenditure in Percent of GDP in EU-15, Japan and the USA

J.3.3 Acceleration of Innovation Dynamics

The OECD countries have witnessed considerable differentiation in economic growth in the 1980s and 1990s on the one hand, on the other hand the rate of innovation – as measured by patent applications – has increased in the US and Europe in the 1990s (COUNCIL OF ECONOMIC ADVISERS, 2000; WELFENS/AUDRETSCH/ADDISON/GRIES/GRUPP, 1999). The US has achieved a considerable lead in economic growth and technological progress vis-à-vis the EU in the 1990s which was characterized by an unusual increase in labor productivity in the second half of the economic cycle in the US (COUNCIL OF ECONOMIC ADVISERS, 2001). US labor productivity growth in the period 1973-1995 was 1.4% p.a., but in 1995-2000 it reached 3.1%. It is unclear what the reasons for the robust US productivity growth is. The Council of Economic Advisers has argued that falling computer prices and rising computer expenditures of wholesale trade, banking and the ICT sector itself play a crucial role for US growth in the 1990s. Moreover, there was a strong rise of multifactor productivity growth in the 1990s, and to a considerable extent this is related to information and communication technology (ICT); in the US both the production of ICT and the use of ICT – this is associated with ICT investment – have contributed to a strong growth of labor productivity in the 1990s. The picture for EU countries is heterogeneous: There are countries in which labor productivity growth in the services sector is more affected by ICT dynamics than in manufacturing industry (OECD, 2003).

The growth of the information and communication technology sector (ICT) in the 1990s has considerably contributed to growth in the US, especially in the second half of the 1990s. According to estimates by the US Department of Commerce (see the study DIGITAL ECONOMY) the ICT sector represented 8.3% of US output in 2000, but the sector contributed almost 1/3 of real GDP growth in the period 1995-99. Even more impressive is the contribution of ICT to investment in the US; it is noteworthy that computer prices have fallen strongly in the 1990s. In 1999 business spending for ICT equipment and software represented more than ¾ of the 12 percent real growth in total equipment and software spending. The contribution of the ICT sector in percentage points increased from 0.8% in 1994 when overall US growth was 4.2% to 1.6% in 1999 when the overall growth rate was close to 5%. In Europe only Finland and Sweden as well as Ireland, have an ICT sector which directly contributes significantly to economic growth. In 1989 Swedish Ericsson stood for about ½ percent of total Swedish GDP, but in 1999 the company stood for 2.6% of GDP and contributed 0.5 percentage points to economic growth. In Finland Nokia stood for 4% of GDP – and 1/5 of Finnish exports - and contributed a full percentage point to growth in 1999 (EUROPEAN COMMISSION, 2000).

The ICT sector (as defined by EITO, 2000) consists of IT-spending which reached 2.7% of GDP in the EU in 1999, but 4.5% in the US. Telecommunications accounted for 2.8% of 3.1% of GDP in the EU in 1999, for 2.8% in the US. Assuming that prices in the EU for telecommunication equipment and services are slightly higher than the US one may argue that the transatlantic differential in ICT spending is almost zero in telecommunications, but that the EU is far behind in the IT sector.

The use of telecommunications has contributed considerably to economic growth in the 1970s and 1980s in Germany, and the expansion of the internet could lead to a similar effect if it contributes to accelerating diffusion of information and knowledge, respectively (WELFENS/JUNGMITTAG, 1998, 2000; 2001; WELFENS, 2001). Network effects play a role both in the use of telecommunications and PCs (the internet).

As regards the US GORDON (1999) has argued that US growth acceleration in the second half of the 1990s – ignoring the cyclical effects – can fully be explained by the growth of output and productivity growth, respectively, in the computer producing sector and in the output of other durables. GORDON argues that there were no spillover effects in productivity to other sectors. GORDON argues that falling computer prices signal a falling marginal product of computer equipment. Subsequently, we will raise some doubts about this view. We also will look into the problem of modelling certain spillovers in a straightforward way. Indeed, we will address several aspects of the new economy and emphasize the potential role of spillover effects and network effects. One may also consider the GORDON (2000) argument about the limited role of computer expenditures in the US as flawed: He argues that the expenditure on computers as a share of nonfram private business has stagnated at 1.3% in the late 1990s, however, he completely overlooks that the US is the leading country in terms of software expenditures which accounted for 2.7% of GDP in 1995 – for comparison France 0.9% (OECD, 1998). Analyzing the role of computers – and semiconductors - without taking into account software expenditures obviously is inconsistent.

The 2003 European Innovation Scoreboard (EUROPEAN COMMISSION, 2003; SEC (2003) 1255) – the fourth Scoreboard realized, namely as part of the Lisbon strategy – has shown that the EU lags the US for ten out of eleven indicators available in both the EU and the US. Only in the field of science and engineering graduates did the EU beat the US. Fields with a gap were:

- high-technology patents at the US Patent and Technology Office (USPTO)
- USPTO patents
- Early stage venture capital in percent of GDP
- high-tech patents at the European Patent Office (EPO)
- Population with tertiary education
- High-tech manufacturing value-added
- Business R&D expenditures in percent of GDP
- Expenditures on information and communication technology (ICT) in percent of GDP
- Public R&D expenditures in percent of GDP
- EPO patents

On the basis of an Overall Summary Innovation Index which combines a look at the average change in SII trend indicators with the level of the indicator – in the range 0-1 – for the respective country Finland and Sweden are clear leaders while Germany, Netherlands and France are losing momentum; Italy is falling behind. The fact that except for the UK all large EU countries are facing problems raises serious worries. An important field in which, however, the EU is indeed catching up with the US concerns ICT as is noted in the 2003 European Innovation Scoreboard (EUROPEAN COMMISSION, 2003; SEC (2003) 1255, p. 10): "The only encouraging example of a long lasting catching-up process is in ICT expenditures (gap cut by 50% since 1996). Reaping the full benefits of this positive trend would require acceleration of organisational innovation following investment in ICT hardware." The 2003 summary innovation index (SII-2 which covers the 12 most widely available indicators from the Community Innovation Survey) shows that Greece, Portugal and Spain are catching up while the Netherlands, France and Germany are losing momentum. Another interesting finding is that there is a rising role of R&D expenditures in the services sector: For the overall EU the share of services in business R&D was 13% in 1999 which was 5 percentage points above the 8% in 1992. In Japan R&D in services represented 2% in 2000, up from 0.2% in 1992. In the US the share of business R&D has increased from 24% in 1992 to 34% in 2000. EU-25 countries which were found to rank high in terms of innovativeness also ranked high in terms of diffusion. As regards the response time of markets to innovative products the Scandinavian countries had relatively short response periods while Germany, Italy, Spain, France, the UK, Greece and Portugal had long response periods (TELIIS/STREMERSCH/YIN, 2003, in Marketing Science 22, 188-208; data for US and Japan not available).

J.3.4 Specialization in Innovation and ICT Network Perspectives

Analyzing the ICT sector means to look into technological dynamics, output-GDP shares and expenditure-GDP shares. Let us start with the simple observation that ICT is a highly dynamic sector of the economy. Judging by figures from the

European Patent Agency the telecommunication sector has become that sector which has the highest growth rate of all patent groups; the growth rate in the period 1989-97 was 13.6% p.a., the growth rate of advanced electronics was 6.4% which made it No. 7 in the field of the ten fastest growing technology fields. This means that ICT is rather technology intensive and has some potential for technology spillovers (in the sense of the New Growth Theory à la Romer or else). The US plus Canada, the UK, Sweden and the Netherlands are positively specialized in telecommunications; they should strongly benefit from the global telecommunications boom which, however, will face some saturation problems in the long term when almost everybody has a mobile phone. In advanced electronics we find the US plus Canada and the Netherlands again, but also and strongly Japan.

Table 21. Specialization (Relative Patent Share in Interval -100, +100) in 1995-99 in Technology-Intensive Fields with High Growth Rates in Patents*

	Growth	USA	Japan	Germany	France	UK	Switzerland	Canada	Sweden	Italy	Netherlands
Telecommunication	13,6	0	-3	–	-7	7	–	5	0	–	8
Turbines	10,6	-8	–	34	8	8	75	0	-7	67	52
Railway Systems	8,5	74	74	40	9	–	3	84	19	96	26
Paper-Making Equipment	7,6	-4	41	7	71	67	8	22	5	0	62
Automobiles	6,7	47	88	8	5	43	54	0	12	41	56
Medi. Sector, Instruments	6,6	6	14	7	3	31	84	71	2	0	29
Advanced Electronics	6,4	18	80	38	36	-7	8	64	52	20	8
Power Distribution	6,4	20	6	1	21	18	52	2	3	44	36
Agrochemicals	6,1	5	59	0	4	23	27	53	53	13	69
Medi. Sector, Electronics	5,8	2	31	47	64	-9	48	19	0	65	5

Source: FhG-ISI, Karlsruhe, preliminary

*Average Annual Growth of Patent Applications at the European Patent Agency in 1989-1997

According to these figures the US, Canada and the Netherlands stand to gain particularly from the ICT boom worldwide. Japan is likely to benefit mainly on the electronics side. In the New Economy, there is, however, one caveat with respect to patent figures; many internet-based services cannot be patented – copyrights and trade marks play an important role here.

Network Effects

As is well known the use of computers and modern telecommunication equipment often is characterized by network effects. For the initial users the network becomes more useful with additional users linked to it. Therefore users might actively promote the use of their network, but more importantly, networks – say AOL, MSN or YAHOO (giving some incentive to existing users) – have an incentive to encourage users to convince friends and family to also use the network. Network effects also can play a role in industry, especially if there are strategic technology alliances in technology intensive industries. Indeed, the number of technology alliances is particularly strongly in the US in the 1990s (COUNCIL OF ECONOMIC ADVISORS, 2001, p. 117).

A logistical function can be used to model network effects in the new economy, that is we can use the standard innovation diffusion model. Assume that Z(0)=1, the adoption rate for the innovation Z is given by the differential equation:

$$dZ/dt = aZ(L-Z) \qquad (1)$$

L is the exogenous population, Z the number of persons using the innovation - say a mobile phone, a PC or the internet - and L-Z the number not using it. Whenever pioneer users meet nonusers there is an "infection" effect which is desribed by the positive parameter a. In an economy which also is a heavy producer of the innovative product the diffusion parameter a is likely to be higher than in a setting where the innovative product is only used.

The solution of the above equation is given (see BECKMANN/KÜNZI, 1984, p. 130) by a logistical equation for the stock variable Z(t):

$$Z(t) = L/[1 + (L-1)e^{-at}] \qquad (2)$$

Note here that in an open economy the parameter a might be influenced by both the export-GDP ratio (x) and the import-GDP ratio (j) to the extent that the "infection" rate in the tradables sector is more intensive than in the nontradables sector; a simple suitable function could be a= $a_0(1+x+j)$. If the presence of foreign direct investment (FDI) at home and abroad reinforces international diffusion of knowledge an FDI stock proxy K"/Y and K"*/Y* for the stock of FDI at home and abroad relative to GDP might also affect the diffusion rate. Moreover, one could study an export function with standard products (1...n) and innovation products (m...z) where the innovation products are ranked according to novelty – with novel products assumed to fetch higher prices than standard products; innovation products are increasingly adopted by firms in the export sector. After some critical time T innovation products become standard products with no premium in the world market, that is prices are equal to marginal costs. The terms of trade thus will depend on the percentage of innovation products in the overall basket of export goods. We will not look in these special problems here. Rather we will continue with the above equation 2. Denoting Z/L as z we have

$$z(t) = 1/[1 + (L-1)e^{-at}] \qquad (2')$$

Assume that there is a dual use good (dual here refers to its double nature as consumption and investment good) – here mobile telecommunication devices that are first bought as consumption gooods – whose diffusion is described by (1) and (2), respectively; we use the following modified production function in which positive spillover effects from mobile telecommunication devices Z are entering:

$$Y = K^{\beta}L^{1-\beta}Z^{\sigma} \qquad (3)$$

The basic assumption here is that the use of computers in households has positive spillover effects in industry; there are knowledge spillover effects into output of firms whose aggregate value-added is Y. A special case which is easy to handle is where σ=1:

$$Y = K^{\beta}L^{1-\beta} L/[1 + (L-1)e^{-at}] \qquad (4)$$

In per capita terms we have (with y=Y/L and k=K/L):

$$y = k^{\beta} Lz(t) \qquad (4')$$

Interestingly, the size of the country plays a positive role for per capita income here. From this perspective there could be an advantage for large countries – with large markets (US or EU or other regional integration areas) – in the era of the New Economy. In such a model setup the size of the country matters. Comparing the NAFTA and Europe there is no reason to believe that Europe cannot benefit from size effects as much as North America plus Mexico.

An important aspect concerns the impact of the ICT boom on the wage-real interest rate-ratio. If ICT is partly Solow-neutral capital augmenting technological progress the ratio of wages to interest rates will increase which will stimulate US firms to relocate ICT production abroad. Say to Mexico, Ireland, Hungary or Malaysia. This means that ICT production in low income countries will grow so that the growth-enhancing effects of strong productivity growth in ICT finally arrives outside the pioneer country (US, partly Japan). If the host countries for foreign direct investment in ICT should reflect as small a group of host countries as for FDI in general in the 1980s and 1990s only two dozen countries worldwide will benefit from ICT product cycle trade.

In a Schumpeterian economy there will be a series of innovations coming to the market. If such innovations are not evenly distributed over time they can cause a spurt in growth when a cluster of innovations is entering the diffusion stage, later the growth rate will slow down. If this stimulates entrepreneurs to come up with new innovations – again being realized in a cluster-type fashing at some point t – there will be another economic upswing. Instead of using a single differential equation for one innovation, one will have to use a system of logistical equations for all products i (i=1...n). The new economy is generating logistical diffusion patterns both in the household sector – namely in the case of mobile telecommunication equipment and PCs plus internet use – and in industry (computers, internet use).

The GORDON view of computers and ICT is doubtful for several reasons. But further research is needed. From the human capital growth model it follows: Europe will fall behind the US in terms of per worker income if EU countries are not reducing unemployment rates and reducing tax rates and raising efforts on human capital formation. The most difficult problem in Europe is to finance higher education in private universities. European governments will find it very difficult to generate higher tax revenues in the era of globalization and the internet; unfortunately the idea of private universities (and vouchers) is unpopular in Europe. The competition of private universities would not only mean a higher stock of educational capital but also would stimulate the efficiency of teaching and research efforts in public universities. An economically meaningful investment-output ratio in the knowledge society should be defined as the weighted sum of the traditional investment-output ratio, the R&D-GDP ratio, the software expenditure-GDP ratio and the education expenditure-GDP ratio. In the latter three fields the US has a clear lead over Euroland and Germany, respectively.

J.3.5 Openness, Taxation and Growth

Several authors have dealt with the issue whether openness affects growth. An interesting indirect route is suggested – and empirically tested – by BRETSCHGER (2005). His theoretical point of departure is an optimum taxation framework which aims at equalizing marginal benefits of taxation and marginal costs of taxation. In an open economy overall marginal costs are equal to private marginal costs M' plus marginal capital outflows (M''). If the economy is characterized by a Cobb-Douglas production function $Y=AK^{\beta}L^{1-\beta}$ the marginal product of capital is $\partial y/\partial k = (1-\tau)^{\beta}A^{1/\beta}y^{[\beta-1]/\beta}$ so that inserting this expression in the Keynes-Ramsey rule gives the following expression for the per capita growth rate (g as symbol for growth rate; η is the intertemporal elasticity of substitution): $g_y = [1/\eta][(1-\tau)^{\beta}A^{1/\beta}y^{[\beta-1]/\beta} -(a+ n+\delta)]$. The empirical estimation for 18 OECD countries then proceeds under the assumption that the tax rate is a negative function of economic openness, and the results indeed show such a negative impact and thus indirectly a positive impact of trade on the level of the growth path.

As an alternative we may consider the following – standard – setup which relies on a production function with Harrod-neutral technological progress). We will assume that the income tax rate is a negative function of the sum of the import ratio j at home and abroad (j*); and that the government budget constraint is given by $\gamma Y - \tau Y = \mu[M/P]$ so that $\gamma y' - \tau y' = \mu[M/P]/[AL]$; as we impose money market equilibrium under the assumption that money demand (with m'=: [M/P]/[AL] is given by $m'^{d}=y'\sigma'/i$ (i is the nominal interest rate which is equal to r in the absence of inflation, σ' is a positive parameter) we obviously can write $\gamma = \tau + \sigma'/r$. Hence we get the following differential equation for k'=: Y/(AL) as we use the goods market equilibrium condition $[s(1-\tau) + \tau - \gamma]Y = dK/dt +\delta K$ and assume that the real interest rate is a positive function of j/j* while the tax rate is a negative function of openness (with τ" defined as a positive parameter):

$$dk'/dt = \{s(1-\tau/[\tau"(j+j^*)] + \sigma'/r(j/j^*))\}k'\beta - [n+a+\delta]k' \qquad (5)$$

Hence we have for a central bank with a non-inflationary (and non-deflationary) monetary policy and a progress function $a = a_0 + a'(j+j^*)$– with a' denoting a positive parameter and a_0 autonomous technological progress - the steady state solution for y'=: Y/[AL]:

$$y'\# = \{[s(1-\tau/[\tau"(j+j^*)] + \sigma'/r(j/j^*)]/[n + a_0 + a'(j+j^*) +\delta]\}^{\beta/1-\beta} \qquad (6)$$

The effect of trade openness – the combined effect of j and j* - on the level of the growth path is ambiguous while the impact of trade openness on long run trend growth is positive. It thus depends on the length of the political capitalization horizon whether the positive trend growth effect is sufficiently taken into account. One major challenge for international organizations such as the IMF/the World Bank and the WTO is to help poor countries quantifying the empirical side of the approach presented and to support a political strategy which adequately takes into account both the aspects of changes in the level of the growth path (already requiring a long term view) and in the trend growth rate.

While the US stands for the leading global innovator country and may be expected to build its progress function mainly on domestic sources – the education system, the US innovation system and ICT capital accumulation – small open economies' progress function indeed may be expected to be rather strongly affected by international trade dynamics: in particular if technology-intensive imports on the one hand and on the other hand technology-intensive products with considerable economies of scale play a role.

International Alliances

As regards international alliances the emphasis is more on EU15 countries than on EU accession countries. Strategic R&D alliances played an increasing role in the EU in the late 1980s as globalization and the run-up to the single market programme as well as higher EU funds for cooperative R&D projects stimulated the internationalization of European R&D (NARULA, 1999); the IT sector and biotechnology played a particular role. Moreover, there also have been renewed dynamics in R&D in the form of both asset-exploiting and asset-seeking FDI in the EU and the US (CRISCUOLO/NARULA/VERSPAGEN, 2005) argue that R&D facility's capacity to exploit technological competences is a function not just of its own resources, but the efficiency with which it can utilise complementary resources associated with the relevant local innovation system; the empirical analysis indicates that both EU (US) affiliates in the US (EU) rely strongly on home region knowledge sources, although they appear to exploit the host knowledge base as well. The crucial emphasis on home knowledge suggests doubts about a potential R&D strategy of the EU which would neglect the EU countries as prime locations for leading edge R&D in technologically dynamics sectors, in particular the

ICT sector. One also must raise the issue to which extent the expansion of ICT requires reforms of the innovation system and in particular a stronger role of virtual
research networks and "Digital Universities"; optimal linkages between R&D facilities and firms in technology-intensive sectors are crucial which naturally will
include foreign investors.

J.4 Recommendations for Future EU Innovation Policy

The existing experience with EU framework programmes has shown that they are
an important stimulus for internationalisation of research in the Community. At
the same time it is obvious that the lessons from the mid-term of the 6th framework
raise some doubt in term of efficiency.

One major challenge in terms of research efficiency in the 6th framework programme is that Integrated Projects have been introduced which consists of 15-25
partners and thus are very complex to administer for the coordinator in the research projects. The efficiency of such projects is thus rather limited. The benefit
of integrated projects for the Commission is that it facilitates work for the EU authorities – in the sense that a rather limited number of projects has to be evaluated
– but this is offset by efficiency losses in research itself as a high number of partners implies enormous coordination efforts (unless partners work together over
many years). Therefore very large integrated projects – unless there specific reasons to aim at involvement of many countries and partners, respectively - stand for
a doubtful approach which should be replaced by a new strategy with emphasis
on:

- Specific Large Integrated Groups (SLIG) with a large number of partners
  should be continued; there are clear arguments in favour of a broad network.
  The Commission – and its advisors – should identify a limited number of areas
  deemed as suitable for Specific Large Integrated Projects. Areas earmarked as
  suitable for SLIP should not be exclusive so that other types of projects – in
  particular compact projects – should be allowed to compete.
- Many compact projects with a carefully selected small number of players could
  be quite successful. Small Integrated Projects (SIP) with not more than five
  partners; this requires that the Commission and the European Parliament, respectively, put up more resources for project evaluation. A relatively large
  share of resources should go to those projects. If projects reach high marks in
  evaluation the research group should be allowed to increase the number of
  partners provided that it has indicated such plans in a mid-term report. This
  would then result in two-stage Integrated Projects.
- Networks of Excellence should continue, but start on a rather limited number of
  actors (not more than 10). Research groups applying should indicate a two-
  stage plan for Network Extension in the Final Report; and networks with high
  marks in evaluation should then be allowed to apply for a Large Network of
  Excellence. However, the budget allocation for an enlarged network of excellence should be required to reflect growth in the number of partners underpro-

portionately as the very idea of network effects suggests that efficient networks will be able to exploit economies of scale.

- For both networks of excellence and for integrated projects there should be standardized contracts available for research groups which bring together partners from industry and outside industry. The available experience from NoEs and IPs indicates that legal problems raised by industry partners in prospective international R&D groups impair the realization of both NoEs and IPs.

The proposed organizational improvements will bring enhanced R&D efficiency. However, this is not the most crucial issue when it comes to the topic how the EU could catch up with the USA. There is no doubt that the EU has fallen behind the USA in the 1990s in terms of innovativeness as measured by patent applications and share in high technology trade. A relatively weak performance has been measured in Germany whose poor economic performance after German unification raises many unpleasant questions.

From an EU perspective it is crucial that the transatlantic digital technology gap should be closed relatively quickly. At the same time the EU might want to maintain its lead in mobile telecommunications which seems possible in the medium term provided that UMTS services are quickly rolled out and that the US is not catching up very fast in 2G mobile telecommunication density.

Taking a look at the main budget items of the European Community – with No. 1 agriculture (share about 45%) and No. 2 structural funds (share about 1/3) – we do not find adequate priorities. Agricultural subsidies should be reduced to less than 20% of the EU budget while structural funds should be reformed in a way that would support more strongly retraining, education and support for research and development.

If both the production of ICT and the use of ICT are important for economic growth there could be two ways for high growth. Trying to become a country that has successfully specialized in ICT production or encouraging firms and households to quickly use the new technologies. As regards the use of new ICT and promotion of the diffusion process governments could have a role in countries which are not leaders in ICT production – namely to the extent that government can substitute for the diffusion impulses which come from ICT production in other countries. The Scandinavian countries, the Netherlands and Germany have embraced telecommunication liberalization energetically after 1998, the UK already before. This lets one expect that part of the EU could be a driving force in the European and global ICT revolution. However, while the EU partly looks strong in the field of telecommunications its role in the fields of computer and software looks relatively modest when compared to the US.

It would be useful to study the user patterns of internet users more closely – both with respect to the time budget and the structure of use. Moreover, the size of network effects and the significance of the role of spillover effects from household computer use should be estimated empirically. Part of the problems encountered here will refer to data problems as neither government nor industry has straightforward data which could tell where computers sold finally are used. But the data issue should be solved by survey analysis and other methods.

With EU eastern enlargement there will be pressure on EU-15 countries to move up the technology ladder. This should go along with increasing human capital formation which, however, raises the issue how the system of state-run universities will be able to cope with this challenge. The mixed US system – with private and public universities - has been impressive in its supply side elasticity in the 1990s when more than two million new jobs were created in the education system. Serious problems for EU countries could also emerge in education since the Maastricht criteria have increased the pressure for budget consolidation. This raises some critical questions for an adequate future policy mix in the EU. There is a broader need for more comparative US-EU research – such research certainly could be helpful for identifying policy options to improve economic policy in all relevant fields of Schumpeterian dynamics.

K. Financial Market Integration, Interest Rates and Economic Development

K.1 Introduction

Economic globalization progressed considerably in the 1990s with the opening-up of post-socialist eastern European countries for trade and capital flows as well as with the completion of the single EU market. Part of the single EU15 market introduced in 1993 was the liberalization of services including financial services. With EU eastern enlargement in 2004, there were steps towards an EU25 single market. However, free movement of labour was postponed for most EU15 countries until 2011 (at the latest). In ASEAN countries, financial integration resumed after the 1997/98 crisis, and a broader integration strategy was envisaged. Both the EU and ASEAN are facing economic globalization in the sense that there is a long run increase in the trade of financial services, in foreign direct investment in the banking and insurance sector and a growing influence from global international organizations such as the IMF and the Bank of International Settlements.

Financial markets are important for economic development for many reasons, including the financing of capital accumulation, innovation and human capital formation. In his survey, TSURU (2000) points to several channels through which financial markets can affect growth. Competitive financial markets contribute to

- the efficient allocation of capital;
- efficient intermediation so that savings flow to those investment projects with the highest yield;
- a rise in the savings rate (under certain circumstances).

In their empirical analysis, KING/LEVINE (1993) have emphasized that several traits of the financial market contribute to higher growth. For example, liquidity relative to output and the share of private credits in total credits are important for growth; the emphasis on the share of private credits implicitly is an argument that a high share of public credits is not only crowing out private investment in a way which is neutral to output but that it indeed reduces real income. LEVINE/ZERVOS (1998) have pointed out that several variables affect growth of output:

- stock market capitalization, stock market liquidity and the degree of international capital market integration were found to have a positive impact on real output;
- the volatility of stock returns negatively affects output.

Thus empirical findings suggest that international capital market integration – in particular to the extent that it raises stock market capitalization (relative to GDP) – increases stock market liquidity and reduces the volatility of stock returns – will positively contribute to economic development. There is, however, a causality problem in the sense that we cannot exclude that capital markets stimulate growth, which stimulates the development of financial markets, since one may argue that wealth accumulation typically grows faster than output, leading to a situation in which the long run growth of asset accumulation will naturally stimulate the expansion of financial markets and the respective services (Granger causality analysis could shed some light on this, however, the causation could also be a phenomenon of interdependency).

One also cannot be certain that capital market liberalization and regional capital market integration will go along with reduced stock market volatility. To the extent that the US stock market dominates regional stock markets in the EU and Asia, the key issue is the speed and scope of international transmission of US stock market impulses. Moreover, while the US financial market system is the result of an evolutionary market development in which aspects such as stock markets, bonds markets, banks and prudential supervision interact in a useful way, one should expect that financial market institutions in other countries reflect their own specific evolutionary development. Therefore it would be no surprise if temporarily high US stock market volatility causes few problems in the US or Western Europe, but this can have rather destabilizing effects in eastern Europe, Asian NICs and other regions. Instability in major regions could occur as the consequence of unequal economic globalization so that not modern globalization is the key problem; rather critical international differences in the respective modernization of national financial markets and institutional developments seem to be a critical challenge.

EU countries have recorded sustained growth since the creation of the single EU market at the end of 1992. However, growth was slower than in the US. This broad comparison obscures the more detailed picture in the Euro zone, namely that medium term growth performance was rather different across countries. As regards the late 1990s, this is particularly the case across member countries of the Euro zone which started on January 1, 1999 when the European Central Bank (ECB) and the European System of Central Banks (ESCB=ECB + national central banks) started. The 11 starter countries of the Euro were a rather heterogeneous group in terms of per capita income and debt-GDP indicators; most starter countries faced considerable unemployment problems in 1999, and the large member countries of the Euro zone still had serious unemployment problems in 2005. By contrast, the non-Euro countries in the EU15 group – UK, Denmark and Sweden – had low unemployment rates. Attributing differential unemployment figures to the Euro is not adequate, however, as several countries in the Euro zone had favourable development in terms of employment and growth. Regional monetary integration does, however, require an adequate degree of wage flexibility and labor mobility.

With financial market integration making considerable progress in the Euro zone, visible for instance through the convergence of nominal interest rates, there was hope that economic growth in the Euro zone would accelerate and unemployment be reduced. This has hardly been the case since growth accelerated mainly in small open economies of the Euro zone while it fell in Germany and Italy. – having a high debt-GDP ratio of close to 110% in the run-up to the start of the Euro – was to benefit from falling nominal and real interest rates as well as from interest rate convergence. Hence Italy should benefit from higher growth/ better economic development, as should Germany provided that domestic policies adopted were growth-enhancing and increasing trade with member countries of the Euro area stimulated growth through higher trade dynamics and technology diffusion. From a theoretical perspective, trade creation was to be expected from monetary integration. This holds despite the fact that the Euro area of 11 starter countries (France, Germany, Italy, Austria, Belgium, Netherlands, Luxemburg, Spain, Portugal, Finland, Ireland) could not be considered as representing an optimum currency area as defined by traditional criteria from the literature. There was considerable economic heterogeneity which led to the creation of cohesion funds for the relatively poor countries, Portugal, Spain, Ireland and Greece, with the latter joining the Euro area in 2001. Weak current account positions of Portugal, Spain and Greece indicate that even within a monetary union a country's external position is a useful indicator of economic dynamics and prosperity. Relatively high growth of unit labor costs has been a major problem for several countries in the Euro zone. Between 1995 and 2005 the increase was 4.2% in Portugal, but -14.3% in Ireland; the figures for Spain and Greece were -8.5% and - 2.4%, respectively. The Czech Republic recorded 6.4% which signals incipient competitiveness problems, Poland recorded – 7.9%, Hungary – 9.6%. Germany recorded -4%, but Austria did even better at -8.6%. Sweden and the UK witnessed an increase in unit labor costs, namely 5.8% and 2.3%, respectively. As rise of unit labor costs in industry would not be a problem if the relative degree of product innovations would increase or if the rise of wage costs would be driven by a strong expansion of the services sector; as regards the latter the UK has been rather successful, in particular in the financial services sector.

Table 22. Growth of Unit Labor Costs in Selected OECD Countries

Countries	1995	2000	2005	Change 2006 to 1995
Belgium	100	97,8	96,6	-3,4
Czech Republic	100	104,6	106,4	6,4
Denmark	100	99,8	100,5	0,5
Germany	100	99,6	96	-4
Estonia	100	89,2	88,1	-11,9
Greece	100	99,6	97,6	-2,4
Spain	100	97,2	91,5	-8,5
France	100	98,4	98,3	-1,7
Ireland	100	87,1	85,7	-14,3
Italy	100	94,6	96,9	-3,1
Cyprus	100	95,3	93,9	-6,1
Latvia	100	94,1	90,4	-9,6
Lithuania	100	108,7	101,1	1,1
Luxembourg	100	87,9	94,1	-5,9
Hungary	100	90,5	90,4	-9,6
Malta	100	95,1	95,4	-4,6
Netherlands	100	99	99,3	-0,7
Austria	100	95,2	91,4	-8,6
Poland	100	100,7	92,1	-7,9
Portugal	100	109,1	104,2	4,2
Slovenia	100	92,4	91,4	-8,6
Slovakia	100	99,4	99	-1
Finland	100	94,9	98,9	-1,1
Sweden	100	105,3	105,8	5,8
United Kingdom	100	100,6	102,3	2,3

Source: Ameco Database

Financial Market Integration in Western Europe

Financial market integration was hoped to deliver some of the expected economic benefits through the creation of the Euro and the ECB. Such integration could reinforce specialization in production and exports which should translate into higher productivity and output growth. However, following the KENEN criterion of optimum currency areas such reinforcement of specialization would undermine the case for a common monetary area (the KENEN criterion basically argues that a more diversified economy will be subject to international shocks which more or less cancel out, a strongly specialized economy faces a high risk of external shocks which amount to serious stability problems). JUNGMITTAG (2006) has shown that export structures have converged across EU15 while there is increasing specialization in production across countries. BORBELY (2006) comes up with similar findings for EU accession countries. This difference in international structural convergence of trade and output could explain why business cycles still differ considerably across countries – even within the Euro zone. However, the implication also is that vertical trade (trade within sectors/trade in intermediate products) plays only a limited role since otherwise convergence of trade and convergence of output specialization would occur in parallel.

Monetary integration creates larger markets allowing the exploitation of economies of scale and the reduction of transaction costs. If one defines financial market integration through the weighted nominal interest rate convergence – with the relative share of loans across the spectrum of maturities as the weight for that convergence – one could indeed measure financial market integration. As financial market integration might go along with financial market deepening, which amounts to a yield curve with a longer time horizon than before, we have to take into account an additional aspect. Finally, the whole yield curve might be shifted upwards or downwards through monetary integration so that we have at least one additional aspect to be considered. A downward shift, which amounts to reduced costs of capital and in turn should raise the investment output ratio, should increase real income.

As regards benefits from monetary union, one may emphasize the reduction of international transaction costs within the union, the reinforcement of competition via higher price transparency, the increase in liquidity in bonds markets, benefits from achieving a broader reserve currency status and achieving a high degree of price stability in all member states of the monetary union. ROSE (2000) has argued in an empirical paper that a 1 percent rise in trade between countries in a monetary union will lead to a rise of per capita income of 1/3 of a percent. FARUQUEE (2003) has emphasized that monetary union has raised trade volumes among member countries by 10% so that there should be considerable benefits for countries in the Euro zone. It is, however, less clear which benefits come from increased fiscal policy surveillance and the Stability and Growth Pact which impose new restrictions on fiscal policy. If deficit ratios hover over many years close to the 3% deficit-GDP ratio, member countries might have insufficient room to maneuver in times of slower growth and also might face a long term increase of the debt-GDP ratio whose long term dynamics are determined by the ratio of the long run structural deficit-GDP ratio to the trend output growth rate. To the extent that real interest rates in the Euro zone are reduced one may anticipate higher investment in the overall Euro area, however, this could still go along with asymmetric intra-Euro zone and extra-Euro zone inflows so that economic divergence and lack of social cohesion could be a major effect. Moreover, it is unclear how innovation dynamics and indeed the innovation system is changing under the twin pressure of

- limited fiscal policy options which could impair R&D financing in some countries

- larger capital markets which raise the required rate of return in some countries of the monetary union so that long term innovation financing might become more difficult

Another important effect which concerns both cohesion countries and potential eastern European Euro member countries refers to structural change where financial market integration could reinforce specialization. Increased specialization would be not in line with the KENEN criterion of optimum currency areas, so that entering the Euro zone could bring problems. Moreover, if there are strong Balassa-Samuelson effects – meaning a rise of the relative price of non-tradables along with per capita income – the inflation rate in catching-up countries could be much higher than in the Euro zone/in Euro zone partner countries. The real interest rate could become very low, which in turn could distort the investment and innovation process in a way which weakens productivity gains, profitability and growth in the long run. Bubbles in the stock market and the real estate market also could become more likely.

A rather neglected aspect concerns the issue of increased international bond substitutability in the context of the creation of the Euro zone and the enlargement of the Euro zone. If Euro denominated bonds and $ denominated bonds become closer substitutes one may anticipate lower interest rates and higher stock market prices.

Perspectives of the Lisbon Agenda

The EU's Lisbon Agenda 2010, which put forward the goal of making the EU the most competitive and dynamic knowledge-based economy by 2010 points to the prominence of setting growth goals. Therefore it is important to focus on some of the potential links between information and communication technology and financial markets. From a practical perspective, one may point out that the European Council – here, the heads of governments and presidents of EU member countries – has not raised this topic. Moreover, the European Council has adopted a strange policy goal with the "Lisbon Agenda 2010" in the sense that it has defined a supranational goal for which the European Commission has hardly any power in laying these foundations. It is the EU member countries which have in principle the means to stimulate economic growth (and some countries fail in this respect; notably is Germany which runs a high current account surplus but has achieved only slow economic growth in the decade after 1994 – except for 2000 when growth was 3.1%).

The following analysis describes the stages of financial market integration and monetary integration in the EU and presents basic theoretical reflections on financial market integration and about the links between regional financial market integration and growth. As regards the potential link between financial market dynamics and economic growth, we rely partly on traditional arguments from literature, but we also look at the problem from an endogeneous growth perspective. In principle this requires that we:

- look at the level of the growth path, with the neoclassical growth model suggesting that one examine the impact of financial market integration on the savings rate.
- look at the growth rate of output as explained by various elements of financial market integration.

It seems to be rather unclear as to whether regional financial integration in the Euro area has strongly fostered economic growth in the Euro area thus far. Part of the problem is that regional integration effects are superseded by globalization effects on the one hand. On the other hand, policymakers in some EU member countries have adopted economic policies which did not promote growth and employment. Moreover, interesting effects of financial market integration can also be studied in the context of EU eastern enlargement. From the perspective of accession countries, membership brought with it the advantage of reducing the political risk premium to almost zero so that higher foreign direct investment inflows could be anticipated. High FDI inflows could be particularly stimulating for growth if FDI were significant and entering those sectors crucial for economic modernization, including the financial market sector. Banking and insurances are, however, traditionally considered sensitive sectors so that there are considerable impediments for taking over banks or other financial intermediates.

At the bottom line we must ask which policy options could be useful for promoting growth and employment. We find that financial market integration has not yet been completed in the EU and that both national policymakers and the supranational policy level of the EU could contribute to higher growth. Political interference in goods markets and political obstacles to inward foreign direct investment as well as to outward foreign direct investment are key problems which must be overcome. If the Euro area does not adopt a more coherent set of policy measures, the Euro zone might disintegrate in the long run. The creation of an economic and monetary union in the EU has opened a window of opportunity in Europe, however, it is unclear whether policymakers will come up with consistent policies and the necessary set of reforms to stimulate productivity growth and innovation in the Euro area. Those EU countries which are not yet members of Economic and Monetary Union can be expected to closely watch the dynamics of integration and growth in the Euro area and outside. It also is interesting to focus on issues of future enlargements of the Euro zone which effectively began with German unification in 1990. The negative referenda on the EU constitution – in France and the Netherlands – raise doubts about broad political support for EU deepening and EU widening. It is clear that integration projects normally have the support of broad strata of the population if integration contributes to higher growth and employment. This also reinforces the ability of politicians to pursue EU interests abroad. Thus the question rises as to whether the EU still has a consistent set of goals, strategies and means. Achieving sustained growth will not, however, be easy in an ageing society, which naturally brings about a decline in long term growth rates of the respective country (McMORROW/ROEGER, 2004). Much will depend on the process of financial market integration which in principle could stimulate higher long run growth.

K.2 Financial Market Integration in the EU

K.2.1 From Basic Theory to Endogeneous Growth Approaches

From an economic perspective, globalization is mainly shaped by intensified trade dynamics, rapid growth of capital flows and the expansion of the digital economy. For a better understanding of the links between financial markets and growth, one should take into account standard theoretical elements as well as some new aspects related to, for example, the role of ICT, which is a critical sector in several ways. As regards ICT, one should note that productivity growth in the US banking sector is strongly influenced by sectoral accumulation of ICT capital, while the productivity impact of ICT in the EU is – for unclear reasons – more modest (INKLAAR/O'MAHONY/TIMMER, 2003). Impediments to intra-EU foreign direct investment in the banking sector could be part of the explanation.

Moreover, it is important to consider the link between financial market development and technological progress. In an economic system with innovating firms, there is a basic information asymmetry between the innovating firm and the institution financing the respective project (and related investment). Depending on the type of financial system, it is more or less difficult to finance innovation projects, with small and medium-sized firms having particular problems. In a system with universal banks, it is relatively difficult to finance international innovation projects of a firm unless there is a long term relationship between a major bank and the respective firm, with the bank also being active in those markets/countries – and thus getting relevant information – within which the innovating firm has partners. If the innovating medium-sized firm has high profit rates and retained earnings, it can signal credibly to the banking community that it is willing to adequately share risks in the innovation project.

The alternative to bank-financed innovation projects is to rely on stock markets while building up reputation as a successful innovator. This in principle requires taking a firm public. The more technologically advanced the country is, the more it should rely on stock markets as a source of financing innovation and investment projects. International stock market listings can help innovating firms from small countries get broader access to global risk capital. However, listing a European or Asian company in New York is relatively costly. Regional integration of stock markets is thus an alternative for both EU and ASEAN countries. If the respective firm is a newly-created high technology company, it will not immediately be able to rely on stock markets, rather it will need adequate access to venture capital. As regards venture capital, regional integration of venture capital markets could also stimulate both dynamic start ups and long run growth. However, one should not really expect sweeping economic benefits from financial market integration if this is not embedded in a broader concept. The overall economic system consists not only of financial markets, and therefore benefits cannot be fully realized if there are stumbling blocks for growth in other factor markets. Moreover, one should raise the issue as to whether there is a critical minimum degree of financial market integration – say, as defined by full interest convergence across 2/3 of the maturity spectrum (starting with short term markets), and one may well debate whether there is full integration if mortgage markets are not truly integrated, which national regulations often impair.

From a theoretical and empirical perspective, one may state that output Y positively depends on (WELFENS/JUNGMITTAG, 1996, 2002) not only on the input of capital, labor and technology (technology input as measured by patents and real expenditures on the import of licences), but also on the use of telecommunications which is a proxy for the intensity of the diffusion of new technology.

An interesting empirical approach was conducted by JUNGMITTAG (2004), who finds that not only capital, labor and patents are empirically significant for the growth of output for the EU15, but also the degree of high-technology specialization (Ω'). From this perspective, it is not simply technological specialization – emerging in an open economy under the joint pressure of trade, foreign investment and financial market dynamics – which is relevant for growth, rather it is specialization in high technology sectors.

A standard reference in empirical economic growth analysis is MANKIW/ROMER/WEIL (1992) who explain growth of real income by the investment output ratio and human capital. Their approach is, however, somewhat doubtful, since they impose the assumption that the growth rate of technological progress is the same across all countries of the sample which is highly unrealistic (indeed, the assumption amounts to ignoring the existence of multinational companies whose very existence is related to ownership specific advantages, read: technological advantages!). This is important for the link between financial market analysis and growth to the extent that financial market development or financial market integration contributes to longterm technological progress. The MANKIW/ROMER/WEIL approach– in line with some other studies – points to the relevance of the (net) investment output ratio I/Y. As I/Y times the marginal product of capital $\Delta Y/\Delta K$ is equal to the growth rate of real gross domestic product, one must take into account that I/Y has a trend component and a cyclical component – related to the real interest rate r, the cyclical unemployment rate u^c and expectations about future profits – while the marginal product of capital is determined by capital intensity, technology and human capital.

In the following graph, we can see that output growth rates in the Euro zone went through a cyclical increase in the five years after 1995 but have fallen after 2000. The ratio of the long run interest rate to the short term rate increased after a transitory fall after the start of the both Euro zone and the ECB. After 1995, there was a fall in the real interest rate in the Euro zone and most member countries of the Euro zone. The Netherlands and Spain recorded a strong fall in the real interest rate in the four years after 1999, while Germany faced a temporary rise in the real interest rate; in a trade gravity modelling perspective it is clear that Germany, Austria and Finland – compared to France, Spain or Portugal - will be strongly exposed to import competition from eastern Europe which tends to reduce the inflation rate; hence the real interest rate in Germany (and Austria and Finland) will be higher than in other countries of the Euro zone.

After a temporary real appreciation in the early years of the Euro zone, the Euro faced a period of real appreciation, which reduced the real and nominal interest rate below the US level for some time. With monetary integration, it is also clear that the rest of the world will benefit considerably from higher capital outflows from the Euro zone. The reason for this is that from an investors' perspective, there are no longer opportunities for currency diversification within the Euro zone. This should have contributed to an early depreciation of the Euro in the starting phase of the ECB and the Euro. There is another long term aspect which is related to the ageing of societies in the EU; ageing should raise the savings rate of the population. However, financial market integration could dampen this development in the Euro zone, since households are likely to face less borrowing constraints in integrated markets.

One should also note that empirical findings and most analyses in the literature suffer from a problem in that one rarely makes a clear distinction between the level of output and the growth rate of output. Within the context of a standard macroeconomic growth model (JONES, 1998) in the steady state, output per capita (y) is given by the following formula if one assumes – with Y denoting output, K capital, L labor and ß a parameter in the interval 0,1 – that the macroeconomic production function is $Y = K^{\beta}(AL)^{1-\beta}$ and that the growth rate of the population is n, the exogenous growth rate of the Harrod-neutral factor A is a and the depreciation rate on capital is δ (e' is the Euler number, s the savings rate, A_0 the initial value of A, t the time index, # for steady state):

$$y\# \,(t) = A_0 e'^{at} \{s/[n+a+\delta]\}^{\beta/1-\beta} \tag{1}$$

Taking endogenous growth into account is interesting from a theoretical perspective. If one assumes that the progress rate a(t) is endogenous in the transition to the steady state for the variable real income relative to labor in efficiency units – this is the variable $y'\# =: Y/[AL]$ –, we must ask how financial market integration will affect endogenous growth and innovation dynamics, respectively. It also would be interesting to consider an endogeneous savings rate.

With respect to explaining the progress rate, endogenous growth theory has emphasized the role of human capital (LUCAS, 1988), positive external effects from capital accumulation (ROMER, 1990), R&D expenditures and innovation (GROSSMAN/HELPMAN, 1991) and intermediate products – allowing firms the production of a greater variety of final products which stimulates both demand and real output growth (ROMER, 1990; GROSSMAN/HELPMAN, 1991; BRETSCHGER, 1998).

One may summarize the link between financial market integration and growth as follows:

- Financial market integration may affect the savings rate s and hence the level of the growth path. In principle it could dampen the savings rate as households face less borrowing constraints (a phenomenon obviously relevant in the Euro zone), but it could also stabilize the savings rate to the extent that the monetary union imposes new constraints on government borrowing (such as the constraints envisaged in the Stability and Growth Pact of the Euro area; as they have not been implemented, however, they are likely to undermine the creditability of the Euro zone and may sooner or later trigger a risk premium on international capital flows into the Euro zone. This particularly reflects doubts

about bonds in Italy, Portugal or Greece, which have very high debt-GDP ratios
as well as high internal euro area current account deficits).

• Financial market integration can also affect endogenous growth in various
  ways. Examples of this include facilitating human capital formation (banks facing more competition and becoming more innovative become more willing to
  engage in university studies financing), influencing the share of firms undertaking innovations (and influencing the type of innovations pursued), encouraging
  more foreign investors to come – also more MNCs to emerge within the country – and thus to contribute to international technology transfer and increased
  international outsourcing. Foreign direct investment will contribute to higher
  capital intensity in the host country, and hence to a higher output and a higher
  income per capita, respectively; one thus should not be surprised to find a positive correlation between FDI and trade.

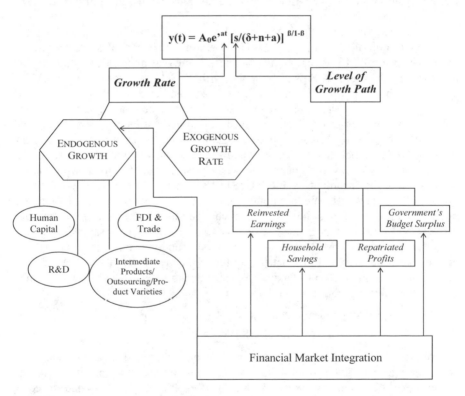

Fig. 93. Financial Market Integration and Growth

As regards empirical findings, it is obvious that we know rather little about the
links between financial market integration and growth. As regards transitory economic catching-up in open economies one should consider the role of temporary

net capital inflows for which relative yields on investment are expected to play a major role.

K.2.2 Current Account Dynamics: A New Approach

The current account Z' is the difference between private savings S plus the government surplus T-G minus investment I.

$$[S+(T-G)] - I = Z' \qquad (2) ()$$

One may consider Z' as a distinct economic function or assume that taking a closer look at the left hand side of the above equation – if specified adequately and if consistent behavior of economic agents is assumed – will finally allow to specify the equation for Z'. We will consider the indirect specification of the equation for Z'.

Assume that savings $S=S(Y', M/P, r, q^*)$ – where Y' is real national income (Y is real GDP and $Y'=Y[1-b]$, where b is the share of the capital stock owned by foreign investors), M/P is real money balances, r the real interest rate r and q^* the real exchange rate eP^*/P. Savings will rise with Y and r and with M/P ($m=:M/P$) as a rise of broad real money indicates financial market development and hence better opportunities to earn high yields. If the country is indebted abroad a real depreciation will raise foreign debt expressed in real domestic terms and hence savings will rise provided we assume an exogenous wealth target (or a target ratio A'/Y where A' is net private sector wealth). Let us assume that the share of the capital stock owned by foreign investors is a positive function of b which is an implication of the arguments of FROOT/STEIN (1991). Moreover we assume that investment I is proportionate to output; and a negative function of the real interest rate r and a positive function of the real exchange rate q^* (the latter reflecting the FROOT/STEIN argument). Thus we can write on the basis of a savings function $s'(r;q^*)Y[1-b(q^*)]+s''[M/P]$ and an investment function $I=z(r,q^*,Y_K/Y_K^*)Y$ – where Y_K is the marginal product of capital, * denotes foreign variables, τ'' the government surplus-GDP ratio and s" a positive parameters - the following equation for the current account:

$$s'(r,q^*)Y[1-b(q^*)]+s''(M/P)y + \tau''Yy +\{-zr +z'q^*y + \qquad (3)$$
$$z''([Y^*/K^*]/[Y/K])\}Y = Z'$$

Note that z, z' are positive parameters. We have assumed that both countries considered produce under Cobb-Douglas functions so that the respective marginal product of capital and the average products of capital are proportionate to each other. The term $\beta[Y^*/K^*]/(\beta[Y/K])$ indicates the international marginal product ratios and hence the capital intensity gap between the rich capital abundant country II and the poor home country I; the latter is a host country for foreign direct investment. FDI inflows thus are a positive function of the marginal product ratios. Assume that both countries are characterized by Cobb-Douglas productions function $Y= K^{\beta}(AL)^{1-\beta}$, $Y^*= K^{*\beta^*}(A^*L^*)^{1-\beta^*}$ We then know that the marginal product of capital in country I is $\beta k'^{\beta-1}$ and in country II it is $\beta^* k'^{*\beta^*-1}$; and $y=Ak'^{\beta}$ and

$y^*=A^*k'^{*\beta^*}$ ($k'=:K/AL$ and A is the level of technology). Denoting per capita income as y we thus can write $z''(y/y^*, A^*/A)$ where z'' is a positive function of y/y^* and of A/A^*:

Dividing the current account equation by Y we get an empirically testable equation for the current account-GDP ratio Z'/Y

$$Z'/Y= s'(r, q^*) + s'm/Y + \tau'' - zr + z'q^* + z''(y/y^*, A^*/A) \qquad (4)$$

Thus we have the missing theoretical basis for an empirical analysis published by DEUTSCHE BUNDESBANK (2006) in its January monthly report, however, in the view presented here (with Eastern Europe standing for country I and Western Europe or Germany being country II) one additionally should include the relative level of technology. The two ambiguous signs from a theoretical perspective is the impact of the real interest rate and the real exchange rate. Let us simply quote from the Bundesbank's research findings which has presented a study on the determinant of current accounts in the eastern European accession countries (the following quote also refers to theoretical underpinnings which, however, are rather opaque; note that the Bundesbank approach uses $1/q^*$ as the real exchange rate):

"As part of a panel analysis, major determinants of the current account balances in the new EU member states of central and eastern Europe (Czech Republic, Estonia, Hungary, Latvia, Lithuania, Poland, Slovakia and Slovenia) were examined on the basis of quarterly data for the years 1994 to 2004. The starting point for this was the following regression equation for the current account balance or savings-investment gap.

$$CAGDP_{i,t} = \gamma_0 + \gamma_1 RELGDP_{i,t} + \gamma_2 FINGDP_{i,t} + \gamma_3 INVGDP_{i,t} + \gamma_4 REER_{i,t} \qquad (5)$$
$$+ \gamma_5 RIR_{i,t} + \gamma_6 M2GDP_{i,t} + \varepsilon_{i,t}$$

CAGDP denotes the ratio of the current account balance to gross domestic product, while RELGDP is defined as a logarithm of relative per capita income in relation to Germany. The government budget balance (FINGDP) and investments (INVGDP) are measured as ratios to gross domestic product and are thus comparable between the countries. The logarithm of the real effective exchange rate (REER) rises in the event of a currency appreciation and falls in the event of a depreciation. The real interest rate (RIR) and the money stock in relation to gross domestic product (M2GDP) were included in the study as financial market variables.

Positive signs are expected for γ_1, γ_2 and γ_5 and a negative sign for γ_3. According to theoretical considerations, the relationship between the real exchange rate and the current account (γ_4) is a priori just as indeterminate as the net effect of a growing financial sector (γ_6). The absolute values of γ_2 and γ_3 should lie between zero and one since the associated variables, as components of the savings-investment decision, have a direct influence on the current account but can be at least partially offset by adjustments to private saving. Panel unit root tests confirm that the variables are stationary.

Two estimation methods are compared. A feasible generalized least squares estimate (FGLS) takes into account fixed country effects, panel-specific autoregressive terms, a heteroscedastic error structure and a contemporary correlation between the countries. By contrast, an instrument variable estimator (IV) allows an explicit modeling of the dynamics by means of a lagged endogenous variable. In this way, the Nickell bias, which arises in the static estimate when calculating the autoregressive terms, can be avoided. Furthermore, selecting the appropriate instruments means that any endogenous results, i.e. repercussions which the current account has on the independent variables, are accommodated in the model. These advantages of the dynamic estimator contrast with it being less efficient than the static model.

Table 23. Macroeconomic Determinants of the Current Account

Determinant	FGLS estimate	IV estimate
CAGDP (– 1)	-	0.4608***
		(2.75)
RELGDP	0.02700***	0.0147***
	(5.40)	(2.75)
FINGDP	0.0831**	0.1420***
	(2.20)	(2.75)
	– 0.2375***	– 0.2891***
INVGDP	(– 6.93)	(– 6.66)
REER	– 0.0381*	– 0.0264
	(– 1.94)	(– 1.15)
RIR	0.0009**	0.0014***
	(2.09)	(2.71)
M2GDP	0.0062	0.0138***
	(1.02)	(3.19)

*** (**) [*] means significant on the 1% (5%) [10%] level; t-values in parentheses

The table shows the results of the FGLS estimate and dynamic IV estimator."

Our theoretical approach presented is consistent with the empirical findings of Deutsche Bundesbank research. Only the relative technology variable is missing here (and our theoretical reflection suggests replacing the investment output ratio through r, q^*, y^*/y and A/A^*); the approach presented clearly suggests that this variable should play a role. It is surprising that γ_2 in the Bundesbank model is not unity, as this is expected on theoretical grounds.

K.2.3 Monetary Integration, Financial Market Integration and Welfare Effects

As regards financial market integration in the Euro zone, we clearly can measure this through interest rate convergence. High interest rate countries should converge to the low interest rate of Germany. (In the period of the Deutsche Mark, Germany almost always had the lowest nominal interest rate in the EU.) Thus, a country previously known for high interest rates (e.g., Italy) will experience a fall in the interest rate as the Euro zone starts and also during the run up to the start of the Euro and the ECB. Let us call Germany country I and Italy country II (with starred variables). Italy will have a considerable once-and-for-all welfare gain as the nominal interest rate falls form $i*_0$ to $i*_1$, which is equal to the (unchanged) German interest rate ($i_0=i_1$). As the real money demand m is a positive function of Y and a negative function of the interest rate, the historically high interest rate country will have a welfare gain equivalent to the area CDEE. If financial market integration and associated financial innovations bring about a higher substitutability of money and bonds in the country with previously high interest rates, there will be an additional welfare gain since the money demand becomes flatter. These additional gains are equal to the area AF'E'. As such, the real money stock M/P=: m in equilibrium would not only rise from $m*_0$ to $m*_1$ but to $m*_2$. Note that a lower nominal interest rate implies a rise of the equilibrium real money stock; if the fall in the nominal interest rate is brought about by a fall of the inflation rate there must be an additional once-and-for-all increase in the real money stock which could be achieved through a lower price level (once-and-for-all fall of the equilibrium level of the price path which might go along with a higher real wage rate which could translate into higher unemployment) or a higher level of the nominal money supply path.

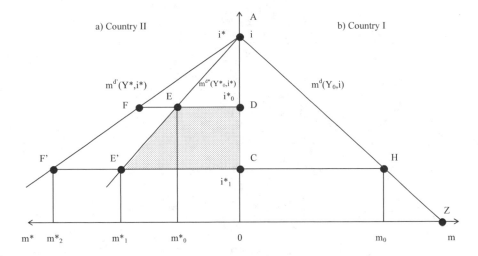

Fig. 94. Static Effects and Medium-Term Effects of Monetary Union

Indeed, the real money stock can increase in only two ways. First, the new central bank can increase the nominal money supply at a given price level, which implies that the European Central Bank could have considerably increased the money stock in the early years of the Euro zone without inflation effects. (The ECB will have to reduce monetary growth at a later date if inflation is not to become a problem.) The associated positive wealth effect should stimulate consumption and investment so that there is a favourable one-off effect on the unemployment rate. The alternative way of raising the real money stock would be a fall of the nominal price level at a given stock of the nominal money stock, which is likely to bring about a rise of unemployment. The two alternative policy options are shown for the simple case of a non-growing economy with constant trend inflation. There will be a one-off increase in real output if the central bank brings about a rise in the real money balances through an expansion in the nominal money supply (b). If the central banks sticks to its pre-monetary union expansion path of the money supply, the monetary union will bring about a one-off rise in unemployment and hence a fall in the equilibrium output level (a) (assuming a given degree of wage flexibility). Hence, a temporary expansionary monetary policy of the ECB is clearly preferable, and it seems that the Euro zone has indeed adopted such a policy – however, obviously not as part of a deliberate strategy. Analysts worried about the allegedly excessive growth in the stock of money simply overlook the analytical aspects discussed here. As regards the empirical analysis of the link

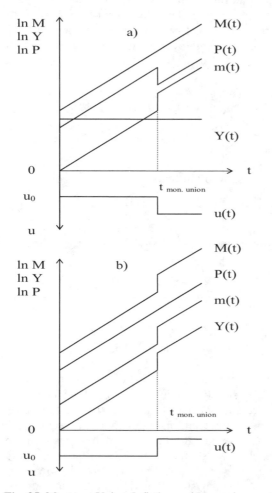

Fig. 95. Monetary Union, Inflation and Unemployment: Structural Break from Switching to Monetary Union

between inflation and the growth of the money stock in the Euro zone (hypothetical Euro zone prior to 1999) in the period from 1980 to 2005, one should expect a statistical break around 1999/2000/2001. Of course, it will be difficult to clearly separate the effect identified from the switch to the new monetary regime as well as the ECB.

In a more medium term perspective it is quite important to focus on real income development. If due to monetary union output in country II in the monetary union would be lower (Y^*_2) than without monetary union (Y^*_0), there is a welfare loss of $BE_1E_3A^*_2$. In country I monetary union could lead to a rise in real output ($Y_1 > Y_0$) so that for the overall monetary union, the net welfare effect is unclear. There would be a clear welfare gain if output in the monetary union were higher in country I and country II (Y^*_1, Y_1). If country I indeed had a higher real output, the existence of positive spillover effects could then indeed raise output in country I to Y_2 (a similar reasoning applies to the analytical framework of a growing economy). Whether output is raised by the switch to a monetary union is an empirical question and depends – from a theoretical perspective – largely on wage flexibility in the monetary union on the one hand and the degree of financial market innovations on the other. With low or even reduced wage flexibility, increasing price competition in the monetary union is likely to increase the unemployment rate (u) and hence reduce output. A higher degree of financial market innovations – particularly if geared towards venture capital markets, commercial paper markets and stock markets – should stimulate the creation and expansion of new firms, thus leading to increased output. Finally, one should raise the question as to whether the European Central Bank takes opportunities to stimulate output expansion more or less than the average national central banks in the pre-Euro area into account. Clearly, a central bank should avoid long term inflationary policy since this will not only raise inflation to critical levels but distort managers' attention from product and process innovations toward more innovative liquidity and asset management in order to exploit inflation dynamics. The crucial point here is that this type of financial engineering does nothing to raise consumption output per capita or the quality of consumption goods available.

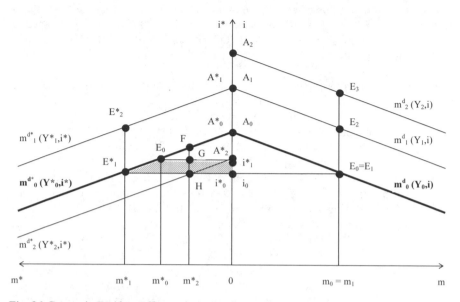

Fig. 96. Dynamic Welfare Effects of Monetary Union

There is one more interesting aspect of monetary union in a dynamic perspective. If per capita income positions differ strongly in the monetary union, there will be considerable differences in the national inflation rate (the price index is composed of tradables and nontradables prices), where differences are on the one hand related mainly to the Balassa Samuelson effect; this means that the relative price of nontradables will rise relative to tradables as per capita income rises. On the other hand, considerable differences in per capita income imply different degrees of intra-industrial trade, which in turn affects the inflation dynamics. A country with high per capita income will have a relatively high share of intra-industrial trade which acts as a disciplinary force on inflation as consumers have a broader choice among domestic and foreign tradables which are close substitutes. This effect is likely to be underestimated in empirical analysis, as a rising share of intra-industrial trade and a rising per capita typically go along with a higher degree of product innovations which will raise prices at face value – but not if improvements in quality are adequately taken into account in the context of hedonic price measurement approaches. By implication, the inflation rate should fall with a rise in per capita income. This perspective is reinforced, if one assumes that stock market capitalization – and stock market turnover – relative to GDP should increase in a more innovative economy. As relatively rising stock market turnover absorbs more liquidity, a given growth rate of the money supply should translate into a lower inflation rate – of newly produced goods – in the long run.

K.3 Integration of Financial Markets in the Euro Zone and Global Dynamics

In both the EU and ASEAN, there is an increasing overlap of regional integration and economic globalization. As regards regional financial market integration, we expect interest rate convergence and actually a fall in the nominal and real interest rate if financial market integration is embedded in a stability-oriented monetary union of countries with a similar per capita income. We also expect maturity deepening in bonds markets and should witness volume growth of bond emissions in the integrated bonds market where economies of scale in intermediation will be easier to exploit than before. All this contributes to lower interest rates. At the same time (see the following figure), there are international impulses possibly leading to higher interest rates. Globalization pressure implies that required rates of return are on the increase in EU and ASEAN stock markets. In particular, banks come under pressure to generate higher profit rates which will – along with the pressure from the BIS's Basel II package requiring more risk-differentiated credit pricing of banks – reduce the growth rate of loans. Medium-sized firms in Europe and Asia facing problems as bank credits become more expansive will consider therefore the option to finance investment and innovation through the bond market with greater interest. (Governments in Europe have not done much to encourage SMEs to take this route, and the ECB as well as the BIS have done much to downplay the impact of Basel II).

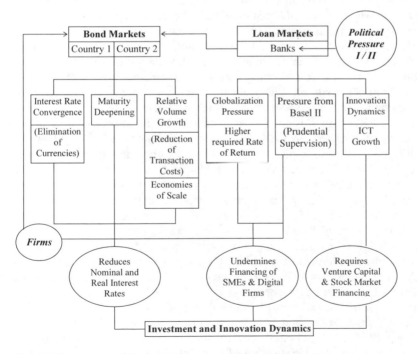

Fig. 97. Integration of Financial Markets and Globalization

Finally, there are increasing global innovation dynamics in OECD countries
and Newly Industrialized Countries on the one hand and an expansion of the ICT
sector largely based on the use of modern computers and software on the other.
The latter is particularly poor collateral from a banker's perspective, which implies that countries with a strong reliance on a universal banking system have disadvantages in financing the expansion of ICT. This could be a major problem in
continental EU countries which heavily rely on universal banking and are obviously lagging behind in ICT expansion relative to the US and the UK (as well as
to Sweden and Finland). A rising role of global innovation dynamics and of ICT
requires a greater role of venture capital financing and a relative expansion in the
role of stock markets. The latter is, however, not without risks, as there are considerable overshooting problems in stock markets and foreign exchange markets.
The standard DORNBUSCH overshooting problem from exchange rate markets
can indeed have mirror effects in the stock market, and both markets are interdependent as has been shown in the empirical analysis by WELFENS/BORBELY
(2004).

K.4 Policy Conclusions

We can draw a number of policy conclusions from our analysis above. Financial
market integration and economic growth are characterized by a number of interesting links on which one should shed more light through empirical analysis.

If one considers the interdependencies of the overall economic system, it is not
very realistic to expect major benefits from financial market integration if there
are blockades to structural change in labor markets. The high unemployment rate
in the Euro area represents a blocking factor in this respect. For example, while
raising factor productivity and the yield on investment might well require outsourcing in many sectors, the resistance of trade unions in countries with high unemployment is likely to slow down such outsourcing in some countries of the
Euro zone (also compared to the US). Uniform minimum wages – without regional differentiation – in France and Italy as well as certain social security elements in Germany seem to be crucial problems for the labor market in the Euro
zone. At the same time, one should take into account that more integrated financial markets – in a period of global financial market liberalization as enshrined in
GATS – could be subject to larger shocks and more extreme bubble problems than
was previously the case. To the extent that stock market bubble problems are related to short-sighted speculations, it is worthwhile to consider strong tax incentives for long term investment while short-term yields could be taxed more heavily. Such a development is unlikely to happen unless OECD countries agree upon
some joint framework in this respect.

In the Euro zone, the governments in Germany, France and Italy should carefully consider their serious and long-lasting unemployment problems. Financial
market integration will be a complementary measure towards full employment if
this integration stimulates the creation of new firms and encourages investment

and innovation in existing firms as well. The latter will, however, not come easily. Governments have many possibilities – including tax policies – to stimulate the expansion of venture capital markets and to encourage the growth of stock markets. Moreover, social security reforms should be done in such a way as to give stock markets a greater role. However, one should not overemphasize the expansion of this pillar for savings toward retirement, since stock markets are quite volatile. An important problem in the Euro zone is the Commission's emphasis that state-owned savings banks in several member states (including Germany) should no longer earn privileged backing by government, since this would not allow for the establishment of a level playing field with private banks. To some extent this is a valid argument, but at the same time it is not really clever for government to throw away the economic benefit of a triple-A rating from which state-owned banks can benefit. Given the rather limited engagement of private banks in start-up financing, one may instead argue that state-owned banks should not only enjoy a privilege with respect to capital costs but also have special obligations in the field of local venture capital financing; such banks should also have an information advantage in this respect. One might well consider allowing private banks to acquire a majority stake in local and regional state-owned banks. However, there could indeed be reasons to require that government keep a certain minority stake in certain regions (say, below 1/3 of overall capital).

It seems quite important that governments in the Euro zone remove barriers to foreign direct investment since there can be no truly integrated financial market if the convergence of capital costs is not facilitated by broad FDI activities. Moreover, there might be FDI diversion effects in the context of EU eastern enlargement and Euro area enlargement toward Eastern Europe. It also seems adequate to encourage foreign investors from outside the Euro zone to invest more in the EU. This, however, requires that the Stability and Growth Pact in the EU truly be respected, which is not the case thus far; one might have to adopt a new Pact. Higher FDI inflows into the Euro zone also depend on a consistent and growth-enhancing policy of the European Central Bank. It is not clear whether the ECB really exploits opportunities to stimulate growth and employment. International confidence in the Euro would benefit from a more consistent framework in prudential supervision in the Euro area. Once the first crisis hits the financial markets in the Euro zone, national governments – which in many member countries are strongly involved in supervision – and the ECB as well as some national central banks involved in supervision will finally want to cooperate (or to cooperate more than in the first seven years of the Euro period). Yet this cooperation will then come at a premium price.

Governments in member countries of the Euro zone should commission studies to highlight not only the problems in venture capital financing but also to better understand the problems of ICT financing. It is naturally a challenge for the universal banking system to finance investment and in particular innovation in an increasingly digital world. The risk that benefits from an innovation will not accrue to the ICT investor but rather diffuse to other countries is only one problem; the lack of collateral in the digital services sector is another.

One can only hope that the Euro zone will proceed slowly with an eastern enlargement of the Euro area. There is still considerable need for exchange rate flexibility in eastern European accession countries. However, at the same time the ECB should carefully analyze the dynamics of financial market development and growth in Eastern Europe, and prudential supervision agencies in the euro area and in accession countries would be wise to cooperate. If there is ever a crisis in Poland its neighbour, Euro country (or Germany) cannot be indifferent to such negative dynamics.

At the bottom line, one may hope that financial market integration in Europe can contribute to both higher growth and a higher level of the growth path. There are many interesting issues for both theoretical and empirical analysis. The necessary bridging between real economics and monetary economics is an enormous challenge, as there has been a long tradition that most researchers in their respective fields have worked in splendid isolation for many years. The contribution presented thus is only a modest step towards building such a bridge.

K.5 FDI and Information and Communication Technology in the Dornbusch Model

K.5.1 Basics of the Dornbusch Model

Overshooting of exchange rates has become an important analytical issue since the seminal paper of DORNBUSCH (1976) who has emphasized that importance of considering differential adjustment speeds in goods markets and financial markets. The implication of this is that the short-term exchange rate dynamics can establish a temporary equilibrium solution in the foreign exchange market which is above the long term exchange rate (overshooting). A key feature of the Dornbusch model is simple: The adjustment speed in financial markets – here the foreign exchange market and the bond market – is high, while prices in goods markets are sticky. The analysis of the DORNBUSCH model is interesting not only in terms of money supply shocks which imply overshooting but also in terms of supply shocks, where the former in some cases could bring about overshooting problems.

In the following analysis we use an extended model of DORNBUSCH (1976); we will partly follow the basic setup of GÄRTNER (1997) who considers a small open economy with trade and portfolio capital flows. In addition, we want to focus on the role of foreign direct investment flows. In the following analysis, # denotes long run equilibrium, E the expectation operator, e the nominal exchange rate, P the price level, G real government expenditures, M the nominal money supply and e' the Euler number.

A useful alternative approach is HANSEN/RÖGER (2000) who focus on the asset accumulation dynamics of the current account, a Phillips curve and the aggregate demand side in combination with a price index for tradable and nontradable goods (hence there is an internal relative equilibrium price in both countries). The intersection of the equilibrium locus for external equilibrium and the schedule of internal equilibrium – with zero output gap - then determines the medium term equilibrium real exchange rate which is influenced by the net asset position of the respective country.

The original Dornbusch model ignores the accumulation dynamics and puts the focus on the differential adjustment speeds in goods markets and financial markets. Here we are interested in taking a closer look at the Dornbusch model which we extend in a simple way to include foreign direct investment flows (in a more elaborate model we could combine the modified Dornbusch model with accumulation dynamics where one option would be to replace Y# by the solution of the Solow growth model which). A major problem tackled here is how to state a logarithmically consistent aggregate demand function and to discuss some key aspects of money supply shocks versus supply-side shocks.

We will focus on the role of foreign direct investment flows in the Dornbusch model and also discuss the impact of product innovations as well as information and communication technology (ICT): Both FDI and ICT affect various parameters of the model and thus the dynamics of adjustment and the role of overshooting, respectively. Important results are a consistent formulation of a logarithmically-stated specification of aggregate demand (with the elasticity parameter for Y being negative and not positive as stated in hundreds of articles published in the literature). Moreover, we shed additional light on the overshooting debate.

K.5.2 The Modified Dornbusch Model

Subsequently we consider a simple system of six equations: Equation (1) is a kind of Phillips curve, where Y# is full employment long run equilibrium output: An excess in demand will lead to an increase in price level. Equation (2) is a logarithmically-stated specification of aggregate demand – partly following GÄRNTER (1997); however, we insert several extensions including the impact of product innovations which are assumed to raise net exports; in the original formulation of GÄRTNER there also is a term related to real income lnY (and a term related to trade and the exchange rate); however, the sign of the parameter of lnY is negative – as we will show - and not positive; in spite of hundreds of articles using ad hoc logarithmically stated demand curves where the elasticity of lnY is positive while it actually is ngative as the relevant parameter reflects the impact of a change in lnY on real net exports and imports, respectively. Moreover, there often also is lnG in the aggregate demand but we will replace lnG by the ratio G/Y which is more consistent as will be argued subsequently.

It is assumed that the foreign price level P* is constant and equal to unity so that $\ln(eP^*/P) = \ln e - \ln P$; we define $q^* = eP^*/P$. To the extent that we consider a model with foreign direct investment, the parameter ψ' does not only reflect the link between trade balance (ψ) and the real exchange rate but also the impact (ψ'') of the real exchange rate on foreign direct investment and hence on the overall investment-GDP ratio: A real depreciation will bring about higher net foreign direct investment inflows – relative to GDP - and hence higher overall investment according to the theoretical arguments and empirical findings of FROOT/STEIN

(1991). The perspective suggested here implies that $\psi'=\psi+\psi$". The variable e is the current nominal exchange rate, e# denotes the long run exchange rate.

As regards the logarithmic formulation of aggregate demand ($\ln Y^d$) it is not easy to reconcile the commonly used formulation (e.g. see GÄRTNER) $\ln Y^d =$ $a\ln q^* + a'\ln Y + a''\ln G$ (the parameters a, a', a" all are positive) with the standard expression of the uses side of GDP: $Y = C + I + G + X\text{-}q^*J$ where C is consumption, I investment, X exports and J imports (τ is the tax rate, v product innovations, * for foreign variable). One may, however, consider a consistent setup where C= $cY(1\text{-}\tau)$, $G=\gamma Y$, $I=\lambda Y$; and $\lambda=\lambda(\ln q^*, \gamma, \ln v, \tau)$, the net export function is X' = $x'(\ln[eP^*/P], \ln Y, \ln Y^*, \ln v)Y^*$; we then will use the function $\ln x'(\ldots)$. The investment output ratio λ is assumed to be a positive function of the real exchange rate as we follow FROOT/STEIN (1991) who argue that in a world with imperfect capital markets foreign firms will find it easier to take over companies in country I (host country) since a real depreciation of country I's courrency will raise the equity capital expressed in terms of the potential host country so that a leveraged international take overs will become easier; hence we assume that the overall investment-GDP ratio is a positive function of the real exchange rate eP^*/P (or $\ln q^*$); the partial derivative of λ with respect to $\ln q^*$ therefore is positive (ψ">0). With respect to the government expenditure-GDP ratio γ the partial derivative ω is ambiguous (will be positive if a rise of γ mainly falls on investment goods), with respect to product innovations v the partial derivate is positive ($\eta>0$), and with respect to the income tax rate it is negative (in absolute term ω'). We also define $1+\omega=:\omega$". Furthermore, we assume that $\ln x'$ is a function of all the four arguments shown in the function $x(\ldots)$. Thus we can write a consistent version of the aggregate demand side:

$$Y^d\{1\text{-} c[1\text{-}\tau] - \gamma - \lambda(\ln q^*, \gamma, \ln v, \tau)\}= x'(\ldots)Y^* \qquad (2')$$

Assuming for simplicity that $-c\text{-}\gamma\text{-}\lambda$ is rather small so that we can use the approximization $\ln (1+z)\approx z$ we can rewrite the equation as:

$$\ln Y^d - c[1\text{-}\tau] - \gamma - \lambda(\ln q^*, \gamma, \ln v, \tau) \qquad (2'')$$

$$=\{\ln x'(\ln q^*, \ln Y, \ln Y^*, \ln v)\}+ \ln Y^*$$

Using linearized functions $\lambda(\ldots)$, $\ln x'(\ldots)$ we can write – with three positive derivatives $\partial \ln x'/\partial \ln q^*=:\psi$", $\partial \ln x'/\partial \ln Y^* =:\Omega'$, $\partial \ln x'/\partial \ln v =:\eta'$and $\partial \ln x'/\partial \ln Y=:$ - $\Omega<0$ – the equation as follows:

$$\ln Y^d= c \text{-}c\tau + \gamma + \psi''\ln(\ln e\text{-}\ln P) + \omega\gamma + \eta\ln v \qquad (2''')$$

$$+\omega'\tau + \{\psi(\ln e\text{-}\ln P) -\Omega\ln Y + \Omega'\ln Y^* +\eta'\ln v\} + \ln Y^*$$

This then leads to subsequent equation (2) where $\psi'=: \psi''+\psi$, $\eta''=\eta+\eta'$ and $\Omega^*=1+ \Omega'$; we also define $1+\omega=:\omega$". The money market is characterized (with φ denoting the income elasticity of the demand for money, $\sigma'$the interest semi-elasticity and e' the Euler number) by nominal money demand $M^d= PY^\varphi$ e' $^{-\sigma'i}$ which implies for equilibrium $\ln M = \ln P + \varphi\ln Y - \sigma'i$. While money market equilibrium is fairly standard, the subsequent capital market equilibrium condition is rather unusual as it modifies the interest rate parity condition by taking into account portfolio-theoretical considerations relevant in a setup with foreign direct investment – the latter is not considered in the Dornbusch model. Note that an alternative way to express the aggregate demand in a logarithmically-stated function is based – with j denoting the import –output ratio (imports J=jY) - on $Y^d([1-c-\gamma-\lambda(\ldots)+q*j(lnq*)] = x(lnY, lnq*, lnv*)Y*$ where we have assumed in the spirit of the gravity equation that exports are not only a positive function of real income abroad but of domestic real output or actually of lnY as well (in an empirical context the assumption that $c+\gamma+\lambda-j$ is close to zero is more convincing than assuming that $c+\gamma+\lambda$ is close to zero)

Capital market equilibrium is given by two interacting factors (i is the nominal exchange rate), namely the impact of portfolio investors guided by the interest rate parity (i=i* + E(dlne/dt)) and foreign investors who focus on long run differences in the marginal product of capital; (as we assume that both the home and the foreign country (* denotes foreign variables) produce according to a Cobb Douglas function $Y=K^ß(AL)^{1-ß}$ and $Y*=K*^{ß*}(A*L*)^{1-ß*}$, respectively, the relevant variable for foreign investors is the difference in marginal products of capita $(Y_{K\#,}, Y_K*\#)$ namely ßY#/K minus ß*Y#*/K#* where # denotes long run values. From a portfolio-theoretical perspective, real capital and bonds are complementary in terms of risk as risks faced by holders of K are negatively correlated with that of holding bonds. Hence we state the rather simple equilibrium condition i+ζ(ßY#/K# - $Y_K\#$)= i*+E(dlne/dt). Thus a positive international differential of marginal products in favor of the home country requires for a given sum i* +E(dlne/dt) that domestic interest rates fall. To put it differently, given the domestic and the foreign interest rate the required expected exchange rate depreciation rate E(dlne/dt) must rise along with a positive differential of marginal products since bond investment abroad would otherwise be insufficiently attractive now that holding domestic bonds has become more attractive.

The expected devaluation rate is assumed to be proportionate to the difference between the equilibrium exchange rate e# and the actual exchange rate e; or expressed in logarithms, we have equation (6).

Goods Market

$$dlnP/dt = \pi'(lnY^d - lnY\#) \tag{1}$$

$$lnY^d = c+\psi'[lne-lnP]-\Omega lnY\#+[1+\omega]\gamma-[c+\omega']\tau+\eta''lnv+ \Omega*lnY* \tag{2}$$

Money Market

$$lnMd = lnP + \varphi lnY - \sigma'i \tag{3}$$

$$lnM^s = lnM^d = lnM \tag{4}$$

International Capital Market

$$i+\zeta(\beta Y\#/K\# - Y_K^*\#)= i^* + E(dlne/dt)]$$ (5)

$$E(dlne/dt) = \theta(lne\#-lne)$$ (6)

Note that in the very long run (defined by equality of marginal products of capital across countries), equation (5) boils down to the standard interest rate parity condition. Here we focus on the short term and the long run where the latter is defined by a response of the price level P.

We now can draw in lnP-lne space, the positively sloped equilibrium line for the goods market (ISP; slope is unity). The ISP line is obtained by combining equations (1) and (2) and imposing dlnP/dt=0 which also implies $Y^d=Y^s$. The equilibrium line ISP – the goods market equilibrium schedule – represents the equation:

$$lnP= lne +c/\psi' + \omega''\gamma/\psi'- [(1+\Omega)/\psi']lnY\# - [(c+\omega')/\psi']\tau$$ (7)

$$+ (\eta''/\psi')lnv + (\Omega^*/\psi')lnY^*$$

The slope in lnP-lne space is unity. To the right of ISP, we have an excess demand; above the ISP line there is an excess supply. In the third quadrant, we have drawn money market equilibrium. In the forth quadrant, we have the CME line which indicates international capital market equilibrium.

The LM curve represents money market equilibrium and hence the equation:

$$i = (1/\sigma')[lnP - ln M + \varphi lnY\#]$$ (8)

The CME line is obtained by combining the equations for the capital market which results in

$$i = [i^* + \theta(lne\# - lne)] -\zeta(\beta Y\#/K\# - Y_K^*\#))$$ (9)

The logic of equation (9) basically says – disregarding the term relevant for foreign investment for the moment:

- a rise in the domestic interest rate – given i^* - must go along with a rise in the effective yield of a portfolio investment abroad which requires an expected depreciation rate. Such an expected depreciation rate will occur only if there has been an excessive initial appreciation.
- a fall in the domestic nominal interest rate – given the foreign interest rate i^* - will have to go along with a decline in the effective yield on investments abroad so that the expected rate of change of the exchange rate must be negative. An expected appreciation can, however, only occur if the initial depreciation has been excessive (i.e., stronger than required in terms of the long run equilibrium exchange rate).

Now let us take into account foreign direct investment term. If a positive differential between the domestic marginal product of capital and that of country II (foreign country) emerges for any interest rate differential, a lower expected depreciation rate is required than before. Note also that in the absence of inflation and assuming profit maximization, we will have $Y_K\# = Y_K^*\#$ in the long run.

Assume that we have initial equilibrium in all markets where $i=i^*$, equality of marginal products across countries and that the actual exchange rate is equal to the equilibrium exchange rate e#. Let us consider the short-term and long run impact of an expansionary monetary policy which leads to an upward shift of the LM schedule and a rightward shift of the CME schedule. In the short term the price level does not change so that the adjustment takes place only through the response of the exchange rate and the interest rate. In long run equilibrium, we must have $i=i^*$ again, and points A_2, C_2 and B_2 indicate overall equilibrium. In the short run, however, the excess supply in the money market leads to a strong reduction of the nominal interest rate I (see point A_1) which implies an interim exchange rate of e_1 which is higher than e_2. The phenomenon that the short term exchange rate reaction exceeds that which is required by long term equilibrium is called exchange rate overshooting.

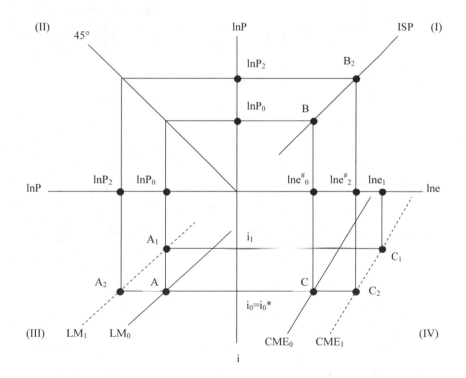

Fig. 98. Goods Market, Money Market, International Capital Market

If we plug equation (9) into (8) – that is combine the capital market with the money market in a financial market subsystem – we get

$$\sigma'i^* + \sigma'\theta(\ln e\# - \ln e) - \sigma'\zeta(\text{ß}Y\#/K\# - Y^*_{K^*}\#) \tag{10}$$

$$= [\ln P - \ln M + \varphi \ln Y\#]$$

$$\ln P = \ln M - \varphi \ln Y\# + \sigma'i^* + \sigma'\theta(\ln e\# - \ln e) - \sigma'\zeta[(\text{ß}Y\#/K\# - Y^*_{K^*}\#) \tag{11}$$

In an economy in which the marginal product of capital exceeds that abroad the long term effect of net foreign direct investment inflows on the price level obviously is negative. Only in the very long run – when there is international equalization of marginal products of capital – will there be no effect of foreign direct investment inflows on the price level. By implication a temporary net inflow of foreign direct investment will dampen the price level in the host country and raise it in the host country.

This equation is crucial in the sense that it represents short-term adjustment dynamics in financial markets. In lnP-lne space we have a negatively sloped FMS curve while the ISP curve is positively sloped. An expansionary monetary policy will shift the FMS curve to the right so that – at given ln P –a new temporary exchange rate equilibrium is immediately established. This is above the long run equilibrium value, and adjustment then continues along the FMS curve.

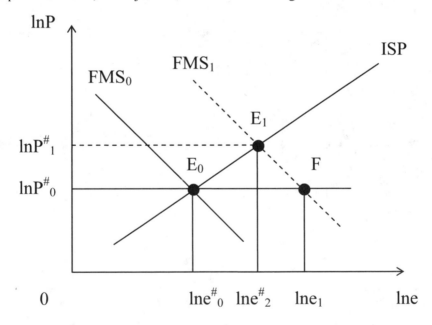

Fig. 99. Financial Market Equilibrium and Goods Market Equilibrium in the Dornbusch Model (slope FMS = $-\sigma'\theta$)

In long run equilibrium, lne#=lne and $Y_{K\#}= Y^*_{K*}\#$ so that the long run financial sector equilibrium can be written as:

$$\ln P\# = \ln M - \varphi\ln Y\# + \sigma'i^* \tag{12}$$

Hence the long run price level is a monetary phenomenon and we can conclude

$$d\ln P\#/d\ln M =1 \tag{12'}$$

Moreover, note that the long run multiplier for an increase of lnY# is given by

$$d\ln P\#/d\ln Y\# = -\varphi <0. \tag{12''}$$

Hence a positive supply shock will reduce the equilibrium price level in the long run.

Inserting the long run solution of equation (12) in equation (7) and assuming e=e#, gives

$$\ln M - \varphi\ln Y\# + \sigma'i^*= \ln e\# + c/\psi' + \omega''\gamma/\psi' \tag{13}$$
$$- [(1+\Omega)/\psi']\ln Y\# - [(c+\omega')/\psi']\tau + \eta''/\psi'\ln v + (\Omega^*/\psi')\ln Y^*$$

$$\ln e\# = \ln M - \varphi\ln Y\# + \sigma'i^* -c/\psi'- \omega''\gamma/\psi' +[(1+\Omega)/\psi']\ln Y\# \tag{14}$$
$$+ [(c+\omega')/\psi']\tau - \eta''/\psi'\ln v - (\Omega^*/\psi')\ln Y^*$$
$$=\ln P\# -c/\psi' - \omega''\gamma/\psi'+[(1+\Omega)/\psi']\ln Y\#$$
$$+ [(c+\omega')/\psi']\tau -\eta''/\psi'\ln v-(\Omega^*/\psi')\ln Y^*$$

Hence dlne#/dlnP =1 and dlne#/dlnM=1. Product innovations will bring about a nominal and real appreciation in the long run. As regards the impact of the government-GDP ratio on the long run exchange rate the model implies a real depreciation as long as we assume that $\omega<1$ and are not considering the need to balance the budget - that is to combine a rise of γ with a rise of the income tax rate. As regards the impact of tax policies a rise of the tax rate will bring anbout a nominal and real depreciation. Note that one might consider within a modified model the case that ζ is a function of q* and the tax rate. If there is a parallcl supply side shock abroad (rise of Y*) and at home (rise of Y#) the net effect is ambiguous.

Moreover, the long run real exchange rate lne#-lnP# thus equal to

$$\ln q^*\#=-c/\psi' -\omega''\gamma/\psi' \tag{14'}$$
$$+[(1+\Omega)/\psi']\ln Y\# + [\omega'+c)/\psi']\tau- \eta''/\psi'\ln v- (\Omega^*/\psi')\ln Y^*$$

Note that product innovation will bring about a real appreciation as:

$$d\ln q^*/d\ln v = - \eta''/\psi' \tag{14''}$$

The short run reaction of the exchange rate can be obtained from equation (11'):

$$\ln e=\ln e\#+[\ln M-\ln P-\varphi\ln Y\#]/(\theta\sigma')+i^*/\theta \tag{11'}$$
$$-[\zeta/\theta](\text{ß}Y\#/K\#-Y^*_{K*}\#)$$

Therefore, we have in the short run the following result which confirms exchange rate overshooting:

$$dlne/dlnM = dlne\#/dlnM +1/(\theta\sigma') = 1 +1/(\theta\sigma')>1. \tag{15}$$

Monetary policy is unanticipated here (if one changes the formation of expectations the impact effects will differ; e.g. one may set $E(dlne/dt)= E(dlnM/dt)$ or switch to adaptive expectations, namely $E_t(lnM_{t+1}) = E_{t-1}(lnMt) + E_{t-1}(lnMt) + \varepsilon$ $[lnMt_t - E_{t-1}(lnMt_t)] = (1-\varepsilon)E_{t-1}(lnM_t) + \varepsilon lnM_t$ we would have a share of ε of monetary policy which is considered as permanent; and the short-term reaction would become $dlne/dlnM = 1 +1/(\theta\sigma') - (1-\varepsilon)/\theta$; the last term indeed then could imply that there is no overshooting at all or that there is indeed an appreciation followed by a depreciation; see GÄRTNER (1997)).

Moreover, note that the long run exchange rate reaction of a supply-side shock is given from equation (14) as:

$$dlne\#/dlnY\# = -\varphi + [(1+\Omega)/\psi'] \tag{15'}$$

As the real exchange rate is lne-lnP and since $dlne\#/dlnP=1$ the change in the equilibrium long run real exchange rate will be given by:

$$dlnq*\#/dlnY\# = [(1+\Omega)/\psi']>0 \tag{15''}$$

A supply-side shock – standing for a kind of process innovation - will cause a real depreciation in the long run. However, as product innovations will bring about a real appreciation a period of intensified innovation dynamics has an ambiguous effect: If product innovations dominate so that the investment-GDP ratio and the net export-GDP ratio increase sufficiently strongly one should expect a real appreciation of the currency of the Schumpter lead country.

Note that if we want to consider the very long run in the sense of equalization of marginal products of capital, the impact of a supply side shock on the nominal exchange rate is only $-\varphi + [(1+\Omega)/\psi']$; without the transitory FDI impact the more likely is a depreciation.

From equation (11'), we have the following short term reaction of the nominal exchange rate (note: for a variable $y=f(x)$ it generally holds: $df/dlnx = [df/dlnx]$ $[dx/dx] = [df/dx] [dx/dlnx] = [df/dx] [1/(dlnx/dx)] =x[df/dx]$ and hence for $f(x)=ax$ we have – with a as a constant parameter - $df/dlnx=ax$):

$$dlne/dlnY\# = dlne\#/dlnY\# - [\varphi/(\theta\sigma')] - [\zeta\beta/\theta K\#]Y\# \tag{15'''}$$

$$= -\varphi[1+(1/\theta\sigma')] + [(1+\Omega)/\psi'] - [\zeta\beta/\theta K\#] Y\#$$

A positive supply-side shock is the more likely to cause a real appreciation in the short term, the larger the income elasticity of the demand for money is and the higher the output elasticity of capital is (and the lower the capital stock is). A positive supply shock is reinforced by the impact of foreign direct investment which reinforces the tendency towards a short term appreciation.

Note that in the context of a supply-side shock the long run change in the real exchange rate is given by $(dlne\#-dlnP\#)/dlnY\#= dlne\#/dlnY\# - dlnP\#/dlnY\#$

which is zero only if the expression $[(1+\Omega)/\psi']$ is zero which requires that ψ' approaches infinity.

As regards the short term reaction of the exchange rate there will be a real appreciation as a consequence of a supply side shock under certain parameter constellations – indeed a sufficiently high role of foreign direct investment in capital markets (parameter ζ) will bring about this result unless expectation formation is characterized by $\theta \to \infty$. Moreover, we should note that foreign direct investment unambiguously reduces $d\ln e/d\ln Y\#$ since the role of FDI is to raise the denominator ψ' (without FDI the denominator would be $\psi = \psi' - \psi''$); and FDI is visible in the expression $-[\zeta\beta/\theta K\#]$.

The comprehensive analysis of monetary policy shocks and supply-side policy shocks leads to an important conclusion: Whether a system of flexible exchange rates brings rather strong instability of the exchange rate depends on the relative weight of monetary policy shocks and supply side shocks. The presence of foreign investment seems to dampen overshooting problems.

Moreover, to the extent that flexible exchange rates stimulate innovations and hence positive supply-side shocks, the system of flexible exchange rates will bring a double benefit: Higher innovations and rather limited exchange rate volatility, provided that monetary policy is accommodating in the sense that positive supply-side shocks are adequately combined with expansionary monetary policy. However, one cannot rule out that a system of flexible exchange rates will bring about less innovation performance than a system of fixed exchange rates. All which we can say here is that empirical analysis is lacking in this regard.

Turning back to the standard analysis of monetary policy: The stronger foreign exchange markets react to a temporary divergence between expected long run equilibrium exchange rate and the current exchange rate and the higher the semi-interest elasticity is, the lower the overshooting effect.

The short-run adjustment dynamics in the goods markets are obtained from combining equations (1) and (2), which results in:

$$d\ln P/dt = \pi'[\psi'(\ln e - \ln P) - (1+\Omega)\ln Y\# + \omega''\gamma + \eta''\ln v + \Omega^*\ln Y^* - (c + \omega')\tau + c \quad (16)$$

From equation (14) we have

$$\psi' [\ln e\# - \ln P\#] = -\omega''\gamma + [1+\Omega] \ln Y\# - \Omega^*\ln Y^* + (c + \omega')\tau - c \quad (17)$$

and therefore we get in combination with (16):

$$d\ln P/dt = \pi'[\psi' (\ln e - \ln e\#) - \psi'(\ln P - \ln P\#)] \quad (18)$$

Inserting (12) in equation (11') gives

$$\ln e - \ln e\# = (\ln P\# - \ln P)/[\theta\sigma'] - (\zeta/\theta)[\beta Y\#/K\# - Y^*_K\#) \quad (19)$$

If we assume that the foreign marginal product of capital is equal to the domestic marginal product we get after inserting this result into (18):

$$d\ln P/dt = -\pi'(\psi'/\sigma'\theta + \psi') (\ln P - \ln P\#) = -\alpha''(\ln P - \ln P\#). \quad (20)$$

Here we have simply defined $\pi'(\psi'/\sigma'\theta + \psi')=\alpha''$. The above equation is (setting P#=1) a homogeneous differential equation of first order and has the solution

$$\ln P(t) = C_0 e^{-\alpha''t} \tag{21}$$

This implies (having solved for C_0 by considering t=0):

$$\ln P(t) = \ln P\# + (\ln P(0) - \ln P\#) e^{-\alpha''t} \tag{22}$$

Note that

$$\ln e(t) = \ln e\# + [\theta\sigma']^{-1} (\ln P\# - \ln P) e^{-\alpha''t} \tag{23}$$

Thus we can state

$$\ln e(t) = \ln e\# + (\ln e(0) - \ln e\#) e^{-\alpha''t} \tag{24}$$

The adjustment speed for the exchange rate variable is therefore the same as for the price level. Obviously, the adjustment speed α'' is faster the higher π' and ψ' are (i.e., the faster goods market react to excess demand and the stronger trade and (foreign direct) investment react to the real exchange rate). The lower the semi-interest elasticity of the demand for money (σ) and the slower the foreign exchange market reacts to divergences between the long run equilibrium value and the current exchange rate (parameter θ), the faster the adjustment process of the price level towards the equilibrium price level. However, we have seen that low parameters θ and σ' imply a large overshooting in case of a monetary supply shock so that these two parameters are ambivalent. If they are low, the overshooting effect will be large, but adjustment to the new equilibrium value will be fast. Foreign direct investment raises the adjustment speed.

International coordination and the intervention rules of central banks will affect the adjustment parameter θ. There are some arguments that governments and international institutions should work in favour of a high parameter θ, since this means only modest overshooting (and a slow adjustment speed). One may also argue that the presence of foreign investors will affect the learning parameter θ.

Information and Communication Technology and the Dornbusch Model

How will the expansion of information and communication technology affect exchange rate dynamics and the overshooting/undershooting effects? The price adjustment speed in goods market is likely to decrease, as the global supply side elasticity in an internationally networked society will be relatively large, in particular in the field of digital services whose share in aggregate demand is likely to increase in time. Since ICT facilitates access to various kinds of financial market instruments, the interest elasticity of the demand for money may be expected to increase. Monetary overshooting problems should thus be reduced unless the learning speed in the field of exchange rate expectations should decrease. However, ICT might indeed facilitate the learning process in markets and hence ICT expansion will go along with a higher adjustment parameter θ (concerns formation of exchange rate expectations). This implies that ICT will lead to reduced over-shooting problems; at the same time the adjustment speed to the new long run exchange rate equilibrium will slow down. From this perspective, the opportunities of an activist monetary policy have improved, namely in the sense that exchange rate overshooting problems are less severe than in the traditionally industrialized OECD countries. This holds all the more since one has to take into account that ICT expansion is equivalent to a positive supply shock which itself implies a dampening exchange rate movement.

K.5.3 Conclusions

Exchange rate overshooting depends on several parameters, including the learning dynamics of exchange rate expectations and the interest elasticity of the demand for money; the adjustment speed to the new equilibrium is influenced by the responsiveness of the trade balance and foreign direct investment. ICT and FDI will affect the nominal and real exchange rate dynamics. There are several arguments why FDI could reduce the problem of overshooting; from this perspective economic globalization – in the sense of a rising share of FDI in overall investment – is likely to contribute to less exchange rate instability. If ICT for technological reasons is raising the learning speed in the foreign exchange market the size of overshooting is reduced, at the same time one might expect that ICT raises the price adjustment speed in goods markets which reinforces the speed of adjustment towards the new equilibrium. Monetary policy would then generate less over-shooting than in the time of the Old Economy so that a more activist monetary policy could be considered.

From an empirical perspective it would be important to find out more about the effect of the exchange rate regime on innovation dynamics. A fixed exchange rate regime basically transmits the domestic price level to those countries which have pegged the currency to the anchor country. If a fixed exchange rate regime helps to diffuse price stability worldwide – under the assumption that the anchor country pursues a stability-oriented monetary policy leading to a low inflation rate – firms in all countries might find it relatively easy to conduct R&D policies which require a long term perspective; bond maturities (as a proxy for the representative time horizon) are known to be relatively long in periods of low inflation rates. The counter-argument in favour of a flexible exchange rate regime is that it establishes full individual responsibility in monetary policy in each country so that the weighted world inflation rate could be lower under flexible exchange rates than in a system of a fixed exchange rate. However, there other aspects which are rather unclear: Will multinational companies be more active innovators in a system of fixed exchange rates than in a system of flexible exchange rates? More research is needed here.

As regards regional integration several parameters of the (modified) Dornbusch model will be affected: The price adjustment parameter in goods markets should increase as this would be natural to expect in a single market – and to the extent that monetary union is reinforcing this adjustment speed the argument is even more valid. From a Eurozone perspective there is the crucial issue whether or not dollar exchange rate volatility in the sense of overshooting risks will be reduced; indeed, less overshooting problems should be expected if regional integration – in particular monetary integration – raises the interest elasticity of the demand for money (in a monetary union one should expect more liquid alternatives to holding money than in fragmented national markets). Moreover, the learning speed (parameter θ) in the foreign exchange market also should increase. The main risk occurring in a monetary union involving countries with high sustained budget deficits is that there is a considerable risk that tax rates will go up. If such tax increases are not mainly invested in the form of higher public investment – relative to GDP - and higher R&D expenditure-GDP ratios the impact on GNP could be negative in the long run; not least because an increasing share of GDP will accrue to foreign investors (from country II) which will benefit from a real depreciation through cheaper access to the stock of capital abroad.

Finally, one should notice that the expansion of ICT is likely to reinforce the role of foreign direct investment as firm-internal transaction and management costs are reduced. Thus the findings with respect to FDI are reinforced through the expansion information and communication technology. The logarithmic formulation of the aggregate demand side suggested here should encourage new options to consistently develop macro models. Supply side shocks and product innovations will affect the exchange rate in the long run, and in a world economy with increased innovation dynamics the respective topics need to further explored and also require additional empirical analysis.

Appendix K.1: Aspects of Transition and Trend Growth in a Setup with Technology Shifts

We consider our refined neoclassical model with the standard Cobb-Douglas production function $Y=K^\beta(AL)^{1-\beta}$ and an exogenous growth rate of technology (A; $dlnA/dt=:a$) and an exogenous growth rate of the population ($n=dlnL/dt$). We make the assumption that savings equals, $S= s(1-\tau)(1-hu)Y$ where u is the structural unemployment rate and h a positive parameter; τ is the income tax rate. Imposing the equilibrium condition that gross investment (δ is the depreciation rate) equals savings, that is $dK/dt +\delta K = S$, we obtain the differential equation for $k'=:K/(AL)$:

$$dk'/dt = s(1-\tau)(1-hu)k'^\beta -(n+a+\delta)k' \qquad (AK.1)$$

The steady state solution for the ratio of capital to labor in efficiency units is:

$$k'\# = \{s(1-\tau)(1-hu)/(n+a+\delta)\}^{1/1-\beta} \qquad (AK.2)$$

As regards transition dynamics of the Bernoulli equation (see Apendix G.4) for k' – and similarly the dynamics for per capita income y - the transitory adjustment speed is given by $(n+a+\delta)(1-\beta)$ provided that we use the simplifying assumption that $\beta=0.5$. If the unemployment rate negatively affects the rate of progress in such a way that we have a progress function $a=a_0-a\#u$ (a_0 is a kind of autonomous progress rate) the implication is that both the speed of adjustment towards the new steady state is reduced and the long run growth rate is reduced. Conversely, countries with high initial structural unemployment stand to benefit twice from reducing unemployment: First by achieving a higher speed of adjustment towards the new steady state and secondly by a higher trend growth rate. There is also a negative effect, namely the reduction in the level of the growth path. In the context of a modified quasi-monetarist Phillips curve this implies that a fall in the natural rate of unemployment will go along with a fall in the inflation rate which is consistent with Milton Friedman's conjecture in his Nobel lecture. At the same time one should expect a one-off rise in the price level since the level of the growth path is reduced.

Appendix K.2: Uncertainty, Savings and Product Innovations

The impact of the expected yield (r) – and of the standard deviation σ of the interest rate - on consumption is ambiguous (DIXIT, 1991, p. 175). DIXIT considers an infinitely long living consumer who owns wealth A' that earns a random total return (principal plus interest) of r per period; there is no other income.

The impact of uncertainty depends on parameters of the consumption function which may differ – as emphasized here - across countries so that a rise of E(r) could raise the optimum consumption-wealth ratio C/A' (C is consumption, A' is net wealth) in country I while country II (foreign country) has a fall of the ratio of C*/A'*.

Before we consider the impact of product innovations we recall here the basic analysis of DIXIT who assumes the following utility function:

$$U(C) = C^{1-\varepsilon}/(1-\varepsilon); \ \varepsilon > 0 \qquad (Z.1)$$

The utility discount factor $\delta' = 1/(1+r)$ and the objective over time is to maximize the mathematical expectation of the discounted present value of utility. In the initial period the household starts with wealth A', if the household consumes C and saves A'-C his random wealth at the beginning of the following period will be r(A'-C). The Bellman Equation then leads to the following optimum:

$$C/A' = \{1 - \delta' E[r^{1-\varepsilon}]\}^{1/\varepsilon} \qquad (Z.2)$$

Thus the optimal rule for consumption out of wealth is a proportional one, but the proportion critically depends on δ and ε and the distribution of the random variable ε. The special case of a lognormal distrubition of r - ln r is normally distributed with standard deviation σ – yields the following result:

$$E[r^{1-\varepsilon}] = \{E[r])^{1-\varepsilon} \exp(-\varepsilon(1-\varepsilon)\sigma^2/2)\} \qquad (Z.3)$$

Hence we get

$$C/A' = \{1 - \delta' E[r])^{1-\varepsilon} \exp(-\varepsilon(1-\varepsilon)\sigma^2/2)\}^{1/\varepsilon} \qquad (Z.4)$$

Let us consider the case $\varepsilon < 1$: A rise of E(r) – with σ fixed – reduces the optimum consumption-wealth ratio; a rise of σ will raise this ratio. The opposite result holds if $\varepsilon > 1$. If country I is characterized by $\varepsilon < 1$ while II has $\varepsilon > 1$ the asymmetric two-country model – in which the large economy (in a system of fixed exchange rates) dominates real interest rates in both countries - implies the following result of a rise of r* and r, respectively: As the desired ratio C/A' has fallen while C*/A'* has increased abroad country I will run a current account surplus and country II a current account deficit: This could mean that country II acquires part of country I wealth through foreign direct investment. In this case monetary policy in country II causes an international reallocation of wealth.

Role of Product Innovation on the Consumption-Wealth Ratio

In addition to the analysis of DIXIT (1991) we may consider the particular role of ε more closely. Here let us assume that ε is below unity in both countries and that there is a wave of product innovations which raises ε so that consumers get a higher benefit from C(t). How will this affect the optimum C/A'? Let us assume that C/A' is close to unity (that is $\delta'\ E[r^{1-\varepsilon}]$ is close to zero) so that we obtain:

$$\ln(C/A') \approx -(1/\varepsilon)\ \delta' E[r^{1-\varepsilon}] = -(1/\varepsilon)\delta'\ \{E[r])^{1-\varepsilon} \exp(-\varepsilon(1-\varepsilon)\sigma^2/2)\} \qquad (Z.5)$$

$$d\ln(C/A')/d\varepsilon = (1/\varepsilon^2)\delta\ \{E[r])^{1-\varepsilon} \exp(-\varepsilon(1-\varepsilon)\sigma^2/2) - (1/\varepsilon)\delta \qquad (Z.6)$$

$$- (1-\varepsilon)(1/\varepsilon)\delta\ \{E[r])^{-\varepsilon} e\ xp(-\varepsilon(1-\varepsilon)\sigma^2/2)\}$$

$$+\varepsilon(1-\varepsilon)\sigma^2/2)(1/\varepsilon)\delta\ \{E[r])^{1-\varepsilon}\exp\ (-\varepsilon(1-\varepsilon)\sigma^2/2)\}$$

$$= \{(1/\varepsilon)-(1-\varepsilon)+\varepsilon(1-\varepsilon)\sigma^2/2)\}\varepsilon^{-1}\delta'E[r])^{1-\varepsilon}\exp\ (-\varepsilon(1-\varepsilon)\sigma^2/2)$$

Therefore the sign of $d\ln(C/A')/d\varepsilon$ depends only on the expression $\{(1/\varepsilon)-(1-\varepsilon)+\varepsilon(1-\varepsilon)\ \sigma^2/2)\}$ and it holds that

$$\{(1/\varepsilon)+(1-\varepsilon)[-1+\varepsilon(1-\varepsilon)\ \sigma^2/2]\}>0 \leftrightarrow d\ln(C/A')\ /d\varepsilon \qquad (Z.7)$$

We can see that $\varepsilon>1$ – the critical case for the impact of a change of $E(r)$ and of σ – is not generally leading to a switch of the sign of $d\ln(C/A)/d\varepsilon$; the sign for this impact multiplier is less likely to be positive than in the case of $\varepsilon<1$.

Let us return to our standard case of $\varepsilon<1$. If the variance of the interest rate becomes critically large the expression (Z.7) always is positive for the assume parameter range $0<\varepsilon<1$. And conversely: if the variance σ^2 is relatively small product innovations will reduce the ratio of C/A'. If we assume that product innovations will go along with a higher expected real interest rate and a higher standard deviation – more product innovations indeed could imply a higher variance of the failure rate of firms (over time) so that the variance of bond prices and hence that of interest rates will increase –the impact of product innovations on C/A' is unclear as three impulses are overlapping. Thus we have an interesting empirical issue where clarification is needed not least with respect to the link between product innovations and E(r) and the variance of r, respectively. As a hypothesis (assuming a priori $\varepsilon<1$) one may state that a higher rate of product innovations raises both r and the variance of r; if the variance effect – raising the ratio C/A' - dominates the effect of the rise of E(r) the net effect would be a rise of the consumption-wealth ratio provided that there is no sufficiently strong offsetting effect through the rise of ε.

Appendix K.3: A Macro-Model with Unemployment and Endogenous Taxation

We now want to focus on an economy with expected unemployment rate u where the unemployed – the difference between (one period ahead) expected supply L'^s and expected labor demand L'^d - get a transfer which by assumption is proportionate to current per capita income $y = y'A$ $(y'=:Y/[AL]$ where A is the level of technology and Y is real income); we basically assume that unemployment insurance pays an income replacement ratio U' is in the interval 0,1. Hence the government budget – with government consumption and tax revenues denoted by G and T, respectively - is given by

$$G + [L'^s-L'^d]U'y'A = T \qquad (X.1)$$

With γ and τ denoting the ratio of G/Y and T/Y, respectively, we can write:

$$\gamma Y + [L^s-L^d]U'y'A = \tau Y \qquad (X.2)$$

Denoting population (or workforce) by L and using the definition u' =: $(L'^s-L'^d)/L$ and y'=:Y/(AL) we get

$$\gamma y' + u'U'y' = \tau y' \qquad (X.3)$$

Therefore we get for the tax rate τ:

$$\tau = \gamma + u''U' \qquad (X.5)$$

The tax rate is the higher the higher γ and the higher the replacement ratio U' and the higher the expected unemployment rate u' is; note that u' is at first considered to be exogenous and basically is determined by past wage policies and productivity dynamics.

We assume that consumption C=cY(1-τ) or equivalently C/[AL]= cy'[1-τ]. The investment output ratio λ=: I/Y (I is investment) is assumed to depend on the expected unemployment rate u' and the real interest rate r (the partial derivative of λ with respect to r is assumed to be negative); as regards the impact of the expected unemployment rate u' we assume that a rise of the expected unemployment rate stimulates capital deepening (positive parameter λ') and hence the investment rate to a certain extent, but that u' also has a dampening effect (parameter λ") on the investment output ratio: Hence we have $\lambda = \lambda'u' - \lambda''\cdot u' - \lambda_r r$. The import function J=jY and the real exchange rate q*=:eP*/P. Therefore the goods market is characterized by the equation

$$Y[1- c(1-\tau)- \gamma- \lambda(u', r)+q*j] = xY^* \qquad (X.6)$$

Y* denotes foreign real income and exports X=x(…)Y* so that we obtain after division by AL:

$$y'[1- c(1-\tau)-\gamma-\lambda+q*j] = x'y'^*(A^*L^*/AL) \qquad (X.7)$$

The level of technology at home and abroad is considered as exogenous as is the population in both countries. Taking logarithms (while assuming that c(1-τ)-+γ-+λ(u', r) -q*j=:z to be close to zero so that we use the approximation ln[1+z] $\approx$z) we can write:

$$\text{'}\quad \ln y' = c[1-\tau] +\gamma +\lambda(…)-q^*j(\ln q^*) + \ln x' +\ln y'^* + \ln(A^*L^*/AL) \qquad (X.8)$$

We can write the condition for a goods market equilibrium as follows (where x"=: $\partial\ln x/\partial u'$>0, x'''= $\partial\ln x/\partial(A/A^*)$; the import ratio j is linearize as j= j'lnq* where j'=:$\partial j/\partial\ln q^*$):

$$\ln y'= c-c(1-\gamma-u'U') + \gamma - \lambda_r r + \lambda''u' - \lambda''\cdot u' -q^*j'\ln q^*+ \qquad (X.9)$$

$$+ x''u'+x'''(A/A^*)+\ln y'^*+\ln(A^*L^*/AL)\text{ISU curve)}$$

The parameters x" and x''' are assumed to be positive; with respect to u' the implication is that firms intensify activities in exports markets as soon as they anticipate a rise of future unemployment and hence less opportunities to sell in domestic markets.

As regards the money market we assume that the demand for money is a positive function of income and the expected unemployment rate (as regards the latter we partly follow ARTUS, 1995: however, here not current unemployment but expected unemployment is relevant) and a negative function of the nominal interest rate. The money market equilibrium is given by

$$[M/P]/[AL] = y'^{\varphi} (1+u')^{\varphi'} e^{'-\sigma'i} \qquad (X.10)$$

Hence

$$\ln M - \ln P - \ln A - \ln L = \varphi \ln y' + \varphi' u' - \sigma' i \text{ MU curve)} \qquad (X.11)$$

The current account equilibrium under flexible exchange rates – with Q' denoting real net capital imports (depending on domestic yield i, foreign yield and A/A*) and J' denoting net imports which are assumed to be a positive function of lnY and a negative function of u, q* and lnY* - is given by

$$Q'(i, i^*+E(dlne/dt), A/A^*) = J'(lnq^*, lny', lny'^*, u) \qquad (X.12)$$

If the expected depreciation rate E(dlne/dt) is assumed to be zero and net capital imports (Q' is assumed to be a positive function of i*, A/A*) and the net imports function (J') are linearized we can write in a world without inflation the condition for equilibrium in the foreign exchange market as:

$$Q'_r r + Q'_r r^* + Q_\alpha A/A^* = J'_{q^*} dlnq^* + J'_y lny' + J'_{y^*} lny'^* + J'_u u' \text{ (ZZU)} \qquad (X.13)$$

lny' space the slop of the ZZU curve is positive.

References

AGHION, P.; HOWITT, P. (1994), Growth and Unemployment, *Review of Economic Studies* Vol. 61, 477-494.

AGHION, P.; HOWITT, P. (1998), Endogenous Growth Theory: Cambridge: MIT Press.

ARNOLD, L.G. (2006), Does the Choice between Wage Inequality and Unemployment Affect Productivity Growth?, *German Economic Review*, Vol. 7, pp 87-112.

ARROW, K.J. (1962) The Economic Implications of Learning by Doing, *Review of Economic Studies,* Vol. 29, 155-173.

ARTUS, P. (1989), Macroéconomie, Paris: PUF.

AUDRETSCH, D.; WELFENS, P.J.J. eds. (2002), The New Economy and Economic Growth in Europe and the US, Berlin: Springer.

BALASSA B. (1964), The Purchasing Power Parity Doctrine: A Reappraisal, *Journal of Political Economy*, Vol.72, No.6, 584-596.

BALASSA, B. (1965), Trade Liberalization and Revealed Comparative Advantage. *Manchester Schoo*l, Vol. 33, 99-123.

BARFIELD, C.E.; HEIDUK, G.; WELFENS, P.J.J., eds. (2003), Internet, Economic Growth and Globalization, Heidelberg and New York: Springer.

BARRO, R. I.; SALA-I-MARTIN, X. (1992), Convergence, *Journal of Political Economy*, Vol. 100 (April), 223-252.

BARRO, R.I.; SALA-I-MARTIN, X. (1995), Economic Growth, New York: McGraw-Hill.

BARRO, RJ.; MANKIW, N.G.; SALA-I-MARTIN, X. (1995), Capital Mobility in Neoclassical Models of Growth, *American Economic Review,* Vol. 85, 103-115.

BAUMOL, W. (1986), Productivity Growth, Convergence and Welfare: What the Long-run Data Show, *American Economic Review*, Vol. 76, 1072-1085.

BEAN, C.; PISSARIDES, C. (1993), Unemployment, Consumption and Growth, *European Economic Review* Vol. 37, 837-859.

BECKMANN, M., KÜNZI, H.P. (1982), Mathematik für Ökonomen III, Heidelberg: Springer.

BEN-DAVID, D. (1996), Trade and Convergence Among Countries, *Journal of International Economics*, Vol. 40 (3/4), 279-298.

BEN-DAVID, D.; LUMSDAINE, R.L.; PAPEL, D.H. (2003), Unit Roots, Postwar Slowdown and Long-Run Growth: Evidence from Two Structural Breaks, *Empirical Economics,* Vol. 28, 303-319.

BERTSCHEK, I. (1995), Product and Process Innovation as a Response to Increasing Imports and Foreign Direct Investment, *The Journal of Industrial Economics*, Vol. 43, 341-357.

BEYER, A. (1998), Modelling Money Demand in Germany, *Journal of Applied Econometrics*, Vol. 13, 57-76.

BLANCHARD, O.J.; FISCHER, S. (1989), Lectures on Macroeconomics, Cambridge: MIT Press

BLIND, K.; JUNGMITTAG, A. (2004), Foreign Direct Investment, Imports and Innovations in the Service Industry, *Review of Industrial Organization*, Vol. 25, 205-227.

BORBÉLY, D. (2004), Competition Among Accession and Cohesion Countries: Comparative Analysis of Specialization within the EU Market, *EIIW Working Paper,* No. 122, Wuppertal.

BORBÈLY, D. (2006). Trade Specialization in the Enlarged European Union, Heidelberg: Springer/Physica.

BRETSCHGER, L. (2005), Taxes, Mobile Capital and Economic Dynamics in a Globalising World, ETH Zurich, mimeo.

BRETSCHGER, L. (1997), International Trade, Knowledge Diffusion and Growth. *International Trade Journal,* Vol. 9 (3), 327–348.

BRETSCHGER, L. (2002), Wachstumstheoretische Perspektiven der Wirtschaftsintegration: Neuere Ansätze, *Jahrbücher für Nationalökonomie und Statistik,* Vol. 222, 64-79.

CANZONERI, M.; CUMBY, R.; DIBA, B. (1999), Relative Labor Productivity and the Real Exchange Rate in the Long Run: Evidence for a Panel of OECD Countries, *Journal of International Economics*, Vol.47, 245-266.

CARACOSTAS, P. (2003), Shared Governance Through Mutual Policy Learning, in: Edler, J.; Kuhlmann, S.; Behrens, M. (eds.), Changing Governance of Research and Technology Policy, Edward Elgar, Chelterham UK, p. 33-63.

CHINN, M., JOHNSTON, L. (1997), "Real Exchange Rate Levels, Productivity and the Real Exchange Rate in long Run: Evidence for a Panel of OECD Countries", *IMF Working Paper* 97/66 (Washington: International Monetary Fund)

CLARIDA, R.; GALI, J.; GERTLER, M. (1999), The Science of Monetary Policy: A New Keynesian Perspective, *Journal of Economic Literature*, Vol. 37, 1661-1707.

COENEN, G.; VEGA, J.L. (2001), The Demand for M3 in the Euro Area, *Journal of Applied Econometrics*, Vol. 16, 727-748.

COUNCIL OF ECONOMIC ADVISERS (2001), Economic Report of the President, Washington D.C..

CRISCUOLO, P.; NARULA, R.; VERSPAGEN, B. (2005), Role of Home and Host Country Innovation Systems in R&D Internationalisation: A Patent Citation Analysis, *Economics of Innovation and New Technology*, Vol. 14, 417-433.

DE GREGORIO, J.; WOLFF, H. (1994), Terms of Trade, Productivity, and the Real Exchange Rate, *NBER Working Paper* No.4807 (Cambridge, MA: NBER).

DE LONG, J.B. (1988), Productivity Growth, Convergence, and Welfare: Comment, *American Economic Review*, Vol. 78 (December), 1139-54.

DEARDORFF, A.V. (1986), Fireless Firewoes: How Preferences Can Interfere With the Theorems of International Trade, *Journal of International Economics*, Vol. 20, No. ½, 131-142.

DEUTSCHE BUNDESBANK (2006), Report January

DIXIT, A.K: (1976), The Theory of Equilibrium Growth, Oxford: Oxford University Press.

DORNBUSCH, R. (1976), Expectations and Exchange Rate Dynamics, Journal of Political Economy, Vol. 84, 1167-1176.

DUNNING, J. (1973), The Determinants of International Production, *Oxford Economic Papers*, Vol. 25, 289-336.

DUNNING, J.; NARULA, R. (1995), The R&D Activities of Foreign Firms in the United States, *International Studies of Management & Organization*, Vol. 25 (1-2), 39-72.

DUNNING, J.H. (1977): Trade, Location of Economic Activity and the MNE: A Search for an Eclectic Approach, in OHLIN, B./HESSELBORN, P.O./WIJKMAN, P.M. (eds): *The International Allocation of Economic Activities*, London.

DURLAUF, S.N.; QUAH, D.T. (1998),The New Empirics of Economic Growth, Centre of Economic Performance, *Discussion Paper* No. 384.

EBRD, Transition Report, various issues.

EICHER, T. S. (1996), Interaction between Endogenous Human Capital and Technological Change, *Review of Economic Studies* Vol. 63, 127-144

EITO (2004), EITO OBSERVARTORY 2000, Frankfurt.

EUROPEAN COMMISSION (2000), European Economy, Supplement A, No. 10/11., Brussels.

EUROPEAN COMMISSION (2003), 2003 European Innovation Scoreboard, SEC(2003) 1255, Brussels

EUROPEAN COMMISSION (2003), Drivers of Productivity Growth, EU Economy Review 2003, Brussels, 63-120.

EUROPEAN COMMISSION. (2003), Enlargement Paper No. 20.

FINDLAY, R.; KIERSZKOWSKI, H. (1983), International Trade and Human Capital: A Simple General Equilibrium Model, *Journal of Political Economy* Vol. 91, 957-978.

FRIEDMAN, M. (1969), The Optimum Quantity of Money, in: FRIEDMAN, M.; The Optimum Quantity of Money and Other Eassays, Chicago: Aldine.

FROOT, K.A.; STEIN, J.C. (1991), Exchange Rates and Foreign Direct Investment: An Imperfect Capital Markets Approach, *Quarterly Journal of Economics*, November, 1191-1217.

GÄRTNER, M. (1997), Makroökonomik flexibler und fester Wechselkurse, 2nd edition, Heidelberg: Springer

GALOR, O.; MOAV, O. (2000), Ability-Based Technological Transition, Wage Inequality, and Economic Growth, *Quarterly Journal of Economics*, Vol.115, 469-497.

GOODFRIEND, M.; KING, R.G. (1997), The New Neoclassiscal Synthesis and the Role of Monetary Policy, in: Bernanke, B.; Rotemberg, J. (eds.), *NBER Macroeconomics Annual* Vol. 12, 231-283, Cambridge: MIT Press.

GOODFRIEND, M.; KING, R.G. (2001), The Case for Price Stability, in: Herrero, A.; Gaspar, V.; Hoogduin, L.; Winkler, B. (eds.), Why Price Stability? Proceedings from the First ECB Central Banking, Conference, Frankfurt: ECB.

GOODFRIEND, M. (2004), Monetary Policy in the New Neoclassical Synthesis: A Primer, *Federal Reserve Bank of Richmond Economic Quarterly*, Vol. 90/3, 21-45.

GORDON, R.J. (1999), Has the "New Economy" Rendered the Productivity Slowdown Obsolete?, Northwestern University and NBER, revised version, June 14, 1999., mimeo.

GORDON, R.J. (2000), Does the "New Economy" Measure up to the Great Inventions of the Past?, Northwestern University, May 1, 2000, *Journal of Economic Perspectives*.

GOULD, D.M.; RUFFIN, R.J. (1995), Human Capital, Trade, and Economic Growth, *Weltwirtschaftliches Archiv*, Vol. 131, 425-446.

GOULD, E. D., MOAV, O. and WEINBERG, B. A. (2001), Precautionary Demand for Education, Inequality, and Technological Progress, *Journal of Economic Growth*, Vol. 6, 285-315.

GRAFE, C.; WYPLOSZ, C. (1999), A model of the Real Exchange Rate Determination in Transition Economies, in: Blejer, M.; Skreb, M., Balance of Payments, exchange Rates, and Competitiveness in Transition Economies (Boston: Kluwer Academic Publishers), .159-184.

GRAHAM, E.M. (2004), Do Export Processing Zones Attract FDI and its Benefits: The Experience from China, *International Economics and Economic Policy*, Vol. 1, No. 1, 87-103

GRIES, T.; SIEVERT, G.; WIENEKE, A. (2004), Interbank market frictions, international banks and growth, *International Economics and Economic Policy*, Vol. 1, Issue 2-3, 157-172.

GRIES, T. and JUNGBLUT, S. (1997), Catching-up of Economies in Transformation, in: WELFENS, P.J.J.; WOLF, H., eds., Banking, International Capital Flows and Growth in Europe, Heidelberg and New York: Springer, 297-313.

GROSSMAN, G.M.; HELPMAN, E. (1991): Innovation and Growth in the Global Economy, Cambridge: MIT Press.

HAAGEDOORN, J. (2002), Inter-firm R&D Partnerships: An Overview of Major Trends and Patterns since 1960, *Research Policy*, Vol. 31 (4), 477-492.

HALPERN, L., and WYPLOSZ, C., (1997), "Equilibrium Exchange Rates in Transition Economies", *IMF Staff Papers*, Vol.44 (December), 430-61.

HANSEN, J.; ROEGER, W. (2000), Estimation of Real Equilibrium Exchange Rates, *Economic Papers* No. 144, European Commission, Brussels.

HAYO, B. (1999), Estimating a European Money Demand Function, *Scottish Journal of Political Economy*, Vol. 46, 221-244.

HOLLINGSWORTH, R.; BOYER, R. (1997), Contemporary Capitalism: The Embeddedness of Institutions, Hollingsworth, R. and R. Boyer (eds.), Cambridge: Cambridge University Press.

INKLAAR R.; O'MAHONY, M.; TIMMER, M. (2003), ICT and Europ's Productivity Performance: Industry Level Growth Accounting Comparisons with the United States. Groningen Growth and development Centre, Research Memorandum GD-68.

JONES, C. (1995): R&D-Based Models of Economic Growth. *Journal of Political Economy*, 759–784.

JONES, C, I. (1998), Introduction to Economic Growth, New York: Norton.

JONES, C.I. (2002), Sources of US Economic Growth in a World of Ideas, American Economic Review, 72, 220-239.

JUNGMITTAG, A.; MEYER-KRAHMER, F.; REGER, G. (1999), Globalisation of R&D and Technology Markets – Trends, Motives, Consequences, in: Meyer-Krahmer (eds.), Globalisation of R&D and Technology Markets: Consequences for National Innovation Policies, Heidelberg, New York: Physica.

JUNGMITTAG, A. (2004), Innovations, Technological Specialisation and Economic Growth in the EU, *International Economics and Economic Policy*, Vol. 1, 247-274.

JUNGMITTAG, A. (2004), Innovations, Technological Specialisation and Economic Growth in the EU, European Commission, DG II ECFIN, *Economic Papers* No. 199.

JUNGMITTAG, A. (2004), Innovations, Technological Specialization and Economic Growth in the EU, *International Economics and Economic Policy*, Vol. 1, No. 2/3, Special Issue.

JUNGMITTAG, A. (2003), Internationale Innovationsdynamik, Spezialisierungsstruktur und Außenhandel – Empirische Befunde und wirtschaftspolitische Implikationen, in: Gries, T.; Jungmittag, A.; Welfens, P.J.J. (eds.), Neue Wachstums- und Innovationspolitik in Deutschland und Europa, Heidelberg: Physica-Verlag, 183-214.

JUNGMITTAG, A., WELFENS, P.J.J. (1998), Telecommunications, Innovation and the Long-Term Production Function: Theoretical Analysis and a Cointegration Analysis for West Germany 1960-1990, EIIW-Discussion Paper No. 52, University of Potsdam.

JUNGMITTAG, A.; WELFENS, P.J.J. (2003), Innovation, Growth and Wage Structure in Transforming Economies, in: LANE, T.; ODING, N.; WELFENS, P.J.J., eds., Real and Financial Economic Dynamics in Russia and Eastern Europe, New York: Springer, 57-86.

KING, R.G.; LEVINE, R. (1993), Finance and growth: Schumpeter might be right. *Quarterly Journal of Economics*, Vo. 108 (3): 717-737.

KHAN, S. R.; BILGINSOY, C. (1994), Industry Externalities Revisited, Kyklos, Vol. 47, 67-80.

KOK, W. (2004), Facing the Challenge, The Lisbon strategy for growth and employment, European Communities, Brüssel.

KORMENDI, R.C.; P.G. MEGUIRE (1985), Macroeconomic Determinants of Growth: Cross-Country Evidence, *Journal of Monetary Economics*, Vol. 16, 141-163.

KRAJNYAK, K.; ZETTELMEYER, J. (1998), Competitiveness in Transition Economies: What Scope for Real Appreciation? *IMF Staff Papers*, Vol.45 (June), pp.309-62

LAMBSDORFF, J. (2005), The Puzzle with Increasing Money Demand – Evidence from a Cross-Section of Countries, *Kredit und Kapital*, Vol. 38, 155-176.

LEONTIEF, W.W. (1953), Domestic Production and Foreign Trade: the American Capital Position Re-examined, *Proceedings of the American Philosophical Society*, Vol. 97; also in Economia Internazionale.

LEONTIEF, W.W. (1956), Factor Proportions and the Structure of American Trade: Further Theoretical and Empirical Analysis, *Review of Economics and Statistics*, Vol. XXVIII.

LEVINE, R.; RENELT, D. (1992), A Sensitivity Analysis of Cross-Country Growth Regressions, *American Economic Review*, Vol. 82, 942-963.

LEVINE, R.; ZERVOS, S. (1998), Stock markets development and long-run growth, *World Bank Policy Research Working Paper No. 1582*

LILIEN, D.M. (1982a), Sectoral Shifts and Cyclical Unemployment, *Journal of Political*

LILIEN, D.M. (1982b), A Sectoral Model of the Business Cycle, Modelling Research Group.

LJUNGQVIST, L; SARGENT, T.J. (2000), Recursive Macroeconomic Theory, Cambridge : MIT Press.

LOFTS, C.; LOUNDES, J. (2000), Foreign Ownership, Foreign Competition and Innovation in Australian Enterprises, *Melbourne Institute Working Paper* No. 20/00, University of Melbourne.

LUCAS, R.E. (1981), Studies in Business Cycle Theory, Cambridge: MIT Press.

LUCAS, R.E. (1988), On the Mechanics of Economic Development, *Journal of Monetary Economics*, Vol. 22, I: 3-42.

LUNDVALL, B.A. (1992), National Systems of Innovation: Towards a Theory of Innovation and Interactive Learning, Lundvall, B.A. (eds.), London: Pinter.

McMAHON, W. (1991), Relative Returns to Human and Physical Capital in the U.S. and Efficient Investment Strategies, *Economics of Education Review*, Vol. 10, 283-296.

MALISZEWSKA, M. (1997), Modelling Real Exchange Rate in Transition: The Case of Poland and Pomania, *CASE Foundation, S&A* No. 131

MANKIW, N.G.; ROMER, D. (eds.) (1991), New Keynesian Macroeconomics, 2 vols., Cambridge: MIT Press.

MANKIW, N.G.; ROMER, D.; WEIL, D.N. (1992), A Contribution to the Empirics of Growth, *Quarterly Journal of Economics*, Vol.107 (May), 403-438.

MANN, C.L. (1998): Globalization and Productivity in the United States and Germany, in: BLACK, S.W. (eds): *Globalization, Technological Change, and Labor Markets*, 17-44, Kluwer: Boston.

MARKUSEN, J.R. (2002), Multinational Firms and the Theory of International Trade, Cambridge, MA, London: MIT Press.

McMORROW, K.; ROEGER, W. (2004), The Economic and financial market consequences of global ageing, Heidelberg and New York: Springer.

NAVARETTI, B.G.; VENABLES, A.J. (2004), Multinational Firms in the World Economy, Princeton: Princeton University Press.

NARULA, R. (1999), Explaining the Growth of Strategic R&D Alliances by European Firms, *Journal of Common Market Studies*, Vol.37, 711-723.

NSF (2004), Industrial R&D Employment in the United States and in U.S. Multinational Corporations, Arlington.

OBSTFELD, M.; ROGOFF, K. (1996), Foundations of International Macroeconomics, Cambridge: MIT Press.

OECD (1998), The Software Sector: A Statistical Profile for Selected OECD Countries, DSTI/ICCP/AH(97)4/REV1, Paris.

PHELPS, E.S. (1961), The Golden Rule of Accumulation: A Fable for Growthmaen, *American Economic Review*, Vol. 51, 638-643.

PLOSSER, C.I. (1989), Understanding Real Business Cycles, *Journal of Economic Perspectives*, Vol. 3, 51-77.

PRESCOTT, E. (1986), Theory Advanced of Business Cycle Measurement, *Federal Reserve Bank of Minneapolis Quarterly Review*, Vol. 10, 9-22.

REITHER, F. (1989), Das Tobin-Paradox, *Wirtschaftswissenschaftliches Studium*, 295-297.

ROMER, P. M.(1986), Increasing Returns and Long-Run Growth, *Journal of Political Economy*, Vol. 94 , 1002-1037.

ROMER, P. M. (1990), Endogenous Technical Change, *Journal of Political Econonomy* 98, 71–102.

ROMER, P. (1990a), Human capital and growth: theory and evidence, Carnegie Rochester conference series on public policy: a bi-annual conference proceedings, Elsevier, 251-286.

ROMER, D. (1993), The New Keynesian Synthesis, *Journal of Economic Perspectives*, Vol. 7, 5-22.

ROOS, W.M. (2005), TV Weather Forecast or Look through the Window? Expert and Consumer Expectations about Macroeconomic Conditions, *Kyklos*, Vol. 58, 415-438.

ROSE, A. (2000), One Money, One Market: The Effect of Common Currencies on Trade, *Economic Policy*, 15, 9-45.

Rother, P. (2000), The Impact of Productivity Differentials on Inflation and the Real Exchange Rate: An Estimation of the Balassa-Samuelson Effect in Slovenia, IMF Staff Country Report 00/56 (Washington: International Monetary Fund), pp.26-38

SACHS, J.; WARNER, A. (1995), Economic Reform and the Process of Global Integration, *Brookings Papers on Economic Activity*, No. 1, 1-118.

SAPIR, A. (2004), An Agenda for a Growing Europe, Report for the European Commission, Oxford: Oxford University Press.

SCHERER, F.M.; HUH, K. (1992), R&D Reactions to High Technology Import Competition, *The Review of Economics and Statistics*, Vol. 74, 202-212.

SEGERSTROM, P. (1998), Endogenous Growth without Scale Effects. American Economic Review 88, 1290–1310.

SHEEHEY, E.M. (1995), Trade, Efficiency, and Growth in a Cross Section of Countries, *Weltwirtschaftliches Archiv*, Vol. 131(4), 723-726.

SIDRAUSKI, M. (1967), Inflation and Economic Growth, *Journal of Political Economy*, Vol. 75 (1967), 796-810.

SIJBEN, J.J. (1977), Money and Economic Growth, Leiden: Martinus Nijhoff.

SINAI, A.; STOKES, H. (1972), Real Money Balances: An Omitted Variable from the Production Function, *Review of Economics and Statistics*, Vol. 54, 290-296.

SLAUGHTER, M.J. (1997), Per Capita Income Convergence and the Role of International Trade, *American Economic Review*, Vol. 87, No. 2, 194-199.

SOLBES, P. (2004), The European Union: Economic prospects, structural reforms and enlargement, *International Economics and Economic Policy*, Vol. 1, 105-110.

SOLOW, R.M. (1956), A Contribution to the Theory of Economic Growth, *Quarterly Journal of Economics*, 65–94.

SOLOW, R.M. (1970), Growth Theory: An Exposition, Oxford: Oxford University Press.

STAMER, M. (1999): Strukturwandel und Wirtschaftliche Entwicklung in Deutschland, den USA und Japan, Aachen: Shaker.

STEIN, J.L.; INFANTE, E.F. (1980), Money-financed Fiscal Policies in a Growing Economy, *Journal of Political Economy*, 88 (1980), 259-287.

STOKEY, N.L. (1991), Human Capital, Product _Quality, and Growth, *Quarterly Journal of Economics*, Vol. 106, 587-616.

STOLERU, L. (1978), L'équilibre et la croissance économique, Paris: Dunod.

SZAPARY, G. (2000), Maastricht and the Choice of Exchange Rate Regime in Transition Countries During the Run-up to EMU, *NBH Working Paper* 2000/7.

TELLIS, G.U.J.; STREMERSCH, S.; YIN, E. (2003), The International Take-off of New Products: the Role of Economics, Culture and Country Innovativeness, *Marketing Science*, Vol. 22, 188-208.

TEMPLE, J. (1999), The New Growth Evidence, Journal of Economic Literature, 112-156.

TOBIN, J. (1965), Money and Economic Growth, *Econometrica*, Vol. 33, 671-684.

TORSTENSSON, J. (1998), Country Size and Comparative Advantage: An Empirical Study, *Weltwirtschaftliches Archiv*, Vol. 134, 590-611.

TSURU, K. (2000), Finance and growth – Some considerations, and a review of the empirical literature. *OECD Economics department working papers No. 228.*

UZAWA, H. (1965), Optimum Technical Change in an Aggregative Model of Economic Growth, *International Economic Review* 6, 18–31.

VALADKHANI, A. (2005), Modelling Demand for Broad Money in Australia, *Australian Economic Papers*, Vol. 44, 47-64.

VANARK, B.; PIATKOWSKI, M. (2004), Productivity, Innovation and ICT in Old and New Europe, *International Economics and Economic Policy*, Vol. 2&3 (special issue edited by D. AUDRETSCH, L. BRETSCHGER and P.J.J. WELFENS), 105-110.

VEUGELERS, R. (2005), Internationalisation of R&D: Trends, Issues and Implications for S&T Policies, Background report for the OECD forum on the internationalization of R&D, Brussels.

WEIZSÄCKER, C. VON (1962), Wachstum, Zins und optimale Investitionsquote, Tübingen: Mohr.

WELFENS, P.J.J. (1997), Privatization, Structural Change and Productivity: Toward Convergence in Europe? in: BLACK, S. eds. (1997), Europe's Economy Looks East, Cambridge: Cambridge University Press, 212-257.

WELFENS, P.J.J. (2001), European Monetary Union and Exchange Rate Dynamics, New Approaches and Application to the Euro, Berlin, Heidelberg and New York: Springer.

WELFENS, P.J.J. (2001), Information & Communication Technology and Growth: Some Neglected Dynamic Aspects in Open Digital Economies, in: AUDRETSCH, D.; WELFENS, P.J.J., eds., The New Economy and Economic Growth in Europe and the US, Heidelberg and New York: Springer.

WELFENS, P.J.J. (2002), Interneteconomics.net, Heidelberg and New York: Springer, 2nd edition forthcoming 2006.

WELFENS, P.J.J. (2004), Macroeconomic Aspects of Opening up, Unemployment and Sustainable Growth in Transition Countries, paper presented at IMF seminar on May 28, Washington DC, mimeo in: Innovations in Macroeconomics

WELFENS, P.J.J. (2005), Information & Communication Technology and Capital Market Perspectives, *International Economics and Economic Policy*, Vol. 2, No.1, Berlin: Springer.

WELFENS, P.J.J. (2001), Aggregation in a Two-Sector Growth Model: A Modified Solow Approach with Cobb-Douglas Production Functions, *EIIW-Paper* No. 89.

WELFENS, P.J.J.; AUDRETSCH, D.B.; ADDISON, J.T.; GRIES, T.; GRUPP, H. (1999), Globalization, Economic Growth and Innovation Dynamics, Heidelberg and New York: Springer.

WELFENS, P.J.J.; JUNGMITTAG, A. (2000), Auswirkungen einer Internet Flat Rate auf Wachstum und Beschäftigung in Deutschland, *EIIW-Discussion Paper* No. 52.

WELFENS, P.J.J.; JUNGMITTAG, A. (2001), Internetdynamik, Telekomliberalisierung und Wissensgesellschaft, Heidelberg and New York: Springer.

WELFENS, P.J.J.; BORBÈLY, D. (2004), Exchange Rate Developments and Stock Market Dynamics in Transition Countries: Theory and Empirical Analysis, Paper presented at CEPS, Brussels, November 18-20, 2004, *EIIW Working Paper*, No. 126.

WELFENS, P.J.J.; WOLF H.C. eds. (1997), Banking, International Capital Flows and Growth in Europe Financial Markets, Savings and Monetary Integration in a World with Uncertain Convergence, Heidelberg and New York: Springer.

WILLIS, R.J. (1986), Wage Determinants: A Survey and Reinterpretation of Human Capital Earnings Functions, in: ASHENFELDER, O.; LAYARD, R., eds., Handbook of Labor Economics, 525-602, Amsterdam: North-Holland.

WOOD, A. (1999), Openness and wage inequality in developing countries: the Latin American challenge to East Asian conventional wisdom, in: BALDWIN, R.E.; COHEN, D.; SAPIR, A.; VENABLES, A. eds., Market integration, Regionalism and the Global Economy, 153-180, CEPR: London.

WOODFORD, M. (2003), Interest and Prices: Foundations of a Theory of Monetary Policy, Princeton: Princeton University Press.

WORLD BANK (2004), World Development Indicators, CD-Rom.

YOUNG, A. (1993), Invention and Bounded Learning by Doing, *Journal of Political Economy*, Vol.101, 443-472.

ZIMMERMANN, K.F. (1987), Trade and Dynamic Efficiency, *Kyklos*, Vol. 40, 73-87.

VAN ZON, A.; MUYSKEN, J. (2005), The Impact of ICT Investment on Knowledge Accumulation and Economic Growth, in: SOETE, L; TER WEL, B., eds., The Economics of the Digital Society, Cheltenham: Edward Elgar, 305-329.

List of Figures

Fig. 1. RCAs for Machinery & Equipment in Selected Countries, 1992-2003 15

Fig. 2. Product Innovations and Changes of Costs 16

Fig. 3. Annual Growth Rate of Real GNP and GNP per Capita, 1980-2005
(US, Ireland and Netherlands) 24

Fig. 4. Growth Rate of Real GNP per Capita and Population in Selected
Countries, 1970-2005 (US, UK, France, Germany, UK, Italy) 25

Fig. 5. GNP (PPP figures) in the US, UK, France, Germany, Italy, 1980-2005 ... 26

Fig. 6. GNP (PPP figures) in the Netherlands, Sweden, Finland, Ireland,
Poland, 1980-2005 26

Fig. 7. Per Capita GDP and Per Capita GNP of the US, Ireland and the
Netherlands, 1980-2005 27

Fig. 8. Foreign Direct Investment Stocks Per Capita in Selected Countries 27

Fig. 9. Empirical Aspects of Economic Development 28

Fig. 10. Ambiguous Effect of Technological Progress on Price Level 36

Fig. 11. Standard Neoclassical Growth Model and Adjustment Path 44

Fig. 12. Government Activity in the TOBIN Monetary Growth Model 53

Fig. 13. Money Supply Dynamics and the Capital Intensity in the
TOBIN Model 54

Fig. 14. Shifts in the Progress Function over Time 56

Fig. 15. Adjustment Path in the Differential Equation 66

Fig. 16. Asset-Seeking FDI 68

Fig. 17. Savings Rates in Selected Countries: USA, Germany, France, UK,
India, China, Poland, Hungary, Russia 70

Fig. 18. Ratio of M1/Nominal National Income and of Broad Money/Nominal
National Income in Selected Countries (USA, Germany, France) 71

Fig. 19. Patent Applications Per Capita of Selected Countries 73

Fig. 20. Real Capital Stock per Capita in Selected Countries,
1980-2005 (figures are unadjusted for quality effect) 74

Fig. 21. Decomposition of Average Growth Rates of GDP in Selected EU
Countries, 1969-1998 77

Fig. 22. Capital Input and Labor Input in an Economy with Unemployment 84

Fig. 23. Wage Structure and Trade Balance 101

Fig. 24. Transitory Equilibrium and Steady-state Equilibrium 114

Fig. 25. Standard IS-LM Model versus Keynes-Solow Model 127

Fig. 26. Medium Term and Long Run Equilibrium 128

Fig. 27. Level vs. Growth Effect 133

Fig. 28. Impact of Foreign Direct Investment on Growth (Short-term Fall of Per-capita-GNP Level and Rise of Growth Rate as a Consequence of FDI Inflows) 140

Fig. 29. Capital Formation under Endogenous Technological Progress 144

Fig. 30. Endogenous Technological Trogress 144

Fig. 31. Capital Formation Constant Technological Progress (progress for 2.5 periods)..145

Fig. 32. Exchange Rate Dynamics, Trade, Structural Change and Growth.........147

Fig. 33. Effect of FDI on the Level of Per Capita Income and the Growth Rate 156

Fig. 34. Real Effective Exchange Rate (p/ep*) Dynamics in Selected EU Countries: Poland, Hungary, Czech Republic, Portugal, Spain, Ireland, 1990-2002 158

Fig. 35. Rise of Product Innovations in the Mundell-Fleming Model.................168

Fig. 36. Direct and Indirect Effects of Product Innovation 171

Fig. 37a. Real Exchange Rate Dynamics 174

Fig. 37b. Model of the Long Term Real Exchange Rate ($dq/dt=bq^n - a^{*'}q$) 174

Fig. 38. Effects of a Real Appreciation 177

Fig. 39. Relative Price of Oil...191

Fig. 40. Balassa-Samuelson Effect, Technological Progress and Quasi Unemployment...200

Fig. 41. Wage Rate Fixing above the Market-Clearing Rate 202

Fig. 42. Net Exports and Unemployment Rate..206

Fig. 43. Exchange Rate and Stock Market Dynamics in the US (3-months moving average) 230

Fig. 44. Exchange Rate and Stock Market Dynamics in Germany (3-months moving average)..231

Fig. 45. Exchange Rate and Stock Market Dynamics in Europe
(3-months moving average) 231

Fig. 46. Exchange Rate and Stock Market Dynamics in Japan
(3-months moving average) 232

Fig. 47. Exchange Rate and Stock Market Dynamics in Hungary (annual data) 232

Fig. 48. Exchange Rate and Stock Market Dynamics in Poland (annual data) ...233

Fig. 49. Exchange Rate and Stock Market Dynamics in the Czech Republic
(annual data) 233

Fig. 50. Financial Market Equilibrium (M'M') and Real Economy (I'S') 235

Fig. 51. Saddle Point Stability in a Perfect Foresight Model 237

Fig. 52. Real Effective Exchange Rates for Selected EU Accession Countries
in the 1990s, Jan 1990=100..238

Fig. 53. Portfolio Equilibrium in the Simple Basic Branson Model 239

Fig. 54. Foreign Bonds Market, Stock Market and Money Market 241

Fig. 55. Effects of an Increase in Capital Productivity in the Modified
Branson Model with Stock Market 242

Fig. 56. International Bonds Market Integration, Stock Market Volatility
and Interest Rate Volatility 256

Fig. 57. Optimum Growth in the Standard Model 262

Fig. 58. Government Consumption and the Steady State in a
Neoclassical Growth Model..263

Fig. 59. Change of the Level of Growth Path vs. Growth Rate...........................264

Fig. 60. One Sector Economy and the Factor Price Ratio..................................279

Fig. 61. Two Sector Economy..280

Fig. 62. EU 15: Growth Rate of Employment and Annual Change of
Investment / GDP Ratio 294

Fig. 63. Germany: Growth Rate of Employment and Annual Change of
Investment / Ratio 294

Fig. 64. Hungary: Growth Rate of Employment and Annual Change of
Investment / GDP Ratio 295

Fig. 65. Poland: Growth Rate of Employment and Annual Change of
Investment / GDP Ratio 295

Fig. 66. Czech Republic: Growth Rate of Employment and Annual Change
of Investment / GDP Ratio..296

Fig. 67. Equilibrium in the (a) Tradables Market (TT) and Nontradables Market (NN) and Interest Parity (b); Model Can Track Fiscal and Monetary Policy & Supply Shocks 298

Fig. 68. Relative Export Unit Value of German Industry (Germany relative to US, Weighted) 300

Fig. 69. Germany – RCA and Export Unit Values 312

Fig. 70. Hungary – RCA and Export Unit Values 314

Fig. 71. UK – RCA and Export Unit Value 314

Fig. 72. Actors and Institutions in the Innovation System 321

Fig. 73. R&D Expenditure in Selected ICT Industries, 2003 or Latest Year Available as a Percentage of Business Enterprise Sector R&D Expenditure 327

Fig. 74. ICT Patents as a Percentage of National Total (EPO) in Selected Countries. According to the Residence of the Inventors, by Priority Year 328

Fig. 75. ICT Employment Across the Economy- Share of ICT-Related Occupations in the Total Economy in Selected Countries 328

Fig. 76. Share of Countries in ICT Patents' at the EPO, According to the Residence of the Inventors, by Priority Year 329

Fig. 77. Product Innovation with Positive External Effects and R&D Promotion 332

Fig. 78. R&D Promotion, Production and Trade 333

Fig. 79. International External Effects of Domestic R&D Promotion (Technology-intensive Inputs for Tradable Products) 334

Fig. 80. Network Effects and Cost-Saving Progress 336

Fig. 81. Expansionary Fiscal Policy Promoting Product Innovations 337

Fig. 82. Expansionary Fiscal Policy with a Focus on Promoting Process Innovations 338

Fig. 83. Product Innovation and Network Effects. 350

Fig. 84. Quality Ladder for Industry j 353

Fig. 85. Correlations Between Contributions of Transferable Technical Knowledge and Technological Specialisation to GDP Growth 362

Fig. 86. Percentage Shares of Patent Applications at the European Patent Office 363

Fig. 87. EU-15, Japan and USA: Number of Patent Applications Per One
Million Inhabitants at EPO...365

Fig. 88. Stock of Patents at the German Patent and Trade Mark Office
(1960 – 2001)...364

Fig. 89. EU 15: Nunber of Patent Applications Per One Million Inhabitants
at the EPO..365

Fig. 90. Central and Eastern European Accession Countries: Number of Patent
Applications Per One Million Inhabitants at the EPO....................................365

Fig. 91. R&D Expenditure Per Capita in EU-15, Japan and the USA (EUR,
Current Prices)..366

Fig. 92. R&D Expenditure in Percent of GDP in EU-15, Japan and the USA....367

Fig. 93. Financial Market Integration and Growth...389

Fig. 94. Static Effects and Medium-Term Effects of Monetary Union...............393

Fig. 95. Monetary Union, Inflation and Unemployment: Structural Break
from Switching to Monetary Union..394

Fig. 96. Dynamic Welfare Effects of Monetary Union...396

Fig. 97. Integration of Financial Markets and Globalization 397

Fig. 98. Goods Market, Money Market, International Capital Market...............405

Fig. 99. Financial Market Equilibrium and Goods Market Equilibrium in the
Dornbusch Model...406

List of Tables

Table 1. Dynamics of Specialization in the Case of Trade in Intermediate Products (1/2 of final product is assumed to be exported)......................18

Table 2. UN Projections of Growth Rates of Population for US, UK, France, Germany, UK, Italy, Turkey, China, India, Pakistan, World, 2000-2050 25

Table 3. Inflation Rates and Unemployment Rates in Selected Countries (moving centered three-year averages) 72

Table 4. Growth Rates of International Patents, 1990-1997 73

Table 5. Growth Accounting: Comparison of Euro Area and US Developments............75

Table 6. Openness (Trade/GDP), Growth and Unemployment in Transition Countries 193

Table 7. Selected Macroeconomic Indicators for EU Accession Countries and Turkey 218

Table 8. Real Interest Rates, Population Growth Rates and Progress Rates in Selected OECD Countries (Annual Average Growth Rates) 272

Table 9. Actual versus Optimal Total Factor Productivity Growth in Selected OECD Countries...272

Table 10. Various Indicators Measuring Structural Change based on Production Data at the NACE 2-digit level 283

Table 11. Features of Structural Change Indicators...303

Table 12. Various Indicators Measuring Structural Change Based on Export Data to the EU 15 at the NACE 2-Digit Level (Difference Between Indicators in the Time Periods 1998-2003 and 1993-1998 304

Table 13. European Innovation Scoreboard, 2003...309

Table 14. Germany – RCA, EUV, EUV Weighted with the Sectoral Export Shares of Manufacturing 313

Table 15. Hungary – RCA, EUV, EUV Weighted with the Sectoral Export Shares of Manufacturing 315

Table 16. United Kingdom – RCA, EUV, EUV Weighted with the Sectoral Export Shares of Manufacturing and of GDP 316

Table 17. France – RCA, EUV, EUV Weighted with the Sectoral Export Shares of Manufacturing and of GDP 317

Table 18. Italy – RCA, EUV, EUV Weighted with the Sectoral Export Shares of Manufacturing and of GDP 318

Table 19. USA – RCA, EUV, EUV Weighted with the Sectoral Export Shares of Manufacturing and of GDP 319

Table 20. R&D Expenditures for PTO's (USD millions) 326

Table 21. Specialization (Relative Patent Share in interval -100, +100) in 1995-99 in Technology-Intensive Fields with High Growth Rates in Patents 371

Table 22. Growth of Unit Labor Costs in Selected OECD Countries 382

Table 23. Macroeconomic Determinants of the Current Account 392

Further Publications by *Paul J. J. Welfens*

M. W. Klein, P. J. J. Welfens (Eds.)
Multinationals in the New Europe and Global Trade
1992. XV, 281 pages. 24 Figs., 75 Tab.,
Hardcover, ISBN 3-540-54634-0

P. J. J. Welfens (Ed.)
Economic Aspects of German Unification
Expectations, Transition Dynamics and
International Perspectives
1996. XV, 527 pages. 34 Figs., 110 Tab.,
Hardcover, ISBN 3-540-60261-5

R. Tilly, P. J. J. Welfens (Eds.)
European Economic Integration as a Challenge to Industry and Government
Contemporary and Historical Perspectives
on International Economic Dynamics
1996. X, 558 pages. 43 Figs.,
Hardcover, ISBN 3-540-60431-6

P. J. J. Welfens (Ed.)
Economic Aspects of German Unification
Expectations, Transition Dynamics and
International Perspectives
2nd revised and enlarged edition
1996. XV, 527 pages. 34 Figs., 110 Tab.,
Hardcover, ISBN 3-540-60261-5

P. J. J. Welfens
European Monetary Integration
EMS Developments and International Post-
Maastricht Perspectives
3rd revised and enlarged edition
1996. XVIII, 384 pages. 14 Figs., 26 Tab.,
Hardcover, ISBN 3-540-60260-7

P. J. J. Welfens (Ed.)
European Monetary Union
Transition, International Impact
and Policy Options
1997. X, 467 pages. 50 Figs., 31 Tab.,
Hardcover, ISBN 3-540-63305-7

P. J. J. Welfens, G. Yarrow (Eds.)
**Telecommunications and Energy
in Systemic Transformation**
International Dynamics, Deregulation and
Adjustment in Network Industries
1997. XII, 501 pages. 39 Figs.,
Hardcover, ISBN 3-540-61586-5

P. J. J. Welfens, H. C. Wolf (Eds.)
**Banking, International Capital Flows
and Growth in Europe**
Financial Markets, Savings and Monetary
Integration in a World with Uncertain
Convergence
1997. XIV, 458 pages. 22 Figs., 63 Tab.,
Hardcover, ISBN 3-540-63192-5

P. J. J. Welfens, D. Audretsch, J. T. Addison,
H. Grupp
**Technological Competition, Employment
and Innovation Policies in OECD Countries**
1998. VI, 231 pages. 16 Figs., 20 Tab.,
Hardcover, ISBN 3-540-63439-8

P. J. J. Welfens, G. Yarrow, R. Grinberg,
C. Graack (Eds.)
Towards Competition in Network Industries
Telecommunications, Energy and
Transportation in Europe and Russia
1999. XXII, 570 pages. 63 Figs., 63 Tab.,
Hardcover, ISBN 3-540-65859-9

P. J. J. Welfens
**EU Eastern Enlargement and the Russian
Transformation Crisis**
1999. X, 151 pages. 12 Figs., 25 Tab.,
Hardcover, ISBN 3-540-65862-9

P. J. J. Welfens
**Globalization of the Economy,
Unemployment and Innovation**
1999. VI, 255 pages. 11 Figs., 31 Tab.,
Hardcover, ISBN 3-540-65250-7

P. J. J. Welfens, J. T. Addison,
D. B. Audretsch, T. Gries, H. Grupp
**Globalization, Economic Growth and
Innovation Dynamics**
1999. X, 160 pages. 15 Figs., 15 Tab.,
Hardcover, ISBN 3-540-65858-0

R. Tilly, P. J. J. Welfens (Eds.)
**Economic Globalization, International
Organizations and Crisis Management**
Contemporary and Historical Perspectives
on Growth, Impact and Evolution of Major
Organizations in an Interdependent World
2000. XII, 408 pages. 11 Figs., 20 Tab.,
Hardcover, ISBN 3-540-65863-7

P. J. J. Welfens, E. Gavrilenkov (Eds.)
**Restructuring, Stabilizing and Modernizing
the New Russia**
Economic and Institutional Issues
2000. XIV, 516 pages. 82 Figs., 70 Tab.,
Hardcover, ISBN 3-540-67429-2

P. J. J. Welfens
**European Monetary Union and Exchange
Rate Dynamics**
New Approaches and Applications to the Euro
2001. X, 159 pages. 26 Figs., 12 Tab.,
Hardcover, ISBN 3-540-67914-6

P. J. J. Welfens
Stabilizing and Integrating the Balkans
Economic Analysis of the Stability Pact,
EU Reforms and International Organizations
2001. XII, 171 pages. 6 Figs., 18 Tab.,
Hardcover, ISBN 3-540-41775-3

P. J. J. Welfens, B. Meyer, W. Pfaffenberger,
P. Jasinski, A. Jungmittag
**Energy Policies in the European Union
Germany's Ecological Tax Reform**
2001. VII, 143 pages. 21 Figs., 41 Tab.,
Hardcover, ISBN 3-540-41652-8

P. J. J. Welfens (Ed.)
**Internationalization of the Economy and
Environmental Policy Options**
2001. XIV, 442 pages. 57 Figs., 61 Tab.,
Hardcover, ISBN 3-540-42174-2

P. J. J. Welfens
Interneteconomics.net
Macroeconomics, Deregulation, and
Innovation
2002. VIII, 215 pages. 34 Figs., 30 Tab.,
Hardcover, ISBN 3-540-43337-6

D. B. Audretsch, P. J. J. Welfens (Eds.)
**The New Economy and Economic Growth
in Europe and the USA**
2002, XII, 350 pages. 28 Figs., 59 Tab.,
Hardcover, ISBN 3-540-43179-9

C. E. Barfield, G. Heiduk, P. J. J. Welfens
(Eds.)
**Internet, Economic Growth and
Globalization**
Perspectives on the Digital Economy in
Europe, Japan and the U.S.
2003. XII, 388 pages. 34 Figs., 67 Tab.,
Hardcover, ISBN 3-540-00286-3

J. T. Addison, P. J. J. Welfens (Eds.)
Labor Markets and Social Security
Issues and Policy Options in the U.S.
and Europe, 2nd edn.
2003. X, 402 pages. 56 Figs., 52 Tab.,
Hardcover, ISBN 3-540-44004-6

T. Lane, N. Oding, P. J. J. Welfens (Eds.)
**Real and Financial Economic Dynamics
in Russia and Eastern Europe**
2003. XII, 293 pages. 50 Figs., 63 Tab.,
Hardcover, ISBN 3-540-00910-8

J. E. Gavrilenkov, P. J. J. Welfens, R. Wiegert
(Eds.)
Economic Opening Up and Growth in Russia
2004. IX, 298 pages. 61 Figs., 70 Tab.,
Hardcover, ISBN 3-540-20459-8

P. J. J. Welfens, A. Wziątek-Kubiak (Eds.)
**Structural Change and Exchange
Rate Dynamics**
The Economics of the EU Eastern
Enlargement
2005. VI, 288 pages. 26 Figs., 58 Tab.
Hardcover, ISBN 3-540-27687-4

E. M. Graham, N. Oding, P. J. J. Welfens (Eds.)
**Internationalization and Economic Policy
Reforms in Transition Countries**
2005. XI, 340 pages. 77 Figs., 28 Tab.
Hardcover, ISBN 3-540-24040-3

P. J. J. Welfens, F. Knipping, S. Chirathivat,
C. Ryan (Eds.)
Integration in Asia and Europe
Historical Dynamics, Political Issues
and Economic Perspectives
2006. VI, 284 pages. 32 Figs., 30 Tab.
Hardcover, ISBN 3-540-28729-9

P. J. J. Welfens, A. Wziątek-Kubiak (Eds.)
**Structural Change
and Exchange Rate Dynamics**
2005. VI, 288 pages. 36 Figs., 58 Tab.
Hardcover, ISBN 3-540-27687-4

H. G. Broadman, T. Paas, P. J. J. Welfens (Eds.)
**Economic Liberalization
and Integration Policy**
2006. VI, 358 pages. 93 Figs., 52 Tab.
Hardcover, ISBN 3-540-24183-3